INTERMEDIATE ECONOMICS

INTERMEDIATE ECONOMICS

JACK HARVEY

FIFTH EDITION

MACMILLAN

First published 1965 by
THE MACMILLAN PRESS LTD
Houndmills, Basingstoke, Hampshire RG21 2XS
and London
Companies and representatives
throughout the world

ISBN 0–333–54551–6 hardcover
ISBN 0–333–54552–4 paperback

A catalogue record for this book is available
from the British Library.

Printed in Hong Kong

Reprinted 1967, 1968 (twice), 1969, 1970
Second edition 1972
Reprinted 1973
Third edition 1976
Reprinted 1977, 1978 (twice), 1980 (twice)
Fourth edition 1983
Reprinted 1985, 1986, 1988
Fifth edition 1991
Reprinted 1992, 1993

Contents

IV   FINANCE AND BANKING

V   THE LEVEL OF ACTIVITY

Preface to the First Edition

This is a textbook for the student, not a popular account of economic affairs for the everyday man in the street. It recognises that there is no short cut to learning, and asks for a conscientious effort by the reader.

Given that, the book will do its part by making that learning as easy and thorough as possible. At all times I have kept in mind the many students who are working without a tutor, particularly students overseas.

First, the scope of the book is strictly limited. (a) It explains simple economic principles and shows how they can be used to throw light on many of the problems which occur in the real world. (b) It covers the requirements of the GCE 'A' Level syllabus, papers in economics set by professional bodies, and first-year university courses.

Secondly, questions are provided at the end of each chapter and form an integral part of the course. They are of two kinds. The first kind has been designed: (a) to test the student's understanding of the text; (b) to ensure that the student thinks about the ideas expounded; (c) to encourage the student to provide his own examples; (d) to emphasise definitions and important points. To derive full value from the book, a conscientious attempt must be made to answer them. Only when he needs a check or runs into difficulties should the student refer to the answers. The second kind, marked †, deals with special problems which would otherwise interrupt the flow of the text, and takes the student a little further. Indeed, in some respects they are an approach towards 'programmed' learning. The student should be able to think out the answers himself, but it is permissible to refer to the end of the book a little earlier than with the first type of question. These answers should be used to amplify notes.

Thirdly, numerous diagrams are included. Not only do these assist learning by the impact of the visual impression, but they are a neat form of expressing relationships. It is a useful exercise for the student himself to construct other diagrams.

Fourthly, the text is divided into headings and, wherever possible, points are placed under subheadings and enumerated. This assists reading and note-taking.

Although the book provides a complete course, certain sections, especially those describing economic institutions, are given in summary form. Some amplification is provided through the questions, but where the student requires further help he is referred to my *Elementary Economics*. On the other hand, a few sections and questions are 'starred' and the student should not worry if he does not fully understand them at the first attempt. They can be omitted for a later reading.

The student is advised to use the book as follows:

1 Read through the whole book quickly.
2 Return to the beginning and study each chapter carefully. Write notes in the margin and underline important points of the text.
3 Answer the questions at the end of the chapter; check answers with those given.
4 Write concise notes covering the chapter material, incorporating examples from the answers to the questions. Tabulate points wherever possible. Such notes will consolidate your understanding, give precision to ideas, and prove invaluable for examination revision. Some practice should also be had in answering the type of question set by the appropriate examining body.

To those critics who may complain that I oversimplify and thus tend towards error, I make little concession. In London I am often asked by a stranger the best way to get to a certain place. The exact answer would be to describe the short cuts which I, a Londoner, would use. In all probability the enquirer would be so confused that, as soon as I was out of sight, he would consult somebody else. So my directions are more likely to be: 'Follow this road to the fourth set of traffic lights, and then ask again'. This is the policy I have adopted for persons starting a study of economics.

It is impossible to thank all who have contributed to this book – firms, nationalised industries, government departments, etc. All have been most helpful when I have sought information. To some persons, however, I am particularly indebted. Mr M. K. Johnson, Lecturer in Economics, Hatfield Polytechnic, has provided many of the questions. The boys of St Clement Danes have proved enthusiastic 'guinea-pigs' for testing purposes, indicating on numerous occasions how the text could be made clearer and the questions and answers improved. My wife has willingly accepted the privations which the writing of this book has entailed. And to my mother and father I owe a special debt. They applied the principle of the division of labour – doing the humdrum chores while I studied.

Preface to the Fifth Edition

This new edition goes much further than bringing facts up to date and revising the text to cover recent changes in institutions, the development of economic theory and the evolution of government policy.

The decision to reset has provided the opportunity to change the whole approach. After an examination of the role of economics and the two main methods, the market economy and the command economy, of organising production, the book concentrates on the market economy and the part that the government can play in improving the way in which it works.

I feel little need to apologise for this 'normative' stance, particularly at a time when 'command' economies are collapsing throughout the world as it has become evident that, in comparison with market economies, they have failed to 'deliver the goods'.

The market economy faces two broad criticisms: (1) it is motivated by self-interest or, expressed in a more extreme form, 'greed'; (2) its attributed efficiency, working through Adam Smith's 'hidden hand', is based on false assumptions.

Admittedly the first is an unattractive feature of the market economy, but in mitigation it does provide a simple motivational objective as opposed to such nebulous alternatives as 'social responsibility' or 'the public good' where everybody's business becomes nobody's business, and where stagnation or even decline can replace the innovation, ingenuity and risk-taking of private enterprise.

The second, market failure, can be identified. Instead of amputating the 'hidden hand', we can direct it. This is the theme of this new edition. Basic economic theory is retained. In examining policies there is nothing so practical as sound theory: it gives coherence in organising thought and provides a means of testing arguments.

This theory is then applied to the various causes of market failure and thus the possible solutions to the major economic problems of the day: the role of the State in the allocation of resources, privatisation policy, monopoly, the activities of trade unions, paying for state-provided goods and services, pollution, conservation, and government action to achieve full employment, price stability, a balanced regional development, a healthy balance of payments, the European Community, the Single Market, the European Monetary System and aid for less developed countries.

An examination of the above topics involves applying recent developments in economic theory and techniques. Thus the student is introduced to elementary 'welfare economics', cost–benefit analysis, criticisms of Keynes, the view of the monetarists, aggregate demand and aggregate supply analysis, supply-side economics and the relationship between expectations of wage bargainers and inflation.

Although government policy and institutions are dealt with in the context of the UK, overseas students should have little difficulty in applying the principles developed to the particular conditions of their own country.

As there are so many excellent workbooks and multiple choice and data-response question-books available, questions at the end of each chapter have been omitted and the space saved devoted to enlarging the text.

Suggested additional reading has also been omitted for the book aims at being a complete text for the targetted level. However the reader who is interested in further study of the application of theory to the British economy is recommended to read *Understanding the UK Economy*, ed. Peter Curwen (Macmillan Education 1990).

Part I

Introduction

1   What Economics is About

1.1   The Economic Problem

Wants and Limited Means

One day a neighbour saw Abraham Lincoln walking down the road with his two sons, both crying. 'What's the matter with the boys?' asked a neighbour. 'Just what is the matter with the whole world', replied Lincoln. 'I have three walnuts – and each boy wants two.'

    That story puts in a 'nutshell' why we have a branch of study which we term 'economics'. For it underlines a salient fact concerning our everyday life – in comparison with all the things we want, our means of satisfying those wants are quite inadequate. Just think of the things that you would like to buy if only you had more money – more meat for dinner, new clothes, a radio, a better house, a car, a video recorder, a yacht. The list has no end. We have to 'cut our coat according to our cloth'.

The Problem of Choice

This then is the problem: unlimited wants, very limited means. Nor can we completely overcome the difficulty. But we can ease the situation by making the most of what we have. In other words, we *economise*.

    In order to see more clearly what is meant by 'economising', we can study the spending decisions of a housewife. Indeed, this illustration is more appropriate than it may seem at first sight, for 'economics' is derived from a Greek word meaning 'the management of a household'.

    Our housewife's task is to make her fixed housekeeping allowance 'go as far as possible'; in other words, from limited resources she seeks to obtain the maximum satisfaction for the family. Certain goods – those she regards as necessities, such as bread, milk, tea and butter – are purchased in regular quantities almost by habit; but this does not mean that she would

3

not vary her spending on them were there to be any significant change in their prices. Nevertheless, what really lies behind her spending decisions can best be seen if we concentrate on those goods to which she gives frequent consideration. As our housewife walks past the shop windows in the high street, a hundred and one different goods compete for the money in her purse. Should she buy beef or chicken for the Sunday dinner? Peas would be nice – but they are still so dear that cabbage will have to do for one more week. But how everybody would love new potatoes? And they've gone down 2p a pound since last week! Yes, she will buy new potatoes instead of old. And so our capable housewife goes on, comparing the prices of different goods and asking herself whether the pleasure her family will obtain from them will be worth their cost – the inroads they make on her limited housekeeping allowance.

Others, too, have to economise – the schoolboy in spending his pocket money, and the businessman in running his factory. Should he produce this good or that, or some of both? Should he employ extra labourers or would it be better to install a machine to do the work? And so on.

Even Shakespeare draws attention to it:

> When we mean to build,
> We first survey the plot, then draw the model;
> And when we see the figure of the house,
> Then must we rate the cost of the erection;
> Which, if we find outweighs ability,
> What do we then but draw anew the model
> In fewer offices, or at least desist
> To build at all? (Lord Bardolph, Henry IV, Part II,
> Act 1, Scene iii)

And so with the government. Turn to the newspaper any morning, and it soon becomes obvious how often the government is forced to choose. More offices, new schools, and better hospitals – all are competing for the materials and capital used by the construction industry. Extra houses, new roads, and conservation areas – all are claiming a share of the limited land available.

Opportunity Cost

Thus we see that economics is really concerned with the problem of choice – the decisions forced upon us by the smallness of our resources compared with our wants (Figure 1.1). And, as we choose, so we have to sacrifice. If the newspaper boy spends his Christmas tips on a bicycle, then it is likely that he will have to go without the air rifle that he also wanted. In deciding to work overtime on a Saturday afternoon, a worker forgoes leisure time

FIGURE 1.1
The Economic Problem

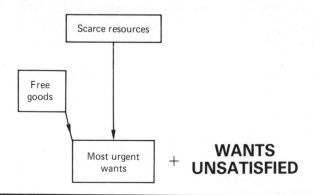

and the football match he would otherwise have watched. When the farmer sows a field with wheat, he accepts that he loses the barley it could have grown. And so with the nation. If extra materials and capital are required to accelerate the building of houses, roads and hospitals, then there will be less left for producing offices, power stations, sport centres, and so on. In all walks of life, having 'this' means going without 'that'. We therefore speak of 'opportunity cost' – the cost of something in terms of alternatives forgone (more accurately, in terms of the *best* alternative sacrificed).

In practice, economising is not so much a complete rejection of one good in favour of another, but rather deciding whether to have a little bit more of one and not quite so much of another. It is principally, as we shall see in Chapter 6, an adjustment at the margin.

'Free' and 'Scarce' Goods

Few goods are so plentiful that nobody will give anything for them. Air, perhaps, is one of the few exceptions. Occasionally, too, there is such an abundant apple harvest that a farmer says 'help yourself'. Such goods are termed 'free' goods. Usually, goods are 'scarce' – they can be obtained only by going without something else. With such goods we have to economise, and so they are often referred to as 'economic goods'. It is worth noting, however, that over time there is no hard and fast dividing-line between economic and non-economic goods. Desert wastes can be transformed into agricultural land by irrigation; coal-mines are left derelict as new fuels are developed. Scarcity is relative to demand.

In future when we speak of 'goods' we shall be referring to economic goods, including, without further distinction, both commodities and services.

The Production-possibility Curve

We can illustrate the economic problem as follows. Suppose that country X produces only agricultural produce and manufactured goods and that it can, with all its resources fully employed, produce during a year the following alternative combinations (in unspecified units).

Agricultural produce	+	Manufactured goods
100		0
80		25
60		40
40		45
20		48
0		50

By plotting these alternative combinations we obtain a 'production-possibility curve' (Figure 1.2). This shows the various combinations of agricultural produce and manufactured goods open to country X with its limited resources and given technology.

The table shows that, with its limited resources, country X can produce either 100 agricultural produce or fifty manufactured goods, or a combination of both. Any larger output is outside the curve and unattainable.

Nevertheless, as resources are transferred to manufacturing from agriculture, an ever increasing quantity of manufactured goods has to be given

---

FIGURE 1.2
A Production-possibility Curve

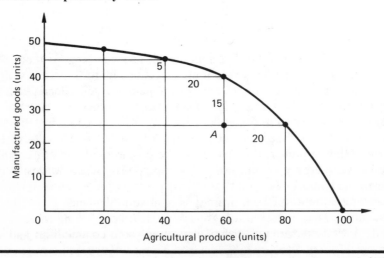

up to obtain an extra twenty units of agricultural produce. For instance, when twenty agricultural produce are produced, the opportunity cost of an extra twenty is only five manufactured goods, whereas when production is sixty agricultural produce the opportunity cost of a further twenty is fifteen manufactured goods.

The reason is that resources are not equally suited to producing agricultural produce and manufactured goods. For instance, factory workers would need training in farm work, while land, tractors, etc. would have to be worked more intensively. The result is that the production-possibility curve is concave to the origin.

1.2 The Scope of Economics

Definition of Economics

Scarcity forces us to economise. We weigh up the various alternatives and select that particular assortment of goods which yields the highest return from our limited resources. Modern economists use this idea to define the scope of their studies. But since there is no definition which is completely satisfactory, we keep ours as simple as possible. *Economics is the study of how people allocate their limited resources to provide for their wants*.

Amplification

Because economics studies how *people act,* it is a social science. As we shall see, this puts it at a disadvantage compared with the physical sciences which examine various aspects of man's environment.

But, although economics is closely connected with such social sciences as ethics, politics, sociology, psychology and anthropology, it is distinguished from them by its concentration on one particular aspect of human behaviour – choosing between alternatives in order to obtain the maximum satisfaction from limited resources. This modern, narrower approach is an improvement on Professor Alfred Marshall's definition – 'a study of mankind in the ordinary business of life' – because this, as it stands, would embrace all forms of human activity.

In effect, the economist limits the study by selecting four fundamental characteristics of human existence and investigating what happens when they are all found together, as they usually are. First, the ends of human beings are without limit. Second, those ends are of varying importance. Third, the means available for achieving those ends – human time and energy and material resources – are limited. Fourth, the means can be used in many different ways: that is, they can produce many different goods.

But no one characteristic *by itself* is necessarily of interest to the economist. If, for instance, you have two wants and you cannot choose between them, you are between the devil and the deep blue sea, and you will never get as far as the problem of allocating resources between them. Similarly, 'free' goods are of no interest to the economist since resources do not have to be allocated to obtain them. Nor is the mere scarcity of means necessarily of significance. Where resources can be used only in one way, e.g. lichen-bearing volcanic land in Iceland for rearing sheep, they do not, although scarce, have to be 'economised'. Using such land for sheep does not mean that the owner has less of other things. Its use therefore gives rise to no problems, and the economist is interested only in the relatively minor point of determining the earnings of such land. Only when all four characteristics are found together does an economic problem arise.

The Difficulties

But, in pursuing such studies, economists face two major difficulties:

1. Economists Cannot Experiment

The task of a science is to formulate laws describing what will happen when there is a change in a given set of circumstances. The physicist and chemist can conduct their investigations by experimenting under controlled conditions in a laboratory. But because economists are dealing with human behaviour rather than with physical properties, their laboratory, it has been said, is the real world.

(*a*)   Since facts concerning people are difficult to ascertain, they can never be quite sure of the initial position.

(*b*)   It is impossible to isolate a group of consumers or business people in a test-tube to see how they would react to a given change. The most the economist can usually do as regards consumers' behaviour, for instance, is to take a sample survey which will suggest how groups as a whole will behave.

(*c*)   The economy is subject to continuous change, and so conditions cannot be held constant while the effect of one particular measure is observed.

(*d*)   Because the economy is so complex, no body of economists could follow through all the results of any given change.

(*e*)   Any measurements are only approximate, and even so take time to collect.

Because of these difficulties, economists can only be approximate in their investigations in real life. Nevertheless, the information available is increasing and becoming more precise, e.g. through market research and government statistical enquiries. Thus economists' predictions are likely to gain in accuracy.

2. Economists Cannot Directly Measure Welfare

Since satisfaction, like love or pain, is personal to the individual, there is no absolute scale for measuring welfare. So the economist, using the best approximation, works on the principle that, because two loaves are better than one, an increase in goods represents an increase in welfare.

Even so, he cannot measure all goods. If he gives a value to the vegetables grown in gardens or to do-it-yourself repairs to cars, should he not logically include also something for housewives' cleaning and cooking services? Because it is impossible to know where to draw the line, the economist simplifies matters by confining attention to those goods which are exchanged against money (see p. 388). Since all these have a 'price' it is possible to make use of exact measurement and total dissimilar goods in terms of the common standard.

Nevertheless, the economist must be careful to include any costs or benefits which are not allowed for by an individual in making a decision. Or, if the project is so large that it is likely to have external effects elsewhere, for example the proposed third London airport, a cost–benefit analysis may have to be used to cover these full effects (see Chapter 18). Moreover, since the economist can only quantify in terms of money, some costs and benefits which are not exchanged directly in a market, e.g. environmental costs and benefits, have to be given 'shadow prices'.

Positive and Normative Economics

Consider how the particulars of different estate agents describe the same room: the first, 'the living room is 4.5 metres by 3.5 metres', the second, 'the living room is deceptively spacious'. One can be verified by measuring; the other is a matter for the eye of the beholder. This leads us to the distinction between positive and normative economics.

Positive economics limits itself to statements that can be verified by reference to the facts. Thus the observation that 'the UK's real national income in 1990 was larger than in 1989' is a positive statement. In other words, positive economics holds that any hypothesis formulated should be testable against empirical evidence.

Normative economics, on the other hand, appreciates that in practice many economic decisions involve subjective judgements; that is, they cannot be made solely by an objective appraisal of the facts but depend to some extent on personal views in interpreting facts. Thus the statement that 'the UK's national income in 1990 should have been larger than it was' is a normative statement. As soon as we introduce the words 'should' or 'ought' we are making subjective valuations, that is normative statements.

Because in practice the distinction between positive economics and normative economics is often blurred, opinion is divided about the exact scope of economics, and so it is instructive to examine their nature in more detail.

1.3 Positive Economics

Positive economics considers that economics can claim to be a science only if it is strictly scientific in its approach, eschewing normative judgements and adopting scientific methods.

First, it does not attempt to set out criteria for determining what is good or bad, what ought or what ought not to be – any more than physics attempts to say that liquids are 'better' than solids. It is concerned only with positive statements and with the consequences of certain actions. That is why, for instance, the economist must accept ends as given, expressing no opinion as to whether those ends are 'good' or 'bad'. On the other hand, he must point out that individual ends have economic implications for society as a whole. A man, for instance, may decide that he wants to get drunk every day. Here the economist must point out the full cost of this end – the cost to the man of getting drunk, plus the cost to society if he eventually becomes a charge on the National Health Service as an alcoholic.

Nor is the economist concerned directly about the physical aspects of the limited means – the mechanical principles of the plough, the chemical properties of the soil or the biological characteristics of the seed. Both ends and resources are accepted as given. The subject of study is how men mobilise these resources to achieve their ends and how efficient are the methods which they choose.

Second, economics science has a particular object in view – the establishment of principles, propositions, theories or generalisations stating the relationship of one thing to another. In this it goes beyond *descriptive economics*, which concentrates on a mere description of an economy – its institutions (firms, banks, government organisations, etc.), its population, its system of taxation, and so on. But studies ended there could hardly be termed 'scientific'. While descriptive economics is desirable, indeed necessary, it merely describes the mechanism. What we really want to know is how the mechanism operates.

That is the task of *analytical economics*, which sets out to establish general principles about the way in which an economic system works. In discovering these principles, economics makes use of the methods of other sciences. These methods are: (1) induction, (2) deduction.

1. Induction

In the inductive approach, the economist observes facts, classifies those facts, and then tries to observe any causal relationship between them. For instance, he may discover that the price of eggs falls in the spring. This would be connected with the increase in the supply of eggs at that time of the year, and from this a generalisation can be established that an increase in supply, other things being equal, leads to a fall in price.

The weakness of the inductive approach is that the scientist can never be sure that the principles established are 100 per cent foolproof. Hence, whenever possible, he will try to substantiate by deduction what has been discovered by induction.

2. Deduction

With deduction, the economist starts from hypothetical assumptions (frequently referred to as postulates). Then, by a process of logical reasoning, he derives propositions from these assumptions. This is often termed 'model-building'. The sequence is as follows:

(*a*) The economic phenomenon to be explained is selected. Of course, if the analysis is to be useful, the problem must be of practical significance.

(*b*) The initial assumptions are made. These should be as close to reality as possible. But, although he is concerned with human behaviour, realistic assumptions are not impossible. In the main he is interested in market, not individual, reactions. Dealing in large numbers means that patterns of behaviour emerge, and it is possible to think in terms of an 'average economic man'. Thus it is quite reasonable to assume that, in disposing of his income, this average consumer will act rationally, seeking to obtain maximum satisfaction from it.

Of course, the economist has to simplify initially, confining himself to broad assumptions from which he can obtain only broad generalisations. Later, the assumptions can be changed according to particular circumstances, and the conclusions modified accordingly.

(*c*) Logical reasoning establishes what follows from the assumptions. Let us take a simple example. The economist wishes to discover what price will prevail in a market. He makes three assumptions:

(i) a high degree of competition, on the basis of price, among buyers and among sellers, and between buyers and sellers;

(ii) more will be demanded the lower the price;

(iii) more will be supplied the higher the price.

Demand and supply thus move in opposite directions for a given change in price. The conclusion he comes to is that the price of the good will settle where the amount supplied equals the amount demanded. Any other price will not be a settled price. If it is above, there will be more offered for sale than is demanded. Stocks will pile up, and some suppliers will lower their prices. As the price falls, so more will be demanded, and this will go on until demand equals supply. Similarly, when the price is below that where demand equals supply, shortages lead buyers to offer higher prices. As the price rises, so more will be supplied, and this goes on until demand equals supply (see p. 58). He has thus built up a model showing how price is determined in a market – a very useful piece of economic theory.

By modifying the assumptions he can make the model closer to real life or show how changes in the economic system work. For instance, suppose that, as a result of an advertising campaign, people's tastes change, so that they want more of the good at the market price than formerly. At the original price, demand now exceeds supply. As before, this will cause the price to rise and supply to expand until a new price is arrived at where once more demand and supply are equal.

(*d*) As far as possible, propositions derived by deduction are tested by observed data. Often, however, such tests will prove impracticable, if not impossible, to undertake. For instance, the economist may be predicting outcomes which have no past parallels; he has therefore to await events before he can test the validity of his propositions.

If the principles established are not disproved by such testing, they can be used to predict what will happen in particular instances, for they show how the different parts of a system are related to one another. It should be noted, however, that such forecasts are not unconditional statements of what will occur. The nature of an economic proposition is simply of the form 'if this occurs, then such and such will result'. For example, if demand increases then, other things being equal, price will rise (see p. 59). When we apply general principles to particular cases, we are in the realm of what is often called *applied economics*.

It is this power to predict which enables firms and governments to plan with some degree of accuracy. The theory of price, for instance, would enable a building firm to make a useful forecast of the effect of an increase in the demand for houses on bricklayers' wages. Or, if there were widespread unemployment in the economy, a knowledge of the principles determining the level of activity could suggest appropriate measures which the government might take to reduce it.

1.4 Normative Economics

Normative economics, or 'political economy' as economics was originally called, accepts the analytical methods of positive economics in formulating theories. But it considers that the rigid scientific stance adopted is defective in two main ways.

First, it holds that it is virtually impossible to avoid value judgements. For instance, since facts have to be used to test hypotheses, the *selection* of those facts depends on the judgement of the economist who may unwillingly let his individual bias creep in. Again, in holding that the preferences and ends of individuals in a society are the ones which count, it overlooks that the State may have different ends. Thus the State may ban certain drugs because their abuse can result in ill-health and crime, incurring costs to society. But which drugs are banned involves a value judgement by the State. Finally, in evaluating growth over a period, the economist holds that 'more is better'. However, this view is based only on a consensus opinion, and is thus a value judgement. In any case, even though there may have been an increase in income per head of the population over time, we have no *objective measure* of welfare to assess whether people are obtaining more satisfaction (see p. 9).

Second, and more fundamental, economics is rather sterile if not applied to policy objectives. Positive economics, by restricting itself simply to predicting all the relevant consequences of alternative policies, ends up by 'sitting on the fence'. In contrast, the earlier economists have pursued their studies chiefly because of the social benefits which can result. 'The compelling motive that leads men to economic study is seldom a mere academic or scientific interest in the movements of the great wheel of wealth. It is rather the sense that, in the world of business and of labour, justice stands with biased scales; that the lives of the many are darker than they need be. In these things lies the impulse to economic investigations.' (Professor A. C. Pigou: *Unemployment*, 1913).

Thus the normative economist, while still seeking to solve problems as scientifically as possible by following the techniques of the positive economist, applies the results to suggest the course of action which appears to be economically more efficient than the others. In doing so, he enters the region of value judgements.

It means also that, because economics studies human behaviour, it is a social science. Thus the economist's judgement is enhanced by taking into account the findings of other social sciences. For instance, most people would consider that the economist should have something to say on the question, 'Should income tax be made more progressive?' But the reply would have to be along the following lines: 'The tax yield would almost certainly increase; but higher-income groups might not work so hard. While I can suggest theoretical reasons for this, you should also consider what the psychologist has to say. Furthermore, the pattern of consumption may change as the rich have less income to spend. For possible social effects, consult the sociologist. Finally, it will also help in making incomes more equal. That concerns me in that it may increase the proportion of total income spent – but ethics and politics have most weight in deciding whether greater equality of incomes is desirable.'

1.5 Conclusions

Why economists disagree

The foregoing discussion throws light on the reasons why economists appear to disagree so often. Take the statement, 'Britain must remain in the European Community (EC) because it leads to a faster rate of economic growth.' Why might economists disagree on this?

First, they may not agree on the facts. Can we be certain that Britain's rate of economic growth has accelerated since she joined the EC? Facts are deficient; for example, calculations of Gross National Product (GNP) over time are not unambiguous (see pp. 396–8).

Second, they may disagree on the causal connection. Even if a faster rate of economic growth has been achieved since joining the EC, can we be sure that membership is the cause of this increase? There may be more than one explanation, e.g. the discovery of North Sea oil or increased capital investment in agriculture and industry. It may be difficult to decide which explanation fits the facts best.

Third, the statement really rests on a value judgement – that economic growth is a good thing. Some economists might consider that other objectives – more leisure, less worry, the avoidance of friction through competition, and so on – are in a fairly affluent society more desirable.

Fourth, they may unconsciously let individual bias creep into their analysis and interpretation of the facts. While, as scientists, economists try to be as objective as possible, they are often examining subjects upon which they have strong personal feelings. Thus an economist who is an ardent supporter of Anglo–American relationships may unconsciously fail to give full weight to evidence supporting an increase in the growth rate of the EC countries.

The Economist as a Consultant

Such imperfections do not mean that the economist is without value. If, for instance, he is employed in a business enterprise, the scope of his work is fairly well defined – to promote the success of the business in terms of profits. As regards government policy, however, the advice the economist can give may be less definite. In any case, the final decision will usually rest on the judgement of the politician. A government is seldom faced with a simple choice, since ends are usually a compromise between alternatives. The first task of the economist is to point out any inconsistency between aims. For instance, the aim of economic expansion could conflict with the aim of balance-of-payments equilbrium.

In any case, the economist can indicate the full implications of a particular policy. For example, if a very high level of employment is the aim, then he should point out that this could make it more difficult to maintain a steady price level.

Finally, he may be able to recommend more economic ways of achieving a given end. This is possible because, although ends may be given, there are economic and non-economic means of achieving those ends. Is it better perhaps to obtain food supplies by importing from abroad or by home production?

For his part, the economist tries to be as objective as possible, establishing principles which, given certain conditions, show how the economy works and how it can be made to work better in real life. Furthermore, the principles can be applied to specific problems. Decision-makers may brush these principles to one side, either because facts necessary for a complete answer are not available or because different weight is given to assumptions. But at least economics provides a reminder of where objectivity ends and subjectivity begins.

2 Methods of Allocating Resources

2.1 Functions of an Economic System

The Conditions of Economic Efficiency

We respond to the economic problem by 'economising'. This means that we have to:

(a) Ascertain what assortment of goods will yield the greatest satisfaction having regard to our limited resources.
(b) Employ those resources as efficiently as possible.

This involves: (i) relating production to the particular assortment chosen; (ii) combining resources in the right proportions; (iii) organising production so that the desired quantity of each type of good is produced with the least cost in scarce resources, e.g. by applying division of labour, considering large-scale production, carefully choosing the location of operations; and (iv) avoiding unemployment of resources.

In terms of Figure 1.2, maximum economic efficiency in the use of scarce resources is achieved when output is at that point on the production possibility curve which reflects the demand for agricultural produce relative to the demand for manufactured goods. If production is technically inefficient or if there is unemployment, production will fall short of the production possibility curve, for example at A.

The Role of the Economic System

In primitive economies, the individual uses his resources directly to provide what he wants. Thus Robinson Crusoe had to decide how much time to spend hunting, fishing, growing corn and relaxing in the sun according to the strength of his preferences for meat, fish, bread and leisure. Similarly, in a subsistence economy the farmer's output is mainly for his own family's needs.

Today, however, decisions as to what shall be produced are linked only indirectly with the actual consumer. Man now specialises in production, obtaining the variety of goods he wants by exchange. Thus answers have to be provided to a multitude of questions. How much wheat shall the farmer grow? How much shall be milled each day? How many leaves shall the baker bake? Thus if the greatest possible satisfaction is to be obtained from limited resources, there must be a link between producers and consumers.

Put briefly, the following questions have to be answered:

  (i) *What* goods and services shall firms produce?
 (ii) *How much* of each good and service shall be produced?
(iii) *How* shall the goods and services be produced?
(iv) How shall products be *divided* between households?

To solve these problems we need some form of economic system.

Broadly speaking, any economic system consists of two parts:

(a) *Firms* – the business organisations which decide what goods and services to produce and who to bring together the different resources required.
(b) *Households* – which consume the goods and services and supply the resources, such as labour, to produce them.

In short, the economic system provides the link between firms and households (Figure 2.1).

Different Forms of Economic System

Man's first exchanges were quite simple: there was a direct swap of one good for another – a 'market' was established (see p. 46). Eventually a 'go-between' – money – was developed, allowing goods to be 'priced' and sold more easily. The subsistence economy had now evolved into the *market economy*, where answers to the above questions follow from people's decisions in the market.

FIGURE 2.1
The Flow of Goods and Resources in an Economic System

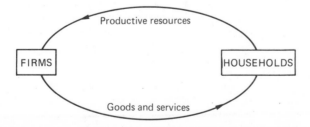

In contrast to the market economy, there is the *command* or *centrally directed economy*, where the State decides what to produce and directs the factors of production accordingly. Furthermore, what is produced is distributed according to the decisions of the central body, the emphasis being 'to each according to his need' rather than on financial ability to pay.

Our task now is to examine in turn the respective strengths of these two systems.

2.2 The Market Economy

Outline of the Market Mechanism

In the market economy, emphasis is laid on the freedom of the individual, both as a consumer and as the owner of resources.

As a consumer he expresses his choice of goods through the price he is willing to pay for them. As the owner of resources used in production (usually his own labour) he seeks to obtain as large a reward as possible. If consumers want more of the goods than is being supplied at the current price, this is indicated by their 'bidding-up' the price. This increases the profits of firms and the earnings of factors producing that good. As a result, resources are attracted into the industry, and supply expands in accordance with consumers' wishes. On the other hand, if consumers do not want a particular good, its price falls, producers make a loss, and resources leave the industry.

Prices therefore indicate the wishes of consumers and allocate the community's productive resources accordingly (Figure 2.2). There is no direction of labour; people are free to work wherever they choose.

FIGURE 2.2
The Allocation of Products and Resources through the Market Economy

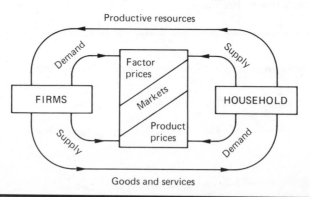

Efficiency is achieved through the profit motive: owners of factors of production sell them at the highest possible price, while firms keep prodution costs as low as they can in order to obtain the highest profit margin.

Furthermore, factor earnings decide who is to receive the goods produced. If firms produce better goods or improve efficiency, or if workers make a greater effort, they receive a higher reward, giving them more spending power to obtain goods in the market.

In this way the *price system* acts, as it were, like a marvellous computer, registering people's preferences for different goods, transmitting those preferences to firms, moving resources to produce the goods, and deciding who shall obtain the final products. Thus, through the motivation of individual self-interest, the four problems inherent in economising are solved automatically.

Defects of the Market Economy

In practice the market economy does not work quite so smoothly as this. Nor are its results entirely satisfactory. We speak of 'market failure'.

First, some vital *community goods*, such as defence, police, justice and national parks, cannot be adequately provided through the market. This is mainly because it would be impossible to charge a price since 'free-riders' cannot be excluded (see p. 311).

Second, the *competition* upon which the efficiency of the market economy depends *may break down* (see p. 181).

Third, in practice the price mechanism may through *imperfect knowledge* or *immobility of factors of production,* function sluggishly (see pp. 220, 302). As a result supply is slow to respond to changes in demand.

Fourth, the private-profit motive does not always ensure that *public* well-being (as distinct from the sum total of *private* wealth) will be maximised. There may be *social benefits or costs* (often referred to as *spillovers* or *externalities* (see chapter 18).

Fifth, the market economy, where individuals decide what to produce, is subject to instability in the overall level of activity and in the rate of growth, with resources remaining *unemployed* because firms as a whole consider that profit prospects are low (see Chapter 28).

Sixth, *competition itself may sometimes lead to inefficiency*. Duplication of research and competitive advertising may waste resources. Uncertainty as to rivals' plans may hold back investment.

Seventh, *consumers' choice may be distorted* by persuasive advertising, sometimes of goods injurious to health, e.g. cigarettes.

Lastly, the consumers with the most money have the greatest pull in the market. As a result, resources may be devoted to producing luxuries for the rich to the exclusion of necessities for the poor. While this is really brought about by the unequal distribution of wealth and income rather than by the market system, the fact is that the latter tends to produce, and even accentuate, such inequality.

2.3 The Command Economy

Central Decision-making

With the command economy, the decisions regarding what? how much? how? and for whom? are taken by an all-powerful planning authority. It estimates the assortment of goods which it considers people want and directs resources accordingly. It also decides how the goods produced shall be distributed among the community. Thus economic efficiency largely depends upon how accurately wants are estimated and resources allocated.

Merits of the Command Economy

The merits of the command economy correspond closely to the defects of the market economy. The central planning authority can: (i) ensure that adequate resources are devoted to community and other goods; (ii) use its monopoly powers in the interests of the community, e.g. by securing the advantages of large-scale production, rather than make maximum profits by restricting output; (iii) introduce more certainty into production by dovetailing plans and improving mobility by direction of resources, even of labour; (iv) allow for external costs and benefits when deciding what and how much to produce; (v) employ workers in order to keep them occupied

FIGURE 2.3
The Allocation of Resources and Products through a Command Economy

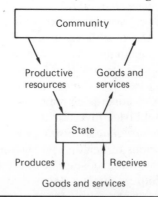

although to do so may be unprofitable in the narrow sense; (vi) eliminate the inefficiencies resulting from competition; (vii) use advertising to inform rather than simply to persuade or brainwash; (viii) allow for the uneven distribution of wealth when planning what to produce and in rewarding the producers.

Defects of the Command Economy

Nevertheless, the command economy has inherent defects which lay it open to criticism on both economic and political grounds.

First, estimating the satisfaction derived by individuals from consuming different goods is impossible – although some help can be obtained by introducing a pricing system through markets, changes in prices signalling changes in wants. Often, however, prices are controlled, supplies rationed or queues form for limited stocks.

Second, many officials are required to estimate wants and to direct resources. In as much as such officials are not needed in a market economy they represent wasted factors of production. Moreover, the use of officials may lead to bureaucracy – excessive form-filling, 'red tape', slowness in coming to decisions and an impersonal approach to consumers. At times, too, officialdom has been accompanied by corruption.

Third, even when wants have been decided upon, difficulties of coordination arise. On the one hand, wants have to be dovetailed and awarded priorities. On the other, factors have to be combined in the best proportions. Usually plans are coordinated through numerous committees, directed at the top by a central planning committee. Yet members of this committee tend to be primarily politicians with little experience of administration, especially in coping with the difficulties of managing a large organisation (see p. 121).

Fourth, it is argued that state ownership of resources, by reducing personal incentives, diminishes effort and initiative. Direction of labour may mean that people are dissatisfied with their jobs; officials may play for safety in their policies (see p. 314). Thus production may be less than under private enterprise.

Fifth, and probably most important, there always exists the danger that the State will make it easier to pursue economic objectives by restricting freedom of action, e.g. peasant farms are collectivised, or even by reducing or stifling political expression, e.g. by setting up a one-party system. Individuals would then exist for the State, and not the State for the individual. Thus the ultimate choice between a market economy and a command economy (in their extreme forms) really hinges on whether people prefer to run the risk of dictatorship or to accept the defects of the market economy which allows them to choose their own jobs.

2.4 The Mixed Economy

The 'Middle Way'

Fortunately, a community does not have to make a complete choice between these two extremes. Instead it can compromise, allowing the State, to act, not as a dictator, but more like a wise parent who gives children much personal freedom but plans ahead to avoid many of the pitfalls into which they may stumble.

Thus, in an attempt to get the best of both worlds, the UK has a 'mixed economy' in which three-quarters of production is carried out by private enterprise through the market (though subject to varying degrees of government control), while for the other quarter the government is directly responsible through the public sector. Moreover, chiefly by income redistribution and subsidies, the government influences the allocation of the goods and services produced.

Summary of the Objectives of Government Economic Policy

The objectives of government economic policy in the UK fall into three broad categories: allocation of resources, stabilisation of the economy and redistribution of wealth and income.

The government may influence the allocation of resources by producing goods and services itself. This occurs when they would not be provided adequately by the private sector, as with community goods, or when they can be produced more efficiently by the State, as with certain nationalised industries, e.g. postal services and activities of local authorities, such as the provision of roads and libraries.

But other defects of the market mechanism are often dealt with by influencing the operation of the price system either by physical controls or by market intervention. The most rigid form of physical control is legislation. For example, pornographic literature (and certain drugs) must not be sold freely, and certain forms of cigarette advertising are forbidden. Controls can be flexible, however, when they are administered by the authorities under general powers conferred by Act of Parliament. Thus under the Town and Country Planning Acts local authorities exercise planning functions which take into consideration the external costs and benefits of various uses of land and of the erection of buildings. As we shall see, other direct controls operate over certain prices, proposed mergers of firms and foreign trade.

Alternatively, the government can avoid the rigidity of physical controls by intervening in the market itself. Thus it can adjust its own demand and supply to affect the price, as with agriculture (p. 66), Treasury bills (p. 375) and foreign exchange rates (p. 544). It may also influence demand, supply and price by indirect taxes and subsidies.

While such intervention is best discussed in terms of the specific topics concerned, other government policy is more in the nature of overall control to achieve stability in the economy, and is therefore considered separately. Thus Chapters 26–34 cover full employment, price stability, regional development, economic growth, international trade and the redistribution of income.

Since satisfaction cannot be measured objectively, the economist cannot analyse fully the effects of government redistribution policy on welfare. Such redistribution is carried out directly by government taxation and expenditure, and indirectly by intervening in the free operation of the price system, e.g. rent control and pressure on building societies to keep mortgage interest rates low. What the economist has to point out is how such redistributive measures may affect economic efficiency. The politician can then weigh the balance of advantage.

Politically, some people would like more government control, and others less. This book tries to avoid taking sides. It simply explains how the price mechanism operates, where the defects occur, and what the government can do to avoid or to mitigate the results of such defects.

The Private and Public Sectors

In examining how a mixed economy works, it is convenient to distinguish between the 'private sector' and the 'public sector'. The former consists of those firms which are privately owned. Here decisions are taken in response to market signals. The latter includes government departments, local authorities, the nationalised industries, and public bodies such as the Property Services Agency. All are distinguished by the fact that their capital is publicly owned and their policies can be influenced through the ultimate supply of funds by the government. Thus the existence of the public sector enables the government to exercise an important measure of control over the economy. Moreover, decisions on what to produce can be based on need rather than demand (see p. 325).

2.5   Micro-and Macroeconomics

Microeconomics

A study of the price system is largely concerned with:

(1) how the supply of a particular good or service is related to the demand for it;

(2) how the demand for a particular factor of production is related to its supply.

As we shall see, this relationship of demand to supply is based upon prices established in the different product and factor markets (Figure 2.2). Since it is largely a study of the decisions of individual consumers and of individual firms in particular markets – small parts of the economy – it is usually referred to as microeconomics (from the Greek word (*mikros* meaning 'small'). Thus if we ask ourselves what forces determine the price of potatoes, the rent of an acre of land in London, or the wage of a Nottingham bus driver, we are dealing with microeconomic questions.

Macroeconomics

However, in addition to studying how resources are allocated to different uses, we have to consider the level at which resources *as a whole* are being employed; that is, the overall level of activity. This gives rise to a series of 'general' questions. How can the total of consumers' demand in the economy change? How do firms in total respond to such a change in demand? What brings about changes in the general level of prices? We are now looking at variables in the aggregate – the aggregate flow of income, aggregate investment, aggregate wages, and so on. Such questions are the concern of macroeconomics (from the Greek word *makros* meaning 'large').

The difference in approach in the construction of models for micro- and macroeconomics is described in Chapter 26.

3 The Population as Consumers and Producers

3.1 Growth of Population

Changes in Population Size

The people of a country are its consumers. They also provide the labour force for production. A study of the population of the UK, therefore, will give us a bird's-eye view of the community for which the economic system must provide, and also of the size and nature of the available labour force.

At any one time the structure of the population is largely the result of demographic factors prevailing some fifty years earlier. It is necessary, therefore, to consider such factors in order to explain the UK's present pattern of population and how it is likely to change in the future. Owing to the difficulty of obtaining consistent figures for Northern Ireland, the discussion concentrates on Great Britain. The basic conclusions, however, apply equally to the UK as a whole.

Table 3.1 and Figure 3.1 reveal that, while the UK's population increased rapidly during the nineteenth century, there was a marked falling-off in the rate of increase in the twentieth century. This poses three main questions. (i) Why was there such a rapid growth during the nineteenth century? (ii) Why did that rate fall so markedly during the twentieth century. (iii) What is likely to happen during the rest of the twentieth century?

Causes of Changes in the Rate of Growth

The factors affecting population changes are shown in Figure 3.2. On the one hand, we have the natural increase – the excess of births over deaths; on the other, migration – the balance between immigration (inwards) and emigration (outwards). In fact, apart from the years 1931–41 and 1951–61, Great Britain has lost by migration about half a million people each

FIGURE 3.1
Population, 1801–1981, Great Britain

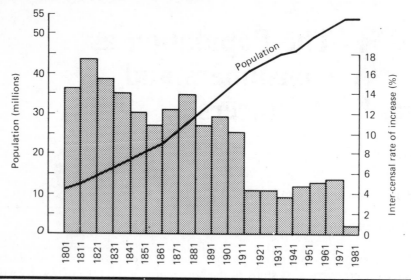

decade. Changes in the rate of growth, therefore, have resulted chiefly from changes in the natural increase.

For our purposes crude rates are adequate for examining changes in the rate of births and deaths. The *crude birth rate* (CBR) is the number of births per year per thousand of the population. For example, if the total population is 50 million and the number of births in the year is 1 million,

FIGURE 3.2
Factors Affecting Population

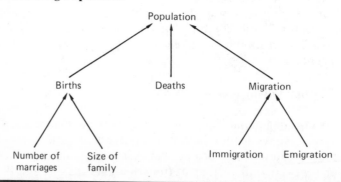

Table 3.1
Population (in 000s) Great Britain and Northern Ireland, 1801–1988

Date	Great Britain (England, Wales and Scotland)	Northern Ireland
1801	10 500	1442
1851	20 817	1237
1901	37 000	1361
1951	48 854	1536
1971	53 979	1539
1981	54 286	1490
1988 mid-year estimate	55 487	1578

Source Annual Abstract of Statistics

Table 3.2
Crude Birth Rate (CBR) and Crude Death Rate (CDR) 1851–1988, England and Wales

Date	CBR	CDR
1851	35.5	22.7
1900–2	28.7	17.3
1950–2	16.0	11.9
1961	17.9	12.0
1971	16.2	11.6
1981	13.0	11.8
1988	13.8	11.7

Source Annual Abstract of Statistics

the CBR is 20. Similarly, the *crude death rate* (CDR) is the number of deaths per year per thousand of the population.

The reason for the high rate of increase during the nineteenth century was that, while the birth rate remained high (Table 3.2), the death rate fell considerably (probably from about 33 in the mid-eighteenth century). This fall was the result of improved medical knowledge, better sanitation and water supplies, and the higher standard of living following the agricultural and industrial revolutions.

But the situation changed in the twentieth century. The death rate did not fall so rapidly. More important, the birth rate fell considerably. The reason was a decrease in the average size of family – from between five and six children to just over two. A variety of factors contributed to this: improved methods and social acceptance of birth control; the increased economic burden of parenthood – due, for instance, to the gradual raising of the school-leaving age; the higher standards which parents generally set themselves for their children's welfare; the growth of competing alternatives to children, such as holidays, foreign travel, the cinema and the motorcar; the emancipation of women, politically, economically and socially, with the consequent desire to be free from home ties; and the momentum which social example, smaller houses and advertisements provided once the movement towards smaller families had started. In 1949 there was a real possibility that Britain's population would have declined in number by the end of the century!

Today, however, such a decline seems less likely. Until recently, people were building slightly larger families, the result of younger marriages, greater economic prosperity, increased government help to families and improved opportunities for young mothers to resume work.

But the 1981 census revealed that the rate of increase of the population over the previous ten years had dropped to a mere 0.3 per cent. While external emigration had been a contributory factor, the fall in the rate of increase 1971–8 was mainly due to a fall in the birth rate. Indeed after the 'baby boom' of the early 1960s, the actual number of births each year fell until 1977. Not only has the marriage rate fallen and people are getting married older, but they are leaving it longer after marriage before starting their families. On the other hand, the first child is now followed more quickly by the second, but those couples having three or more children has halved compared with 1971. This change in the pattern of family building has been brought about largely by the desire of married women to shorten the period when they are not available for work.

As a result, the average size of family has fallen to around the 2.19 level, at which the population would just be replacing itself.

While any projections of population depend upon the reliability of assumptions, especially as regards births and migration, it now seems likely that the population of the UK will be about 59 million at the end of the century. Whether such an increase is desirable or not will now be examined.

3.2 Implications of Changes in the Size of the Population

The Malthusian Theory of Overpopulation

Until the middle of the eighteenth century, the population of Britain grew slowly. But, from then on, growth became more rapid, and in 1798 Thomas Malthus's first essay on *The Principle of Population as It Affects the Future Improvement of Society* made it a major subject of discussion.

Malthus began from two postulates: (i) that the passion between the sexes is necessary and will remain nearly in 'its present state'; and (ii) that food is necessary to the existence of man. Given these two postulates, his arguments forced him to conclude that: (i) the population will, if unchecked, double itself every twenty-five years; and (ii) the means of subsistence can, at a maximum, increase by only the same amount every twenty-five years. In other words, while population multiplies in a geometric progression, food supplies increase in an arithmetic progression.

The first conclusion was based on information collected by Malthus on the populations of various countries. But the second was supported by no evidence whatsoever. In order to substantiate it, Malthus appealed to the 'known properties of land'. Here he was virtually relying on the *law of diminishing returns* (see p. 122) although that was not precisely stated until some fifty years later.

From these two conclusions the important result followed that the power of population to increase was 'infinitely greater than the power of the earth to produce subsistence for man'. In short, the population would always tend to outgrow its food supply.

Since man cannot live without food, what, Malthus asked, kept population within its means of subsistence? The answer he found in certain 'checks'. First, there were 'positive checks', involving misery – famine, war, disease. Second, there were 'preventive checks' – which, with one exception, all involved 'vice', including contraception. The exception was 'moral restraint', by which was meant deliberately refraining from marrying at an early age. Since this was a remote possibility, the outlook for civilisation was gloomy: in the long run mankind could only expect a subsistence level of existence. Moreover, social policies to alleviate poverty would be self-defeating.

Malthus's 'Blind Spots'

Although at the beginning of the nineteenth century Malthus's views were widely accepted, the final tragedy of starvation, the logical outcome of his two conclusions, has not occurred. Where, therefore, did Malthus go wrong?

First, we must note that to some extent his argument was illogical, for he did not deal with the fact, well known at the time, that, in spite of the rapid increase in the population over the previous fifty years, people on the average were no worse off. This showed that the means of subsistence must at least have increased in proportion. Had Malthus possessed a precisely formulated law of diminishing returns, he could have based his argument on a fixed total supply of land which would sooner or later make itself felt as the population increased.

Second, Malthus was preoccupied with people as consumers. He failed to see that, by and large, a consumer is also a producer, for 'with every mouth God sends a pair of hands'. Here again a fixed supply of land with consequent diminishing returns could have overcome this objection.

Third, Malthus did not foresee change. On the one hand the geometric increase in Britain's population did not come about, because of emigration and above all because of the reduction in the size of the family with rising living standards. On the other hand, improved agricultural techniques and the vast increase in imports meant that Britain's food supplies were not limited to increasing in an arithmetic progression.

Thus Malthus's arguments have validity only when there are fixed resources, such as land or energy reserves. It is, for instance, the limited supply of land which brings about a Malthusian situation in the Far East today.

The Concept of an 'Optimum Population'

To Malthus, increasing numbers were a bad thing, as they pressed on the means of subsistence and lowered the standard of living. But his views lost ground towards the middle of the nineteenth century, for, as the capital investment of the industrial revolution began to yield benefits, the standard of living was seen to be keeping pace with the increase in population.

Indeed, at the turn of the century, Professor Edwin Cannan showed that population could be too small to take full advantage of available technical knowledge. For example, a larger population might justify large-scale production, with more use being made of division of labour, specialised machines and technical discoveries. In short, a doubling of the population could lead to more than doubling production.

Since, therefore, population can either be too large or too small, there must be an intermediate point where it is just right: the optimum population at which, given existing technical knowledge, capital equipment and possibilities of exchange with other countries, average output per head is at a maximum. Thus, with reference to Table 7.2 on p. 124, the optimum population for the example given would be four labourers. It follows that any country is over-or underpopulated if its population is respectively more or less than the optimum.

But the concept of an optimum population is not without difficulties. In the first place, it is unjustifiable to specify 'given existing technical knowledge, capital equipment and possibilities of exchange' and then to speculate as to what production would be if the population were larger or smaller. Had the population increased differently, these variables themselves would have been different. The same mistake is apparent in J. S. Mill's argument in the middle of the nineteenth century that the world would have been better off if, with the improvements that had taken place, population growth had been less. The truth is that such improvements would not have materialised, for a large and rapidly growing population accumulates knowledge and equipment differently from a smaller or slowly growing one. Even more important is that, from the practical point of view, the concept is of little help. Any optimum population at which a country was aiming would only remain the optimum so long as technical knowledge, etc., did not change. Thus, before an optimum was achieved, some new figure would have taken its place. All that can be done, therefore, is to consider the present composition of the population, forecast the population which will result from it, and then relate the population to likely changes in capital accumulation and technical discoveries.

We now apply this procedure to a study of Britain's population.

The Advantage to Great Britain of an Increasing Population

An increasing population has certain advantages which stimulate growth:

1. It Increases the Size of the Home Market

The additional output needed for a larger population should benefit industries working under conditions of decreasing costs, e.g. those producing aircraft, computers, nuclear reactors. It should be noted, however, that this applies only if the extra output is provided by existing firms and not by additional firms entering the industry. Moreover, it is possible to obtain large-scale economies by specialising on a narrow range of goods and exporting, as in Switzerland.

2. It Facilitates Labour Mobility

With an increasing population, unemployment resulting from the immobility of labour presents fewer problems. This is because the decline of older industries is slower and can be covered by natural wastage with fewer redundancies, while expanding industries can obtain most of their additional workers from new entrants to the labour force.

3. It Encourages Investment

An increasing population makes it easier to maintain the level of replacement investment. More than that, the extra consumer demand necessitates additional investment in machinery, factories, schools, houses, transport, etc. Consequently, it stimulates improved techniques, thereby accelerating the replacement of existing equipment.

4. It Promotes Vitality

By weighting the age distribution in favour of youth, an increasing population ensures more workers per retired persons and makes for energy, mobility, inventiveness and willingness to accept new ideas.

It should be noted that the disadvantages of a decreasing population could be stated as the opposite of these.

The Disadvantages of an Increasing Population

Against the advantages given above it is necessary to set certain disadvantages which may make it difficult for an increasing population to raise present living standards. Resources have to be used in adding to capital equipment instead of in producing consumer goods or improving existing buildings. Moreover, the saying that 'with every mouth God sends a pair of hands' ignores two important facts. The first is that not every person is a producer – for a time the additional mouths have to be provided with food, education, etc., by the working group. The second is more important: the increase in the number of labourers on a fixed amount of land may well bring the law of diminishing returns into operation, with a consequent fall in living standards.

It is the law of diminishing returns (see p. 125) which pinpoints the problem of increasing numbers. In the Far Eastern countries there is simply a lower output per head, as extra people have to obtain their subsistence from a fixed amount of land. But for Britain the law of diminishing returns does not apply in this basic way. The law assumes no technical improvements, but improved techniques in agriculture have enabled Britain in recent years to raise her self-sufficiency in her principal foodstuffs from 50 per cent to 90 per cent.

As far as Britain is concerned the law of diminishing returns is significant in three ways. First, Britain is still very dependent on imports for the raw materials, special types of machinery, base metals, consumer goods (e.g. cars, cameras) and certain sorts of food and drink (e.g. fruit, wine) that she requires. What Britain has to ask, therefore, is: can exports be increased sufficiently to pay for the extra imports required by the larger population without a severe depreciation of sterling especially when North Sea oil runs out (see p. 577).

Throughout the nineteenth century Britain proved that this was possible. Indeed, a balance-of-payments surplus allowed her to invest heavily abroad. But since then the problem of finding and holding foreign markets has become more difficult.

Second, the growth of population accompanied by increasing real income puts pressure on space for amenity and recreational purposes, as, for example, more houses with spacious gardens are demanded and access to the countryside is sought.

Third, with population growth, environmental problems intensify. As city congestion increases and more open space is required for housing, roads and industry, arguments for conservation and control of pollution gain momentum.

Conclusion

At present Britain is managing to support increasing numbers while improving living standards. But the overall level of the future population must be watched by the government and, if necessary, influenced by immigration policy and the level of child benefits. Social as well as economic considerations have to be taken into account.

In Africa and Asia a Malthusian situation exists. While the death rate is falling through better medical services, the birth rate remains high. By the end of the century an almost doubled population could be seeking to live with little increase in land. Possible solutions are birth control, improved agricultural techniques, the development of export industries, and economic aid from developed countries.

3.3 Age Distribution

Any change in the birth or death rates will affect the age distribution over time. Thus the boom in births after the war and in the early 1960s produced a bulge in new young workers some sixteen years later.

The present overall pattern is of an ageing population brought about by the fall in the rate of increase during the twentieth century (Figure 3.3). In 1988, the 15–64 age-group formed about 70 per cent of the population, and those under 15 years and those over 65 years, 19 per cent and 11 per cent, respectively. By the end of the century, the working age group could form only 64 per cent of the total population; but, through the fall in the number

FIGURE 3.3
Changes in the Age Distribution of the Population of Great Britain, 1851–1988

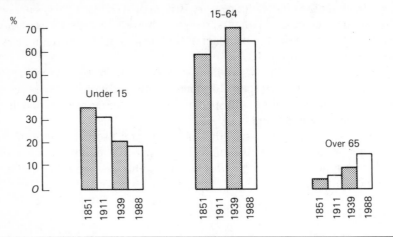

of births after 1964, those under 15 years will account for only 16 per cent, and those over 65, for 20 per cent.

The Effects of an Ageing Population

It should be noted that in part this trend is due to a normal development, the fall in mortality. This means that we have to adjust to the change: trying to prevent it by raising the birth rate will also increase the size of the population – which, as we have seen, presents problems.

It is essential, therefore, to anticipate the possible economic, social and political difficulties resulting from changes in the age structure so that the necessary adjustments can, with planning, occur smoothly.

1. Economic

First, there is an increased dependence of retired persons on the working population. Current wants can only be provided for by current production. An ageing population means that the proportion of workers to consumers is falling. Whereas in 1851 there were over twelve people of working age for every person over 65, in 1988 there were less than four. One particular result will be the increased burden of retirement pensions, more pensioners having to be supported by proportionately fewer contributors. This highlights the importance of economic growth.

Second, a changing pattern of consumption will result. An ageing population means, to take extreme examples, that wheelchairs will be wanted in place of prams, walking sticks in place of hockey sticks, tea in place of milk. For many of these new wants, consideration has to be given well in advance. Today, almost one-quarter of British households consist solely of pensioners and, when planning a housing programme, we have to provide the smaller units and sheltered housing they require. Similarly, the fall in births since 1964 has resulted in fewer school places and teachers being required.

Third, older people make greater demands on the health service, those over 75 years, for instance, costing four times as much per head as the average person. Thus government expenditure has to be increased and diverted towards the special types of medical care and hospitals required by older people, e.g. hip operations, geriatric wards.

Fourth, an older labour force is less mobile. In the past, expanding industries have obtained labour from young people just starting their working lives, while the decaying industries have declined fairly quietly by natural wastage – not replacing workers as they leave or retire. However, where the working population is static in size, expanding industries have to draw older workers from the declining industries. 'Teaching old dogs new tricks' and moving them to new areas is not always easy (see pp. 220–1). A high level of unemployment increases the difficulties, for it is the older workers in the declining industries who are likely to remain out of a job the longest. Thus both the government and firms must provide training schemes and relocation incentives.

Fifth, an older population tends to be less progressive. While older people are more patient and experienced than younger people, the latter excel in energy, enterprise, enthusiasm and the ability to adapt themselves and to learn new skills.

2. Social

Where old people are more numerous and live longer, their children find greater difficulty in caring for them. Thus there is an increasing need for the State to provide home-care services (such as 'meals-on-wheels' and home helps) and old people's homes.

Similarly, there is a greater demand for advice from Citizens' Advice Bureaux, since older people need more help in sorting out difficulties relating to housing, gas and electricity bills, social security benefits and so on.

3. Political

Political decisions have to be made as a result of the disadvantages of an ageing population. To what extent should younger generations be augmented by a liberal immigration policy, bearing in mind the social stresses which could arise? Can adequate defence be provided by the use of more sophisticated weapons, or will the falling proportion of young people necessitate conscription? Should TV and radio programmes give greater weight to the type of entertainment preferred by old people? And, since older people own the larger share of the nation's capital but are averse to taking risks, should the State assume responsibility for providing funds for the riskier types of enterprise, such as North Sea oil prospecting and development, the building of nuclear power stations and the exploration of outer space?

Indeed, the ageing population may even influence the election of governments, for older people tend to be more conservative.

3.4 The Industrial Distribution of the Working Population

The Working Population

The UK's population in 1988 was estimated to be 57 065 000 persons. Of these 28 211 000 persons (16 383 000 males and 11 828 000 females) are described by the Department of Employment as 'the working population'.

The working population consists of persons over school-leaving age who work for pay or gain or are claiming unemployment benefit. It therefore includes both employees and self-employed persons, even if they are over retirement age or are working only part time, and members of the armed forces. Excluded are: (a) children under 16 years of age and students above 16 years of age who are receiving full-time education; (b) persons, such as housewives, who do not work for pay or gain; (c) persons who, having private means, e.g. from investments or gifts, do not need to work; (d) retired persons; (e) work-seekers who do not claim benefit, e.g. house-wives who are ineligible.

The size of the working population depends upon:

(i) The numbers within the 16–65 age-group.
(ii) The activity rates within this group, especially as regards young people and female workers. The tendency over the last twenty years has been for a higher proportion of young people to remain in further education, thus reducing their activity rate. On the other hand, a higher proportion of women are now entering the working population. The expansion of the service and light manufacturing industries has provided increased job opportunities for women, while the changed attitude to women workers is reflected in the Equal Pay Act 1970 and the Sex Discrimination Act 1975. Above all, the smaller family, the availability of crêches and school dinners, the development of part-time employment opportunities and new labour-saving

domestic appliances have allowed married women to work. About 66 per cent of women in the 16–60 age group are economically active.
(iii) The extent to which people over retiring age continue to work, something which is largely influenced by the level of pensions.
(iv) The employment opportunities available – the tendency being for the working population to contract in a depression (mainly through withdrawal of married women.)

Table 3.3
Total Working Population, UK, 1975–88 (000s)

	1975	1980	1988
Total employees in employment	22 710	22 458	22 226
HM Forces	336	323	316
Self-employed persons	1 993	1 950	2 986
Unemployed	838	1 444	2 341
Government work-related trainees			343
Total working population	25 877	26 839	28 211
of whom: Males	16 162	16 320	16 383
Females	9 715	10 520	11 828

Source Annual Abstract of Statistics

The main changes in the working population since 1975 are:

(1) An overall increase of nearly $2\frac{1}{2}$ million (9 per cent). Thus today the working population covers one-half of the total population.
(2) Of this increase, 2 million have been in female workers. Here the main cause has been the expansion in the service industries. Forty per cent of female workers are part time (compared with only 5 per cent males). In the UK, the activity rate of women of 16–60 years of age is 66 per cent, higher than all other countries except for Japan and the Scandinavian countries.
(3) Self-employment has increased by 993,000 (50 per cent), largely through the active support of the government. It occurs mostly in agriculture, construction, distribution, catering and other services.
(4) As regards occupation, the movement has been from traditional craft and semi-skilled jobs towards more highly skilled technicians and technologists.

Changes in the Industrial Distribution of the Working Population

Table 3.4 shows significant changes in the industrial distribution of employees between 1971 and 1988:

(1) a 27 per cent decrease in the primary (extractive) industries – agriculture, mining and fishing;
(2) a 30 per cent increase in services;
(3) a 35 per cent decrease in manufacturing industries.

Table 3.4
Employees in Employment by Industry: UK, 1971–88

	1971		1988	
	Total (000s)	Per cent	Total (000s)	Per cent
Agricultural, forestry and fishing	450	2.0	313	1.4
Energy and water supply	798	3.6	487	2.2
Manufacturing industries	8 065	36.5	5 215	23.5
Construction	1 198	5.5	1 043	4.7
Distribution, hotels, catering and repairs	3 686	16.6	4 427	19.9
Transport and communication	1 556	7.0	1 324	6.0
Banking, insurance and other financial services	1 336	6.0	2 467	11.0
Other services	5 049	22.8	6 949	31.3
All industries and services	22 139	100.0	22 226	100.0

Source Annual Abstract of Statistics

The basic explanation of the first two changes is an increase in real income over the period, and in this respect it is merely a reflection of a continuous trend. As a result, spending moves to those goods having a high income elasticity of demand. In 1901, for example, the average worker spent 60 per cent of his income on food; by 1988 it had fallen to 21 per cent, of which nearly one-quarter went on meals bought outside the home. Today the provision of services now covers three-fifths of all employees.

The decrease in manufacturing has largely been the result of the uncompetitiveness of British products in world markets brought about by (a) the greater technical efficiency of Japan, (b) the inability to contain wage costs relative to competitors, (c), the appreciation in the value of the £ sterling after 1979 as the result of the export of North Sea oil.

Technical advances and increased mechanisation also help to explain the relative falls in agriculture, energy supply, construction, transport and communications (e.g. increased car ownership), and manufacturing. In contrast, services are more labour intensive and less highly capitalised.

3.5 The Geographical Distribution of the Population

Geographically, the population of the UK is dominated by two features: it is *concentrated*, and it is *urban*. Both are the result of moving from an agricultural to an industrial economy.

The Concentrated Nature of the Population

As a result of the Industrial Revolution industry migrated to the coalfields in the Midlands and north of England. And today, even though electricity frees industry from being located on the coalfields and the basic industries of these areas have declined, they still remain important centres of industry and population (Figure 3.4). There are two main reasons for this. First, many industries remain because of acquired advantages, particularly the availability of labour (see p. 112). Second, new industries have been attracted by the government's Development Area policy (see p. 472).

During the twentieth century, the main areas of natural expansion have been the Midlands and south-east England, particularly in the counties around London. The Midlands expanded with the demand for light engineering and electrical products and for motor vehicles, but the area has recently suffered some stagnation with the decline in the motor and other manufacturing industries. On the other hand, London, always a relatively wealthy area, has expanded outwards as production of goods having a high income-elasticity of demand has moved nearer to their main markets. In addition, the development of government and financial services has attracted population, and this tends to have a multiplier effect as other industries move in to provide for their needs. The proximity of south-east England to the Continent has also attracted industry and population, especially since 1973 when Britain joined the EC.

Certain rural counties, although not of high density, have also shown a high rate of growth, particularly Norfolk, Suffolk and Cornwall.

FIGURE 3.4
Geographical distribution of the Population of the UK

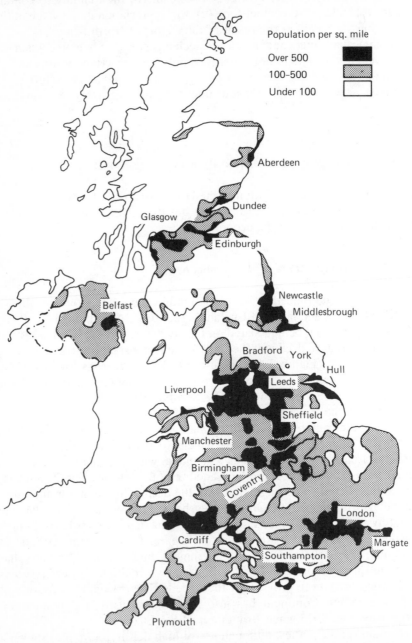

The Urban Nature of the Population

This concentration of population is in towns (unlike the Nile and Ganges deltas which consist mainly of concentrated rural communities). Over three out of every four persons in Britain live in an urban area. Moreover, 30 per cent of the population lives in the seven conurbations (continuous built-up areas) of Greater London, south-east Lancashire (Manchester), west Midlands (Birmingham), central Clydeside (Glasgow), west York-shire (Leeds and Bradford), Merseyside (Liverpool) and Tyneside (New-castle).

Nevertheless, over the last thirty years, the proportion of the total population in rural areas has increased, reversing the trend towards town life of the previous 150 years. As cities grow, retailing and commerce compete for central sites. The consequent rise in land values pushes the residential population outwards. Moreover, as real income increases, people can afford houses with more space in the suburbs. Thus *inner*-city areas have been losing population.

Indeed, in the conurbations the population is moving beyond the green belt into rural areas. Long-term factors are bringing this about: (a) the growth in real income which covers the higher costs of transport; (b) the mobility provided by the car and faster rail travel; (c) the improvement in public utility services; (d) the direct stimulus of the new towns policy; (e) the expansion of new light industries in rural towns; (f) a greater appreciation of rural life.

Problems Resulting from the Concentration of Population in Urban Areas

The concentration of population in large urban areas has certain advant-ages. Such areas can offer better and more specialised schools, shops, entertainment and other services. Fast road, rail and air communications facilitate travel between cities. They can usually provide a variety of employment opportunities, enabling firms to recruit the different types of labour they require. But conurbations often involve travelling long dis-tances to work within the urban area, putting a heavy stress on the transport system. There are also problems of inner-city decay, with poor housing, inadequate schools, pollution and lack of open spaces. Moreover, there are fewer social ties, and the lower community spirit results in vandalism and petty crime. Above all, where these areas are faced with the decline of major local industries, there is the problem of regional unemployment. Not only do government organisations have to respond to these conditions, but the development of urban areas may itself lead to the reorganisation of local government.

Part II

The Market Economy

4 How Price is Formed in the Market Economy

4.1 Value and Price

As soon as we wish to know what to produce, there immediately arises the question: 'How can people indicate what they want?'. A mere statement of want is meaningless, for, as we showed in Chapter 1, people always *want* something. A want is significant in economics only when a person is prepared to give up something in order to satisfy it. As the strength of the different wants varies, so will the amounts which people are willing to give up. In other words, different goods have a different *value* to them. Value is measured in terms of 'opportunity cost'. For example, if Ms A is willing to work five hours for the money which will buy a hat, we say that the value of the hat to her is greater than the value of the five hours' leisure forgone. Value therefore means the rate at which a particular good or service will exchange for other goods. It is important to note, however, that, while to have value a good must be capable of satisfying a want, a good which satisfies a want need not necessarily have value. For example, air satisfies a want; but, in normal circumstances, the supply is so great that nobody will give anything in exchange for it. Because it has no power to command other goods in exchange, it has, in economics, no value.

In modern economic systems we rarely exchange goods directly against other goods. We make use of a 'go-between', or, as it is usually said, a medium of exchange. This medium of exchange is money and the values of goods are expressed in terms of money. In other words, we *price* the goods and services. Price can be defined, therefore, as the value of a commodity or service measured in terms of the standard monetary unit. By comparing prices, we can compare the *rates* at which different goods can be exchanged.

Changes in *relative* prices, if supply conditions have not changed, indicate a relative shift in the importance of those goods. Thus price changes can signal a change in what people want. We must therefore

45

examine the mechanism by which the signals are flashed up. We begin by looking at the 'market' – where values are established by exchange.

4.2 Markets

Definition

'I am offered £650 for this heifer. No more offers? For the last time of asking, any advance on £650? Going at £650, going, gone.' Down comes the hammer. 'Sold at £650 to Mr Giles on my right.'

This is the local cattle market. On his stand above the cattle ring is the auctioneer. Inside the ring, a black and white heifer is appraised by local farmers and dealers. Some are buyers, some sellers. The market fixes the price at which those who want something can obtain it from those who have it to sell.

Note that it is only exchange value which is significant here. The farmer selling the heifer may have felt that it ought to have made more than £650. Or, as it was the first calf reared by his son, it may have had great 'sentimental value' to him. Such considerations, however, mean little in the market economy.

Of course, prices are not always fixed by auction. This is the method usually employed where there are many buyers but the seller only comes to the market infrequently, or wishes to dispose of his goods quickly. If there are few buyers and sellers, e.g. in the purchase of a house or a secondhand car, the final price may be arrived at by 'higgling' – the seller meeting the prospective buyer personally and bargaining with him.

But where goods are in constant demand the above methods take too long. Thus most goods, such as foodstuffs, clothing and household utensils are given a definite price by the shopkeeper. But buyers will still influence this price. If it is too high, the market will not be cleared; if it is too low, the shopkeeper's stocks will run out.

A market need not be formal or held in a particular place. Second-hand cars are often bought and sold through newspaper advertisements. Second-hand furniture may be disposed of by a card in a local shop window. Foreign currency, gold, base metals, raw cotton and other goods which can be accurately described are dealt in over the telephone.

However, in studying the market economy it is essential to understand how price is determined. Since this is done in the market, we can define the market simply as *all those buyers and sellers of a good who influence its price*. Within the market there is a tendency for the same price, allowing for costs of transport, to be established for the same commodity.

1. World Markets

Today modern transport allows many commodities to have a world market – a price change in one part of the world affects the price in the rest of the world. Examples of such commodities are wheat, coffee, oils, basic raw materials (such as cotton and rubber), gold, silver and base metals. What conditions must a commodity fulfil to obtain a world market?

First, there must be a wide demand. The basic necessities of life (e.g. wheat, vegetable oils, wool, cotton) answer this requirement. In contrast, such goods as national costumes, books translated into little-used languages and postcards of local views have only a local demand.

Second, commodities must be capable of being transported. Land and buildings are almost impossible to transport. Personal services are limited by the distance the consumer can travel. Labour, too, is particularly immobile, especially when it comes to moving to a different country (see Chapter 14). Furthermore, governments may, by import taxes and quotas, effectively prevent the entry of certain commodities into the country.

Third, the costs of transport must be small in relation to the value of the commodity. Thus the market for diamonds is worldwide, whereas that for bricks is local. Similarly, wheat and oil are cheap to transport compared with coal because they are more easily handled – although, as sea transport is relatively cheap, coal mined near the coast can be sent long distances.

Last, the commodity must be durable. Goods which perish quickly, such as milk, bread, fresh cream and strawberries, cannot be sent long distances. Nevertheless, modern developments, such as refrigeration and air freight transport, are extending the market even for these goods.

2. Perfect and Imperfect Markets

In any market the price of the commodity in one part affects its price in another part. Hence the same price tends to be established. Where price differences are eliminated quickly, we say the market is a 'perfect' market. (Note that this is not quite the same as 'perfect' competition – see chapter 8.)

For a market to be perfect certain conditions have to be fulfilled. First, buyers and sellers must have exact knowledge of the prices being paid elsewhere in the market. The development of communications, particularly telecommunications, has facilitated this. Second, both buyers and sellers must base their actions solely on price, and not favour one particular person out of loyalty or mere inertia. Thus, if one seller puts up the price of his good, his customers immediately go to another who is cheaper. Alternatively, if he lowers his price, customers will so flock to him that he would sell out quickly unless he raises his price to that asked elsewhere.

Examples of perfect markets are the precious stones market of Hatton Garden in London, and above all the organised produce markets and the stock exchange (see below). In these markets the two essential conditions are fulfilled, for prices are watched closely by professional dealers. As a result of their operations, variations in price are quickly eliminated.

But such conditions are rarely satisfied in other markets. Buyers and sellers neither have perfect knowledge nor act solely on the basis of price. The ordinary housewife, for instance, cannot afford the time to go from one shop to another in order to compare the prices of her everyday purchases, though she is usually much more careful when spending on the more expensive goods bought at infrequent intervals. Similarly, shop-keepers do not always know what competing shopkeepers are charging for their goods. Moreover, purchasers may be influenced by considerations other than price. Thus they may continue to deal with one particular trader, even though he is charging a slightly higher price, because he has given them good service in the past. Finally, although two goods may be virtually the same physically, by 'product differentiation' and advertising the merits of his own brand a producer may convince the consumer of its superiority. Such 'persuasive' advertising, makes the market less perfect, and must be contrasted with 'informative' advertising, which increases knowledge and thus helps to make the market more perfect.

Where price differences persist, markets are said to be 'imperfect'. As we have already hinted, such markets are often found in retailing.

3. Organised Produce Markets

As explained above, the market for certain commodities is worldwide. Moreover, many of these commodities are in constant demand, either as basic raw material or as mainfoods or beverages for a large section of the world's people. They therefore figure prominently in international trade, and are the subject of the following discussion.

England's foreign trade began with the export of raw wool in the thirteenth century, and it was extended by the subsequent development of the chartered companies. These were based in London, and it was there that merchants gathered to buy and sell the produce which the companies' ships brought from abroad.

The big change, however, came about with the expansion of inter-national trade following the industrial revolution. The UK became the greatest importing and exporting nation in the world. London, her chief port and commercial city, not only imported the goods which were required for the people of her own country but built up an important entrepôt business, acting as a go-between in the distribution of such commodities as tea, sugar, hides, skins and wool to many other countries, particularly those of western Europe.

Hence formal 'organised markets' developed. These markets are dis-tinctive in that buying and selling takes place in a recognised building, business is governed by agreed rules and conventions, and often only certain persons are allowed to engage in transactions. They are thus a highly developed form of market. Today, London has exchanges or auction centres for such commodities as rubber, wool, tea, coffee, furs, metals (tin, copper, lead and zinc), grain, and shipping freights (the Baltic Exchange). It must not be thought, however, that such organised produce markets exist only in London. Liverpool has exchanges for cotton and grain, and most of the other large trading countries have exchanges too. Although today many of the goods go directly to other countries, the earnings of London dealers are part of the UK's income from 'invisible exports ' (see p. 527).

Broadly speaking, organised markets fulfil three main functions. First, they enable manufacturers and wholesalers to obtain supplies of commodities easily, quickly and at the competitive market price. Because they are composed of specialist buyers and sellers, prices are sensitive to any change in demand and supply. Thus they are perfect markets.

Second, 'futures' dealings on these markets enable people to protect themselves from heavy losses through price changes. Thus a cotton grower prefers to know what price he will receive before his output is actually delivered to the market. On the other hand, a cotton spinner has to protect himself from a rise in the price of raw cotton between the time he quotes a price for his yarn and the time of its actual manufacture. Where a good is bought today for delivery today, the deal is known as a 'spot' transaction and the price is the 'spot price'. With many goods, however, it is possible to buy today for delivery in the future. The price agreed upon is the 'future' or 'forward' price. For a commodity to be dealt in on a futures market certain conditions must be fulfilled: (i) the commodity must be durable, thereby enabling stocks to be carried; (ii) the commodity must be described in terms of grades which are internationally uniform; (iii) dealings must be frequent enough to occupy professional dealers; and (iv) the commodity must be subject to price fluctuations.

In futures dealings the dealer uses his expert knowledge to make a profit on what he considers will be the future price of the commodity. At any time a dealer will quote a price (according to the view he takes of the future movement of prices) at which he is prepared to buy or sell at some future date. Thus a cotton grower can cover himself against a possible fall in price by selling his produce forward, while a cotton spinner can quote a weaver a price for yarn and guard himself against loss by buying the raw cotton forward.

Such dealing usually performs the third function of organised markets – evening out price fluctuations. At a time when an increase in supply would cause the price to fall considerably, the dealer adds his demand to the normal demand in order to build up his stocks, and thereby keeps the price up. On the other hand, when the good is in short supply he releases stocks and so prevents a violent rise in price. The difficulty is that speculation on the future price may dominate the real forces which influence it, prices fluctuating violently in response to changes in optimism and pessimism.

4.3 Forces Determining Price

Demand and Supply

'That animal was cheap,' remarks Phil Archer as the auctioneer's hammer falls. 'And no wonder,' replies Brian Aldridge. 'This has been a long winter. We're now in the middle of April, and the grass is hardly growing. Hay's running short, and breeders are being forced to sell sooner than expected. Old Giles is about the only farmer who'll take the risk of buying extra cattle.'

What can we learn from Brian Aldridge's observations? Simply that the £650 at which the heifer was sold was not really determined by the final bid. The real factors producing the relatively low price were the reluctance of farmers to buy and the number of young animals being offered for sale. In short, the price was determined by the interaction of the forces of demand and supply. We shall look at each in turn.

Preliminary Assumptions

First, we examine how these forces work in an imaginary market – for eggs. To simplify, we shall assume:

  (i) All eggs are exactly the same in size and quantity.
 (ii) There are no transport costs within the market.
(iii) The market consists of so many small buyers and sellers that there is keen competition.
(iv) That it is a perfect market: price differences are quickly eliminated because buyers and sellers (1) have complete knowledge of prices and conditions in other parts of the market, and (2) act solely on the basis of price.
 (v) There is no interference by the government in the operation of market forces, e.g. by price control, regulating supply, etc.

Demand

Demand in economics is the desire for something *plus* the willingness and ability to pay a certain price in order to possess it. More specifically, it is how much of a good people in the market will buy at a given price over a certain period of time.

It is helpful if we separate the factors affecting demand into (i) price, and (ii) the conditions of demand, the determinants of demand other than price.

1. Price (the conditions of demand remaining unchanged)

Normally a person will demand more of a good the lower its price. This is because, once you have some units of a good, you have partly satisfied your want and so will only buy more at a lower price. This conforms to our everyday observations. 'Winter sale, prices slashed' announce the shops when they wish to clear their stocks of clothing.

We can draw up a table showing how many eggs a person would be willing to buy at different prices. If they are very expensive, other foodstuffs will, as far as possible, be substituted; if they are cheap, people may even buy them to pickle. By adding up the demand from all buyers of eggs in the market at different prices over a given period of time, it is possible to obtain a *market demand schedule* (Table 4.1).

Note that this schedule does not tell us anything about the actual market price or how much is in fact sold. It is an 'if' schedule. All it says is: 'If the price is so much, then this quantity will be demanded.' Plotting this schedule on a graph, and assuming that demand can be obtained for intermediary prices, gives the demand curve *D* in Figure 4.1.

Table 4.1
Demand Schedule for No-Such Market for the Week
Ending 26 January 1991

Price (pence per egg)	Eggs demanded (thousands)
12	3
10	9
8	15
6	20
4	25
2	35

* what buyers would take at each price

FIGURE 4.1
Quantity Demanded and Price

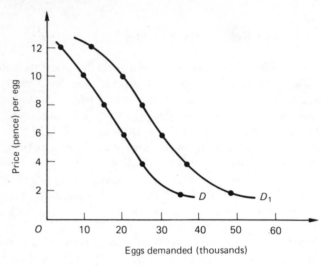

Eggs demanded (thousands)

2. *The Conditions of Demand*

Something may occur to cause housewives to demand more eggs at a given price. In other words, the demand schedule alters. Suppose, for instance, farmers unite in an advertising campaign describing tasty egg dishes. As a result more eggs are demanded at all prices (Table 4.2).

Table 4.2
An Increase in Demand

Price (pence per egg)	Eggs demanded (thousands)
12	12
10	20
8	25
6	30
4	37
2	49

Plotting this revised demand schedule gives curve D_1 to the right of D. Had conditions so changed that demand decreased, the new demand curve would have been to the left.

The influence of both (1) price, and (2) the conditions of demand, on the quantity demanded is thus shown on the graph. The former determines the shape of the demand curve – its slope downwards from left to right. The latter determines the position between the axes – an increase in demand shifting the curve to the right, a decrease to the left. For clarity's sake, a change in demand resulting from a change in price will in future be referred to as an *extension* or *contraction* of demand; a change in demand due to new conditions of demand will be described as an *increase* or *decrease* in demand.

Conditions of demand may change in a *short* period of time through:

(1) A CHANGE IN THE PRICE OF OTHER GOODS
Goods compete for our limited income and are thus, to some extent, substitutes for each other. When the prices of other goods fall, the particular good under discussion becomes relatively dearer and therefore less of it is demanded. When the prices of other goods rise, it becomes relatively cheaper, and so more of it is demanded.

But the effect on the demand for a particular good is more pronounced when the price of a close *substitute* changes. Suppose that fried tomatoes are an alternative to eggs for breakfast. If the price of tomatoes falls, housewives will tend to buy them rather than eggs. Thus, although there has been no initial increase in the price of eggs, demand for them has decreased. Similarly, where goods are *complements*, a change in the price of one good has a pronounced effect on the demand for the other. For example, a fall in the price of cars results in more cars being purchased, leading eventually to an increase in the demand for petrol and tyres (see also p. 66).

(2) A CHANGE IN TASTES AND FASHION
A campaign advertising eggs would increase demand; a scare that eggs were the source of infection would decrease it.

(3) EXPECTATIONS OF FUTURE PRICE CHANGES OR SHORTAGES
The fear that the price of eggs may rise considerably next week may induce people to increase their demand now in order to have eggs in stock.

(4) GOVERNMENT POLICY
A tax on eggs paid by the consumer would raise the price and lead to a decrease in demand; a rebate paid to the consumer would have the opposite effect (see Chapter 21).

Over a *longer* period the conditions of demand may change through:

(5) A CHANGE IN REAL INCOME

If there were an all-round increase in real income (that is, money income adjusted for any change in the price level) people could afford more eggs, and demand would probably increase. Or it might now be possible to afford mushrooms for breakfast, and these would take the place of eggs.

(6) GREATER EQUALITY IN THE DISTRIBUTION OF WEALTH

The wealth of a country may be so distributed that there are a few exceptionally rich people whereas the remainder are exceedingly poor. If many poor people felt they could not afford eggs, greater equality of wealth would be likely to increase the demand for eggs.

(7) A CHANGE IN THE SIZE AND COMPOSITION OF THE POPULATION

Additional people coming into the market will, with their extra income, increase demand, especially if eggs figure prominently in their diets.

Supply

Supply in the economics refers to how much of a good will be offered for sale at a given price over a given period of time. As with demand, this quantity depends on (i) the price of the good, and (ii) the conditions of supply.

1. Price (the conditions of supply remaining unchanged)

Normally, more of a good will be supplied the higher its price. The real reason for this is explained in Chapter 6. But even a brief consideration of how the individual farmer reacts to a change in price will show that it is likely to be true. If the price of eggs is high, he will probably consume fewer himself in order to send as many as possible to market. Moreover, the higher price allows him to give his chickens more food so that they can lay a few extra eggs. When we extend our analysis to the market supply it is obvious that a higher price for eggs enables other farmers – the less efficient – to produce.

Hence we are able to draw up a *market supply schedule* – the total number of eggs supplied at different prices by all the sellers in the market over a given period of time (Table 4.3).

Once again it must be noted that this is an 'if' schedule, for all it says is: 'If the price is so much, then this quantity will be offered for sale.'

We can plot this schedule (Figure 4.2); assuming supply for all intermediate prices, a supply curve *S* is obtained.

However there is a fundamental difference between demand and supply. Whereas demand can respond almost immediately to a change in price, a period of time must usually elapse before supply can be fully adjusted. For

Table 4.3
Supply Schedule for No-Such Market for the Week
Ending 26 January 1991

Price (pence per egg)	Eggs supplied (thousands)
12	40
10	32
8	25
6	20
4	13
2	7

* what sellers would offer at each price

the first day or two the only way in which the farmer can send more eggs to market is by eating fewer himself. By the end of the week he may have increased output by giving the hens more food or by leaving the light on in the hen-house all night; the higher price covers the extra cost. But to obtain any sizeable increase the farmer must add to his hens; if all farmers

FIGURE 4.2
Quantity Supplied and Price

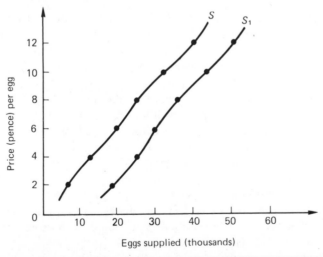

are following the same policy, this will take about five months, the period required to rear laying hens from chicks.

These different periods of time are dealt with more fully in Chapter 6.

2. The Conditions of Supply

The number of eggs supplied may change even though there has been no alteration in the price. In the spring, for instance, chickens lay more eggs than in winter. Thus more eggs will be supplied at all prices in the spring, and fewer in winter as shown in Table 4.4.

Table 4.4
An Increase in Supply in the Spring

Price (pence per egg)	Eggs supplied (thousands)
12	50
10	43
8	36
6	30
4	25
2	19

Table 4.4 shows that compared with winter when only 25 000 eggs were supplied at 8p each (table 4.2), during the spring 36 000 were supplied. Or, looked at in another way, 25 000 eggs can be supplied in the spring at 4p each compared with 8p in the winter. When plotted, the revised supply schedule gives a curve S_1 to the right of the old one (Figure 4.2). Had supply decreased, the new supply curve would have been to the left.

Like demand, therefore supply is influenced by both (i) price, and (ii) the conditions of supply. The former determines the shape of the curve – its upward slope from left to right. The latter determines its position between the axes – an increase in supply shifts the curve to the right, a decrease to the left. To distinguish between the two we shall refer to a change in supply resulting from a change in the price of a commodity as an *extension* or *contraction* of supply; a change in supply due to new conditions of supply will be described as an *increase* or *decrease* in supply.

In general, conditions of supply may change through:

(1) PRICE EXPECTATIONS

Where a commodity is durable and the relative cost of storage low, e.g. gold, wheat, antiques, price expectations can, as with consumers' demand, affect supply. Thus if the price is expected to rise, stocks will be held or even augmented. If the price is expected to fall, stocks will be depleted. Supplies of perishable goods such as eggs are at a disadvantage here.

(2) A CHANGE IN THE PRICES OF OTHER GOODS, ESPECIALLY WHEN IT IS EASY TO SHIFT RESOURCES INTO PRODUCING THOSE GOODS

Suppose, for instance, that there is a considerable increase in the price of chicken meat, including boiling fowls. It may pay the farmer to cull more of his older hens. Thus fewer eggs are supplied at the old price.

(3) A CHANGE IN THE PRICES OF FACTORS OF PRODUCTION

A fall in the cost of pullets or of their food would reduce the cost of producing eggs. As a result more eggs could be supplied at the old price, or – looked at in another way – the original quantity could be produced at a lower price per egg. A rise in the wages of workers on chicken farms would have the opposite effect.

(4) CHANGES RESULTING FROM NATURE

(e.g. the weather, floods, drought, pest) and from *abnormal circumstances* (e.g. war, fire, political events).

(5) GOVERNMENT POLICY

A tax on the output of eggs or an increase in employers' national insurance contributions would result in fewer eggs being offered for sale at the old price. That is, the supply curve moves to the left. On the other hand, a subsidy, by decreasing costs, would move the supply curve to the right (see p. 68).

Other changes in supply take longer, occurring through:

(6) IMPROVED TECHNIQUES

Technical improvements reduce costs of production, shifting the supply curve to the right. Thus improved automatic feeding devices might be developed, or selective breeding producing hens which lay more eggs.

(7) THE DISCOVERY OF NEW OR THE EXHAUSTION OF OLD SUPPLIES OF RAW MATERIALS

(8) THE ENTRY OF NEW FIRMS INTO THE INDUSTRY

4.4 The Determination of Price: Market Clearing

The demand and supply curves can be combined in a single diagram (Figure 4.3).

Let us see how this analysis helps as a first approach to understanding how the market is cleared. The assumptions we have made so far are:

(i) Many buyers and sellers.
(ii) Keen competition between buyers, between sellers, and between buyers and sellers.
(iii) More will be demanded at a lower price than at a higher price.
(iv) Less will be supplied at a lower price than at a higher.

Given assumptions (iii) and (iv), the two curves slope in opposite directions. Thus they cut at a single point – in our example, where the price is 6p. It can be predicted that in No-Such Market, where these conditions of demand and supply exist, the price of eggs will move towards and eventually settle at 6p. This is the *market* or *equilibrium* price, the price where the plans of both buyers and sellers are consistent.

This proposition can be proved as follows. Suppose that initially the price of eggs is fixed at 8p. Here 15 000 will be demanded but 25 000 supplied. There is thus an excess supply of 10 000. But some sellers will want to get rid of their surplus, and therefore reduce the price being asked.

FIGURE 4.3
The Determination of the Equilibrium Price

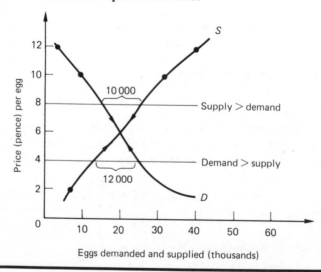

Eggs demanded and supplied (thousands)

As this happens some supplies are withdrawn from the market, and there is an extension of demand. This continues until a price of 6p is reached, when 20 000 eggs are both demanded and offered for sale. Thus 6p is the only price at which, given existing demand and supply, the market is 'cleared'.

Similarly, if the initial price is 4p, 25 000 will be demanded, but only 13 000 offered for sale. Because of this shortage, housewives queue to buy eggs, and sellers see that their supplies will quickly run out. Competition among buyers will force up the price. As this happens, more eggs are supplied to the market, and there is a contraction of demand. This continues until a price of 6p is reached, when demand equals supply of 20 000 eggs.

4.5 Changes in the Conditions of Demand and Supply

The equilibrium price will persist until there is a change in the conditions of either demand or supply.

Let us begin with our market price of 6p. Suppose tastes alter, and people eat more eggs. The conditions of demand have now changed, and the demand curve shifts to the right from D to D_1 (Figure 4.4).

At the original price of 6p we now have an excess of demand over supply – 30 000 eggs are demanded, but only 20 000 are supplied. As explained in the previous section, competition between buyers will now force up the

FIGURE 4.4
The Effect on Price of a Change in the Conditions of Demand

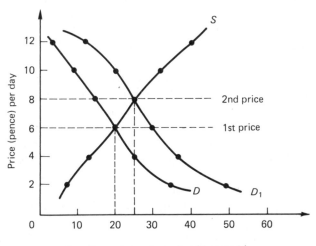

Eggs demanded and supplied (thousands)

price to 8p, a new equilibrium where 25 000 eggs are both demanded and supplied.

Similarly, a decrease in demand – resulting, for instance, from a significant fall in the price of tomatoes – would cause the curve to shift to the left and the price of eggs to fall.

Alternatively a change may occur in the conditions of supply. At any given price more eggs can be produced during the spring, when the supply curve shifts to the right from S to S_1 (Figure 4.5).

FIGURE 4.5
The Effect on Price of a Change in the Conditions of Supply

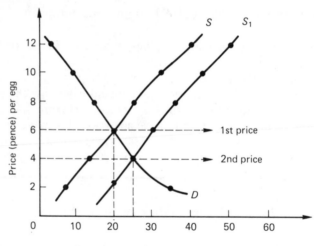

Eggs demanded and supplied (thousands)

At the original price of 6p we now have an excess of supply over demand – 30 000 eggs are supplied, but only 20 000 are demanded. Here competition amongst sellers will mean that the price falls to 4p, where 25 000 eggs are both demanded and supplied.

Similarly, a decrease in supply, resulting for instance, from higher costs of feedingstuffs for hens, would cause the curve to shift to the left and the price of eggs to rise.

Later we have to allow for the time element when looking at the response of supply to a change in the conditions of demand.

5 Applications of Demand and Supply Analysis

Our analysis can be applied to practical problems, especially those relating to government policy. First, however, we use it to examine the role of price in the market economy.

5.1 Functions of Price in the Free Market

In a free market, price both *indicates* and *motivates* by conveying information to buyers and sellers and evoking a response.

Price 'Rations Out' Scarce Goods

At any one time the supply of a good is relatively fixed. It therefore has to be apportioned among the many people wanting it. This is done by adjusting price. As price rises, demand contracts; as it falls, demand expands. At the equilibrium price demand just equals the supply. Should supply increase, the total quantity can still be disposed of by lowering the price; should supply decrease, the price would have to be raised.

We can illustrate how price works by considering, with much simplification, two current problems.

1. How Can Parking-meters Help to Solve the Problem of Traffic Congestion in City Centres?

So long as parking in city streets is free, people going to work in their cars suffer no penalty for monopolising kerbside space throughout the day. At zero price, all kerbside space is occupied, demand exceeding supply in the vicinity of the offices by MM_1. In addition, it often means that off-street car parks and garages cannot pay through lack of demand.

The introduction of parking-meters: (1) makes parkers pay for the space they occupy; (2) helps the police to limit parking to one side of the street or prohibits it in busy roads; (3) discourages the all-day parker by limiting the time which can be spent at one meter; (4) induces the motorist to travel to work by public transport or to park off the street or out of the city centre; (5) causes the demand for off-street parking to increase, thereby encouraging expansion of supply.

In Figure 5.1 when a price *OP* is charged, demand for parking-space just equals the total supply (kerbside and off-street).

2. *Why do Ticket Touts Obtain Such High Prices for Cup Final Tickets?*

To ensure that the regular football supporter can afford a Cup Final ticket, prices are fixed by the Football Association. Let us simplify by assuming that the FA has one price, £10, for the 100 000 tickets, but that a free-market price would be £30. In Figure 5.2, when the price is £30 demand equals the available supply, but at the controlled price of £10 demand exceeds supply by 150 000.

But some tickets are obtained by touts, who resell at a profit in a free market where demand and supply determine price. Keen club supporters, not lucky enough to have been allocated a ticket, are willing to pay more than £10. As the price rises, some people possessing tickets may be induced to sell them to the touts. Thus the demand and supply curves are roughly as shown in Figure 5.3, giving a 'spiv-market' price of £100.

FIGURE 5.1
'Rationing' Car-parking Space

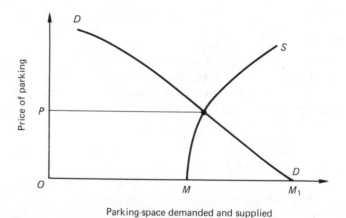

Parking-space demanded and supplied

FIGURE 5.2
Excess Demand for Cup Final Tickets

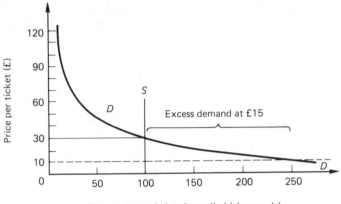

FIGURE 5.3
The Black-market Price of Cup Final Tickets

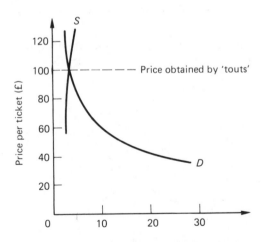

An important conclusion can be drawn from this example: where price is controlled below the market price, only some form of rationing can ensure that everybody gets a share of the limited supply. Normally this is achieved by the FA, which after allocating a certain number of tickets to each finalist, limits each affiliated club to approximately two. One alternative would simply be a 'first come, first served' method of distribution, penalising those who could not queue and increasing the scope for tout activity.

Price Indicates Changes in Wants

Prices are the signals by which households indicate the extent to which different goods are wanted, and any changes in those wants.

Consider how the demand for owner-occupied houses in south-east England has increased over the last ten years through the pressure of population, higher real incomes, tax concessions, etc. As a result, prices have risen from OP to OP_1 (Figure 5.4).

Price Induces Supply to Respond to Changes in Demand

When demand increases, price rises and supply extends: when demand decreases, price falls and supply contracts. Thus in Figure 5.4 the increase in price has made it profitable for extra houses MM_1 to be supplied by new building, by transferring houses from the rented sector, etc.

FIGURE 5.4
The Effect on House Prices of an Increase in Demand by Owner-occupiers

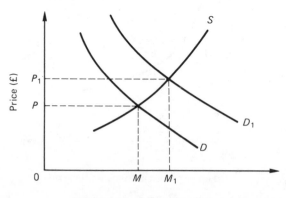

Houses demanded and supplied

In Chapters 8 and 9 we explain in more detail how supply responds to changes in demand.

Price Indicates Changes in the Conditions upon Which Goods Can Be Supplied

If the cost of producing a given commodity rises, this should be signalled to consumers, who can then decide to what extent they are prepared to pay these higher costs by going without other goods. Again this is achieved through price. Assume in Figure 5.5 that the cost of producing good X has increased because raw materials have risen in price. Where demand is depicted by D, most consumers pay the higher costs (price rises by PP_1) rather than do without the good. Where demand is depicted by D_1 consumers tend to go without the good as its price rises (demand falls by MM_1), substituting other goods for it.

FIGURE 5.5
The Effect of a Change in the Conditions of Supply on Price and Quantity Traded

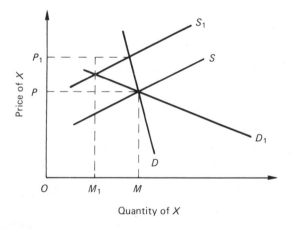

Price Rewards the Factors of Production

Payments for factors of production give their owners spending power. The relative size of this spending power determines the division (usually termed 'distribution') of the cake produced. If the price of a good rises, producers can afford to offer higher rewards in order to attract factors from other uses.

FIGURE 5.6
Stabilising Price through Buffer Stocks

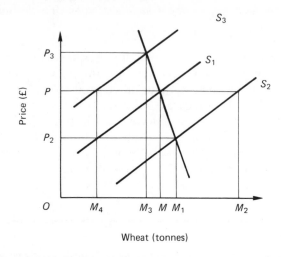

Wheat (tonnes)

5.2 Further Applications

How Can the Government Use Buffer Stocks to Stabilise Commodity Prices?

The government can use a stockpile in order to stabilise the price of basic commodities where demand or supply fluctuates.

In Figure 5.6, it is assumed that the demand for wheat remains constant, but that the conditions of supply change from one period to another. S_1 is the supply curve for period 1, S_2 for period 2 and S_3 for period 3. The government has a stockpile by means of which it stabilises the price of wheat at OP a tonne. This it does by adding MM_2 to the stockpile in period 2 and withdrawing M_4M in period 3.

It should be noted that while the price has been stabilised, farmers' income fluctuates. In period 1, revenue is $OP \times OM$; in period 2, $OP \times OM_2$; in period 3, $OP \times OM_4$.

Application of the same principle allows foreign currency reserves to be used to maintain a stable exchange rate (see p. 544).

How Would an Increase in the Demand for Cars Affect the Price of Tyres?

Cars and tyres are 'jointly demanded'. When there is a change in the conditions of demand for cars, the price of tyres moves in the same direction. This can be seen in Figure 5.7. The increased demand for cars leads to an increased demand for tyres, and the prices of both rise.

Suppose, however, that new techniques allow more cars to be supplied at all prices, Figure 5.7 (iii). There is now an extension of demand in response to the price *fall*. Figure 5.7 (ii) still applies, but prices have moved in opposite directions.

FIGURE 5.7
Joint Demand

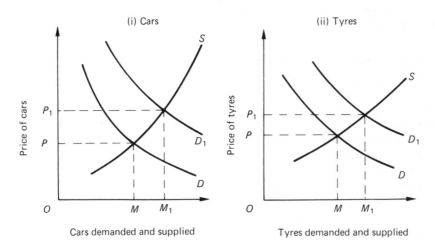

(i) Cars

Cars demanded and supplied

(ii) Tyres

Tyres demanded and supplied

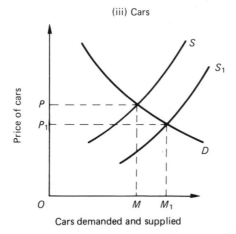

(iii) Cars

Cars demanded and supplied

How would an Increase in the Price of Petrol Affect the Price of Paraffin?

Petrol and paraffin are 'jointly supplied': increased production of one automatically increases production of the other. Suppose that demand for petrol increases but that there is no change in the demand for paraffin. The price of petrol rises from OP to OP_1 and supply expands from OM to OM_1 5.8(i). But this means that the supply of paraffin increases, although there has been no change in price. Thus the supply curve for paraffin moves from S to S_1, and the price of paraffin falls from OR to OR_1 (Figure 5.8ii).

How Could the Government Secure Greater Use of Coal in Order to Conserve the Stock of North Sea Oil?

Here the government must operate to alter the relative prices of coal and oil, reducing the former and increasing the latter. To reduce the price of coal it could give the producer, the National Coal Board, or consumers, such as National Power, a subsidy. In contrast, a high tax could be imposed on the producers or consumers of oil.

The effect is shown in Figure 5.9. Assume the NCB is given a flat-rate subsidy per tonne. This allows more coal to be supplied at all prices, the supply curve moving to S_1. Price falls to OP_1 and demand expands by MM_1. On the other hand, suppose a flat-rate tax is levied on consumers of oil. Their demand is reduced to allow for the tax, the curve falling to D_1. Price, including the tax, rises to OP_1, and the amount sold contracts by MM_1.

FIGURE 5.8
Joint Supply

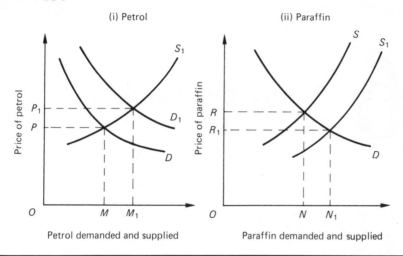

(i) Petrol

(ii) Paraffin

Petrol demanded and supplied

Paraffin demanded and supplied

FIGURE 5.9
The Effect on Quantity Bought of a Subsidy and Tax

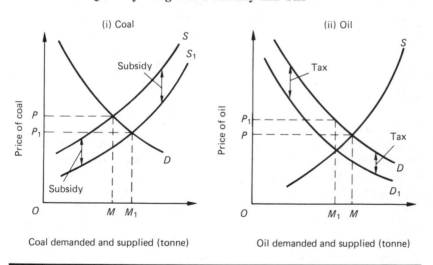

(i) Coal

(ii) Oil

Coal demanded and supplied (tonne)

Oil demanded and supplied (tonne)

6 A Further Look at Demand

6.1 Why the Demand Curve Normally Slopes Downwards: The Marginal Utility Theory

Maximising Satisfaction

Our assumption in Chapter 4 that more of a good will be demanded the lower its price was based solely on our everyday observations. However, by examining a little more closely how the individual consumer 'economises', we can explain why this is normally so.

Our method of approach will be as follows. Our main interest is in the market demand curve. But the market demand is made up of the demand of all the individuals who comprise the market. If, therefore, we study the behaviour of the individual buyer as he spends his income, and it can be said that other buyers act similarly, we can conclude that the market and individual patterns of behaviour are similar.

We assume that every individual has limited resources – represented by a limited money income – and that each acts 'rationally'. 'Rational' must not be interpreted in a value sense as being 'sensible'. It might not be sensible for someone to spend a large part of his income on cigarettes, but that is up to him. All the economist means by 'rational' is that the individual is consistent in his behaviour in the sense that he tries to get the most out of his limited resources. This is a reasonable assumption. There may be the odd consumer who acts frivolously, but since we are dealing with a relatively large number of consumers in the market we can think of a typical consumer who does act 'rationally'.

Because resources are limited, buying one good involves going without something else. In disposing of incomes, therefore, people weigh up the various 'opportunity costs', and try to obtain the maximum satisfaction from their expenditure. Normally their choice does not necessitate making an absolute decision between one good and another, but rather presents itself as whether to have a little more of this by sacrificing a little bit of that.

Here again it might be questioned whether the consumer really does follow this careful procedure. How many people when purchasing a good weigh up its pros and cons and compare it, according to its price, with other goods? Surely, most expenditure is purely automatic? Admittedly, much expenditure is habitual – but this does not mean that people give no thought to it. Our immediate reaction to a selective increase in tax on petrol or cigarettes, for instance, is to ask whether we cannot make do with less. In any case, following a routine for minor matters (including everyday purchases) allows more time for thinking about those things which are outside the usual run of events. Thus while we may not consciously consider the satisfactions to be obtained from other goods every time we buy a packet of tea, we are careful when furnishing a home to weigh up the merits and price of a refrigerator as opposed to a washing machine.

Preliminary Assumptions

 (i) Our consumer is a housewife
 (ii) She has a limited housekeeping allowance per week.
(iii) She acts so as to obtain the maximum satisfaction from her limited income.
(iv) During the period of time under consideration, income, tastes and the other conditions of demand do not change.
 (v) She knows how much satisfaction each unit of a good will give.
(vi) She is one of a large number of buyers and her demand does not directly affect the price of the good.

Questions to Be Answered

Three basic questions have to be answered. First, what conditions will hold when the consumer has obtained the maximum satisfaction from her limited resources? In other words, what are the equilibrium conditions? Second, how does she achieve this equilibrium? Third, what happens when the equilibrium is disturbed by a price change? We deal with each in turn.

1. The Equilibrium Condition

Our housewife will be in equilibrium when she would not switch a single penny of her expenditure on one good to another.

We can be more explicit by introducing the term 'utility'. In economics this simply means that a good has the power to satisfy a want, irrespective of whether it is useful. Note, too, that we cannot measure utility objectively; it is purely subjective to the individual for 'only the wearer knows where the shoe pinches' (see p. 9).

However, our housewife knows in her own mind how much satisfaction each good affords her. She is in equilibrium, therefore, when she has obtained the greatest possible utility from her income: that is, *she maximises total utility*.

She achieves this by careful allocation of her spending – say between cheese and margarine. All the time she is asking: 'If I spend a penny more on cheese, will I obtain more or less utility than if I spent the penny on margarine?' Only when the satisfaction she obtains from the last penny spent on cheese (in the sense of the penny she only just decided to spend) is equal to that from the last penny spent on margarine will she be in equilibrium. That is, her spending adjustments take place at the margin.

Note that we did *not* say that she obtained the same utility from the last pound of cheese as she obtained from the last pound of margarine. If for instance, a pound of cheese were four times as expensive as a pound of margarine, that would obviously be unreasonable; we would expect four times the amount of utility.

Sometimes, however, we cannot buy goods in 'pennyworths' – the good is 'lumpy' and we have to take a whole 'lump' of it or nothing at all. Can we restate our equilibrium condition to allow for this? Yes, but first we must define more carefully the concept of the margin and what we mean by 'marginal utility'.

Each small addition to a given supply of a good is called the *marginal increment*, and the utility derived from this increment is known as the *marginal utility*. Our original condition of equilibrium can therefore be stated in general terms:

$$\text{The marginal utility of 1p spent on good } A \quad = \quad \text{The marginal utility of 1p spent on good } B$$

But the marginal utility of 1p spent on good A depends on how much of a unit of good A you get for 1p. Thus:

$$\text{The marginal utility of 1p spent on good } A \quad = \quad \frac{\text{The marginal utility of one unit of good } A}{\text{The number of pence it costs to buy a unit of good } A}$$

Similarly with good B. Thus our original equilibrium condition can be rewritten as:

$$\frac{\text{The marginal utility of one unit of good } A}{\text{Price of a unit of } A \text{ in pence}} = \frac{\text{The marginal utility of one unit of good } B}{\text{Price of a unit of } B \text{ in pence}}$$

That is:

$$\frac{\text{Marginal utility of good } A}{\text{Price of } A} = \frac{\text{Marginal utility of good } B}{\text{Price of } B}$$

The argument can be extended to cover more than two goods.

2. How Does the Consumer Achieve This Equilibrium?

The question must now be asked: how can our housewife arrange that the utility of the last penny spent on different goods is the same? The answer is to be found in the so-called *law of diminishing marginal utility*. Although wants vary considerably in their nature, they all possess the underlying characteristic that in a given period they can be satisfied fairly quickly. Thus, if a boy drinks lemonade to quench his thirst, the first glass will yield him a great amount of satisfaction. Indeed, the second glass may be equally satisfying. But it is doubtful whether he will relish the third glass to the same extent, since his thirst has now been partially quenched. If he continues to drink the lemonade, there will come a time when a glass gives him no additional satisfaction whatsoever and, in fact, it might be that he would be better off without it – there is a 'disutility'.

Different goods are imperfect substitutes for each other in satisfying a particular want; they therefore yield a smaller satisfaction if transferred to other uses. But, as above, when they continue to be used to satisfy the same want, eventually additions to the supply will yield ever smaller satisfactions. From these two facts – the imperfect substitution of different goods and the satiability of human wants – we can deduce the law of diminishing marginal utility: the utility derived from any given addition to a consumer's stock of a commodity will eventually decline as the supply increases. W. S. Gilbert puts it thus:

> When you have nothing else to wear
> But cloth of gold and satins rare,
> For cloth of gold you cease to care –
> Up goes the price of shoddy.
> *The Gondoliers*

This means that our housewife can arrange that equal utility is derived from the last penny spent on each good by varying the quantity she buys. If she buys more of a good, the stock of other goods remaining fixed, its marginal utility relative to other goods falls. Similarly, if she reduces the quantity she buys, the marginal utility of the good relative to other goods rises. She goes on making these marginal adjustments until she is in equilibrium.

3. What Happens When the Equilibrium is Disturbed by a Price Change?

Suppose the price of cheese falls from 130p to 110p per pound while the prices of other goods remain unchanged. How will this affect her demand for cheese, assuming that she could still do with some more? We can proceed in either of two ways:

(1) The fall in the price of cheese will enable her to obtain more cheese than before for every penny, including the last, which she was spending on it. More cheese usually implies greater satisfaction. The last penny she spent on cheese, therefore, now yields greater satisfaction than the last penny being spent on other goods. Hence she reduces the utility obtained from the last penny spent on cheese by buying more cheese.

(2) The alternative form of the equilibrium condition is:

$$\frac{\text{The marginal utility of the last lb of cheese}}{\text{Price of lb of cheese}} = \frac{\text{The marginal utility of one unit of good } B}{\text{Price of one unit of good } B}$$

A fall in the price of cheese destroys this relationship; the marginal utility of cheese to its price is now higher than with goods *B*, *C*, etc. To restore the equilibrium relationship, the marginal utility of cheese must be decreased. Hence our housewife buys more cheese.

The reasons for this expansion in the demand for cheese can be analysed more closely. A reduction in the price of cheese means that our housewife is now able to purchase all the cheese she had before and still have money left over. This is an *income* effect of a price fall – she can now buy more of all goods, not only cheese. But, in addition to this income effect, more cheese will tend to be bought because of a *substitution* effect. At the margin this means that a penny spent on cheese will now yield more satisfaction than a penny spent on other foods. Thus cheese is substituted for other foods. If cheese is a good substitute, marginal utility will diminish comparatively slowly as the consumption of cheese increases. A given price fall, therefore, will lead to a considerable increase in the quantity of cheese demanded.

Although we have explained the behaviour of only one consumer, it is reasonable to expect other buyers in the market to act similarly, demanding more of a good as its price falls. Since the *market-demand curve* is made up of the demand schedules of all the individual purchasers, we can conclude that more of a good will be demanded the lower its price.

Difficulties of the Above Explanation

While the marginal-utility approach can explain consumers' behaviour in response to price changes, it does present two major difficulties:

(1) It assumes that the housewife knows how much utility she will derive from each unit of all goods bought and then acts almost like a calculating-machine to equalise their marginal utilities relative to price.

(2) It assumes *money income* is fixed, but ignores the fact that a fall in the price of a good, other prices and money income remaining unchanged, represents an increase in *real income*. As we see in the next section, this becomes significant when the fall in price occurs for a good on which the housewife spends a high proportion of her resources. These difficulties are largely avoided by the indifference-curve approach (see pp. 77–88).

6.2 Exceptional Demand Curves

Normally the demand curve slopes downwards from left to right, showing that demand expands as price falls. It is possible, however, to envisage circumstances in which the reverse occurs – a fall in price bringing about a contraction of demand, and a rise in price an extension.

Inferior Goods

Certain goods can be termed 'inferior' in that less is spent on them as income increases, people preferring other goods as incomes rise. Bread, cheap cuts of meat and low-quality floor-coverings are examples.

Now with most goods, e.g. strawberries, demand is likely to increase with a rise in income. The income effect on demand of a price fall will therefore be positive, reinforcing the substitution effect which is always in a positive direction. But with inferior goods the income effect on demand is negative, working in the opposite direction to the substitution effect. Take the case of cheap meat. A fall in its price would result in a tendency to substitute it for better cuts, such as steak, but the income effect would work in the opposite direction, people tending to replace cheaper meat with steak. If the income effect were greater than the substitution effect, the net result would be that less cheaper meat would be demanded at the lower price.

The income effect of a price fall will be more significant the greater the proportion of one's income which is spent on the good. And, if a large part of one's income is spent on an 'inferior' good (as may happen when income is low), the income effect may be so considerable as to outweigh the positive substitution effect. Suppose, for instance, that a person is so poor that 40 per cent of income has to be spent on bread in order to obtain the necessary calories to live. Now suppose that a loaf of bread falls in price from 40p to 20p per lb. The same amount of bread can now be obtained for only 20 per cent of money income, the other 20 per cent being available for spending on different goods. In other words, there has been a substantial increase in real income. As the person is now better off, it is quite likely that a more varied diet will be sought. Foods, other than bread, will be bought but, since they will yield calories formerly provided by bread, they will tend to replace bread, the demand for which will thus contract even though its price has fallen (see also pp. 87–8).

The above is really an extreme case. What is an 'inferior' good depends largely upon one's level of income. Take a cheap joint of meat, for instance. To a particular person this may be an 'inferior' good, the negative income effect of a price fall outweighing the substitution effect. But there would also be poor people who could not have afforded this joint at the old price. For them both the income effect and the substitution effect of a price fall would be positive. Thus, when we look at the *market* demand curve (as opposed to an individual's demand curve), we could find that it follows the normal shape, showing that more is demanded as price falls.

Price Movements are Linked with Expectations

With certain goods, expectations are an integral part of demand. The best example is securities bought and sold on the Stock Exchange where a person's current demand is largely determined by what he thinks will be the price of the security in the future. In this case, a rise or fall in the price of a security may well be associated with a larger or smaller quantity respectively being demanded if people think that the rise or fall will continue.

Goods Having 'Snob Appeal'

Certain goods, e.g. diamonds, model gowns, and mink coats, may be wanted chiefly for ostentation – the desire to impress others. Should the price of such a good fall so much that it comes within the reach of many more people, original purchasers may no longer want it. However, we must distinguish between the individual and market demand curves. Although 'snob' buyers may leave the market when the price of the good falls, it is likely that large numbers of new buyers would enter, thereby adding to demand at these lower prices.

6.3 The Indifference Curve Approach

The great merit of the marginal utility theory is that it focuses attention on how our consumer actually thinks when she is considering whether to buy one good (or an extra unit of it) rather than another. She decides how much satisfaction she will derive from each good and compares this with its price – what it will cost her in terms of other goods which her money could buy. But this marginal utility theory has two main defects:

(a) it assumes that a person can directly measure the utility to be obtained from each unit of all goods bought;
(b) it ignores implicit real income changes resulting from a change in price. For instance, a fall in the price of a commodity, other prices and money income remaining unchanged, is equivalent to an increase in a buyer's real income. Such a change in real income may be significant when a high proportion of income is spent on the commodity whose price has fallen.

The indifference curve approach overcomes these difficulties.

The Construction of an 'Indifference Curve'

We assume that each individual can and does put different goods in a certain order according to the satisfaction each affords. Moreover, because commodities can be substituted for each other, it is possible to find different combinations of them which will yield equivalent satisfaction.

Consider an individual possessing definite quantities of goods, *A, B, C* . . . etc, who is allocating the rest of his income on two other goods *X* and *Y*. (For our exposition it matters little whether *X* and *Y* represent broad categories, such as food and clothing, or specific commodities, such as dwelling space and garden space.) Let us select a random combination of *X* and *Y*, say $4X + 5Y$.

From our assumptions, there must be other combinations of *X* and *Y* that our consumer will regard as giving equal satisfaction to $4X + 5Y$. Table 6.1 suggests a schedule of different combinations of *X* and *Y* which, because they each give equal satisfaction, our consumer can be regarded as being 'indifferent' between.

Table 6.1

X	units	Y
2		11
3		7
4		5
6		3
8		2
12		1

We can plot the combinations of X and Y on a graph (figure 6.1) and join up the points. Since, if X and Y are perfectly divisible, the number of possible equivalent combinations is limitless, we have a continuous curve (I). This is called an *indifference curve* for it represents various combina-

FIGURE 6.1
An Indifference Map

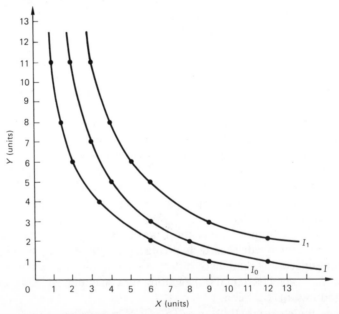

tions of X and Y between which our consumer is indifferent, that is, he does not mind which combination he has.

The Psychological Facts: The Indifference Curve 'Map'

It is possible to envisage other combinations of X and Y which are preferable to any of those indicated by I. For example, $6X + 5Y$ would be preferable to our first combination because it contains 2 more X but just as many Y.

Extending the notion of indifference to this second combination we can envisage other combinations each equivalent to the consumer of $6X + 5Y$ (I_1 Table 6.2). These, too, can be plotted as an indifference curve, I_1 with every combination on I_1 being preferable to any combination on I.

Table 6.2
Combinations of X and Y yielding equivalent satisfactions

I_1		I_0	
X	Y	X	Y
3	11	1	11
4	8	$1\frac{1}{2}$	8
5	6	2	6
6	5	$3\frac{1}{2}$	5
9	3	6	3
12	2	9	2

Similarly, I_0 represents combinations which are inferior to I.

In principle we can fill the whole plane YOX with an infinite number of indifference curves each denoting a higher level of satisfaction as we move north-easterly from O. Lacking a third dimension for measuring satisfaction, we are in fact adopting the technique of the geographer. If the plane YOX represents the horizontal surface at sea level, and the points on any given indifference curve as 'height above sea level', indifference curves are really contours on a 'hill of consumer satisfaction'. If we could measure satisfaction cardinally we could read off such heights. But since we can only rank utility ordinally (that is, in terms of more or less) the most we can say is that I is 'higher on the hill' than I_0, and I_1 higher than I.

Properties of Indifference Curves

1. They Slope Downwards from Left to Right and Are Convex to the Origin

Since the consumer obtains the same satisfaction at any point on the same
indifference curve, it means that as he moves along the curve obtaining
more of one commodity, he must relinquish some of the other commodity.
Thus in Figure 6.2, the consumer in moving from M to M_1 obtains $2Y$ by
giving up $1X$. But it must be emphasised that this is a *marginal*, not a total,
substitution.

Any movement between two points on an indifference curve depicts
such a marginal adjustment. It means that a little bit (usually written Δ) of
one commodity is being given up in order to obtain a little bit more of
another. Thus, if we move from M to M_1, $\Delta X = 1$ and $\Delta Y = 2$; in other
words, 2 extra Y will compensate for the loss of $1X$.

The *marginal rate of substitution* is defined as the increment of Y which
will just compensate for the loss of one unit of X so that the consumer is in

FIGURE 6.2
The Marginal Rate of Substitution

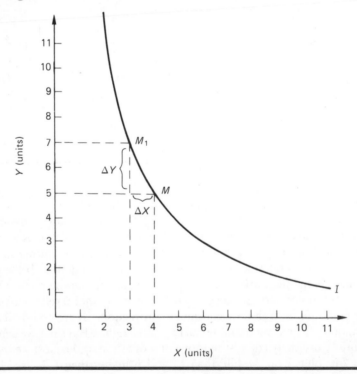

neither a better nor a worse position. At M_1, therefore, the marginal rate of substitution of Y for X (written MRS_{yx}) is $\frac{2}{1}$ or, in general terms, $\frac{\Delta Y}{\Delta X}$. If ΔY and ΔX become small enough, the MRS at a particular point becomes the slope of the tangent to the indifference curve at that point.

It will be seen that, as we move downwards along the indifference curve, less Y has to be given up for an extra unit of X. In other words, there is a *diminishing* MRS_{yx}. This is the reason why the indifference curve is convex to the origin.

2. Commodity Substitutability is Shown by the Slope of the Curve

If Y were an extremely good substitute for X, the MRS would change little as X was substituted for Y. Conversely, if X and Y were poor substitutes, the MRS would change significantly as substitution occurs. These facts would, following the reasoning in (1) above, be reflected in the convexity of the respective difference curves. The shallower the convexity (the closer is the indifference curve to a straight line), the better substitutes are the two commodities for one another. Thus Figure 6.3a might represent different brands of standard tennis balls. The greater the convexity, the worse substitutes they are. Thus Figure 6.3b could represent left- and right-hand gloves which must be used in fixed proportions.

The Economic Facts; the 'Price-Budget Line' Constraint

Indifference curves simply describe consumer preferences, and if these preferences change the curves have to be redrawn. They also presume that

FIGURE 6.3
Substitution Between Goods

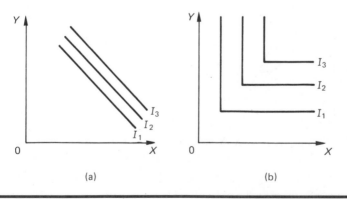

(a)   (b)

the consumer's stock of goods other than X and Y remains constant; again, any change in this stock may change the preference map.

But to obtain the consumer's equilibrium position in his spending on X and Y the psychological data (the indifference curves) has to be related to the economic facts – how much the consumer has to spend and the market prices of X and Y.

Both these facts can be graphed, and both are defined by a single straight line. Suppose, for instance, that our consumer has altogether £10 to spend on both X and Y, and that the prices of X and Y are £2 and £1 respectively. If he spends all his income on X, he can buy 5 units of X; if he spends it all on Y he can buy 10 units of Y. Or he can buy $4X + 2Y$, or $2X + 6Y$, and so on. Using the scale as in Figure 6.1, a graph of these possible quantities gives the straight line AB (Figure 6.4).

FIGURE 6.4
The Price–Budget Line

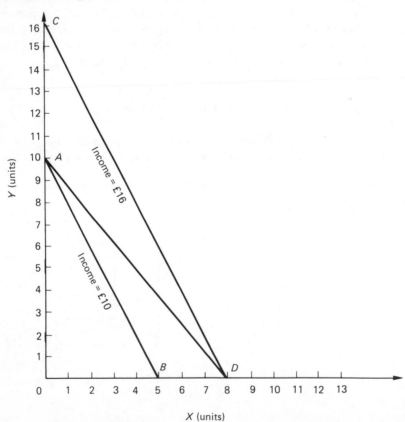

The distance of this *price budget* line from the origin indicates the total amount which the consumer can spend on X and Y. Thus if this amount increased to £16, 60 per cent more of both X or Y could be bought, and so the line moves to CD. Thus a parallel movement of the budget line north-easterly from the origin indicates an increase in income.

The *slope* of the budget line defines the market rate at which X can be exchanged for Y, i.e. it indicates opportunity cost. When X costs twice as much as Y it is AB; if the price of X falls to £1.25, the price line moves to AD for now $8X$ can be bought for £10.

The Equilibrium of the Consumer

In order to see how our consumer allocates his £10 income between X and Y we have to relate his preferences to the market data by combining Figures 6.1 and 6.4 on one graph, Figure 6.5.

Now the greater the satisfaction received from commodities bought, the further is the indifference curve from the origin. On the other hand, our consumer is limited by his income to combinations of X and Y on the budget line AB. Thus the highest indifference curve he can attain is I_0 which the budget line AB just touches at P. Thus his most preferable possible combination is $2X + 6Y$. Here the indifference curve and budget line are tangential – their slopes are equal. In general terms, the consumer is in equilibrium when his MRS of Y for X is equal to the rate (relative prices) at which X can be exchanged for Y.

How Does a Change in the Price of a Commodity Affect Demand for It?

As we have already shown, changes in the relative prices of X and Y are represented by a change in the slope of the budget line. Thus in Figure 6.5 when the price of X falls from £2 to £1.25 the budget line moves from AB to AD. The result is that the consumer moves to a new equilibrium E where he buys $4X$ and $5Y$. In short, because X has become relatively dearer, he buys fewer Y replacing them by X which have become relatively cheaper.

If we join the equilibrium positions P and E and so on for other equilibrium positions for a change in price of X, we shall trace out a line which shows how the consumption of X and Y varies as their relative prices change. We can call this the 'price consumption curve' (PCC, Figure 6.6).

From the above we could construct the demand curve for X (Figure 6.6). Let Y represent money income. We can now obtain the price of X in money terms, since the opportunity cost of X as represented by the scope of the 'price–budget' line, can be related directly to money income. As the price of X falls, more is demanded. Since consumers generally act in this way, it gives us the normal downward-sloping market demand curve.

FIGURE 6.5
Consumer Equilibrium

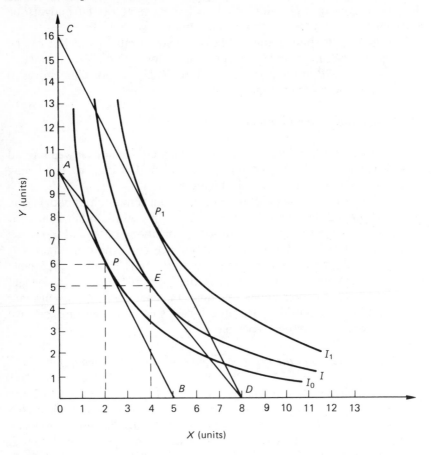

How Does a Change in Income Affect Demand?

As we have seen, if the consumer's income increases from £10 to £16, the budget line moves outwards from the origin while retaining its slope (Figure 6.4). The consumer can now get on to a superior indifference curve (i.e. from I_0 to I) and his equilibrium position will be P where he buys $4X$ and $8Y$ (Figures 6.5 and 6.7). We could imagine a further increase in income, e.g. to £20, which would give another equilibrium position P_1; and so on. Thus in Figure 6.7, the point P traces out a line which shows the way in which the consumer's consumption of X and Y varies as his income increases (the prices of other goods remaining unchanged). We can call this

FIGURE 6.6
The Effect of a Relative Change in Price on Demand

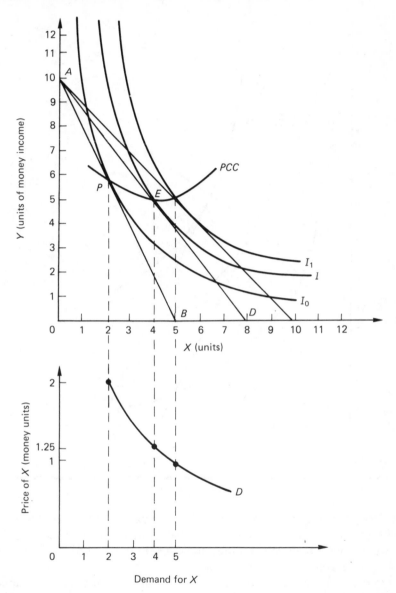

FIGURE 6.7
The Effect on Demand of a Change in Income

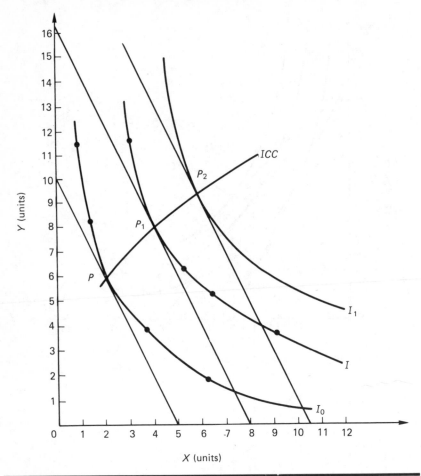

an 'income consumption curve' (ICC). Normally it slopes upwards to the right (as in our example) showing that, when income increases, the consumption of both commodities increases. In other words, for a normal good, the income effect is positive.

On occasions, however, one good may be an 'inferior good' – consumed when the level of income is low but replaced, or partially replaced, by goods of higher quality when income rises. This could happen, for instance, with margarine and butter, when the slope of the indifference curves would be approximately as shown in Figure 6.8. The result is that

FIGURE 6.8
Inferior Goods

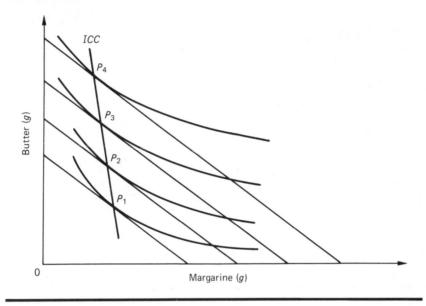

more butter but less margarine are consumed as income increases. The ICC slopes backwards because the income effect is negative.

The 'Giffen Case': Demand Contracts as Price Falls

Figure 6.6 shows that when the price of X falls to £1 the PCC turns upwards – more Y is obtained as well as more X. This is because the fall in the price of X (with the price of Y remaining unchanged) represents a rise in real income.

This distinction between the substitution effect and the income effect can be used to analyse the 'Giffen case' (named after the nineteenth-century economist who first drew attention to it with respect to bread) where *less* of a good is demanded as its *price* falls (see p. 76).

In Figure 6.9, commodity X is an inferior good – the ICC curve slopes backwards showing that, as income increases, less of commodity X is bought (also see Figure 6.8). In other words, the income effect is negative. The ICC is obtained as follows. The price fall from AB to AD puts the consumer on a higher indifference curve, and therefore represents an increase in income from AB to CF. If there were just an increase in

FIGURE 6.9
The 'Giffen Case'

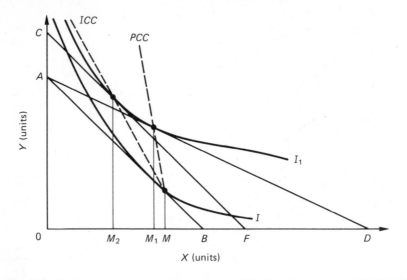

income, he would buy OM_2 of commodity X – less than before because it is an inferior good.

But apart from the negative income effect, there is a positive substitution effect (at the new price of AD) along the indifference curve equal to M_2M_1. This is less than the negative income effect, and the net result of the price fall is that demand drops by MM_1.

Conclusions

Indifference theory is an improvement on marginal utility theory in that:

1. it is simpler in its assumptions – all the consumer is required to do is to prefer one good to another;
2. it shows how changes in the demand for a commodity resulting from a price fall can be separated into two categories – those which arise because the commodity is being substituted for other commodities which are relatively dearer, and those which arise from the increase in real income resulting from the price fall;
3. the psychological data concerning the consumer is kept distinct from the factual data concerning his income and the market.

6.4 Price Elasticity of Demand

Measure of Elasticity of Demand

Consider Figure 6.10. At price OP, demand for both commodities A and B is OM. But when the price of both falls by PP_1, demand for A expands by only MM_1, whereas that for B expands by MM_2. It is possible, therefore, to refer to differences in the 'price elasticity' of demand. This always refers to the elasticity at a particular price, and in what follows when we talk about 'elasticity' it will be assumed that there is some price in mind.

(1) Elasticity of demand is defined by comparing the *rate* at which demand expands to the rate at which price falls. If the former is greater than the latter, we say that demand is *elastic*; if it is smaller, we say that demand is *inelastic*. When they are equal, elasticity of demand is said to be equal to *unity*. Using this definition, elasticity of demand can be measured in two ways. One is direct, showing the degree of elasticity: the other is indirect, merely indicating whether the demand for the good is elastic or inelastic.

Elasticity of demand is the proportionate change in the amount demanded in response to a small change in price divided by the proportionate change in price. That is:

$$\text{Elasticity of demand} \ = \ \frac{\text{Proportionate change in demand}}{\text{Proportionate change in price}}$$

FIGURE 6.10
Elasticity of Demand

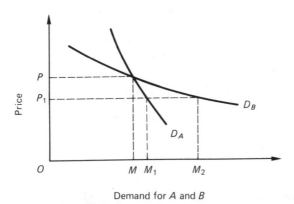

Demand for A and B

$$= \frac{\dfrac{\text{Change in quantity demanded}}{\text{Original quantity demanded}}}{\dfrac{\text{Change in price}}{\text{Original price}}}$$

$$= \frac{\dfrac{\text{New quantity} - \text{Old quantity}}{\text{Old quantity}}}{\dfrac{\text{New price} - \text{Old price}}{\text{Old price}}}$$

We can illustrate by an example from the demand schedule, Table 4.1 (see p. 51). When price falls from 10p to 8p, demand for eggs expands from 9 000 to 15 000. Elasticity of demand is thus equal to

$$\frac{\dfrac{6{,}000}{9{,}000}}{\dfrac{2}{10}} = \frac{\dfrac{2}{3}}{\dfrac{1}{5}} = 3\tfrac{1}{3}$$

Similarly, for a rise in price from 8p to 10p, elasticity of demand equals $1\tfrac{3}{8}$. The difference in the two results occurs because we are measuring from two different points and the change in price is relatively large. Where the price change is infinitely small, measurement of elasticity of demand is at the same point, and there is only one elasticity.

(2) *Point elasticity* at say P (Figure 6.11) can be measured as follows. Take another point P_1 on the curve, and join P and P_1 by a straight line cutting the *y*-axis at t and the *x*-axis at T.

At price PM, demand is OM; at price P_1M_1, demand is OM_1. PF equals the fall in price, and MM_1 the amount by which demand has expanded as a result of this fall in price.

Hence, elasticity of demand

$$= \frac{\dfrac{MM_1}{OM}}{\dfrac{PF}{PM}} = \frac{MM_1}{OM} \times \frac{PM}{PF} = \frac{MM_1}{PF} \times \frac{PM}{OM}$$

But the little $\triangle PFP_1$ is similar to the large $\triangle PMT$.

FIGURE 6.11
Point Elasticity

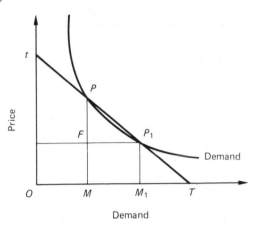

Therefore,

$$\frac{MM_1}{PF} = \frac{MT}{PM}$$

Substituting, elasticity of demand $= \dfrac{MT}{PM} \times \dfrac{PM}{OM} = \dfrac{MT}{OM} = \dfrac{PT}{tP}$

If the distance between P and P_1 is diminished indefinitely, the two points coincide, and tT becomes the tangent to the demand curve at P.

Thus elasticity of demand at a point P on a demand curve equals $\dfrac{PT}{tP}$

where tT is a tangent at that point cutting the y-axis at t and the x-axis at T.

It should also be noted that it is conventional to ignore the minus sign which results from the fact that the typical demand curve has a negative slope.

Conclusions which follow from the above are:

(*a*) A straight-line curve with constant slope does not have constant elasticity. (Although constant slope indicates the same expansion of demand for a given fall in price, we start from *different* prices and quantities when we remeasure, and so the *proportionate* expansions in demand are different.) Thus the $\dfrac{PT}{tP}$ measure above gives the elasticities shown in Figure 6.12:

FIGURE 6.12
Elasticity of a Straight-line Demand Curve

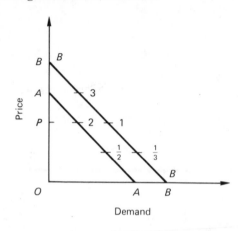

(*b*) Usually we cannot compare the elasticities of demand of different goods by comparing the slopes of the respective demand curves. Thus in the above diagram, at the same price the elasticity of demand at OP of A is 2, while of B it is 1. The reason is that original quantities are different and thus the proportionate changes are different.

(*c*) Elasticity usually varies at every point on the demand curve. The three important exceptions are: demand infinitely elastic (Figure 6.13(a)) demand absolutely inelastic (Figure 6.13(b)), and elasticity of demand equal to unity, where the curve is a rectangular hyperbola (Figure 6.13(c), for rectangles showing total expenditure, e.g. $AOCB$ and $PORQ$, are always equal in area.

(3) For the purpose of economic analysis, it is usually sufficient to refer to elasticity of demand in broad terms. Where elasticity is greater than 1 (the change in the quantity demanded is more than proportionate to the change in price), we say demand is elastic. Where it is less than 1 (the change in the quantity demanded is less than proportionate to the change in price), we say demand is inelastic. If it is 1 (the change in the quantity demanded being proportionate to the change in price), elasticity is described as being equal to unity.

FIGURE 6.13
Constant Elasticities of Demand

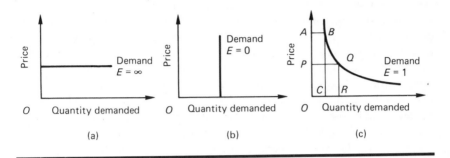

(a) (b) (c)

This broad approach can be used to measure elasticity in a slightly different way. If the proportionate expansion in demand is greater than the proportionate fall in price, the total amount spent on the good will increase. In other words, demand is elastic when, in response to a fall in price, total outlay increases; or, in response to a rise in price, total outlay decreases. Similarly demand is inelastic when, in response to a fall in price, total outlay decreases; or, in response to a rise in price, total outlay increases. Elasticity of demand is equal to unity when, as price changes, total outlay remains the same. Thus, using the same demand schedule, we have elasticities as shown in Table 6.3.

Table 6.3
Elasticity of Demand and Total Outlay

Price of eggs (pence)	Demand (thousands)	Total outlay (pence)	
10	9	90 000 ⎫	Elastic demand
8	15	120 000 ⎭	
6	20	120 000 ⎫	Inelastic demand
4	25	100 000 ⎭	

NOTE
Between 8p and 6p, elasticity of demand equals unity.

Factors Determining Elasticity of Demand

1. The Availability of Substitutes at the Ruling Market Price

As a good falls in price, it becomes cheaper relative to other goods. People are induced to buy more of it to replace goods which are now relatively dearer. How far they can carry out this replacement will depend upon the extent to which the good in question is, in their own minds, a substitute for the other goods. Goods within a particular class are easily substituted for one another. Beef is a substitute for lamb. Thus, if the price of beef falls, people will buy more beef and less lamb. Between one class and another, however, substitution is more difficult. If the price of meat in general falls, there will be a slight tendency to buy more meat and less fish, but this tendency will be very limited because meat is not nearly so perfect a substitute for fish as beef is for lamb.

We must be careful, however, over labelling the demand for the accepted necessities of life as 'inelastic' and the demand for luxuries as 'elastic'. With both, the substitution factor may be more important. Thus, although bread is a necessity, at a high enough price demand for it might be elastic because it has to compete with potatoes or cake. Similarly, a Rolls-Royce is a luxury, but demand for it will be inelastic if no substitute gives a similar prestige. In any case it is difficult to state categorically which goods are necessities and which luxuries. But we can use the concept of elasticity of demand to help, saying that where the demand for a good is very inelastic over a wide price range, that good can be regarded as a necessity, and vice versa.

2. The Number of Possible Substitute Uses

Where a good can be substituted for another good, its demand tends to be elastic. And the more goods it can be substituted for, so the more will demand for it extend as its price falls. Thus reductions in the price of plastics have led to large extensions of demand as they have been substituted for materials used in such articles as enamel bowls, galvanised buckets, paper wrappings, glass garden cloches, wooden toys and tin containers.

3. The Proportion of Income Spent on the Good

When only a very small proportion of a person's income is spent on a good, as (for example) with pepper, salt, shoe polish, newspapers, matches and toothpaste, no great effort is made to look for substitutes when its price rises. Demand for such goods is therefore relatively inelastic. On the other hand, when the expenditure on a good is fairly large, as (for example) with most groceries, a rise in price would provide considerable incentive to find substitutes. Thus supermarkets have succeeded because, when they cut prices, large numbers of customers are attracted from other retailers who are selling the same good at a higher price.

4. The Period of Time

Since it takes time to find substitutes or to change spending habits, elasticity may be greater the longer the period of time under review. In practice, many firms try to overcome the ignorance or conservatism of consumers by advertising, giving free samples, or making special offers.

5. The Possibility of New Purchasers

In discussing the possibility of substitution above, we have looked at elasticity of demand from the point of view of the individual consumer. But when we are considering the market demand curve, we must allow for the fact that, as price falls, new consumers will be induced to buy the good. In fact with many goods, such as cars, video recorders, washing machines, etc., of which people require only one, it is the fall in price bringing the good within the range of the demand of new consumers which leads to the increase in demand. Hence a fall in price which induces people in a numerous income group to buy will result in a considerable elasticity of demand. A fall in price which affects only the higher and smaller income groups, however, will not produce many new customers and hence the market demand schedule tends to be inelastic in this price range.

Uses of the Concept of Elasticity of Demand

The concept of price elasticity of demand figures prominently in both the theoretical analysis of the economist and the practical decisions of the businessman and government. The following are a few examples.

1. Theoretical Economics

(A) TO DEFINE 'PERFECT COMPETITION' IN SELLING A GOOD

The economist, in order to explain the working of the economy, usually begins by constructing a model of how it works under theoretical conditions known as 'perfect competition' (see pp. 134–7). On the selling side, one essential requirement of perfect competition is that everybody in the market produces so small a quantity of the total supply that no one seller can influence the price of the good by the amount he puts on the market. He has to accept market price as given for any output he might produce. That is, he sees the demand for his good as perfectly elastic (*see* p. 135).

(Similarly, on the buying side, no one purchaser must be able to influence the price by the size of his demand – **see** p. 136).

(Similarly, on the buying side, no one purchaser must be able to influence the price by the size of his demand – **see** p. 136).

(B) AS A HELPFUL TOOL IN ANALYSING PROBLEMS CONNECTED WITH CHANGES IN SUPPLY

Many problems analysed by the economist can be tackled adequately only by making use of the concept of elasticity of demand. Consider, for example, the question: 'What effect will a rise in wages have on the numbers employed in the car industry?' The answer hinges largely on the elasticity of demand for the product made by that labour. An increase in wages will move the supply curve of the product to the left (Figure 6.14). Output will contract – but how much it contracts depends upon the elasticity of demand. If demand is elastic, it will contract to OM_1; if inelastic, to OM_2.

The general rule is that where demand is elastic, a change in supply will cause the quantity sold to change rather than price; where demand is inelastic, price changes rather than the quantity sold. Thus a trade union will find it more difficult to obtain a wage increase for its members without creating unemployment where the elasticity of demand for the product made is high (see pp. 229–30).

2. Business Decisions

(A) THE SUPERMARKET

The policy of the supermarket rests largely on the high elasticity of demand for its products. When it cuts the price of a good, the supermarket expects

---

FIGURE 6.14
Elasticity of Demand and a Change in the Conditions of Supply

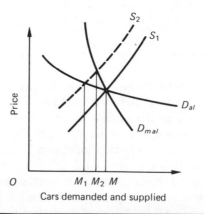

a considerable expansion in demand by winning customers from retailers selling at a higher price. Thus it is most successful in selling standardized goods, such as branded groceries, but less successful where customers form a personal attachment to the shopkeeper, as with butchers, tailors, etc.

(B) BRITISH RAIL

If at the existing fare, demand is elastic, a fare increase would reduce total revenue. Only if, through carrying fewer passengers, operating costs fell more than revenue would the fare increase be justified. On the other hand, if demand were inelastic, raising fares would be bound to increase total revenue without adding to operating costs.

In practice, British Rail discriminates in its charges between commuters and casual travellers. The former have to travel at peak periods. Their demand, therefore, is relatively less elastic than that of casual travellers, who can choose their time and particular mode of travel. If the demand of casual travellers is elastic, offering them a lower fare outside peak hours will be profitable provided the extra revenue exceeds any additional operating costs.

3. Government Policy

(a) TAXATION

If the Chancellor of the Exchequer wishes to raise revenue, he would tax goods having an inelastic demand. This can be shown diagrammatically (Figure 6.15).

At price OP the demand curve D_e is more elastic than D_i. Levying a fixed tax per unit has the effect of reducing demand at all prices by the amount of the tax (see p. 503). This gives new demand curves, $D_e + t$ and $D_i + t$ respectively. To simplify the model, we assume that costs are constant at OP whatever the output, giving a horizontal supply curve. This results in price rising by the full amount of the tax to P_t (see p. 506). The shaded area represents the extra yield of D_i over D_e

(B) BUFFER STOCKS CAN BE USED TO STABILISE FARMERS' INCOME

We can assume that the total revenue received from the sale of agricultural produce roughly represents farmers' incomes. Inelastic demand for agricultural produce means that any change in the conditions of supply can lead to wide fluctuations in farmers' incomes (Figure 6.16). The government can use its stockpile to stabilise incomes. In doing so, it also dampens price fluctuations, thus giving greater price stability for consumers.

We start with an equilibrium price OP and farmers' income $POME$. Price can change, but income will only be stable if the price received lies on the unitary elasticity of demand curve.

FIGURE 6.15
Elasticity of Demand and Tax Yield

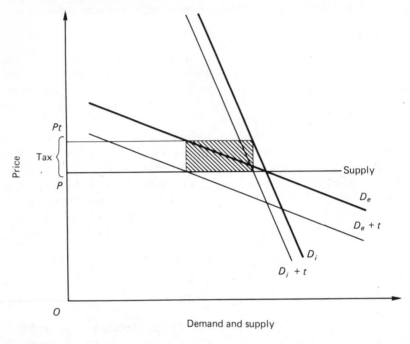

Suppose S increases to S_1. The government must now purchase $M_1 M_2$ (i.e. increase demand). Price falls only to OP_1 instead of to P_M, but farmers' incomes remain unchanged since by definition rectangle $P_1 O M_2 E_1$ = rectangle $POME$.

Similarly, for a decrease in supply to S_2, the government must use its stockpile to increase supply by $M_4 M_3$ to give a price of OP_2 rather than the market price of P_N.

Other examples of government interest in elasticity of demand are: (c) How will a tax on its products affect the size of the industry? (p. 504); (d) How is the burden of a selective indirect tax shared betwen the consumer and the producer? (p. 506); (e) Can the terms of trade be improved by an import duty? (p. 522); (f) Would devaluation or depreciation be successful in improving the balance of payments? (p. 546); (g) Will an improvement in the terms of trade improve the balance of payments? (p. 519).

FIGURE 6.16
Maintaining Farmers' Incomes

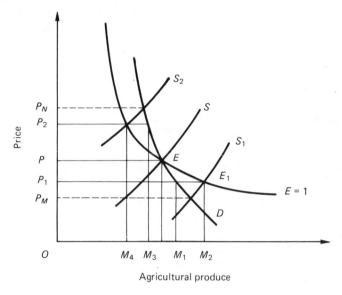

6.5 Other Elasticities of Demand

When we refer to 'elasticity of demand' without qualification, we are speaking, as above, of what is more precisely *'own-price* elasticity of demand'. But the concept has other applications.

Income Elasticity of Demand

An increase in real income usually increases the demand for goods, but to a varying degree. It is thus possible to speak of *income elasticity of demand* – the proportionate change in demand divided by the proportionate change in real income which has brought it about. If demand increases 20 per cent, for instance, as a result of a 10 per cent increase in real income, income elasticity of demand equals 2. Which goods have a high income elasticity of demand depends upon current living standards. Thus in Western Europe today, it is the demand for such goods as cars, washing machines, dish washers, central-heating appliances, new houses, and personal services which expands the most as income increases. In contrast, necessities, such as potatoes, salt, eggs, and soap, have a low income elasticity of demand. With 'inferior' goods (see p. 86), income elasticity of demand is negative.

Cross-elasticity of Demand

Where two goods are related, e.g. as substitutes or complements, a change in the price of one will lead to a change in demand for the other. Thus a rise in the price of oil leads to an increase in the demand for coal, while a fall in the price of video recorders leads to an increased demand for video tapes.

The extent to which the demand for a good changes in response to a price change of another good is known as *cross-elasticity of demand:*

$$\text{Cross-elasticity of demand} = \frac{\text{Percentage change in the quantity demanded of good } X}{\text{Percentage change in the price of good } Y}$$

With substitutes, cross-elasticity is positive. For example, an increase in the price of Y would lead to an increase in the demand for X (as with oil and coal in the example above). With complements, cross-elasticity is negative, since a fall in the price of Y leads to a rise in the demand for X (as with video recorders and tapes above). The closer the substitutes or complements, the larger will be the figure for cross-elasticity. A cross-elasticity near zero signifies that there is little relationship between the two goods:

Cross-elasticity

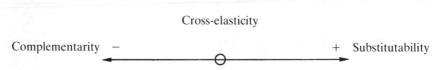

Complementarity −   + Substitutability

7 Supply (1): Organising Production

7.1 The Role of the Firm

So far we have given only a very approximate explanation of how supply responds to a change in price. For the next three chapters our task will be to examine the supply curve a little more closely. As with demand, we have to study the actions of individuals, in this case *firms*, the units which hire productive resources in order to produce goods and services.

By considering the decisions a firm has to make, we try to establish general principles governing its behaviour. This chapter will be concerned mainly with the decisions on hiring and combining the factors of production. Chapters 8 and 9 will look at problems connected with output. First, however, we must consider what economists are really referring to when they talk about the different 'factors of production' and 'production'.

The Factors of Production

The classical economists divided the factors of production into four groups – land, labour, capital and organisation. The rewards going to these factor groups were called rent, wages, interest and profit, respectively.

Such a classification, based on physical characteristics has serious weaknesses, e.g. the training of a worker represents an input of capital. Thus present-day economists conduct much of their analysis by talking about factors of production generally – resources which cooperate in the production of goods and services wanted by the community. But they also recognise that certain factors do have some common, broad and important characteristics which permit a general classification useful for purposes of analysis and so the old classical economists' terminology has been retained.

Land now refers solely to the resources provided by nature, e.g. space, rain and minerals. In practice, it is treated as a separate factor of production in order to examine the nature of the earnings of any factor which is fixed in supply.

Labour refers to the actual effort, both physical and mental, made by human beings in production. It is this 'human' element which distinguishes it from other factors, for it gives rise to special problems regarding mobility, unemployment and psychological attitudes.

Capital, as opposed to land, is man-made. Goods can be classified as:

(*a*) *Consumer goods:* those goods which directly satisfy customers' wants and are in the hands of the consumer, e.g. a loaf, a bicycle, a table.

(*b*) *Producer goods:* those goods which are not wanted directly for their own sake, but for the contribution they make to the production of consumer goods, e.g. buildings, machines, tools, raw materials. Sometimes the same good may be either a consumer good or a producer good, depending on its use. A car, for instance, may be used simply for pleasure, or by a sales representative for business.

Capital, as a factor of production, consists of producer goods and stocks of consumer goods not yet in the hands of the consumer. It is treated as a separate factor of production in order to emphasise (*a*) the sacrifice of present enjoyment which is necessary to obtain it, and (*b*) the fluctuations in economic activity which occur because its use extends over a period of time (see Chapters 28 and 29).

Enterprise refers to the acceptance of the risks of production which arise through uncertainty. This is a somewhat narrower meaning than that given by the classical economists to the *entrepreneur* – the person or persons who decided what goods to produce and brought the factors of production together to produce them.

Today the role of organising the factors of production is regarded as a managerial function which can be performed by a paid manager, i.e. by a highly skilled form of labour. What really distinguishes enterprise from other factors is that it has to carry all the *risks of production*. How these risks arise will be examined in more detail later. Briefly, they occur because production takes time. The entrepreneur engages labour and buys raw materials and machinery now in order to produce a good which will not be sold until some time in the future. Whether costs are recovered will depend upon the demand for the good when it comes to be sold. There may be a change in tastes in the meantime; or a rival may, through a better process, be putting the good on the market at a lower price. In such ways, an expected profit may turn out to be a loss.

Profit or loss is the reward of uncertainty-bearing. Whoever accepts this ultimate risk is the true entrepreneur – the farmer working on his own account, the doctor who starts his own practice, the persons who buy shares (the 'risk' capital) in a company, or the citizens of a state (who gain should a nationalised industry achieve a profit, but ultimately bear any losses made).

Production

Early economists, such as the French Physiocrats of the eighteenth century, considered that only work in the extractive industries (agriculture, mining and fishing) was productive. In his *Wealth of Nations* in 1776, Adam Smith added manufacturing, but he was specific in excluding workers who merely rendered services.

This was illogical. People work, and production takes place, in order to satisfy wants. Consequently, people who render services must be regarded as being productive. The soldier, actor and footballer are all satisfying wants. Similarly, in a factory, the clerk who calculates the wages is just as productive as the man who makes the nuts and bolts. All are helping to produce the final product, a good satisfying wants.

Wants can take different forms. Most people like a newspaper to read at the breakfast table; thus the boy who takes it from the shop to the customer's letterbox is productive. Most people, too, prefer to buy their potatoes weekly; thus the farmer or merchant who stores them through the winter is satisfying the wants of consumers, and is similarly productive. Utility is created by changing not only the *form* of our scarce resources, but also their *place* and *time*.

For certain purposes it may still be useful to classify industries broadly. *Primary industries* cover the first steps in the productive process – agriculture, fishing, mining and oil prospecting. *Secondary industries* use the raw materials of the extractive industries to manufacture their own products – flour, clothing, tinned salmon, steel girders, petrol and so on. *Tertiary industries* are concerned with the provision of services – transport, communications, distribution, commerce, government, and professional and other services.

The Objectives of the Firm

In a market economy a firm has to cover its costs if it is to stay in business. Thus regard must be paid to 'profitability'.

But in practice are firms always single-minded in seeking to *maximise money* profits? The answer is no; there is a range of possible objectives.

Personal motives may be important, especially where the manager is also the owner of the firm. Thus emphasis may be placed on good labour relations, the welfare of the workers, the desire for power, political influence, public esteem or simply 'a quiet life'. To cover such objectives profit would have to be interpreted in a wider sense than 'money profit'.

With major companies there is in practice a gap between the ownership and its administration. The business is run by professional managers, and is too complex for shareholders to be able to exert effective control. This applies even to the institutional shareholders, who avoid being directly involved in the running of the business. Thus the motives of the full-time executive managers tend to override the shareholders' desire for maximum return on capital invested. Managers may be anxious for the security of their own jobs and, instead of taking the calculated risks necessary to earn maximum profits, tend to play for safety. More likely, they will be motivated by personal desires for status. Provided they achieve a level of profit which keeps shareholders content, their positions and salaries can be enhanced by expanding the firm to where it *maximises sales* rather than profits. Alternatively, the rate of growth may be maximised. Either objective becomes a possibility when competition is imperfect.

Even when there is an emphasis on money profit, a firm may stress its long-term position rather than immediate maximum profit. Security of future profits may be the dominating motive for mergers and takeovers as an alternative to developing new products and techniques. Moreover, where there is an element of monopoly, a firm can follow its own pricing policy rather than have it determined by competitive market conditions (see Chapter 12). In such circumstances it may not adjust prices to short-term changes in demand and supply conditions. For one thing, there are the administrative costs of printing and distributing new price lists. For another, frequent changes in price tend to offend retailers and customers.

Again a firm enjoying a degree of monopoly has always to assess what effect the pursuit of maximum profit may have on its overall position in the long term. Will a high price attract new entrants or encourage the development of a rival product? Will it lead to adverse publicity and eventually to government intervention by a reference to the Office of Fair Trading?

Finally, a firm has often to modify its objectives in deference to government policy. Thus it may be expected to follow government guidelines regarding wage increases, to have regard to the environment in the disposal of its waste products and even to retain surplus workers for a time rather than add to an already high level of unemployment.

Yet, while we must take account of these other objectives, our analysis cannot proceed far if any are seen as the main motive force of the firm. In any case, they merely supplement the profit objective, for profits have to be made if the firm is to survive. Thus the best general assumption is that firms seek to maximise profits. We can then establish principles concerning how resources should be combined and what output should be produced.

The Decisions of the Firm

The firm has to decide on policies to secure its profit objective. In broad terms, these cover assessing the demand of potential customers and organising production accordingly. If it is seeking to maximise its profits, a firm will have to produce that output which secures the largest possible difference between total receipts and total costs. It will therefore always have an incentive to keep the cost of producing a given output to a minimum. This means that it must answer the following questions:

  (i) What shall it produce?
 (ii) How shall it raise the necessary capital?
(iii) What techniques shall be adopted, and what shall be the scale of operations?
 (iv) Where shall production be located?
  (v) How shall resources be combined?
 (vi) What shall be the size of output?
(vii) How shall it deal with its employees?

We consider the first five problems in the remainder of this chapter; the rest are examined in Chapters 8 and 14.

7.2 What to Produce

The First Approach

Other things being equal, a firm will produce those goods which enable it to make the greatest return on capital. However, in practice, this usually means that it has to choose a line of production within the limited range of its specialist knowledge. Let us assume that the firm is manufacturing light farm machines and that it is contemplating producing lawnmowers.

Since it is likely that some firms are already producing lawnmowers, the market economy throws up two guidelines. First, there is the current price of mowers. The firm would have to estimate its own costs for producing similar mowers, the number it could expect to sell at this price, and its likely profits, and thus calculate the return on capital employed. Second, the accounts of companies have to be filed with the Registrar of Companies, and the profit earned by public companies is publicised in the financial pages of leading newspapers and specialist journals. If existing producers of lawnmowers were shown to be earning a high rate of profit, the prospects for a new competitor would look favourable.

Market Research

Where the proposed market is new or different from that for existing products, the above indicators are not so useful. Here the firm must fall back on some form of market research.

Initially, it may be producing similar goods, e.g. light agricultural machinery, and some indications of potential demand may come from wholesalers, retailers or even customers in conversation with the firm's representatives. Such suggestions can be cross-checked with those of other distributors.

Where the reaction is generally favourable, more thorough market research can be carried out, probably through a specialist market research organisation. Market research can cover desk research, field studies and test marketing.

Desk research examines the broad determinants of the potential demand by using (i) published material, e.g. government statistics, and (ii) the firm's own sales records. As we saw in Chapter 4, these determinants are price and the various conditions of demand. More specialist facts could be obtained from relevant periodicals and trade journals, e.g. *Gardeners' World* (where circulation figures indicate the number of keen gardeners). Membership figures for the Royal Horticultural Society could also be used.

More precise information on potential sales necessitates a planned, consumer-oriented *market research programme* in potential markets. This would cover many aspects of market behaviour, particularly consumer reaction to the product – especially with regard to its quality, packaging, delivery dates and after-sales service, and to price cuts.

Before a national or major sales campaign is undertaken, some form of *test marketing* would probably be carried out so that modifications could be made to correct any deficiencies. For instance, such a test might reveal that certain features of the product were unnecessary, thus permitting greater standardisation. Moreover, not all potential customers have identical preferences. The firm would therefore consider (i) a 'marketing mix' – producing different models at different prices – and (ii) varying sales methods and channels of distribution.

7.3 Raising the Necessary Capital

After deciding what to produce, the firm must consider what legal form its business shall take and how to raise finance in order to employ the desired factors of production. It may be that the two decisions are closely linked from the beginning. But it must be remembered that a business has to be fairly successful before it can induce outsiders to subscribe finance on a large scale for its development. Hence initially it is likely that the legal form of the business will rest primarily on the degree of control which the entrepreneur wishes to exercise personally and the various legal and tax advantages which different types afford. The position is summarised in Figure 7.1.

The finance required by a firm is usually classified as (a) working capital, and (b) fixed capital.

FIGURE 7.1
Forms of Enterprise and the Raising of Capital

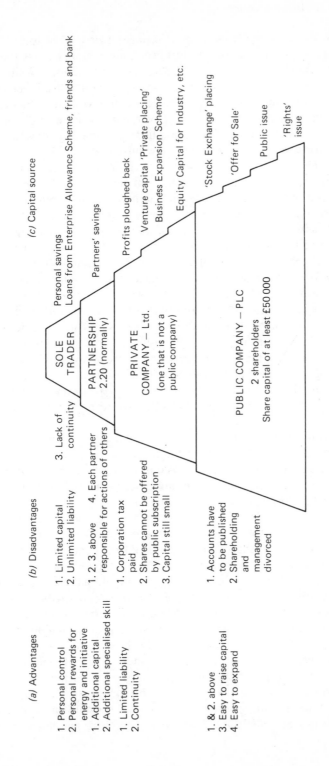

(a) *Working capital* is for purchasing 'single-use' factors – labour, raw materials, petrol, stationery, fertilisers, etc – more or less the factors we refer to in Chapter 6 as 'variable factors'. Finance for working capital can be obtained from a variety of sources: banks, trade credit, finance companies, factor houses, tax reserves, intercompany finance, advance deposits from customers and the government (e.g. through the Enterprise Allowance Scheme which on conditions provides an allowance of £40 per week for a year when starting a new business).

(b) *Fixed capital* covers factors which are used many times – factories, machines, land, lorries, etc. Some finance for fixed capital is therefore required initially for advance payments on factory buildings, machinery and so on before the firm is earning revenue, though it is possible to convert fixed capital into working capital by renting buildings, hiring plant and vehicles or by leasing or buying on deferred payments through a finance company. Normally, fixed-capital requirements are larger than those for working capital. Moreover, lenders recognise that they part with their money for a longer period and accept a greater risk. Thus finance for fixed capital tends to be more difficult to raise than for working capital.

This could mean that unless the business starts as an offshoot of a parent company, the businessman will probably be limited to his own or his friends' savings, for only persons who know him well will lend money. As he progresses, he may be able to obtain a long-term loan from his bank, a merchant bank, or, if he has a building to mortgage, from a building society. But normally expansion will have to rely on the reinvestment of profits.

This is a lengthy process. If he operates as a *sole trader*, accepting full responsibility for the debts of the business, he may even find it easier to obtain a loan. Forming a *partnership* or a *private company* may initially bring in little extra capital. In any case, additional capital could only be secured by losing some of his control.

Many businesses do, however, start their existence as companies. This is to secure limited liability – only the capital of the company and not the personal assets of shareholders can be taken to meet the company's debts. But even with a sole trader, as business expands, a *company* will most likely be formed in order to obtain the additional capital required.

Nevertheless, because the shares of a *private company* are illiquid in that they cannot be offered for sale by public advertisement, a difficult stage in its growth may be reached when its capital is in the region of £250 000, for it is still too small to make a public issue. The gap can be bridged in four main ways. First, as part of the government's desire to encourage growth of the economy through the development of small businesses, new sources of 'venture capital' have arisen. Banks and other institutions have been more willing to provide medium-term loans especially as, under the Loan Guarantee Scheme, the Department of Industry guarantees 80 per cent of loans up to £75 000. More important is the Business Expansion Scheme by which individuals enjoy tax relief on up to £40 000 share capital each year. Second, a stockbroker may effect a 'private placing' of shares or debentures with a life insurance company or an investment trust, who are usually in a position to ignore the disadvantages of holding securities of private companies. Third, help might be obtained from the new issue market, where both issuing houses and merchant bankers assist firms to raise capital even providing some themselves. Fourth, there are a number of specialised finance corporations, e.g. 3i (formerly known as Investors in Industry). Fifth, the commercial banks have now entered the medium-term loan field, particularly through their merchant bank branches.

When a large amount of capital is required, the first step is usually to form a *public company*. But it is the second step which is really important – getting its shares 'quoted' on one of the Stock Exchange markets – the Unlisted Securities Market or the Stock Exchange.

The capital required can be raised by a 'placing', an 'offer for sale' or a 'public issue by prospectus'. The first is the usual method when only about £1 million is required, for the costs of underwriting and administration are less. An issuing house, licensed dealer or investment company agrees to sell blocks of the shares privately to persons who it knows are likely to be interested in them.

For larger amounts of up to £5 million an offer for sale is a likely method. The shares are sold *en bloc* to an issuing house, which then offers them for sale to the public by advertisement similar to a public issue. The above two methods are the only ones available to companies whose shares are dealt in on the Unlisted Securities Market.

For more than £10 million, a public issue by prospectus is the method usually employed. Here the company's object is to obtain from the public in a single day the capital it requires. Hence it must advertise well and price its shares a little on the cheap side. The advertisement is in the form of a prospectus which sets out the business, history and prospects of the company together with its financial standing and the security offered. In practice, the sale is usually conducted through an issuing house.

Later, when the company is well established, it can generally meet its extra requirements of capital by a *rights issue* to existing shareholders, who obtain the shares on bonus terms.

Where Does Capital Come From?

The market for capital is usually classified into two main parts:

(1) The *Money Markets*, dealing with short-term finance and centred on the joint-stock banks and discount houses (Chapter 23).

(2) The *Capital Market*, which is concerned with the provision of medium- and long-term capital to industry, the government, agriculture,

and house-building. Funds are collected from a variety of sources by different institutions. Some of these are quite specialised, e.g. the Agricultural Mortgage Corporation, building societies, finance companies (which deal with hire-purchase capital), and the National Savings Bank (which invests mostly in government stock).

New issues, both of industrial and government securities, are subscribed for by the public and institutions – insurance companies, investment trusts, unit trusts, pension funds, banks, etc. – through issuing houses, brokers, bankers, etc.

7.4   Where to Produce

In deciding where to produce, a firm has to weigh the advantages of a particular locality against the rent or land costs it will have to pay there compared with elsewhere.

Location Advantages

The advantages of producing in a particular locality can be classified as: (i) natural, (ii) acquired and (iii) government-sponsored.

1. Natural Advantages

Costs are incurred both in assembling raw materials and in distributing the finished product. With some goods the weight of the raw materials is far greater than that of the finished product. This is particularly true where coal is used for heat and power, e.g. in iron and steel production (Figure 7.2). Here transport costs are saved by producing where raw materials are found, e.g. on coal- and iron-ore fields, or where they are easily accessible, e.g. near a port.

On the other hand, in some industries the costs of transporting the finished product are greater than those of assembling the raw materials. e.g. with ice cream, mineral waters, furniture and metal cans. With these it is cheaper for a firm to produce near the market for its goods. Thus Walls has ice cream factories close to most large concentrations of population.

What is really important as regards transport costs is their ratio to the value of the product. Thus sand and gravel are excavated locally, whereas special types of brick are transported long distances.

Generally speaking, transport improvements and new developments (e.g. electrical power, lighter materials) have helped firms to move away from their sources of raw materials. The tendency now is, therefore, for firms to concentrate, not on the coalfields, but on the outskirts of areas of

FIGURE 7.2
The Production of Pig Iron – a Weight-losing Industry

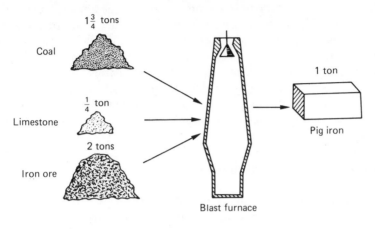

Blast furnace

high population which provide both a supply of labour and a market for the finished good.

A river estuary or coastal location may be essential when huge quantities of water are required by an industry (e.g. chemicals, atomic power), and this may also be important for waste disposal.

Besides accessibility to raw materials and nearness of markets, suitability of climate is a further natural advantage which may have to be considered when locating production. Indeed, in agriculture, it is usually decisive, provided soil conditions are not adverse.

Under 'natural advantages' we can also include an adequate supply of the type of labour required. Thus high technology industries have been attracted to the south-east of England by the skilled labour available, while the abundance of cheap labour has been important for the development of mass production in Taiwan and Hong Kong.

2. Acquired Advantages

Improved methods of production, the development of transport, inventions and new sources of power may alter the relative importance of natural advantages and so change an industry's location. Thus, as high-grade iron-ore fields have become exhausted and improved techniques have reduced coal consumption, it is now cheaper to transport the coal than the iron ore to produce pig iron, and so the industry has shifted from the coalfields to the low-grade iron-ore fields of the east Midlands.

Similarly, improved transport may upset the relative pulls. Finally, new inventions, such as humidifiers and water softeners, can make an industry less dependent upon a particular locality.

Yet we must not overstress the importance of the above changes. Even when natural factors have disappeared, an industry often remains in the same region because of the 'man-made' advantages it has acquired, e.g. steel or cotton. A skilled labour force, communications, marketing and commercial organisations, nearby ancillary industries (to achieve economies of scale or to market by-products), training schools and a widespread reputation for the products of the region all help to lower the costs of production, thereby making the locality attractive to new firms (see also p. 118).

3. Government-sponsored Advantages

Unemployment in such highly localised industries as coal, cotton and shipbuilding, and environmental problems (traffic congestion, pollution, housing stress) in regions attracting new and expanding industries, have led the government to offer firms financial inducements to set up plants in Development Areas (see Chapter 31).

The Level of Rents in Different Areas

Location advantages have to be weighed against the cost of land (or, where it is hired, rent). This cost varies from one locality to another and is determined by the market mechanism. Since other firms, possibly from other industries, may be looking for the same site advantages, competition will fix the price of land at the highest which the keenest firm is prepared to pay. This will be the firm which puts the greatest value on the land's advantages compared with those of land elsewhere.

In the final analysis, therefore, it is not the absolute advantages of a district which decide where a firm locates, but the advantages relative to those of other districts. Thus an industry whose outlay on unskilled labour forms a high proportion of its production costs would, other things being equal, be able to bid more for land in an area of cheap labour than one whose spending on such labour was minimal. And in town centres we see the same principle at work – shops oust other businesses, and houses are converted into offices.

Other Influences on Location

A firm will normally choose the site where the advantages are greatest compared with its cost. But even for a comparatively new industry, where natural advantages are important, we cannot assume that they will be decisive. Thus it is largely historical accident which accounts for the presence of the Austin Rover plant at Cowley on the outskirts of Oxford, for the old school of William Morris came up for sale just as the production of cars at his original cycle works was being expanded.

Moreover, electricity has now practically eliminated dependence on a coalfield site. Yet firms may still go to the original areas because of the advantages acquired over time. Others may choose to be nearer their markets. Some 'footloose' firms have even located in certain districts, particularly south-east England, largely because the managing directors (or their wives) have preferred living there!

The various factors influencing location are summarised in Figure 7.3.

FIGURE 7.3
Factors Influencing the Siting of a Business

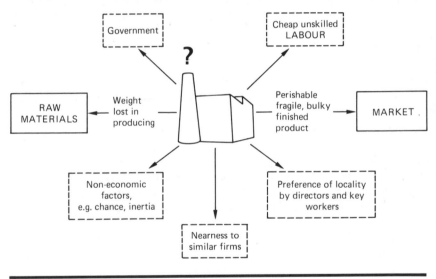

7.5 How to Organize the Factors of Production

In organising its factors of production, the firm will have to consider the advantages of specialisation and of producing on a large scale.

Specialisation: The Division of Labour Advantages of Specialisation

Specialisation is the fundamental principle of modern production. Here we examine it with particular reference to labour – although, as we shall see, it is equally applicable to machines, localities and even countries.

Where workers are organised so that each specialises on a particular task, increased production results. This is because:

1. Each Man is Employed in the Job in Which His Superiority is Most Marked

Rudyard Kipling puts it thus:

> And some can pot begonias and some can bud a rose,
> And some are hardly fit to trust with anything that grows;
> But they can roll and trim the lawns and sift the sand and loam,
> For the Glory of the Garden occupieth all who come.

We shall return to the advantage of specialisation when we consider international trade (p. 512).

Even if, initially, workers were equally proficient at the different jobs, it might still pay to specialise, for the following reasons.

2. Learning is Facilitated

Not only is less time taken in learning a particular job, but 'practice makes perfect' so that skills are developed by repetition of the same task.

3. Economy in Tools Allows Specialised Machinery to be Used

This is illustrated in Figure 7.4 where in (b) division of labour has been introduced. Not only are specialised tools in constant use but their output is much greater. Thus division of labour sets free talented men for research – and allows their inventions to be used profitably.

4. Time is Saved Through not Having to Switch from One Operation to Another

5. The Employer Can Estimate His Costs of Production and Output More Accurately

Disadvantages of the Division of Labour

While the division of labour leads to lower costs of production, it may have disadvantages both for the workers and for society. The worker may find his job monotonous, and this could affect the quality of work. With some occupations such as paint spraying there is a risk of occupational disease. Moreover, the skilled specialist may face redundancy if demand falls, while

FIGURE 7.4
Economy in Tools Through Specialisation

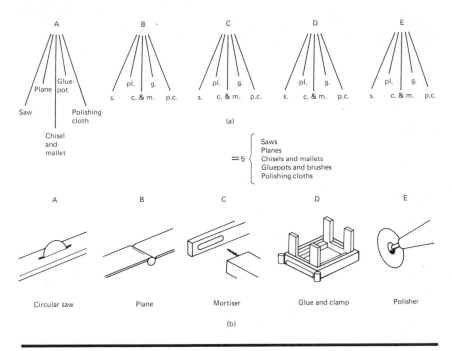

a strike by a few key workers can lead to widespread unemployment. Finally, standardised products tend to replace individual craft work.

Limitations on the Division of Labour

Naturally, the scope for the division of labour varies from one industry to another. Countries like Switzerland which have too few workers to permit much specialisation concentrate on manufacturing a narrow range of products. Again, in industries such as agriculture and building where the same operations are not taking place each day, many 'Jacks of all trades' are required. Moreover, an exchange system is essential: we must first unite in exchange before we can divide in production. Finally, the division of labour has to be related to current demand for the product. It is no use specialising in making something which nobody wants; conversely, minute division of labour is only possible when there is a large demand. The complex organisation of car production, for instance, rests on a mass demand for a standardised product made up from a multitude of small parts.

7.6   The Advantages of Large-scale Production

As a firm's output increases, costs per unit may fall as a result of the advantages of large-scale production. These are often referred to as 'internal economies' to distinguish them from 'external economies', which arise indirectly from the growth of the industry (see p. 118).

Internal Economies

Internal economies are of five main kinds:

1. Technical Economies

In making a good, as distinct from distributing it, increased output permits more division of labour, greater specialisation of machines, the economy of large machines (e.g. a double-decker bus can carry twice as many passengers as a single-decker, though neither the initial cost nor running costs are doubled) and the linking of processes (e.g. in steel-making, where re-heating is avoided).

Generally, technical economies fix the size of the unit actually producing, e.g. a supermarket, rather than the size of the firm, which may consist of many units, e.g. Tesco. Where technical economies are great, the size of the typical unit will tend to be large – as, for example, in the production of cars, sheet steel, gas and electricity. Where, however, increased output merely means duplicating and reduplicating machines, the tendency will be for the unit to remain small. For instance, in farming at least one combine harvester is necessary for about 500 acres. Thus farms tend to remain small, for as yet there are no great technical economies to be derived from large machines. Where few technical economies can be gained and yet the firm is large, consisting – as with chain stores – of many operating units, it is usually because other types of economy are possible, as follows.

2. Managerial Economies

When output increases, division of labour can be applied to management. For example, in a shop owned and run by one man, the owner, although having the ability to order supplies, keep accounts and sell the goods, has yet to do such trivial jobs as sweeping the floor, weighing articles and packing parcels – tasks within the capability of a boy who has just left school. His sales, however, may not warrant employing a boy. The large business overcomes this difficulty: a brilliant organiser can devote all his time to organising, the routine jobs being left to lower-paid workers.

The function of management can itself be divided, e.g. into production, sales, transport and personnel. These departments may be further subdivided – sales, for instance, being split into sections for advertising, exports and customers' welfare.

3. Commercial Economies

If a bulk order can be placed for materials and components, the supplier will usually quote a lower price per unit, since this enables him also to gain the advantages of large-scale production.

Economies can also be achieved in selling the product. If the sales staff are not being worked to capacity, the additional output can be sold at little extra cost. Moreover, the large firm often manufactures many products, so that one acts as an advertisement for the others. Thus Hoover vacuum cleaners advertise their washing machines, dishwashers and steam irons. In addition, a large firm may be able to sell its by-products, something which might be unprofitable for a small firm.

Finally, when the business is sufficiently large, the division of labour can be introduced on the commercial side, with expert buyers and sellers being employed.

Such commercial economies represent real gains to the community, reducing prices through better use of resources. On the other hand, where a large firm uses its muscle to *force* suppliers into granting it favourable prices, it will simply result in higher prices to other buyers.

4. Financial Economies

In raising finance for expansion the large firm is in a favourable position. It can, for instance, offer better security to bankers – and, because it is well known, raise money at lower cost, since investors prefer shares which can be readily sold on the Stock Exchange.

5. Risk-bearing Economies

Here we can distinguish three sorts of risk. First, there are those which can be insured against, enabling large and small firms alike to spread risks.

Second, certain businesses usually bear some risk themselves, saving some of the profits made by the insurance company. Here the large firm has a definite advantage. London Transport, for instance, can cover its own risks, while a large bank can call in funds from other branches when there is a run on the reserves in a particular locality.

The third kind of risk is one that cannot be reduced to a mathematical probability and thus cannot be insured against – risk arising from changes in demand for the product or in the supply of raw materials: this is usually referred to as risk arising from 'uncertainty'. To meet fluctuations in demand the large firm can diversify output (like British American

Tobacco) or develop export markets. On the supply side, materials may be obtained from different sources to guard against crop failures, strikes, etc.

External Economies

While the firm can plan its internal economies, it can only *hope* to benefit from external economies which arise as the *industry* grows.

First, the concentration of similar firms in an area may produce mutual benefits: a skilled labour force; cooperating in providing common services, such as marketing and research; better roads and social amenities; technical schools catering for the local industry; product reputation; ancillary firms supplying specialised machinery, collecting by-products, etc. The firm must take into account such economies when deciding where production shall take place, for the lower costs may outweigh any diseconomies which arise through traffic congestion, smoke, etc. (see p. 147).

Second, external economies can take the form of common information services provided either by associations of firms or even by the government.

Finally, as an industry grows in size, specialist firms may be established to provide components and services for all producers thereby extending economies of scale.

7.7   The Size of Firms

Horizontal, Vertical and Lateral Combination

The advantages of large-scale production provide firms with a strong impetus to combine (Figure 7.5).

Horizontal integration occurs where firms producing the same type of product combine. Thus Nestlé took over Rowntree, and Ford acquired Jaguar.

Vertical integration is the amalgamation of firms engaged in the different stages of production of a good. Thus Britoil, an oil exploration company was taken over by BP. Vertical integration may be 'backward' towards the raw material; or 'forward' towards the finished product.

Both the above can lead to lower costs per unit, and therefore to increased profits. Thus horizontal integration can allow greater specialisation, commercial economies and a saving on administrative overheads. Vertical integration facilitates linked processes and reduces risk by increasing direct control over the supply and quality of raw materials and components. Moreover, all parts can be manufactured to an integrated

FIGURE 7.5
Horizontal and Vertical Integration

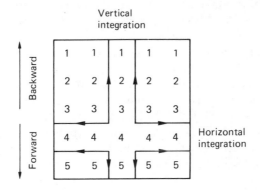

design, and there is direct control over the distribution of the final product (see below).

Lateral integration occurs where a firm increases the range of its products. Concentration on one product may make a firm vulnerable to a change in fashion, a switch in government policy or a recession. Thus the firm diversifies, often by taking over other firms producing completely different products. For instance, P & O is engaged in shipping, cross-Channel ferries, road transport and construction through its subsidiary companies.

Apart from increasing profits through economies of scale, integration can achieve other objectives, such as prestige and security of profits. One other aim, however, must not be overlooked – monopoly power. This is discussed in Chapter 12.

Integration may result from internal development or combination with existing firms. Combination may be secured by a complete takeover, when a company buys all the shares of a smaller firm and absorbs it completely, or by the formation of a holding company in which the parent company owns enough shares of a subsidiary company to give it effective control, though the smaller company preserves its identity and enjoys considerable independence of action. Many large companies, e.g. Unilever, GEC and Great Universal Stores, hold such controlling interests in subsidiary companies.

The Predominance of the Small Firm

In spite of the advantages enjoyed by the large firm, we must not conclude that every firm has to be large to be competitive. Indeed the small firm still predominates in all forms of production. In agriculture two-thirds of all holdings are less than fifty acres in size, while in retailing nearly three-quarters of all firms consist of only one shop. Even more remarkably, the same is true of manufacturing where one would have thought that technical economies of scale would be all-important. Table 7.1, which shows the size of the establishment – the factory or workshop – in manufacturing, reveals two important features: (i) the small establishment is typical of manufacturing in the UK, over nine-tenths employing less than 100 people; (ii) these small units employ only one-third of the labour force.

Any explanation of this predominance of the small firm has to deal with two salient facts: (i) small firms are especially important in certain industries, such as agriculture, retailing, building, and personal and professional services; (ii) variations in the size of firms exist even within the same industry. Both result from the nature of the conditions of demand and supply.

Table 7.1
Size of Manufacturing Establishments in the UK, 1989

Employees	Number of firms	Percentage of total firms	Number of employees (000s)	Percentage of total employed
1–9	107 155	67.3	319	6.6
10–99	42 477	26.7	314	27.4
100–999	9 173	5.7	2 322	48.3
Over 1,00	433	0.3	851	17.7
TOTAL	159 238	100	4 806	100

SOURCE *Annual Abstract of Statistics*

1. Demand

Large-scale production may be only *technically* efficient; it is not *economically* efficient unless a large and regular demand justifies it.

The market may be small because demand is local (e.g. for personal services and the goods sold by the village store), or limited to a few articles of one pattern (e.g. for prestige luxury goods and highly specialised and individually designed machine tools) or because transport costs are high (e.g. for bricks and perishable market garden produce), or because product differentiation divides it artificially (see p. 204).

Where demand fluctuates (e.g. in construction), the overhead cost of idle specialised equipment is heavy – but the smaller the firm, the less the burden.

2. *Supply*

Even if demand is large, factors on the supply side may make for small firms. While in certain industries, e.g. retailing and building, it is possible to start with little capital or supported by franchising (e.g. McDonald's) or by joining a wholesale chain (e.g. Spar), the difficulty of obtaining further funds and the taxation of profits are obstacles to expansion. Furthermore, government monopoly policy may prevent mergers (see p. 195). Alternatively, where vertical dis-integration is possible, firms need not expand internally but simply employ specialist firms for advertising, research, supplying components and selling by-products. Important, too, is the fact that many small owners do not have the drive to expand or the ability to manage a large concern. Or, as in farming and retailing, they will work long hours (that is, accept a lower rate of profit) simply to be their own bosses.

Above all, as the size of the firm increases (Figure 7.6), management difficulties occur. If management is vested in heads of department, problems of coordination rise and rivalries develop. This means that one person must be in overall command – yet people with such capabilities are in very limited supply. In certain industries these difficulties may soon occur. Rapid decisions are required where demand changes quickly e.g. in the fashion trades, or supply conditions alter, e.g. through the weather in agriculture. Or care may have to be given to the personal requirements of customers, e.g. in retailing and services. This may necessitate the close supervision of management, and thus the firm has to be small.

7.8 Combining the Factors of Production

Even the simplest form of production requires at least two factors of production. Thus the manna which fell from Heaven, although a free gift of Nature, needed labour to collect it (Exodus 16). But since factors can usually be combined in different proportions, a firm has to decide how much of each it will hire. In other words, how will it allocate its spending in order to obtain the greatest possible output from a given outlay? For example, the same amount of concrete can be mixed by having many men with just a shovel apiece or by having only one man using a concrete-mixer. Can we discover any general principle governing the firm's decision? We

FIGURE 7.6
Factors Influencing the Size of a Firm

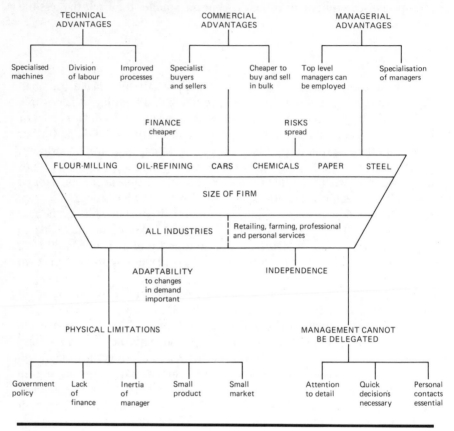

can begin by seeing what happens to output when one factor is held fixed while the amount of another factor is increased. From this we derive the law of diminishing returns.

The Law of Diminishing (or Non-proportional) Returns

The present-day formulation of the law is as follows: provided that all units of the variable factor are perfect substitutes for each other and that techniques or organisation do not change, if one factor is held fixed, but additional units of the varying factor are added to it, eventually the extra output resulting from an additional unit of the varying factor will become successively smaller. Since the additional output resulting from an extra unit of the varying factor is known as the 'marginal product', the law refers to eventual diminishing marginal productivity.

The law can be illustrated as follows. Assume: (i) production is by two factors only, land and labour; (ii) all units of the variable factor, labour, are equally efficient; (ii) there is no change in techniques or organisation.

Table 7.2 shows how the output of potatoes varies as more labourers work on a fixed amount of land. Until 3 men are employed, the marginal product of labour is increasing – the third labour, for instance, adding thirty-eight bags. Here there are really too few labourers for the given amount of land. Thereafter the marginal product falls, the fourth labourer adding only twenty-six bags, and so on; total output is still increasing, but at a diminishing rate. The maximum return per labourer occurs when there are four labourers to the plot. If we increase the number of labourers to eight, the maximum return per labourer can only be maintained by doubling the amount of land. When eleven labourers are employed they start to get in one another's way, and from then on total output is declining absolutely.

In order to avoid any misconceptions, it is helpful to call attention to certain fundamental points.

1. The units of the variable factor are homogeneous. The marginal product of labour does not fall because less efficient labourers are being employed. Diminishing returns occur because more labourers are being employed on a fixed amount of land – and, through physical considerations, labour is an imperfect substitute for land. (If it were otherwise, all the world's food supplies could be grown on a garden plot: extra land would not be necessary, since output could be increased merely by adding labourers.)

2. The law applies only if one factor is held fixed. (If both factors can be varied, we have a change of 'scale'.)

3. The law is not applicable if the factors can only be combined in fixed proportions. If, for instance, you must have one labourer to one shovel to obtain any output, then merely increasing the number of labourers by one will add nothing to output; the marginal product is nil. For the law to hold, the proportions in which the factors can be combined must be variable. For this reason, the law is often referred to as the law of variable proportions.

4. The law does not formulate any *economic* hypothesis or theory; it merely states physical relationships. While the physical productivity of an extra labourer is important to a farmer in deciding how many men to employ, it will not *determine* his decision. He must also know the relative costs of factors; that is, he requires economic data as well as technical facts.

5. There are no changes in techniques.

Table 7.2
Variations in Output of Potatoes Resulting from a Change in Labour Employed

Number of men employed on the fixed unit of land	Total output	Output (50-kilo bags) Average product	Marginal product	Stage
1	2	2.0	2	
2	16	8.0	14	I
3	54	18.0	38	
4	80	20.0	26	
5	95	19.0	15	
6	108	18.0	13	
7	120	17.1	12	II
8	130	16.2	10	
9	138	15.3	8	
10	142	14.2	4	
11	142	12.9	0	III
12	132	11.0	−10	

NOTES
(a) *Total output* is the total output (bags) from all factors employed.
(b) *Average product* refers to the average output per man. It therefore equals

$$\frac{\text{total output}}{\text{number of men employed}}$$

(c) *Marginal product* refers to the marginal output (bags) to labour, and equals the addition to total output which is obtained by increasing the labour force by one man. That is, marginal output equals total output of $(n + 1)$ men minus total output of n men.
(d) There is a fundamental relationship between average product and marginal product. Marginal product equals average product when the latter is at a maximum (Figure 7.7). This relationship is bound to occur. So long as the marginal product is greater than average product, the return to an additional labourer will raise the average product of all labourers employed. On the other hand, as soon as the marginal product falls below average product, the additional labourer will lower the average product. Hence when average product is neither rising nor falling, that is, at its maximum, it is because marginal product equals average product.

   This relationship can be made clearer by a simple example. Suppose Botham has played 20 innings and that his batting average is 60 runs. Now if in his next innings he scores more than 60, say 102, his average will increase – to 62. If, on the other hand, he scores less than 60, say 18, his average will fall – to 58. If he scores exactly 60 in his twenty-first innings, his average will remain unchanged at 60.

The Practical Applications of the Law of Diminishing Returns

The law is significant both in our everyday life and in the theoretical analysis of the economist.

First, it helps to explain the low standard of living in many parts of the world, particularly the Far East. Increasing population is cultivating a fixed amount of land. Marginal product, and thus average product are falling – and so, therefore, is the average standard of living.

Second, it shows how a firm can adjust the marginal physical products of factors by altering the proportion in which they are combined. Thus few labourers to the plot gave a high return per labourer; after four labourers, the average product began to fall. So the law is often referred to as 'the law of varying proportions'. The firm will choose that combination of factors which yields the maximum output from a given outlay, as follows.

The Optimum Combination of Variable Factors

So far we have assumed that there are just two factors, land and labour, and that land is fixed. But suppose that there is another variable factor, say capital. Now the farmer will have to decide how he will combine labour

FIGURE 7.7
The Relationship between the Number of Labourers Employed, Average Output and Marginal Output

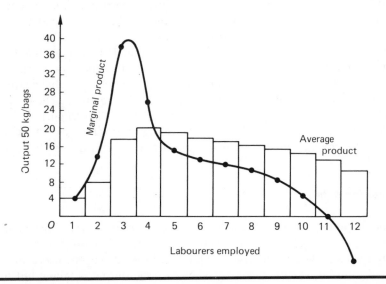

with capital. The problem is similar to that of the consumer seeking to obtain the maximum satisfaction from the expenditure of limited income.

How much of each he employs will depend upon its productivity relative to its price, since he will alter the combination until, for the last pound spent on both labour and capital, he obtains the same amount of product. Suppose, for instance, the last pound's worth of labour is yielding more potatoes than the last pound spent on capital. It will obviously pay the farmer to transfer this pound from capital to buying more labour, for this will increase his total physical yield.

But labour and capital are obtained in different units, their units being different in price. Thus we cannot directly compare the productivity of one man with that of one unit of capital, say a mechanical hoe; we must allow for their respective prices. If the cost of one man is only one-third of the cost of a mechanical hoe, then the marginal product of a man need only be one-third of the hoe's to give the same yield for a given expenditure. Thus the farmer will be in equilibrium in combining factors when:

$$\frac{\text{Marginal product of labour}}{\text{Price of labour}} = \frac{\text{Marginal product of capital}}{\text{Price of capital}}$$

A corollary of this is that, like the housewife in purchasing her goods, the entrepreneur will tend to buy more of a factor as its price falls, and less as it rises. Suppose the wage-rate rises but the marginal product of labour remains unchanged. The fundamental relationship stated above has now been destroyed. To restore the position it is necessary to raise the marginal product of labour and to lower that of capital by combining less labour with more capital: in short, a rise in wages without a corresponding increase in the productivity of labour will, other things being equal, tend to bring about the replacement of labour by machines.

The above argument helps to explain why in Britain more capital is combined with a given amount of labour in agriculture compared with Ireland; relative prices are different. Similarly, if land is variable as well as labour, agriculture will be extensive where land is relatively cheap (as in Canada) and intensive where it is relatively dear (as in Britain).

A third application of the law of diminishing returns is to show how costs vary with changes in output when one or more factors are fixed (see pp. 130–1).

Increasing Returns

In our example it is possible to trace three separate stages of production. Stage I, when average output is increasing, occurs when no more than four men are employed on the plot of land. (Marginal output, however, has already started to fall.) Stage II, when average output is falling but total output is still increasing, ranges from four to eleven labourers. Stage III, when total output is decreasing absolutely, occurs when twelve or more men are employed. Let us examine these stages in more detail.

Total output is decreasing absolutely in Stage III because so many men are employed on the plot of land that they get in each other's way. Any labourer above eleven has a negative marginal output! Nobody but a fool would produce under such conditions. What is not so obvious is that a similar situation exists in Stage I, except that here too much land is being employed per unit of labour. For the purposes of our argument we assumed that the plot of land was fixed in size, that is, 'indivisible'. In practice, a farmer who owned the land and had fewer than four labourers available would not farm the whole plot; by decreasing the amount of land under cultivation he could increase output. Suppose, for example, that he had only two labourers. Were he to farm the whole plot, his total output would be 16 bags of potatoes. But, by confining cultivation to half the plot, he could combine land and labour in the same proportion as when four men were employed on the whole plot, obtaining 40 bags, a gain of 24 bags. In short, over Stage I, the men waste their time walking over surplus land; here the marginal product of land, if it were divisible, is negative.

It might easily be concluded that the ideal combination occurs where four men are employed, for here the average output per labourer is at a maximum. But, as just shown, if the plot of land is divisible its marginal product (not labour's) up to this point is negative. As more labourers are employed, so the marginal output of the land increases and by the time four labourers are working, it has ceased to be negative and is nil. Now a factor will be used to the point where its marginal output is nil only if it is superabundant, and therefore costs nothing, or if it is completely specific, that is, it has no use in any other line of production. In the case of land, both situations are rare. Hence farming usually takes place somewhere in Stage II (where average output of both land and labour are falling), the exact position depending, as already shown, on the relative prices of land and labour.

But many factors, unlike land, are not easily divisible. It is often impossible for a firm to equip itself to produce one unit of a commodity without immediately providing capacity to produce more than one unit. Any output of pig iron, for example, necessitates the prior provision of an expensive blast furnace capable of producing many millions of tonnes in the course of its life. Such indivisible equipment represents factors fixed in size as opposed to varying factors, such as labour and raw materials, which can be increased as output expands. Until a certain output is reached, the situation is similar to Stage I, where the whole plot of land is being used. The plant is being worked to 'less than capacity'; average output increases as variable factors are added. In short, indivisibilities produce for a time increasing returns.

8 Supply (2): Deciding on the Most Profitable Output

8.1 The Costs of Production

Opportunity Costs and Profit

Suppose a man sets himself up as a shopkeeper selling sweets. He invests £2 000 of his savings in the business, and in the first year his receipts are £40 000 and his outgoings £22 000. The accountant would say that his profits over the year were £18 000. The economist, however, would disagree.

The reason for this is that the economist is not so much concerned with money costs as with 'opportunity cost' – what a factor could earn in its best alternative line of production. This concept of cost has a bearing on (i) the economist's concept of 'profit', and (ii) how long production should continue when total costs are not covered.

'Implicit Costs'

The £22 000 money outgoings of the shopkeeper above can be regarded as 'explicit costs'. But when we look at costs as alternatives forgone we see immediately that the shopkeeper has certain 'implicit costs' – the rewards his own capital and labour could earn elsewhere. If, for instance, his capital could be invested at 12 per cent, there is an implicit cost of £240 a year. Similarly with his own labour. His next most profitable line, we will assume, is to be a shop manager earning £11 760 a year. Thus a total of £12 000 in implicit costs in addition to the explicit costs should be deducted from his receipts.

Normal and Supernormal Profit

But we have not finished yet. The shopkeeper knows that, even in running a sweet shop, some risk arises through uncertainty – a risk which he avoids if he merely works for somebody else. The shopkeeper must therefore anticipate at least a certain minimum profit, say £2 000 a year, before he will start his own business. If he does not make this minimum profit, he feels he might as well go into some other line of business or become a paid shop manager. Thus another type of cost (which we call 'normal profit') has to be allowed for – the minimum return which keeps a firm in a particular industry after all other factors have been paid their opportunity cost. Normal profit is a cost because, if it is not met, the supply of entrepreneurship to that particular line of business dries up.

We have, therefore, the following costs: explicit costs, implicit costs and normal profit. Anything left over after all these costs have been met is 'supernormal' profit. In terms of our example, we have:

	£	£
Total revenue		40 000
Total costs: explicit	22 000	
implicit	12 000	
normal profit	2 000	
		36 000
Supernormal profit		4 000

Fixed Costs and Variable Costs

For the purpose of our analysis, we shall classify costs as either *fixed* or *variable*.

Fixed costs are those costs which do not vary in direct proportion to the firm's output. They are the costs of indivisible factors, e.g. buildings, machinery and vehicles. Even if there is no output fixed costs must be incurred, but for a time, as output expands, they remain the same.

In short, fixed factors cannot be engaged currently with their use and in proportion to output. The entrepreneur has to pay for them in advance, and if what he makes turns out to be a 'white elephant', there is little he can do about it short of selling up for what he can get. With such costs, 'bygones are forever bygones'.

Variable costs, on the other hand, are those costs which vary directly with output. They are the costs of the variable factors, e.g. operative labour, raw materials, fuel for running the machines, wear and tear on equipment. Where there is no output, variable costs are nil; as output increases so variable costs increase.

In practice it is difficult to draw an absolute line between fixed and variable costs; the difference really depends on the length of time involved. When current output is not profitable, the firm will have to contract production. At first overtime will cease; later, workers will be paid off. In time, more factors, e.g. salesmen, become variable, and if receipts still do not justify expenditure on them they too can be dismissed. A factor becomes variable when a decision has to be taken on whether it shall be replaced, for then its alternative uses have to be considered. Eventually machines need renewing; even they have become a variable cost. A decision may now be necessary on whether the business should continue.

The distinction between fixed and variable factors and costs is useful in two ways. First, in economic analysis it provides a means of distinguishing between differences in the conditions of supply which result from changes in the time period. The *short period* is defined as a period when there is at least one fixed factor. While, therefore, supply can be adjusted by labour working overtime and more raw materials being used, the time is too short for altering fixed plant and organisation. Thus the firm cannot achieve its best possible combination for a given output. In the *long period* all factors are variable; they can therefore be combined in the best possible way. Thus supply can respond fully to a change in demand.

Second, as we shall see later, the distinction is fundamental when the firm is considering whether or not to continue producing. In the long period all costs of production, fixed and variable, must be covered if production is to continue. But in the short period fixed costs cannot be avoided by ceasing to produce; they have already been paid for, simply because it was necessary to have some 'lumpy' factors even before production could start. Only variable costs can be saved; and so, provided these are covered by receipts, the firm will continue to produce. Anything that it makes above such costs will help to recoup its fixed costs (see p. 140).

Changes in Costs as Output Expands

In our discussion of the law of diminishing returns we referred to quantities of factors and yields in physical terms. But in deciding how to maximise profit, the firm will be concerned with those quantities translated into money terms. It can then see directly the relationship between costs and receipts at different outputs and is thus able to decide what output will give the maximum profit (see Table 8.1). Our first task, therefore, is to consider how costs are likely to change as output increases. We shall assume perfect competition in buying factors of production – the demand of each firm is so small in relation to total supply that any change in demand will not directly affect the price of those factors.

In the short period there are, by definition, bound to be fixed factors. And when considering the law of diminishing returns we found that when a variable factor was added to a fixed factor the marginal product might increase for a time but would eventually diminish. How will this affect costs as output expands?

Let us assume that two factors are being used, one of them fixed. If each unit of the variable factor costs the same, but the output from additional units is increasing, the firm is obtaining an increasing output for any given addition to expenditure. In other words, the cost of each additional unit of output is falling as output expands. On the other hand, if the marginal product of the variable factor is diminishing, the cost of an additional unit of output is rising. This cost of an additional unit of output is known as *marginal cost* (MC).

The above conclusions are represented diagrammatically in Figure 8.1, where average product = total product of n units of the variable factor/n and average variable cost = total variable costs of n units of output/n.

FIGURE 8.1
The Relationship between Returns and Costs

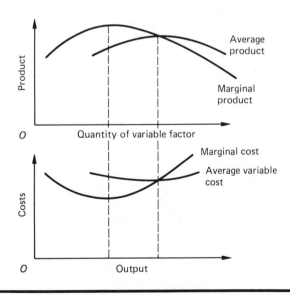

Cost Schedules

Table 8.1 illustrates this relationship between output and costs. The figures, which have been kept as simple as possible, are for an imaginary firm, Rollermowers, manufacturers of lawnmowers. Fixed costs (FC) amount to £10 000, and, as variable factors are added, output expands. At first, there is an increasing marginal product; as a result MC is falling. This has its effect on average total cost (ATC) until approximately 75 units are being produced. From then onwards, as the fixed factors are being worked more intensively, diminishing returns cause the ATC curve to rise. These figures can be plotted on a graph (Figure 8.2).

The following relationships between the curves should be noted:

(i) AFC and AVC added vertically give ATC.
(ii) The MC curve cuts both the AVC and ATC curves when they are at a minimum, the same reason applying as in Table 8.1, note (d).

FIGURE 8.2
Cost Curves

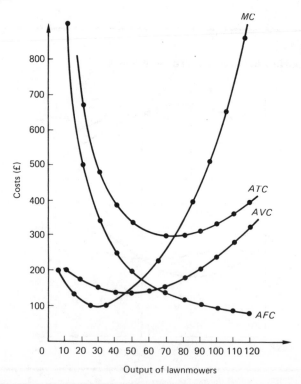

Table 8.1
Costs, Revenue and Profits of Rollermowers (in £)

Output per week (units)	Fixed cost (FC)	Total variable cost (TVC)	Total cost (TC)	Marginal cost (MC)	Average fixed cost (AFC)	Average variable cost (AVC)	Average total cost (ATC)	Total revenue (TR)	Profit, super-normal (TR-TC)
0	10 000								
				200					
10	10 000	2 000	12 000		1 000	200	1 200	4 500	−7 500
				140					
20	10 000	3 400	13 400		500	170	670	9 000	−4 400
				100					
30	10 000	4 400	14 400		333	146.7	480	13 500	− 900
				100					
40	10 000	5 400	15 400		250	135	385	18 000	2 600
				135					
50	10 000	6 750	16 750		200	135	335	22 500	5 750
				185					
60	10 000	8 600	18 600		167	143.3	310	27 000	8 400
				240					
70	10 000	11 000	21 000		142.9	157.1	300	31 500	10 500
				300					
80	10 000	14 000	24 000		125	175	300	36 000	12 000
				390					
90	10 000	17 900	27 900		111.1	198.9	310	40 500	12 600
				510					
100	10 000	23 000	33 000		100	230	330	45 000	12 000
				660					
110	10 000	29 600	39 600		91.1	269.1	360	49 500	9 900
				840					
120	10 000	38 000	48 000		85	316.7	400	54 000	6 000

NOTES
(a) TC of n units = FC + VC of n units.
(b) MC is the extra cost involved in producing an additional unit of output. That is, MC of the nth unit = TC of n units – TC of $n - 1$ units. Here output is shown in units of 10, so that this difference in total costs has to be divided by 10.

(c) AFC of n units = $\dfrac{FC}{n}$

(d) AVC of n units = $\dfrac{TVC \text{ of } n \text{ units}}{n}$

(e) ATC = $\dfrac{TC \text{ of } n \text{ units}}{n}$

8.2   How much to Produce: Output of the Firm Under Perfect Competition

In order to ascertain whether a firm is maximising profits, we have to know (i) the price at which it can sell different outputs and the price at which it can buy different quantities of factors, and (ii) whether it is free to enter another industry where it can make higher profits. Both questions involve us in a study of the extent to which competition prevails.

First, we build up a model assuming that the conditions of 'perfect competition' – the highest form of competition – apply. Later we show how relaxing these conditions leads to imperfect competition, forms of which prevail in real life.

The Conditions Necessary for Perfect Competition

For perfect competition to exist the following conditions must hold:

1. A Large Number of Relatively Small Sellers and Buyers

If there are a large number of sellers relative to demand in the market, any one seller will know that, because he supplies so small a quantity of the total output, he can increase or decrease his output without having any significant effect on the market price of the product. In short he takes the market price as given, and can sell any quantity at this price. He is a *price-taker*.

This is illustrated in Figure 8.3, where (a) shows market price OP determined by the demand for and supply of the goods of the industry as a whole. But the industry supply, we will assume, comes from a thousand producers, each of about the same size. Each producer therefore sells such a small proportion of the total market supply that he can double his output from ON to OM or halve it from OM to ON without affecting the price – Figure 8.3b.

In other words, in perfect competition a seller is faced with an infinitely elastic demand curve for his product. If, in our example, he charges a higher price than OP, nobody will buy from him; if he charges less than OP, he will not be maximising his revenue, for he could have sold all his output at the higher price, OP.

In contrast, the producer in Figure 8.4b sells such a large proportion of the market supply that a change in his output affects the price he receives for his product. When he supplies OM, the price is OP. If he increases his supply to OM_2, the price falls to OP_1. Similarly, if he decreases his supply to OM_2, the price rises to OP_2. Alternatively, such a producer can decide

FIGURE 8.3
The Firm's Demand Curve under Perfect Competition

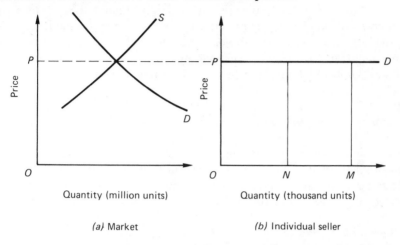

(a) Market   *(b)* Individual seller

on the price he charges, leaving it to the market to determine how much is sold at that price. But he cannot fix both price and quantity at the same time. We can call such a producer a *price-maker*. Any change in market conditions is reflected in the quantity the firm can sell at the price it has fixed. Here the firm can respond by changing the price it charges.

FIGURE 8.4
The Firm's Demand Curve under Perfect and Imperfect Competition

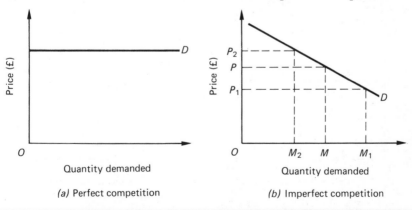

(a) Perfect competition   *(b)* Imperfect competition

Similarly, on the buying side, purchasers of goods and of factors of production are faced with an infinitely elastic supply curve. For example, one producer can increase his demand for a factor of production but the price of the factor does not rise as a result (Figure 8.5a). Here the producer's demand is so small relative to the market supply that he can buy all the labour he requires at the prevailing market wage rate *OW*. On the other hand, in (b) the producer employs such a large proportion of the market supply of labour that when he takes on more workers the wage rate rises.

2. Homogeneous Product

Buyers must regard the product of one producer as being a perfect substitute for that of another, and purchase solely on the basis of price, switching to a competitor if one producer raises his price. Where goods are graded, e.g. wheat and cotton, there is identity of product in the same grade.

Such identity of product does not exist where there is a real or imaginary difference (e.g. a special wrapping or brand name) or where reasons other than price (e.g. goodwill) influence buyers. Here an individual producer can raise his price without necessarily losing all his customers. In short, product differentiation leads to some downward slope in the demand curve.

3. A Perfect Market, Especially Perfect Knowledge of Market Conditions

There are two aspects of perfect knowledge:

FIGURE 8.5
The Supply of a Factor under Perfect and Imperfect Competition

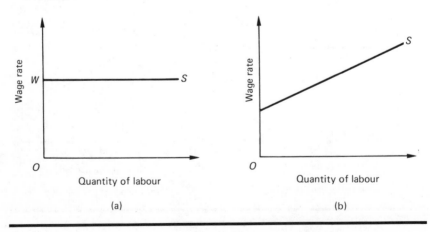

(a)   (b)

(a) sellers and buyers must know the prices being asked in other parts of the market, both product and factor, so that they can act accordingly;

(b) in order to make free entry effective, a would-be producer must also know what profits are being made by other producers and the profit he could reasonably expect to make.

The above conditions give a perfectly competitive market. For a situation of perfect competition to exist we must also have:

4. Free Entry

(a) If the number of sellers is to remain large, there must be free entry to the industry for other producers, otherwise existing firms could combine to influence price or they could grow in size as existing firms leave the industry.

(b) Free entry allows the profit motive to function. If demand increases, causing the price of a product to rise, the possibility of profits will attract other firms into that industry. Likewise, if the demand falls, losses sustained by some firms will cause them to leave the industry.

5. Perfect Mobility of the Factors of Production in the Long Period

A change in the demand for a product must, in the long period, result in factors of production being transferred from one line of production to another. Moreover, all factors, including entrepreneurship, must be equally available to all firms. In real life, however, this does not occur (see p. 149).

In practice these conditions never apply simultaneously, and perfect competition must be regarded primarily as an analytical device which enables us to arrive at some fundamental conclusions.

Maximising Profit

Since the objective of the firm, we have assumed, is to maximise its profits, it will seek to produce that output where the difference between total revenue and total costs is greatest. The firm, therefore, will be concerned with two broad questions: (i) How much will it obtain by selling various quantities of its product? (ii) How much will it cost to produce these different quantities?

At first sight it may seem that maximum profit will occur at the minimum average cost output. But this is unlikely to be so. The real question which the entrepreneur will be continually asking is: 'If I produce another unit, will it cost me less or more than the extra revenue I shall receive from the sale of it?' That is, he concentrates his attention at the margin: if an extra unit of output is to be profitable, *marginal revenue* (the addition to total revenue received from the last unit of output) must at least equal *marginal cost* (the cost of producing the last unit of output).

Under perfect competition the producer will obtain the market price for his goods, whatever his output. In other words, marginal revenue (MR) equals price, with the price line horizontal (Figure 8.6). On the other hand, although under perfect competition the firm can buy increasing quantities of its factors at a given price, marginal cost (*MC*) eventually rises because of diminishing returns.

The Equilibrium Output of Rollermowers

Let us return to our imaginary firm, Rollermowers, and its cost curves (Table 8.1). These curves are plotted in Figure 8.6. Assume that the market price of mowers is £450. We can impose this *MR* curve on the cost curve diagram.

Now at any output where MR (price) is above MC, Rollermowers can increase profits by expanding output. Where MC is above MR (price), it can increase profits by contracting output. Its equilibrium output, therefore, is where MR (price) equals MC: that is, at an output of 90 units. Here ATC is £310. Thus supernormal profit equals total receipts (£40 500) − total costs (£27 900) = £12 600 = shaded area *PDAC* (Figure 8.6). (The reader can check this by seeing whether, from the total costs given in Table 8.1, the difference between total revenue and total costs would be greater at any other output.)

Two provisos should be noted:

(1) The MC curve must cut the MR curve from below. (It is possible for the MC curve to cut the MR curve at a smaller output while it is falling, but in this case the firm would increase profit by expanding output.)

(2) Current revenue must cover current costs overall. Now 'current revenue' is simply the number of goods currently produced times their price. But as we have seen, 'current costs' depend upon whether we are dealing with the short or the longer period.

Alternatively, we can plot TR and TC at different outputs (Figure 8.6, lower part). Profit is maximised at 90 mowers where the slopes of the two curves are equal. Here the *rate* of change of TR, that is MR, equals the *rate* of change of TC, that is MC.

The Short-period 'Shut-down' Price

A firm will only *start* to produce if it expects that total revenue will be sufficient to cover (i) the cost of fixed factors, (ii) the cost of variable factors, e.g. labour, raw materials, and (iii) normal profit.

FIGURE 8.6
The Equilibrium Output of the Firm under Perfect Competition

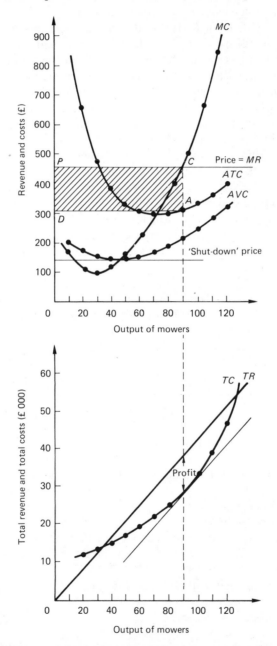

We will imagine that the firm does think it can make a go of it. It buys highly specific machinery (fixed costs) which, we will assume for the sake of simplicity, has no value to any other firm, together with labour and raw materials (variable costs), and starts producing.

But as time goes by it finds that its original expectations are not being fulfilled. Although the cost of variable factors is being covered, the firm sees that, unless price rises the margin between the two is too small to provide sufficient cash to replace machines when they wear out. In other words the business as a whole will prove unprofitable.

But what will our firm save by stopping production forthwith? Obviously its variable costs, for these vary directly with output. But what of its machines, which, since they have no alternative use, have no resale price? These are fixed factors which have already been paid for, and ceasing to use them now cannot recoup past expenditure. Their opportunity cost is zero.

Consequently our firm takes a philosophic view of the situation. It has some perfectly good machines which, if used, will add nothing to costs. So, provided the cost of the variable factors is being covered, it goes on producing. Anything earned above such cost will help to recoup the cost of the fixed factors.

How can we tell if variable costs are being covered? Simply by looking at the AVC curve. If we take Rollermowers as an example, a price of £135 for a mower would just enable it to produce in the short period. Here MC would equal MR and, with an output of 45 units, TVC would just be covered. Any price lower than this, however, would mean that, for any output where MC = MR, total receipts (price times output) would be less than TVC (AVC times output). Rollermowers could not make a 'go' of it even in the short period; and so we can call £135 the 'shut-down' price.

8.3   The Long-period Equilibrium of the Firm and Industry

In the long period, all factors are variable. This has two effects:

1. The *firm* can vary the size of its plant in order to obtain a given output at the lowest possible cost.
2. New firms can obtain plant in order to enter the *industry*; or alternatively firms need not renew plant and can leave the industry.

We shall develop each of these effects in turn.

Returns to Scale

The firm must have started off with some plant, and, in deciding on its size, have taken into account the advantages of producing on a large scale. But it may have misjudged its future sales. They may be larger than originally expected; as a result, plant capacity is too small. On the other hand, sales may have been overestimated; as a result, plant capacity is too large.

Let us assume that Rollermowers has underestimated what it can sell. As a result of starting with too small a plant for its output, it has had to work it more intensively by increasing its variable factors – labour, etc. That is, it is working under conditions of diminishing returns.

But in the long period it can remedy this situation. It decides to enlarge its *capacity* to combine more capital with labour. This gives it the chance to acquire more specialised machines, for those are justified by the larger output. Probably, too, it will be able to introduce more division of labour and even secure commercial and other economies.

Thus, as we saw in Chapter 7, as the *scale* of output increases, costs per unit fall. In other words, up to a certain point (an output of OM in Figure 8.7), additions to plant produce new short-run cost curves for any given capacity, each lower than the other. Here there are increasing returns to *scale*.

Beyond output *OM*, decreasing returns to scale set in. This could arise through the increased difficulties of making decisions, or, in other words, through the fixed nature of entrepreneurship. And, from *OM* onwards, these diseconomies resulting from the fixed nature of management out-weigh any economies still being achieved of a technical, commercial, financial or risk-bearing nature. Thus, although plant is adjusted to cope with a larger output, the minimum average cost per unit possible is still higher, even in the long period, than at a smaller output.

FIGURE 8.7
Increasing and Decreasing Returns to Scale

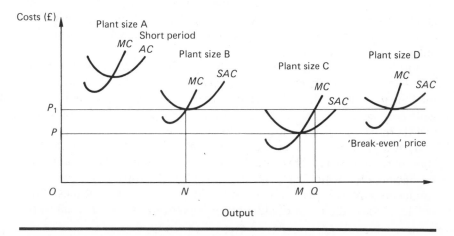

The Optimum Size of the Firm

In the above example, the firm's long-period costs of production per unit are at a minimum when output is OM. This is known as the optimum size of the firm; it is its *most efficient* size.

As we have seen, this 'most efficient' size varies from one industry to another. When technical economies of scale are important, as (for instance) in the production of steel and cars, decreasing costs occur over a large output. On the other hand, in some industries, such as farming and retailing, reductions in average cost which may be obtained by working with large machines are exhausted at a relatively small output. From then onwards, only economies of a commercial, financial, risk-bearing, or managerial nature can be secured. But as output increases, management problems are more likely to arise. Personal attention to detail is impossible, quick decisions are more difficult, and flexibility is lost. As a result, diseconomies occur, and eventually these diseconomies outweigh the economies of increased size, thereby producing increasing costs. The optimum size is thus a compromise of forces pulling in opposite directions.

In practice, the optimum size of a firm is not a fixed one. Not only do the relative prices of different factors of production change (resulting in changes in the shape of the cost curves), but techniques are improved (again changing the position of the curves). Hence the concept of an optimum size of firm is theoretical; it is, as we shall see, the size to which firms *tend* to conform in the long period as, in their efforts to survive, they compete with other firms.

The Industry

We now consider the effects of competition between firms. In the long period not only can existing firms alter the size of their plant to secure greater efficiency, but new firms, observing the supernormal profits being earned by firms already producing, will be able to obtain plant to enter the industry. Output will increase.

But this increased supply by the industry will cause the market price to fall. That is, the horizontal price line facing the individual firm will fall in the long period, e.g. from OP_1 (Figure 8.7). Furthermore, this adjustment will continue until no super-normal profits are being made, for only then will there be no incentive for firms to enter the industry.

If one firm is more efficient than the others, it will be making supernormal profits. This could occur, for instance, because it was producing OQ with plant size C, when other firms were each only producing ON with plant size B. In the long period, some of these firms would increase their size of plant towards plant size C. As a result of the increased supply, price would fall. Firms failing to adjust towards the more efficient size would be forced out of business.

Thus competition forces existing or new firms towards plant size *C*, and increased output forces price down to *OP*. If there were a higher price, some firms could be making supernormal profits, and new firms entering would increase supply and force down the price. On the other hand, if price were less than *OP*, no firm could break even in the long period when all factors had to be paid their current price. *OP* is therefore referred to as the 'break-even price'.

To summarise: in the long period and assuming conditions of perfect competition, each firm will be producing at the 'optimum' size *OM* and the price of the product will be *OP*. Each firm, too, will be in equilibrium at output *OM* because price equals marginal cost. The industry is in equilibrium because: (a) each firm is in equilibrium; (b) there is no incentive for firms to enter or leave the industry, because no supernormal profits or losses are being made.

We can illustrate the above from Rollermowers' cost curves (Figure 8.1). Let us assume that it chose the optimum size of plant in the first place – all firms have to conform to its cost curves in the long period or go out of business.

In the long period, all costs must be covered – but with no super-normal profits if the industry is to be in equilibrium. This will occur when Rollermowers' output is 75 units and the market price of mowers is £300. Here total revenue (£300 × 75) equals total cost (average cost × output, £300 × 75). £300 is thus the 'break-even' price.

9 The Supply Curve of the Industry under Perfect Competition

9.1 Introduction

So far we have concentrated our attention on the behaviour of the firm. But the individual firm is only one of a large number comprising the industry. To obtain the supply curve of the industry, therefore, we have to add together the supply curves of these firms. This will give us the market supply curve, the one which interacts with the demand curve to fix price.

In practice, the term 'industry' presents difficulties. In everyday speech 'industry' includes firms producing goods which differ slightly, e.g. cars, washing-machines, furniture, etc. But the reader is reminded that, when we defined perfect competition, we assumed a homogeneous product. Our definition of an industry must therefore be the group of firms producing the total amount of an identical good supplied to the market. Variations in this definition can be allowed for later (see Chapter 14).

We total the output of the individual firms at different prices to obtain the market supply schedule. Generally speaking, more is supplied the higher the price. But why this is so differs in principle according to whether we are considering the short or the long periods. Each must therefore be examined separately.

9.2 The Short Period

Consider, for example, Rollermowers' cost schedules, Table 8.1. Any price below £135 per mower will stop production, because TVC are not covered. At higher prices, however, it will produce an output where price = MC. The part of the MC curve above the AVC curve (see Figure 8.6), therefore, is its short-period supply curve as follows:

144

Price (£)	Outputs (units)
135	45
185	55
240	65
300	75
390	85

In the short period, no new firms can enter the industry because, by definition, they cannot obtain fixed factors. The supply curve of the industry, therefore, is obtained simply by adding the output of all existing firms at each given price.

Suppose, for the sake of simplicity, that the industry consists of four firms, the other three being less efficient than Rollermowers. Their outputs (*starting from minimum AVC*) are given under A, B and C in Table 9.1.

Table 9.1
Short-period Supply Schedule

Price (£)	Output (units)				
	Firm A	Firm B	Firm C	Rollermowers	Total
135				45	45
185			45	55	100
240		45	55	65	165
300	50	55	65	75	245
390	55	65	75	85	280

This is shown graphically in Figure 9.1. The MC curves of the four firms are summed horizontally to obtain the short-period supply curve of the industry. Since all firms under perfect competition must produce where MC is rising, their output will be greater the higher the price. Thus the short-period market supply curve rises from left to right, showing that more is supplied the higher the price. It will be influenced by any change which affects the firms' MC curves, e.g. the prices of factors, productivity, taxes.

It will be observed that the supply curve derived above is not smooth, but stepped. This is because we have taken only four firms. If there had been very many firms each differing only slightly in efficiency, we should have had a much smoother curve.

FIGURE 9.1
The Short-period Supply Curve of the Industry

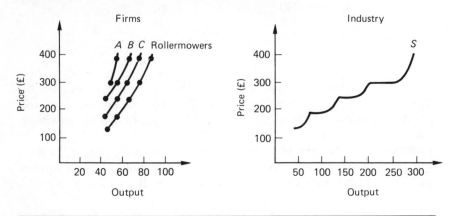

9.3   The Long Period

The Long-period Equilibrium of the Firm and Industry

The long-period supply curve of the industry must be derived from
conditions where the industry itself is in equilibrium, for it represents the
supply offered, given no change in demand or techniques, when all factor
adjustments have been made.

This requires two conditions:

(a) Each and every firm must be in equilibrium. That is, there must be no
incentive for a firm to change its output. In both the short and the long
periods, this occurs when marginal revenue equals marginal cost (with
provisos as to a minimum price of the product).

(b) There must be no incentive for firms to enter or leave the industry
(which they can do in the long period if they so wish). This means that,
for the industry to be in equilibrium, no supernormal profits are being
made by any firm. Given our assumptions regarding perfect competition, the forces of competition will bring this about in the long period.

Our discussion of the firm showed that, in the long period, each existing
firm (including any attracted into the industry) will be producing at its
optimum size *OM* and at a price *OP* where total costs are just covered
(Figure 8.7). Since new firms can now come into the industry on identical
terms, there would be a long-period supply curve for the industry which

will be perfectly elastic at price *OP*. In other words, the supply curve would be horizontal.

But such a conclusion can be arrived at only on the very theoretical assumptions of perfect competition. In particular, this assumed that:

(a) each firm is so small that its demand for a factor does not affect the price of that factor;
(b) there is perfectly free entry into the industry.

A rigid acceptance of these conditions, however, is impossible. First, it creates a theoretical difficulty – if all firms are at the peak of efficiency since they are operating at a minimum average cost, which goes out of business if the price of the goods falls slightly? Second, it leads to a conclusion – that supply can be increased indefinitely at constant cost – which is most unlikely. We can overcome both objections by making either of the above assumptions more realistic.

The Price of Factors of Production and the Size of the Industry

While an individual firm may be so small that its demand will not affect the price it has to pay for factors of production, the collective action of all firms in the industry will have repercussions. In the past, we have referred to these 'industry results' as *external* economies and diseconomies of scale.

Now it could happen that, as the industry expands, there are external economies of scale – growing reputation, skilled labour availability, transport improvements, etc. These will tend to lower the cost curves for individual firms as the output of the industry expands. On the other hand, there may be diseconomies which will raise costs. One such likely result of the expansion of the industry will be an increasing price of the factors of production. Given full employment, as the size of the industry's output expands, higher rewards will have to be paid to attract factors from other industries.

In practice, therefore, at the same time as the increased supply resulting from the entry of new firms tends to lower the price of the product, the cost curves of the firm are tending to be pushed down by external economies and pushed up by external diseconomies of scale. In other words, external economies will make for increased supply at a lower cost – there are decreasing costs to the industry; external diseconomies will make for increased supply at a higher cost. The actual slope of the long-period supply curve – downwards or upwards – will depend upon the balance between the two.

Suppose, for instance, that the entry of a fourth firm, D, to the industry in Figure 9.2 drives up the prices of the factors of production without giving any external economies. As a result the cost curves of all firms moves from

FIGURE 9.2
The Long-period Supply Curve of the Industry

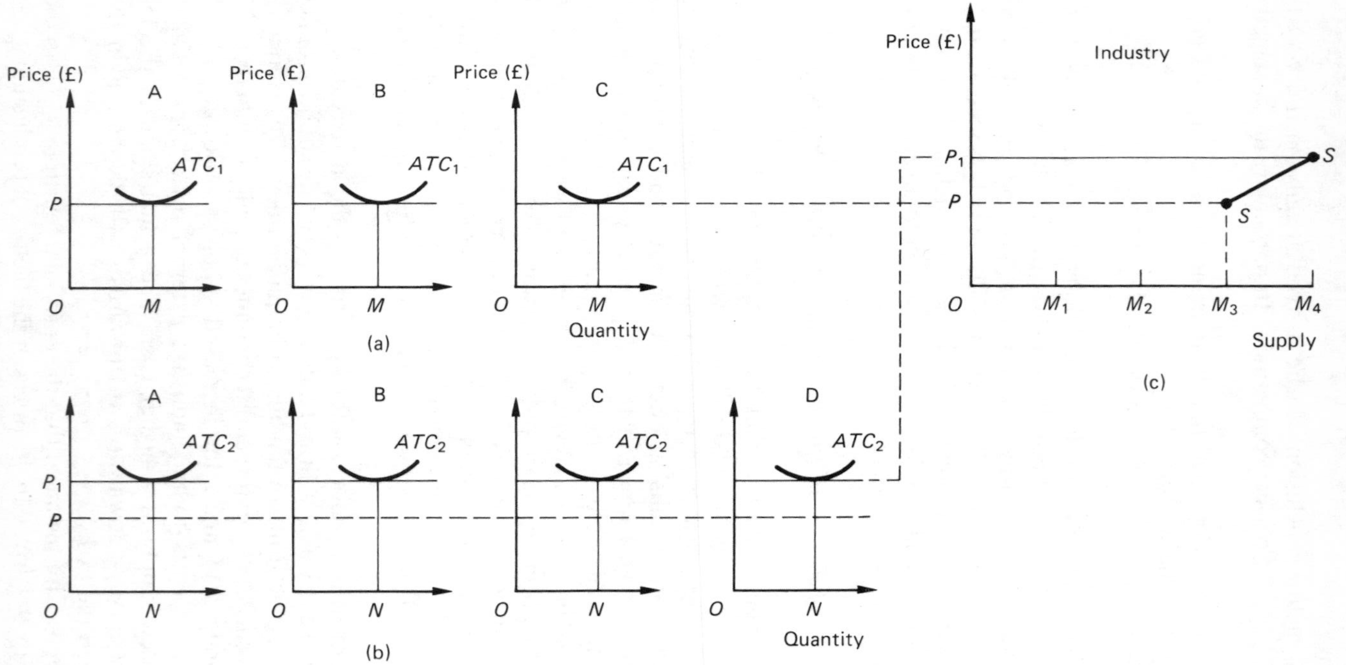

(a) to (b), each firm in (b) having a higher minimum average total cost. This gives a new supply for the industry, M_4, at a higher price OP_1, as compared with the previous supply, M_3 at a price OP (Figure 9.2c). That is, there is an upward-sloping industry supply curve.

Perfectly Free Entry

Even if there were no institutional barriers to entry into an industry (e.g. through cartel or other agreements or through conditions imposed by the government), the condition of free entry is effective only if:

(a) there is perfect knowledge
(b) factors of production are perfectly mobile and equally available to all firms.

As soon as either of these conditions is relaxed, firms of differing degrees of efficiency will result.

Is it likely that these conditions will apply as regards entrepreneurship? The answer is 'no'. Our assumption of 'perfect knowledge' means that entrepreneurs outside the industry are aware of any supernormal profits being earned by existing firms, of the prices of all factors of production, and of all the different ways in which the good can be produced.

Obviously, the extent of such knowledge is so vast that entrepreneurs must differ in the degree to which they possess this knowledge. And this disparity becomes even more marked when we introduce dynamic considerations. Fluctuations in demand, improvements in techniques and changes in the relative prices of factors of production are continually giving rise to changes in the conditions of demand and supply. Entrepreneurs therefore have to plan ahead according to their estimates. Some entrepreneurs will make more accurate estimates than others.

What this means is that equally efficient entrepreneurs are not available to all firms. At any one time, therefore, some firms are making supernormal profits of varying degrees, while others are marginal in that they are just making normal profits. The situation is shown diagrammatically in Figure 9.3.

Firm D, the highest-cost firm, is also a marginal firm – it is only just induced to stay in the industry by the present price, OP, and it will be the first to leave the industry if the price falls, e.g. to OP_1. If the price falls below OP_1, firm C will leave the industry, and so on. Once again, therefore, we can plot the supply of the industry at different prices. This will give a supply curve sloping upwards from left to right.

FIGURE 9.3
Differences in Efficiency of Entrepreneurs

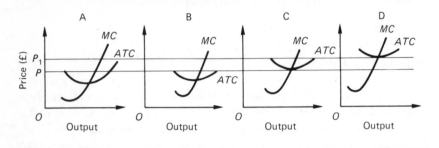

9.4 Elasticity of Supply

Definition of Elasticity of Supply

Consider Figure 9.4. For a rise in price from OP to OP_1, supply extends from OM to OM_1 with S_1 and to OM_2 with S_2. At price OP, therefore, S_2 is said to be more elastic than S_1.

More precisely, the elasticity of supply of a good at any price or at any output is the proportional change in the amount supplied in response to a small change in price divided by the proportional change in price. In the

FIGURE 9.4
Elasticity of Supply

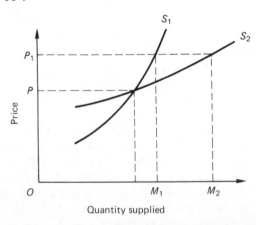

supply schedule on p. 55, for instance, when the price of eggs rises from 10p to 12p supply expands from 32 000 to 40 000. Elasticity of supply is therefore equal to:

$$\frac{\frac{8}{32}}{\frac{2}{10}} = 1.25$$

As with elasticity of demand, we say that supply at a given price is elastic if elasticity is greater than 1, and that it is inelastic if elasticity is less than 1.

Limiting Cases

There are two limiting cases of elasticity of supply which are of economic significance:

1. Elasticity of Supply Equal to Infinity

The main uses of this concept are: (a) where a single firm demands so small a proportion of a factor of production that it can obtain an infinite amount at a given price – that is, there is perfect competition in buying factors of production; (b) where production takes place at constant cost. In both cases, the supply curve is horizontal (Figure 9.5a).

2. Supply Absolutely Inelastic

Here a good is fixed in supply whatever the price offered (Figure 9.5b). It applies to rare first editions and Old Masters, and, by definition, to fixed factors in the short period.

FIGURE 9.5
Extremes of Elasticity of Supply

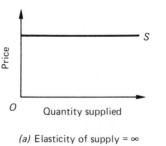

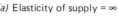

(a) Elasticity of supply = ∞

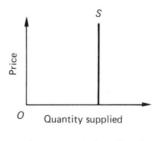

(b) Elasticity of supply = 0

Whereas elasticity of demand equal to 1 was significant because it described the case where total expenditure on the good remained constant at all prices, unitary elasticity of supply has no such significance. (Any straight line passing through the origin will give a supply curve with a constant elasticity of 1, for such a line describes a situation where supply always changes in the same proportion to a given price change.)

Factors Determining Elasticity of Supply

Elasticity of supply is determined by: (i) the period of time under consideration; (ii) the relationship between the individual firms' minimum-supply points; and (iii) the cost of attracting factors from alternative uses. We shall consider each in turn.

1. Time

We distinguish three main periods:

(1) MOMENTARY EQUILIBRIUM
Here the supply is fixed and elasticity of supply = 0. An example is Christmas trees on Christmas Eve. With many goods, some increase in supply can take place by drawing on stocks or switching factors of production from one product to another (where a firm makes two or more different products).

(2) SHORT-PERIOD EQUILIBRIUM
Usually varying supply requires a change in the factors of production employed. Unless there is surplus capacity this takes time – and the period differs for each factor. In the short period, as we have seen, it is possible to adjust supply only by altering the variable factors (raw materials, labour, etc.).

(3) LONG-PERIOD EQUILIBRIUM
Other factors – the fixed factors, e.g. land already sown and capital equipment – can be altered in the long period, allowing supply to adjust fully to a change in price. Thus elasticity is greater in the long period.

This is because the difference between the short and the long periods has an important effect on costs. Since, in the short period, supply can be expanded only by adding to the variable factors, it means that, unless there is surplus capacity, the best possible combination of the factors of production cannot be achieved. Too many of the variable factors are being applied to the fixed factors, and the law of diminishing returns operates. Increased production, in other words, is obtained only by decreased efficiency, and we have increasing marginal cost.

In the long period, because all factors can be varied, the optimum combination can be achieved. Increased efficiency produces a smaller rise in costs per unit as output expands. But it may take a long time before this position is reached. Expanding rubber production, for instance, takes seven years while new trees mature.

It follows that, because the supply curve of an industry consists of the *MC* curves of the firms in it, a given rise in price will produce a smaller expansion of supply in the short period than in the long period. The longer the period of time under consideration, the greater elasticity of supply will tend to be. If we refer to Figure 9.4, S_1 could well represent the short-period supply curve, and S_2 the long.

2. The Relationship Between the Firms' Minimum-supply Points

The supply curve is obtained by aggregating the supply of individual firms. If these firms each offer a supply to the market at more or less the same minimum price, supply will tend to be elastic at that price. Similarly, as price rises, the greater the number of firms coming in, the greater is the elasticity of supply.

3. The Cost of Attracting Factors of Production

In order to expand production additional factors have to be attracted from other industries. For an industry as a whole, this means that higher rewards will have to be paid. What we have to ask, therefore, is how much of a factor will be forthcoming in response to a given price rise. In other words, what is the elasticity of supply of factors of production? And, of greater significance, what influences determine this elasticity?

In answering this question we can first consider what happens when one particular industry, e.g. office-building, wishes to expand. Let us concentrate on one factor: labour. With increased demand for building labourers, wages rise. But they rise not only for the office-building industry but for all other industries employing such labourers – house-building, road construction, public works, etc. How will it affect these industries?

First, they will try to substitute other factors, e.g. cement mixers, bulldozers, etc., for the labour, which now costs more. Is such substitution physically possible? If so, how elastic is the supply of these alternative factors? Will their prices rise sharply as demand increases? If physical substitution is fairly easy and the supply of alternative factors is elastic, it will mean that a small rise in wages will release much labour for the office-building industry.

Second, higher wages will lead to increased costs in building houses, constructing roads, etc. The supply curve of these products, therefore, moves to the left; and, the higher the proportion of wages to total costs, the further will it move. The extent to which this leads to a reduced production of these alternative goods will depend upon the elasticity of demand for them. If elasticity is high, the small rise in the price of the good will cause a considerable contraction of demand, and labour will be released for office-building. If, on the other hand, demand is inelastic, even a considerable rise in wages will have little effect on the output of houses, etc., and the increase in the supply of labour to office-building will be correspondingly small.

We see, therefore, that the two main influences affecting the elasticity of supply of a factor to a particular industry are (1) the extent to which other factors can be substituted, and (2) the elasticity of demand for the alternative goods it produces.

Practical Uses of the Concept of Elasticity of Supply

1. The Elasticity of Supply of a Good is a Major Factor in Determining How Much Its Price Will Alter When There is a Change in the Conditions of Demand

This is apparent in the following examples:

(a) *Why does a crisis in the Middle East lead to a sharp increase in the price of gold?* The threat of war in the Middle East leads holders of assets, particularly the local oil-rich rulers, to seek a store of wealth which will hold its value. Because of its general acceptability, such an asset is gold. There is thus an increased demand for gold, D_1, and, since supply is almost inelastic, the price rises from OP to OP_1 (Figure 9.6).

(b) *Given free markets how would the price of cane sugar be affected in the short period and the long period if the demand for sugar increased?* Once again we can assume a fairly inelastic demand curve for sugar. The original price is OP (Figure 9.7). Demand then increases from D to D_1. The supply of cane sugar in the short run is inelastic, for supply can be expanded only by adding labour, fertilisers, etc. Price therefore increases to OP_1. But in the long period more land can be planted with sugar cane.

Supply is therefore more elastic, and is represented by the curve S_1. The long-run price falls to OP_2.

(c) *Given free markets, why is the price of butter likely to fluctuate more than the price of margarine?* Generally speaking, the prices of primary products tend to fluctuate between wider limits than the prices of manufactured goods. This is because (i) demand is often more inelastic for primary products, and (ii) supply is usually more inelastic, particularly in the short period. We shall concentrate on supply.

Margarine is processed chiefly from vegetable oils. If the price of margarine falls, these oils can be transferred to other uses, e.g. soap

FIGURE 9.6
The Effect of a Middle East Crisis on the Price of Gold

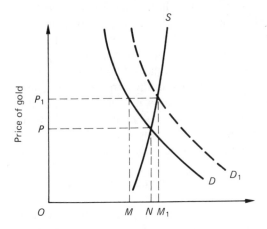

Quantity of gold demanded and supplied

FIGURE 9.7
Changes in the Price of Sugar Cane over Time in Response to a Change in Demand

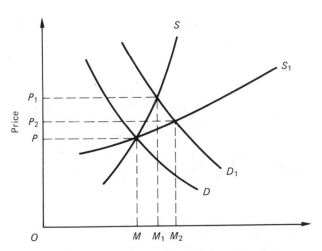

Quantity of cane sugar demanded and supplied

manufacture. The supply of butter, on the other hand, depends chiefly on the number of cows. If the price of butter falls, roughly the same amount of milk still has to be processed into butter, for other outlets are very limited. No real change can take place in the number of cows for some time. This would still apply should the price of butter rise. In short, the supply of butter is more inelastic than the supply of margarine, and the price varies more for a given change in demand (Figure 9.8). The price of margarine rises from OP to OP_1, whereas that of butter moves from OP to OP_2.

The general rule is: a change in the conditions of demand or supply will tend to produce wide fluctuations in price but small fluctuations in the quantity bought where supply or demand respectively are inelastic; and small fluctuations in price but wide fluctuations in the quantity bought where supply or demand respectively are elastic.

2. The Elasticity of Supply is Significant with Regard to Taxation

(a) Where the supply of a good is inelastic, the Chancellor of the Exchequer can impose a tax on the producer without it having a great effect on the amount of the good offered for sale. Suppose, for instance, that a person owns a field which is suitable only for sheep-grazing, and that the most any farmer will pay for the use of this field is £10 a year, which the owner accepts. Now suppose that the government puts a tax of £5 a year on this type of land. This means that the owner will have to pay the tax, for the

FIGURE 9.8

Changes in the Prices of Margarine and Butter in Response to a Change in Demand

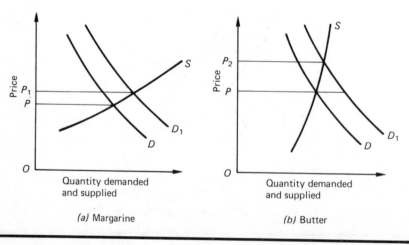

(a) Margarine

(b) Butter

farmer will pay no more, and the land cannot be put to any other use. In fact, the government could tax almost all the rent away before it would make any difference to the number of sheep being grazed on it; but, if all the rent went on tax, the owner might leave the land standing idle (see p. 247).

(b) The relative elasticities of demand and supply determine the proportion of a selective indirect tax borne by the producer as compared with the consumer (see p. 506).

10 Factor Markets: The Marginal Productivity Theory of Distribution

10.1 Introduction

Factor Rewards

Factors of production cooperate together to produce the national product. Each of these factors is owned by somebody. How much of the cake each individual in the country obtains depends upon (i) how much of the factors is owned, and (ii) the reward each factor receives.

Differences in individual incomes therefore depend upon both inequalities of ownership and inequalities in earnings. It is the latter, concerned with the theory of distribution, which is the subject of this chapter.

Before proceeding, however, two important points must be made:

(1) Some factors are consumed in one use (e.g. raw materials), while others are durable, rendering services over a period. In what follows we are examining the price of the *service* rendered by a factor, not the factor itself, though of course the two are directly related. This proviso must be borne in mind when, in what follows, we abbreviate by talking about the 'price of a factor of production'.

(2) Here we are concerned only with the reward to factors in a given industry, occupation or district. In other words, we examine how the price of a factor is fixed in a particular market. Analysis by ordinary demand and supply curves is therefore possible. When, as in Chapter 26, it becomes necessary to examine the economy as a whole, we have to abandon this partial-equilibrium analysis for a more general one, and we then speak of labour, capital, investment, wages and the rate of interest in broad terms.

Our approach will be as follows. The price of a factor service is, in a free market, determined, like that of a good, by demand and supply. First, therefore, we look at the demand for and supply of factor services in general.

But, as we have seen, factors can be classified according to certain broad and important characteristics. In Chapter 14–17 therefore, we examine how these special characteristics influence the return to these different factors.

The Marginal Productivity Theory

The marginal productivity theory is primarily concerned with what determines the *demand* for factors of production. It shows that, *under perfect competition*, an employer will always pay a reward to a factor equal to the value of its contribution to the product. Its most serious weaknesses are that in the real world perfect competition seldom prevails and that it tends to ignore the supply side. Nevertheless, it does give precision to what determines the demand for a factor, and thus some examination of the theory is a necessary preliminary to a more detailed discussion of the rewards of individual factors in the real world. It is a general theory applying to all factors of production. Illustration, however, is usually in terms of labour and wages, and we shall adopt this practice.

The Marginal-revenue Product (MRP)

The demand for labour is made up of the individual demands of all the firms using it. It is a *derived* demand – the factor is not wanted for its own sake, but simply because it can contribute to the production of particular goods. Hence the actual price which a firm is willing to pay for a factor depends upon the addition to its receipts which results from the employment of a particular unit of that factor. By examining this in more detail precision can be given to what constitutes the demand for a factor.

We do this by developing our earlier analysis of the law of diminishing returns. Let us assume that (i) there is perfect competition in the market where the product is sold, (ii) there is perfect competition in buying labour – each firm is so small that it cannot, by varying its demand, alter the wage-rate which it has to pay, and (iii) in changing output, only the quantity of labour employed is varied; all other factors remain fixed.

The law of diminishing returns (see pp. 122–4) showed that, as additional quantities of a variable factor (labour) are added to a fixed factor (land), the marginal return (physical product) of that variable factor would eventually decline. The analysis was conducted in terms of the physical returns to factors (Table 7.2, p. 124), and columns (1) and (2) of Table 10.1 are extracted from the earlier table.

But when demanding labour (or any other factor) the firm is not so much interested in the marginal physical product as in the amount of money it will receive from the sale of that product. What it has to ask, therefore, is: 'How much will total revenue increase if an additional worker is employed?' The value of this contribution to total revenue of an additional factor is known as its *marginal-revenue product* (MRP).

The MRP depends not only on the marginal physical product, but also on the price at which the product sells. Under perfect competition, the producer can sell any quantity at a given price. Hence the MRP is equal to the marginal physical product × the price of the product. Thus, in Table 10.1, by assuming that potatoes sell at £10 per 50 kg bag, we can arrive at the MRP in column (3). For example, when 2 labourers are employed, the total physical product is 16 bags, which at £10 a bag yields a total revenue of £160. When 3 are employed, the total physical product is 54 bags, giving a total revenue of £540. The MRP of the third worker is thus £380. Table 10.1 gives the MRP for each additional labourer, and the figures are plotted in Figure 10.1. The MRP curve shows the increase in total revenue as each extra worker is added to the labour force.

Table 10.1
Schedules of Marginal Physical Productivity and Marginal-revenue Productivity of Labour–Product Sold under Conditions of Perfect Competition

Number of labourers employed (1)	Marginal physical product (50 kg bags potatoes) (2)	Marginal-revenue product (£) (3)
1	2	20
2	14	140
3	38	380
4	26	260
5	15	150
6	13	130
7	12	120
8	10	100
9	8	80
10	4	40
11	0	0

How the farmer decides on the number of labourers to employ can be seen from this example. An extra labourer will be employed so long as the resulting additional total revenue is greater than the cost of employing the

FIGURE 10.1
Changes in the Marginal-revenue Product as the Number of Labourers is Increased

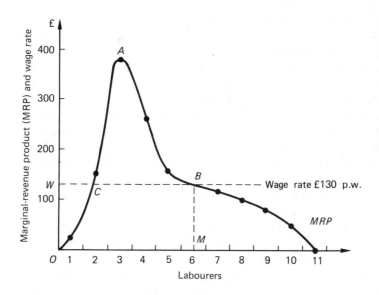

additional worker. In our example, because labour is the only variable factor, the farmer is equating MR and MC.

MR is shown by the MRP curve. But what of MC, the cost of engaging each additional labourer? Here it must be remembered that we have postulated perfect competition in buying factors of production. This means that the farmer's demand for labour is so small relative to the market that he cannot directly influence the price of labour. He has to accept the market wage-rate as given, and, at this ruling wage rate, the supply of labour is perfectly elastic. MC and AC are one and the same thing, and are represented by a horizontal straight line equal to the wage rate (Figure 10.1).

The firm therefore equates MRP and the wage rate. Thus, in Figure 10.1, if the wage rate were £130 per week, the farmer would engage six workers. If fewer, say five, were employed, the farmer could add more to receipts than to costs by taking on another worker, for the MRP (£150) would exceed MC (£130). On the other hand, if seven were employed, the farmer would be paying the seventh worker £10 more than he was contributing to receipts.

Some Difficulties Examined

It might be asked whether the firm can always estimate the marginal-revenue productivity of each factor of production. The following two cases are particularly difficult.

First, with certain factors, such as secretaries, teachers, etc., there is no definite and immediate physical product resulting from their work. How, then, can the marginal physical product, and thus their marginal-revenue productivity, be measured? The answer is simply that they cannot be – but that does not alter the fact that, in practice, a firm proceeds to engage factors as though it can so estimate.

Second, how do we separate the contribution of factors when, for technical reasons, they have to be combined in fixed proportions? In our example this difficulty does not arise. Because labour is the only variable factor, the physical product of an additional worker is measured simply by seeing the difference made to total product. Even when there is more than one variable factor, the marginal product of one factor can be estimated if it is possible to hold the other factors fixed while the one is varied. But where a driver and a lorry, or a carpenter and a plane, have always to be combined together in a fixed ratio, there is the difficulty of distinguishing how much of the additional total product should be attributed to the extra labourer and how much to the extra machine or tool employed.

In practice, this problem arises only in the case of labour, for it is usually possible to vary the proportion of capital employed by such means as giving the driver a larger lorry or providing the carpenter with a mechanical plane. But where an addition to labour necessitates an automatic addition to capital equipment, the marginal productivity theory comes up against a real obstacle. All we can do is measure the MRP to each factor in turn by deducting from the MRP of the whole unit the cost of all the other factors. This will give us what we can call the 'marginal net revenue product' of the particular factor.

One further point needs looking into. The value of the total product when there are six labourers employed is £1,080 equivalent to the area *OMBA* in Figure 10.1. The total wage bill, however, is £780, equivalent to the rectangle *OMBW*. We have to ask, therefore, what happens to the surplus £300 over and above the total wage bill (equivalent to the triangle *ACB* minus the triangle *WOC*).

The answer is that although we have been considering specifically the return to labour, that labour, in order to produce, has had to be combined with another factor, land. (We will ignore the farmer's effort.) £300 represents the return to land. In the long period, this £300 is not a surplus in the true economic sense. Land can be transferred to other uses. Its return, on the demand side, is determined, as with labour, by its marginal-revenue productivity. We could show this by imagining an isolated farm where labour was fixed in supply and land was variable. The farmer would then demand land until the cost of an acre equalled its marginal-revenue product. Thus if there is perfect competition and all firms are producing at the position of minimum average cost (that is there are no supernormal profits and constant returns to scale), the sum of the marginal-revenue products of all factors will just exhaust the total product.

10.2 The Determination of the Price of a Factor Service

Like all other prices, the price of a factor service is determined by demand and supply.

Demand

The concept of marginal-revenue productivity gives precision to what determines the *shape* of the demand of an individual firm for a factor. The analysis takes a different form for the short period and the long period.

1. The Short Period

As we have seen, the individual entrepreneur demands factors according to their marginal-revenue productivity. Thus in Table 10.1, if the wage rate (the price of the factor) is £120 per week, seven men would be employed by the farmer; if the wage rate were £100, eight men would be wanted; and so on. We can therefore draw up a demand schedule for each individual farmer, and the demand curve would be that part of the marginal revenue product curve lying below the average revenue product – for above the wage rate would be higher than the average revenue product, entailing a loss. More labourers are demanded the lower the price – the demand curve slopes downwards from left to right.

2. The Long Period

Our analysis so far is applicable only to the short period. The falling marginal-revenue-product curve is the result solely of a diminishing marginal *physical* product. But the latter, in its turn, occurred simply because land was assumed to be fixed in supply as labourers were added. What happens in the long period when there are no fixed factors and firms can enter or leave the industry?

If we assume that there is an infinite number of equally efficient entrepreneurs available, then competition ensures that the wage rate will in the long period be equal, not only to the marginal-revenue product of labour, but to its average-revenue product.

Let us consider Figure 10.2, which includes the average-revenue-product curve calculated from Table 7.2. The wage rate could be below *W* (£200) only in the short period. If, for instance, it was *W'* (£100), eight men would be employed. Here the average cost of employing the factor would be less than the average-revenue product (£162.50). In other words, the total wage bill – £800 – is less than the total revenue received from their labour – £1 300. Because there is perfect competition we can assume that the other factors employed in the production of potatoes are receiving their average-revenue product. Hence the firm would be making supernormal profits. This would attract other firms into the industry. With more potatoes being supplied to the market, the price of potatoes would fall. Revenue-productivity curves would correspondingly fall until the average-revenue product equalled average cost – the wage rate. (In practice, the extra demand for labourers would also raise the wage rate – see below.)

In the same way, if the wage rate were *W"* (£380), farmers would be losing money on their production because the average-revenue product (£180) is less than the wage rate; that is, receipts are smaller than the wage bill. Farmers would therefore go out of business. With fewer potatoes being supplied to the market, the price of potatoes would rise. Con-

FIGURE 10.2
The Equilibrium Wage-rate under Perfect Competition

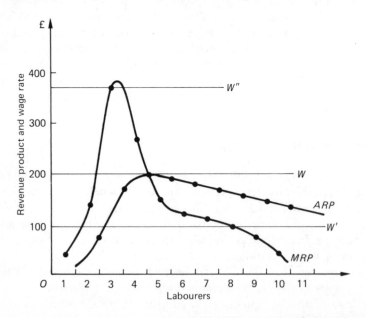

sequently, revenue-productivity curves would rise until the average-revenue product equalled average cost – the wage rate.

Our argument shows that, in the long period when all firms are making only normal profits, each firm would demand four labourers at a wage rate of £200 (*W*). Any higher wage is impossible, for this would result in losses; any lower wage attracts firms into the industry, forcing it up. In the long period every firm is at the optimum size, supernormal profits have been eliminated, and workers are being obtained at a wage rate of *W*, that is, at a constant cost.

The *industry's demand curve* for a factor service is the sum of the demands of the individual firms. It would seem, therefore, that the demand curve of the industry for labour is a horizontal straight line.

But the argument, like the earlier one concerning the supply curve of the industry, comes up against difficulties.

First, we have to allow that entrepreneurs are not homogeneous. Some are marginal – only just managing to survive when the price of labour equals its average-revenue product. If the wage rate should now rise, they would find it impossible to survive; the higher the rise, the more firms would be forced out. Thus the higher the wage rate, the less is the demand for labour.

Second, it is necessary to re-examine our original assumption regarding the price of the product – that the price received by each farmer when selling his potatoes was independent of his output. Such an assumption is really valid only when we are considering the output of an individual farmer. When we are dealing with the potato-growing industry as a whole (as we must do when discussing the total demand for a particular type of labour), it is more realistic to assume that, as its output expands, so the price of the product falls. In other words, revenue productivity falls as output increases, and the demand for labour consequently decreases.

For both these reasons – the existence of entrepreneurs of varying abilities and a falling price as the output of the industry increases – the demand curve for labour, even in the long period, is likely to slope downward from left to right (Figure 10.3).

The *position* of the demand curve of the individual firm will depend upon the following.

1. The Physical Productivity of the Factor

Productivity could be increased through: (a) additional capital being combined with labour, though in the short period some labour might be displaced; (b) technical progress and improved organisation, e.g. increased division of labour, though here again there may be some initial unemployment; (c) higher wages increasing the efficiency of undernourished or discontented workers ('the economy of high wages').

2. The Price of the Product that the Factor is Producing

A rise in the price of the product resulting from an increase in demand would raise the marginal-revenue productivity of labour (see p. 225).

3. The Prices of Other Variable-factor Services Employed by the Firm

In our example above we assumed that there was only one variable factor. But most firms employ, even in the short run, many variable factors – skilled workers, unskilled workers, fuel, raw materials, etc. In order to obtain the maximum return from a given outlay, the firm has to combine its variable factors so that:

$$\frac{MRP_A}{Price\ A} = \frac{MRP_B}{Price\ B} = \cdots = \frac{MRP_Z}{Price\ Z}$$

(See p. 126) It is obvious, therefore, that if the prices of other services, e.g. *B*, rise, the demand curve for *A* (when *A* can be substituted for *B*) will move to the right. Similarly, if the price of *B* falls, the demand curve for *A* will shift to the left.

Supply

By the supply of a factor we mean the amount which is offered as the reward is varied. Usually we should expect a higher price to extend supply, for factors would be attracted from other industries and occupations. Thus the supply curve normally slopes upwards from left to right (Figure 10.2).

Nevertheless, the actual shape of the supply curve, i.e. the elasticity of supply, will vary according to (a) the nature of the factor, (b) the institutional background and (c) the period of time involved. It is considered in Chapters 14–17 which follow, where each class of factor is dealt with separately.

Demand, Supply, and the Price of the Factor

The reward of a factor, in this case the wage rate, is determined by the interaction of demand and supply. Thus in Figure 10.3, with demand curve *D* and supply curve *S*, the wage rate is *OW*.

A change in the price of the product will affect the marginal-revenue productivity of the factor. This will be reflected by a change in the position of the demand curve. Suppose, for instance, that the price of the product rises. This will mean that the demand curve for labour will shift to the right, say from *D* to D_1. As a result, the wage rate is higher, OW_1, and the number employed increases from *OM* to OM_1

FIGURE 10.3
The Determination of the Price of a Factor

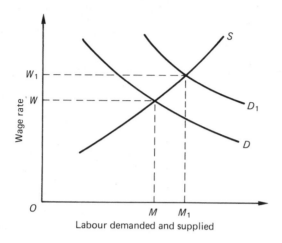

Labour demanded and supplied

10.3 Weaknesses of the Marginal Productivity Theory

The marginal productivity theory shows that, given perfect competition, each factor receives a reward the size of which depends upon the total supply of the factor and the value of its contribution to the finished product. The latter depends upon the price placed by the market on the particular product made. The wage rate, for instance, will increase if the supply of labourers decreases or if the price of the product rises; similarly, it will decrease if the supply of labourers increases or the price of the product falls.

However, although the marginal productivity theory gives precision as to how the demand for a factor arises, it has to be modified for the conditions of the real world, largely because many of its assumptions do not hold strictly.

First, it assumes that a producer knows the value of marginal products whereas at best he may only know the *expected* value.

Second, prices, particularly wages, are not flexible.

Third, time-lags in adjusting supply through the immobility of factors mean that, in the short period, factor earnings may contain an element of 'economic rent' (see p. 250).

Fourth, there may be less than full employment.

Fifth, and most important, the theory ignores imperfections in the market, both for goods and services.

Part III

The Government and Allocation Intervention

11 Economic Efficiency Through the Market Economy

11.1 Welfare and Economic Efficiency

Maximising Welfare

In Chapter 1 we put forward the proposition that society's aim is to maximise its satisfaction or welfare. Two factors which will influence welfare are: (a) how society uses its limited resources; and (b) the distribution of income.

The first is the subject matter of positive economics; it is possible to analyse it scientifically. Economic efficiency is achieved when society has secured the best allocation of its limited resources, in the sense that the maximum possible satisfaction is obtained.

The second, the distribution of income, does not lend itself to scientific analysis. Satisfaction is personal to the individual and cannot be measured on any objective scale. Thus, while distributional efficiency is necessary to maximise welfare, it cannot be dealt with scientifically, and decisions on income redistribution ultimately rest with the politician.

The Pareto Criterion

To avoid the fundamental problem of inter-personal welfare comparisons, economic analysis goes as far as it can without making any. Hence the following idea is frequently used: any change in resource allocation or of final product composition that makes at least one individual better off and none worse off is an improvement in social welfare. A change which makes none better off and some worse off is a worsening of social welfare. No statement is attempted about a change which makes some better off and some worse off.

We can put this in the form of what is known as the *Pareto-optimality condition:* welfare is maximised when no one can be made better off without somebody else being made worse off. Thus, any improvement in economic efficiency which involves nobody losing will represent an increase in welfare.

For instance, in Figure 11.1 we start from the initial income position X, with A's income equal to OA and B's equal to OB. A movement to Y would represent an increase in welfare for both A and B; a movement to Z would increase B's welfare without reducing A's. Both Y and Z therefore represent Pareto improvements. It is impossible, however, to say whether position R represents an overall gain or loss since A's income has increased but B's has fallen.

Consumer Surplus

Consider Figure 11.2, in which DD_1 represents the market demand curve for eggs and SS_1 the supply curve. The price of eggs is therefore OP and total expenditure in $POMT$.

Some consumers would be prepared to pay more than OP, some even going as high as OD. Thus the total satisfaction (welfare) derived by consumers is equal to the area $DOMT$, although their expenditure (the opportunity cost) is only $POMT$. Consumers therefore enjoy a surplus satisfaction equal to DPT. This surplus is termed consumer surplus.

Producer Surplus

We can apply a similar argument on the supply side. Some producers would be willing to supply at less than OP, some even going as low as OS. Thus, in total, producers receive a surplus of PST – producer surplus.

FIGURE 11.1
Pareto and non-Pareto Improvements

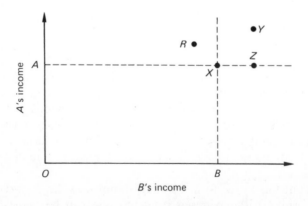

FIGURE 11.2
Consumer Surplus and Producer Surplus

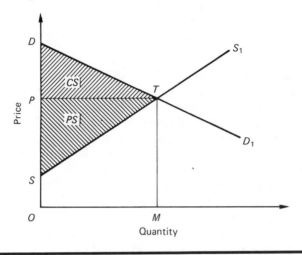

11.2 The Allocation of Resources Through the Market Economy

The Conditions of Economic Efficiency

In Chapter 2 we stated that the function of an economic system was to allocate resources *efficiently* according to the preferences of consumers. We now have to ask: 'To what extent does our analysis in the previous chapters help us to assess the performance of the market economy in this respect?'

The weakness of the Pareto-optimality condition is that it is limited to cases where only gainers and no losers result from a reallocation of resources. Even so, it does enable us to specify three conditions which are essential to economic efficiency. First, no improvement can be achieved by an exchange of goods between persons. Second, no increase in output can be obtained by producers substituting one factor for another. Third, from the maximum overall output of goods which can be obtained when society's limited resources are combined efficiently, that assortment is produced which gives society the greatest possible satisfaction.

These conditions can be abbreviated to *exchange* efficiency, *technical* efficiency and *economic* efficiency. We will explain each in turn.

Exchange efficiency is achieved by consumers relating their preferences to market prices in order to maximise satisfaction from their limited resources. There is equilibrium within and between markets when all consumers have arranged their purchases so that:

$$\frac{\text{Marginal utility of good } A}{\text{Price of } A} = \frac{MU \text{ of good } B}{P_B} = \frac{MU \text{ of good } Z}{P_Z}$$

which can be rewritten $\dfrac{MU_A}{MU_B} = \dfrac{P_A}{P_B}$ (11.1)

But since in competitive markets there is a *single price* for each good and all consumers seek to maximise satisfaction, it follows that each consumer will buy that quantity of the good which will make the marginal utility he obtains from it equal to that obtained by other consumers. Should, for instance, one consumer have a higher marginal utility for good A, he will demand more of A and less of other goods, i.e. he offers 'other goods' to other consumers in exchange for good A. As a result, an adjustment in the set of relative prices takes place until all consumers are in equilibrium.

A similar argument can be applied to the way in which factors are combined in order to achieve *technical efficiency* in production. Individual producers combine resources, e.g. land and capital, to obtain maximum output of a given good from a limited budget. Demand and supply in the factor market will establish prices at which resources are exchanged, the demand for each factor being dependent upon its productivity and the price of the finished product. Each producer employs that quantity of a factor where:

$$\frac{\begin{array}{c}\text{marginal physical product}\\ \text{of factor } M\end{array}}{\text{Price of factor } M} = \frac{MPP_N}{P_N} = \ldots \frac{MPP_Y}{P_Y}$$

which can be rewritten $\dfrac{MPP_M}{MPP_N} = \dfrac{P_M}{P_N}$ (11.2)

Since there is only one price at which one factor exchanges for another, and since each producer adopts for his limited resources the same profit-maximising criterion, it follows that in equilibrium the marginal physical product of a factor is the same in all lines of of production. If the marginal product is higher in one particular line, producers there will demand more of that factor, substituting it for other factors. As a result the relative factor prices change until the equilibrium condition is fulfilled.

While exchange efficiency and technical efficiency are necessary conditions for the optimum allocation of resources, they are *not sufficient*. There must also be *economic efficiency* in the sense that the actual assortment of goods produced is the one which gives maximum satisfaction. This necessitates relating the total individual preferences (marginal utilities) to the conditions of supply (the marginal costs). Relative prices determined in the market provide the link, as follows.

The opportunity cost of producing a good is its cost in terms of the best alternative sacrificed. Given perfect competition and no external costs, this cost is reflected in money terms by marginal cost.

Now as we saw in Chapter 8, in perfect competition, a producer of good A will produce that output where the price of A (P_A) equals the cost of producing an additional unit of A (MC_A). Similarly, a producer of good B will produce that output where $P_B = MC_B$. Since we are dealing with equalities, we can divide the first equation by the second, giving:

$$\frac{P_A}{P_B} = \frac{MC_A}{MC_B} \tag{11.3}$$

That is, the relative prices of A and B are equal to their relative marginal costs, the opportunity cost of supplying an addition unit. Combining equations (11.1) and (11.3) we have:

$$\frac{MU_A}{MU_B} = \frac{P_A}{P_B} = \frac{MC_A}{MC_B}$$

Therefore,

$$\frac{MU_A}{MU_B} = \frac{MC_A}{MC_B} \tag{11.4}$$

That is, the extent to which people prefer one good to another is equal to the relative cost of supplying those goods. Thus economic efficiency in the allocation of resources is achieved through the system of relative prices established in the market economy.

11.3 The Basic Assumptions

So far so good. But how then do the weaknesses of the market economy mentioned in Chapter 2 arise? The answer lies in the fact that, in order not to interrupt the flow of argument, no assumptions were made. For the market economy to achieve the efficiency outlined above certain conditions must apply.

1. Perfect Competition

For market prices to reflect both consumers' satisfaction and producers' costs, certain conditions must exist:

(a) *There must be a perfect market*, so that any price differences are quickly eliminated. Consumers and producers must seek to maximise utility and profits respectively and, in doing so, be unhampered by legal and other constraints.

(b) *There must be perfect knowledge* in that consumers are aware of any price differences which temporarily exist in the market and entrepreneurs of any supernormal profits being made by other firms, the costs of producing different outputs, production costs using different techniques, etc. Moreover, there should be no costs of obtaining knowledge, no ostentatious buying and no 'brain-washing' advertising. Even such 'static' assumptions as these are impossible in real life.

But the difficulties are magnified when allowance is made for dynamic conditions – something outside the simple price-mechanism model. Dynamic conditions, for instance, produce uncertainty as regards the size of future demand, the nature of competitors' plans and changes in government policy. Thus perfect competition really involves perfect foresight of the future.

Only if conditions (a) and (b) apply will there be common prices throughout the market for each product or factor of production.

(c) $P = MR = MC$. Producers maximise profits by producing that output where $MR = MC$. But this will only represent economic efficiency if $MR = P$, since production must proceed to the point where the satisfaction which the consumer derives from an additional unit of the good equals the cost to society of producing that unit, that is $P = MC$.

However, price will only equal marginal revenue under conditions of perfect competition (see Figure 8.3). Here the producer is a 'price-taker', accepting the market price as given. For this situation to occur there must be many producers each supplying so small a quantity to the market that no single producer can influence the market price. Furthermore, there must be freedom of entry into the industry. Similar conditions must apply in selling factors of production.

In contrast, where there is imperfect competition, marginal revenue is less than price (see Chapter 12).

(d) *There must be increasing costs.* For perfect competition to exist, the MC curve must be rising to cut the horizontal demand curve from below (see Figure 8.5). However, certain industries, chiefly those that have to produce on a large scale, have decreasing costs (a falling MC curve) at the relevant part of the demand curve. This means that, to obtain an equilibrium output, the MR curve would have to be downward-sloping in order to cut the MC curve (Figure 11.3). Thus at the equilibrium output (OM), price (OP) is greater than marginal cost (OC) and so the conditions of economic efficiency are not fulfilled.

(e) *There must be perfect mobility of factors of production.* The price system operates imperfectly if factors of production do not move in response to changes in relative prices. However, such movement takes time, and this is particularly so with labour and land resources.

FIGURE 11.3
Equilibrium Output under Conditions of Decreasing Cost

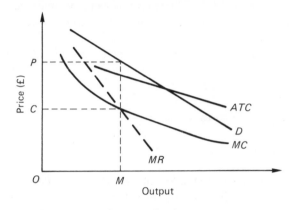

Immobility may also give rise to imperfect competition and supernormal profits.

(f) All the necessary conditions for perfect competition should exist everywhere in the economy simultaneously.

2. No External Benefits or Costs

In the market, private consumers and producers seek to maximise their own benefits and profits. However, this assumes that their decisions impose no indirect benefits or costs on others. In practice, this is often not so. For example, the design of a new house may destroy the architectural harmony of a whole street. In the decision-making process allowances should be made for such spillover benefits and costs, referred to later as 'externalities'.

3. All Economic Goods Can be Priced in the Market

The pure price system implicitly assumes that all economic goods are capable of being priced in the market, but this is possible only if the enjoyment of a good or service can be confined to those people willing to pay for it. With some goods and services, such as defence, street-lighting, common land and National Trust open spaces, it is impossible or impractical to exclude non-payers since anybody can be a 'free-rider'. Goods from which the community benefits, therefore, have to be provided collectively and financed, not by charging individuals as they use them, but by subscription (e.g. the Royal Society for the Protection of Birds), by advertising and sponsorship (e.g. commercial television) or, more usually, by taxation (e.g. defence, street-lighting, common land). Indeed, as we shall see in Chapter 21, a Pareto improvement may be effected by providing collectively, rather than privately, goods where exclusion *is* possible.

The above conditions apply to the efficient allocation of resources. But regard must also be paid to the overall performance of the economy. We have to further assume therefore:

4. Full Employment of Resources

5. No Price Inflation

Inflation could undermine stability of the economy, distort relative prices or have undesirable effects on the distribution of income.

It must also be emphasised that even if the economy is working efficiently it is only doing so within the existing distribution of income.

11.4   The Value of the Assumption of Perfect Competition

The conditions of perfect competition are so stringent that they are rarely met with in real life. It might be asked, therefore, why economists should choose to assume it for purposes of analysis.

The first reason is that model-building has to start at a simple level. From this first step modifications can be made to the original assumptions to make the model conform more closely to real life. We can illustrate by an example from the physical sciences. The physicist tells us that a body falling freely to earth will accelerate at 32 feet per second. But, by inserting the world 'freely', there is eliminated any resistance by the air or other force. Yet such a condition does not apply to the real world; it can only be produced artificially. On the other hand, it provides the fundamental 'benchmark'. From it the physicist can proceed to work out the rate at which different objects, e.g. a parachute, would fall when allowance is made for air resistance, etc. In exactly the same way the analysis of a private enterprise economy operating under conditions of perfect competition provides a simple jumping-off board from which more complex situations can be analysed as the conditions – such as rationality, profit-maximisation, perfect knowledge, perfect mobility, etc. – are relaxed.

The second reason for assuming perfect competition follows from the first. Since certain assumptions have to be made when beginning to build a model, it is desirable to be as realistic as possible, even though they will be modified later. Now, an alternative model could start from monopoly – one seller. Yet, as we shall see later, there can be no absolute monopolist, since all goods are to some extent competitive with one another. In real life, too, a deviation from perfect competition is probably a much nearer approximation than a deviation from monopoly.

Lastly, perfect competition does provide some indication of economic efficiency. Production, for instance, takes place where price (what consumers are prepared to give up at the margin) equals marginal cost (what it costs in factors of production to produce this marginal increment). Moreover, in the long period, production also takes place at minimum average total cost; no supernormal profits are being made.

On the other hand, we must not go so far as to say that complete perfect competition would provide maximum economic efficiency. For one thing, it considers only private costs and benefits. But there are likely to be external costs and benefits.

Furthermore, to achieve maximum efficiency, perfect competition would have to rule throughout the economy: promoting it in just one direction may not necessarily be a step towards greater efficiency. Thus marginal cost pricing may only be the right policy for the public sector (see p. 313) if the principle is applied generally throughout the private sector. In short, we have to recognise that we have to settle for the 'second-best' as the best attainable in practice.

11.5 The Economic Functions of Government

The Role of Government

The strength of the market economy is that it decentralises decision-making. Households and firms act according to prices which reflect demand and the conditions of supply. Private profit provides the incentive for efficiency and innovation.

Even so the market economy could not function without some form of government interference. At the very least the government must provide a framework of rules for protecting private property, enforcing contracts and settling disputed claims.

But the government can go further and play an active part in improving the efficiency of the system. Our earlier discussion has indicated how deficiencies can arise in the allocation of resources. More than that the economy may not, for various reasons, be consistent over time in achieving its full employment output.

Nor does the market economy ensure that the distribution of wealth which results from the way in which it works is equitable.

The economic functions of the government, therefore, fall under three broad headings: the allocation of resources, stability of the economy, the distribution of income.

The Allocation of Resources

Our discussion of the possible reasons why defects in the allocation of resources can occur, suggest that the government must be concerned with:

(a) imperfect competition, particularly with regard to monopoly and the immobility of resources;
(b) external costs and benefits;
(c) imperfect knowledge, both in the present and as regards the future;
(d) community goods, where the market cannot respond to demand.

Stability

Stability of the economy involves the government taking measures to achieve:

(a) full employment;
(b) a stable price level;
(c) a balanced regional development
(d) a healthy balance of payments;
(e) a steady and acceptable rate of growth.

As we shall see, the government faces difficulties in achieving all these objectives simultaneously.

The Distribution of Income

While voluntary bodies play a part in the redistribution of income, their efforts are limited and concentrated mostly on sectional interests. Only the government can achieve the degree and fairness of redistribution which is acceptable.

The government may carry out redistribution by deliberate policy measures (as with public spending and taxation). In contrast redistribution may take place only as an adjunct of measures designed to achieve other objectives e.g. parking meter charges. The economist's task is to reveal where such redistribution occurs and suggest the likely economic effects; the ultimate decision has to be left to the politician.

The remainder of this book deals with economic theory in more detail especially with regard to the various reasons for market failure. How the government can use this theory in pursuing its economic objectives is also considered.

12 Imperfect Competition (1): Monopoly

12.1 Forms of Imperfect Competition

In Chapter 11 we stated the assumptions of perfect competition and examined their implications. What happens if *any* of these assumptions is broken? For instance:

(i) A seller may be so large that the quantity he supplies affects the price. Similarly, a large buyer may affect the price by the quantity he demands.
(ii) Products may not be homogeneous, because product differentiation or goodwill allows a producer to raise his price somewhat while still retaining some customers.
(iii) Lack of knowledge, barriers to entry or immobility of factors of production result in imperfect elasticity of demand or supply. Consumers, for instance, may not have complete knowledge of prices ruling elsewhere – as, for example, in retail markets. Thus sellers can raise their prices without losing all their custom. Similarly, there may not be free movement into the industry. This may arise when again outside firms do not have complete knowledge of the profits being made by existing firms. Or entry may be legally prohibited or made impossible by the inability to obtain essential factors of production. In such cases, existing firms can combine to exert some control over the market supply.

Thus whenever any of our conditions for perfect competition is broken, some form of 'imperfect competition', indicated by a downward-sloping demand curve or an upward-sloping supply curve facing the individual seller or buyer, results.

There are many 'shades' of imperfect competition. At one extreme, we have a single producer of a certain product; at the other, the only difference from perfect competition is that firms in the industry are each producing a slightly different brand. The first we call 'monopoly', the second 'monopolistic competition'. In between, we can have just a few sellers of the same or of a slightly different product – 'oligopoly'. The broad market forms are shown in Figure 12.1.

12.2   The Nature of Monopoly

Definition of 'Monopoly'

Under perfect competition, there are many sellers each producing a very small amount of the total supply of a homogeneous product. The result is that each producer is faced with an infinitely elastic demand curve. It would be nice, therefore, if, at the other extreme, we could define a monopolist, which literally means 'one seller', as a producer who is faced with an absolutely inelastic demand curve.

Unfortunately this is impossible. Because income is limited, goods

FIGURE 12.1
Market Forms

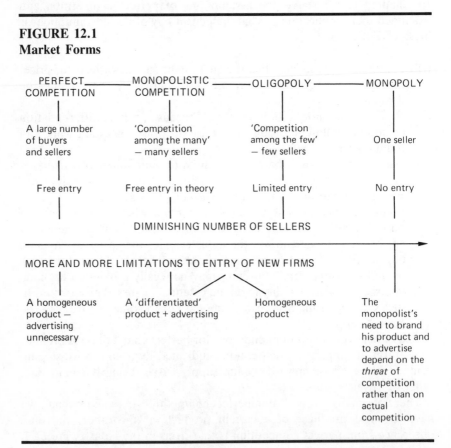

compete with one another for this income. To a greater or lesser degree, therefore, all goods are substitutes for each other.

It has been suggested, therefore, that the only true monopolist is one who sold all goods and therefore obtained all consumers' spending. The demand curve facing him would then be of unit elasticity at all prices. Any rise in the price of goods would simply mean that, although less were bought, total expenditure was unchanged.

But if we follow this argument through we can see that this definition is untenable for two reasons:

1. Any reduction in output will result in the same receipts, but lower costs. Where, then, does the reduction stop?
2. What the monopolist pays to the factors of production (his costs) is also the income of households which they spend on the goods he produces (see Chapter 28). If he goes on reducing output (in order to lower costs), where do receipts come from?

Since, therefore, a theoretical definition of monopoly is impossible, we have to consider the situation from a practical point of view. While to some extent all goods are substitutes for one another, there may be essential characteristics in a good or group of goods which give rise to gaps, as it were, in the chain of substitution. If one producer can so exclude competitors that he controls the supply of such a good, he can be said to be a 'monopolist' – a single seller.

Foundations of Monopoly Power

Possible sources of a monopolist's power to exclude competitors are:

1. Immobility of the Factors of Production

Such immobility means that existing suppliers cannot be challenged by new entrants. It may arise through:

(a) *Legal prohibition of new entrants* – as with public utilities, where many firms would create technical difficulties, e.g. gas, electricity, and postal services.
(b) *Patents, copyrights and trademarks*, where the object is to promote invention and the development of new ideas.
(c) *Government policy of establishing single buying and selling agencies*, e.g. marketing boards.
(d) *Control of the source of supply by one firm*, e.g. diamonds (De Beer), specialist workers (e.g. dress designers), trade unions and professional associations.
(e). *Restrictions on imports*, by tariffs, quotas, health controls, etc.

2. Ignorance

A monopoly may persist largely through the ignorance of possible competitors. They may not know about the supernormal profits being made by the existing firm, or they may be unable to acquire the necessary know-how, e.g. for involved technical processes.

3. Indivisibilities

Whereas the original firm may have been able to build up its size gradually, new firms may find it difficult to raise the large capital required to produce on a scale which is cost-competitive, e.g. with cars, drugs, computers.

In some cases, too, the efficient scale of plant may be so large relative to the market that there is only room for one firm. These 'natural' monopolies cover many of the public utilities, e.g. gas supply, water, electricity generation.

4. A Deliberate Policy of Excluding Competitors

Restriction of competition falls into two main groups. On the one hand, we have the sources of monopoly power described so far. These have, as it were, resulted indirectly rather than from any deliberate action by producers. Such 'spontaneous' monopolies must be contrasted with 'deliberate' monopolies – those which are created specifically to restrict supply.

It is essential to distinguish between the two when formulating policy. While the 'spontaneous' monopolies may still abuse their fortunate position in order to make high profits, to a large extent they are inevitable, and usually policy should seek to control rather than destroy them. On the other hand, monopolies solely designed to follow restrictive practices detrimental to the consumer should, where possible, be broken up. In practice, however, it is often difficult to draw a distinct line between the two. While firms may increase production or combine in order to reduce costs through economies of scale, the effect may still be that competitors are forced out.

Deliberate action to exclude competitors takes various forms. Firms producing or selling the same good may combine, or a competitor may be subject to a takeover bid. Monopolies are often formed in the sale of services. Trade unions are primarily combinations of workers formed with the object of obtaining higher wages (see Chapter 14). Certain professions, such as medicine and the law, have their own associations which regulate qualifications for entry, professional conduct, and often the fees to be charged.

Some practices designed to exclude competitors are highly questionable – vicious temporary price-cutting, collusion in submitting tenders, collective boycotts, intimidation of rivals' customers by threats to cut off the supply of another vital product, etc.

12.3   The Equilibrium Output of the Monopolist

The Effect of the Downward-sloping Demand Curve on Marginal Revenue

Consider Figure 12.2. In (a) the producer is selling under conditions of perfect competition. His marginal revenue is equal to the full price, since all units sell at this. Thus, for the fourth unit, MR is the shaded area *A*.

In (b), however, the producer is selling under conditions of imperfect competition. If he wishes to sell a fourth unit, he must lower his price from £5 to £4. But this lower price applies not only to the fourth unit but also the first three units. Thus his net addition to receipts is equal to what he gets for the fourth unit, *A*, less what he loses on the three previous units, *B*. Under imperfect competition, therefore, MR is always less than price at any given output.

The Relationship Between the Costs, Revenue and Output of a Monopolist

Let us consider another imaginary manufacturer of lawnmowers, Airborne Mowers. To simplify, we shall assume that it has identical cost curves to those of Rollermowers, but differs in that it has a patent for its particular mower, thereby excluding competitors. In short, Airborne Mowers is a

FIGURE 12.2
Marginal Revenue under Conditions of Perfect and Imperfect Conditions

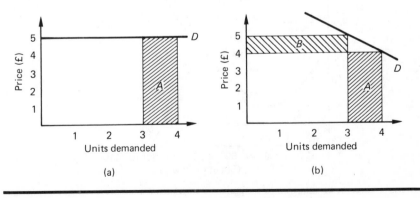

(a)   (b)

monopolist. Since its output is also the market supply, the number of the mowers which it puts on the market affects the price. Thus if it produces only twenty mowers a week, each will sell at £790; if total output is increased to ninety, the price drops to £440.

Airborne Mowers has the same problem as Rollermowers – to decide which output yields maximum profit. But it has an extra complication on the revenue side – as output increases, price falls for the *whole* of the output. The result can be seen in the marginal receipts (Table 12.1). These figures are plotted in Figure 12.3.

By inspection we can see that the maximum profit is made when sixty-five Airborne mowers are produced each week. At this output MR = MC (both £240), as in perfect competition. But MR is no longer equal to,

---

FIGURE 12.3
The Equilibrium Output of a Monopolist

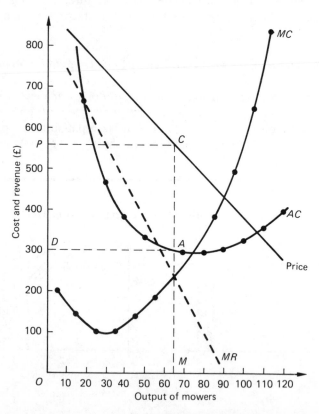

but is less than price (£565). Total weekly receipts are £36 725 and total costs £19 825 (by interpolation), giving a maximum profit of £16 900.

Alternatively, we can use the price and ATC at an output of 65 units to calculate profit. In Figure 11.3, total receipts equal the rectangle *OMCP* (output times price) = 65 × £565; total cost equals the rectangle *OMAD* (output times average cost) = 65 × £305. Thus profit is the difference between the two: the rectangle *DACP* equals 65 × £260, i.e. £16 900.

Table 12.1
Costs, Revenue, and Profits of Airborne Mowers (in £)

Output per week (units)	Total	Costs Average total	Marginal	Price per unit	Revenue Total	Marginal (per unit)	Profits
0	10000						−10000
			200			840	
10	12000	1200		840	8400		−3600
			140			740	
20	13400	670		790	15800		2400
			100			640	
30	14400	480		740	2200		7800
			100			540	
40	15400	385		690	27600		12200
			135			440	
50	16750	335		640	32000		15250
			185			340	
60	18600	310		590	35400		16800
65	19825	305	240	565	36725	240	16900
70	21000	300		540	37800		16800
			300			140	
80	24000	300		490	39200		15200
			390			40	
90	27900	310		440	39600		11700
			510			−60	
100	33000	330		390	39000		6000
			660			−160	
	39600	360		340	37400		−2200
110			840			−260	
	48000	400		290	34800		−13200
120							

Some Important Analytical Points Concerning the Monopolist

1. MR is Related to Elasticity of Demand

As we have seen, demand is elastic when, as a result of a fall in price, total expenditure increases. In terms of MR, demand is elastic when MR is positive. Similarly, demand is inelastic when MR is negative. This is shown in Figure 12.4, where we have assumed a straight-line demand curve for simplicity.

From Figure 12.4 we can draw the following conclusions:

(a) A monopolist will never produce at a price where demand is inelastic. (Here MR is negative; so the monopolist can increase total revenue by reducing output.)

(b) Where a monopolist has no marginal costs (e.g. the owner of a mineral spring gushing from the earth), the MC curve will be horizontal along the x-axis. Production will therefore take place where elasticity of demand equals unity for here $MR = 0$.

(c) Where a monopolist firm has marginal costs, it will always produce at a price where demand is elastic. (If MR = MC, MR must be positive, too.)

FIGURE 12.4
Elasticity of Demand and the Monopolist's Output

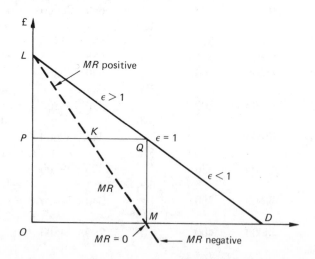

2. With a Straight-line Demand Curve, the MR Curve bisects the Horizontal Distance between the Price Axis and Quantity Demanded

This can be proved as follows:

Total revenue = Sum of revenue for each unit of output = *LOM* at output *OM*
Total revenue =   Price × Output   = *POMQ* at output *OM*

Therefore $LOM = POMQ$

But area *POMK* is common. Therefore *LPK* is equal in area to *KMQ*. But identical angles are equal. Therefore, Δ *LPK* is congruent with Δ *KMQ*. Therefore, $PK = KQ$, and thus *OM* = MD. This also means that $LQ = QD$. Thus the mid-point of a straight-line demand curve is where elasticity of demand equals 1, with MR = 0.

3. The Greater the Absence of Substitutes, the Greater the Power of the Monopolist to Make Profits

While the monopolist will never produce at an output where demand is inelastic, the greater the inelasticity of demand, the greater will be monopoly power – a higher price will drive fewer purchasers elsewhere. This can be seen from Figure 12.5.

FIGURE 12.5
Elasticity of Demand and Monopoly Profits

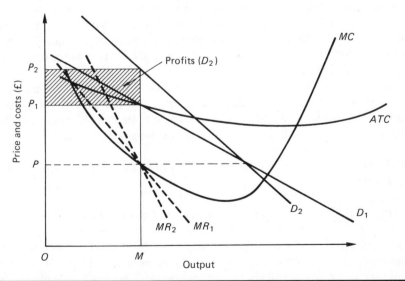

At any given price above *OP*, D_1 is more elastic than D_2. Since these demand curves cut each other at price *OP*, the MR of each must be the same at output *OM* (from proposition (2) above). Suppose the monopolist's MC curve cuts these MR curves at output *OM*. This will give the same equilibrium output for both D_1 and D_2. But the price charged will be OP_1 for D_1, and OP_2 for D_2. Profits are therefore greater for D_2 (shaded) than for D_1 (nil).

4. The Monopolist Can Produce at an Output Where MC is Falling Even in the Long Period

At an output where MC is falling, AVC must be greater than MC (see Figure 8.1). Under perfect competition, therefore, an output where price = MC (falling) must mean that TVC are greater than TR. There will thus be no production.

With monopoly, however, MR is below price. Thus a profit is still possible provided ATC at the equilibrium output, e.g. *OM* (Figure 12.5), is less than the price at which the monopolist sells.

5. It is Impossible to Derive a Supply Curve for the Monopolist

Under perfect competition, MC is equated with MR to obtain equilibrium output. Since the producer is faced with a demand curve of infinite elasticity, MR also equals price. There is thus a direct relationship between the amount supplied and price.

A monopolist, too, equates MC and MR, but now MR is less than price. But the MR corresponding to a given price depends upon the elasticity of demand at that price. It is possible, therefore, to have many different outputs at the same price, or many different prices for the same output. Thus we cannot show a *unique* supply at any given price as we can under perfect competition.

This can be illustrated from Figure 12.5, for at the output *OM* different elasticities of demand give different prices. The reader can construct a similar diagram showing different quantities supplied by the monopolist for the same price according to differences in elasticity of demand.

6. Even in the Long Period, the Monopolist Can Retain Supernormal Profits

Under perfect competition, the existence of profits in the short period attracts new entrants, and supernormal profits are competed away. Under monopoly, the producer is the industry, and, by definition, no new firms can enter. Thus, even in the long period, the monopolist's profits remain. Indeed, his profits are likely to increase because he can now combine his factors to produce his profit-maximising output at the lowest possible average cost.

12.4 Public Policy and Monopoly

Monopoly is an emotive word; it is often assumed that in seeking to maximise his profit the monopolist will always follow policies harmful to the consumer. The argument runs as follows.

Where there is perfect competition, output for all firms in the industry will take place where price equals MC, i.e. at *OM* (Figure 12.6). In other words, production is carried to the point, *OM*, where the cost of producing an extra unit, MP, just equals the value which consumers place on that extra unit in the market. Moreover, in the long period, this will be the output where, for all firms, ATC is at a minimum. There are no supernormal profits.

Now suppose a cartel formed from all the individual firms becomes responsible for selling the product. In order to maximise profits the cartel will sell an output where MC = MR, i.e. *OM*$_1$ at price *MP*$_1$. Thus consumers get less of the product and at a higher price than under perfect competition. It means, too, that demand for factors of production in this particular activity is lower than it would be in the absence of monopoly, and so there is a distortion of factor prices – which has its repercussions on more competitive sectors of the economy.

But the above analysis is not infallible. For one thing, it makes certain implicit assumptions; for another, it ignores dynamic considerations.

FIGURE 12.6
Output under Perfect Competition and Monopoly

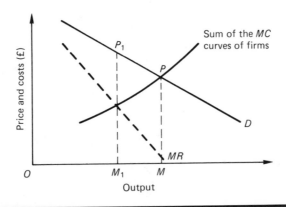

First, it rests on the assumption that the competitive industry's supply curve will be the same as the *MC* curve of the monopolist. But this is unlikely to be so. A single firm may be able to achieve economies of scale which are not open to the comparatively small firms which comprise the competitive industry. In addition its investment may be higher since there is now no fear of over-capitalisation of the industry through rival firms carrying out similar investment.

It is probable, therefore, that the monopolist will, at the relevant market output, have lower costs than the firms producing under conditions of perfect competition. Indeed, we can envisage a situation where, even though the monopolist is producing at the maximum profit output, the consumer nevertheless obtains more of the product and at a lower price than under perfect competition. Thus, in Figure 12.7, perfect competition between firms would give an output of *OM* at price *OP*. But, since the monopolist has lower cost curves, OM_1 would be produced at a price OP_1 (and there would still be supernormal profits!)

Second, our competitive model was purely static in its approach. Profits were maximised on the basis of *given* prices of products and factors. No consideration was given to other influences on the growth of firms over time.

FIGURE 12.7

A Monopolist Producing a Larger Output and at a Lower Price than a Perfectly Competitive Industry

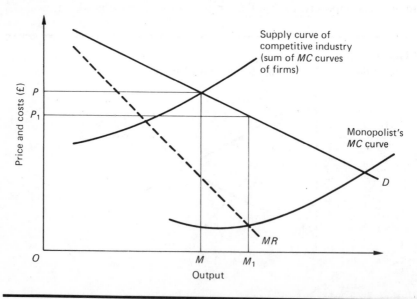

But the *development* of firms depends upon innovation and investment in research. Thus we have to ask the question: 'Are firms more likely to innovate and spend on research if, by being granted monopoly powers, they can be assured of the rewards?' In short, are monopolies more conducive to growth than perfect competition? We cannot develop the argument here, but the mere existence of the Patents Acts suggests that there is some truth in it. On the other hand, there have been instances where monopolies have bought up patents in order that they would *not* be developed in competition with them.

Third, price and output may be more stable under monopoly. Where there are many competing producers, as in agriculture, the reactions of each can bring about sharp swings in the total supply and price of the commodity. In contrast, the monopolist can view the market as a whole in assessing likely future demand, probably finding that only marginal adjustments to supply are necessary. Partly for this reason Marketing Boards have been set up as selling monopolies in certain branches of agriculture.

Finally, in criticising monopoly, we must remember that restriction of output may permit a discriminating monopolist to charge prices which will allow certain markets to be supplied (see pp. 202–3).

12.5 The Control of Monopoly

Monopolies can be divided into two groups: (a) the 'spontaneous' which arise through indivisibilities or through government policy, e.g. the Patents Acts, nationalisation, rationalisation; (b) the 'deliberate', which have come into being with the principal object of eliminating competition in order to make supernormal profits.

But such a division does not make the first group 'white' or the second 'black'. In the first place, our analysis has shown that, no matter how the monopoly has arisen, it will restrict output if its aim is to maximise profits. Second, while a monopoly may be 'deliberate', there may still be benefits for reasons given above. All we can say is that some control of monopoly is desirable, but that it must usually be done on an empirical basis. The degree of monopoly power has to be established and the benefits weighed against the possible economic and social disadvantages – restriction of output, a waste of resources in maintaining the monopoly position (e.g. by advertising), a lack of enterprise through the absence of competition, the exertion of political pressure to secure narrow ends (e.g. by trade unions), and a redistribution of wealth from consumers to the monopolist.

As a result, monopolies in the UK are regulated rather than prohibited. Yet any policy is fraught with difficulties. An exact assessment of the public benefits and disadvantages resulting from a monopoly is impossible.

Very often, too, the decision as to whether a monopoly is useful or anti-social in character depends on circumstances and therefore varies from one period to another (note the fostering of monopolies in the 1930s). Moreover, if legislation is proposed, the term 'unfair competition' has to be closely defined by lawyers, though, for the purposes of control, it really requires an elastic interpretation based on economic issues. Last, government policy in another field may influence the problem of monopoly. Thus tariff protection, by restricting competition from abroad, enhances the possibility of establishing monopolies in the home market.

Broadly speaking, policy can take three main forms:

1. State Ownership

When it is important not to destroy the advantages of monopoly, the State may take it over completely; the public then appears to be effectively protected. Freed from the objective of maximising profit, there should be no tendency for the state-owned industries to use their monopoly position to make high profits. Should, however, such profits be made they would eventually be passed on to the public in lower prices, or in reduced taxation.

In practice, however, lower profits may mask inefficiency in operation or the payment of wages to employees above those in comparable occupations elsewhere. Consequently, provision must be made for the prices charged to be examined by an independent body and for efficiency checks to be carried out by independent experts.

2. Legislation and Administrative Machinery to Regulate Monopolies

This method is usually employed when it is desired to retain monopolies because of their benefits but to leave them under private ownership.

The Monopolies and Restrictive Practices Act 1948 (since amended) set up a Monopolies Commission to investigate monopoly situations. Upon the Commission's report, a ministerial order can declare certain arrangements or practices illegal. Subjects investigated have included: supply of household detergents, breakfast cereals, bricks, asbestos, wire and fibre ropes, plasterboard, cross-channel sea-ferries, frozen foodstuffs; London rail services for commuters; and proposed mergers, e.g. GEC and Plessey.

3. Breaking up or Prohibition of the Monopoly

Where the monopoly is, on balance, detrimental to consumers, policy can take the form of breaking it up or prohibiting it by legislation. Thus the State could reduce the period for which patents are granted or make their renewal more difficult. When the owner of a particular site uses his monopoly power to frustrate a comprehensive city centre development, the site can be compulsorily purchased by the local planning authority.

Alternatively, it could outlaw attempts to eliminate competition, whether by unfair practices, the formation of cartels or restrictive agreements. Total prohibition was the policy at one time followed in the USA.

In the UK, an investigation by the Monopolies Commission led to the Restrictive Trade Practices Act 1956. This (1) allowed manufacturers and traders to enforce *individual* resale price maintenance through the ordinary civil courts; (2) banned the *collective* enforcement of resale price maintenance through such practices as private courts, stop lists and boycotts; (3) required other restrictive pacts, such as common-price and level tendering, to be registered with a new Registrar of Restrictive Trading Agreements, appointed by the Crown; and (3) set up a new Restrictive Practices Court. The court sits as three-member tribunals, each consisting of at least one judge and two lay members. For a practice to be allowed it must be justified as being 'in the public interest' according to one of seven closely defined 'gateways'. The tribunal's decision is made on a majority basis.

But the 1956 Act still permitted individual suppliers to enforce resale price maintenance for their own products. This was amended by the Resale Prices Act 1964, which made minimum resale price maintenance illegal, except for goods approved by the court. So far only minimum prices for books and proprietary medicines have been authorised.

The Monopolies and Mergers Act 1965 strengthened and extended the legislation on monopolies. A merger or proposed merger can be referred to the Monopolies Commission where it would lead to a monopoly or would increase the power of an existing monopoly. The act also increased the government's powers to enforce the findings of the Commission (for example, by allowing it to prohibit mergers or dissolve an undesirable monopoly).

The Fair Trading Act 1973 introduced a new concept with regard to monopoly and consumer protection. Unlike the earlier Monopolies Acts, whose primary concern was whether monopolies might be harmful to economic efficiency and thus not in the public interest, the object of this new Act was stated to be to 'strengthen the machinery of *promoting competition*'. The Act:

(*a*) created an Office of Fair Trading under a Director-General. Not only did the Director-General take over the functions of the Registrar of Restrictive Trading Agreements, but he now also has the responsibility for discovering probable monopoly situations or uncompetitive practices. Thus the Office of Fair Trading provides ministers with information and advice on consumer protection, monopoly, mergers and restrictive practices.

(*b*) empowered the renamed Monopolies and Mergers Commission to investigate local as well as national monopolies and extended its powers of enquiry to the nationalised industries and even to restrictive labour practices (though with limited follow-up powers).

(*c*) reduced the criterion for a monopoly situation to a one-quarter (minimum) market share.

These powers were strengthened by the Competition Act 1980, the government seeking to place greater emphasis on the promotion of competition. The Director-General can investigate any business practice in both the public (e.g. the nationalised industries) and private sectors which may restrict, distort or prevent competition. If found to be uncompetitive, he may accept an undertaking from the business responsible, or in default refer the practice to the Monopolies and Mergers Commission to establish whether it operates against the public interest.

Furthermore, new legislation is proposed to deal with weaknesses in current restrictive trade practices legislation. The registration system (which firms have evaded) is to be scrapped. Agreements and concerted practices with anti-competitive effects or purposes will be prohibited outright.

Looking forward to the single market in 1992, British law on monopolies and restrictive trade practices will have to be made compatible with EC law so that UK firms operating in Europe do not have to deal with two fundamentally different forms of legislation.

4. Price Control

The object here is to remove the monopolist's power of influencing price. Thus if the government controls the maximum price at OP (Figure 12.8) the demand (MR) curve facing the monopolist is perfectly elastic up to that price, and the equilibrium output is OM_C instead of OM_M. Here $P = $ MC, but it is only a second-best solution because, although price is lower and output greater, supernormal profit could still be made. This solution should be compared with that where production takes place where costs are decreasing (see p. 198).

The Conservative government of the 1980s, with its preference for market solutions rather than regulation, has introduced three new methods for dealing with monopolies, chiefly those monopolies given more independence as a result of privatisation.

1. FRANCHISING

With respect to independent television programmes, for example, companies will be required to tender for the right to broadcast programmes, the idea being to foster competition and divert at least a part of the profits to

FIGURE 12.8
Monopoly and Price Control

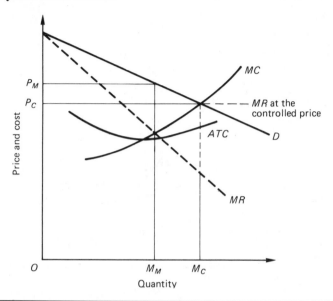

the State. However, some device seems to be required to ensure that quality programmes, for example the existing Channel 4, are not completely ousted by the more profitable low-brow shows.

2. CONTESTABLE MARKETS

This method introduces competition into the natural monopolies. With these decreasing-cost monopolies the initial fixed capital required is so high that would-be entrants could not accept the risk, for in the event of failure they would be left with irrecoverable sunk costs. But suppose those high initial costs can be circumvented. Firms would then be willing to compete because withdrawal would be easier should the venture prove unprofitable.

We can illustrate the method and its results from British Gas (BG). The Oil and Gas (Enterprise) Act 1982 permits independent gas producers to negotiate a contract direct with large consumers and deliver supplies through the BG pipelines system. This the independent supplier would do were BG making a monopoly profit $P_M LRS$ (Figure 12.9). An independent supplier could now use the pipeline to negotiate a price OP_C which would enable it to break even. In fact when a large American oil company proposed to do this, BG cut its own contract price. Thus the *threat* may be sufficient to avert monopoly pricing, though it should be noted that $P = AC$ (rather than $P = MC$) and so is again only a second-best solution.

FIGURE 12.9
Price and Output under a Contestable Market

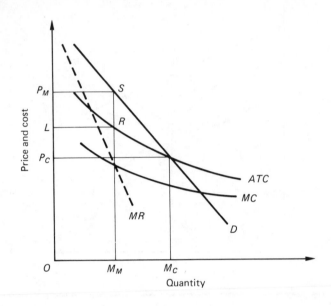

However it does succeed in a lower price (P_c rather than P_M) and increases output by $M_M M_C$.

This is the best that can be achieved, without government subsidy, in a decreasing MC situation. Of course, a watchdog body would have to ensure that BG's *pipeline* charges to the independent supplier were not excessive, covering only a reasonable rate of return on its investment.

3. PRICE REGULATION BY FORMULA TO CONTROL PROFITS

To prevent these newly privatised monopolies charging a profit-maximising price and yet give them an incentive to be efficient, price increases have been regulated according to a formula. BG, for instance, can increase its price to the tariff section – those consumers using less than 25 000 therms a year – only by the increase in the Retail Price Index less 2 per cent. To this BG can add increases in the average price it has to pay for its gas. This means that 2 per cent is the productivity increase target and leaves BG with an incentive to do better since any surplus revenue can be retained.

12.5 Discriminating Monopoly

A discriminating monopolist is one who can, and does, sell the *same* product at different prices to different consumers.

Examples of discriminating monopoly are: (a) a doctor who varies fees for the same treatment according to estimates of the wealth of the patients; (b) a car manufacturer who sells cars in export markets at a lower price than on the home market (even allowing for differences in taxation); (c) electricity taken during the night for heat-storage and charged at a lower tariff than that consumed during the day; (d) a small builders' merchant who charges the professional builder less for paint and wallpaper than the 'do-it-yourself' amateur; (e) British Rail fares.

The Necessary Conditions for Discriminating Monopoly

For discriminating monopoly to be practicable, certain conditions must be fulfilled:

1. There Must be Some Imperfection in the Market

Under conditions of perfect competition, discrimination is impossible. But where there are different markets, or where parts of the market are separated by transport costs, consumers' ignorance, or national barriers, sellers can exercise some control over each market, or each part of the market, separately.

2. Elasticities of Demand in the Markets Must be Different

This means that different prices can be charged by the monopolist in order to maximise his profits.

3. No 'Seepage' is Possible Between Markets or Different Parts of the Market

If an exporter in one country, for instance, sells his good much more cheaply in another country, then either transport costs or physical controls must prevent reimport to the country of origin.

The Equilibrium Position of the Discriminating Monopolist

Suppose that a discriminating monopolist is faced with two markets, A and B. The demand curves for each of these markets are shown in Figure 12.10. In order to maximise his profits he will have to decide: (1) the total output he will produce; (2) how to divide this output between the two separate

FIGURE 12.10
The Equilibrium Output of a Monopolist Who Sells in Different Markets

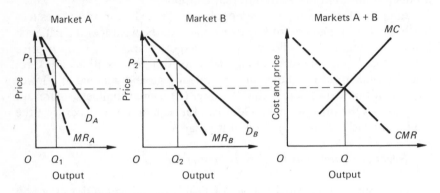

1 For simplicity, straight-line revenue and cost curves have been assumed.
2 Demand is more elastic in market B at all prices.

markets; (3) what price to charge in each market. We shall examine each problem in turn.

1. What Shall be His Total Output?

Since we assume that the product is homogeneous, the monopolist must consider the MC for the *whole* output irrespective of which market it is sold in. This MC he will equate with the combined MR curve of the two markets (CMR). This curve is found by adding the two MR curves – the output of market A for any given MR is added to the output of market B for that MR. This is repeated for all values of MR. Thus in Figure 12.10 the monopolist will produce OQ. At that output the addition to this cost of producing the last unit just equals the addition to his revenue from selling that unit in either market.

2. How Shall He Divide This Output Between the Two Markets?

The monopolist will maximise profits by equating the MC of the *whole* output with the MR in market A (MR_A) and the MC of the *whole* output with the MR in market B (MR_B). This means that he will sell OQ_1 in market A and OQ_2 in market B, for the combined output OQ (where CMR equals marginal cost) is obtained by summing the output in A and in B. MR must be the same in both markets, for it has to be equated with MC for the total output. If it were not the same, the monopolist could increase profits by transfering output from where marginal revenue was lower to where it was higher.

3. *What Will be the Price in Each Market?*

This, too, can be seen from the diagram. An output of OQ_1 in market A will sell at OP_1; an output of OQ_2 in market B will sell at OP_2. Since demand is less elastic in market A than in market B, a smaller quantity is sold and at a higher price in A than in B.

Can Price Discrimination be in the Interest of Consumers?

The term 'discrimination' suggests that consumers are exploited in order to increase the profits of the monopolist. Now price discrimination will enable the monopolist to obtain a higher total revenue (and thus higher profits) than if he merely charged a single price for the whole of the market. But this means he must produce a larger output than with a single price. He is able to do this because, by being able to separate the markets, he does not force down the price in one market by selling extra goods in another market. Indeed, if there were different markets for all units of his product (that is, 'perfect discrimination'), the marginal revenue for each good would be the price at which it sold. The monopolist's output would then be identical with the perfectly competitive output (Figure 12.11), but with producer surplus replacing consumer surplus entirely.

   Two points of significance to the consumer follow from this.

FIGURE 12.11
Receipts under 'Perfect Discrinination'

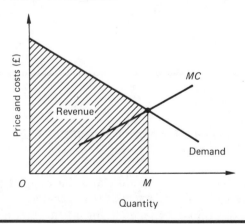

1. Price Discrimination May Make it Possible to Supply a Particular Market

Two examples come to mind. British Rail charges all passengers at so much per mile. Main line services are profitable at the standard rate; many local services are not. Local lines are therefore closed down. It is possible, however, that local passengers would be willing to pay higher fares to maintain the service.

Or we can consider a doctor whose services are demanded by both wealthy and poor patients. Their demand curves, D_1 and D_2 respectively, will, with price differentiation, allow the monopolist doctor to supply OM_1 at price OP_1 to the wealthy patients and OM_2 at price OP_2 to the poorer patients. But if he has to charge a single price (and wishes to maximise his profits), he will supply OM at a price OP – and this only to his wealthy patients. This is because his total demand curve is still D_{1+2} but, without price discrimination in separate markets, a negative MR_1 outweighs increased revenue from D_2 at the price and output where that becomes effective, K (Figure 12.12).

FIGURE 12.12
The Possibility Allows an Extra Market to be supplied

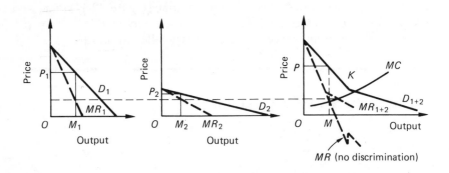

---

2. Price Discrimination May Make it Possible to Supply a Good when no Single Price would Cover Total Costs

Suppose the demand for the product and the costs of producing are as shown in Figure 12.13. Where a single price is charged, no firm could cover its total costs. But it may be possible for a firm (e.g. a public utility) to

FIGURE 12.13
How Price Discrimination Allows an Extra Market to be Supplied

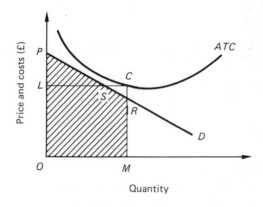

charge discriminating prices and thus cover its costs. If the monopolist could discriminate perfectly between every purchaser, he could produce an output up to the point where $\Delta\ SRC = \Delta\ PLS$, for $LOMC$ are his total costs and $POMR$ would be his total revenue.

The firm might be able to cover its costs by imposing a fixed standing charge on consumers irrespective of the quantity bought. But, if this is impossible, without price discrimination the firm would either have to close down or have its revenue shortfall covered by a subsidy.

13 Imperfect Competition (2): Other Forms

Perfect competition and monopoly represent two extreme market forms. The first, we have seen, occurs where identical goods are made by a large number of producers and there is completely free entry to the industry. The opposite market condition, monopoly, is possible where a good which has no close substitutes is made by a single producer who can prevent competitors entering the industry.

In the real world, however, there is more likely to be a situation somewhere between the two where many firms or perhaps just a few compete *imperfectly* in the market.

13.1 Monopolistic Competition: Imperfect Competition with Many Firms

The Nature of Monopolistic Competition

An industry may consist of many firms each making a product which differs only in detail from that of its rivals. Each firm, since its product is not homogeneous with that of other firms, enjoys some monopoly power. On the other hand, because there is no real gap in the chain of substitution, there is competition from other firms. What we really have is a number of small 'monopolists' competing with one another – 'monopolistic competition'. How does this come about?

Conditions Giving Rise to Monopolistic Competition

On the demand side, we have a situation which is closely akin to monopoly. Few goods are completely homogeneous. Indeed, nearly every firm tries deliberately to give its product some distinction from those with which it competes. This 'product differentiation', as it is called, takes

various forms. Special characteristics of the good are extensively adver-
tised, competitions are run periodically, free gifts are offered, distinctive
wrappings are used. Or, quite simply, the brand name is splashed across
television screens and street hoardings in the hope that constant repetition
will lead consumers to prefer the good. Apart from product differentiation,
a seller may depend upon 'goodwill' (arising through habit or social
contacts), rather than the actual price charged, to retain customers.

Whichever method is used, product differentiation or goodwill, the
result is the same. The producer is not faced with a market demand which
is beyond control. If the firm raises its price, some customers will buy
competitors' brands. But not all customers will do this. Some will consider
other brands inferior, and only a large price rise will induce them to
change. Similarly, if the firm lowers its price, it will attract only a limited
number of customers from rival producers. In short, the producer of a
brand good or a seller possessing goodwill is, like a monopolist, faced with
a demand curve which slopes downwards from left to right. Nevertheless,
demand tends to be elastic. Although there are not perfect substitutes
available, there are fairly good ones – the different brands of rival
producers.

On the supply side, because entry to the industry is possible, the
situation is similar to perfect competition. Where one producer is seen to
be making supernormal profits, existing producers tend to copy the
product and new competitors start producing a somewhat similar brand.

The Equilibrium of the Industry under Monopolistic Competition

We simplify the analysis by making two important assumptions: (a)
individual producers can obtain all their supply of any factor at a given
price; (b) external economies do not affect costs as the number of firms in
the group increases. While the latter can be allowed for by subsequent
modification, the former is to some degree unrealistic. The industry
consists of many but not an infinite number of firms. The demand of one
firm for a factor of production may therefore be sufficient to affect its
price. Nevertheless, our assumption enables us to analyse a situation where
all firms can, in the longer period, achieve identical cost curves, and where
cost curves will not rise as new producers enter.

1. The Short Period

In the short period existing firms cannot increase production by employing
additional fixed factors, nor can new firms enter. Each firm, therefore, is a
little 'monopolist', having a downward-sloping demand curve for its
product and producing where MC equals MR. Because there are many
firms, each firm can set its price without having to consider the reactions of

competitors. This price will be greater than MR, and supernormal profits are made.

2. The Long Period

In monopolistic competition the full long-period equilibrium position is possible only when both firms and the industry are in equilibrium. Whereas for each firm the condition of equilibrium (MR = MC) will apply whatever the output, for the industry we must allow, as with perfect competition, for the entry of new firms and for increased production by existing firms. This is where monopolistic competition differs essentially from monopoly; with the latter, *one* firm is *the* industry.

The increase in supply in the long period will lead to a fall in the price of the good, and the demand curve facing each producer shifts its position downwards to the left, for more producers are now dividing up the total market. At the same time, it is likely that the demand curve will become more elastic, for all products of the group will tend to become more similar to that of the most successful. In other words, each brand becomes a better substitute for other brands.

This will continue until supernormal profits have disappeared. Each firm will be earning only normal profits. (In practice the full equilibrium position is unlikely to be reached. Differences between firms will persist, and most will be earning small supernormal profits.)

A comparison of the equilibrium position of the firm in the short period and the long period under monopolistic competition is shown in Figure 13.1. In the short period, output is *OM*, where MR = MC. But the inability to add to fixed factors means that supernormal profits exist, equal to *ABCD*. In the long period, the entry of close substitutes causes the AR curve to fall. Supernormal profits disappear, and the equilibrium output is OM_1, where MC = MR, and AC = AR.

Certain points regarding this long-period equilibrium output should be noted:

(a) No supernormal profits are made; as in perfect competition, there is free entry to the industry.
(b) The same conditions of full equilibrium hold as in perfect competition – MC = MR (equilibrium of the firm), and AC = AR (equilibrium of the industry). That both conditions hold at the same output is due simply to a mathematic relationship. At an output less than OM_1, AC is falling more rapidly than AR. This means that MC must be pulling down AC more than MR is pulling down *AR*. In other words, MC must be less than MR. At any output greater than OM_1, *AC* is rising more rapidly than AR. MC must therefore be greater than MR. The only point where AC and AR are falling at the same rate is at output

FIGURE 13.1
Monopolistic Competition: Equilibrium of Firms in the Short and Long Periods

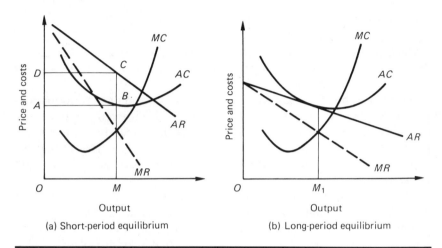

(a) Short-period equilibrium   (b) Long-period equilibrium

OM_1 where they are tangential, and here MC is neither less nor greater than MR – it is equal to it.

(c) Price is greater than MC and MR – a result of the falling AR curve.

(d) The equilibrium output is less than that under perfect competition. This again is the result of the downward-sloping AR curve, which can be tangential to a U-shaped average-cost curve only at an output less than the minimum average cost.

The Economic and Social Effects of Monopolistic Competition – the 'Wastes of Competition'

1. Even in the Long Period Firms Operate at less than the Optimum Size

Under perfect competition, not only are supernormal profits eliminated, but in the long period each firm is producing where AC is a minimum – the optimum output. At this output factors of production are combined in the correct proportions and the full advantages of large-scale economies are achieved. What happens under monopolistic competition is that firms operate at less than their optimum size and thus there is some waste in the way in which factors of production are used.

But we should not assume from the above argument that monopolistic competition is necessarily a 'bad' thing. Not every consumer will want to buy goods which are identical with those bought by other consumers. Different individuals have slightly different tastes. Thus waste in the use of the scarce resources can be regarded as the part of the price that has to be paid for variety of choice.

2. Costs are Incurred in Competitive Advertising

Perfect competition assumes perfect knowledge and homogeneous goods. Advertising is therefore unnecessary. If any one firm incurred costs in this way, it would benefit no more than its rivals.

In practice, however, knowledge is not perfect, and most firms marketing a new product have to spend money in bringing its merits to the notice of the public. Such costs are as justfiable as those incurred in the actual production of the good. Indeed, they may even be beneficial in that, by expanding demand, they allow the advantages of large-scale production to be achieved.

But 'informative' advertising forms only a small proportion of modern advertising. The main object is to *persuade*. Firms, having made their product somewhat different, then incur large costs in advertising this difference and in persuading the customer that their brand of good is superior to other brands. Put in economic terms, they aim at decreasing the elasticity of demand for their particular product as well as shifting the demand curve to the right. In reality, there may be little basic difference between brands – but labour and other scarce resources are wasted in trying to convince the public that it is otherwise. The *AC* curve includes this cost of advertising, so raising the final equilibrium price (Figure 13.1b).

In practice it is not always easy to draw the line between informative and persuasive advertising. What is 'one person's meat is another person's poison'; and if you adhere to the principle of allowing people to exercise freedom of choice, then you must accept what follows – that they are open to be persuaded. What consumers lack is knowledge of the good, and they are thus easy victims to the pressures of advertising. Today there is only a private body, the Consumers' Association (publishers of *Which?*), to report on goods to subscribers.

13.2   Oligopoly: Imperfect Competition with Few Firms

Pricing Where There are Few Firms

In real life many goods and services are produced by just a few firms, e.g. cigarettes, cars, petrol, tyres, screws, detergents, electric cable, kitchen tiles and lawnmowers. Here we have 'oligopoly', where pricing and output policy conforms to no given principles. Sometimes one large firm is a 'price leader', setting the price which will maximise its profit and taking its share of the market. Smaller firms have to take this price as given and consider themselves as operating in a competitive market.

In other cases, firms may be of fairly equal strength but, since their number is small, no one firm can set a price *without considering the likely reaction of its competitors*. If, for instance, it reduces its price, it cannot guarantee that it will win a greater share of the market since other firms may retaliate and cut their prices.

It is impossible, therefore, to predict the exact behaviour of the oligopolist. Whereas with monopoly and monopolistic competition the relationship of marginal revenue and marginal cost determines price and output, the oligopolistic firm has the added dimension of having to make a guess about the reaction of its competitors to a change in price. There are many different assumptions it can make, and each will give a different solution.

Thus, there is no single theoretical model to cover the oligopolist's pricing policy. A likely assumption by firms is that price cuts will be matched by competitors, but not price increases. From this has developed the theory of the kinked demand curve.

The Kinked Demand Curve

The oligopolist firm reasons that if it cuts prices, its competitors will follow suit in order to avoid losing customers. On the other hand, if it raises its price, its rivals will do nothing, being content to pick up the extra customers driven away by the price increase. This means that its demand curve is relatively inelastic for price cuts, but relatively elastic for price increases. Thus in Figure 13.2, if the original price is P, the firm would expect to move down along the curve towards D and upwards towards D_1.

For two reasons, the kinked demand curve makes for price stability. First, the oligopolist firm is likely to be conservative in its pricing policy, not changing its price from P. Second, even though its costs change, the firm would not change its price or output. This is the result of the broken marginal revenue curve, MR, which follows from the kinked demand curve. Thus marginal cost can change between MC to MC_1 without exerting any pressure on the firm's policy. Only if costs change more would the firm consider risking the loss of customers by raising its price or risk a price war by lowering its price.

The model, however, does have weaknesses in that: (a) it cannot explain how price P was originally determined; and (b) there is little empirical evidence to support the assumption that a price cut, but not a price rise, will be matched by competitors – though provided the oligopolist *acts* on this assumption it makes no difference to the outcome.

FIGURE 13.2
The Kinked Demand Curve

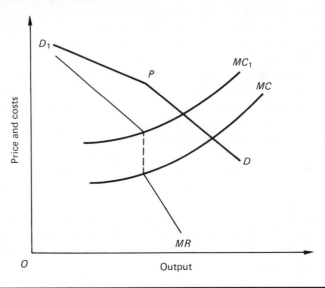

Oligopoly Policy in Practice

Since in an oligopolistic market situation firms are reluctant to engage in price-cutting, other policies are often pursued in practice.

First, the few firms concerned are able and usually willing to come to a tacit agreement on price in order to achieve joint profit maximisation. Often this takes the form of following the price set by the largest firm. Thus Brooke Bond Oxo appears to give the lead in tea prices. The extent to which such an understanding is possible depends on the ability to exclude new firms, for example because production has to be on a large scale from the outset.

Second, non-price competition is prevalent, e.g. through extensive advertising, free gift stamps, competitions, temporary special offers, low interest rates (cars), better after-sales service, etc.

13.3   Pricing Policy in the Real World

Difficulties of the MC = MR Principle

Following the above brief discussion of oligopoly, we have to admit that in many other cases the strict principle of fixing a price where MC equals MR may not be rigidly adhered to. For one thing the optimum output may be unobtainable because of cash-flow difficulties, the result of the capital market not being perfect. For another, few markets are so perfectly competitive that individual producers have no control over their price and have such an exact knowledge of the shape of their demand curve that MR can be equated with MC at all outputs.

Pricing policy therefore usually follows more pragmatic methods. Sometimes, for example with government contracts, the firm may follow a 'cost-plus' approach, being allowed what is considered to be a fair percentage addition to basic costs to cover overheads and normal profit; or the firm will, by a process of trial and error, seek to charge 'what the traffic will bear', e.g. the 'black-market' ticket seller.

Mark-up Pricing

More usually where a producer has some control in fixing a price, pricing is on a 'mark-up' basis. Only the cost of manufacturing is calculated accurately, and to this is added a rather arbitrary percentage for overheads in order to arrive at the final selling price. Thus, in selling a book, the publisher calculates the cost of printing and binding, adds a percentage (say 40 per cent) to cover overheads and normal profit, and fixes a final bookshop price which covers these costs plus the author's royalty and the bookseller's margin based on the retail price.

Indeed, this may be the only practicable method when, as is usual, firms are producing more than one product. A publisher, for instance, could not

FIGURE 13.3
The Product Life-cycle

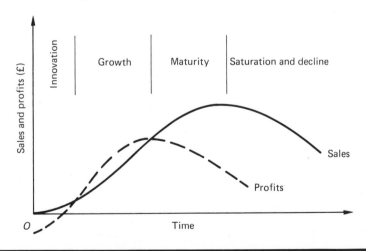

exist on the sales of one book and, in any case, would want the extra security of publishing different types of books. Furthermore, in order to survive, producers have to pay regard to what is known as 'the product life-cycle', which consists of innovation, growth, maturity, saturation and decline (Figure 13.3). In the growth period the product shows increasing profitability, for the firm enjoys almost a monopoly position. With time, competitors enter: sales increase, but only at the expense of rising advertising costs. Threafter the market becomes oversupplied or competitors produce improved models, and sales decline. Thus the go-ahead firm will always be planning new products so that one replaces another as each passes through its life-cycle.

With a many-product firm the exact share of overheads attributable to any one product would be difficult, if not impossible, to ascertain. The mark-up method sidetracks this difficulty. Furthermore, it allows control by the cost accountant, especially as regards maintaining cash flow and assuring profitable production. Where pricing is on the MC = MR principle, there is no certainty that total costs are covered.

14 Labour and Wages

In Chapter 10 we discussed in broad terms the theory of distribution in conditions of perfect competition. We now have to consider the rewards which the different factors receive in practice, allowing where necessary for imperfect competition and immobility, and for the effects of unequal distribution of wealth and income.

14.1 The Nature of the Labour Force

Special Features of Labour

Labour is the effort, both physical and mental, made by human beings in production. It is the 'human' element which is important.

Because people have feelings and emotions their response to economic forces is different from that of machines. First, whereas a machine which proves profitable can be reproduced fairly easily and quickly, the overall supply of labour does not depend upon its earnings. Other factors are more important in deciding how many children parents have (see p. 28). Second, the effort of labour is not determined solely by the reward offered. The method of payment may affect effort, while raising wages may result in less work being offered. Above all, a contented worker will produce more than an unhappy one; thus job satisfaction or loyalty to a firm, rather than a high rate of pay, may be decisive in inducing an employee to work overtime. Third, labour does not move readily, either occupationally or geographically, in response to the offer of a higher reward. Often such 'immobility' results from strong human contacts. Fourth, workers can combine together in trade unions. Finally, if unemployed for long periods, workers deteriorate physically and mentally.

Both firms and government must have policies which take account of these special characteristics. Training schemes are essential to improve the

213

skill of workers and thus their productivity. Firms must pay particular attention to psychological and social factors in an effort to motivate workers, e.g. by profit-sharing schemes and participation in decision-making. Furthermore, they must endeavour to cooperate with the workers' trade-union representatives. Above all, firms have to comply with the constraints imposed by government policy.

The government is vitally concerned with labour. It lays down the requirements of the employment contract, supervises working conditions and prescribes the terms under which a worker may be dismissed. Moreover, it exerts pressure in wage negotiations in order to avoid inflationary wage increases. Most important, it pursues a variety of policies aimed at securing a high and stable level of employment.

This chapter examines these special features, though postponing the problem of full employment to Chapter 28.

The Overall Supply of Labour

By the supply of labour we mean the number of hours of work offered. There are two separate problems to be considered: the total overall supply of labour available, and the supply of labour to a particular industry, occupation or locality. Here we consider the first.

The total supply of labour in an economy depends upon:

1. The Size of the Population

The size of the population sets an obvious limit to the total supply of labour. But while it is influenced by economic factors, e.g. through the birth rate and immigration, it is doubtful, especially in more advanced economies, whether economic factors are of paramount importance.

2. The Proportion of the Population which Works

In the UK, the proportion of the population which works is 48 per cent of the total population (somewhat higher than most European countries). It is determined chiefly by:

(a) The numbers within the 16–65 age group.
(b) The activity rates within this group, especially as regards young people and female workers (see pp. 36, 37).
(c) The extent to which people over retiring age continue to work, something which is largely influenced by the level of pensions.
(d) The numbers who can live on unearned incomes.
(e) The employment opportunities available – the tendency being for the working population to contract in a depression (mainly through withdrawal of married women).

FIGURE 14.1
The Relationship between the Wage-rate and Hours Worked

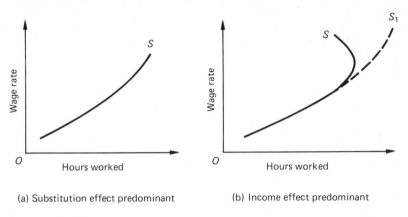

(a) Substitution effect predominant   (b) Income effect predominant

3. The Amount of Work Offered by Each Individual Labourer

Higher rates of pay usually induce a person to work overtime, the increased reward encouraging a substitution of work for leisure. But this is not always so. In addition to the substitution effect, there is also the income effect, and the latter may outweigh the former (see p. 75). A higher wage rate enables the worker to maintain the existing material standard of living with less work, and extra leisure may be preferred to more goods. Thus while it is usual to depict the supply curve of labour as in Figure 14.1a, it is possible that, in the short period, it may follow the shape of the curve in Figure 14.1b (see p. 218).

Nevertheless, as we shall see, more significant than the overall supply of labour are the obstacles to mobility which divide up the labour market.

14.2   The Determination of the Wage-Rate

Methods of Rewarding Labour

Some people are self-employed – window-cleaners, plumbers, solicitors, etc. As such they are really entrepreneurs, securing the rewards when demand is high but accepting the risks of being unemployed or working for a low return. Nevertheless, most workers contract out of risk, accepting a wage which is received whether or not the product of their labour is sold – although some element of risk-bearing may be incorporated in the wage agreement, e.g. by commission payments, bonus schemes, profit-sharing arrangements and the profit-related pay scheme introduced in 1986.

In what follows, reference will be mainly to the *wage-rate* – the sum of money which an employer contracts to pay a worker in return for services rendered. This definition includes salaries as well as wages, and makes no distinction between time- and piece-rates.

Earnings are what the worker actually receives in his pay-packet (his 'take-home' pay) *plus* deductions which have been made for insurance, income tax, superannuation, etc. In practice earnings over a period often exceed the agreed wage-rate, additions being received for overtime working, piece-rates and bonus payments.

Where the nature of the work allows workers to be paid on a piece-rate basis as an alternative to time-rates, the firm has to consider their respective merits.

1. Time-rates

Time-rates are more satisfactory than piece-rates where:

(*1*) A high quality of work is essential, e.g. in computer programming.
(*2*) The work cannot be speeded up e.g. in bus driving and milking cows.
(*3*) There is no standard type of work, e.g. in car repairs.
(*4*) Care has to be taken of delicate machinery, e.g. in hospital medical tests.
(*5*) Output cannot be easily measured, e.g. in teaching and nursing.
(*6*) Working long hours may undermine health, e.g. in laundry work.
(*7*) The labour is by nature a fixed factor which has to be engaged whatever the output, e.g. secretarial and selling staff.
(*8*) Periods of temporary idleness necessarily occur, e.g. in repair work.

On the other hand, time-rates have certain disadvantages:

(*1*) There is a lack of incentive for better workers.
(*2*) Supervision of workers is usually necessary.
(*3*) Agreements can be undermined by working to rule and 'go-slow' tactics.

2. Piece-rates

Where output is both measurable and more or less proportionate to the amount of effort expended, piece-rates are possible. It is not essential that each individual worker's output can be measured exactly. So long as the output of his group can be assessed he can share in the group's earnings.

The advantages of piece-rates are:

(*1*) Effort is stimulated.
(*2*) The more efficient workers obtain higher rewards.
(*3*) The need for constant supervision and irksome time-keeping is eliminated.
(*4*) Interest is added to dull, routine work.
(*5*) Workers can proceed at their own pace.
(*6*) A team spirit is developed where workers operate in small groups.
(*7*) Workers are encouraged to suggest methods of improving production.
(*8*) The employer's costing calculations are simplified.
(*9*) Output is increased, and the more intensive use of capital equipment spreads overheads.

We see, therefore, that piece-rates have advantages for both employee and employer. Moreover, the lower prices which result benefit the community as a whole. Nevertheless, for the following reasons they are often disliked by trade unions:

(*1*) Workers may overexert themselves.
(*2*) Where piece-rates have to be varied according to local conditions or different circumstances, e.g. capital per employee, negotiations for a national wage-rate are difficult.
(*3*) Variations in piece-rates from one place to another undermine union solidarity.
(*4*) The union may lose control over the supply of labour, and this makes it difficult to take strike action or to apportion work in periods of unemployment.
(*5*) Piece-rates are subject to misunderstanding, e.g. a firm which instals a better machine may be accused of cutting the rate if it does not attribute all the increased output to the effort of labour.
(*6*) Workers may resist being shifted from tasks in which they have acquired dexterity (and which therefore produce high piece earnings) even though the current needs of the factory organisation require such a transfer. Thus employers find that piece-rates lead to a loss of control over their employees, and many prefer to pay high time-rates to avoid this.

3. Combined Time- and Piece-rates

When deciding the basis of the wage-rate, both employees and employers want certain guarantees. Workers have a minimum standard of living to maintain, and they desire protection against variations in output which lie outside their control, e.g. weather conditions. On the other hand, employers providing expensive equipment must ensure that it is used for a minimum period of time. Thus piece-rates are usually incorporated in a wider contract which provides for some basic wage and a stipulated minimum number of hours.

14.3 The Determination of the Wage-rate and Conditions of Employment in the Real World

The Wage-rate in a Particular Industry, Occupation or Locality

In theory, the wage-rate in a particular industry, occupation or locality will be determined as shown in Chapter 10 by demand and supply. Demand is shown by the MRP curve. Its position can shift with changes in: (a) the price of the final product, (b) the price of substitute or complementary factors, and (c) the productivity of labour (e.g. owing to a change in the amount of capital supplied). Supply depends upon the wage-rate offered compared with that in other industries.

In practice this merely provides a first approach. In the real world the actual wage-rate and conditions of employment are influenced by immobilities which split up supply, worker's psychological attitudes, imperfect competition in both the product and labour markets, the strength of the relevant trade union and government intervention.

Workers' resistance to a cut in the money wage-rate, their desire to preserve time-honoured wage differentials and notions regarding the status of their occupation all serve to prevent 'market clearing' with the workers preferring unemployment at least in the short run.

The Wage-rate and the Immobility of Labour

The main weakness of the *MRP* theory is that, in concentrating on what determines the demand for labour, it underplays conditions on the supply side.

The supply of labour to an industry depends on:

1. The Response of Existing Labour to a Higher Wage-rate

In the short period an industry may find that the supply curve of labour corresponds to curve S in Figure 14.1b. This has been the case in coal-mining, where, as wages have increased, miners have preferred to enjoy more leisure. In the long period, however, higher wage-rates should attract labour from other industries, with the result that the long-period supply curve follows the dashed line, S_1.

2. The Cost of Attracting Labour from Alternative Uses or Localities

Unless there is unemployment, the supply of labour in a particular use can be expanded only by increasing the wage offered. This will attract labour of the same or of a nearly similar kind from other industries, occupations or localities. The extent to which this happens depends upon the elasticity of demand for the products in these alternative uses. If demand is inelastic, higher wages can be offered to hold on to labour, and thus the supply of labour will expand little in response to the wage rise (see p. 230).

3. The Mobility of Labour

A rise in the price of a factor should attract it from alternative uses or localities. This may take time, but it is achieved in the 'long period'. With labour, however, there are particular obstacles to moving, and these may mean that the long period is delayed indefinitely. Such obstacles provide frictions to the full and efficient operation of the price system. When they cannot be overcome, the effect is to split up the market into a number of separate occupations and localities with barriers around each.

Take the wages of plasterers, for instance. The demand for plasterers depends upon the price at which houses sell (a derived demand) and the productivity of plasterers. The supply of plasterers is the number offering their services at different wage-rates. This will vary with the length of time under consideration. But in the long period more will be forthcoming the higher the wage-rate, since they will be attracted from lower-paid areas or occupations.

For example, if the conditions of demand and supply are different in different parts of the country, the wages of plasterers will differ. If there were perfect geographical mobility, plasterers would move from low-wage districts to high-wage districts, until eventually a common equilibrium wage-rate would be established. Similarly, where different wage-rates existed for different occupations, perfect occupational mobility would eventually eliminate these differences.

In practice, geographical and occupational mobility are not perfect, so that differences in wage-rates persist. A typist earns more in London than in Norwich; a doctor earns more than a docker. In short, immobilities result in the labour market's being divided into a number of separate smaller markets according to locality and occupation.

Thus differences in the wage-rates between occupations, or between localities for the same occupation, can frequently be explained by differences in the supply rather than by differences in demand. We are dealing not with one market for labour but with a number of fairly distinct markets.

What are these major barriers? What are the causes of the 'immobility of labour', as it is usually termed?

Workers may be required: (a) to shift from one industry to another; (b) to change occupation; (c) to move home to a different district. Often conditions dictate that all three types of change take place at the same time, but this is not necessarily so. Each presents its own obstacles to workers in their efforts to change jobs.

(*a*) *Obstacles between industries.* Provided that it does not involve a change of occupation or district, a worker can usually move job from one industry to another fairly easily. Secretaries, lorry drivers and porters, for example, are found in most industries. But middle-aged and older workers may experience difficulty. Prejudice or tradition in certain industries may also prove to be obstacles. Women drivers, for instance, would find it difficult to become taxi drivers in London. Moreover, a worker's loyalty to a particular firm may prevent him or her from looking for another job, even though a cut in wages has been suffered (though obviously this does not apply if the worker is made redundant).

(*b*) *Obstacles to a change of occupation.* In changing occupations, obstacles may be encountered in both moving out of the old occupation or in entering a new one. They arise because:

(i)   a high natural ability is required in certain occupations;
(ii)   training may be costly and take time.
(iii)   stringent entry conditions are sometimes prescribed by trade unions and professional associations.
(iv)   the new job may be repugnant; and, equally, some occupations, e.g. the Church, art and acting, are so pleasant that workers are not drawn into another occupation by the offer of a higher wage rate;
(v)   through a high division of labour, only limited skills have been acquired;
(vi)   workers may be reluctant or too old to learn a new job;
(vii)   workers may prefer to remain unemployed rather than accept a wage below a 'recognised minimum' in an alternative occupation;
(viii) in spite of prohibiting legislation, there is discrimination on account of sex, colour, social class or religion;
(ix)   workers are ignorant of wage-rates and opportunities in other occupations.

Of the above, the greatest obstacle to occupational mobility is natural ability. In this respect it should be noted that there can be more mobility between occupations, e.g. storeman and clerk, requiring the same level of innate ability than between doctors and dockers, where there are marked differences in the natural ability and training required. The first is sometimes termed 'horizontal' occupational mobility; the second, where there are non-competing groups of workers, 'vertical' mobility.

(c) Obstacles to a change of district. When it comes to moving from one part of the country to another, workers have to overcome both real and psychological obstacles. These include:

(i) the costs of moving, which to many workers represent a considerable capital sum and are incurred even if workers own their own homes;
(ii) the difficulty of securing acommodation elsewhere on comparable terms, particularly for council and rent-controlled tenants but also for owner-occupiers having to move into the more expensive housing in southern England;
(iii) social ties of friends, clubs, Church, etc.;
(iv) family ties, such as the children's education:
(v) imperfect knowledge of vacancies or wages paid in other localities;
(vi) prejudice against certain parts of the country, e.g. people at present generally prefer to live in the south-east rather than in the industrial north.

Such immobility of labour means that wage-rates can often be more easily explained by supply conditions rather than by demand. Even if there is competition between employers, differences in supply produce differences in the wage-rates between occupations, and between localities even for the same occupation. Thus solicitors earn more than their clerks because, on the demand side, the services of solicitors are valued more highly and, on the supply side, the supply of solicitors is small compared with clerks, for more natural ability and longer training are required.

Immobility is also one of the major causes of unemployment, and in Chapter 31, we consider some of the ways in which the government tries to reduce occupational and geographical immobility.

Imperfection in the labour market arises where one firm is the major employer in a locality (see above). But mainly it is due to trade unions, which (through the closed shop) can establish what is virtually a monopoly in the supply of a given type of labour. We therefore analyse the economic background to trade-union activity with reference to its strength in negotiating wage increaes.

14.4 Functions of Trade Unions

It would be wrong to regard trade unions primarily as a disruptive influence in the economy. For one thing there must be a means by which workers can communicate with employers. For another, by making the worker more contented, they enhance productivity. We can summarise their most important functions as: (i) improving working conditions; (ii) providing educational, social and legal benefits for members (iii) improving standards of work; (iv) obtaining pay increases; and (v) cooperating with governments in order to secure a workable economic policy and to improve working and living conditions generally. The remainder of this chapter is concerned with (iv).

The Process of Collective Bargaining

Collective bargaining is the settlement of conditions of employment by employers negotiating with the workers' trade unions. For its smooth working, certain conditions should be fulfilled. First, it must be pursued with good sense on both sides. This is enhanced where the industry has a tradition of good labour relations and where there is some accepted objective measure to which wage-rates can be linked (e.g. the Index of Retail Prices, wage-rates paid in similar trades, the level of profits in the industry). Second, both sides should be represented by strong organisations. Where all employers are linked in an association, there is no fear of outsiders stealing a march by negotiating independent wage bargains, while, if the union can speak for all its members, employers know an agreement will be honoured. Unofficial stoppages damage the union's reputation, and to avoid them there must be regular contact between employer and union and prompt investigation of grievances on the shopfloor. Third, there must be an understood procedure for settling disputes. While this must not be so prolonged as to fray patience, it should exhaust all possibilities of reaching agreement before a strike or lock-out is called.

In short the procedure of collective bargaining covers (i) negotiation and (ii) the settlement of disputes.

1. Negotiation

Broadly speaking the machinery for negotiation falls into three categories:

(1) VOLUNTARY NEGOTIATION
Generally, the government has left it to the unions and employers' organisations to work out their own procedures, and today voluntary machinery covers nearly 70 per cent of the insured workers of the UK. Because union organisation varies, the recognised procedure differs between industries and trades.

(2) JOINT INDUSTRIAL COUNCILS
Most industries have some national joint council or committee which, without outside assistance, thrashes out agreements. Usually it follows the

system of Joint Industrial Councils, composed of representatives of employers and workers in the industry. These consider regularly such matters as the better use of the practical knowledge and experience of the workpeople, general principles governing the conditions of employment, means of ensuring workers the greatest possible security of earnings and employment, methods of fixing and adjusting earnings, technical education and training, industrial research, improvement of processes and proposed legislation affecting the industry. Although Joint Industrial Councils are sponsored by the government, they are not forced upon any industry, and some important industries, such as iron and steel, engineering, shipbuilding and cotton, which had already developed their own procedure for negotiation, have not formed Joint Industrial Councils. Nevertheless, in 1990 there were some 400 Joint Industrial Councils or bodies of similar character.

(3) WAGES COUNCILS

In some industries and trades where the organisation of workers or employers or both is either non-existent or ineffective, the government has had to intervene. This started in 1909 when Trade Boards were set up to fix minimum time- and piece-rates for the 'sweated' trades. In 1945, they were renamed Wages Councils and today (1990) there are twenty-six covering a variety of industries, such as retailing, catering, hairdressing, clothing and textile manufacturing. The Councils are appointed by the Secretary of State for Employment and are composed of equal numbers of employers' and workers' representatives together with not more than five independent members. Their wages orders are enforceable by law.

Recently Wages Councils have been increasingly criticised as having little relevance to today's employment climate; for instance, the government considers that the ability to pay lower rates to trainees will encourage employers to take on more. Consequently the scope of Wages Councils has now been limited to setting minimum hourly and overtime pay rates for workers over twenty-one years. Furthermore, Councils now have to consider the impact on jobs of the minimum pay rates set, particularly in areas where pay is below the national average.

In agriculture, wages are fixed by the Agricultural Wages Board, similar to the wages councils' system. Thus about 10 per cent of insured workers are covered by schemes of statutory wage regulation.

2. Settlement of Disputes

Where the negotiating machinery fails to produce an agreement, it is a help if agreed procedures exist for ending the deadlock. Three methods can be employed: conciliation, arbitration or special inquiry.

(1) CONCILIATION

In 1974 the Secretary of State for Employment set up an *independent* Advisory Conciliation and Arbitration Service (ACAS), controlled by a council whose members are experienced in industrial relations. When efforts to obtain settlement of a dispute through normal procedures have failed, ACAS can provide conciliation if the parties concerned agree.

(2) ARBITRATION

ACAS can, at the joint request of the parties to a dispute, appoint single arbitrators or boards of arbitration chosen from a register of people experienced in industrial relations to determine differences on the basis of agreed terms of reference.

Alternatively the Terms and Conditions of Employment Act 1959 allows claims that a particular employer is not observing the terms or conditions of employment established for the industry to be referred compulsorily to an industrial court for a legally binding award.

(3) INQUIRY AND INVESTIGATION

The Secretary of State for Employment has legal power to inquire into the causes and circumstances of any trade dispute and, if he thinks fit, to appoint a court of inquiry with power to call for evidence. Such action, however, is chiefly a means of informing parliament and the public of the facts and causes of a major dispute, and is taken only when no agreed settlement seems possible.

The minister's power of inquiry also allows for less formal action, by way of setting up committees of investigation, when the public interest is not so general.

Neither a court of inquiry nor a committee of investigation is a conciliation or arbitration body, but both may make recommendations upon which a reasonable settlement of a dispute can be based.

Trade Union Arguments for Wage Increases

A trade union is likely to base its claim for a wage increase on one or more of the following grounds.

1. A Rise in the Cost of Living

Because inflation reduces their real incomes, workers seek an increase in money wages. But difficulties have arisen. First, wage demands have become an annual event. Second, they are often pitched higher than the rate of inflation, thereby fuelling further inflation (see Chapter 2).

2. A Higher Wage-rate in Comparable Grades and Occupations

The trouble here is that wage differentials are often ingrained in workers' attitudes, whereas they should reflect changes in the demand for and supply of particular types of labour. Furthermore, it is often difficult, indeed impossible, to assess 'comparability', e.g. between a social worker and a computer programmer. On the other hand, if there is a shortage of nurses in national health hospitals owing to the higher pay offered in private hospitals, there is a strong argument for increasing the wage of the state-paid nurse.

3. Profits Have Increased

Trade unions feel that they should share in extra profits and here they may be in a strong position (see pp. 228–232).

4. Productivity Has Increased

Where output per worker is increasing, there is a rise in the MRP curve, and firms can grant a wage increase (see p. 226). But there may be difficulty in apportioning the increased productivity between the workers' efforts and investment in new machines, research, etc. Capital has to receive its share if investment is to continue.

Trade Union Bargaining Limitations

The question must now be answered – how, and to what extent, can trade unions secure increases in the wage rate for their members in conditions of free collective bargaining? We shall assume that the trade union is a 'closed shop' with 100 per cent membership, making it virtually a monopolist in selling its particular type of labour.

Broadly speaking, there are three ways in which a trade union can secure a wage increase:

1. It Can Support Measures Which Will Increase the Demand for Labour

An increase in the demand for labour will come about if the *MRP* curve rises, either through an improvement in the physical productivity of the workers or through an increase in the price of the product. Thus the National Union of Mineworkers not only supports the National Coal Board's exhortation to miners to improve output per man-shift, but backs the campaign advertising the advantages of solid fuel for central heating.

The situation is illustrated in Figure 14.2. As marginal revenue productivity rises from MRP to MRP_1, wages of existing workers, *ON*, rise from

FIGURE 14.2
The Effect on the Wage-rate of a Change in Marginal Revenue Productivity

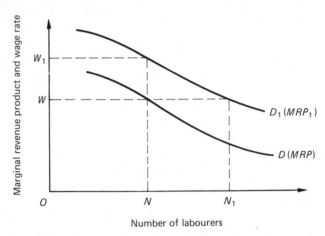

Number of labourers

OW to OW_1. Alternatively, if there were unemployment, extra men, NN_1, could be employed at the previous wage-rate.

2. It Can Restrict the Supply of Labour, Allowing Members to Compete Freely in Fixing Remuneration with Employers

A trade union or professional association may be sufficiently strong to restrict entry by apprenticeship regulations (e.g. plumbers and electricians) or high professional qualifications (e.g. solicitors, doctors, accountants and surveyors). While a minimum wage-rate or scale of fees may be suggested, many members work on their own account and these are left to negotiate their own rewards.

We can therefore analyse this method of securing a wage increase by the simple demand-and-supply approach (Figure 14.3). If the trade union reduces the supply of workers in an occupation from S to S_1, the wage-rate rises from OW to OW_1.

3. It Can Fix a Minimum Wage-rate

Where wages are raised by restricting entry, the trade union does not have to worry about unemployed members. It works simply on the principle that, assuming demand remains unchanged, greater scarcity leads to a higher reward.

FIGURE 14.3
The Effect on the Wage-Rate of Trade-union Restriction of the Supply of Labour

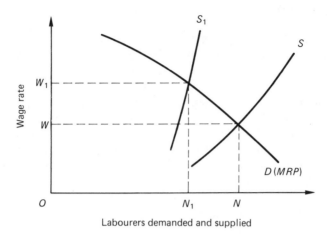

Most trade unions, however, are faced with a more difficult problem. While they may secure higher wage-rates for their members, their success may be double-edged if, as a result, many members are sacked. What we really have to ask, therefore, is: *Under what conditions can a trade union obtain higher wages for its members without decreasing the numbers employed?*

This means that we have to consider conditions of competition in both the product and factor markets. There are four main combinations:

(*a*) *Perfect competition in both selling the product and buying labour.* In the short period, even if there is perfect competition, an entrepreneur may be making supernormal profits. Here a strong trade union could, by threatening to withhold all its labour, force the employer to increase wages to the point where the whole of his supernormal profits disappear.

But this could not be permanent. The long-period equilibrium position is one in which there are no supernormal profits and the wage rate is equal to the MRP. A higher wage will represent a rise in costs. Some employers will now be forced out of business (see p. 149) and remaining firms will have to reduce their demand for labour until once again the MC of labour (the wage rate) is equal to the marginal-revenue product. Thus, in Figure 14.3 we will assume that OW is the original wage rate fixed by competition and ON the number of men employed – the trade-union membership. Suppose the trade union stipulates a minimum wage of OW_1. In the long-period, employment will then be reduced to ON_1. Given a downward-sloping MRP curve, this will always be true. Where there is perfect competition both in selling the product and in buying labour, a trade union can successfully negotiate an increase in wages only if there has been increased productivity; any increase without this will merely lead to members becoming unemployed.

The amount of unemployment resulting from such a rise in wages depends upon the elasticity of demand for labour. This will vary according to:

(i) *The physical possibility of substituting alternative factors*. As the price of one factor rises, other factors become relatively cheaper and the tendency is to substitute them for the dearer factor. Thus, if wages rise, entrepreneurs try to install more machinery and labour-saving devices; that is, they replace labour by capital. But because different factors are imperfect substitutes for each other, such substitution is limited physically. Indeed, if they have to be employed in fairly fixed proportions, little or no substitution is possible. As we saw in Chapter 6, the extent to which substitution can take place largely determines the elasticity of demand.

The degree of substitution is shown by the slope of the MRP curve. Where labour is added to another factor, but is a poor substitute for it, marginal productivity falls steeply; where it is a fairly good substitute, marginal productivity falls more gently. Thus in Figure 14.4(a), labour is not a good substitute for land, and marginal-revenue productivity falls steeply as the number of men employed increases. Demand for labour is therefore inelastic, and a wage rise of WW_1 leads to only NN_1 extra men being unemployed. Compare this with Figure 14.4(b), where labour and land are better substitutes. Here the same wage rise leads to a much larger number of men being unemployed.

It should be noted that, since the possibility of substitution increases over time, the longer the period under consideration, the greater will be the change in the labour force.

(ii) *The elasticity of supply of alternative factors*. Under conditions of perfect competition, the cost of a factor to an individual firm will not rise as the firm's demand for that factor increases (see p. 136). But when we are analysing a rise in the wage-rate of the workers of an *industry*, we must recognise that the whole industry will now be demanding the alternative factors in order to substitute them for labour. This increased demand will affect the price of the alternative factors, and a higher price will have to be paid in order to attract a greater supply. This increase in price of the alternative factors also limits the extent to which substitution is carried out. Thus if the supply of the alternative factor is perfectly elastic, only the physical considerations referred to above will affect the demand for it; if, on the other hand, supply is inelastic, then it is likely that the quick rise in its price will soon make it uneconomic to substitute it for labour. Once

FIGURE 14.4

The Relationship of Substitutability between Labour and Land and Numbers Employed

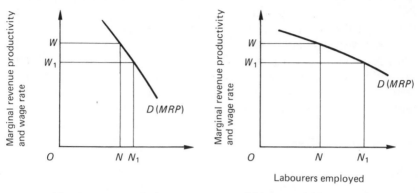

(a) Labour a poor substitute –
    cultivation already intensive

(b) Labour a fairly good substitute –
    cultivation extensive

again, the elasticity of supply of the alternative factors will be greater the longer the period of time under consideration.

Where unemployed labour exists, two conditions prevail that make it difficult for a trade union to obtain a wage increase without reducing the level of employment: (i) a high degree of substitution existing between the union labour and the alternative factor, unemployed labour, particularly if the work performed is unskilled; (ii) an infinite elasticity of supply of the alternative factor, unemployed labour, at least for a time. Hence trade unions are relatively weaker in periods of unemployment.

(iii) *The proportion of labour costs to total costs.* The proportion of labour costs to total costs has two effects. First, if labour costs form only a small percentage of total costs, demand for labour will tend to be inelastic, for there is less urgency in seeking substitutes (see p. 94). Second, if labour costs form a small percentage of total costs, as in steel production, a rise in wages will produce only a small movement of the supply curve of the product to the left. The opposite applies in each case, e.g. with government services, which are labour intensive.

(iv) *The elasticity of demand for the final product.* The effect of a rise in the wage-rate will be to decrease the supply of a good at each price; that is, the supply curve moves to the left. Hence the market price of the good rises. We have to ask, therefore: 'How much will the demand for the good contract as a result of this rise in price?' Once again we are back to the practical application of elasticity of demand.

If demand is elastic (D_{el}), the quantity of the good demanded will contract considerably, from OM to OM_1 (Figure 14.5). This will mean a large reduction in the numbers employed. On the other hand, if demand is inelastic (D_{inel}), there will be no great contraction in the quantity demanded – only to OM_2. Here people are willing to pay a higher price for the good (OP_2), and this will cover the increase in wages. In other words, the marginal-revenue productivity of labour has risen.

Elasticity of demand depends mainly on the availability of substitutes. Thus demand in export markets is usually more elastic than in the home market for with the former there are often many competing alternative sources of supply from firms in other countries. Consequently, if an industry sells a high percentage of its output abroad, e.g. electronic equipment and aircraft engines, the trade union is limited in its ability to secure a wage increase.

(*b*) *Monopoly in the product market, competition in buying labour.* Here the employer has a marginal-revenue curve similar in shape to that for perfect competition, except that it falls more quickly because the price of the product falls as output increases. Hence, because he is faced with a horizontal wage curve, the same conclusion holds as with perfect competition – raising the wage rate will reduce employment.

(*c*) *Perfect competition in the product market, monopsony in buying labour.* Imperfect competition can exist not only in selling the product but also in buying the factor. A firm may be the sole buyer – a 'monopsonist' –

FIGURE 14.5
The Extent to which Demand for the Product Contracts as a Result of a Wage Increase

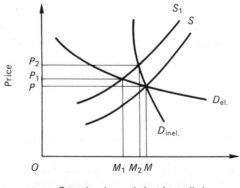

of a particular factor in a given locality. This applies to labour, for instance, where a large factory is the main source of employment in a district. In such a case, the size of an employer's demand for labour will affect the wage-rate. If more labour is engaged, a higher wage will have to be paid to all the labourers hired.

The result is that the wage-rate, the average cost of engaging labour, is no longer represented by a horizontal straight line. Instead the wage-rate increases as more labour is employed – the curve rises to the right. But as he hires more labour, the monopsonist firm has to pay the additional wage to *all* workers engaged. Hence the marginal cost of an extra labourer, that is, the addition to the total wage bill, will be greater than the average cost, that is the wage-rate. The position is shown in Figure 14.6. The firm would engage *ON* men at a wage of *OW*. Here the marginal-revenue product is higher than the wage-rate, and thus, to some extent, there is exploitation of labour. If now a trade union fixes a minimum wage-rate for all workers, this minimum at once becomes the marginal cost of labour. The firm has to pay this wage-rate or have no labour at all. Hence it ceases to be able to influence the wage-rate by the amount of labour it demands; average cost and marginal cost of labour are the same. It can be seen, therefore, that a union can fix a wage of up to OW_1 without there being any reduction in the

FIGURE 14.6
The Effect of Trade-union Action in Raising Wages where the employer is a Monopsonist

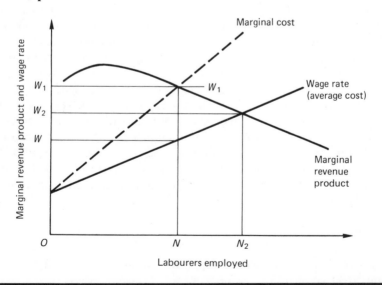

numbers employed, for W_1W_1 now becomes the new marginal-cost curve. Indeed, at any wage rate of less than OW_1, the trade union will not only be able to raise wages, but also to increase the numbers employed. Thus with a wage rate of OW_2, ON_2 men are employed.

(d) *Monopoly in the product market, monopsony in buying labour.* The result here is merely a combination of (b) and (c). So long as the wage-rate is not increased above the former marginal cost (OW_1 in Figure 14.6 above), both wages and employment can be increased.

It can be seen from the above analysis that a trade union stands the best chance of successfully negotiating a wage increase in situations (b) and (d), where there is an element of monopsony in buying labour. But even in situation (b), (monopoly in selling the product), if a trade union is a monopolist in the supply of labour, it can insist that the firm employ *all* or none of its members at a wage-rate which is higher than the MRP. The higher wages would come from the supernormal profits being made from the monopoly sale of the product, with the firm working on the principle that 'half a loaf is better than no bread'.

In these circumstances there is a whole range of possible wage-rates between the minimum which workers will accept and the maximum which employers are prepared to give rather than lose all their labour. The success of the trade union will depend, therefore, upon (1) the extent to which it can maintain its monopoly position by preventing employers from engaging blacklegs – non-union workers, or other substitute labour – and (2) the bargaining ability of its leaders relative to that of the employers. On the one side, the union leaders have to estimate how high they can push the wage rate without employers allowing a strike to take place; on the other, the employers must judge the lowest rate acceptable without a strike. As each is by no means certain of the other's strength, bluff will play a large part in the negotiations. Such factors as a large order-book for the firm's products, costly equipment's standing idle, a wealthy strike fund or increased profits, will obviously strengthen the union's hand. Considerations which could enlist public sympathy are a rise in the cost of living, a higher wage paid elsewhere in comparable occupations and an increase in productivity. Should a strike actually take place, it is usually because of misjudgement by one side; it is doubtful whether either really gains in the long run by strike action. Thus the strike is a form of 'blood-letting', allowing one or both sides to reassess the position before further negotiations take place.

Conclusions

The above analysis leads to two important conclusions. First, in both cases of imperfect competition the demand for the factor is less than it would have been had perfectly competitive conditions existed. From the point of view of government policy, this may have important implications. Suppose, for instance, that there is unemployment through lack of effective demand. If the government wishes to alleviate the situation by itself placing orders for goods, it should, for the maximum effect, concentrate on those industries where competitive conditions prevail.

Second, in both cases of imperfect competition some 'exploitation' exists. For instance, if there is monopoly in the product market but perfect competition in the factor market, factors receive the competitive reward. But supplies of the product are restricted. Here it is chiefly the consumer who is exploited, though it must be remembered that, indirectly, the factor suffers in that demand for it is less than it would be were there perfect competition. Where there is monopsony in hiring a factor, exploitation is more direct, for the reward is less than the marginal-revenue product irrespective of whether that product is sold under perfectly competitive conditions.

14.5 The Government and Wages

Influence on Wage Determination

The government influences the wage-rate through: (1) its minimum-wage regulations for industries covered (see p. 223), (ii) the legal protection it affords to workers with regard to conditions of work. e.g. stipulating a written statement of the conditions of employment, prohibiting discrimination on account of sex or race, protecting employees against unfair dismissal, providing for redundancy payments and regulating conditions for health and safety at work; (iii) its efforts to break down illogicalities, etc. sanctioned by custom; (iv) guidelines for wage settlements which it may lay down from time to time in its efforts to combat inflation (see p. 460).

Curbing Trade-union Power

With one main exception trade unions are similar to other pressure groups which seek to influence the government to further the interests of their particular causes. The exception is that trade unions can reinforce political means by economic sanctions. Moreover, in the case of key industries, just a small group of workers may, by strikes, go-slow tactics or working-to-rule, disrupt the whole economy.

The Thatcher government of 1979 took the view, therefore, that if it was to achieve its major role of stabilising the economy it could not allow its policies to be undermined by trade unions misusing their current extensive legal advantages. Thus it has promoted a succession of legislation which has progressively removed trade-union privileges. It should be noted that to a large degree there is now a consensus of opinion, for the present opposition Labour Party has suggested that much of the legislation would be retained should it be returned to power.

In brief, the main changes effected are:

(a) Trade unions may be fined and their assets seized for offences committed by them or their members.
(b) Before industrial action can be taken, approval must be obtained by means of a secret ballot of its members.
(c) Picketing by employees must be confined to their place of work.
(d) Sympathetic strikes by workers not directly involved in the particular strike are illegal.
(e) A majority of members of a trade union must approve by secret ballot:
    (i) the setting up or continuance of a closed shop; (ii) any use of funds for any political purposes; (iii) the election of executive committees at least every five years.

15 Capital and Interest

15.1 Capital

What is 'Capital'?

A schoolmaster earns, say, £250 a week. He also has £900 in the National Savings Bank, yielding him £54 per annum interest (or about £1 a week). We can say, therefore, that his total *income* is £251 *a week*, or £13,054 *per annum*; his *capital* assets are £900.

Thus we see that, whereas *income* is a *flow of wealth* over a *period of time, capital* is a *stock of wealth* existing at any one *moment of time*.

This broad definition of capital, however, has slightly different meanings when used by different persons. The ordinary individual, when speaking of his 'capital', would include his money assets, holdings of securities, his house, and possibly many durable goods, such as his car, television, cine camera, etc. (sometimes referred to as 'consumer's capital'). The businessman would count not only his real assets (such as his factory, machinery, land, stocks of goods, etc.), but add any money reserves ('liquid capital') held in the bank and titles to wealth (such as share certificates, tax-reserve certificates, government bonds, etc.).

But the economist considers capital chiefly as a form of wealth which contributes to production. In other words, he is concerned with capital as a *factor of production*, that is, as something real and not merely a piece of paper. It is the factory and machines, not the share certificates (the individual's entitlement to a part of them), which are vital to him.

This has two effects. First, in defining capital, the economist concentrates on all producer goods and any stocks of finished consumer goods not yet in the hands of the final consumer. Second, in calculating the 'national capital', the economist has to be careful to avoid double-counting. Titles to capital – shares, bonds, National Savings deposits and certificates, Treasury Bills, other government securities, etc. – must be excluded. Share certificates merely represent the factories, machinery, etc. which have already been counted. Government debt refers to few real assets, for most has been expended on shells, ships, and aircraft in previous wars. Its effect is really to establish a debt from one person in the country to another, with taxation redistributing income (in the form of interest) to those who hold government bonds. The only exception regarding titles to wealth is where a share or bond is held by a foreign national, or conversely, where a British national holds a share or bond representing an asset in a foreign country. We then have to subtract the former and add the latter when calculating national capital. Foreign shares or bonds held by British nationals, for example, can always be sold to increase our real resources.

Naturally, 'social capital' (roads, schools, hospitals, municipal buildings, etc.) which belongs to the community at large is just as much capital as factories, offices, etc. And, in order to be consistent, owner-occupied houses have to be included, for they must be treated in the same way as houses owned by property companies (Figure 15.1).

Capital as a Factor of Production

When the economist refers to 'capital', it is usually in the sense of *wealth which has been made by man for the production of further wealth*. This is because capital plays such an important part in increasing production, and, therefore, in improving living standards. It is in this sense that the term is used from now on.

Increased production occurs because capital – tools, machines, irrigation works, communications, etc. – greatly assists persons in their work. Indeed, with modern electronic equipment, machines often take over the actual work. As the use of capital increases, there are three possible gains. First, more current goods can be produced. Between 1979 and 1989 the output of agriculture increased by 12 per cent, although the labour force *fell* by 13 per cent. There was thus an increased output per worker, due largely to more efficient machines and improved techniques resulting from capital investment in research. Second, instead of simply producing more current goods, people can be released to produce new goods. And, third, people can, as an alternative to more goods, enjoy increased leisure.

The Accumulation of Capital

If capital is so important in adding to our well-being, why do we not have more of it? The answer is simply that we can accumulate capital only by postponing current consumption. In everyday language, more jam tomorrow means less jam today. The accumulation of capital represents an

FIGURE 15.1
'Capital' in the Economy

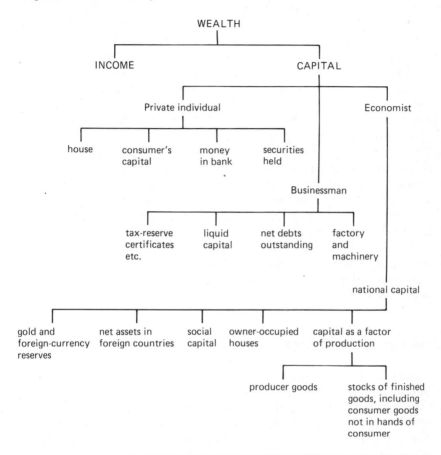

opportunity cost over time – consumption now or greater consumption later? A simple example will make this 'trade off' clear.

Suppose a peasant farmer has been tilling the ground with a primitive spade. By working twelve hours a day he can cultivate one hectare in a year. Obviously, if he had a plough which could be drawn by his oxen it would help him considerably. How can he obtain it? Three ways are open to him:

1. He could reduce the land he cultivates to $\frac{3}{4}$ ha. This would reduce his tilling time by three hours, and he could use this time to make the plough.

2. He could reduce his leisure and sleeping time from twelve to eight hours a day. This would give him an extra four hours for making the plough.
3. He might decide not to consume some of the produce already harvested, exchanging it instead for a plough.

Whichever method is chosen, some present sacrifice is necessary. With (1) and (3) he has to reduce his standard of living by having less to eat. With (2) he has to forgo some leisure. In short, he has either to draw in his belt or work harder. But the reward of such sacrifice comes when he has the plough at work. Then, with the twelve hours' work a day he can cultivate 2 ha in a year; his standard of living has doubled. We take up this point of output growth again in Chapter 32.

One other point emerges from this illustration. If, owing to the poverty of the soil, sixteen hours were required to dig his hectare, our farmer would have found it much more difficult to find time to make his plough. He would not reduce his food consumption below subsistence level, nor go without essential sleep. In other words, the more fertile his land, the easier it is for him to increase his income. In economics the maxim 'to him that hath shall be given' often holds. Thus a country with a very low standard of living finds it difficult to build up the capital which would improve its living standards and it is for this reason that any aid which can be given to poor countries is so valuable.

Maintaining Capital Intact

Naturally our farmer will have to devote a part of his time to repairing the plough. So long as his capital equipment is capable of cultivating 2 ha, we can say that it is being 'maintained intact'. If it is being increased or replaced in a more efficient form so that more land is cultivated, it is said that capital is 'being accumulated'. Where it is not being maintained (as in wartime), capital is being 'run down' or 'depreciated'.

In practice it is unusual for the same people to devote so much time to producing consumer goods and so much to the production of capital. Instead, production is organised by applying the principle of the division of labour – some people specialise in consumer goods and others in capital goods.

We can now see why most governments encourage investment, the process of producing capital. Where the proportion of productive capacity devoted to investment falls, there may be serious consequences for living standards in the future. More important, the poverty of many countries is chiefly the result of their lack of capital. Hence the USSR, China, India, and Cuba have directly restricted present consumption so that capital development may proceed rapidly under Five-Year Plans.

15.2   Interest

Investment, i.e. adding to capital goods or stocks, usually first involves obtaining liquid capital. Interest, expressed as a rate, is the price which has to be paid for this liquid capital. What we shall examine here is the rate of interest which has to be paid for liquid capital in a *particular* use or *industry*. We shall *not* discuss what determines the *general* level of interest in the economy.

The *demand for liquid capital* arises because it is necessary or advantageous to use capital in production. The farmer who sows seed in the autumn and harvests the crop in the summer is using capital in the form of seed. Similarly, a manufacturer needs capital in the form of a factory and machines because, provided demand is large enough, it is cheaper to produce in this way.

Now, as we saw when examining the peasant's decision to make a plough, the accumulation of capital can come about only by postponing present consumption. This can be done directly by the producer himself. The farmer could have obtained seed by putting aside a part of the previous year's harvest; the manufacturer could have secured capital by retaining rather than distributing profits. However, such retentions may be inadequate. In this case funds may be borrowed from other persons who have so saved (that is, forgone current consumption), repaying them later when the product is sold.

The actual demand of the farmer or manufacturer will depend upon the MRP of capital – the addition to profit which, for instance, a farmer thinks will result from adding an additional cow to his herd. Suppose he calculates that profit can be increased by spending £500 on a cow now. To avoid complications, let us also assume that he considers that in eight years' time, when the cow ceases to be worth milking, he will be able to sell it for beef for £500. Assume that the increase in profit (yield from the extra milk less labour and feeding costs) is estimated to be £200 for the year. He would then be willing to borrow the money to buy that cow so long as the interest he had to pay was not more than £200, i.e. not more than 40 per cent. If he bought another cow, the net addition to receipts might be only £190, for the third cow £180, and so on. It is possible, therefore, to draw a curve showing the expected addition to profit which the farmer estimates will be received through adding one more cow. We can call this curve the 'marginal revenue productivity of capital' curve, and the farmer will go on borrowing capital until the rate of interest equals the marginal-revenue product of capital. Hence at different rates of interest, different quantities of capital will be demanded.

Thus in Figure 15.2, when the rate of interest is OR, the farmer will borrow capital to buy eight cows. If the rate falls to OR_1, he will borrow sufficient capital to buy eleven cows. One point must be emphasised.

Because he is producing in advance, the farmer has to base his demand for capital on the *prospective* money yield resulting from its use. His expectations are thus all-important, and we shall have more to say on this subject later.

The sum of the demand curves for liquid capital from all the firms in the industry gives the demand curve for the industry, though some allowance could be made for a fall in the price of the good produced by the capital equipment (see p. 165).

The *supply* of liquid funds for *one* use can only be obtained by bidding them away from alternative uses. How much has to be paid for a given quantity relative to other uses will depend upon:

1. whether lenders consider more or less risk is involved:
2. the period of the loan, people preferring to lend for a short period rather than a long one;
3. the elasticity of demand for the alternative products to which capital contributes in their production.

Generally speaking, however, we can expect more liquid capital to be forthcoming for a particular use the higher the rate of interest offered. We therefore have an upward-sloping supply curve. Thus the rate of interest is fixed by the interaction of the demand and supply curves (as in Figure 15.2).

Once again, however, we must point out that this is only a *partial* explanation of the determination of a rate of interest. It does not tell us how the *general* level of the rate of interest is determined. To discover what determines this benchmark we have to look at the nature of money and government policy (see Chapters 22 and 28). But it is helpful if we first look briefly, by way of contrast, with the loanable funds theory of the Classical economists.

15.3 A Note on the Loanable Funds Theory of the Classical Economists

The Rate of Interest as the Price of Savings

To the Classical economists the benchmark rate of interest was the price of savings – loanable funds. Like any other price, therefore, it was determined by the demand for and supply of loanable funds.

Because investment is profitable, firms *demand* funds for investment. The lower the rate of interest, the greater the number of investment projects which are profitable. Thus total demand for liquid capital consists

FIGURE 15.2
Demand for Capital, the Marginal-revenue Product of Capital and the Rate of Interest

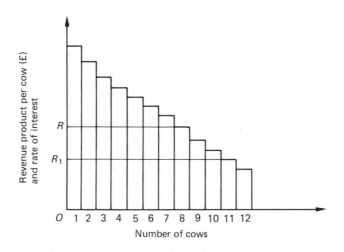

Note: each cow costs £500.

of the sum of the demands of the individual firms at different rates of interest (Figure 15.3).

The *supply of loanable funds* comes from persons willing to forego present consumption in order to enjoy it at some future date. To most people, 'a bird in the hand is worth two in the bush'. The Classical economists argued, therefore, that in order to persuade people to overcome the inclination to consume immediately a reward in the form of interest had to be offered. The higher the rate of interest, the greater would be the inducement to postpone current consumption, and so the greater would be the supply of loanable funds. Thus we have a supply curve of loanable funds, S, sloping upwards to the right.

The rate of interest, i, the price of liquid capital, is fixed by the interaction of demand and supply.

Criticisms of the Classical Theory

For the following reasons the Classical economists' explanation of the rate of interest is too simple.

FIGURE 15.3
The Classical Economists' Theory of the Determination of the Rate of interest

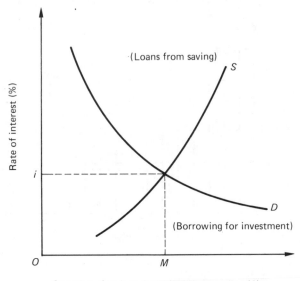

Quantity of savings demanded and supplied (£)

1. The demand for loanable funds is not confined to the demand of firms for new capital. Households want funds to purchase houses, securities, cars and other durables. The government needs funds to cover its Public Sector Borrowing Requirement (see p. 326).
2. It ascribes to the rate of interest a greater influence on the volume of investment than is justified. Other factors, notably the level of income and the degree of confidence, are more important (see pp. 412–8). In addition, investment carried out by the public sector is influenced by political and social factors as well as by the rate of interest.
3. Saving does not respond automatically to changes in the rate of interest. Again the level of income is likely to be more important, while in any case much saving is contractual (see pp. 406–9).
4. Since investment and saving as conceived by the Classical economists would be fairly stable, their theory cannot explain why fairly short-term variations in the rate of interest occur.
5. It ignores the influence of the government especially on the short-term rate of interest.

6. *Most important*, it assumes that the whole of income saved is actually lent to entrepreneurs. But besides being reluctant to save, people are reluctant to lend. They prefer to keep their assets liquid in the form of money. It is money as a *liquid* asset that is the starting-point of Keynes's theory of the rate of interest (see Chapter 22).

16 Land and Rent

16.1 Land and Rent in General Terms

Land

Land has already been defined as the resources provided freely by nature – fresh water, sunshine, rain and space to employ the other factors of production and to dispose of waste.

These resources can be classified as being renewable or non-renewable. With *renewable resources*, e.g. fish and tropical rainforests, we have to make arrangements, often by international agreement, to preserve an adequate stock to provide a supply sufficient for future needs. In contrast, with *non-renewable resources* e.g. coal, fossil oils, minerals, supplies are finite and so will eventually run out. Here the problem is one of eking out the supply over time bearing in mind future needs and the possibility of discovering substitutes (see Chapter 20).

The Determination of 'Commercial Rent'

To the economist, the terms 'land' and 'rent' have a special meaning. This is just as well, for in everyday speech each can imply different things. Thus, if I buy land for farming it will probably include buildings, fences, a water supply and a drainage system, all of which are really capital. Similarly, I can rent things other than land – a house, a television set, a gas meter, building equipment, shooting rights, etc. Rent in this sense simply means a periodic payment for the use of something. It can be termed 'commercial rent'.

Usually, however, rent does refer to payment for the use of a piece of land, and before we consider 'land' and 'rent' in their special economic sense, we must ask what determines how much rent is paid to a landlord.

The problem is similar to the determination of the return on any factor service. The demand for land depends on its marginal revenue productivity and the curve slopes downwards from left to right for the reasons given in Chapter 10. On the supply side, land, like labour, can usually be put to alternative uses – building factories or houses, growing wheat or barley, raising cattle or sheep, and so on. A given piece of land will be transferred to its most profitable use. If, for instance, the price of cattle rises and that of wheat falls, some land will be transferred from arable to pasture farming. Thus the supply curve for land in a particular use slopes upwards from left to right. The interaction of the demand and supply curves will give the rent actually paid (as in Figure 10.3).

Of course, this assumes (i) that the landlord can vary the rent charged any time the demand for and supply of his particular type of land alters, and (ii) that land can be transferred fairly quickly to a different use. The first assumption is complicated by the fact that rents are usually fixed for a period of years. Only when the contract expires is the landlord free to adjust the rent. The second assumption implies that we are concerned only with the long period in our analysis. But what of the short period, when land is a fixed factor? An analysis of this situation is basically what we are concerned with in the remainder of this chapter.

16.2   Economic Rent: Land and Rent to the Economist

Ricardo's Views on 'Land' and 'Rent'

To explain the special meaning which economists today give to the terms 'land' and 'rent', we have to examine the views of Ricardo, a Classical economist of the early nineteenth century. He was concerned not with the rent paid to land for a particular purpose, but with the rent paid to land as a whole. Moreover, he was referring to land in the economist's sense – as the resources provided by nature (see p. 101) – and, as such, its total supply was fixed.

In this respect, he argued, land was different from the other factors of production, labour and capital, where more would be supplied the higher the price and, if no price at all were offered, there would be no supply. But with land as a whole – in the sense of space and natural resources – the same amount is available whatever the price offered. An increase in price cannot bring about an expansion of supply; and if the price fell to zero the same amount would still be available. Thus land as a whole has no supply price.

The return to land, therefore, was merely a 'residual' – the difference between, on the one hand, what was received for the product, and, on the other, the payments of wages and interest to labour and capital respectively. If the price received for the product was high, there would be more left over as rent; if the price was low, there would be less for rent. Rent did not determine the price of the good produced; instead, the opposite was true – rent was determined by price.

'Land' and 'Rent' in Economic Theory Today

On the ambiguities of Ricardo's reasoning we need not dwell. First, it can be argued that the total supply of land is fixed only in the short period; in the long run improved farming techniques and developments in transport are constantly increasing the amount of land which can be put to economic use. Indeed, in this respect there is little difference between land and other factors of production, which likewise can only be increased in the long period. Over a certain period of time – the short period, whatever that may be in months or years – all are fixed in total supply. Second, land, like other factors of production, has alternative uses. It can be used to produce different crops, or as a site for different buildings. The cost of putting it to one use is the yield that could have been obtained had it been employed in another way. Thus, in order to secure it for one purpose, a producer will have to pay a sufficient price to attract it from its best alternative use. It is this allocation of land between its different uses which is the main concern of the economist.

The Nature of the Return to a Fixed Factor

But Ricardo did point out an essential truth – that the return to a factor fixed in supply, i.e. whose supply is absolutely inelastic, will vary directly with variations in the price of the good produced by it. We can illustrate this more clearly by a simple example.

Let us assume: (i) a given plot of land on which only potatoes can be grown; (ii) that only land and labour are necessary to grow potatoes; and (iii) that the supply of labour for growing potatoes is perfectly elastic because only a small proportion of the total labour force is required.

The return to this plot of land will depend entirely on the price of potatoes. This can be seen from Figure 16.1. When the marginal revenue product of labour is shown by the curve QN, at a wage of OP, OM men are employed. The value of the total product is $OMNQ$: the wage bill is $OMNP$ and the return to the plot of land PNQ. If now the price of potatoes increases, the marginal-revenue product of labour rises to Q_1N_1. OM_1 men are now employed at a wage bill of OM_1N_1P. (Each worker still receives the same wage, OP, because the supply of this type of labour is perfectly elastic). But the return to the given plot of land has increased to PN_1Q_1. The opposite would apply if the price of potatoes fell.

FIGURE 16.1
The Effect of the Price of a Product on the Rent of Land

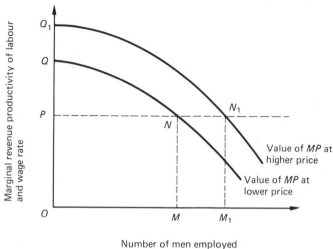

Number of men employed

Certain practical conclusions follow from the above analysis:

(a) Because the plot of land will grow only potatoes, it will be cultivated so long as the value of the total product is sufficient to pay the wage bill. In other words, at the lower price a lump-sum tax on the plot up to *QPN* could be levied without affecting the output. This is the theoretical basis of the often-proposed tax on land. Unfortunately, in practice it is impossible to distinguish precisely between economic rent and other factor earnings.

(b) The return to land as we have analysed it above – rent in its economic sense – is purely a surplus. It arose because, by definition, our plot of land was confined to one particular use – growing potatoes. The supply of this land offered for sale or hiring will not be affected by a price, simply because nobody has any other use for it. In short, it has no opportunity or transfer cost.

(c) Once land has been built on, it is largely specific to a given use, and the return to the land and building will be dependent on demand.

(d) Because land is really space, it is impossible to increase the area of sites in city centres except by building upwards, e.g. as in Oxford Street and the City of London. Such fixity of supply means that rent is largely determined by current demand. Thus in Figure 16.2 it is assumed that the supply of land is fixed at OM.

FIGURE 16.2
The Determination of Rent When Land is Fixed in Supply

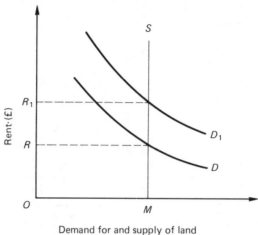

Demand for and supply of land

This means that the rent is determined by demand: an increase from D to D_1 raises rent from OR to OR_1. For instance, rents in Oxford Street depend upon the demand for shops there (which in its turn depends upon people's spending) and rents in the City of London depend on the demand for offices there (which in turn depends upon the level of business activity).

Economic Rent

Economists have generalised Ricardo's concept of land to cover all factors which are fixed in supply. 'Economic rent' is the term used to describe the earnings of any factor over and above its supply price. Put in another way, it is any surplus over its transfer earnings – what it could obtain in its next most profitable use (its 'opportunity cost', in our earlier terminology). How this idea can be applied generally will now be explained.

The actual rate of return to a factor is the price per period of time at which it is selling its services. For example, the return to a plasterer is his wage, say £180 per week. But what is the opportunity cost? Simply what has to be paid to retain it in its present use – that is, sufficient to keep it from going to the best alternative use. Take our plasterer, for instance. His next-best occupation may simply be plasterer's labourer, earning £90 per week. He would offer his services as a plasterer, therefore, at anything above £90 per week.

A second plasterer, however, may be a competent bricklayer, and as such earn £120 per week. He will only offer his services as a plasterer, therefore, if at least £120 per week is offered. And so we could go on. The supply curve of plasterers to the industry is thus an 'opportunity cost' curve (Figure 16.3).

If in Figure 16.3 we now insert the demand curve, we can obtain the current wage-rate to the industry, £180, when *OM* plasterers will be employed. But all plasterers receive this wage-rate. Thus the first plasterer receives an economic rent of £90, the second £60, and so on. The total economic rent received by plasterers as a whole is shown by the shaded area.

What Determines the Size of Economic Rent?

The size of economic rent earned by a particular type of factor depends upon the elasticity of supply of the factor and how the particular type of factor is defined.

1. The Elasticity of Supply

Elasticity of supply is determined largely by the period of time under consideration and by immobilities, some of which cannot be eliminated even in the long period. Both will affect economic rent.

FIGURE 16.3
Economic Rent

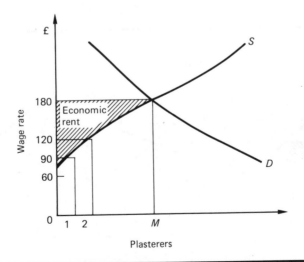

Let us assume that, in the short period, the supply of plasterers is fixed: there is insufficient time for them to move into alternative occupations or for others to move in. In short, there is no alternative occupation – they can either work as plasterers or not at all. Thus all their earnings are economic rent – Figure 16.4a.

In the long period, however, other occupations can be trained as plasterers, and existing plasterers can move elsewhere. Sufficient has to be paid – the opportunity cost – to retain plasterers. Thus we have a long-period supply curve of plasterers, and economic rent is smaller (Figure 16.4b).

In the long period, however, other occupations can be trained as plasterers, and existing plasterers can move elsewhere. Sufficient has to be paid – the opportunity cost – to retain plasterers. Thus we have a long-period supply curve of plasterers, and economic rent is smaller (Figure 16.4b).

If the supply of plasterers became perfectly elastic, economic rent would disappear (Figure 16.4c). Thus economic rent depends upon a less than perfectly elastic supply curve to the industry.

Sometimes the degree of immobility between different uses or occupations persists indefinitely. Building sites for offices in the City of London, for instance, earn rents far in excess of what they could obtain in their best alternative use, say for houses. Simply because such sites are very limited in supply, competition for office accommodation has forced up the rents of these sites far beyond the possible price which houses could offer. A large part of their earnings, therefore, is 'economic rent'.

Occasionally, too, we refer to the 'rent of ability'. Many footballers, pop singers, film stars, barristers and surgeons have talents which, to all intents

FIGURE 16.4
Economic Rent and Elasticity of Supply

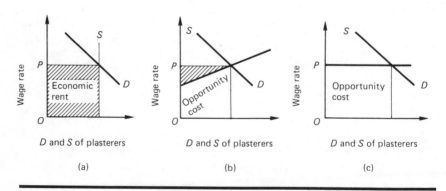

and purposes, are unique, for they cannot be duplicated by training others. Their high earnings, therefore, are almost wholly in the nature of 'economic rent'.

2. The Definition of an 'Occupation', etc.

If we adopt a wide definition of our factor, e.g. land as a whole, the distinction is between employing it or idleness, and thus the whole of its earnings is economic rent. This is what Ricardo had in mind.

If, however, our definition is narrower, e.g. covering only land for a particular use, such as growing wheat, then the opportunity cost (e.g. growing barley) will be larger and the economic rent smaller. Similarly, we could distinguish between cabinet-makers and carpenters, surgeons and doctors, and so on. Each would give a smaller 'economic rent' than if the distinction were simply between cabinet-makers and labourers, surgeons and teachers, etc.

Likewise, economic rent will be different whether we are looking at it from the point of view of the industry or the firm. The industry is unlikely to have a perfectly elastic supply curve; thus there will be some element of economic rent in its payment to the factors it hires. The firm, however, will face, in perfect competition, a perfectly elastic supply curve. In this case it will pay the transfer cost to all factors (whose best alternative is another firm); there is thus no economic rent.

Quasi-rent

For fixed factors, particularly capital equipment, what the firm has to pay to retain them will vary according to the period of time.

In the short period, capital equipment is, by definition, fixed in supply. There is no transfer price. More capital equipment cannot be added; nor can existing equipment be diminished. The entrepreneur will continue to work his capital equipment so long as total earnings just cover the cost of his variable factors (see Chapter 8). Any earnings above variable costs will be in the nature of a residual which helps towards the cost of the fixed factors. The size of this residual depends upon the price at which the product sells.

This can be seen immediately if we refer to Figure 8.6. Were the demand for mowers to increase, the price would rise, say to £600, and production would be expanded to the point where once again price equalled marginal cost – that is, to 100 units. The increased cost of such production would be equal to the increase in total cost – that is, £5100. But total receipts would have increased by £19 500, and so, through the fixed factors, the share-holders of Rollermowers earn an additional return – the increase in 'supernormal profit', equal to £14 400.

As time passes, however, we move into the long period. If the product has been selling at a high price, the high return to the capital equipment will induce firms to produce and instal additional equipment. On the other hand, if the price of the product was low, existing capital equipment will either be transferred to its next most profitable use or, when it wears out, simply not be replaced. In the long period, therefore, earnings of fixed factors are, under perfect competition, equal to their transfer cost: economic rent is eliminated.

To distinguish between economic rent which is more or less permanent and that which disappears over time, the latter is often referred to as 'quasi-rent'. It is not a true rent, for the high return earned by such factors leads to an increase in their supply, and this eliminates the economic rent they earn. True rent refers only to factors which are fixed in supply; even if their earnings are high, identical factors are not forthcoming, and so economic rent persists.

17 Entrepreneurship and Profit

17.1 Entrepreneurship

The Identity of Entrepreneurship and Risk-bearing

For production to take place, resources must be brought together and set to work. Whoever undertakes this task is often described as 'the entrepreneur'. Usually, however, a somewhat narrower meaning is given to the term.

Organising production can be broken down into two parts. First, there is the task of coordination – bringing factors of production together and setting them to work. Second, there is accepting the risk of buying factors to produce goods which will not be sold until sometime in the future – when receipts may not cover costs.

In practice, it is not always easy to separate coordination and risk. A farmer, for instance, not only manages and runs the farm, but also accepts the risk involved in deciding what to produce. On the other hand, in a joint-stock company most of the work of coordination is left to a paid board of directors, with a manager playing the major role. Here the risks of the business are borne by the ordinary shareholders. With a public corporation, they are carried by the taxpayers. But neither shareholders nor taxpayers take part in running the business except in a most remote way.

The function of coordination, therefore, can be fulfilled by a paid manager. In this respect, management is simply an exceptionally highly skilled form of labour. Thus we narrow our concept of enterprise to cover only bearing those risks of the business associated with ownership.

The Nature of Risks

A firm is always open to the risk of fire, accidents, burglary, storm damage, etc. But these risks are calculable. A mathematician can work out, for instance, the chances of a building catching fire during the course of the year. One cannot say which building will be destroyed in this way, but information is available which states that on average, say 1 out of every 10 000 will be. Such risks can therefore be insured against. They are thus reduced to a normal cost – what the firm has to pay to contract out of the risk involved.

Certain risks, however, cannot be calculated according to a law of averages. Nobody, for instance, can forecast with certainty how many cold drinks will be sold in Britain next summer. That will depend upon the weather. Similarly, it might be thought that a new 'mini' car would sell profitably. But again there is a chance that this will not be so. The risk of demand being different from that estimated cannot be reduced to a mathematical profitability. Such a risk, therefore, cannot be insured against; it must be accepted by those persons whose money is tied up in producing goods for an uncertain demand.

These uninsurable risks are inherent in a dynamic economy. Modern methods of production take time. When an entrepreneur engages factors of production, therefore, it is an act of faith – faith in the estimate of the demand for the product some time ahead. But demand can never be completely certain. People have freedom of choice, and their tastes may change. Many of the factors affecting demand fluctuate even over a relatively short period of time. It is similar on the supply side. Techniques do not stand still; new methods discovered by a rival may mean that, by the time a firm's product comes on the market, it is undersold by a cheaper or better substitute.

Thus there is always some degree of uncertainty, and this involves risk. It is a risk which must be shouldered by those who back with their money the decision as to what shall be produced. The true entrepreneurs, therefore, are those who accept the risks of uncertainty-bearing.

17.2 Profit

How Profit Differs in Nature from Other Rewards

The reward of uncertainty-bearing is 'profit'. But profit differs from the earnings of other factors of production. First, profit may be negative. Whereas wages, rent and interest are paid as part of a contract at the time of hiring, profit is received in the future, and then only if expected demand has materialised. Where the entrepreneur has been far too optimistic, a loss is made. Second, profit fluctuates more than other rewards. Thus its size is uncertain, for it feels the immediate impact of booms and slumps. In a boom profits rise faster than wages, while in a slump they fall more severely. Third, unlike wages, interest, and rent, which are contractual and certain payments, profit is simply a residue.

Differences in the Concept of the Term 'Profit'

We must be careful to distinguish four different concepts of 'profit':

1. Profit in its Everyday Meaning

To the accountant, profit means simply the difference between total receipts and total costs (see p. 128). But because the economist defines costs in terms of alternatives forgone, this idea of profit is amended by deducting, first, the return which would have been received on capital had it been used elsewhere, and second, the value of the entrepreneur's skill in the best alternative line of business (see also p. 129).

2. Normal Profit under Perfect Competition

Because uncertainty cannot be eliminated from a dynamic economy, there must be a return to induce people to bear uncertainty. This is true even in the long period. Thus there must be a rate of profit – the price which equates the demand for and supply of entrepreneurship. In the long period under perfect competition, any rent element from profit is eliminated. We then have 'normal profit' – the cost which has to be met if the supply of uncertainty-bearing is to be maintained.

Two modifications should be noted. First, industries differ as regards the uncertainty involved. Where fashions or techniques change frequently, for instance, uncertainty is greater. This would tend to reduce the supply of entrepreneurship in such industries at any given level of normal profit, and thus for them normal profit must be higher. Second, the elimination of the rent element in profit in the long period is only possible if one assumes that entrepreneurs of equal ability are available. In practice, this is not so. Thus there will always be some entrepreneurs earning a rent of ability (supernormal profit) even in the long period, simply because their forecasts and decisions are more accurate.

3. Supernormal Profit

Under perfect competition the entrepreneur is able to make supernormal profit for a period because new firms cannot enter the industry. Certain factors such as key workers and machines are for a time fixed in supply, and entrepreneurs already possessing them will make supernormal profit. In other words such profit is really the return to fixed factors in the short period; it is the 'quasi-rent' earned by such factors.

4. Monopoly Profit

With monopoly, competitors can be excluded. Certain factors, e.g. diamond-mines, know-how, patents and copyrights, are fixed to the monopolist. Even in the long period, competitors cannot engage such factors, and so supernormal profits persist. The profits of the monopolist are therefore closer to economic rent than to quasi-rent.

17.3   The Role of Profit in the Market Economy

'Profit' tends to be an emotive word, and firms which make large profits are often frowned upon. But usually there is little justification for this, since it is through profits – and losses – that the market economy works. We must emphasise, however, that we are discussing only profits under competitive conditions. But, given such conditions, profit fulfils the following functions:

1. Normal Profits Induce People to Accept the Risks of Uncertainty

Because uncertainty is implicit in a dynamic economy, a reward – normal profit – is essential for entrepreneurs to undertake production. Thus normal profit is a cost, as essential as the payment of wages. The level will vary with the industry; thus it will be higher for oil exploration than for selling petrol.

2. Supernormal Profit Indicates Which Industry Should Expand and Which Should Contract

When a firm produces a good which proves to be popular with consumers, it probably makes supernormal profit. This indicates that output should be expanded. On the other hand losses show that consumers do not want the good, and production should contract.

3. Supernormal Profit Encourages Firms to Increase Production

Profits not only indicate that consumers want more of a good: they are also the inducement to firms to produce those goods. As we saw in Chapter 9, supernormal profits act as the spur for existing firms to increase capacity and for other firms to enter the industry. On the other hand, when losses are being incurred, firms go out of production and the industry contracts. Thus losses are as important as profits in the operation of the market economy.

4. Supernormal Profit Provides the Resources for Expansion

An industry making supernormal profit can secure the factors necessary to expand. First, profits can be ploughed back, while shareholders will respond to requests for further capital, usually through rights issues. New firms can enter the industry, because investors will subscribe to a company intending to operate where the level of profits is relatively high. Second, profits allow expanding firms to offer higher rewards to attract factors. In this way resources are moved according to the wishes of consumers.

5. Supernormal Profit Encourages Research, Innovation and Exploration

Research, e.g. for new drugs, and exploration e.g. for oil, carry a high risk of failure and therefore of wasted capital expenditure. But the possibility of high returns if successful induces firms to engage in research, especially if new developments are protected for a period from competitors by patents.

6. Profits Ensure that Production is Carried on by the Most Efficient Firms

In a competitive industry the firm making the largest profit is the one whose costs are lowest. It will have an incentive to expand production and, if necessary, can afford to pay more for factors to do so. Less efficient firms must copy its methods to retain factors. In any case the increased output of the more efficient firm will eventually lower the price of the product. As a result inefficient firms make losses: profits have become negative.

To sum up, profits and losses are the means by which the process of natural selection occurs in the market economy. The drive is provided by profits – and the fear of losses. Whether the desire for personal gain is the best of motives may be open to doubt. But, human nature being what it is, it is still the most effective. Uncertainty exists in any dynamic economy, and so there is bound to be scope for profits whether production is organised by private enterprise or by the State. What we have to ask, therefore, is: 'When no personal gain or loss is involved, is there the same incentive to maximise profits or to avoid losses?'

It must be pointed out, too, that under perfect competition, profits are self-destructive. Thus where there is competition it is wrong to regard profits as being somehow immoral. The exception is monopoly profits, which are not eliminated even in the long period. Entry into the industry is not free; consequently profits are not competed away. It may be that such monopoly profits stimulate research and allow an industry to expand. But where scarcity has been deliberately brought about, they simply represent an economic rent earned at the expense of consumers by the monopolist owners. Moreover, an efficient allocation of resources according to the wishes of consumers does not take place.

18 Externalities

18.1 The Nature of Externalities

Definition

Resource allocation in the market economy is decided by the decisions of consumers (households) and producers (firms) who seek to maximise the difference between benefits and incurred costs. We refer to these as *private benefits* and *private costs*.

But one weakness of the market economy is that it may fail to take account of any additional benefits or costs which 'spill over' from the original decisions. A person who keeps honey-bees, for instance, confers a benefit on the local fruit-grower in pollinating the flowers, while at the same time the orchard owner provides the bees with nectar. If we add these spill-over benefits (and costs) to the private benefits (and costs) of a transaction we have the full *social benefits* (and costs) involved. It is usual to refer to these 'spill-overs' as 'externalities' – the costs or benefits additional to those which are the immediate concern of the parties to a transaction and which are not provided for directly in the market price.

Diagrammatic Representation

We can present the problem of allowing for externalities diagrammatically. Suppose, for instance, that a farmer applies nitrates to his field up to the point where the marginal revenue product (in terms of the value of the extra grass which will result) equals the marginal cost. Thus in Figure 18.1, given no government control over the use of nitrates, OC kilos per hectare will be applied.

However, some of the nitrate may not be taken up by the grass, but finds its way into the water supply. There is now an external cost to be taken into account which increases as the application of nitrate per hectare increases.

FIGURE 18.1
The External Cost of Nitrates Applied to Land

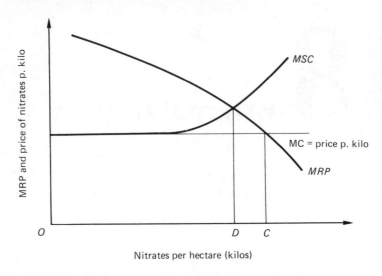

Nitrates per hectare (kilos)

This external cost has had to be added to the private cost (MC) to obtain the true marginal social cost, shown by the curve MSC, and the socially efficient application of nitrates is reduced to OD per hectare.

18.2   Methods of Dealing with Externalities

If there is to be an economically efficient allocation of resources, spill-over costs and benefits must be allowed for. Of course, certain external costs may be too trivial to consider, e.g. a slight increase in traffic noise as a town increases in size. But in practice it is often debateable where the line should be drawn, e.g. as regards traffic congestion.

Externalities and the Price System

To some extent externalities may be allowed for in the market price. For instance, shops where traffic congestion is a serious problem will, other things being equal, command lower rents than shops having nearby parking facilities.

However, leaving the price mechanism to deal with externalities is not usually a satisfactory solution. For one thing there may be heavy frictional costs before a new equilibrium pattern of shop rents is established. How much congestion has to be suffered in the meantime? For another, passively leaving the price system to deal with externalities may produce an inferior net social product (see below). Some positive means of dealing with externalities is therefore usually necessary.

Providing for Externalities by Private Negotiation

Private negotiation often deals with external costs. Thus within a local community rules may be drawn up governing car-parking, standards of house maintenance, children's play areas, etc. Alternatively, such matters may be covered more rigidly by covenants in the leases. Similarly, owners of the fishing rights on the Hampshire chalk-streams mutually agree to confine weed-cutting to two specified weeks during the fishing season.

Taking this a stage further, persons adversely affected by a building proposal can form a pressure group and subscribe on a voluntary basis towards the cost of opposing the scheme. Alternatively, where possible losers are few in number, they could join together to forestall building. Thus two or three house-owners on one side of a road who enjoy an exceptional view across farmland of a valley may prevent building by collectively buying land from the farmer.

Nevertheless, negotiation is usually an impracticable solution. Not only may the costs of negotiation be exorbitant relative to the benefits to be shared, but where 'free-riders' cannot be excluded, it may be impossible to organise sufficient collective bargaining strength to negotiate effectively. In any case, costs (or benefits) are often so far-ranging e.g. the detrimental effects of exhaust fumes, that not all the losers (or beneficiaries) can be identified. Finally, uncertainty and selfishness may prevent a satisfactory solution by private action. Usually, therefore, some form of government action is necessary.

Possible Government Action to Allow for Externalities

Because there are a variety of methods by which externalities can be allowed for the government can choose according to the particular case.

First, it may introduce a pricing system to bring externalities into the reckoning. For example, to deal with traffic congestion, parking-meters may be installed, with even local residents charged for reserved parking permits.

Second, taxation and subsidies may take the idea of 'charging' a stage further. Thus the rating of empty houses can be regarded as a tax imposed to offset the external costs resulting from homelessness and the overall shortage of accommodation. On the other hand, external benefits may be allowed for by subsidies, e.g. towards the costs of repairing ancient monuments and listed buildings where, because private costs of upkeep exceed private benefits, rapid deterioration and eventual demolition would otherwise result.

Third, externalities may be covered by physical controls. Most evident are the consents required under the Town and Country Planning Acts (see below).

Fourth, externalities may be internalised by widening the area of control. The National Trust, for instance, harmonises the interest, both of farmers and walkers in order to secure maximum benefits from its Lake District properties.

Fifth, the government may itself assume responsibility for providing certain goods and services. This is usual when externalities are: (a) so extensive that only government authority can adequately allow for them, e.g. providing a major airport; (b) cumulative, e.g. a slum area.

Conclusion

The concept of externalities is central to many of the problems confronting governments today. Indeed, externalities are not now confined to national boundaries, e.g. acid rain, nuclear fall-out from Chernobyl. By way of illustrating alternative policies, we consider three current problems; control over building, pollution and traffic congestion.

18.3 Building Controls

Where the total effect of the externality is important but spread so thinly that persons affected cannot be identified for purposes of coordinated action, state intervention is necessary. Those conditions apply in particular to land use. The type of building erected and the use to which it is put affect the welfare not only of neighbours but also of passers-by. Thus both the design of the building and its use are subject to public intervention through planning control.

Planning as applied to urban areas is broadly on two levels:

(1) The *overall structure plan* drawn up by the county council for the area. This envisages the broad lines of development by designating zones for different types of use.

(2) *Planning consents* for a specific development which the developer has to obtain from the local planning authority – the district council – before he can proceed. In contrast to structure plans and building regulations which represent control by general regulation, planning consents are made on a case-by-case basis, though decisions are normally required to conform to the overall structure plan.

By imposing conditions on proposed development they seek to minimise external costs arising, for example, from road congestion, fire hazards, pollution, noise, or a building out of harmony with its surroundings. But planning can secure benefits additional to those estimated by the private developer. For instance, in a comprehensive city centre redevelopment, it can arrange complementary uses, siting car-parks, bus termini and shops in strategic proximity to each other.

18.4 Pollution

Aspects of Pollution

Pollution is not a new phenomenon. In the sixteenth century, for instance, the shortage of wood led to coal, mainly from Newcastle, being used for fires in London. The resulting smoke that hung over the capital provoked such a public outcry that eventually the burning of 'sea coles' was prohibited by Act of Parliament. Nor is pollution confined to urban areas of advanced industrialised societies. For example, rural Indian villages have untreated sewage flowing into water-courses and garbage rotting in the streets.

What is new is the recognition of the *problem* of pollution. On the one hand, economic growth through rapid industrialisation has been accompanied by external costs – acid rain, river pollution, oil slicks, nuclear radiation and waste. On the other hand, people are now enjoying a standard of living where they can afford to question whether material growth is not being achieved at too high a cost to the environment. Parodoxically, while economic growth may cause pollution, growth may be an essential prerequisite of environmental improvement. Economic poverty often compels us to accept visual squalor, poor buildings and pollution. It is prosperity which enables us to buy a better environment. Thus the EC's excess production of foodstuffs has made it easier to switch attention to preserving the landscape.

Pollution occurs when man introduces waste matter into the environment directly or indirectly causing damage to persons other than himself. Such waste is created both in production (e.g. acid rain, smoke, gases, toxic chemicals, pesticide contaminants, liquid effluents, noise, oil spillages) and in consumption (e.g. litter, household refuse, scrapped consumer durables). It is harmful to agriculture, e.g. resulting in lower yields or poorer quality; to human health, e.g. through carbon monoxide fumes; to buildings, e.g. in corrosion of stonework; to amenity, e.g. causing damage to fish, fauna and flora; and to the life of the whole planet through the greenhouse effect produced by carbon dioxide discharged into the atmosphere.

Here we are not concerned with the technology of pollution control, e.g. the substitution of other goods, greater technical efficiency in production to reduce waste, on-site treatment or controlled disposal of waste. We simply show how economic analysis can contribute to a solution of the problem.

This means that the emphasis has to be on *marginal* decisions. While everybody likes clear air, pure water, a peaceful environment, clean pavements, roads free from congestion, etc., pollution abatement incurs costs. Thus the choice is not the simple one between clean air and polluted air, but between various levels of dirty air. In short, we have to apply the marginal principle and accept that level of pollution where the cost of further abatement exceeds the extra benefit which results.

Why Does the Market Economy Fail to Control Pollution?

In most cases pollution represents external costs. The right to peace and quiet, the right to enjoy a landscape unspoiled by electricity pylons, the right to swim from an oil-free beach are not private legal rights which can be easily enforced. Often, therefore, no *private* cost is incurred for infringing those rights. Thus in Figure 18.2 if there is no cost to a chemical manufacturer of discharging effluent into the river, he will produce chemicals up to the point *OC*. But when we take into account the poisoning of fish, the destruction of vegetation which provides a habitat for insects and birds and the overall loss of visual beauty for ramblers, such

---

FIGURE 18.2
Efficient Output with External Costs

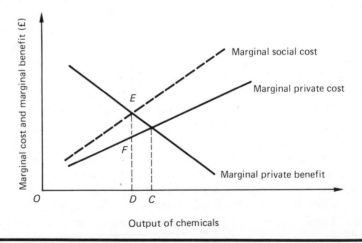

spill-over costs have to be added to private costs to obtain the aggregate social cost. This means that while *OC* is the efficient level of production from the point of view of the chemical manufacturer, the *socially* efficient level of production is *OD*, because here marginal private cost equals marginal social benefit (assuming marginal private benefit equals marginal social benefit).

Policy Difficulties

While this analysis of the nature of the problem is fairly straightforward, difficulties occur in devising and applying an appropriate policy.

First, although the costs of pollution control can be measured in money terms, the benefits are 'intangibles', having no price-tag since they are not traded in the market. Take as an example the chemical factory which discharges effluent into a river. While the value of the fishing rights lost can be measured by market information, the value of the loss suffered by bird-watchers and ramblers has no direct market price. This means that the techniques of shadow pricing, with all their weaknesses, have to be employed (see Chapter 10).

Second, most economic assessments of damage are made after the pollution has occurred. But adjustments in response to such pollution may already have been made. For example, the cabbage yield in a market garden may be 20 per cent below that which could have been expected in a clean-air environment. Yet this loss would understate the damage if, in an environment originally free from smoke, more profitable tomatoes would have been grown. In practice, it is extremely difficult to ascertain and measure this 'adjustment factor'.

Third, since pollution occurs in different forms, circumstances and scale, it is necessary to apply different policies to deal with the problem.

Policy Alternatives

1. Direct Regulation

Here the government decides what each polluter must do to reduce pollution, and enforces it under penalty of law, e.g. no discharge of oil waste by ships within so many miles of the coast. Such a policy, however, provides little incentive to install anti-pollution devices, involves constant inspection and tends to impose national (sometimes international) standards instead of allowing for different local circumstances. Nevertheless, rigid control is essential where: (a) pollution is a threat to existence, e.g. blue asbestos dust in workshops; and (b) pollution is cumulative and becomes dangerous at a certain level, e.g. cadmium absorption by the soil and smoke from straw-burning blowing across main roads.

2. Subsidising the Reduction of Pollution

Where it is impossible or too costly to identify the polluters (e.g. litter louts) the government itself takes responsibility for pollution control, the cost being covered from the proceeds of taxation. Alternatively, the government may decide that specific compensation is adequate to deal with the particular pollution, especially where this is localised. Thus in clean-air zones, people are given subsidies to install smokeless fuel appliances. On the other hand, losers may be compensated, e.g. grants to provide double-glazing to reduce noise from aircraft. The difficulty is that such public schemes for pollution control simply mean that polluters are passing on the cost to the taxpayer. Often, therefore, where polluters can be identified, control has to be enforced through individual penalties imposed by the courts, e.g. for dropping litter.

Alternatively, the government could seek to reduce pollution by subsidising: (a) the development of new techniques to reduce pollution; (b) the production of cleaner substitutes; or (c) the recycling of waste, e.g. bottles.

3. Taxing Pollution

A charge or tax can be imposed on polluters according to the level of pollution. In terms of Figure 18.2 a tax of *EF* would induce the factory-owner to limit his production to *OD*. Such a policy has the merit of flexibility, and is thus particularly desirable where the benefits of pollution abatement can only be ascertained by trial and error or where the aim is to achieve a progressive reduction over time since it allows charges to be adjusted accordingly. Moreover, charges have the effect of 'internalising externalities', and so a profit-maximising polluter would install his own pollution control to the point where the marginal cost of doing so was less than the tax saved. Furthermore, the proceeds of a tax can be used to compensate those losing by the residual pollution. Finally, in as much as the charge raises the price of the product, the actual consumer now pays the full opportunity cost of production – a fairer solution than passing on the external costs to society at large.

Even so, a charges policy has its limitations. First, there are distributional implications if the product whose price rises is one which is bought mainly by poor persons. Second, a tax can only be imposed if the individual polluter can be identified and his degree of pollution measured, e.g. the quantity of toxic waste being pumped into a river by a factory, the amount of sulphuric and nitric acids being discharged into the atmosphere by a power station, the number of hectares of straw being burned by a farmer, the number of litres of leaded petrol used.

4. *Impose an Acceptable Minimum Standard of Pollution*

Where a pricing policy to control pollution cannot be effectively pursued the laying-down of minimum standards – e.g. the level of exhaust smoke emitted by lorries – is necessary. The difficulty is that the specified standard becomes the target since there is no incentive to reduce pollution still further. But the policy could allow the polluter to find the cheapest means of achieving the specified minimum.

18.5 Urban Traffic

The Benefits and Costs of Motor Transport

In the twentieth century motor transport has increased accessibility for both resources and people through the mobility, flexibility and convenience it affords. It has thus contributed to the improvement of living standards.

Unfortunately as the use of road vehicles has increased, the benefits they afford have been progressively diminished by external costs. The greater mobility afforded by the car has enabled workers to live some distance from their place of employment and has thus been a major cause of urban sprawl. Moreover, people still have to travel from the suburbs to the city centre for work, shopping and leisure activities. Whereas traffic increases as we approach the centre, road capacity decreases. The resulting concentration of traffic imposes external costs on non-car users by exhaust-fume pollution, noise, the danger of accident, visual blight, inconvenience to pedestrians and loss of time to bus travellers. More than that, the expansion of motor transport has led to the demand for road space exceeding supply so that one road-user imposes on other road-users the extra costs of congestion – higher petrol consumption, reduced speed and time spent in traffic jams – now estimated to cost £15 bn per annum. Indeed, the problem is likely to become more acute as income and population increase and the use of cars and commercial vehicles expands.

The Urban Traffic Problem

The major external cost is congestion for this undermines the chief advantage – accessibility – which motor transport affords. It is necessary, therefore, to analyse the problem and to consider possible ways of dealing with it.

Two salient points should be noted. First, it is basically a peak-hour problem, confined to approximately five hours a day on fewer than 250 working days of the year. Second, it is largely the result of the increased use of the private car for journeys to work. The former tends to restrict the amount of investment which can be profitably undertaken in the transport system. The latter indicates that some effort should be directed towards making the road-user pay the full costs (including external costs) of taking his vehicle on the road.

Bearing these principles in mind, actual policy can follow six main lines:

(1) do nothing;
(2) increase investment to cope with motor traffic;
(3) impose physical controls to improve traffic flows;
(4) restrict parking;
(5) use the price system to allocate existing road space;
(6) adopt pricing policies to achieve a better distribution of the means of travel as between the car and public transport.

1. Do Nothing

Some people argue that trying to improve movement on the roads is self-defeating: the easier it is to travel, the more people use their cars. As congestion increases, there comes a point where the cost in terms of wasted time and frustration is such that motorists switch to public transport.

But such a policy has snags. First, it provides no *incentive* for motorists to switch to public transport. There should be such an incentive since those who do switch make travelling easier for those who do not. Second, the high level of congestion envisaged would become a permanent feature, penalising equally the essential car-users and the optional users, those for whom using public transport would impose no severe hardship. Third, the congestion would affect non-road users, e.g. pedestrians.

2. Invest in More Roads

The long-term solution is increased investment to improve the urban environment and the circulation of traffic. This could take the form of comprehensive redevelopment of existing city centres and improved town planning, e.g. siting industry away from city centres.

The main thrust, however, would be to build more roads linking the suburbs and city centre. But by-passes also play a part in that through traffic is siphoned off.

It is doubtful, however, whether this would be a complete solution.

(*a*) As it is difficult to impose tolls on short-run roads, they have to be financed from taxation and made freely available to all wishing to use them. But as the amount which can be devoted to public investment in general is limited, roads have to compete with defence, health care, social welfare, the modernisation of public transport, etc. Yet, without direct pricing of road use, there is no precise indication of what people are prepared to pay for more roads and therefore no firm basis for comparing the rate of return with that of alternative capital projects (though cost–benefit analysis may help). Thus there is no answer to the basic questions of whether vast investment in new urban road systems is economically viable bearing in mind that it is largely to provide only for peak-hour travel between the suburbs and the city centre.

(*b*) Investment in roads, as opposed to extending public transport, involves an income redistribution since public transport is used mainly by poorer persons. The result is that the decision on whether to invest in more roads is eventually a political one and pressure groups in favour may be successful in spite of the very high cost of urban road construction.

(*c*) It would take many years for a complete road network to be built. In the meantime, movements in industry and population and transport developments could change needs considerably.

(*d*) The demand for road space seems to respond to supply, with better roads generating more motor transport. Demand and supply, therefore, are never in equilibrium. This means that we are always faced with a short-term situation of making the best possible use of existing road-space, as follows.

3. Manage Traffic Flows

Some immediate improvement in traffic flows can be achieved by clearways, reversible lanes, linked traffic signals, bus lanes, mini-roundabouts, etc. Such adaptation can often be combined with schemes which improve the environment e.g. designating pedestrian-only areas, constructing culs-de-sac in residential districts or simply restricting the movement of heavy vehicles in residential zones.

In the longer term attempts can be made to spread the flow of rush-hour traffic over a longer period (e.g. by staggering working hours) or to reverse the flow (e.g. by encouraging offices to locate in the suburbs and the building of out-of-town shopping centres). Nevertheless care must be taken to ensure that the commercial heart of the city is not destroyed.

It must be noted, however, that traffic management can only increase the capacity of the road network when the initial *pattern* of movement is suboptimal. Even then it only provides a short-term relief from congestion since, unless entry is restrained, improving the traffic flow eventually generates additional traffic.

4. Restrict Parking

Perhaps the greatest advantage of the motor vehicle is the convenience of door-to-door travel. This needs parking facilities. Yet, paradoxically, too many facilities lead to congestion, and so an appropriate balance between parking and movement has to be sought. Indeed the old Greater London Council proposed taxing each private office parking space provided to divert commuters to public transport.

Parkers are of two sorts: the 'long-term' parker (the commuter) and the 'short-term' parker (the shopper and the business visitor). The problem is largely one of removing the 'long-term' parker from the streets, so that there will be sufficient accommodation for 'short-term' parkers to pursue their shopping or business activities. Two approaches are possible: physical control and road pricing. Both involve costs of adequate administration.

Physical controls take various forms, from the restriction of parking to certain days, time, side of street or type of vehicle (e.g. taxis only) to the complete prohibition of all kinds of waiting, including the loading and unloading of commercial vehicles. Permits may also be issued to give priority to essential users and residents. Furthermore, planning consents for new buildings usually stipulate the minimum number of parking spaces to be provided.

While physical controls are unrelated to ability to pay, they lack the subtlety of the price mechanism's rationing function. Where parking is possible, charges can be imposed to bring demand into line with the limited number of spaces available. In order that street parking shall be confined to short-term parkers it is usually linked with the physical control of limiting the time which can be spent at any one bay.

Kerbside parking has to be supplemented by off-street parking, especially for the long-term commuter. Since the cost of this is high, it is more likely to be provided where meter charges are also high. Local authority car parks are mostly hardstands and tend to be for short-term parkers only. Multistorey and underground garages are expensive to build. Since demand drops off at night, they are largely dependent financially on there being sufficient day-time parkers to pay the relatively high economic cost. On the other hand, if high charges induce commuters to travel by public transport, there is a net benefit to the community through reduced congestion and less cost of road construction, and so any shortfall in projected revenue could be underwritten by the local authority.

5. Use the Price System to Allocate Scarce Road Space

The principle of allocating limited parking space by charges can also be applied to moving vehicles by imposing a tax to reduce the use of vehicles and so relieve congestion.

In addition to his running costs, the private motorist allows for the time his journey will take. The greater the traffic flow, the longer this time. There is thus a rising cost curve, MPC (Figure 18.3). The demand curve, *D*, also takes account of this time factor: the greater the congestion, the longer the time journey, so that demand falls as the intensity of traffic-flow increases. Thus, left to the private motorists' decisions, the flow of traffic will be *OP*, where private marginal cost equals marginal benefit (price).

But while the private motorist allows for the time-cost of a heavy traffic-flow, the very fact of his taking his car on the road will add to the time–cost of others. Congestion can be defined as occurring when the private use of his car by a motorist 'impedes' the movement of other road-users, that is, at *OC* (Figure 18.3). There is a marginal external cost which, if added to the marginal private cost, gives the marginal social cost curve, MSC. Applying the principle that output should take place where MSB = MSC the economically efficient flow of traffic would be *OS*.

This could be achieved by imposing a charge equal to *LM*. Ideally, such a charge should reflect the time, miles covered on the road, the size of car and the location and direction of the journey in relation to the city centre. The difficulty lies in devising a single tax which covers all these requirements and is practical. A petrol tax reflects only mileage and size of car, and is thus unfair to the country-dweller. Requiring the motorist to buy a permit to enter a congested area does not take account of the degree of

---

FIGURE 18.3
Allowing for the External Cost of Traffic Congestion

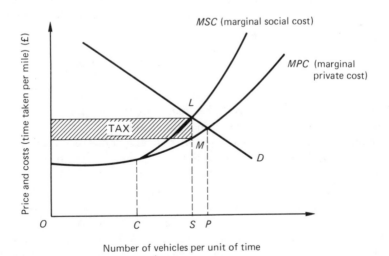

congestion or the extent of use within the congested area. The most appropriate method of charging is to fit each car with a meter which would electronically register 'units' as certain control points were passed. These control points could be located more closely to each other as the city centre was approached, and the number of units could be varied according to the time of day.

Some economists consider that an additional advantage of such road-pricing is that it would establish 'road values' and thus rates of return to guide future road investment. But metering faces difficulties:

(a) While it is economically valid and technically possible, it is only practical if the cost of installation, the periodic reading of the meter and the payment of charges are accepted by the motorist. The costs of administration and enforcement could be high.

(b) Since this meter does not catch the parker, there would have to be additional parking charges.

(c) It raises a distributional problem in that the wealthier motorist would be able to travel on the now uncongested roads, while the poorer *non*-motorist would enjoy better public transport. The relatively-low income motorist, who now has to resort to public transport, would lose most. But why should the price mechanism be unacceptable on account of income differences in the road price market and not elsewhere in the economy?

(d) Unless MC pricing is imposed in all sectors of the economy and, in particular, on all modes of transport, an optimal allocation of road use will not be achieved (see p. 179).

(e) It has to be decided how the tax yield should be disposed of. Returning it to motorists would simply increase their income so that they could reclaim the road-use given up.

6. Pricing Policies to Improve the Split Between the Private Car and Public Transport

We have to consider the respective merits of the private car and public transport from both the demand and supply sides.

On the demand side, the car affords a convenient door-to-door means of transport and, in comparison with public transport, is comfortable. Even traffic jams can be made tolerable by listening to the radio or cassette player. In contrast, public transport may be irregular and incur the discomfort of standing. Its great merit is speed, especially with rail travel for the long-distance commuter. Moreover, the method of charging for car travel as opposed to public transport favours the former. Much of the car's costs are fixed costs – the initial purchase price, the motor vehicle tax, insurance etc. The cost of actually using the car – the variable cost – is the cost of petrol and wear and tear (though motorists are inclined to ignore the latter). Thus the private motorist adopts a marginal-cost basis of pricing when deciding to use his car.

In contrast, apart from any subsidies given, fares on public transport tend to cover both fixed and variable costs: that is, the fare per mile tends to equal *average* total cost. The price system cannot yield an efficient allocation of resources between private and public transport when different principles are adopted as the basis of pricing.

Moreover, since fixed costs, particularly for the railways, are high, public transport tends to operate under conditions of decreasing cost. This means that the principle of marginal-cost pricing cannot be used if total costs are to be covered (Figure 18.4). Instead public transport seeks to cover total costs by price discrimination, charging higher fares to passengers whose demand is least elastic. Such passengers tend to be commuters and businessmen – and higher fares simply induce them to switch to travelling by car. The alternative is to make good the shortfall by government subsidy.

On the supply side, consideration has to be given to the respective cost patterns of the car and public transport. Figure 18.5 shows that when a relatively small number of passengers have to be coped with, the car has a cost advantage. Since the initial fixed costs to put a car on the road are so small compared with the bus and train, for exposition purposes average cost per passenger can be regarded as constant.

However, as the number of passengers increases, the higher fixed costs of the bus are spread more thinly, so that eventually at *OB* average cost per

FIGURE 18.4
The Effect of High Fixed Costs on Public Transport

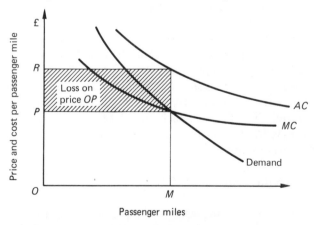

FIGURE 18.5
The Differences in Average Costs per Passenger Mile of a Car, Bus and Rail Transport

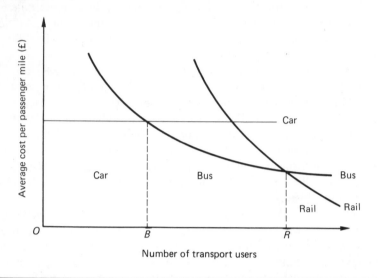

passenger mile falls below that of the car. Rail transport has to incur even higher fixed costs in maintaining tracks, stations, expensive rolling stock, etc., and so costs per passenger mile are only below those of the bus at a high level of passenger use, *OR*. In addition, house density should be high so that the number travelling from a single station is large. Hence urban rail travel is limited to very large cities.

One further point should be noted: the bus is more flexible in use than the train both in routing and in dealing with small variations in the number of passengers. In its turn, the car is more flexible than the bus, especially for cross-commuting to employment in suburban offices, etc.

It must again be emphasised that while the bus and train have a *cost* advantage over the car in dealing with passenger-users above *OB* and *OR* respectively, relative prices for each mode of travel will also depend upon demand. It may be that people's preference for car travel is so high that this mode prevails even at a high transport-user level.

A Policy for Traffic Congestion

The foregoing analysis suggests that on cost considerations rush-hour travel is most economically provided by public transport since this follows the predominantly radial flow to the centre and causes less congestion per passenger carried than the private car.

The logical first step, therefore, would be to tax the private car-user as described earlier. This tax, supplemented by funds from general taxation, could be used to subsidise public transport. The subsidy would:

(a) enable public transport to cover its fixed costs:
(b) recognise the 'fall-back' or 'option' benefit which everybody enjoys simply from there being available public transport facilities;
(c) allow for the external benefits conferred by not increasing road congestion and other environmental costs, and
(d) redistribute income in favour of the poorer sections of the community who are most dependent on public transport.

In addition, price discrimination must be applied to the fare structure to allow for differences in the time and direction of travel so that passengers travelling in the direction of the traffic flow during the rush hours pay more.

But there are difficulties. First, the policy is dependent upon the extent to which travellers would respond to the change in relative prices and switch to public transport. People seem wedded to their car, and public transport is regarded as an inferior good. In other words, there is a low price-elasticity of demand for the private car and a high income-elasticity of demand. Indeed, it can be argued that the decline in the use of public transport is a result more of inconvenience and discomfort (e.g. draughty bus-stops and overcrowding) than of cost. If this is so, in fairly affluent societies, more convenient and better transport even at *higher* prices would attract more customers than cheaper transport of the traditional type.

Second, the equity of public transport subsidies have to be considered. A subsidy financed by general taxation is unfair to the person who does not use public transport.

Conclusions

There are many approaches to the traffic problem and considerable controversy as to the most appropriate 'mix' of policies. A system which relies on any *one* mode of transport, or on one single approach, is unlikely to be satisfactory. There is a need for facilities which permit all types of transport; walking, cycling (through the provision of cycle tracks or lanes), car, minibus, bus and rail transport.

The cost of providing new roads to cater for the increasing number of private motorists may be such that some form of congestion tax may have to be imposed. But eventually an integrated city system could be introduced, with some flexibility to allow for individual preferences. The car would be used to get people from places where demand was insufficient to justify the fixed costs of providing public transport. Such people would be taken to collecting points from which they could transfer to public transport, as with 'park and ride' and 'kiss and ride' (where the wife returns home with the car) commuters. In the absence of adjustments through the price system, methods of diverting travellers to public transport will have to be effected by physical controls, such as banning cars and goods vehicles from certain areas, extending parking restrictions and creating bus lanes. In the long term, large cities may find that the solution to their traffic problems lies in building new underground railways.

Finally, the traffic problem cannot be solved in isolation from the location of urban activities. In the long run, one of the most effective ways of dealing with it may be to reduce the need for travel by so organising cities that work-places and residences are nearer each other.

19 Cost–Benefit Analysis (CBA)

19.1 Purpose of CBA

The Allocation of Resources in the Public Sector

In the market economy, resources are allocated through the interaction of demand and supply in the market. Prices are the signals which coordinate the wishes of consumers with the cost of supplying goods.

But market signals may be either non-existent or defective especially where the government is responsible for providing goods and services, such as roads, bridges, airports, parks, amenity land, education, health services, new urban areas and housing.

Without firm market signals, decisions on the desirability of a project may rest mainly on subjective political considerations. For instance, in order to obtain a 'social mix', council housing may be provided in an expensive residential area where land costs are high.

Allocating resources largely by means of the ballot-box, however, has serious defects in dealing with public investment. First, the one-man, one-vote principle does not weight votes according to the intensity of welfare gained or lost. Thus, the simple majority decision might allow two voters marginally in favour of a scheme to outvote one who strongly opposes it in spite of the fact that the sum of their benefits is less than the costs inflicted on the single opponent. Second, political decisions are essentially subjective. Economic efficiency in resource allocation requires that objective criteria should be used as far as possible. Third, the extension of government involvement in the economy has increased the burden and complexity of public-sector decisions. Many would argue that decentralisation of decision-making is desirable.

Functions of CBA

CBA is a technique which seeks to bring greater objectivity into decision-making. It does this by identifying all the relevant benefits and costs of a particular scheme and quantifying them in money terms so that each can be aggregated and then compared. While it can be applied in the private sector, its main use is connected with the public provision of goods and services.

First, price signals are inadequate to guide investment decisions. For one thing, goods may be provided free (e.g. hospital care, education, street lighting). For another, market prices merely indicate value in exchange – by ignoring consumer surplus, they do not measure the full benefit, that is value in use', which the consumer enjoys. This is particularly important when comparing the benefits and costs of large public sector projects (see below).

Second, with these projects, externalities are important because of the magnitude of the schemes. For instance, the usual cost–revenue criterion may be inappropriate when there are unemployed resources for then the real cost of government spending to employ them may be zero.

Third, because of its undying nature, the State has to allow for the welfare of unborn generations.

Welfare and Pareto Optimality

Our early statement of the Pareto criterion (p. 171) indicated that a reshuffling of resources will result in a *definite* welfare improvement where at least one person is made better off without anyone being made worse off. From a welfare aspect, this statement is perfectly safe.

For practical purposes, however, it is too restrictive. Securing benefits for some persons almost invariably incurs costs to others. We can allow for this by saying that a *potential* Pareto improvement exists when those who gain from a change can fully compensate those who lose. The improvement is only 'potential' because welfare may be affected by the inherent income redistribution underlying the change when compensation is not actually paid (see p. 285).

But the justification of this extension is that it allows us to set off costs and benefits. Naturally, the actual policy decision will have to take into account the possible redistributive effects.

19.2 The CBA approach

Quantifying in Money Terms

Since welfare is subjective to the individual, it cannot be measured cardinally in order to aggregate the welfare of individuals. The nearest we can come to surmounting this difficulty is to say that benefits are commensurate with willingness to pay (WTP) in terms of money. This can be justified as follows.

A consumer maximises benefits from his expenditure when:

$$\frac{MU_A}{MU_B} = \frac{P_A}{P_B}$$

If, for instance, the marginal utility (MU) of the last unit of A is five times that of the last unit of B, he will buy an extra unit of A provided that the price of A is less than five times the price of B. Thus benefits derived are indicated by WTP, i.e. the sum of money which a person will pay for a good or service rather than go without it. The area under a market demand curve measures the aggregate of individuals' WTPs.

Benefits as measured by WTP are shown in Figure 19.1. DD_1 is the demand curve. Assume that average costs are constant: the supply curve PS is thus perfectly elastic. The price will then be OP, and people will buy OM. Benefits derived equal $DOMR$, but total expenditure will be $POMR$, giving consumers' surplus of DPR. Consumer surplus should therefore be included with benefits, especially with large indivisible projects. However, because of the difficulties involved in obtaining a complete demand curve, it is usual to value the benefits simply in terms of total expenditure, thus ignoring any consumer surplus.

Benefits have to be compared with the costs of obtaining them – that is, the cost of the factors which have to be diverted from the best alternative

---

FIGURE 19.1
Measuring 'Willingness to Pay' (WTP)

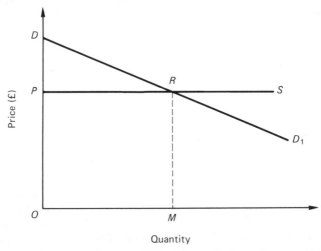

project (*POMR* in Figure 19.1). In practice, costs also are measured in terms of quantity times price.

A Simple Public Investment Problem

Assume that a large area of sandy beach can be reached only by a narrow lane branching off the main road some five miles away. As a result, visitors, even though they are mostly local, find it necessary to travel to the beach by car. No parking is permitted on the approach lane, but the local farmer has converted a field adjacent to the beach into a car park.

A parking fee is charged which the farmer feels maximises his profits. The car parking fee is £1, at which 10 000 cars park annually, leaving considerable spare capacity. The only cost, which is incurred irrespective of the number of cars parking, is £2 000 for two attendants employed for four summer months to collect parking fees and clean the toilets. The farmer is currently asking £80 000 for the car park.

Because the lane to the car park is so narrow, all waiting is prohibited by double yellow lines each side. The council has to employ two wardens, costing £5 000 a year, to ensure that the no waiting restriction is observed. Even so, frequent hold-ups mean that the return journey averages thirty-two minutes.

The council estimates that if it took over the car park and made parking free, the cars using the park would increase by 10 000 a year. The increased visitors would require extra toilets costing £20 000, but these could be supervised and cleaned by the existing two men since they would not be needed to collect parking fees. The extra traffic would also necessitate widening the approach lane at a cost of £170 000. After the road improvements the return journey to the beach would only take twenty minutes. It is estimated that the twelve minutes saved is worth 20p per car journey. Moreover, the two traffic wardens would no longer be necessary.

The scheme has a further advantage for the council: enlarging the town's recreation park some eight miles distant at a cost of £50 000 need no longer be proceeded with since people are likely to prefer the beach once car parking is free. Finally, it is assumed that there is full employment and no inflation.

The CBA Approach

In all cost–benefit analysis it is necessary to:

(1) *List all relevant items.* These will include spill-over effects of the proposal, e.g. the cost of extra toilets and road-widening, the saving on the extension to the town's recreation park. Care must be taken to avoid double-counting; thus the farmer could not include the loss of his

land and the loss of parking fees, because the former is simply the capitalised value of the latter.

(2) *Value expected benefits and costs*, deciding whether any allowance is to be made for the more distant future.

(3) *Discount the future flow of benefits and costs* in order to obtain their capitalised present value. This involves choosing an appropriate rate of discount (see pp. 294–7).

(4) *Appraise the project* by setting off aggregate benefits against aggregate costs. This can be done either by showing which different parties gain or lose (the 'Pareto balance sheet') or by a direct comparison of additional benefits and additional costs.

The Pareto Balance Sheet

The parties to this public investment in a car park are the farmer, the existing parkers, the additional parkers and the taxpayer. What are their respective gains and losses?

The *farmer* receives £80 000, but loses a net income of £8 000 a year.

Existing parkers save £10 000 a year on fees, and twelve minutes on the return journey valued at £2 000 a year.

New parkers have so far provided no firm indication of the value of car parking benefits to them. It is therefore necessary to estimate their WTP. Let us assume that the demand curve is linear. Since the farmer is a monopolist, Figure 19.2 depicts the situation. We know that all his costs are fixed costs: thus $MC = 0$ up to the full capacity of the car park, and therefore the MC curve is coincident with the quantity axis up to this point. The monopolist farmer would thus maximise profits from car parkers by changing 100p (OF) where $MR = MC$. At this price there are 10 000 parkers.

Since at M, $MR = 0$, at A elasticity of demand $= 1$. Therefore $DA = AD$, and $OM = MD_1$. Thus with free parking total demand would be 20 000 and their WTP would be measured by the area AMD_1, equal to £5 000 a year. If we assume that this represents their demand when the journey takes thirty-two minutes, the saving in time through the road improvements provides these additional 10 000 car parkers with an extra benefit of £2 000 a year.

Taxpayers have to bear the costs of the investment: £170 000 for widening the road and £20 000 for the additional toilets. But there are gains: £50 000 is saved through not having to enlarge the town's recreation park, and the two traffic wardens at £5 000 a year will no longer be required; since full employment has been assumed, they can find jobs elsewhere.

Annual future revenues and costs have to be expressed in terms of their current capital value. To simplify, let us assume that they are valued at a

FIGURE 19.2
Demand for Car Parking

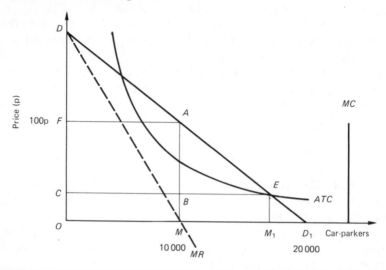

Table 19.1
A Pareto Balance Sheet

	Gains (£)		Costs (£)
Farmer		Profit lost	80 000
Sale proceeds	80 000		
Existing parkers			
Fees saved	100 000		
Time saved	20 000		
New parkers			
Parking benefits	50 000		
Time saved	20 000		
Taxpayers		Land	80 000
Saving on town park			
extension	50 000	Toilets	20 000
Traffic wardens	50 000	Road widening	170 000
Total benefits	370 000	Total costs	350 000

ten times purchase basis. We therefore have the Pareto balance sheet shown in Table 19.1

Since those who gain can compensate those who lose and still show a net increase in benefits of £20 000, the local authority should undertake the project. Two points should be noted, however. First, the viability of the scheme arises only because spill-over benefits, chiefly the saving on enlarging the town's recreation park, have been included. Second, there are distributional effects (see p. 285).

Additional Benefits and Costs Approach

In practice, CBA usually concentrates on net *additional* benefits and costs without identifying their incidence (Table 19.2). The net increase in benefits is still, of course, £20 000.

Table 19.2
CBA Net Additional Benefits and Costs

	Benefits (£)		Costs (£)
Existing parkers	100 000	Road-widening	170 000
New parkers	50 000	Land	80 000
Costs saved:		Toilets	20 000
Parkers' time	40 000		
Traffic wardens	50 000		
Town's recreation park	50 000		
Total	290 000	Total	270 000

Further Problems

A CBA itself involves costs of calculation and therefore should not be undertaken if such costs are likely to be greater than the possible net benefits.

But even if CBA shows a favourable balance, the project may run up against obstacles. Thus the council's car park scheme above could only go ahead if funds were available. In practice, there may be *budget constraints*. Public-sector borrowing may be limited, or financing the scheme through taxation may be difficult. Where there is a budget constraint, projects have to be ranked and available funds apportioned between them so as to secure the maximum net benefit possible.

Some projects may be subject to *legal constraints*, involving, for example, easements, covenants or even the responsibilities of public bodies as laid down by statutes, e.g. for common land. A costly and time-consuming private bill procedure may be necessary in order to proceed with the scheme.

More important, the project may encounter *administrative or political difficulties*. Where more than one local authority or public body is involved they may be motivated by different interests or·political views. Thus the National Trust would probably oppose an electricity scheme which took pylons over land for which it was responsible.

Finally, the project may be opposed on *distributional* grounds.

Difficulties with a CBA

Our simple example of the car park obscures conceptual and practical difficulties which are inherent in any CBA. These include:

(a) allowing for the distributional effects of a project;
(b) adjusting market prices to allow for indirect taxes, price controls, and so on;
(c) estimating the 'willingness to pay' for intangibles which are not priced in the market;
(d) incorporating intangibles;
(e) choosing the appropriate discount rate; and
(f) providing for risk and uncertainty in estimates of future benefits and costs.

We now examine these in more detail.

19.3   The Problem of Distributional Effects

It would be rare for a public project to qualify on the strict Pareto principle of some gainers but no losers. We can adapt the car park scheme above as an example. Suppose the farmer knows the demand curve, DD_1 (see Figure 19.2). His costs as stated are all fixed, with the average total cost curve a rectangular hyperbola (ATC) and the marginal costs nil up to the point of capacity (MC). Profits are maximised at a parking charge of OF (100p) with the number of cars restricted to OM (10 000), where $MC = MR$. Now assume the council faces the same demand curve and the same cost conditions. It could purchase the site from the farmer and extend car parking to OM_1, charging price OC where revenue just covers the same total costs. This produces a net benefit increase given by the triangle *ABE*. Moreover, since the farmer has been fully compensated in money, no problem of income redistribution arises.

However, in our original example, car parkers, although willing to pay, were given the benefit free, the cost being borne by taxpayers. The former gain; the latter lose. There is thus some redistribution of income.

The difficulty is that the gainers may be rich people having, as is generally assumed, a lower marginal utility of income than poor people: on the other hand, the losers may be poor people with a high marginal utility of income. In the car park project, for example, the gainers were car owners who had sufficient leisure time to take a trip to the beach, whereas the losers, the taxpayers, may include many old people who could ill-afford an increase in local taxation.

While we cannot completely overcome this difficulty of income redistribution, it is possible to deal with it up to a point. If the change in income redistribution is small relative to the net benefit gain, it can be ignored. Alternatively, a weighting system, which will necessarily have an element of subjectivity, can be used. Thus, to assess the welfare of the car park scheme, we should apply a low weight to the richer car parkers' benefit and a higher weight to the poorer taxpayers' losses in order to reflect their relative differences in marginal utility of income.

This problem of distributional effects crops up in various forms. Country lovers may lose pleasure through electricity pylons intruding on the landscape. If they were fully compensated, there is no loss of income so the problem of measuring their marginal utility of income does not arise. The difficulty (a frequent one) of identifying such losers means that compensation is not actually paid, and there are thus distributional effects. Similarly, when comparing the benefits of a project to future generations with its costs to the present population, some allowance should be made for the fact that future generations are likely to have a higher income.

19.4 Adjusting Market Prices

Possible Deficiencies in Market Prices as Reflecting Opportunity Costs

CBA expresses benefits and costs in money terms. To do this it has to give a price to identifiable units. But do observed market prices reflect the true opportunity cost to society of employing resources in a particular way (even assuming no externalities)?

In the real world it has to be recognised that this may not be so. This may be the result of imperfect competition, indirect taxes and subsidies, or controls which interfere with the free operation of the market mechanism.

Imperfect Competition

Under perfect competition, price = marginal revenue = marginal cost = the cost of an additional unit of the good to society. Where there is imperfect competition, however, price is higher than marginal revenue, though the latter is still equated with marginal cost. Thus, price exceeds marginal cost – the measure of opportunity cost to society. Similarly, in factor markets the value of the marginal product at the quantity employed is higher than the factor reward when the firm is a monopsonistic buyer of factors.

Suppose in our example of the car park that the tarmac for the road was supplied by a monopolist. In order to maximise his profits, he would charge price *OP* per ton – the benefit to society (Figure 19.3). On the other hand, marginal cost – the opportunity cost to society – would be only *OC*, and this is the price at which we should value the tarmac.

But even marginal cost is not acceptable when, in a situation of decreasing costs, total costs are not covered. It has been suggested for such a case, therefore, that the principle of a two-part tariff pricing system should be followed, a sum being added to marginal cost by way of a fixed standing charge (see p. 329).

FIGURE 19.3
A Monopolist's Price and Marginal Costs for a Given Output

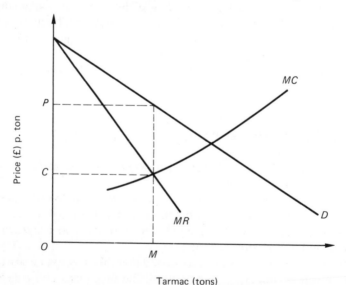

Indirect Taxes, Subsidies and Market Controls

Opportunity cost is represented by factor cost. It is argued that market prices should be adjusted by subtracting indirect taxes, e.g. for petrol saved by the construction of a motorway, and adding subsidies, e.g. for the value of agricultural produce lost. The snag with this procedure, however, is that taxes 'deducted' in this way should really be 'recouped' on other goods, thereby distorting *their* prices. There is thus a case for calculating benefits and costs at current market prices.

Similarly, physical controls may keep prices below market price, e.g. rent control. Such controlled prices cannot therefore be used for CBA purposes.

Moreover, prices may be distorted by controls elsewhere, e.g. through quotas. Suppose, for instance, that a land-reclamation project allowed a crop of potatoes to be grown. In valuing this crop it should be remembered that the price of potatoes is to some extent the result of the Potato Marketing Board's policy of restricting the potato acreage. Similarly, prices of imports may be artificially lowered by a protection policy aimed at maintaining a higher exchange rate than that which would prevail in a free market.

Should Adjustments be Made to Market Prices?

While market prices may not reflect true opportunity costs, the obstacles to making adjustments are formidable. The cost of obtaining the information necessary to estimate marginal cost may be too high to be worth while, and consistency in the adjustment made would be difficult to attain throughout the public sector. We are thus back to the problem of the 'second best' (see p. 179).

Because of such problems, some economists have rejected correcting market prices. Others, however, consider that adopting a straight marginal-cost pricing rule gives consistency to accounting procedures and corresponds more closely to the costs which CBA is seeking to measure.

19.5 Pricing Non-market Goods

Market prices may not be available. This occurs with:

(1) *Community and public goods*, where 'free riders' cannot be excluded (e.g. street-lighting, land, radio programmes) or where it is decided to make no charge (e.g. public parks, bridges). Here the cost is covered by taxation which is unlikely to reflect true 'willingness to pay'.

(2) *Intangible externalities*, e.g. noise and congestion cost, human lives saved, the pleasure derived from a walk in a park.

Since both enter into CBA calculations, it is necessary to ascribe 'shadow' prices to them so that benefits and costs can be quantified in money terms. Such an exercise, however faces formidable difficulties as the following specific examples reveal.

Recreation

In our example of the car park we were able to estimate the benefits (WTP) of a trip to the beach from an existing market. However, for many recreational facilities, e.g. the Lake District, Hadrian's Wall, the National Gallery, there has been no previous market. How, then, do we derive a demand curve?

One method would be to devise a questionnaire in which people state how much they would be willing to pay for the facility. Nevertheless, difficulties may arise in obtaining a representative sample, while replies may lack accuracy because of respondents' subjectivity.

A second possibility is to adapt prices from a parallel facility where charges are made, e.g. for admission to the grounds of a stately mansion. But for many activities, e.g. fell-walking, such an alternative is not available.

The usual method, therefore, is to see how demand varies with travel costs, both in money and time. The greater the distance travelled for such recreation, the greater the travel costs; thus demand should fall with distance. To allow for differences in density of population in the catchment area being studied, the number of trips per thousand of the population for different zones is derived. Suppose the following figures are obtained:

Zone	Trips per 1000 population
1	300
2	100
3	60

To simplify, let us assume that: (i) travel costs from zone 1 average £1; (ii) an outward movement to zones 2 and 3 each adds £1; and (iii) there are 1,000 people in each zone. We can now derive a demand curve as follows:

Price (£)	Trips made from zone			Total trips
	1	*2*	*3*	
1	300	100	60	460
2		100	60	160
3			60	60

From the demand curve we can estimate WTP.

This approach, although based on revealed market behaviour, presents difficulties:

(a) What should be the unit priced – whole-day trips, half-day trips or hours spent enjoying the facility?
(b) If the car is the main mode of travel, then the number of trips should be related to every 1000 *car-owners* of the population.
(c) Some allowance ought to be made for the average number of persons brought by each car.
(d) Where the journey is made by car, the assessment of cost presents problems. If the car is used mainly for business, then only the marginal cost (chiefly for petrol) will be the real cost of the journey. On the other hand, if the car is used exclusively for recreation, a proportion of overheads should also be included.
(e) At what price should travel time be valued (see below)?
(f) How should costs be adjusted if the actual journey to the facility also gives pleasure?
(g) How is the cost to be apportioned if more than one recreation centre is visited on the journey?

Valuing Time Saved

Transport improvements usually result in reducing the time spent in making a journey. What price do we put on this benefit?

Where it is working time saved, e.g. deliveries by lorry, and it results in extra work being done, the employer's valuation should be accepted: that is, it would include savings on overheads as well as on wages.

But time saved may simply mean that people get to work quicker, thereby increasing their leisure time. For people who choose how many hours they work, the marginal utility of leisure and work time would be equal, so that again time saved should be at the earning rate. But for most people a straight choice between an extra hour's work and an extra hour's leisure is not available. In practice, therefore, leisure time has to be valued arbitrarily as a proportion of the earning rate, and in fact 25 to to 50 per cent is usually taken as being the value of time saved.

An alternative approach is to take the value which people put on time indirectly when they incur higher costs in order to save it. This value may be indicated in different ways.:

(a) People may pay a higher price for their housing in order to be nearer their work. The snag here is that the higher price may reflect quality differences or nearness to non-work facilities.
(b) The route chosen may reduce time but at a higher cost, e.g. the toll paid to cross an estuary by ferry. To be accurate, however, the

assessment would have to be confined to regular users having perfect knowledge.
(c) Car drivers may rate speed against petrol consumption, etc. However, they may not know the exact extra cost involved, may enjoy driving at speed, or choose their speed for safety considerations.
(d) One mode of travel may be faster than another but more expensive, e.g. a taxi as opposed to a bus. Comfort considerations, however, may enter into such a choice.

Some allowance should also be made for the fact that as productivity increases over time so will the wage rate: thus the value of leisure time will tend to increase over time.

Human Life

Such projects as road improvements reduce deaths and accidents: others such as airports may increase them for people in the vicinity. How can a money value be given to human life? More specifically, how do we value loss of life? Here again there are alternatives, each presenting its own difficulties.

First, the present value of future expected earnings can be calculated, with additions for suffering endured and the grief experienced by the family. However, this ignores the consumer's surplus a person enjoys in spending his income.

The second alternative measures the present value of *net* output of the dead person, i.e. the flow of future earnings less consumption. This method, however, presents moral difficulties, for it implicitly assumes that society's objective is maximising total GNP. Fortunately, society does not require a person to justify his existence on economic grounds. People living on state pensions are not disposed of because their death would represent a net gain to society! Society takes human feelings into account.

A third method assesses the value placed on human life by society through its political decisions. For instance, if compulsory safety belts costing £X saved in total Y lives, the value of human life is at least $£\Sigma X/Y$. However, the fundamental objection to this approach is that it is a circular argument: the economist should really be justifying the cost of compulsory safety belts in terms of the value of lives saved!

A fourth measure, the sum for which a person insures his life, does not measure the value of life, but simply reflects a man's concern for his family's future in the event of his death. A bachelor, for instance, might have no life insurance, but he still values his life!

A fifth measure may be derived from people doing dangerous jobs. But information about risks may be incomplete and the labour market may be imperfect.

The real difficulty with all these methods is that they break with the criterion for a potential Pareto improvement: that there is still a gain after all losses have been compensated for. The second method highlights this snag, for the fact that society could gain from the death of a retired person arises simply because the latter receives no compensation for the loss of his life. Since such compensation is probably infinite, any project which saved one life would cover its costs!

However, it must be remembered that, in practice, we are not concerned with *one* person's certain death. What we have to compensate for is the extra *risk* of death to which all affected persons are exposed, e.g. as the result of the increased traffic of a new airport. Those concerned are: (i) the additional air passengers; (ii) their relatives; and (iii) people living around the airport. The value of the risk to the first can be disregarded, since it can be assumed that travellers have allowed for this in buying an air ticket. Indeed, as regards the third group, care must be taken to avoid double-counting since compensation may already have been carried out through the price system, e.g. in a lower price for houses near the airport which has induced residents to accept the risks involved. Otherwise, an insurance figure can be accepted as the necessary compensation required by the second and third groups except that, since people tend to underestimate, this figure may be somewhat inadequate.

19.6 Dealing With Spill-over Effects and Intangibles

Spill-over effects present practial problems. Which spill-overs should be included? In aggregating costs and benefits, how much weight should be attached to the shadow prices of intangibles compared with true market prices?

The problem of which spill-overs should be included is concerned, first, with the difficulty of distinguishing between real changes and distributional effects, and, second, on deciding the cut-off point.

Real Changes and Distributional Effects

Real changes are those that affect the performance of other inputs (e.g. an additional large office building in the City of London could increase traffic congestion and thus lower the efficiency of road transport) or the pleasure of others (e.g. a motorway, which creates a noise nuisance to nearby residents). Obviously such effects should be taken into account.

Distributional or transfer effects refer to those effects of individual projects which result in shifts in *prices* to other parties. Thus an increased demand by tourists for hotels in London will lead to higher wages of catering workers, not only in hotels but also in restaurants and cafés. Other things being equal, profits of the latter will be reduced. Are these effects part of the cost to society of increasing hotel services? Consider what has happened. The higher wages of catering workers will cause restaurants and cafés to reduce their demand for them. The restaurant itself will now earn a lower economic rent, while variable factors will drift to more profitable uses. But what all this means is simply that maximising consumers' economic welfare has pointed to a better 'basket' of products from a reshuffling of resources. Although painful for some, such readjustments must occur in a changing economy. In any assessment of the costs and gains of public development, there is no reason why the government should consider distributional effects except that, on grounds of equity, it may feel some compensation is called for.

Similarly, does an allowance have to be made for changes in the prices of substitute and complementary goods and services which result from some public development? For example, road and rail transport are to some extent substitute products. If the government, by instituting a new road-building programme, reduced the economic viability of British Rail, should this be allowed for in assessing the economic viability of investment in new roads? A private monopolist with many lines of production would obviously take into account such interactions when introducing changes. Should not the government do the same? Quite apart from the obvious difficulty of trying to trace the endless chain of effects throughout the whole field of government action, the answer is not entirely clear. The action of the monopolist may not be the appropriate criterion for the maximisation of consumers' economic welfare since there may be other spill-over effects which he does not take into account. Thus the government may require the price of North Sea gas to be raised relative to that of coal in the interests of full employment, conservation of reserves and a long-term fuel policy dependent on coal reserves.

To sum up, the gains and costs of a project should include the value of any *real* spill-overs. But changes in price which merely reflect relative changes in the conditions of demand and supply are beside the point. Thus, in choosing between alternative public projects, the government should not act like a giant monopoly, seeking to maximise overall profits from its many activities, but should assess each case on its merits, taking into account real spill-over effects. Pure redistribution effects are outside the question of economic efficiency, though the government can make a political decision to allow for them on the grounds of equity.

The Cut-off Point for Spill-overs

In considering spill-overs there is also the difficulty of deciding the cut-off point and whether any allowance should be made for unforeseen costs and benefits.

In Figure 19.4, for example, a motorway is built from *A* to *B*. Do we include only the benefits of travellers from *A* to *B*? It is likely, however, that it could reduce congestion for travellers from *B* to *C* and from *E* to *B*. Indeed, such routes could be extended, so where do we stop? The further we go, the more difficult it is to distinguish all beneficiaries. Moreover, certain spill-overs have to be decided by reference to what would generally be regarded as 'reasonable'. Thus while environmental spill-overs from the motorway would certainly qualify, the envy which some people not owning a car might feel as they saw others using the motorway to get to the seaside would have to be excluded.

Nor can all spill-overs be foreseen. The motorways around Los Angeles have saved the white-tailed kite from extinction. The reason is that the shrubs and grass of the broad shoulders and central dividers provide relative safety for the mice and lizards, the staple diet of the kite, for no man in his right mind ever sets foot in these areas. Alternatively, there could be unforeseen external costs. The Aswan Dam, for instance, reduced the flow of fish food from the Nile into the Mediterranean, giving rise to the real costs of fewer fish and, by affecting the livelihood of fishermen, having distributional effects. Moreover, since this was not confined to Egyptian fishermen, it raises the problem of whether, in a world where countries are becoming increasingly dependent on one another, spill-over effects should be limited to the national economy.

FIGURE 19.4
Effects of a Motorway on Surrounding Roads

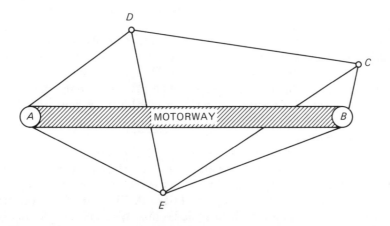

The Weighting of Intangibles in Aggregating Benefits and Costs

In so far as there is perfect competition, market prices at factor cost reflect true opportunity costs. In comparison, shadow prices are derived indirectly, and to that extent are somewhat suspect. Should we therefore, when aggregating, treat market and shadow prices equally? The difficulty becomes more real when shadow prices form a high proportion of total costs and benefits. Thus, in our example of the car park, the £70 000 benefits obtained by new parkers was based on an estimated demand curve derived from the price paid by existing car parkers. Should this shadow price represent an overestimate of 30 per cent, the scheme would not be viable. Actual CBAs have shown the crucial margin of error is usually much smaller. Thus, while the Roskill Commission estimated that the Cublington site for the Third London Airport would be £158 to £197 million cheaper than Foulness, only a 1 per cent error in total benefit or total cost figures could have made Foulness the lower-cost site.

In some cases, no quantitative estimate can be given for the value of intangibles. But they can still be noted on the Pareto balance sheet so that the decision-takers can weigh up both the tangible and intangible aspects of the project.

19.7 Choosing the Appropriate Discount Rate

The 'Real' Rate of Interest

If we postpone current consumption, resources can be used for investment in capital equipment. This produces greater output in the future: that is, there is growth. The gain is increased future consumption. We can thus speak of a rate at which current consumption can be transformed into future consumption.

However, future consumption is valued less highly than present consumption. This is because (i) people generally suffer from myopia; (ii) future income is less certain since there is always the risk of death: and (iii) future income is likely to be greater than present income, and thus the marginal utility of present income is higher. This preference which people generally have for present as opposed to future consumption is referred to as *time preference*.

A function of an economic system is to bring people's time preference into line with the actual opportunity cost of transforming current consumption into future consumption. Given a perfect market, perfect competition, perfect knowledge and no externalities, the free market system can produce a rate of interest which achieves this. We shall refer to this as the 'real' rate of interest. It is a unique rate which equates the time preference of society (the individuals comprising the market) with the profitability of available investment opportunities.

Complications

In practice, the conditions necessary for a unique, equilibrating rate of interest are not fulfilled.

First, many different rates exist, reflecting differences in risk (the small private company would have to pay a higher rate of interest than a large public company) or in imperfections in the capital market (the only source of funds to the small private company may be a bank, whereas the large company could float a loan on the capital market).

Second, money rates of interest may be affected by monetary influences as opposed to being determined solely by real forces – the return on investment and time preference. Monetary influences would include external pressure on the exchange rate or changes in the demand for money for liquidity purposes.

Third, actual money rates of interest may be higher than the real rate, because the reward for saving is reduced by taxation and inflation.

Selecting from the Rates Offered in the Capital Market

With different rates to choose from, which is the most appropriate for assessing public-sector projects?

One view is that discounting should be at the rate of interest at which the government can borrow to finance such schemes: that is, the yield on long-term gilt-edged securities. However, the government borrowing rate tends to be low because it is a 'riskless' rate. But public projects are not free from risk, e.g. *Concorde*, and the rate of discount should reflect this. Even if the project is financed from taxation, the opportunity cost is the rate which the taxpayer could have obtained had the money been left with him to invest.

Therefore, it is argued that because resources for investment are not unlimited the opportunity cost of a public project is the equal-risk project in the private sector which has to be forgone. Thus the appropriate rate of interest is what a large public company would have to pay for funds to finance such investment, e.g. the current debenture rate.

Only if lower risk is inherent in public projects should a lower interest rate be used. It can be argued that this lower risk does in fact exist. Because so many public projects are undertaken, risks are spread: losses on one project can be averaged out by gains on others. Thus the government (as it were) carries its own 'insurance' by diversification. Moreover, not only are risks spread over projects but also the cost of any error in estimation is distributed among so many taxpayers that the actual risk borne by each is so small as to be acceptable. Thus discounting projects at a slightly lower rate than in the private sector is justified.

Projects Financed out of Taxation

It should also be noted that many projects are financed, not out of borrowing, but out of taxation. Here the true opportunity cost of capital would necessitate tracing the taxes back to their source and discovering the value of them to the original owner – a formidable task. Suppose, for example, that firms paying corporation tax could obtain a 25 per cent rate of return by ploughing back their profits. This would be the opportunity cost of capital raised by such taxation. Alternatively, if taxes force firms to borrow in order to carry out investment, then the opportunity cost of funds to the government is the cost of such marginal, private market borrowing.

The Social Time Preference Rate

Apart from allowances for differences in risk between public and private projects, the problem is complicated by time-preference considerations.

First, society's time preference is not the same as the sum total of individual time preferences. It can be held that individuals suffer from myopia, a deficient 'telescopic faculty', so that they fail to appreciate how much they would benefit from future as opposed to current consumption. This difficulty is covered where society acts for individuals.

Second, society as a whole is an undying institution, and the government, which is responsible for society's decisions, is therefore concerned with the welfare of future generations, making decisions (as it were) on behalf of those still unborn. Such decisions are of particular importance when a project has an 'irreversible' cost, such as the demolition of a historic building, the destruction of the natural beauty of the Lake District, the complete exhaustion of a mineral stock or the wiping out of a particular species of animal, bird or plant. As the Green Party puts it: 'We do not inherit the land from our fathers: we borrow it from our children.' Thus in comparison with individuals, who have a limited time horizon, society has a lower time preference.

Both the above arguments therefore give further justification for discounting public projects at a lower interest rate than that arrived at through the market.

Providing for Risk and Uncertainty Through the Rate of Interest

While all the usual methods of allowing for risk and uncertainty in appraising projects can be applied to public-sector schemes, the above discussion suggests that one based on choosing an appropriate rate of interest will be the one usually followed. In practice, governments fix a minimum rate of return which must be achieved for public-sector investment to be acceptable.

However, if public projects are discounted at a lower rate than in the private sector, it will divert resources towards public investment, e.g. producing energy from coal (a public project) rather than from oil (mainly private-sector investment).

19.8 An Appreciation of the Role of CBA

Applicability of CBA in the Public Sector

It is essential, since resources are limited, that public-sector expenditure obtains 'value for money'. The difficulty is that financial criteria may be either non-existent or inadequate for assessing the viability of projects. CBA is designed to assist such decision-making. Public projects often involve the allocation of land resources; thus the technique of CBA can be applied to evaluating planning applications, comprehensive redevelopment proposals, motorway construction, the siting of an airport, and so on. In particular, spill-over benefits and costs are fully allowed for.

Limitations of CBA

Nevertheless, as our analysis has indicated, CBA runs up against conceptual and practical difficulties. These weaken its effectiveness as a tool for decision-making. The following considerations are of particular importance.

First CBA cannot be used where political decisions dominate. For instance, how much is spent by Britain on defence may depend upon subjective views as to how far the Soviet Union's expansionary aims are a threat to Britain and to what extent such expenditure can be trimmed in order to extend the social services. Similarly, proposals for comprehensive education are advanced, at least partly, on the subjective grounds that they promote a more integrated society, while expensive local authority housing may be provided in areas of high land values, e.g. Hampstead, in order to achieve a 'social mix'. Although social factors can be identified, it is often impossible to measure them satisfactorily.

Second, CBA may be difficult to apply to certain decisions. Consider, for instance, a local authority which has £1 million to spend on a swimming pool. The decision rests between: (i) one swimming pool of Olympic standards which, while it could also be used by local people, would bring prestige to the town; (ii) three smaller swimming pools, suitable for inter-school galas; and (iii) six very small pools specifically designed for children learning to swim. The advantages of each are largely immeasurable by CBA techniques, the result being that councillors would have to decide subjectively by voting at a council meeting.

Similarly, a firm CBA decision cannot be applied to a project involving irreversible decisions, e.g. the survival of a species of animal or plant. In such cases it is impossible to estimate a current economic cost since it would deny the opportunity to choose to future generations.

Third, CBA cannot deal objectively with the redistribution of income which results from a project.

Fourth, CBA encounters formidable difficulties both in measuring and aggregating intangibles. Its validity is enhanced as the number of values obtained directly from the market increases, particularly if they are determined under conditions of near-perfect competition.

Fifth, there is always the problem of the cut-off point in deciding the benefits and costs to be included. The viability of a project could rest on this decision, and interested parties may be tempted to extend the cut-off point in order to justify their particular preferences.

Finally, what passes as CBA is often in reality merely a 'cost-effectiveness' study comparing different methods of achieving a given end. CBA should not only examine the method of achieving an objective but should compare the likely returns from alternative uses of the resources. Thus, in the Roskill study, the decision to build a Third London Airport had been predetermined; the Commission merely examined the costs and benefits of alternative sites.

Conclusion on the Role of CBA

CBA provides a rational technique for appraising projects where market information is either non-existent or deficient. But it must not make false claims for objectivity by dealing in precise sums. While it is an aid to decision-making, it is not a substitute for it. Its role is to present systematically all the information relevant to a decision, indicating the weight which can be placed on the accuracy of the calculations submitted. Drawing up such an agenda ensures that the claims of rival pressure groups are assessed and that all the relevant issues are fully debated before the ultimate political decision is taken.

Finally, because resources are limited, the aim of policy should be to maximise total net benefits, the difference between gains and costs. CBA should really, therefore, enable the government to rank projects in order of net benefit. In practice, however, the cost of evaluating all competing projects would be prohibitive, and so CBA is confined to ascertaining whether the benefits of a particular scheme exceed costs.

Examples of the Use of CBA in Actual Land-use Decisions

While CBA as outlined above can be used in all public investment decisions, it has particular application to the allocation of land resources, where externalities are likely to loom large. Thus CBA studies have been undertaken for:

(a) the construction of the M1 motorway;
(b) the siting of the Third London Airport:
(c) the resiting of Covent Garden Market.

19.9 Cost–Benefit Studies of the New Covent Garden Market

The defects of CBA as a method of arriving at firm policy decisions is highlighted by two separate studies of resiting the old Covent Garden Market at Nine Elms.

The first was undertaken by A. J. Le Fevre and J. F. Pickering (1972) who used 1973 as the base year for their figures. They estimated that as a result of the growing direct links between the multiple retail chains and growers and the trend towards 'convenience' foods, the volume of trade passing through Covent Garden Market in 1973 would be only 75 per cent of that in 1959–60, and in 1981 it would be only 66 per cent. This assumption was then used as the basis for assessing future labour and equipment requirements.

Their figures for the main costs and benefits were as shown in Table 19.3. Certain items are not given because the costs and benefits were assumed to balance within the heading. Nor did the study claim to be fully comprehensive – reduced congestion costs, environmental effects on residents and the loss of the individual character of the old site were considered to be of too small a magnitude to affect the general conclusion.

Discounting costs and benefits at 8 per cent (then the current test rate for public-sector investment), and allowing for some reduction in annual equipment costs after 1981, gave a NPV under Table 19.3 assumption (a) of – £7.6m and under assumption (b) – £6.03m. Thus Le Fevre and Pickering concluded that on the basis of the assumptions made, 'the investment of £30m in a new market at Nine Elms falls a long way short of proving a viable investment'.

How far has this conclusion been borne out in practice? The New Covent Garden Market transferred to Nine Elms in 1974 and the Covent Garden Market Authority commissioned Professor J. H. Kirk and Mr M. J. Sloyan to ascertain the position in 1976 after nearly two years of operation. As a preliminary to assessing their study, however, it should be emphasised that

Table 19.3
1972 CBA of Resiting Covent Garden Market

Costs	(£)
Land and building	30 m.
Capital equipment (assumption a)	100 000 p.a.
(assumption b)	260 000 p.a.

Benefits

Sale of old site	10 m.
Saving in:	
Labour costs:	
assuming (a) a 10% reduction in the labour force	142 000 p.a.
assuming (b) at 25% reduction in the labour force	338 000 p.a.
Transport costs	207 000 p.a.
Waiting costs	705 000 p.a.
Wastage	126 000 p.a.

Kirk had previously disagreed with the conclusion of Le Fevre and Pickering, chiefly on the grounds that they had underestimated the value of the old Covent Garden site (which he put at £23m, to produce a net gain rather than a loss).

Valuation of the 15-acre Covent Garden site was complicated by the delay in deciding planning use and the listing of some 250 buildings. But largely on the basis of sale of 4.6 acres of land adjacent to the old market hall at the end of 1974, Kirk and Sloyan (1978) estimated the value of the released land at Covent Garden as £24.3 m. Their other figures were based on costs actually incurred during the two years' operations and on empirical studies. For easy comparison with the Le Fevre and Pickering analysis, their figures are set out in Table 19.4 under similar headings.

Using an eight-year purchase basis. Kirk and Sloyan estimated the annual value of the old site as £3m. The project therefore produced an annual return of £5.7m on an outlay of £36.2m, equivalent to just under 16 per cent, an acceptable yield. Alternatively, if we discount the total annual net benefits of £2 724 000 at 10 per cent (a higher figure being chosen for 1976) the scheme shows a NPV of approximately £15m.

Table 19.4
1978 CBA of Resiting Covent Garden Market

Costs	(£)
Land and building (net of the cost of that part of Market Towers let to non-market users)	36.2 m.
Capital equipment	660 000 p.a.
Benefits	
Value of the old site	24.3 m.
Saving in:	
Labour costs:	804 000 p.a.
Transport and waiting costs	1 100 000 p.a.
Wastage and pilfering	1 420 000 p.a.

It will be observed that for all items Kirk and Sloyan's figures are higher than those of Le Fevre and Pickering. This is partly due to the rise in prices between 1973 and 1976. But Kirk and Sloyan were able to base their figures on observed costs, and these would reflect the fact that the volume of traffic actually increased by nearly 10 per cent during the Nine Elm site's first year of operation (compared with Le Fevre and Pickering's assumption of a gradual reduction in trade).

Postscript

In the event the Covent Garden Market has proved economically viable, but for reasons not covered by the CBA studies.

Of the £36.7 million owed to the Ministry of Agriculture in 1977, £13 million was written off. The subsequent appreciation of London office property allowed Market Towers, the office block built on the corner of the new site, to be sold for £20 million, and the remainder of the debt was repaid in 1990.

The Authority's pre-tax operating profit is now approximately £1.5 million a year, and the market value of the land exceeds considerably its £6 million book value. Hence proposals are now afoot for the Covent Garden Market Authority to be privatised.

20 Imperfect Knowledge

20.1 Defective Market Information

Forms of Imperfect Knowledge

Imperfect knowledge leads to imperfect competition and so the efficiency of the market economy is impaired. In practice such imperfect knowledge may occur for the following reasons.

(1) Buyers and sellers cannot obtain complete market information. Thus housewives shopping in retail markets do not have the time to acquaint themselves with the price being charged for the good by all the sellers. Similarly, an unemployed worker may not be aware of a local job vacancy.

(2) Buyers have difficulty in ascertaining the qualities of certain goods, e.g. second-hand cars, houses, antiques and works of art.

(3) Firms may not be aware of supernormal profits being made by other firms, of the costs of producing different outputs or of using different techniques, and so on.

(4) There is uncertainty of future market prices.

(5) Decisions may depend upon the actions being taken by others, but these are not known. Thus a firm's investment which is duplicated by competitors could result in oversupply by the industry concerned. The resulting inability to sell at the expected price could mean that no firm can produce profitably.

(6) Although they cannot be provided for, external benefits may arise in the course of time. Similarly, unforeseen external costs may occur.

(7) Individuals may have a restricted time-horizon resulting in inadequate conservation of existing resources.

(8) Instability in the economy generally, e.g. changes in the rate of inflation and in the balance-of-payments position, produces uncertainty, affecting the decisions of both households and firms.

The Government and Imperfect Knowledge

Usually the government leaves it to consumers and firms to improve knowledge. Thus consumers can subscribe to *Which?* (the Consumer's Association) which reports on the quality, safety and relative prices of goods. Experts can be employed on an individual basis. Second-hand cars can be tested by the Automobile Association, houses examined by a surveyor, and antiques and works of art reported on by the leading auction houses. Firms, too, can obtain professional advice through, for example, their own accountants, economists or outside specialist consultants. Indeed, as regard future price uncertainties, the price system may respond by setting up special 'futures' markets, where the cautious can exchange 'risk' with the more adventurous.

Today, however, the government is taking an increasingly active part in improving knowledge, e.g. by collecting and publishing statistics covering most facets of the economy, setting up Jobcentres, advertising the advantages of Development Areas (see p. 473), advising firms on preparation for the 1992 Single Market.

How the government can achieve a better allocation of resources by improving knowledge, mainly through the removal of some uncertainty, can be shown by examining its role in the use of land and in conservation. Its 'stabilising' functions are covered in Chapters 29–39.

20.2 Land-use Planning

In the UK, local authorities are responsible for overall planning of land use. This coordinating function has certain advantages.

First, the local authority has probably better information than the private developer regarding future demand. By its planning controls it can direct development so as to avoid over- or undersupply.

We can illustrate by office development in a city area. In Figure 20.1, D, D_1 and D_2 represent the demand curves for offices at different time periods, and S the long-period supply curve. In period 1, demand increases from D to D_1 but, because it takes some time for supply to expand to OM_1 the number of offices remains fixed at OM. Competition, therefore, leads to higher rents which rise to OP_1. Office developers respond to this higher price, starting to build offices irrespective of the fact that others are doing likewise. When all their building programmes have been completed supply has increased to OM_2. In order to clear the market, price has to fall to OP_2 unless demand increases to D_2 or inferior office accommodation is taken off the market. Here the planning authority can impose a scheme which coordinates the proposals of separate developers.

FIGURE 20.1
The Effect of Time-lags in the Supply of Offices

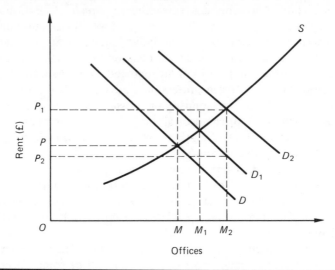

Second, the planning authority can do something to remove the uncertainty arising from the imperfect knowledge of the intentions of others. This can be explained in terms of 'the prisoner's dilemma'. The police suggest to prisoner A that, in return for confessing and implicating his accomplice B, they will do their best to ensure that A's sentence is limited to one year's imprisonment, although B will get five. However, prisoner A senses that the police do not have a strong case and, that, if neither confesses, there is a chance that they will both be acquitted. He has no means of communicating with B, and so his problem is to assess how B is likely to react to the same offer. Will he remain silent, relying on A to do likewise in order to give them both a good chance of going free? Or will he act selfishly and settle for one year, leaving A to do five years?

This situation can be related to owners' decisions on whether to improve their property in a run-down inner-city area. One owner is contemplating spending £20 000 on improving his property. If the owners of adjacent properties do likewise, there is a beneficial spin-off because the value of all properties would each increase by £30 000. On the other hand, if fellow owners fail to renovate their properties, the first owner's expenditure could be largely wasted in terms of adding to the value of his property since it may eventually have to be demolished. While the local authority also does not have direct knowledge of owners' intentions (since no planning permission is required here), it can create greater certainty by policy action –

announcing a definite plan to renovate the whole area. This would stimulate owners to improve independently, secure in the knowledge that those who failed to do so would be brought into line. A similar situation would occur if individual retailers could only be induced to move from a central position to a peripheral area more accessible to shoppers (e.g. a shopping centre) if they were sure that the external benefits of concentration would be retained by fellow retailers making the same move.

Third, it can be argued that at times people may not be the best judges of their own welfare. For instance, their preferences expressed through the market might make inadequate provision for open space, such as parks and playing fields. Through planning, a paternalistic policy is followed by allocating land to such uses. On the other hand, permission to build on cheap land near a motorway may be refused because the authorities consider that prospective purchasers of houses would underestimate the noise nuisance.

Finally, in their present utilisation of land resources, individuals might make insufficient allowance for future needs. The government, however, has a longer time-horizon (see p. 296). Thus it designates green belts around towns to safeguard amenity land for unborn generations.

20.3 Conservation

The Nature of Conservation

Conservation is only one aspect of the larger problem of protecting the quality of the environment in the midst of change. It is not limited to more preservation but seeks *creative continuity* by promoting vitality of use of the environment while ensuring that change is sympathetic to the quality of life for both present and future generations.

Thus conservation embraces a wide field – green belts around towns, national parks, public bridle ways and footpaths, fauna and flora protection, Sites of Special Scientific Interest, National Trust property, mineral and oil reserves, museums, buildings of special architectural and historial interest, and so on. All have common features as follows.

The first which must be emphasised is that there is an *opportunity cost* of a better environment. A 'green belt', for instance, keeps land in agriculture – a lower use compared with housing – and also extends the journey to work of those city workers who live beyond it.

The second, because in essence conservation is synonymous with the optimum use of resources over time, reflects many of the problems concerned with investment in general. But, largely on account of the distant time-horizon involved and its far-reaching effects on the community at large, there are special aspects of conservation which make it unsuitable to be left entirely to market forces – difficulties of estimating future conditions of demand and supply, choosing an appropriate discount rate, allowing for externalities and the possible irreversibility of wrong decisions.

We can illustrate the problems by analysing just one aspect of conservation – preserving historic buildings – but the approach is applicable to the conservation of resources generally.

The Market Solution

The historic building (which we will assume is a house in the centre of town) will be demolished when the site can be put to a more 'profitable' use. This necessitates calculating its present capital value, obtained by totalling the discounted flow of net benefits expected in the future. It is likely that, ignoring inflation, the value of the house will fall over time as it becomes increasingly unsuitable for modern living requirements. This is shown by the curve *PP* (Figure 20.2).

In contrast, the capital value of a new office block (*RR*) will eventually be such that, even allowing for the cost of rebuilding, the cleared site is worth more than the historic house. If left to market forces, therefore, demolition of the historic house occurs in year D.

FIGURE 20.2

Adjustments to the Present Value of a Historic Building for Different Uses

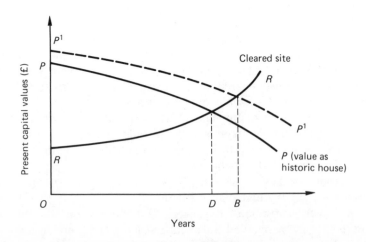

Possible Weaknesses of the Market Solution

On what grounds may *economics* justify interference with this market solution?

First, it is unlikely that the curve *PP* reflects the true opportunity cost of the historic house at any one time. For one thing, certain benefits are likely to have been ignored.

Apart from *external benefits* (such as the pleasure which the view of a historic house gives to passers-by), we should recognise the existence of an 'option demand'. Where decisions are irreversible (as with the destruction of a historic building), many people would pay something just to postpone such a decision. The difficulty lies in quantifying such 'option demand', but its existence is evident in the fact that many people subscribe voluntarily to the National Trust and the World Wildlife Fund, for example. The rest enjoy the option as 'free riders', but their demand should also be included.

Furthermore, because the rate of social time preference is lower than that of private time-preference (see p. 296), a present capital value derived from the lower rate of discount appropriate to the social time-preference would be higher than one based on a rate of discount which merely reflected *private* time-preference.

These additional benefits and the lower discount rate would give the historic house a higher capital value curve, P^1P^1, with demolition being postponed until year B.

Second, and even more important, we have to recognise that, when dealing with the future, knowledge is not perfect. Thus a decision to demolish a building may be based on a defective assessment of the future conditions of demand and supply. This is not serious when we are dealing with *flows*, such as the services provided by offices, since new offices can always be built if demand increases in the future. But demolishing a historic building diminishes a stock which cannot be replaced. The situation is illustrated in Figure 20.3.

In period t, the historic building has a low value, OH. On the other hand, an office block would command price OP_1. Over time, however, the value of the historic building increases relatively to that of offices. This is because, with higher incomes and more leisure, people take a greater interest in historic buildings. Increased demand means that in period $t + 2$ the price of the historic building has risen to OH_2. On the other hand, the demand for offices is not likely to increase so quickly, income-elasticity of demand being lower. Moreover, with technological improvements in construction, the supply curve shifts to the right over time. As a result, in period $t + 2$ the price of offices falls to OP_2.

The situation is transferred to Figure 20.4. We can assume that the price of the office block in period t gives a cleared site value of FD, so that demolition of the historic building and redevelopment of the site as offices

FIGURE 20.3
Changes in the Future Relative Prices of Historic Buildings and Offices

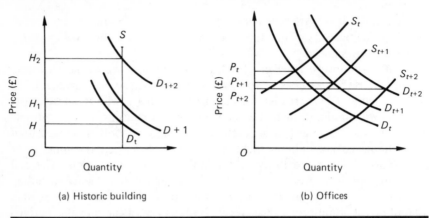

(a) Historic building   (b) Offices

has become a viable economic proposition. Eventually, however, the value of the historic building starts to rise, while the rate of increase in the value of the cleared site declines. Indeed, if demolition in year D could be prevented, by year E the present value of the historic building once again exceeds the value of the cleared site.

Government Policy for Preserving Historic Buildings

The above analysis suggests that the government must intervene in the free operation of the price system in order to preserve historic buildings. Its action can take a variety of forms.

First, the building could be brought under public ownership. Such a policy would usually be followed where the cost of excluding free-riders would be prohibitive, e.g. Hadrian's Wall. Equally important, it would allow welfare to be maximised (see pp. 313, 326). Finally, public ownership would automatically allow external benefits to be internalised.

Second, the historic building could be left in private ownership but a subsidy given through repair grants or tax concessions on the grounds of the external benefits conferred. Such a subsidy would increase net benefits to the owner and so raise the present value (as shown by the dotted line in Figure 20.4). However, there are difficulties. Many external benefits cannot be quantified while shortage of funds could mean that the subsidy was insufficient to raise the present-use value curve permanently above the cleared-site curve so that demolition is only postponed to year B, unless other action is taken.

Third, any building of special architectural or historic interest may be 'listed'. This means that it cannot be altered or demolished without the consent of the local planning authority. While this gives protection against positive acts of demolition, it may not cover destruction by the neglect of the owner. Such neglect occurs because high maintenance costs result in negative net benefits. Even though in such circumstances the local authority can appropriate the building, there is reluctance to do so since the cost of maintenance now falls on public funds. Thus, in practice, 'listing' in year D may be only a 'stop-gap' measure, bridging the years between D and E (Figure 20.4) until increasing demand raises the value of the historic building above that of the cleared site. More frequently, 'listing' simply imposes a prohibition on demolition until an alternative policy can be formulated.

Fourth, giving permission for the building to be adapted to a more profitable use provides such a policy. Thus stables may be converted into a dwelling, and houses into offices. This has the effect of increasing net benefits and thus raising the present value curve so that it is above the cleared-site curve. This change of use is shown as taking place in year D and the new present value product is depicted by the line *FCP'* (Figure 20.4).

FIGURE 20.4
Methods of Preserving a Historic Building

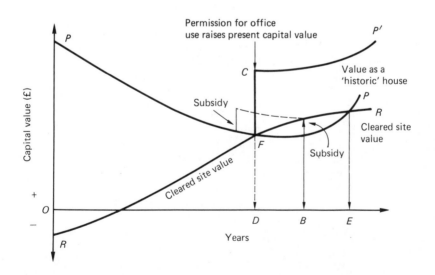

In consenting to a change of use of a historic building, the objective of the authorities must be to retain as many of the original features as possible. Thus some flexibility of building regulations is necessary, for example, as regards height of rooms, window space and even fire precautions. As in Figure 20.3a the distinctive character of the converted building may produce increasing rentals over time, e.g. for prestige reasons, so that not only is it preserved but there is no charge on public funds.

21 The Provision of Goods and Services by the Public Sector

21.1 Public Sector Goods and Services

Why Public Sector Provision?

As we saw in Chapter 11, in order to achieve a more efficient allocation of resources, the government has to intervene in the market economy. Such intervention may take the form of administrative regulation, e.g. by rent control and anti-monopoly measures, or simply influencing relative market prices, e.g. by indirect taxes and subsidies. Alternatively, the government may itself provide certain goods and services. Economic reasons for this direct provision are:

1. *Community goods*, such as defence, police, street lighting and flood control, have the following characteristics:
   (a) they are indivisible in the sense that supply must be a complete package or nothing;
   (b) one consumer's use does not deprive others of its simultaneous use;
   (c) once produced, the opportunity cost to additional consumers is nil;
   (d) a price cannot be charged on the basis of use. This means that it is impossible to supply such goods through the market.

2. *Collective goods*, similarly, satisfy people's collective needs, e.g. parks, motorways, bridges, water supply, refuse collection and drainage, but they are distinguished from community goods in that it is possible to exclude free-riders and so charge on the basis of use, eg. by entrance fees, tolls, meter recording, etc.
   But these goods entail such high fixed-capital investment that production takes place under conditions of decreasing cost. Some monopoly

311

element is therefore inevitable (see p. 176), but while a private monopolist will endeavour to limit supply to where marginal cost equals marginal revenue, a public body can secure a better allocation of resources.

We can illustrate with reference to a public garden in the centre of a town. Let us assume that: (i) people derive pleasure from the flower gardens and would be willing to pay for this benefit; (ii) the garden can be fenced round so that, by excluding 'free-riders', a price can be charged; and (iii) the only cost is the initial price, which includes a capitalised sum for future maintenance, giving marginal cost of zero up to the capacity of the gardens to take visitors. The situation is depicted in Figure 21.1, where the ATC curve is a rectangular hyperbola and the capacity of the gardens is *OZ* after which more visitors involve serious overcrowding. Thus production, in terms of number of visitors, takes place under conditions of decreasing cost. As a result, some form of imperfect competition is inevitable.

If the gardens were provided privately by a monopolist, he would charge an admission price of *OP*, limiting visitors to *OM*, where marginal cost equals marginal revenue and where elasticity of demand equals unity.

Suppose now that the gardens were taken over by the local authority. By

---

FIGURE 21.1
Public Provision of Collective and Public Goods

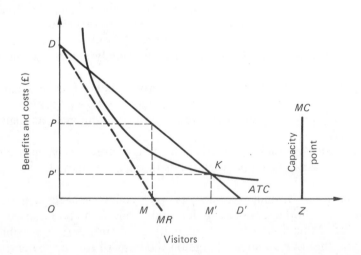

Visitors

lowering the price to OP', a larger number of people OM' could enjoy the gardens at no extra cost, and total costs would be covered.

3. *Public goods* are those whose enjoyment by an extra person imposes no sacrifice on others because marginal cost is nil, e.g. parks, bridges, motorways, art galleries. With these maximum benefits can be enjoyed only if they are provided by the State at no charge, the cost being met from taxation. Thus, in the above example of the garden, limiting admission to OM' visitors would not be a Pareto-optimal situation. If the principle of MC pricing were adopted (see p. 179) and no charge was made (because MC = 0), benefits could be increased by $KM'D'$ at *no extra cost*. But the total cost would have to be covered out of taxation for the gardens are now being provided in exactly the same way as community goods.

4. *Merit goods*, e.g. housing, education, medical care, would be inadequately consumed if left to market forces, with possible external costs. In selecting such goods, the government makes a subjective judgement, for they are provided free or below cost.

5. *External costs and benefits* may be so widespread that only the government can take full account of them, e.g. urban renewal, new town development, new airport construction.

6. *A project may be so large that only the government can provide the initial capital*, particularly where it is doubtful whether revenue will cover total costs, e.g. coal-mine modernisation, the development of nuclear energy, the supply of natural gas. Here the government can either make good any shortfall out of taxation or exercise its monopoly powers to impose a pricing structure which will generate sufficient revenue to cover total costs (see below).

Accountability versus Economic Efficiency

Even after it has been decided that the State should provide goods and services, consideration has still to be given to two fundamental principles which pull in opposite directions.

The first, 'public accountability', arises because British democracy requires that where the State is granted powers it shall be answerable, in some form or another, for the way in which those powers are exercised. The citizen requires some assurance that powers granted to the State to produce goods and services are not abused by authoritarianism, inefficiency or monopolistic exploitation.

The second principle is 'economic efficiency'. The difficulty is that, by insisting on strict public accountability, we may so tie the hands of those running the state services that they cannot operate efficiently.

21.2   Forms of Public Sector Organisation

The result of the above clash of principles is that the provision of goods and services through the public sector may be undertaken by a government department, local authorities, nationalised industries, quasi-government bodies (variously termed authorities, boards, commissions, councils or committees).

The *government department* form of organisation achieves a high degree of public accountability because the minister in charge is directly responsible to Parliament for all aspects of the department's work. He is subject to examination in Parliament, having to explain general policy in debate and to answer questions on even minor details of administration. Over finance, too, there is strict control: the Treasury ascertains that money is spent economically and within the limit authorised by Parliament.

But such accountability has inherent snags. First, Parliament is basically a forum for discussing major political issues rather than for dealing with administrative details. In any case, MPs are laymen without the necessary technical knowledge to supervise. Second, Parliament would be overworked if it tried to exercise detailed control. Third, frequent questions in Parliament on the decisions of civil servants can lead to their taking a 'play-for-safety' attitude or the line of least resistance. The opposition probes mainly with political ends in view; civil servants are therefore hardly likely to follow a bold, imaginative policy which, should it fail, could excite considerable criticism, when by taking an alternative middle-of-the-road line they can settle for a less troubled life. Fourth, Treasury control over finance is restrictive in character. Whereas private enterprise only requires proposed expenditure to be justified by overall profits, the Treasury insists that each individual item of service be provided at the lowest possible cost.

To sum up, accountability clashes with economic efficiency. Thus the *government-department* form of organisation is most appropriate for dealing with community and public goods which are of national importance and where local differences in the standard of provision would be unacceptable, e.g. defence, trunk roads, health care. Their cost is covered, therefore by taxation. Such expenditure, however, does enable the government to consider its effects on stabilising the economy and, through taxation, on the distribution of income, two objectives which by and large should be left to the central government. Other functions of the government department are basically concerned with supervision or control or both, e.g. in foreign affairs and tax collection.

Local authorities carry out functions, delegated by Parliament, chiefly where economies of scale and spill-over effects are relatively weak. Services are divided between the *counties* and *districts*. As a general rule the *counties* provide those services which are best administered over a wide area or which are most economically provided on a large scale and therefore for a large population, e.g. education, police, roads, structure planning and fire services. The *districts* are basically local planning, refuse collection, sanitation and housing authorities.

Provision of such services by local authorities has certain advantages:

(a) those who run local services are local people responsive to local needs and attitudes;
(b) it allows close contact between the governed and those who govern;
(c) it provides for division of power between Whitehall and town hall, reminding the central government that its decisions must respect local feelings and loyalties.
(d) it reduces the burden of central government administration.

Because the strict accountability of the government department form of organisation may conflict with economic efficiency, the *nationalised industries* have been organised as 'public corporations'. The minister concerned exercises control over their broad policies, but not their day-to-day operations. They are fairly free to choose their own pricing policies but have to submit an annual report to Parliament. Thus some accountability is sacrificed in the interests of economic efficiency. We discuss these nationalised industries in more detail below.

Quasi-government bodies have usually been formed to operate particular services where only minimum accountability is required, e.g. the National Parks Commission, the Countryside Commission. In practice the degree of accountability varies. Thus, in their composition, certain official representatives may have to be included; or there may be the simple requirement that an annual report be laid before Parliament. These bodies are usually set up to administer services which have social overtones and where spill-over effects are extensive or economies of scale can be secured.

21.3 The Nationalised Industries

Reasons for Nationalisation

In addition to providing community, public and merit goods, the State has in the past taken over the production of certain goods from the private sector, nationalising such industries as coal, gas and electricity supply, iron and steel, shipbuilding, rail transport, aerospace, cable and wireless and the Bank of England. Many, however, have been returned to private enterprise (see later).

Nationalisation, however, does not automatically solve the problem of allocating resources; it simply means that the ultimate economic decisions are taken by the government. But in making those decisions the government can allow for external benefits and costs (e.g. by keeping the shipyards working at a loss because the men would otherwise be idle), overcome the temptation of a monopoly industry to maximise profits by restricting output (e.g. by producing up to the point where price, not marginal revenue, equals marginal cost) and redistribute income through its pricing policy (e.g. by providing low-priced transport for senior citizens).

While the precise arguments for nationalisation depend upon the industry concerned, the following are those which have been most generally advanced.

1. Single Control over All Firms in the Industry Enables the Full Advantages of Large-scale Production to be Achieved

2. State Ownership is Essential for the Necessary Capital Investment

Private owners may not have the resources or may be unwilling to commit themselves to long-term capital outlays. Thus, for security and technical reasons, atomic energy has been developed by the State, while the railway modernisation programme would have been too risky for private enterprise. Moreover, losses may possibly be justified by external benefits, e.g. less congestion on the roads, maintaining jobs (e.g. shipbuilding), or strengthening social contacts (e.g. postal services in rural areas).

3. State Ownership is a Means of Controlling Monopoly

Public utilities in particular are 'natural' monopolies in that competition would lead to a considerable waste of resources. It is argued that control by state ownership ensures that they will work in the public interest and not merely for high profits.

4. A Pricing Policy Can be Adopted Which Allows a Highly Capitalised Industry to Cover Its Costs

Where initial fixed costs are very high – e.g. in electricity supply – it is impossible to charge a single price which will generate sufficient revenue to cover total costs (see p. 328). However, by creating a monopoly which can discriminate between customers by charging different prices to each according to what they are willing to pay, total revenue can be increased. But since such monopolies are essential public utilities, it is held that they should be under direct state control.

5. The Efficiency of Key and Strategic Industries Must be Guaranteed

There are certain industries, e.g. iron and steel, coal and power, upon which most other production depends. Others, e.g. atomic research, are vital for defence. Such industries, it is argued, should be run by the State in the wider interests of the nation rather than by private enteprise for profit.

6. Productivity will Increase Through Improved Attitudes of Employees

It is argued that, because workers will enjoy better working conditions and be motivated by being employed by the State and not a company striving for its own profit, increased worker productivity will result.

The Public Corporation as a Form of Business Organisation

When the government embarked on its nationalisation programme in 1945, the disadvantages of the government-department form of organisation discussed above were highlighted. The industries being transferred from the private sector were concerned with economic functions, not the administration of particular policies. As such they served the everyday needs of the whole community, and so their contact with people was much greater than in traditional fields of government. This meant that the House of Commons, as a supervisory body, would have been overworked by parliamentary questions. Moreover, accountability through Parliament would have made it difficult to pursue long-term objectives because the minister in charge could change with a reorganisation of government. Finally, civil servants are not chosen to provide the dynamic and imaginative management required for large commercial undertakings.

The answer to these defects was to make the nationalised industries the responsibility of public corporations. The objective was to get the best of both worlds: on the one hand the world of energetic industrial enterprise found in the market economy; on the other the world of accountability to the public, to whom it belongs and whom it serves.

Organisation of the Nationalised Industries

The organisation of the nationalised industries, based on the principles outlined above, presents some common features.

(i) The boards are 'bodies corporate'. This means that they have a legal identity and therefore, like a company, have a life of their own, can own property and can sue and be sued in the courts.

(ii) Assets of the industry are vested in the board, and the nationalising act usually gives the board instructions as to its general responsibilities. Thus the National Coal Board is charged with:

(1) Working and getting coal in Great Britain.
(2) Securing the efficient development of the industry.
(3) Making supplies of coal available in such quality, size, quantity and price as may seem to be best calculated to further the public interest in all respects.

(iii) A minister is given overall control. He exercises, as it were, the shareholders' rights in a company, the 'shareholders' being the community. It is the minister, therefore, who appoints the board's members, though the nationalising act usually specifies their general qualifications. In addition the minister may give the board general directions as to how it is to perform its functions with regard to matters which appear to him to affect national interests, e.g. by authorising capital development, supervising borrowing and appointing auditors.

In this way the boards enjoy freedom in their day-to-day operations but possible subordination in general policy. While they are not subject to parliamentary questioning on details of administration, they are required to submit annual reports to parliament, which are usually debated for a day.

(iv) In financial and staffing matters the boards are free from Treasury control. Originally, they were expected to pay their way, taking one year with another, but with some, e.g. British Rail, shipbuilding and iron and steel this proved impossible. They engage their own staff, arranging pay and conditions of service through employees' organisations.

(v) To provide some direct representation for consumers, *consumers' councils* have been established for the coal, electricity, and railway industries. They consist of twenty to thirty unpaid members appointed by the minister. Nominations for membership are from bodies he selects as being representative of consumers, e.g. women's organisations, professional associations, trade unions and trade associations. These councils (1) deal with complaints and suggestions from consumers, and (2) advise both the boards and the minister of the views of consumers. Unfortunately, because of ignorance, remoteness from the offices or general lack of confidence, consumers have so far made little use of these councils.

To sum up, public corporations are made accountable through:

(i) the responsibility of the minister for appointing board members and ensuring that the board's policies harmonise with the government's overall economic strategy;

(ii) Parliament, which examines how the minister exercises his responsibilities and debates the boards' annual reports;

(iii) consumers' councils.

The detailed organisation of boards has varied; we can illustrate from
the coal and electricity industries.

The Coal Industry Nationalisation Act 1946 set up the National Coal
Board, and this determines the rest of the organisation of the coal
industry.

Collieries are grouped in areas, each under an Area Director responsible to the NCB. The day-to-day working of the collieries is under the
direction of colliery managers.

It seems, however, that originally the problem of size was underestimated, for later nationalising acts have tended towards decentralisation. Thus the Electricity Council, established in 1948, is really only a
central representative body for the industry as a whole, and is composed
mainly of the chairmen of the twelve area boards, with an independent
chairman or vice-chairman appointed by the minister. The area boards
were themselves set up by the nationalising act, and the assets of the
industry were vested in them. They were also given the *statutory*
responsibility for the distribution of electricity. Each board adopted its
own pattern of organisation and arrangements for fulfilling its statutory
obligations.

Economic Problems of Nationalisation and Efficiency in the Public Sector

Apart from the constitutional problems – internal organisation, the
minister's exact responsibilities, the extent of and opportunities for parliamentary review – many economic problems still remain to be resolved.

First, problems arise because often nationalised industries are monopolies. On the demand side there can be some loss of consumers'
sovereignty since the ultimate sanction – taking his custom elsewhere –
may not be practicable. On the supply side, too, there are grounds for
concern. Prices are fixed with the object of covering costs, but what
guarantee is there that costs are kept to a minimum by efficient operation?
Nevertheless, the introduction of some form of competition may help.
Thus in the power industries, gas, oil (the private sector), coal and
electricity (the public sector) all compete to some degree with each other.

Second, problems of coordination arise in managing these vast industries. However, these same problems exist in the private sector, and there
seems little reason why state industry should be inferior in its ability to
solve them.

Third, some economists have criticised investment decisions in many of
the nationalised industries, arguing that there has been overinvestment,

e.g. in the coal industry, with the result that alternative, and probably more profitable, investments have been 'crowded out'. Although some error is bound to occur in a dynamic economy (the discovery of natural gas, for instance, upset the NCB's projections of future demand for coal), there is a feeling that initially the nationalised industries were favoured in the allocation of capital because the government had a vested interest in their success. The present requirement is that any investment project should show a minimum return of 10 per cent on capital.

Finally, although the industries were expected to pay their way, taking one year with another, some have failed to do so. Partly this has resulted from a miscalculation of demand and costs; partly it has been due to the government's use of the nationalised industries to promote wider aims, such as price stability (e.g. by restricting increases in the price of gas, coal, electricity, fares, etc.), income redistribution (e.g. by encouraging free travel for senior citizens), social policy (e.g. by retaining loss-making rural railway lines), and full employment and regional balance (e.g. by support-ing shipbuilding on Clydeside and the north-east coast).

As a result, the government has had to write off accumulated deficits (e.g. on coal and railways) or subsidise heavily (e.g. shipbuilding). More than that, those wider policy objectives have prevented some nationalised industries from following pricing policies which would have enabled them to break even. The difficulty with many nationalised industries, as we saw above, is that fixed costs are so high that no *single* price can generate sufficient revenue to cover total costs. While the electricity-supply indus-tries has used price discrimination and a two-part tariff to enable it to break even, other industries, notably the railways, have been allowed to operate price discrimination only in a downward direction, fares being reduced where demand is elastic (e.g. on the part of students and senior citizens) but not raised where demand is inelastic (e.g. on the part of commuters and rural passengers). Generally speaking, those who use the services should bear the cost; this is fair and also makes for economy in consump-tion. Only where there are identifiable external benefits are subsidies to cover deficits justified.

21.4   Privatisation

Nature of Privatisation

'Privatisation' implies more than the movement of assets from the public to the private sector. Rather it embraces all the different means by which the disciplines of the free market in the provision of goods and services can be applied to the public sector. Thus this 'pushing back the frontiers of the state' covers:

(a) the transfer of the nationalised industries to private ownership, e.g. British Telecom, British Gas, British Airways, British Airports Authority;

(b) selling óther state assets, either completely (e.g. Britoil, Rolls-Royce, motorway service areas) or partially (e.g. woodlands owned by the Forestry Commission, British Petroleum shares, council housing);

(c) opening-up state monopolies to outside competition, e.g. relaxing licensing restrictions to allow private bus firms to compete with publicly owned services;

(d) 'contracting-out' to the private sector services paid for out of public funds, e.g. refuse collection, street cleaning, hospital ancillary services;

(e) charging beneficiaries for publicly provided goods and services, e.g. museums, medical prescriptions, school meals, council housing.

Reasons for Privatisation

Although the Labour government initiated a form of privatisation when in 1977 it sold a part of the State's British Petroleum shares in order to be less dependent on borrowing to cover its Public Sector Borrowing Requirement (the excess of government current spending over revenue), privatisation is really based on the market economy philosophy of the Conservative Party. Thus while Mrs Thatcher's first term of office still concentrated on the PSBR objective, privatisation was extended by returning to the private sector firms which had been recently acquired (e.g. British Aerospace and Cable and Wireless) and by encouraging contracting-out of services. But during her second term beginning in 1983 privatisation measures were extended and integrated in line with her private enterprise views and supply-side policies (see pp. 449–51). It is in this context, therefore, that the advantages claimed for privatisation have to be analysed.

1. Reduced Burden on the Public Purse

As a one-off, short-term measure the proceeds from state asset sales have helped to cover a worrying PSBR. Indeed, where state industries have had recurrent deficits (with debts eventually having to be written off, e.g. coal, railways, airways), there is a long-term relief to the public purse. On the other hand, it can be argued that such 'write-offs' can be regarded as subsidies for external benefits, e.g. the relief of unemployment.

2. Freedom from Detailed Political Control

Some political control over general policy and the scale of borrowing is necessary to achieve a degree of accountability. But some governments have seen public enterprises as legitimate instruments of macroeconomic policy, e.g. countenancing overmanning to preserve jobs in periods of unemployment, holding prices to combat inflation, and restricting investment spending to reduce the PSBR.

Thus managers of the nationalised industries have felt frustrated at not being able to pursue pricing and long-term investment strategies unencumbered by government interference, preferring to reap the rewards for success and carry the consequences of failure.

3. Improved Efficiency Through Competition in the Market

Economic efficiency must be considered from both the demand and supply sides. The market indicates consumer preferences (e.g. for ownership of council housing as opposed to renting), while competition promotes efficiency in supplying consumer goods and services.

As monopolies, however, the nationalised industries have tended to take some profits in the form of a 'quiet life' since competition does not force Boards to respond to the changing wishes of consumers or to push the industry to the highest possible supply efficiency. Even at the lower levels, managers may seek to maximise their own empires and budgets.

4. Greater Resistance to Trade Union Power

Where the State is the ultimate provider of funds, wage demands can more easily be pressed by trade unions and conceded even though not justified by profits. Moreover, especially in the basic industries such as coal, rail and steel, wage rises have been granted on a *national* basis. It is suggested that privatisation undermines the ability of militant public sector trade unions to secure high wages and protection of employment through such subsidies from the taxpayer.

5. Creation of a Property-owning Democracy

The sale of shares has been so arranged that they have as broad an appeal as possible both as regards price and allocation. Special encouragement has been given to employees to buy shares. Although many purchasers have subsequently sold, a much wider public has been introduced to share ownership, some 9 million holding shares in 'privatisation' issues.

It is claimed that those who have retained their shares reflect the current movement towards private ownership (e.g. in the success of the sale of council houses), and the private provision of services (e.g. medical and pension schemes).

Difficulties of Privatisation

Earlier we discussed possible reasons for nationalising certain industries. It must be recorded, however, that few of those industries have, in practice, justified the claims of those who advocated nationalisation. Some such as coal and steel, have been over-capitalised, largely because funds were available at relatively low rates of interest or because the industries were given priority for political reasons. This has led to 'crowding-out' of investment in the private sector. Moreover, profit targets have been missed with persistent regularity and, even after the government has written off debts, the sequence of losses is repeated. Nor have the energy industries in particular shown a high sensitivity to such external considerations as air pollution or the protection of the rural environment. Estimates of future demand, e.g. for coal, ships and steel, have been over-optimistic, while monopoly powers have enabled them to base prices on costs with consequent lack of efficiency.

Even so privatisation is no guarantee that these problems will be eliminated, but steps have been taken to introduce some form of competition wherever possible or to introduce devices to ensure that regard is paid to the 'public interest'.

The major difficulty is that while privatisation eliminates direct government involvement in decision-making and responsibility for particular industries, many, especially the 'natural monopolies' (chiefly public utilities) have retained their monopolist and monopsonist positions. This can result in exploitation of consumers by monopoly pricing and inefficiency through lack of competition.

Consequently, where possible, indirect competition has been fostered. For example, gas still has to compete with coal, oil and electricity, while Mercury has been granted a licence to compete in telecommunications with British Telecom. Similarly, Racal's Vodafone is a major competitor in car telephones with British Telecom's Cellnet. The most striking progress has been in the rapid growth of express coach services with reduced fares after competition with the National Bus Company was allowed.

An alternative arrangement has been to grant independence to firms on a franchise basis for a limited period, e.g. regional television companies. Provision is made to prevent mergers and, in reviewing the franchise, consideration can be given to past conduct as regards quality of service and sensitivity to the wishes of the public as well as to the price tendered. The difficulty with this method is that investment may be inhibited by lack of certainty of long-term future operations.

Where some form of competition is difficult to devise, the responsibility for protecting the public interest may rest with a regulatory body. Thus the Office for Telecommunications (OFTEL) acts as a watchdog to ensure fair competition by restraining British Telecom from behaviour to weaken competing firms, e.g. by delaying the installation of other firm's equipment. Furthermore, price rises are limited to 3 per cent *less* than the rate of inflation. This ensures that the consumer receives some benefit of technical improvements, but encourages efficiency in that the company is allowed to retain any additional cost savings.

Another problem in deciding on privatisation is that it is not always easy to separate regulatory, strategically vital or welfare functions from those appropriate to provision through the market. Thus privatisation has been carried out on a pragmatic basis, selecting industries which are making profits but which are not natural monopolies, e.g. British Telecom, British Airways. In contrast, the decision on privatising the Water Authorities was less clear-cut.

Difficulty has also been experienced in fixing a satisfactory price at which the industry's shares are offered to the public. If the offer is oversubscribed, the government is accused of not realising the full potential of public assets; if shares are left with the underwriters, the object of achieving a wide ownership is defeated for eventually they are bought by the institutions. A different method (British Airports Authority) was to offer a proportion of the shares at a fixed price, and the rest by tender. The device of offering a bonus royalty share for every ten shares held for the first three years has not been so successful as hoped for, since many small purchasers have taken their profits by selling.

In spite of these difficulties, however, we must recognise the radical nature and achievement of the Thatcher government. Until 1977 the public sector was growing and this seemed to be generally accepted. What the Thatcher government has done is to reopen the debate on the proper role of the State in the economy, for reducing the size of the public sector has become an end in itself.

Yet not all government activities can be satisfactorily privatised, e.g. education and medical treatment for the majority of people. For these there must be a continuing process of improving their management and accountability by efficiency scrutinies and by monitoring their progress within the financial limits imposed.

21.5 The Problem of Assessing 'Needs'

Differences Between 'Demand' and 'Needs'

Whereas goods and services are supplied by private-sector firms in response to effective demand, government departments and local authorities provide goods and services according to 'needs', a social rather than an economic concept since it cannot be defined objectively. As a result 'needs' are more difficult to assess than demand.

For example, in the private sector owner-occupied houses are built according to the price which people are able and willing to pay for them. *Demand* will depend upon the price of the house, the prices of other goods and services (particularly near-substitutes), the level of income, the distribution of wealth and all the other factors mentioned in Chapter 4 as influencing the conditions of demand. Supply responds automatically to this demand; the number and type of houses supplied depends ultimately on the equilibrium price determined in the market.

In contrast, in providing housing according to *needs* the public-sector authorities regard housing as a social obligation. Consequently, price signals are either inadequate or non-existent. This increases the difficulties of decision-making. Consider the factors which have to be borne in mind in planning a housing programme based on needs. First, the authorities have to estimate the number of households seeking accommodation according to the sizes of the family units, the ages of their members, their location, their preferences as between houses and high-rise flats, and so on. Moreover, since houses are very durable, some consideration has to be given to future requirements. Second, the authorities have to decide arbitrarily on the standard of an adequate housing unit. Third, they have to get the dwellings built, either through a private contractor or by their own direct-labour building organisations.

Subjective Assessment of 'Needs'

The task of estimating needs is made more difficult because there is no price system in operation to provide reliable criteria. Thus rents charged by local authorities are less than the open-market rent. This means that demand exceeds supply, and the only indication of needs thrown up by this restricted-price system is the number of households waiting their turn on the housing list.

And, all the time, the authorities must be conscious of dealing with limited resources – more spent on housing may mean less available for the health services. In the last resort, therefore, the standard of goods and services provided on the basis of needs is determined by the political views of the central government and local councils.

21.6 Pricing Policy in the Public Sector

The problem arises as to how goods and services provided by the public sector are to be paid for. There are three sources of funds: borrowing, taxation and user-charges.

Borrowing

In principle, long-term *government borrowing* should cover only spending on capital items, e.g. the provision of motorways, loans to nationalised industries. In practice, however, the government's yearly expenditure is so vast that what would normally be regarded as capital items are included in current expenditure. For example, the cost of warships built for the Royal Navy is met from the annual sum voted by Parliament for defence expenditure. In any case, from the point of view of control of the economy, it is the *total* spending of the government relative to revenue which is of major significance.

What happens, therefore, is that any excess of public sector expenditure over current income is covered by borrowing – the Public Sector Borrowing Requirement (PSBR). For the past ten years the size of the PSBR has proved embarrassing for government economic policy since additional borrowing increases interest charges on the National Debt besides forcing up interest rates.

Borrowing by the *nationalised industries* follows more conventional lines, being mainly to cover capital expenditure. Loans are obtained from the government and also through the open capital market, including overseas sources. Even so, for some industries, e.g. coal, iron and steel, the government has had to write off accumulated deficits, thereby adding to its own borrowing needs. To control its liability the government has imposed financial limits on borrowing by public corporations.

Local authorities borrow both short-term and long-term, the former mainly to cover shortfalls between revenue and current expenditure, the latter to meet the cost of capital projects, e.g. school and housing construction. However, because the central government must retain overall control of public sector spending, the amount which local authorities can borrow is subject to government approval, and usually in accordance with a projected programme for long-term capital expenditure. Short-term funds are obtained through the money markets, but long-term projects are financed mainly through the Public Works Loans Board, supplemented by issues on the open market.

Taxation

With *community goods*, where free-riders cannot be excluded, no price can be charged, since nobody will pay when private rights to them cannot be granted, e.g. with defence, street lighting and flood control. Here the cost has to be covered entirely from taxation.

Charges can be levied on *collective* and *public goods* (see p. 311, 313). But if their marginal cost is nil, welfare can only be maximised if no charge is levied (see p. 313) e.g. for crossing bridges, visiting museums and public parks.

With *merit* goods in particular, it may be desirable to recognise the uneven distribution of income when considering charges. For instance, charges for essential education would be highly regressive on low-income families with children of school-age. Alternatively, the regressive impact of charges can be modified by price discrimination. Thus low-income families are given housing benefits, while persons over retirement age do not pay prescription charges.

Where demand for a public service is not likely to be too high at zero price, the choice between tax financing and user-charging could reasonably rest on the question, who benefits from the service? Where the community as a whole benefits – e.g. street lighting and by-pass roads – tax-financing is appropriate. In contrast, if certain individuals benefit, the cost is best covered by individual fees (e.g. public tennis courts and swimming pools), or if a particular group benefits, a special levy can be imposed e.g. for street-making charges. User-charges levied on this principle are generally accepted as being fair in that the direct beneficiaries pay.

User-charges

For goods other than community goods, the choice between charges, taxation or a combination of both is governed by technical, economic and political considerations. Thus while motorways could be financed by toll charges, the effect on the traffic flow, especially during vital rush hours, has led the UK to adopt the principle of paying for them from general taxation, both central and local. However, users contribute heavily through motor-vehicle licences and petrol duties, while charges are imposed on motorists in minor matters, such as parking fees. On the other hand, while public transport could be financed from taxation, economic factors favour charges, for elasticity of demand is such that, at a zero price (financed wholly from taxation), demand would be so high that a mis-allocation of resources would result. This applies to many other services, e.g. postal services. National Health prescriptions, dental treatment, sight testing and spectacles.

One other advantage of charges is that they can throw up a valuable guideline for investment. For example, metered water charges reveal demand at the current price and thus provide a datum line from which future demand can be estimated.

In practice, the choice between charges and taxation is likely to be decided politically, especially where income redistribution figures promi-nently. But there are economic constraints on charging less than the free market price for an extended demand may impose a heavy burden on taxation generally, especially as consumers who benefit most press for extensions of the service, as with subsidised public transport and housing. The result of this constraint on taxation is that some form of administrative rationing according to need may have to be imposed, e.g. the 'points' system for allocating Council dwellings. More seriously, hidden rationing may prevail through depreciation of the quality of service provided, e.g. State medical services and education.

In the course of time, methods of covering expenditure may be changed, as the history of road financing illustrates. Tolls were satisfactory when there were few roads, but they had to give way to special levies (for example, Road Fund revenues) as the government assumed responsibility for a rapidly growing road network. Eventually the Chancellor of the Exchequer realised that expenditure on motor vehicles could be a major source of tax revenue, and the idea of the Road Fund was replaced by covering the full cost of roads out of general taxation. However, the attributes of user-charges outlined above suggest that a return to toll financing for motorways and, if technical difficulties can be overcome, the introduction of some form of pricing for the use of urban roads (see Chapter 18) may now be appropriate.

Determining User-charges

Even when it has been decided to cover the cost of a service by charges, difficulties may arise where there are relatively very high fixed costs, e.g. as with public transport, electricity, and natural gas, for supply by competing firms would mean that no one firm could be financially viable. In any case, for technical reasons, a monopoly may be necessary. For instance, only one firm can be given the right to acquire land for laying a gas main or for running a water pipe under the roads, while, for public transport, competing firms cannot be allowed to 'skim' the profitable commuter traffic with none providing a service at other times or on other routes.

The necessity of having to create a monopoly because of decreasing costs or of special technical conditions of supply has strengthened the case for the provision of certain services by local authorities, e.g. passenger transport, or by nationalised industries.

Two major difficulties arise. First, the criterion may be laid down (as with the nationalised industries) that over time revenue should cover costs. It then becomes impossible to produce up to the point where price equals marginal cost – the principle of marginal cost pricing (see p. 176). Thus in Figure 19.2, in order to break even, the price would have to be set at *OC*.

Second, fixed costs may be so high that total cost can never be covered by a single price. Thus in Figure 12.13 where average total cost and demand are as depicted by curves ATC and *PD* respectively, it is impossible to cover total cost at a single price since at all outputs ATC will always exceed average revenue.

In practice the problem has been overcome in three ways:

(i) The difference has been covered by a *subsidy*, either directly, e.g. for city transport, or indirectly, through writing off accumulated deficits from time to time, e.g. for coal and railways.

(ii) A *standing charge* is levied irrespective of units consumed, e..g for electricity. The standing charge goes to meet fixed costs; the price per unit consumed covers marginal costs.

(iii) The industry is allowed to exploit its monopoly position by *price discrimination*. This is possible where different customers, having a different elasticity of demand for the product, can be kept separate, each being charged the price he is willing to pay. By 'charging what the traffic will bear', total revenue is increased. Such price discrimination by consumer category is used by British Rail where, for example, cheap-day trippers, senior citizens and students are charged lower fares than commuters.

The highest degree of charging 'what the traffic will bear' is where the undertaking could discriminate perfectly between every consumer and charge different prices to each (Figure 12.13). While this is impractical, a modified form, 'block pricing', separates additional amounts of the product and charges them at decreasing prices.

Thus in Figure 21.2 total revenue from a single electricity price OP would be $POMR$. But if a consumer is charged OP_1 for the first OM_1 units, OP for the second block of M_1M units, and OP_2 for the third block of MM_2 units, the extra revenue realised is shown by the two shaded areas.

FIGURE 21.2
Increasing Revenue by 'Block Pricing'

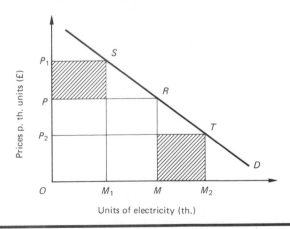

Part IV

Finance and Banking

22 Money and the Rate of Interest

22.1 The Functions of Money

What is Money?

It is possible to exchange goods by a direct swap. But barter, as direct exchange is usually termed, is comparatively rare in the modern world. Consider this advertisement in the *Exchange and Mart*: 'Ever Ready battery portable in exchange for any pedigree bitch up to two years.' The formidable difficulties in the way of such an exchange are obvious.

In an economy where there is a high degree of specialisation, exchanges must take place quickly and smoothly. Hence we have a 'go-between' – money – a common denominator for all goods. The product of specialised labour is sold, that is, exchanged for money, and this money is then used to buy the many different goods and services required.

Anything which is generally acceptable in purchasing goods or settling debts can be said to be money. It need not consist of coins and notes. Oxen, salt, amber, woodpecker scalps, and cotton cloth have at times all been used as money.

In fact, the precise substance, its size and shape, are largely a matter of convenience and custom. But whatever is used, it should be immediately and unquestionably accepted in exchange for goods and services.

Legal Tender

Sometimes an attempt is made to confer acceptability by law. In the United Kingdom, notes have full 'legal tender', in that a creditor must accept them in payment of a debt. But a commodity does not have to be legal tender for it to be money. Nor does legislation ensure that it will be acceptable. In Germany, after the Second World War, cigarettes were preferred to the

333

Reichsbank mark in payment for goods. A commodity will only be accepted as money if people feel confident it will retain its value.

Precious Metals as Money

Most commodities used as money in the past have proved unsatisfactory, especially as exchange economies have developed. Oxen, for instance, were bulky to transport, deteriorated over time, and were costly to store. Moreover, not only were they rarely uniform in size or quality, but they could not easily be divided to purchase goods of small value.

Hence, precious metals eventually replaced other goods as money. Later, in order to simplify transactions, metals were minted into coins of different weights and shapes. The exact amount of money required could now be found by counting (see Genesis 37 v. 25) instead of by weighing (Genesis 23 v. 16).

Paper Money

In England, precious metals and coins were used almost exclusively as money until the middle of the seventeenth century. However, in 1640, Charles I appropriated £130 000 worth of gold held for merchants in the Tower of London. Thereafter gold and silver bullion plate were kept in the strong rooms of the goldsmiths. Eventually receipts for these deposits were accepted in exchange for goods, and so withdrawal of the actual gold and silver became unnecessary.

This was the origin of the bank-note, and paper currency soon began to form an increasing proportion of British money. The paper from which notes are made is comparatively worthless. But people who receive notes are confident that others too will accept them. Notes possess, therefore, the essential characteristic of money – general acceptability. This is true even though, since 1931, it has not been possible in the United Kingdom to exchange notes for gold at the Bank of England.

The Functions of Money

Money, it is usually stated, performs four functions:

(1) It is *a medium of exchange*, the oil, as it were, which allows the machinery of modern buying and selling to run smoothly.

(2) It is *a measure of value and a unit of account*, making possible the operation of a price system and automatically providing the basis for keeping accounts, calculating profit and loss, costing, etc.

(3) It is *a standard of deferred payments*, the unit in which, given stability in its value, loans are made and future contracts fixed. Without

money, there would be no common basis to allow for dealing in debts – the work of such institutions as insurance companies, building societies, banks, and discount-houses. By providing a standard for repayment, money makes borrowing and lending much easier.

(4) It is *a store of wealth*, the most convenient way of keeping any income which is surplus to immediate requirements. More than that, because money is also the medium of exchange, wealth stored in this form is completely liquid: it can be converted into other goods immediately and without cost. Since this 'liquidity' is the most distinctive characteristic of money, we can also define money as anything which confers complete liquidity on its holder. As we shall see, such liquidity results in money's playing an active rather than a merely neutral part in the operation of the economy.

22.2   The Demand for Money

What Do We Mean by the 'Demand for Money'?

Most people would regard a miser as a crank. To the ordinary person, money is wanted not just for counting or to be gloated over, but to be spent on food, clothes, holidays, a car, and all the other things which can be enjoyed. In short, it would seem that money is useful only when we are getting rid of it.

But there is somewhat more to it than that. Money was defined as anything generally acceptable in settling debts. But why is it 'generally acceptable'? Simply because everybody has confidence that other people will accept it *immediately* whenever they wish to buy something. In other words, money is perfectly liquid.

Moreover, no other form of wealth is liquid to the same degree as money. Assets kept in the deposit account of a bank are subject to seven days' notice of withdrawal. Equities and bonds have to be sold before anything else can be bought, and this involves payment of broker's commission and maybe a capital loss. Or, if a house, car, or piano are to be exchanged for something else, it usually means first finding a cash purchaser. Only money can be changed into some other form of wealth without cost or delay.

People want money, therefore, because it is a perfectly liquid asset. It is in this sense that there is a 'demand' for money – *to hold perfectly liquid reserves*. We must now examine more closely why people should want such reserves.

Why People Demand Money

Lord Keynes gives three main reasons for holding money:

1. The Transactions Motive

Both consumers and businessmen hold money to facilitate current transactions.

Most consumers receive the bulk of their income weekly or monthly. On the other hand, payments for food, travel, and pleasure have to be made each day. Thus a part of money income has to be held throughout the week or month to cover these everyday purchases. How much will this be?

Suppose that a man is earning £224 a week, all of which is being spent. He receives £224 on the Friday which begins the week, and by the following Friday he will have nothing left. Thus his average holding of money is £112. Should it now be decided to pay him monthly, and his spending habits remain the same, his average holding of money, either in cash or in his current account a the bank, would rise to £448. In the same way, if his income doubled but was still fully spent, the amount of money he held would double.

Similarly, a businessman requires a money balance because he has to pay wages, purchase raw materials, and meet other current expenses before he sells his goods, i.e. he has a 'cash flow' requirement.

There may be special reasons why the demand for money for the transactions motive may suddenly increase; it does, for instance, at Christmas and holiday periods, or if there is a flurry of activity on the Stock Exchange. Usually the underlying determinants are fairly stable. With consumers, these are the length of the time between successive pay-days and the level of income and prices; with businessmen, it is the size of turnover. It can be seen, therefore, that the community's demand for money for transactions purposes will be roughly in proportion to the size of national income.

It should be noted that the value of transactions for which money is required is much greater than the value of money national income. For instance, if the cost of goods to a shopkeeper (including shop expenses) is £100, and these goods are sold for £110, the income from the transaction is £10, whereas £210 in money was required to effect the necessary exchanges. In addition, money is required for what are basically non-income-creating transactions, e.g. switching securities.

2. The Precautionary Motive

Apart from expenditure on regular, everyday purchases, money is also required to cover events of a more uncertain nature which may easily occur

– illness, accident, unemployment, defects in the car or household appliances, and snap decisions to obtain a cash bargain. Hence both consumers
and businessmen usually keep some extra reserve of cash for a 'rainy day'
or to make a favourable purchase. The amount held will depend mainly on
the outlook of the individual, how optimistic he is both as regards events
and the possibility of borrowing at short notice should the need arise. But,
taking the community as a whole, the amount set aside for the precautionary motive is, in normal times, likely to be tied fairly closely to the level of
national income.

Keynes termed the money held for the transactions and precautionary
motives as 'active' balances. The size of such balances is chiefly dependent
on the level of income.

3. The Speculative Motive

Usually the amount of money in existence exceeds that necessary to satisfy
the demand for active balances. But any surplus must be held by
somebody, for it must be somewhere! Why, however, should people wish
to hold 'idle' balances?

The immediate response of the reader might be 'why not?' As we have
seen, money has no carrying costs (e.g. storage, maintenance) and is
perfectly liquid. Of all assets, only money confers complete manoeuvrabil-
ity.

But holding wealth in the form of money has the disadvantage that *it
does not provide a yield*. (In periods of inflation, there is the added
disadvantage that the value of money is falling, but we can ignore this
complication for the time being.) Furniture, jewellery, works of art, etc.,
afford pleasure; a house can be lived in or rented out. With shares, there is
usually a dividend; with bonds, a fixed rate of interest. There is thus an
oppportunity cost of being liquid – the yield forgone. To simplify, let us
refer to this yield as 'the rate of interest'.

Thus, while people might desire liquidity, they have also to think of the
cost involved. The higher the rate of interest, the greater the cost of
remaining liquid. As the rate rises, so fewer people will be prepared to pay
the 'price'; in other words, they will be tempted out of holding money.
Thus demand for idle balances is closely related to the rate of interest – the
higher the rate, the greater the cost of holding money and so the less will
money be demanded.

But the complete answer is less simple than this. Keynes considered that
the main reason why people hold idle balances is to guard against a
possible capital loss. He termed this the 'speculative' motive.

On any given day it is quite usual for the prices of some securities to rise
while those of others fall. But there are periods when the prices of almost

all securities move in more or less the same direction. To simplify our explanation, however, we shall concentrate our attention on undated government bonds (fixed-interest-bearing securities); this eliminates time and risk complications.

If people think that the price of bonds is going to rise, they will buy bonds now. Should their forecast prove correct, they will make a capital gain. Similarly, if they think that the price of bonds is going to fall, they will sell bonds. Now the lower the price of bonds, the more will people think that the next likely move will be in an upward direction. As the price rises, so more people will gradually come round to the view that the price is so high that a fall is likely to occur. It follows, therefore, that when the price of bonds is low, people prefer bonds to liquidity; but as the price rises, people move out of bonds in order to hold money.

However, the price of bonds varies proportionately but inversely with the rate of interest. Thus if the current rate of interest is $2\frac{1}{2}$ per cent, £100 $3\frac{1}{2}$ per cent War Loan would be worth £140 on the Stock Exchange, but if the rate were 14 per cent it would be worth only £25.

Thus it is possible to relate the demand for money, not only to the price of bonds, but also to the rate of interest. When people are speculating against the future price of bonds they are speculating against the future rate of interest. Hence we can rewrite our original proposition as follows: when the rate of interest is low (the price of bonds is high), people will prefer to hold money; when the rate of interest is high (the price of bonds is low), people will not wish to hold money. This relationship between the current rate of interest and the demand for idle balances is shown in Figure 22.1.

Keynes's term 'speculative' in this situation is rather unfortunate in that it tends to misrepresent the asset-holder's objective. Some 'speculation' must occur where there is an element of uncertainty, and persons in charge of funds, e.g. pension funds, have, as a minimum, to take precautions to avoid capital loss. In doing so they have to take a view as to the future movement of 'bond' prices generally. The bondholder will compare the interest likely to be earned on the bond over a period with the possibility of any loss in its capital value. If the latter outweighs the former, the bondholder will prefer to hold money.

Whereas the level of income, the main factor influencing the demand for money for the transactions and precautionary motives, is fairly stable, people's expectations of the future rate of interest, the determinant of liquidity preference for the speculative motive, is far more liable to change. It is this speculation, therefore, which Lord Keynes considers exercises the dominating influence on the level of the rate of interest.

More recently however, economists have cast doubts on the justification for separating the three motives. Above all, criticism has been levelled at the view that increases in the supply of money will be absorbed in idle speculative balances rather than be spent (see p. 458).

FIGURE 22.1
The Relationship between the Rate of Interest and the Demand for Money

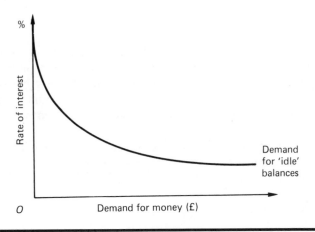

The Demand for Money and Saving

It must be emphasized that the demand for money and saving are quite different things. Saving is simply that part of income which is not spent, and the influences determining it are analysed in Chapter 29. Saving adds to a person's wealth. Liquidity preference is concerned with the form in which that wealth is held. The motives for liquidity preference explain why there is a desire to hold some wealth in the form of cash rather than in goods affording utility or in securities earning income.

22.3   The Supply of Money

The supply of money consists of the following:

1. Coins

These are insignificant in volume, being issued for the convenience of small, everyday transactions.

2. Notes

From the seventeenth century, paper currency began to form an increasing proportion of British money and eventually Parliament had to exercise a strict control over the 'fiduciary issue' – the note issue in excess of the value of gold held by the Bank of England. Today, however, notes, like coins, are regarded as the small change of the monetary system, and so sufficient are always made available for the practical convenience of the public.

3. Bank Deposits

While purchases of everyday goods – bus rides, newspapers, drinks etc. – are usually paid for in coins or notes, about 80 per cent (in value) of all transactions are effected by cheque or credit card. When a person writes a cheque, the bank is instructed to transfer deposits standing in his or her account to the person to whom money is owed. Bank deposits therefore act as money.

A large part of these deposits are 'created' by the bank. How banks create deposits and how they can be controlled will be described in the following two chapters.

Other Forms of Money

There is really no hard and fast dividing line between what is money and what is not. 'True money' confers complete *liquidity* on its holder and, in the last resort, only banknotes and sovereigns do this, for other coins are limited in legal tender. But when considering what serves as money in our economy, the more practical approach is to start from the idea that 'money is what money does'. Is it accepted in payment for goods? If so, it is acting as money. Cheques, as we have seen, are money for this reason, though they represent nothing more than current deposits in a bank. Yet, in advanced economies, cheques form the major part of 'money' in use.

Indeed, although deposits held by bank customers in deposit accounts are subject to seven days' notice of withdrawal, such notice will in practice be waived by the bank with the loss of some interest. Thus sums in deposit accounts can be regarded as 'near' money.

And, in pursuing our argument in the same direction, we find other instruments of credit which, although not 'true money' in the sense that they can be spent anywhere in their present form, nevertheless fulfil the functions of money, if only within a limited sphere. But we must be careful to see clearly how and when they add to the money supply. Deposits can be 'created' by banks only because their clearing system enables them to economise in cash (see Chapter 24). In this the banks hold a unique position; other forms of credit add to the money supply only when they are not covered by cash held idle to an equal amount. Thus, when a person buys a postal order to cover his 'pools' entry, the cash he pays in may be put into circulation again by the Post Office before the order is presented by the pools firm. Thus, to some extent, postal orders can form an addition to the money supply, for they are doing the work of money. This is true, too of other instruments of credit – credit cards (until the bank account is settled), bills of exchange (especially those 'negotiated', i.e. passed on to a third party to settle a debt), trade credit (particularly when deals between firms are allowed to cancel credit, or if the entitlement to payment is transferred to a third party) and book-entry settlements replacing cash (as occurs, for example, when there is a vertical amalgamation of firms.)

'Near' Money

We can carry the above idea further. Any assets possessed can usually be turned into money eventually. Liquidity, therefore, is largely a matter of degree, often depending upon the organisations which exist to make such assets as building society deposits, government securities, shares in public companies and insurance policies liquid. Thus in recent years traders have become more liquid by the development of factor houses to which trade debts can be sold immediate for cash. While assets may have to be sold at some capital loss, they do afford some degree of liquidity to the holder. People possessing first-class shares, for instance, would not need to keep so large a cash balance for the precautionary motive, for they could always sell some in an emergency. Indeed ownership of a house can serve to raise cash through a second mortgage. In short, the existence of 'near' money means that the demand for 'true' money can be correspondingly less. We shall assume that this has been allowed for in our demand for money curves, which therefore depict the demand for 'true' money.

The Official Definition of the Supply of Money

While there may be no hard and fast dividing line between money and certain other assets, the acceptance by the government of the view that the money supply is an important influence in the economy has required that it be defined so that it can be measured and monitored as a guide to policy. There are two broad classifications.

Narrow money refers to money balances which are readily available to finance current spending, that is, for transactions purposes. The chosen monetary target is now M0 which consists of notes and coin held by the public and banks, plus banks' holding of cash (till money) and their balances at the Bank of England.

But, as pointed out above, the distinction between current and deposit accounts is blurred by the ease with which funds can be switched from one to the other. This has to be allowed for if we want an indicator of aggregate monetary expansion in the economy. Thus *broad money* reflects the private sectors holdings of assets which could be converted with relative ease and without capital loss into spending on goods and services. Here the chosen target has been Sterling M3 (£M3) which consists of notes and coin held by the public plus all private sterling deposits (sight and time) held by UK residents in UK banks (see also pp. 580–1).

22.4   The Rate of Interest

We are now in a position to consider the problem postponed in Chapter 15: 'What determines the overall level of interest rates in the economy?' Or, as it is more usually put: 'What determines the *pure* rate of interest, the benchmark around which interest rates fluctuate?'

The Rate of Interest as a Monetary Phenomenon

Income not spent by an individual is said to be 'saved'. But even after some income has been saved, the choice still has to be made as to what assets will be held. This is because assets differ in the qualities they possess, particularly as regards lender's risk, liquidity and yield.

The greater the lender's risk, the higher the yield required, other things being equal. The exact difference in yield between different types of risk will be decided in the market. We can eliminate this complication by concentrating attention at the extreme end where risk of non-payment of interest and capital is nil – government securities.

Liquidity and yield, too, are usually related inversely. Illiquidity has to be compensated for by a high yield. Complete liquidity, conferred only by money, involves total loss of yield.

But since liquidity is a desirable attribute of an asset, money can be regarded as an acceptable way of holding wealth in comparison with interest-yielding assets. Individuals, therefore, have to arrange their portfolios of assets according to the emphasis they put on liquidity as opposed to interest yield. To eliminate the complication of loans of different periods, we shall assume that all securities are undated government stock, which we shall term 'bonds'. Thus there are only two kinds of asset which individuals may hold in storing their wealth – bonds and money (Figure 22.2). The price of bonds will also give us the rate of interest on riskless, undated securities (see p. 338).

On the capital market there will be bonds offered for sale. Some will come out of the existing stock held by people; others will be new bonds arising from current government borrowing, but the former far outnumber the latter. Their price will be determined by demand and supply, just as the price of rubber, tin, wool, cotton and any other commodity is in their respective markets.

People holding money bid on the capital market for the bonds offered. How much money they have will depend upon the total supply of money in

FIGURE 22.2
The Alternative of Holding Wealth as Money or 'Bonds'

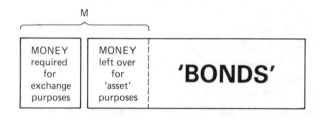

the economy and how much they want to hold for the transactions and precautionary motives. At the end of a day's dealing, all bonds may have changed hands. But this need not be so. If the price of bonds is low, some would-be sellers may prefer to hold on to them. On the other hand, if the price of bonds is high, some would-be purchasers may prefer to retain their money.

But, at the end of the day's dealings, a price will have been found at which people have finished dealing – nobody will wish to exchange more bonds against money, and nobody will wish to exchange more money against bonds. There is equilibrium at the price. This price is the inverse of the current 'pure' rate of interest – the benchmark referred to earlier.

The Keynesian Emphasis on Particular Determining Factors

It can be seen from the above that a change in the demand for money relative to bonds, given the stock of money and of bonds, will bring about a change in the rate of interest. Thus if it becomes less attractive to hold money, the rate of interest will fall.

But changes in the relative quantities of money and bonds, i.e. in the sizes of the stocks of each, will also produce variations in the rate of interest. If, for instance, the quantity of money increased and the demand for money and the stock of bonds remained unchanged, it would mean that more money was being offered against bonds, with the result that the price of bonds would rise. Looked at in an alternative way, the owners of wealth could not, at the given rate of interest, be induced to hold the whole stock of money. Thus there would have to be a reduction in the inducement not to hold money, i.e. in the rate of interest. Similarly, if the quantity of bonds increased, the demand for bonds and the supply of money remaining unchanged, the price of bonds would fall. Looked at in an alternative way, at the given rate of interest owners of wealth could not be induced to hold the whole stock of bonds. Hence the inducement to hold bonds, i.e. the rate of interest, would have to rise. In practice, stocks, both of money and of bonds, are not subject to great variations except over fairly considerable periods of time.

The supply of money is controlled by the government through the banking authorities (see Chapter 25). The supply of bonds coming on to the market comes chiefly from existing stocks of old bonds. In comparison, the flow of new bonds on to the market is small. Current government borrowing, unless it were very large, would therefore have little impact on the rate of interest. Thus, Keynes considered, it is much more realistic to analyse the rate of interest from the point of view of the variable most likely to change over the short period – the demand for money. And here he stressed the role of speculation.

In the market for bonds there will be many people whose main interest will be in their future price. Indeed, as we have seen, Keynes thought that the speculative element dominated all other considerations. If so, then the demand for bonds is largely the result of the present price of bonds. Or, viewing it from the other angle, demand for money is primarily a function of the rate of interest (see p. 338).

Instead of approaching the rate of interest through the demand and supply of bonds, therefore, it is possible to approach it through the demand for and supply of money, the alternative asset.

The demand for money depends upon the level of income (transactions and precautionary motives) and the rate of interest (speculative motive), though modern thought would not separate them completely, for people can economise on active balances when the rate of interest is high. But we can combine the demand for each in a single demand curve, adding the demand for active balances (which is largely unaffected by the rate of interest) to the demand for idle balances (which is influenced by the current rate of interest).

This is shown in Figure 22.3. The demand for money for active balances is shown by the distance of the vertical sections of the demand curve from the y-axis. Thus if income increases from Y to Y_1, the increase in the demand for active balances is equal to the horizontal difference between the two. To this demand for active balances must be added the demand for idle balances – the sloping portion of the curve.

Suppose the supply of money is equal to ON. If the level of income Y, is low, there is less demand for active balances and thus more available for idle balances. The rate of interest is therefore only 8 per cent. With a higher level of income, Y_1, more money is demanded for active balances. This leaves less for idle balances and the rate of interest rises to 12 per cent. And so on.

A smaller supply of money, ON_1 would produce a rate of interest of 12 per cent with Y.

FIGURE 22.3
The Determination of the Rate of Interest

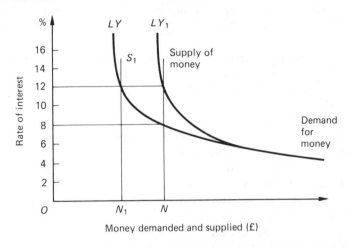

Money demanded and supplied (£)

As we shall see, the level of income is influenced by the level of saving and investment. It is through their effect on income that saving and investment have an impact on the rate of interest.

The Structure of Interest Rates

It merely remains to remove our earlier simplification that the only type of security in existence is bonds. In practice, people can put their money into a range of securities each varying in the degree of liquidity and lender's risk involved. These securities can, however, be regarded as fairly close substitutes for one another, and there will be a rate of return on each depending on the demand for that type of security and the supply of it. These rates will be interrelated because, since they are close substitutes, the demand for one type of security will be affected by the rate of return on the security most similar to it. For instance, a rise in the rate of return on short-dated government stock will cause a movement of funds to it from its immediate close substitutes, such as Treasury bills. This sets up a ripple running through the whole structure of interest rates until eventually equilibrium has been restored. Of course, this ripple could easily start by a change in the demand for or supply of money. It is likely to have its first effect on short-term (three-month) securities, and eventually the long-term rate is brought into line, though this may occur only over a considerable period of time.

Allowing for Inflation

By assuming a stable price level, Keynes was able to concentrate on liquidity and the choice between money and bonds. But when inflation enters into people's expectations, a dynamic element is injected into the situation.

First, we must distinguish between a once-for-all increase in the money supply and a continuous increase. The former lowers the rate of interest, as the analysis suggests. The latter, however, will eventually cause people to expect further inflation. It can occur, for example, by the need to finance a recurrent high PSBR.

Second, the expectation of inflation leads people to widen their choice of wealth-holding assets. Apart from bonds, they can hold equities (shares in companies), real property or simply goods. Like bonds, all these incur a loss of liquidity. But whereas bonds valued in terms of money are bound to fall in real terms with inflation, equities, real property and goods have some degree of inflation-hedge. Thus people are likely to switch to holding these alternatives. Equities and real property also afford a yield, but this now tends to be *below* the rate of interest on bonds because investors bid up their prices to obtain the advantage of the inflation-hedge. This difference is referred to as the 'reverse yield gap'.

Smaller holders of wealth are likely to invest in owner-occupied houses, antiques, works of art and, to some extent, goods in general, for these too are expected to carry a 'yield' through inflation. Thus prices of goods rise; in such circumstances, money *does* matter, as the monetarists claim.

In contrast, bonds are not wanted, and their price falls, people requiring a margin to allow for inflation, i.e. a higher yield. In recent years, therefore, although the supply of money has been increased, the rate of interest has risen – in contrast to the Keynesian theory outlined above!

The Weakness of Keynes's 'Idle Balances' Concept

In his theory of interest Keynes implicitly assumed that, given no change in income, any increase in the supply of money would automatically be absorbed in 'idle' balances where it would be available for spending on capital assets.

But what if extra money encouraged spending on actual goods and services rather than on bonds, because people regard all money simply as a temporary abode of purchasing power? In recent years this has proved to be a distinct possibility and we return to it in Chapter 30.

23 Financial Markets

23.1 The Provision of Liquid Capital

The Need for Liquid Capital

Where expenditure exceeds the receipts of firms or of the government, the deficit has to be bridged by borrowing. Such funds come from the community, which lends savings. Saving represents refraining from spending on consumer goods, thereby setting free resources for the production of capital goods required by firms or for additional expenditure by the government.

Markets for Liquid Capital

The market is the institution which brings borrowers and lenders together, making funds available to firms and the government at a price – the rate of interest. But, because finance is required by different types of firm, by the government and by the nationalised industries, for different purposes and for different periods of time, there is a great variety in the types of loan available and in the institutions providing or arranging such loans. Nevertheless, markets can be classified into two broad groups: (i) the *money markets* (dealing in short-term loans) and (ii) the *capital market* (where medium- and long-term capital is raised). The joint-stock banks (the major source of firms' working capital) and the Bank of England (which exercises a general control over the availability of finance) are discussed in Chapters 24 and 25.

None of the money markets nor the capital market are formal organisations in that buyers and sellers meet regularly in a particular building to conduct business. Instead they are merely a collection of institutions which are connected, in the case of the money markets by dealing in bills of exchange and short-term loans, and in the case of the capital market more loosely – through channelling medium- and long-term finance to those requiring it. Moreover, as we shall see later, within each market there is a high degree of specialisation.

Because it is such a large borrower, the government's requirements tend to dominate these markets, affecting the rates which have to be paid on short- and long-term loans. The complete structure is shown in simplified form in Figure 23.1

23.2   Money Markets

The Discount Market

Bills of exchange are an important source of short-term finance – the commercial bill for firms, the Treasury bill for the government. The discount market comprises the institutions linked by dealings in bills – discount houses, merchant banks acting as acceptance houses, commercial banks and the Bank of England.

It is customary in foreign trade for an importer to be allowed a period of grace, usually three months, to pay for goods. This is arranged through a *commercial bill of exchange*.

Suppose A in London is exporting cars worth £10 000 to B in New York. When he is ready to ship the cars, he draws up a bill of exchange, as shown in Figure 23.2. This is sent to B, together with copies of the shipping documents to prove that the cars are on the ship. B accepts the bill by writing 'Accepted' and his signature across the face of the bill, and then returns it to A. This acceptance of the bill by B is necessary before the original *bill of lading*, the documentary title to the cars, is handed over.

A can now do one of three things: (i) hold the bill until it matures; (ii) endorse the bill and then get a merchant to whom he is indebted to take it in settlement; or (iii) sell the bill, usually to a discount house.

1. Discount Houses

Probably A will choose the latter course. So, after endorsing it, he takes it to one of the *London discount houses*. The exact amount paid for the bill will depend on the length of time to maturity, the prevailing short-term rate of interest and the opinion of the discount house as to B's financial standing. If the bill still has three months to run and the prevailing rate of interest on that class of bill is 12 per cent, the discount house will pay about £9700 for it. The process is known as 'discounting'. Thus, while A quickly regains liqudity by selling the bill, B obtains three months' credit, during which time he will probably sell the cars.

FIGURE 23.1
The Provision of Finance in the United Kingdom

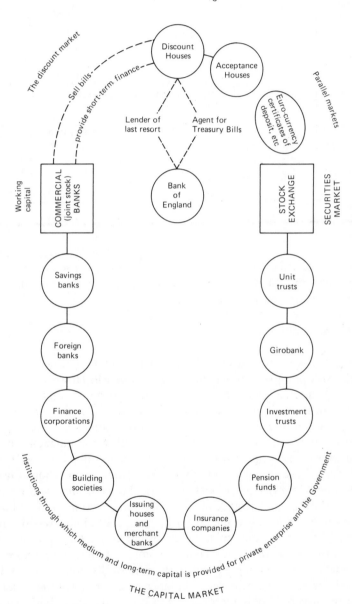

MONEY MARKETS

The discount market

Sell bills

provide short-term finance

Discount Houses

Acceptance Houses

Parallel markets

Euro-currency certificates of deposit, etc

Lender of last resort

Agent for Treasury Bills

Working capital

COMMERCIAL (joint stock) BANKS

Bank of England

STOCK EXCHANGE

SECURITIES MARKET

Savings banks

Unit trusts

Foreign banks

Girobank

Finance corporations

Investment trusts

Building societies

Issuing houses and merchant banks

Insurance companies

Pension funds

Institutions through which medium and long-term capital is provided for private enterprise and the Government

THE CAPITAL MARKET

FIGURE 23.2
A Commercial Bill of Exchange

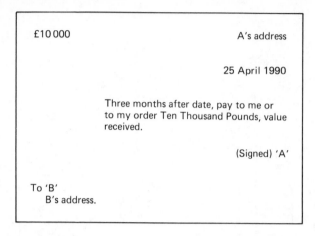

Bills are not usually held for the full three months. Instead after about a month, they are sold in 'parcels' to the commercial banks, who like to have so many maturing each day.

2. Acceptance Houses

If B is a well-known firm of high financial standing, the accepted bill is, from the risk point of view, almost as good as cash. However, as bills are drawn on firms in all parts of the world, little may be known about B. Thus the discount house is either reluctant to discount the bill or will only do so at a high rate of interest. The difficulty can be overcome by getting a firm of international repute to 'accept' responsibility for payment should B default. It is obvious that any firm accepting such a bill must have adequate knowledge of the creditworthiness of the trader upon whom the bill is drawn. Such knowledge is possessed by the *merchant banks*, such as Lazards, Barings and Rothschilds, who commenced as traders but later specialised in financing trade in particular parts of the world. In their capacity of accepting bills such merchant banks are known as *acceptance houses*. For the service, they charge a small commission of about $\frac{3}{4}$ per cent, which is paid willingly because the rate of discount on a 'bank bill', i.e. one bearing the name of an acceptance house, is lower than on a 'trade bill' (a bill accepted only by a trader) or on a 'fine trade bill' (where the merchant is of good standing).

FIGURE 23.3
Operations of the Discount Market

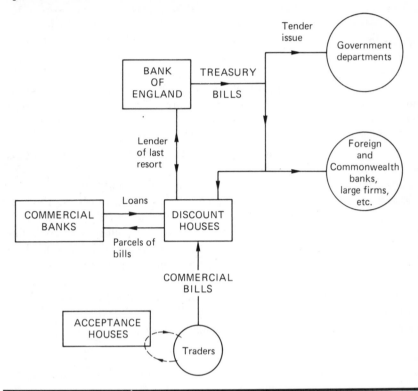

The business of accepting has now declined. Originally this was the result of the diminished use of the trade bill in international trade as the commercial banks competed through the cheaper method of the 'reimbursement credit'. With this, B, an importer in New York, asks his own bank to obtain an acceptance credit in London by making itself responsible for payment. Thus the London bank or acceptor there has only to satisfy itself as to the financial standing of the New York bank. This simpler procedure means that reimbursement credits can be granted at very low rates. Today the commercial bill is mainly used as a means of raising finance internally (see below).

The decline in the use of the commercial bill in international trade initially coincided with a large increase in government borrowing through Treasury bills. A *Treasury bill* is really a bill of exchange drawn by the Treasury on itself, usually for a period of three months (ninety-one days), though occasionally two-month bills (sixty-three days) are issued. Treasury bills are only issued in high denominations and so are primarily for institutional investors.

Recent developments have had repercussions on both the discount houses and merchant banks. The restrictions on the lending powers of the banks before 1971 led to the development of other means of short-term borrowing, e.g. internal commercial bills, local authority bills, certificates of deposit, etc. Furthermore, the government has reduced its dependence on short-term borrowing through Treasury bills. Indeed the PSBR has been *over*funded by the sale of gilt-edged stock, the proceeds being used to purchase internal commercial bills which are more limited than Treasury bills as a liquid asset base.

Dealings in these short-term instruments are now, therefore, the mainstay of the *discount houses*, though they still tender for the reduced weekly offering of Treasury bills.

The functions of the *merchant banks* have also changed. The work of accepting is not required for Treasury bills or for most of the new short-term instruments since the standing of the borrower is generally known to be first class. Instead, they arrange and underwrite new issues, advise on the terms of 'take-overs' and mergers, and pay dividends to stockholders as they fall due. They compete in specialist fields, e.g. property development, in domestic banking business, and also act as trustees and manage investment portfolios. Other functions have resulted from their overseas trading connections. Thus they have important business in the bullion and foreign exchange markets.

3. The Commercial Banks

The commercial banks fulfil two main functions in the discount market – providing the discount houses with funds and holding bills to maturity.

The discount houses do not themselves have sufficient finance to buy all the bills, commercial and Treasury, offered them. They overcome this difficulty, however, by borrowing money from the commercial banks at a comparatively low rate of interest. Then, by discounting at a slightly higher rate, they make a small profit. The banks are willing to lend at a low rate because the loans are of short duration, often for only a day, and need not be renewed if there is a heavy demand for cash from their ordinary customers. For the discount houses, the trouble involved in the daily renewal of this money at call and the slight risk of its non-renewal are compensated for by the comparatively low rate of interest charged.

The commercial banks can earn a higher rate of interest by themselves holding bills for a part of their currency. However, except on rare occasions, they do not bid for them directly but buy them from the discount houses when they still have about two months to run.

4. *The Bank of England*

The Bank of England enters the discount market as follows.

First, it is the agency by which the government issues Treasury bills. This issue is achieved by two methods, 'tap' and 'tender'. Government departments, the National Savings Bank, the Exchange Equalisation Account, the National Insurance Fund and the Bank of England Issue Department, all of which have funds to invest for a short period, can buy what bills they want at a fixed price, i.e. 'on tap'. This price is not published.

The discount houses and other purchasers (such as Commonwealth and foreign banks) can obtain their issue by 'tender'. Every Friday, the Treasury, acting through the Bank of England, invites tenders for a specified amount of bills, usually £100 million each week.

Second, the Bank of England is the 'lender of last resort'. When the discount houses are pressed for money because the commercial banks will not renew their 'call money', the Bank of England will make finance available to them (see p. 377).

Parallel Money Markets

As a result of restrictions placed on bank lending, new markets in short-term loans developed to meet the specific requirements of particular borrowers and lenders. Indeed the existence of such markets has encouraged funds to be lent short-term, since they have made it easier for lenders to regain liquidity.

The following are the most important of these comparatively new markets:

1. *Interbank Deposits*

This is a market bringing together all banks, including merchant banks. British overseas banks and foreign banks, so that those having funds surplus to their immediate requirements can lend to those having outlets for short-term loans or requiring greater liquidity.

2. *Local Authority Deposits*

Local authorities borrow on the open market and are willing to make use of very short-term money. Brokers now exist for placing with them short-term funds of banks, industrial and commercial companies, charitable funds, etc. Such brokers also deal in longer-term local authority bonds.

3. Negotiable Certificates of Deposit

Certificates of deposit enable the banks to borrow for periods from three months to five years. They are like bills of exchange drawn on banks by themselves. For the bank they are for a longer period than an ordinary time deposit, thus facilitating medium-term lending. For the lender they offer a higher rate of interest, while the market in them means that they can be sold whenever cash is required.

4. Eurocurrency Balances

Eurocurrency deposits are simply funds which are deposited with banks outside the country of origin but which continue to be designated in terms of the original currency. The most important Eurocurrency is the dollar. As a result of the USA's continuing adverse balance of payments, branches of European banks have built up dollar balances as customers were paid for exports. These balances are offered to brokers in London (where interest rates have been higher than in New York), and are placed mainly with companies or banks (e.g. Japanese) operating on an international scale to finance foreign trade or investment. While the dollar still dominates the market, other European currencies are now dealt in, chiefly the Deutschmark, the Swiss franc and the Japanese yen.

5. Other Markets

Smaller specialist markets have developed in *finance-house deposits* and *intercompany deposits*. Thus finance houses have obtained funds by issuing bills which are accepted by banks and discount houses. Similarly, in periods of tight credit, firms which are short of finance turn to other companies which temporarily have funds to spare.

23.3 The Capital Market

Whereas the money markets developed to supply short-term finance to trade and the government, industry obtains most of its 'working' capital from the commercial banks (see Chapter 24). But long-term capital for both the public and private sectors is obtained through the capital market. As can be seen from Figure 23.4, this consists of, on the one hand, the suppliers of long-term capital and, on the other, those requiring such capital, the two being connected by a number of intermediaries, usually of a specialist nature. Some of these intermediaries have already been described; here we look briefly at the others.

FIGURE 23.4
The Capital Market

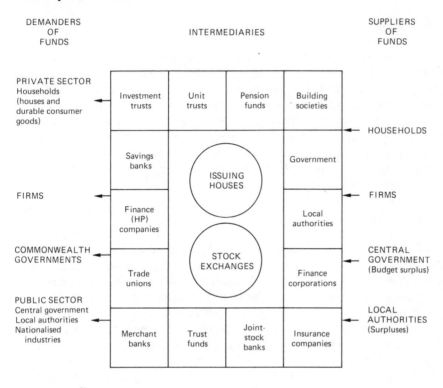

Notes:
(1) Arrows merely indicate direction, not particular intermediaries.
(2) Intermediaries collect relatively small amounts of capital which are channelled to where they are wanted.
(3) Some intermediaries are mainly concerned with old issues.
(4) Issuing houses assist the movement of funds, stock exchanges provide a market in old securities and thus encourage the provision of new funds.

(a) Insurance Companies

Insurance companies receive premiums for insuring against various risks. Some of these premiums, such as those for insuring ships and property, are held only for relatively short periods – having, apart from the profit made, to be paid out against claims. But with life insurance, endowments and annuities, premiums are usually held for a long time before payments are made. Hence insurance companies have large sums of money to invest in long-term securities. These investments are spread over government and other public stocks, the shares and debentures of companies, property and mortgages. Today 'institutional investors', of which insurance companies are the most important, supply the bulk of savings required for new issues.

(b) Investment Trusts

Investors usually try to avoid 'putting all their eggs in one basket' and therefore buy securities in different types of enterprise. However, this requires knowledge of investment possibilities and, above all, sufficient resources. The small investor can overcome these difficulties by buying shares in an investment trust. This invests over a wide range of securities, and after paying management expenses the net yields from these investments are distributed as a dividend on its own shares. Thus investment trusts are not 'trusts' in the legal sense but merely companies formed for the purpose of investment.

(c) Unit Trusts

Unit trusts are a development of the investment-trust idea, but they differ in two main respects. First, they are trusts in the legal sense of the term. Trustees are appointed, while the trust deed often limits investments to a specified range of securities. Second, the aggregate holding is split into many 'units' of low nominal value. Thus even a small investment covers a range of securities, though it is possible to concentrate on a particular group, e.g. minerals, financial securities, property, energy, European growth, capital accumulation, high income, etc.

Many unit trusts have schemes linked with insurance, to which savers subscribe on a regular basis. While most of the funds are used to purchase existing securities, trusts do make capital available for new investment, particularly when they take up 'rights' issues of companies whose shares are already held.

(d) The National Savings Bank

The National Savings Bank operates mainly through Post Offices. It is the government's 'retail' means of collecting relatively small deposits from the public by providing savings facilities of different kinds, e.g. a Savings Book, National Savings Certificates, Savings Bonds and Premium Bonds. Although holdings are limited, these sums, when aggregated, make a significant contribution towards covering the PSBR.

(e) The Girobank

The Girobank carries out all essential banking services, mostly for private customers. Its strength is that it operates through the countrywide network of Post Offices. All records are kept at the computerised centre in Bootle, Lancashire.

(f) Foreign Banks

Branches of over 400 foreign banks are now located in London. Early on they thrived because they were free of the strict credit controls imposed by the government on the clearing banks. Their more recent expansion reflects the development of the international banking system. While they carry out normal banking functions, their work is heavily concentrated on foreign exchange dealing.

(g) Trust, Pension and Trade-union Funds

All these accumulate income which is re-invested in government securities, shares, property, etc.

(h) Building Societies

The main functions of building societies are still the collection of retail deposits from the general public and the granting of long-term loans for the purchase of dwellings for owner-occupation. In recent years they have supplied cheque-books, credit cards and other services to depositors, thereby competing with the banks.

The Building Society Act 1987 allowed them to convert into companies, own property (mostly residential), grant second mortgages and unsecured loans up to 10 per cent of their total lending and to provide a variety of financial services connected with house purchase, e.g. arrange surveys, insurance.

(i) Finance Corporations

Apart from 3i (see p. 108) owned by the clearing banks and the Bank of England, there are a number of similar consortiums, e.g. the Agricultural Mortgage Corporation, the Export Credits Guarantee Department of the Department of Trade, and the British Screen Finance Consortium which provide finance in their specialist fields.

(j) Finance Houses

These were originally independent companies set up to borrow from the public and banks in order to finance hire purchase of both consumer goods and machinery. Today the industry is dominated by the larger commercial banks. For instance, Mercantile Credit is now part of Barclays Bank, and the United Dominion Trust a part of the Trustee Savings Bank.

23.4 Markets in Securities: The Stock Exchange

History

By the second half of the seventeenth century there was a recognisable market for dealing in securities. This was gradually formalised and in 1773 the Stock Exchange occupied its first settled premises and from 1803 published its *Official List* of prices. From 1908 its organisation was based on a separation between 'brokers' and 'jobbers'. Brokers acted on behalf of their clients buying from and selling shares to jobbers, the dealers in the shares. This 'single capacity' requirement was designed to protect clients. Whereas brokers worked on a commission basis, jobbers relied on profits from their dealings.

Recent Influences

This cosy arrangement was jolted in the early 1980s by two developments. First, in 1970 government policy put greater emphasis on extending competition throughout the economy, and the Office of Fair Trading frowned upon fixed commissions as a monopolistic practice. Furthermore, the government was keen to maintain and even develop London's invisible earnings capacity (see p. 527). The abolition of fixed commissions in New York in 1979 made dealing costs for British institutions lower there than in London, while the ending of exchange control in the same year meant that British investors were unhampered in investing in foreign securities.

The second development was technological – the introduction of electronic information and communication systems. This meant that changes in security prices in a dealing centre in one part of the world could be transmitted and indicated visually on screens in other centres. Thus the three leading centres, Tokyo, London and New York, became one market in which, because of the time difference, dealing took place over almost the twenty-four hours of the day.

Thus the pressure was on the Stock Exchange to revise its fixed commission arrangements and to adopt a less parochial outlook. The actual changes took place on 27 October 1986 and produced such an immediate upheaval that it was referred to as 'Big Bang'.

'Big Bang'

The Stock Exchange agreed to end fixed commissions. But since this would have forced many brokers out of business it was necessary to end the 'single capacity' rule and allow members to act in a dual capacity as agents for both clients and dealers. The main dealers are termed 'market-makers'.

Market-makers negotiate their own commissions for buying and selling shares, and on the larger orders put through by the institutions can offer attractive terms. While private investors can also negotiate terms, the size of their business is not deemed profitable by the market-makers and commission rates remain much as they were before 'Big Bang'. This leaves room for brokers to earn a respectable living by acting as the retailer for the private investor, providing a personal contact and offering advice and even research.

Further Developments

'Big Bang' proved to be the catalyst for even more far-reaching developments. The government's desire to establish London as an international trading centre necessitated making dealing costs more competitive and so stamp duty on shares was reduced to $\frac{1}{2}$ per cent. But to trade in competition with the larger Japanese and American firms UK dealers had to have access to considerably more capital in order to carry stocks of securities. Thus firms had to merge or, more usually, were taken over by larger financial institutions, such as the merchant banks.

In this, however, 'Big Bang' simply gave impetus to the movement which was already taking place of linking related services in one firm. We can take the major clearing-banks as an example. As mentioned above, they have already acquired an interest in hire purchase finance and have now followed up their provision of loans for house purchase by acquiring firms of estate agents. The idea has been extended into stock-broking. Market-making, however, has been left to the merchant banks who are less interested in the retail side of finance.

We still refer to the 'Stock Exchange' although dealing is no longer on the 'floor of the House'. Instead there is the Stock Exchange Automated Quotation system (SEAQ) which is the electronic market-place of the London stock market. Information from the sixty-four market-makers on prices and deals made is fed into SEAQ and displayed on screens. This enables the market-maker to quote a selling price and a lower buying price. The difference will be larger when the shares are only dealt in infrequently or where the sale of comparatively few shares can lead to a large fall in price. Unfavourable news, such as a poor monthly balance of payments figure, will cause him to lower prices as a precautionary measure. These new prices would be recorded on the SEAQ screen for the rest of the market.

There are two main markets:

(1) the Stock Exchange, the main market;
(2) the Unlisted Securities Market (USM), a market for smaller companies seeking moderate sums of outside finance.

The government has a strong interest in the integrity of the market but opted for allowing the City to regulate itself rather than impose centralised control. The Secretary of State for Trade and Industry appointed a Securities and Investments Board (SIB) which oversees six Self-Regulating Organisations (SRO) and City dealers have to belong to one of these. The Stock Exchange, as a SRO, issues guidelines to members and ensures that these rules are adhered to.

Economic Functions

As the two main UK markets in securities are still subject to the discipline and regulations of the Stock Exchange Council, both are included under the omnibus term of 'the Stock Exchange'.

Critics of the Stock Exchange tend to ignore its real functions and to concentrate on its speculative aspects. It is true that the facilities offered do provide openings for speculation. The fortnightly account allows a speculator to buy securities at the beginning and sell within fourteen days without ever having to put up any money. A speculator who buys securities because he thinks the price will rise is said to be a 'bull'; he hopes to sell them at a profit before the end of the account. On the other hand, a 'bear' sells securities he does not possess because he expects the price to fall before they have to be delivered.

The difficulty concerning speculation is that both optimism and pessimism are contagious and so the market becomes extremely susceptible to both overconfidence and panic. Indeed, expectations are 'self-fulfilling': people who expect the price of securities to rise bid for them, thereby sending up their price, and vice versa. The result is that the prices of stocks and shares may be written up or down not through changes in their earnings prospects but simply through waves of confidence or mistrust.

Even so, we must not forget that some speculation may be advantageous. Expert professional operators tend to steady prices through their function of holding stocks (see below). This also permits securities to be bought and sold at any time, thereby making them more liquid. The great difficulty occurs in distinguishing harmful speculation from genuine investment, for with all investment there is a certain element of risk. In any case the magnitude of the speculative business must not be overestimated. Most purchases represent genuine investment conducted on behalf of investment trusts, insurance companies, pension funds, building societies and private individuals.

The truth is that, for the following reasons, an organised market in securities is an indispensable part of the mechanism of a capitalist economy.

1. It Facilitates Borrowing by the Government and Industry

If people are to be encouraged to lend to industry and the government by the purchase of securities, they must be satisfied that they will subsequently be able to sell easily those investments which they no longer wish to hold. Such an assurance is afforded to any holder of a fairly well-known security by the Stock Exchange, for it provides a permanent market bringing together sellers and buyers.

Thus, indirectly, the Stock Exchange encourages savers to lend to the government or to invest in industry. Indeed, if a new issue receives a Stock Exchange quotation, the chances of its success are considerably enhanced.

2. Through the Market-makers, It Helps to Even Out Short-run Price Fluctuations in Securities

By holding stocks of shares, a dealer provides in the short run a buffer against speculation by outsiders. This is because he does not merely 'match' a buyer with a seller but acts like a wholesaler, holding stocks of securities. Since he usually specialises in dealing in certain securities, he obtains an intimate knowledge of them. Thus when the public is pessimistic and selling, he may be more optimistic in his outlook and consider that the drop in price is not likely to continue. He therefore takes these securities on to his book. Similarly, when the public is rushing to buy he will, when he considers the price has reached its zenith, sell from his stocks. The effect in both cases is to even out the fluctuations in price, for, in the first case, he increases his demand as supply increases, and, in the second, he increases supply as demand increases.

3. It Advertises Security Prices

The publication of current Stock Exchange prices enables the public to follow the fortunes of their investment and to channel their savings into profitable enterprises.

4. It Protects the Public Against Malpractices and Fraud

With dealers acting in a dual capacity, the previous safeguard of a client that his broker acted solely on his behalf was lost. Under the new arrangements there are two safeguards, the open display of prices on the SEAQ screen and the regulations of the Stock Exchange Council as a SRO. The Council insists on a high standard of professional conduct from its members. Should any authorised member default, the investor is indemnified out of the Securities Association Compensation Fund.

The *Official List* of securities indicates that the Stock Exchange considers shares are reputable. Permission to deal is withdrawn if any doubts arise about the conduct of a company's affairs.

5. It Provides a Mechanism for the Raising of Capital by the Issue of Securities

While the Stock Exchange is essentially a market for dealing in 'old' securities, the success of a new issue to raise capital is enhanced if a promise can be made of a Stock Exchange quotation for it. More directly, brokers and dealers will actively arrange for certain clients to provide capital for firms wishing to expand (see p. 108).

6. It Reflects the Country's Economic Prospects

The movement of the market acts as a barometer which points to the economic prospects of the country – whether as 'set fair', or otherwise!

24 Clearing Banks

24.1 Types of Banks in the UK

Banks vary, both in the type of function they perform and in size. They can be classified as:

1. The Central Bank

This is the Bank of England, which, on behalf of the government, exercises ultimate control over the financial system (see Chapter 25).

2. The Commercial or Joint-stock Banks

These banks are dominated by the 'Big Four' (Lloyds, Barclays, the National Westminster and the Midland) but have now been joined by the Trustee Savings Bank. They operate through a network of branches throughout the country. Their importance in the financial system stems from the fact that most of their business is conducted by way of cheques which, through their central steering arrangements, enables them to economise in cash and so 'create' credit (see pp. 365–7).

3. Merchant Banks (see pp. 350–2).

4. Foreign and Commonwealth Banks Having Branches in the UK
(see p. 357).

5. The National Savings Bank (see p. 356).

6. The Girobank (see p. 356).

The joint-stock clearing banks are the subject of the rest of this chapter.

24.2 The Creation of Credit

The Cheque System

Banks are companies which exist to make profits for the shareholders. They do this by borrowing money from 'depositors' and relending it at a higher rate of interest to other people. Borrowers are private persons, companies, public corporations, the money market and the government. The more a bank can lend, the greater will be its profits.

People who hold a current account at a bank can settle their debts by cheque. This is a very convenient form of payment. Cheques may be sent safely through the post, can be written for the exact amount, obviate carrying around large sums of money and form a permanent record of payment.

Credit cards possess somewhat similar attributes, and in addition can be used to pay for goods ordered over the phone but usually only up to a stipulated limit.

But the use of cheques and credit cards, is, as we shall see, advantageous to banks. Thus, to advertise their business, to induce customers to pay by cheque rather than by cash, and to encourage people to keep sums of money with them, banks perform many services outside their main business of borrowing and lending money – keeping accounts, making standing-order payments, providing night-safe and cash dispenser facilities, paying bills by credit transfers, purchasing securities, transacting foreign work, storing valuables, acting as executors, etc.

The Cheque as a Substitute for Cash

Cheques lead to a reduction in the use of cash. Suppose that I have paid £1000 into my banking account. Imagine, too, that my builder banks at the same branch and that I owe him £500. I simply write him a cheque for that amount, and he pays this into the bank. To complete the transaction, my account is debited by £500, and his account is credited by that amount. What it is important to observe, however, is that in the settlement of the debt no actual *cash* changes hands. A mere book entry in both accounts has completed the transaction.

Perhaps my builder will, towards the end of the week, withdraw some cash to pay workers' wages. But it is likely that most payments, e.g. for building materials, petrol and lorry servicing, will be by cheque. Similarly, while from the £500 still standing to my account I may withdraw some cash to cover everyday housekeeping expenses, the probability is that many of my bills, e.g. club subscription, half-yearly rates, hire-purchase instalments on the car, mortgage repayments, will be settled by cheque or by transfer directly from my account. Furthermore, even where cash is withdrawn, it is often compensated for by cash being paid in.

With the development of the cheque system, the proportion of cash which is required for transactions has decreased. Let us assume a simple model in which the banks operate free of government control but have discovered that in practice only 10 per cent of their total deposits need be retained in cash to cover all demands for cash withdrawals. In short, only £100 of my original deposit of £1000 is needed to form an adequate cash reserve.

The Creation of Credit

It is obvious, therefore, that £900 of my original cash deposit of £1000 could be lent by the bank to a third party without me or anybody else being the wiser. What is not quite so obvious is that the bank can go much further than this – and does!

Let us assume that there is only one bank and that all lending is in the form of advances (see p. 369). When a person is granted a loan by a bank manager, all that happens is that the borrower's account is credited with the amount of the loan, or, alternatively, he is authorised to overdraw his account up to the stipulated limit. In other words, a deposit is created by the bank in the name of the borrower.

When the loan is spent, the borrower will probably pay by cheque. If this happens, there is no immediate demand for cash. There is no reason, therefore, why the whole of my cash deposit of £1000 should not act as the safe cash reserve for deposits of a much larger sum created by the bank's lending activities. But the bank must not overdo this credit creation. To be safe, our model has assumed, cash must always form one-tenth of total deposits. This means that the bank can grant a loan of up to £9000. Because it is the only bank, there is no need to fear that cheques drawn on it will be paid into another bank and eventually presented for cash. In general, the deposit to cash multiplier equals

$$\frac{1}{\text{the reserve asset ratio}}$$

The process of credit creation is illustrated in Figure 24.1. X pays £1000 in cash into the bank. This allows the bank to make a loan of £9000 to B who now settles debts to C and D of £4000 and £5000 respectively by sending them cheques. These cheques are paid into the bank. C withdraws cash rather heavily, £700; but this is compensated for by D, who only withdraws £200 in cash. This leaves £100 cash – enough to cover the average withdrawal which X is likely to make. At the same time as these cash withdrawals are being made, other cash is being paid in, thereby maintaining the 10 per cent ratio.

In practice, there are many banks, but for the purpose of credit creation they are virtually one bank, because they are able to eliminate a large demand for cash from each other by their central clearing arrangements.

FIGURE 24.1
How a Bank Creates Credit

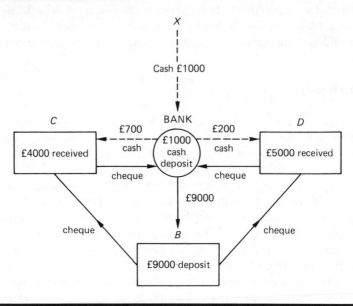

Moreover, banks keep in line with one another as regards their credit creation. Were one bank to adopt, say a 6 per cent cash ratio, it would find that because its customers were making such a large volume of payments to persons who banked elsewhere, it would be continually called upon to settle a debt with the other banks in cash at the end of the day's clearing, so that its cash reserve would fall below the safe level.

The Effect of Lending on the Bank's Balance-sheet

Suppose that the receipt of the £1000 in cash and the loan to *B* are the sole activities of the bank so far. We ignore shareholders' capital. Its balance sheet would then be as follows:

Liabilities	£	*Assets*	£
Deposits:			
deposit account	1 000	Cash in till	1 000
current account	9 000	Advances	9 000
	10 000		10 000

The advance to *B* is an asset; it is an outstanding debt. On the other hand, *B*'s account has been credited with a deposit of £9000 – just as though *B* had paid it in. It can be seen, therefore that *every loan creates a deposit*.

We have assumed that *X* has paid to £1000 into his deposit account. Such deposits are referred to as 'time deposits' since technically they are subject to a seven-day withdrawal notice (though banks usually waive this subject to loss of interest). The loan to *B* would be credited to *B*'s current account and, since it is available for immediate spending, is known as a 'sight deposit'.

24.3   Bank Lending

Considerations Determining a Bank's Lending Policy

In practice, the structure of the bank's assets is more varied than that above. This can be explained as follows.

Creating deposits in order to lend at a profit entails certain risks. In the first place, the loan may not be repaid. Second, and more important, there may be a run on the bank for cash, *X* (the original depositor) wishing to withdraw the £1000, or *B*, *C* and *D* requiring between them an abnormally large amount of cash. Any suggestion that the bank could not meet these demands would lead to such a loss of confidence that other depositors would ask for cash, and the bank would have to close its doors.

Hence, although a permanent cash reserve ratio must always be retained, a bank must have a second and third line of defence so that in an emergency it can raise cash easily and quickly. This means, therefore, that it must not lend entirely by means of advances, for these are usually required by the borrower for a minimum of six months and even longer. Some loans must, if possible, be made for a shorter period – even for as little as a day at a time.

On the other hand, the shorter the period of the loan, the lower will be the rate of interest that the bank can charge. Yet it wants profits for its shareholders to be as high as possible.

The bank is therefore limited in its lending policy both quantitatively and qualitatively. Not only must credit be restricted to a multiple of the liquid reserves, but it must afford adequate *security, liquidity* and *profitability*.

As regards security, the bank endeavours not to lend if there is any risk of inability to repay. Default on a loan represents a serious error of judgement by the bank manager. While it usually requires collateral, e.g. an insurance policy, the deeds of a house, or share certificates, this is regarded more as a weapon to strengthen its demand for repayment against an evasive borrower than as a safeguard against default. Collateral therefore really assists liquidity; if there were a risk of outright default, the bank would not lend.

Liquidity and profitability pull in opposite directions – the shorter the period of the loan, the greater the bank's liquidity, but the less it will earn by way of interest. The difficulty is resolved by a compromise: (a) loans are divided among different types of borrower and for different periods of time; (b) the different types of loan are kept fairly close to carefully worked out proportions. In short, the bank, for financial prudence, maintains a 'portfolio' of assets.

The Distribution of a Bank's Assets

How in practice a bank reconciles the aim of liquidity and profitability can be seen by studying its sterling assets. This is possible because, apart from its cash, buildings and goodwill, loans represent its sole assets. Just as 'sundry debtors' appears on the asset side of a firm's balance sheet, so debts outstanding to a bank represent assets to it. The position is shown in Figures 24.2 and 24.3.

Cash covers coin and notes in its tills to meet customers' demands and its cash reserve at the Bank of England (see p. 373).

Bills, which are Treasury bills, local authority and trade bills, are obtained chiefly from the discount houses (though some may be discounted directly for customers) and are held for the remainder of their currency – usually two months.

FIGURE 24.2
The Nature and Distribution of a Bank's Main Assets

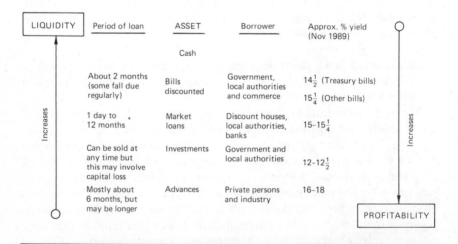

FIGURE 24.3
The Pyramid of Bank Credit

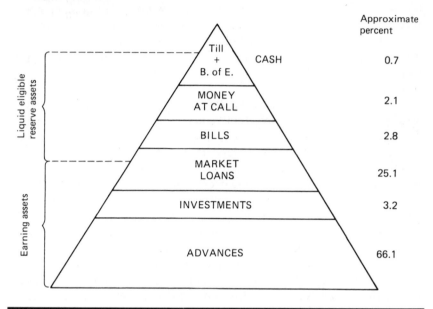

Approximate
percent

Till + B. of E. — CASH	0.7
MONEY AT CALL	2.1
BILLS	2.8
MARKET LOANS	25.1
INVESTMENTS	3.2
ADVANCES	66.1

Liquid eligible reserve assets

Earning assets

Market loans consist mainly of: (a) money at call and short notice which enables the discount houses to discount bills and hold them for a month or so before passing them on to the banks (see p. 352); (b) loans of less than a year to local authorities; (c) certificates of deposit (see p. 354); (d) short-term loans to other monetary authorities.

Investments are medium- and long-term government securities bought on the open market.

Advances, to nationalised industries, companies and personal bor- rowers, are the most profitable (1 to 3 per cent above base rate) but also the least liquid of all the bank's assets. The main object of advances is to provide the working capital for industry and commerce. The type of loan preferred is 'self-liquidating' within a period of about six months. A good example is a loan made to a farmer, who borrows to buy seed and fertilisers and to pay wages, and repays the loan when the harvest is sold. Similarly, a manufacturer may borrow to employ additional labour and raw materials just prior to Christmas in order to increase production. When payment is received for those goods he can repay the overdraft. Borrowers are often allowed to 'roll over' their overdrafts.

Banks also make a large number of 'personal loans', usually modest sums to cover exceptional items of personal expenditure. Repayments are spread over the term of the loan, though interest is charged at an agreed rate on the full amount of the loan for the whole of the period.

At one time banks refrained from providing long-term capital leaving this to the capital market. In recent years, however, they have competed successfully in financing such long-term projects as the building of additional factory accommodation and the purchase of farms and owner-occupied houses. These fixed assets are the security required, though the bank's main consideration is whether or not the venture is likely to succeed.

It must be emphasised that, apart from cash and bank buildings, these assets are covered only by credit created by the bank. For example, Treasury bills and government securities are paid for by cheques which will increase the accounts of the sellers. If they are new issues, there is an addition to the government account at the Bank of England; if they are old issues, the bank is virtually taking over from somebody else a loan already made to the government. In writing these cheques, the bank increases its liabilities, for book-entry deposits have to be created to cover them. This 'pyramid of credit', created to buy earning assets and to make loans upon a minimum liquid assets basis, is shown in Figure 24.3.

Furthermore, apart from maintaining its prudent cash ratio, the bank can only expand credit up to the limit in response to a new cash deposit if: (a) existing cash was already fully used to create credit; (b) no cash leaked out of the clearing banks as a result of a loan; (c) there is a demand for loans.

24.4 Modification of the Cash-ratio Approach

The Importance of Liquid Assets as a Whole

Our explanation of how a bank creates credit has followed traditional lines: credit bears a fixed relationship to the cash reserves. This approach is the easiest to understand and underlines the main principles involved.

However, while the basic principles of credit creation still hold true, some modification is necessary to allow for modern banking practice.

Today, banks are more concerned with the general liquidity position when deciding on their lending policy than with one item, cash. This tendency of cash to lose significance originally stemmed from the introduction of the Treasury bill, which, through government support, became almost as good as cash. Improved markets for loans e.g. the parallel money markets described in Chapter 23, also increase liquidity and, as a result, such loans can be regarded as 'near money'.

External Limitations on the Banks' Lending Policy

Indeed, the monetary authorities (that is, the Bank of England acting as agent for the Treasury) now regard cash simply as the small change of the monetary system, and so they vary it according to the needs of trade.

It follows, therefore, that, if the authorities wish to control the amount of credit which can be created by banks, their attention will have to be directed to the size of the total assets which the banks hold. It is to these external limitations on the banks' lending ability to which we now turn.

25 The Bank of England

For the past 200 years, the Bank of England has followed policies which have placed the needs of the country as a whole before its own financial interests. Nationalisation in 1946 merely formalised its position as a 'central bank' – the institution which, on behalf of the government, exercises the ultimate control over the policies of the joint-stock banks and other financial institutions. In the words of the Radcliffe Report, 'The Bank of England stands as the market operator between the public sector (to which it belongs) and the private sector'.

25.1 Functions of the Bank of England

We need deal only briefly with most of the Bank's functions.

1. It Issues Notes

The Bank of England is the only ultimate source from which the private sector can obtain cash. The *Fiduciary Issue* (the amount by which the note issue is allowed to exceed the Bank's holding of gold) has ceased to have any relevance. Since 1939, the gold reserves of the Bank have been held in the Exchange Equalisation Account, and thus today the notes issued are backed almost entirely by Treasury bills, other marketable government securities and commercial bills.

While in England and Wales the Bank of England is the sole note-issuing authority, Scottish and Northern Ireland banks can issue their own notes, though most of these have to be covered by Bank of England notes.

2. It is the Government's Banker

The government has always been the most important customer of the Bank of England. As a result the Bank has acquired the functions of a 'central bank' (see later). But it also performs many tasks for the government which spring from the normal banker–customer relationship:

(*a*) It keeps the central government account (the Consolidated Fund and the National Loans Fund) and the account of many government departments.
(*b*) It gives overnight assistance by means of 'Ways and Means' advances if the account goes temporarily 'into the red'.
(*c*) It manages the government's borrowing through the issue of Treasury bills and government stock. This involves arranging new issues and conversions, paying interest, keeping the registers, and recording transfers.
(*d*) It advises the government on financial matters.

3. It is the Banker's Bank

The next most important customers of the Bank of England are the joint stock banks who use the Bank very much as a private customer uses his bank. In particular, they:

(*a*) hold about half their cash reserves at the Bank in order to: (i) provide a working balance to set off the net payment which may have to be made to other banks as a result of the day's clearing; and (ii) to conform with the Bank's 0.45 per cent cash to liabilities requirement;
(*b*) draw cash from their balances at the Bank as required;
(*c*) take advice on financial matters from the Bank.

4. It Manages the Exchange Equalisation Account (see p. 544)

5. It Holds the Gold and Foreign Currency Reserves

The importance of these reserves is that, for a time, they can take the strain when sterling is under pressure. Until 1979 the reserves were protected by various degrees of exchange control administered by the Bank of England. Today, the Bank mainly operates by varying the UK short-term interest rate (see p. 584) but, where necessary, it will also arrange loans from other central banks.

6. It has Financial Responsibilities Internationally

(*a*) The Bank of England maintains close contact with other central banks and monetary authorities and cooperates with them chiefly with the aim of bringing greater stability to international monetary affairs.
(*b*) It provides banking services for the central banks of non-sterling countries, e.g. holds and manages their holdings of sterling.

(c) It participates in the work of certain international financial institutions, such as the Bank for International Settlements, the International Monetary Fund, the International Bank for Reconstruction and Development.

7. It Supervises the Banking System

Regulations of the Bank of England are designed to ensure stability in the banking system. All recognised banks must submit monthly acounts to satisfy the Bank that they can meet depositors' demand for cash. To provide the Bank with income to finance its supervisory duties, banks with eligible liabilities of £10 million or more have to deposit with it 0.45 per cent of such liabilities interest free.

Furthermore, only bills accepted by approved banks – eligible banks – are eligible for rediscount by the Bank (see below).

8. It Manages the Monetary System of the UK in Accordance with Government Policy

The Bank of England is the central bank of the UK. It is therefore responsible for seeing that the monetary system of the country is working in harmony with government economic policy. In broad terms, this means varying the cost and availability of credit.

Where households and firms can obtain credit on relatively easy terms, the demand for goods (both consumer and producer goods) will normally increase. If there is unemployment, this is a good thing, for the economy will expand and idle resources be put to work (though there is some disagreement as to whether this will be permanent – see pp. 455–60). But expansion may be accompanied by rising prices and this becomes more serious as we approach full employment.

The Bank of England, therefore, has frequently to adjust the supply of credit to the prevailing economic situation as seen by itself and the Treasury, though the latter will have the last word. We now examine how the Bank seeks to achieve this.

25.2 Principles of Monetary Control

Approaches to Monetary Policy

When the Conservative government took over in 1979, greater emphasis was placed on monetary policy as a means of controlling inflation (see pp. 578–84).

Monetary policy can be approached in two main ways: (1) by controlling the supply of credit quantitatively – that is, restraining lending by financial institutions; (2) by controlling the *demand* for credit by manipulating its price – that is, varying the rate of interest.

The Old System of Competition and Credit Control (CCC)

The system of CCC initiated to 1971 put the emphasis on controlling the supply of credit quantitatively. There were four main weapons:

1. The Minimum Reserve Assets Ratio

The foundation of the policy rested on the ability of the Bank of England to dictate to the banks and other lending institutions their minimum liquidity ratio.

Each bank was originally required to observe a minimum reserve ratio of $12\frac{1}{2}$ per cent of 'eligible reserve assets' (liquid assets, as defined by the Bank of England) to 'eligible liabilities' (broadly net bank deposits).

2. Open Market Operations

By buying or selling government securities on the open market, the Bank of England can vary the ability of the banks to create credit. Suppose it sells long-term securities. The increase in the supply offered lowers their price (that is, raises the rate of interest) until the total offering has been bought by the banks or by their customers. But cash will be necessary to pay for them, and so the banks' cash balances at the Bank of England fall. In other words, the liquid reserve assets held by the banks are reduced and, if previously banks had made loans to the maximum possible extent, they would be forced to squeeze their advances, the exact amount depending on the credit multiplier.

Alternatively, the Bank of England may put the pressure on the short end of the market by varying the weekly offer of Treasury bills. Inasmuch as these bills are bought initially outside the banks, the cash balances of the bank's customers can be made to fall, and hence the cash held by the banks likewise falls.

3. Special Deposits

The supply of credit can be influenced by calls for special deposits, requiring banks to deposit with the Bank of England a prescribed percentage of their total eligible liabilities. Such special deposits reduce the bank's liquid assets and thus the bank's ability to make loans.

4. Minimum Lending Rate

The minimum lending rate (MLR) was the rate of interest at which the Bank of England would help the discount houses as lender of last resort. Although the rate was announced each Thursday, it was only changed for compelling reasons and so its effect was to give some stability to interest rates in general.

At various times the above weapons were supplemented by *requests* to the banks to restrict or discriminate in their lending, *funding operations* to reduce overall liquidity by converting government short-term borrowing into long-term debt, and *supplementary deposits* (the 'corset') which required a bank whose interest-bearing deposits had risen faster than a specified rate to place with the Bank of England a given proportion of the excess.

The Present System

The main purpose of quantitative controls under CCC was to reduce the need to raise interest rates, at least in the short term, by causing banks to ration their lending. In practice, quantitative controls only postponed the rise in interest rates needed. At the same time, they not only tended to reduce competition but caused funds to move from the controlled banking sector to uncontrolled institutions, such as the merchant banks, foreign banks and finance houses. Furthermore, the creation of money substitutes, e.g. the commercial bill of exchange, weakened the role of sterling M3 as a monitor of the money supply. Above all, quantitative controls ceased to be effective in 1979 when exchange controls were abolished for funds could now be obtained from overseas sources, e.g. through the Eurocurrency market.

Instead of following a monetary base policy of requiring a $12\frac{1}{2}$ per cent ratio of eligible reserve assets to eligible liabilities, the Bank now adjusts the supply of credit by influencing the short-term rate of interest. But with the ending of exchange control and the internationalisation of the market in finance, the actual rate is *determined* in the wholesale markets, such as the large interbank market. Only when the market is short of cash does the bank have the whip hand, as a *lender of last resort*. This arises as follows:

Because the operations of financial markets depend largely on the creation of credit, any jolt to confidence can have a cumulative destabilising effect. It is recognised, therefore, that the Bank of England will always act to prevent the financial chaos which would otherwise result. For example, it supported the BP privatisation share price following the stock market crash in October 1987.

FIGURE 25.1
The UK Banking Sector

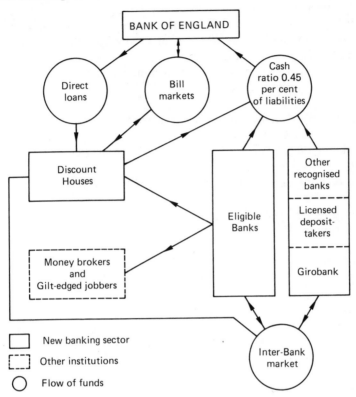

Although its earlier practice of regularly announcing a MLR has now been discontinued, it has the right to indicate in advance the minimum rate at which it will lend for a short period ahead. The kind of situation where this could happen is when a major economic package is announced where interest rates are an important element in the changes envisaged.

Normally, the Bank operates on a daily basis and without prior warning through the discount market. If the discount houses are short of cash to repay money at call, they will have to offer bills, either Treasury bills or eligible bank bills, to the Bank of England and state their price. The Bank of England aims to keep interest rates within an undisclosed band which is moved from time to time in accordance with policy considerations. If, therefore, the Bank does not like the price, it turns them down and the market responds to the Bank's signal, the commercial banks' base rates being adjusted accordingly. Thus while it is the market which proposes short-term interest rates, it is the Bank which has the final word. Twice a day the Bank announces the rates which it has bought and sold bills. The Bank publishes a list of banks and other institutions whose bills are eligible for discount at the Bank.

Although *special deposits* have been retained and extended to all institutions with eligible reserves of over £10 million, they are only called for in most exceptional circumstances.

In conclusion it should be noted that monetary policy now embraces a wider monetary sector covering:

(a) all recognised banks and licensed deposit-takers;
(b) the National Giro Bank;
(c) banks in the Channel Islands and Isle of Man that opt to joint the cash-ratio scheme;
(d) the banking department of the Bank of England.

How monetary policy is in practice used to regulate the economy is described on pp. 578–86.

Part V

The Level of Activity

26 From Micro- to Macro-Economics

26.1 Differences in the Methodology of Micro- and Macroeconomics

The Choice of Goods and the Allocation of Resources

The production-possibility curve in Figure 2.2 shows that: (a) we can choose between manufactured goods and agricultural products in employing our limited resources; and (b) unless we produce a combination of manufactured goods and agricultural products which lies on the production possibility curve, some of our limited resources are being wasted.

So far we have concentrated our analysis on the choice of goods and services (that is, where on the production-possibility curve we wish to be) and how resources are allocated to produce them. We have regarded the economy as being divided into a number of comparatively small parts, and have examined how each part functions – the demand of consumers in a particular market for a particular good, the behaviour of the individual firm in supplying that good, the supply of a given commodity to a market at different periods of time, and so on.

Since we are dealing with only a small part of the economy, we can assume that any change in a particular variable, e.g. the demand for pencils or tennis balls, the supply of potato crisps or kettles, and so on, does not give rise to any *significant* feedback on the operation of the economy as a whole. *Microeconomic* models simplify, therefore, by assuming 'other things being equal' (*ceteris paribus*) when isolating the effects of a change in one variable.

The Overall Level of Activity

Until the 1930s, economics concentrated on the problem of allocating resources according to consumers' choice of goods and services. Little

381

attempt was made to explain why some productive resources remained unemployed; that is, in terms of Figure 1.2, production was taking place between the origin and the production possibility curve, say at *A*.

The Classical economists held that such unemployment would eventually be eliminated through the market by the operation of the price system. If there were unemployed factors of production, competition between them would lead to a fall in their price, and this would make it profitable to employ them.

Experience of unemployment towards the end of the nineteenth century, and particularly in the 1930s, convinced economists that this need not happen. John Maynard Keynes highlighted the major cause – a breakdown in the flow of money income (see his *The General Theory of Employment, Interest and Money*, Macmillan, 1936). The basic elements of this theory are outlined in Chapter 28. Here we concentrate on the nature of the model which has to be used.

In brief, general unemployment can occur because the flow of receipts which firms obtain from spending by households on goods and services at *A* (Figure 26.1), falls short, for some reason or the other, of the payments, *P*, that firms have made to households for the resources used in producing those goods.

But here we are looking at the receiving and spending of income for the economy as a whole. Why this requires a different method of model-building will now be explained.

FIGURE 26.1
Real and Money Flows in an Economic System

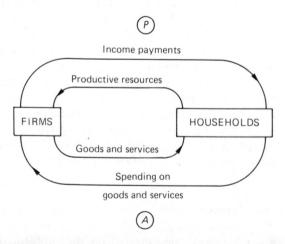

26.2 Simplifying with Macroeconomic Models

The Difficulties of Macroeconomic Analysis

A simple analogy will make clear why simplifying in a macro model must take a different form from that used in microeconomics.

We can investigate the working of a motorcar by examining its different parts in isolation from one another. Thus we look at the wheels, then the gearbox, the engine, the carburettor, the electric fuel pump, and so on. In this way we can find out how each part of the car works in detail.

Now, while such an examination is very important and useful, it has its limitations. This is because we just spotlight one component and see how it operates, *ignoring the rest of the car*. It will not enable us to predict what will happen if, for instance, we replace a one-litre engine by a two-litre engine. We cannot assume that, 'other things being equal', the larger engine will make the car run faster. There will be certain 'feedbacks' on the other parts of the car which will affect its running efficiency as a whole. Thus the larger engine may be too powerful for the gearbox; the carburettor may be unable to supply sufficient fuel; the suspension may not be capable of withstanding higher speeds; and so on. It is not enough to examine how one part of the car works in isolation; we have also to consider how the various components are interrelated, and the relative importance of each.

The same applies when we study how an economic system works. The micro approach will only take us a certain distance, for it merely examines how small parts of the economy operate in isolation. Changes which are simultaneously taking place in other parts of the economy and in the level of activity in general are ignored by inserting the phrase 'other things being equal'. So are the repercussions – the feedbacks – which may result from the single change being analysed.

Now this is legitimate enough if we are analysing a comparatively insignificant part of the economy, for example a small industry. Thus if we wish to discover the effects of an increase in the demand for pencils, we are unlikely to make serious errors by assuming 'other things equal', for such a change is unlikely to cause repercussions on the economy as a whole.

But what if we are examining the effects of a considerable increase in the demand for cars? The car industry is a significant part of the whole economy, and so we cannot merely analyse the effects in isolation, stopping at the point where the price of cars rises or the wages of car workers increase. To indicate the full economic results, we shall have to consider (i) possible 'feedbacks' on the demand for cars, and (ii) repercussions on the economy as a whole – which in turn can produce further feedbacks. For one thing, we shall have to know the level of employment in the economy. If this is low, the increased demand for cars may lead to a considerable expansion of activity throughout the economy, leading to a further increase in the demand for cars. On the other hand, if the economy is already running at full employment, the increased demand may merely cause higher prices.

Simplifying by Aggregating

Although, when dealing with changes in the economy as a whole, we cannot assume 'other things being equal', we still need to simplify if we are to build up a satisfactory model. This we do by 'aggregating' variables into a few broad groups.

The main aggregates we examine in macroeconomics are national income, national output and national expenditure. But we can also deal with subaggregates and analyse the factors that determine these. Thus, in analysing national expenditure, we examine consumption spending, investment spending, government spending, export receipts, spending on imports, etc. Similarly, when looking at national income, we consider wages, rent, and profits (see Chapter 27). Aggregating in this way enables us to handle all the different variables so that we can bear in mind the effects which a change in any one of them will have on the other groups and upon the level of activity as a whole (see Chapter 28).

The Economic System

What we have said so far must not be taken to imply that particular markets and the economy as a whole are mutually exclusive. To return to our analogy of the car, all the parts of a car are 'ticking over' when the car is running. Each bit of the carburettor and gearbox, and the way each is functioning, affect the overall running of the car. And how the car is driven will influence the performance of the individual parts – the engine, the suspension, the wheels, and so on. So it is with the economy. The millions of independent decisions made by individual firms and consumers affect the overall functioning of the economy. For example, each decision of an individual firm regarding alterations to its factory, plant or stocks affects the amount of investment spending which the economy as a whole is undertaking. And the firm's decisions will also be influenced by the price of its product – which in its turn depends upon the demands of individual purchasers.

Both micro- and macroeconomics are necessary, therefore, to an understanding of how the economy functions. Indeed, in recent years, economics has paid more attention to the integration of micro- and macroeconomics. First, microeconomic changes can often give a lead in explaining a macro variable. Thus how the average worker responds to a rise in wages could indicate the likely effect on the overall flow of spending on consumer goods and services which will result from an increase in the income flow brought about chiefly by higher earnings throughout the economy. In short, we can obtain information on the macroeconomic aggregate variables from ordinary markets.

Second, from the point of view of government policy, more emphasis is now placed on the fact that macro aggregates consist simply of the lumping together of what is happening in all the micro markets. These in turn are the result of individual decisions. As we shall see (Chapter 29) governments are now increasingly looking at solving this problem of achieving full employment without running into inflation by putting less emphasis on expanding demand and giving much more weight to the lowering of costs by increased efficiency and productivity on the supply side. Thus taxation on incomes has been reduced, while encouragement, including financial incentives, has been given to small firms to set up in order to harness the drive and innovative skills of the individual owner-manager.

The Objectives of Government Stabilisation Policy

While Keynes's theory was concerned chiefly with solving the problem of cyclical unemployment, the implementation of his policies had repercussions in other directions. This means that today the government's macro objectives can be summarised as:

(1) full employment;
(2) price stability;
(3) a healthy balance of payments;
(4) a balanced regional development
(5) adequate long-term growth.

These are the subjects which are studied in the chapters which follow.

Here it is necessary to issue a word of warning. The fact that the different objectives are dealt with under separate chapter headings is simply to aid the reader's understanding by proceeding in stages. But, as we shall see, the various objectives are interrelated, and to some extent incompatible. This means that, when the government is in practice deciding policy, it has to consider how all different objectives will be affected by a particular strategy.

27 Measuring the Level of Activity: National Income Calculations

27.1 The Principle of National Income Calculations

Fluctuations in the level of activity are monitored by quantitative informa-tion on the national income. Although the collection of statistics proceeds continuously, the principal figures are published annually in *The United Kingdom National Accounts (The CSO Blue Book)*.

The principle of calculating national income is as follows. Income is a flow of goods and services over time: if our income rises, we can enjoy more goods and services. But for goods to be enjoyed they must first be produced. A nation's income over a period, then, is basically the same as its output over a period. Thus, as a first approach, we can say that national income is the total money value of all goods and services produced by a country during the year. The question is how we can measure this money value.

We can tackle the problem by studying the different ways in which we can arrive at the value of a table.

Figure 27.1 shows that the value of the table can be obtained by taking the value of the final product (£100) or by totalling the value added by each firm in the different stages of production. The output of the tree-grower is what he receives for the tree (£30) which, we will assume, cost £20 in wages to produce, leaving £10 profit. The output of the sawmiller is what he receives for the timber (£50) less what he paid for the tree. Again, this output (£20) is made up of wages and profit. And so on. The total of these added values equals the value of the final table. Thus we could obtain the value of the table by adding the *net outputs* of the tree-grower (forestry), the sawmiller and the table-maker (manufacturing) and the retailer (distribution).

Alternatively, instead of putting these individual outputs in industry categories, we could have added them according to the type of factor

FIGURE 27.1
The Value of the Total Product Equals the Sum of the Values Added by Each Firm

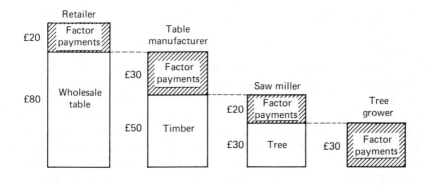

payment – wages, salaries, rent or profit. This gives us the *income* method of measuring output.

Thus, if we assume (i) no government taxation or spending and (ii) no economic connections with the outside world, we can obtain the national income either by totalling the value of final output during the year (i.e. the total of the value added to the goods and services by each firm) or by totalling the various factor payments during the year – wages, rent and profit.

There is, however, a third method of calculating the national income. The value of the table in Figure 27.1 is what was spent on it. If the table had sold for only £90, that would have been the value of the final output, with the final factor payment – profit to the retailer – reduced to £10. Thus we can obtain the national income by totalling *expenditure* on final products over the year.

It must be emphasised that the money values of output, income and expenditure are *identical by definition*. They simply *measure* the national income in different ways. This was shown by the fact that factor payments were automatically reduced by £10 when the table sold for £90 instead of £100.

Before we proceed to examine in more detail the actual process of measuring these three identities, it is convenient if we first consider some of the inherent difficulties.

27.2 National Income Calculations in Practice

General Difficulties

Complications arise through:

1. Arbitrary Definitions

(1) PRODUCTION

In calculating the national income, only those goods and services which are paid for are normally included. Because calculations have to be made in money terms, the inclusion of other goods and services would involve imputing a value to them. But where would you draw the line? If you give a value to jobs which a person does for himself – growing vegetables in the garden or cleaning the car – then why not include shaving himself, driving to work, and so on? On the other hand, excluding such jobs distorts national-income figures, for, as an economy becomes more dependent on exchanges, the income figure increases although there has been no addition to real output! (see pp. 397, 398).

An imputed money value is included for certain payments in kind which are recognised as a regular part of a person's income earnings, e.g. food, etc. provided for the armed forces.

(2) THE VALUE OF THE SERVICES RENDERED BY CONSUMER DURABLE GOODS

A TV set, dishwasher, car, etc., render services for many years. But where would we stop if we imputed a value to such services? A toothbrush, pots and pans, for example, all render services over their lives. All consumer durable goods are therefore included at their price when bought, subsequent services being ignored.

The one exception is owner-occupied houses. These are given a notional rent to keep them in line with property owned for letting, whose rents are included, either directly or as profits of property companies. This also prevents national income falling as more people become owner-occupiers!

(3) GOVERNMENT SERVICES

Education and health services, although provided by the State, are no different from similar services for which some persons pay. Consequently, they are included in national income at cost. But what of certain other government services? A policeman, for instance, when helping children to cross the road is providing a consumer service. But at night his chief task may be guarding banks and factories, and in doing so he is really furthering the productive process. To avoid double-counting, this part ought to be excluded from output calculations. In practice, however, it would be impossible to differentiate between the two activities, and so all the policeman's services – indeed all government services (including defence) – are included at cost in calculating national output (see p. 397).

2. Inadequate Information

The sources from which data are obtained were not specifically designed for national-income calculations. For instance, the Census of Production and the Census of Distribution are only taken at approximately five-year intervals. As a result many figures are estimates based on samples.

Information, too, may be incomplete. Thus not only do income tax returns fail to cover the small-income groups, but they err on the side of understatement.

But it is 'depreciation' which presents the major problem, for what firms show in their profit and loss accounts is affected by tax regulations. Since there is no accurate assessment of real depreciation, it is now usual to refer to gross national product (GNP) rather than to national income (see Figure 27.3).

3. The Danger of Double-counting

Care must be taken to exclude transfer incomes when adding up national income (see p. 390), the contribution to production of intermediary firms when calculating national output (see Table 27.1) and indirect taxes when measuring national expenditure (see p. 392).

A fourth way in which a form of double-counting can occur is through 'stock appreciation'. Inflation increases the value of stocks, but although this adds to firms' profits it represents no increase in real income. Such gains must therefore be deducted from the income figure.

4. Relationship with Other Countries

(1) TRADE

British people spend on foreign goods, while foreigners buy British goods. In calculating national *expenditure*, therefore, we have to deduct the value of goods and services imported (since they have not been produced by Britain) and add the value of goods and services exported (where income has been earned in Britain).

(2) INTERNATIONAL INDEBTEDNESS

If a father increases his son's pocket-money, it does not increase the family income. Instead it merely achieves a redistribution, the father having less and the son more. But if the boy's aunt makes him a regular allowance, the family income is increased. Similarly, with the nation: while transfer incomes, e.g. retirement pensions and student grants, do not increase national income, payments by foreigners do. These payments arise chiefly as interest on loans and dividends from investments made abroad. In the same way, foreigners receive payments for investments in Britain. Net property income from abroad (receipts less payments) must therefore be added to both domestic expenditure and output.

Government Calculations of the National Income

We start off by measuring Gross Domestic Product (GDP). The GDP is simply the money value of the final output of all resources located within a country irrespective of whether their owners live there or abroad. Hence in order to obtain Gross National Product (GNP) we have to add the balance of *net* property income from abroad (Figure 27.2).

Figures for GNP are calculated for income, expenditure and output. Because information is incomplete and derived from a variety of sources, results are not identical. In practice the expenditure figure is taken as the datum, income and output differences being treated as a residual. This is done to allow identical totals to be presented and does not imply that the expenditure estimate is necessarily more accurate than income and output estimates.

1. National Income

National income is the total money value of all incomes received by persons and enterprises in the country during the year. Such incomes may be in the form of wages, salaries, rent, or profit.

In practice income figures are obtained mostly from income tax returns, but estimates are necessary for small incomes. Two major adjustments have to be made:

(1) TRANSFER INCOMES
Sometimes an income is received although there has been no corresponding contribution to the output of goods and services, e.g. unemployment-insurance benefit and interest on the National Debt. Such incomes are really only a redistribution of income within the nation – chiefly from taxpayers to the recipients. Transfer incomes must therefore be deducted from the total. Other forms of transfer income which must be excluded are private money gifts and receipts from the sale of financial assets and of second-hand goods, e.g. a house, furniture, a car.

(2) INCOME FROM GOVERNMENT ACTIVITIES
Personal incomes and the profits of companies are obtained from tax returns. But since dividends and interest payments are already included in profits, to avoid double-counting they are not shown separately.

FIGURE 27.2
Summary of Gross National Product Calculations

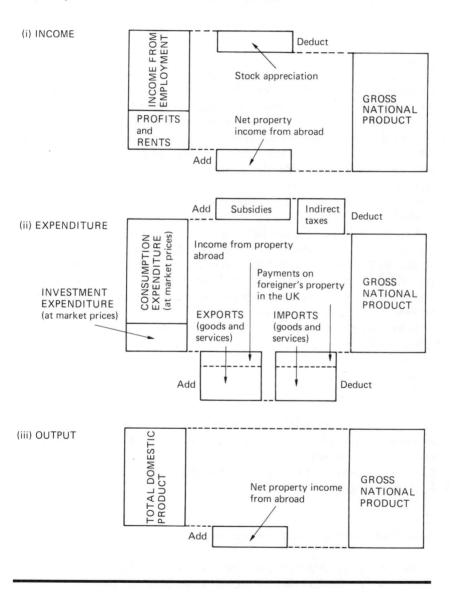

Trading activities of public corporations, e.g. the Post Office, National Power, the BBC, and of local authorities e.g. housing, transport, may also show surpluses which have to be added in, while an imputed rental value in given to the property owned and occupied by the government and local authorities (non-trading income).

2. National Expenditure

National expenditure is the total amount spent on final goods and services by households and central and local government and by firms on net additions to capital goods and stocks in the course of the year.

Figures for calculating national expenditure are obtained from a variety of sources. The *Census of Distribution* records the value of shop sales, while the *Census of Production* gives the value of capital goods produced and additions to stocks. But these censuses are not taken every year, and gaps are filled by estimates from data provided by the *National Food Survey*, and the *Family Expenditure Survey*.

Market prices are swollen by indirect taxes on goods and services, e.g. VAT, and reduced by subsidies, e.g. on council housing. What we are trying to measure is the value of the national expenditure which corresponds to the cost of the factors of production (including profits) used in producing the national product. This is known as 'national expenditure at factor cost' and is obtained by deducting indirect taxes from and adding subsidies to national expenditure at market prices.

Adjustments necessary for exports and imports have already been referred to (see p. 389).

3. National Output

National output is the total of consumer goods and services and investment goods (including additions to stocks) produced by the country during the year. It can be measured by totalling either the value of the *final* goods and services produced or the *value added* to the goods and services by each firm, including the government.

Gross National Product and National Income

In the course of production, machinery wears out and stocks are used up. This represents depreciation of capital. If we make no allowance for this but simply add in the value of new investment goods produced, we have *gross national product*. But, to be accurate, the calculation of total output should include only net investment – that is, the value of new investment goods and stocks less depreciation on existing capital and stocks used up. This gives the net national product, which is the true national income for the year (Table 27.1 and Figure 27.3).

Summary

GDP at market prices

> – indirect taxes
> + subsidies
> ──────────
> = GDP at factor cost

>> + net property income from abroad
>> ──────────────────
>> = GNP

>>> – depreciation
>>> ────────────
>>> = NI

FIGURE 27.3
Gross National Product and National Income

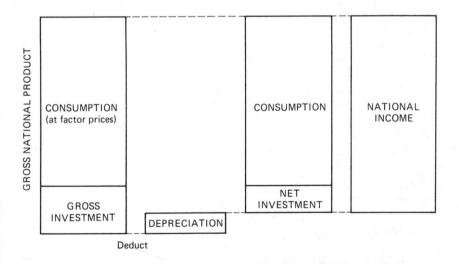

Table 27.1
Calculations of the National Income of the UK, 1988

INCOME	£m
Income from employment	249 775
Income from self-employment	42 617
Gross trading profits of companies	70 242
Gross trading surplus, public corporations	7 286
Gross trading surplus, general government enterprises	−70
Rent	27 464
Imputed charge for consumption of non-trading capital	3 408
Total domestic income	400 722
less stock appreciation	−6 116
GROSS DOMESTIC PRODUCT (income based)	394 606
Statistical discrepancy	181
Net property income from abroad	5 619
GROSS NATIONAL PRODUCT	400 406
less capital consumption	−54 769
NATIONAL INCOME	345 637

EXPENDITURE	£m
Consumers' expenditure	293 569
General government final consumption	91 847
Gross domestic fixed capital formation	88 751
Value of physical increase in stocks and works in progress	4 371
Total domestic expenditure	478 538
Export of goods and services	108 533
Total final expenditure	587 071
less imports of goods and services	−125 194
Statistical discrepancy	2 056
GROSS DOMESTIC PRODUCT (at *market prices*)	463 933
less taxes on expenditure	−75 029
plus subsidies	5 883

GROSS DOMESTIC PRODUCT (at *factor cost*)	394 787
Net property income from abroad	5 619
GROSS NATIONAL PRODUCT	400 406
less capital consumption	−54 769
NATIONAL INCOME	345 637

OUTPUT

Agriculture, forestry, and fishing	5 625
Energy and water supply	21 845
Manufacturing	93 433
Construction	25 745
Distribution, hotels and catering: repairs	55 131
Transport and communication	28 657
Banking, finance, insurance, business services and leasing	76 922
Ownership of dwellings	21 407
Public administration, national defence and compulsory social security	27 023
Education and health services	35 237
Other services	25 785
Total	416 810
Adjustment for financial services, etc	−22 023
GROSS DOMESTIC PRODUCT (income based)	394 787
Net property income from abroad	5 619
GROSS NATIONAL PRODUCT	400 406
less capital consumption	−54 769
NATIONAL INCOME	345 637

SOURCE Annual Abstract of Statistics.

Personal Disposable Income

For some purposes, e.g. as an indication of people's current living standards, a measurement of personal disposable income, that is, what people actually have to spend, is more significant. The necessary adjustments to gross national product to obtain personal disposable income are shown in Figure 27.4.

FIGURE 27.4
The Relationship between Gross National Product and Personal Disposable Income

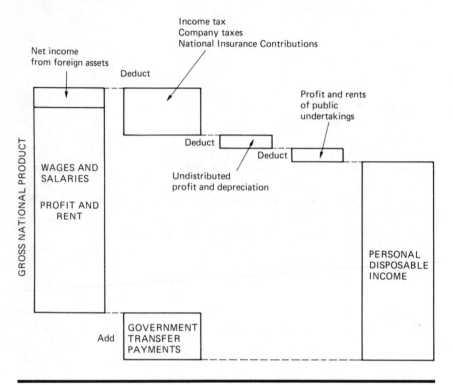

27.3   Uses of National Income Calculations

1. To Indicate the Overall Standard of Living

Welfare is not identical with wealth (see p. 9), but wealth bears the closest single relationship to it. Income, the flow of wealth, is therefore the nearest indication of welfare.

Nevertheless, the national income figure cannot be accepted solely at its face value. Thus, although the national income of the UK was £172 361 million in 1980 and £345 637 million in 1988, it does not automatically follow that everybody had doubled his standard of living over that period. The following qualifications have to be made:

(*a*) Some of the increase may be due to inflation (see Chapter 30), whereas what is relevant is real national income. One way of handling the difficulty is to re-value all money national incomes at 'constant prices' by applying the prices prevailing in a common base year.

(*b*) The national income figure must be related to the size of population; thus average income per head is a better indication of well-being.

(*c*) A person's standard of living depends upon the quantity of consumer goods and services he enjoys. But the increase in national income may have come about mainly through an increase in the production of producer goods. While these goods enable a higher standard of living to be enjoyed in the future, they do not increase *present* welfare. Thus average personal disposable income might provide a better indication of current living standards, though national income per head is the more satisfactory in the long run.

(*d*) The increase in national income may have come about through a surplus of exports over imports. This represents investment overseas, and thus (*c*) above applies.

(*e*) The average-income-per-head figure is merely a statistical average. It does not indicate how any increase in national income is distributed; it may go mostly to a few rich people (as in the oil sheikhdoms), perhaps leaving the others little better off.

(*f*) National income figures do not reflect the 'quality' of life. An increase in national income may be the result of longer working hours, inferior working conditions, longer journeys to work, or the presence of more housewives at work (with less comfort in the home). The national income does not value leisure time.

(*g*) All government spending is included at cost in national income calculations, no distinction being made between expenditure on consumer services and expenditure on defence. As a result, if spending on the social services were cut to pay for rearmament, national income would be unchanged!

(*h*) The national income figure is swollen when people pay for services which they previously performed themselves. Thus a married woman who returns to teaching but pays a woman to do her housework adds to the national income twice – although the only net addition is her teaching services. Indeed, even an oil spillage can increase national income by the costs of cleaning up, unless these are covered by the polluting shipping company.

(*i*) Because national income figures are based on private costs and benefits, external costs or benefits do not enter into the calculations. Thus the erection of electricity pylons would be included at cost, no allowance being made for the social cost of spoiling the landscape.

(*j*) The increase in national income may have incurred an excessive consumption of irreplaceable resources, e.g. fossil fuels.

(*k*) National income figures do not include the 'black' economy (some estimates would add 10 per cent) where services are exchanged for cash in order to evade taxes.

(*l*) National income includes payments for services necessitated by the stress of modern living, e.g. anti-depressant drugs, clinics for alcoholics.

2. *To Compare the Standards of Living of Different Countries*

Comparisons of the national incomes of different countries are often necessary for practical purposes. How much help should be given by the rich countries to the very poor? Which are the very poor countries? What contribution should be made by a country to an international body, such as the United Nations, the Red Cross and NATO? What is the war potential of a country?

But, when used to compare countries' standards of living, national income figures must be subjected to qualifications *additional* to those mentioned in *1* above.

(*a*) Because figures are expressed in different currencies they have to be converted into a common denominator. Using the exchange rate for this purpose is not entirely satisfactory, for the rate is determined by factors other than the internal purchasing powers of currencies, e.g. capital movements. More satisfactory is the use of a conversion rate based on the purchasing power parity for a common basket of goods.

(*b*) Different people have different needs. The Englishman has to spend more on heating than the Indian. Obviously, the Englishman is no better off in this respect – though the national income figures, by valuing goods at cost, would indicate that he is.

(*c*) The proportion of national income spent by different countries on defence varies. Countries which spend less can enjoy consumer goods instead, but average national income does not indicate the difference.

(*d*) Countries vary as regards the length of the average working week, the proportion of women who work, the number of jobs which people do for themselves, the degree to which goods are exchanged against money and the accuracy of tax returns. Some allowance must be made for each of these factors.

3. *To Calculate the Rate at Which a Nation's Income is Growing*

Is the national income growing? Is it growing as fast as it should? Are the incomes of other countries growing faster? Is there sufficient investment to maintain future living standards? The answers to these and similar questions can be found by comparing national income figures, though for the reasons given above some caution must be observed.

4. To Establish Relationships Which Arise Between Various Parts of the Economy

If, for example, national income figures revealed a relationship between the level of investment and growth, or between educational expenditure and growth, or between profits and the level of investment, such information would be useful in planning the economy.

The figures might also indicate trends, e.g. the proportion of national income which is taken by the government.

5. To Assist the Government In Managing the Economy

Some central government planning is now regarded as essential for achieving full employment, a stable currency and a satisfactory rate of growth. But this requires having figures for the various components of the national income, such as consumption spending, investment, exports and imports. How they can be used will be explained later.

6. To Assist Businesses, Trade Unions, Financial Journalists, etc. to Ascertain Economic Trends and Forecast Future Movements

7. To Indicate Changes in the Distribution of Income

While, as a scientist, the economist is not concerned with the 'fairness' of the distribution of income, the government is, for taxation and political considerations. National income figures provide the statistical basis when deciding on such matters.

27.4 Factors Determining a Country's Material Standard of Living

Since people can enjoy only what they produce with their limited resources, the production-possibility curve shows the limit to their material standard of living. Because income is not evenly distributed, however, what we are talking about is an average standard of living, usually measured by the national income per head of the population.

The factors which limit the standard of living can be classified as internal and external, the latter resulting from economic relationships with the rest of the world.

The most important *internal* factors are:

1. Original Natural Resources

Obviously, 'natural resources' cover such things as mineral deposits, sources of fuel and power, climate and the fertility of the soil and fisheries around the coast, but also included are geographical advantages, such as navigable rivers or lakes, which help communications.

While national output increases as new techniques or transport developments allow national resources to be exploited, the exhaustion of mineral resources works in the opposite direction. Moreover, where a country's economy is predominantly agricultural, variations in weather may cause its output to fluctuate from year to year.

2. The Nature of the People, Particularly of the Labour Force

Other things being equal, the standard of living will be higher the greater the proportion of workers to the total population and the longer their working hours.

But the quality of the labour force is also important. This will depend upon the basic characteristics of the people – their health, energy, adaptability, inventiveness, judgement and ability to organise themselves and to cooperate in production – together with the skills they have acquired through education and training.

3. Capital Equipment

The effectiveness of natural resources and of labour depends almost entirely upon capital equipment. Thus machinery is necessary to extract oil and minerals, a turbine generator to harness a waterfall, and hotels to exploit Spanish sun and beaches. Similarly, the output of workers varies almost in direct proportion to the capital equipment and power at their disposal. Indeed, the most important single cause of material progress is investment, the addition to capital.

4. The Organisation of Resources

To achieve the maximum output from scarce factors of production, they must be organised efficiently. Have we the correct proportion of machinery to each worker? Is the production of the particular good being carried on in the best possible locality? Could the factors be better deployed within the factory? Such questions have to be answered by those organising production.

5. Knowledge of Techniques

Technical knowledge is acquired through capital expenditure on research and invention. Further capital expenditure is necessary to develop discoveries, e.g. to utilise our present knowledge of nuclear energy. Nevertheless, the rapid increase of the standard of living of the UK over the last hundred years has largely been due to the development and application of new inventions such as the steam engine, the internal combustion engine, electrical power and electronics.

6. Political Organisation

A stable government promotes confidence and thereby encourages saving and investment in long-term capital projects.

To the above we have to add what can be termed *external* factors:

7. Foreign Loans and Investments

A net income from foreign investments means that a country obtains goods or services from other countries without having to give goods and services in return, and vice versa. Generally speaking, welfare from this source is only likely to fluctuate over a long period.

8. The Terms of Trade

In the short run, fluctuations in the terms of trade are likely to be far more important in changing material welfare, especially if the country has, like the UK, a high level of imports and exports.

By the *terms of trade* we mean the quantity of another country's products which a nation gets in exchange for a given quantity of its own products. Thus, if the terms of trade move in a nation's favour, it means that it gets a larger quantity of imports for a given quantity of its own exports. This happens because the prices of the goods that are imported have fallen relative to the prices of those exported. Thus the 1973 increase in the price of oil reduced the standard of living of the importing countries and raised that of the oil producers.

9. Gifts from Abroad

Aid to countries for purposes of economic development and defence improve the standard of living of the receiving countries.

28 Determination of the Level of Activity: The Keynesian Explanation

28.1 The Link Between Spending and Production

The Circular Flow of Income

We begin by repeating in simplified form the identity which exists between income and expenditure. Take a simple example. A teacher buys a table from a carpenter. With the money he receives, the carpenter pays the timber merchant for the wood, who in turn pays the man who cut the wood. But where did the teacher obtain the original money to buy the table? Simply from the carpenter, the timber merchant and the tree-feller, who each use part of their receipts to pay fees to the teacher for instructing their children. So with the other goods the teacher buys. Thus there is a circular flow of income – one person's spending becomes another person's income. Spending is therefore necessary for earnings.

The same applies to the economy as a whole; at any one time spending equals income. Suppose, for instance, that all production in the economy is in the hands of a giant firm which owns all the land and raw materials and employs all the labour. The firm's income consists of the receipts from the sale of its product. Since it owns all the raw materials and land, these receipts must equal what it pays out in wages and what it has left in profits. This was the principle upon which we measured national income.

Since spending on goods determines the receipts and thus the profits of firms, it is of vital importance in deciding the level of their output and thus of the aggregate level of activity. To explain more fully, we use Figure 28.1, which shows the money flows which correspond to the movement of factors and goods in the outer ring of Figure 26.1 – payments by firms for factors and expenditure of households on goods. The first represents income of households; the second represents receipts of firms.

If spending on goods and services is maintained, factor payments can be maintained; in other words the profitability of production is unchanged

402

FIGURE 28.1
The Circular Flow of Income

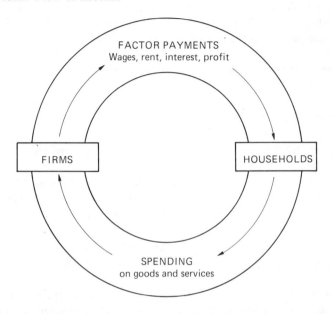

and thus firms have no cause to vary output. If, however, for some reason or another, spending should fall, some of the goods produced by firms will not be sold, and stocks accumulate. As a result output is curtailed. On the other hand, if spending on goods and services increases, stocks will be run down. Production has become more profitable and output is expanded.

Three important points emerge from our discussion so far:

1. There is no impetus towards a contraction or expansion of production if spending on goods and services equals spending (including normal profits) by firms on factors of production. In short, the economy is in equilibrium.
2. The level of production, and therefore of employment, is closely related to the level of spending.
3. There is nothing to guarantee that spending will be sufficient to ensure a level of production where all factors are fully employed.

Definitions and Assumptions

Before we show how changes in spending occur, we must make simplifying assumptions.

We define net profit as gross profit less retentions for depreciation. We assume:

1. *All retentions for depreciation are actually spent on replacement invest-ment.* Thus, when in future we speak of 'investment' it refers solely to net additions to fixed capital and stocks, i.e. net investment.

2. *All net profit is distributed to the owners of the risk capital.* This means that there is no 'saving' by firms.

3. *There is no government taxation or spending.*

4. *There are no economic connections with the outside world; it is a 'closed' economy.*
From the above assumptions it follows that: (1) the sum of the factor payments is equal to national income (equals national output) as defined in Chapter 27; and (2) income equals disposable income.

5. *There are no changes in the price level.* Thus any changes in the money value of national income reflect changes in real output.

6. *The level of employment is directly proportionate to the level of output.* In practice this may not be strictly true: existing machinery, for example, may be able to produce extra output without additional labour. But until there is full employment, the simplification does allow the level of employment to be linked directly with the level of national income.

28.2 Reasons for Changes in Aggregate Demand

Aggregate Demand

Our task, therefore, is to discover why changes occur in the national income (hereafter symbolised by Y). Now, as we have just shown, Y depends upon the level of spending, which we shall refer to as aggregate demand (abbreviated to AD). Thus we can find out why Y changes by discovering why AD changes.

Changes in AD

Let us return to our example of the teacher. Suppose he earns £14 000 in a given year. Most of it will be spent on consumer goods and services – but not all. Some will probably be put aside for a 'rainy day'. That part of income which is not spent we can say is 'saved'. What happens to it? The money could be hidden under the mattress; in that case it is obviously lost to the circular flow of income. But the teacher is more likely to put it in a bank, where it is safer and earns interest. Nevertheless, at this point it is still lost to the circular flow. Saving represents a 'leak' from the flow of income.

So far we have looked only at spending on consumer goods. But spending may also be on capital goods. Firms borrow money from their banks (and other institutions) for such purchases. Thus the sum deposited by the teacher stands a good chance of being returned to the circular flow of income by being 'invested', i.e. spent on capital goods or additions to stocks. Investment, therefore, can be regarded as an 'injection'. And, if exactly the amount of money saved by households is spent by firms on investment, the level of AD is maintained (Figure 28.2), and Y is unchanged.

But suppose that the amount saved does not coincide with what firms wish to invest. This can come about either by a change in the amount invested or by a change in the amount spent by consumers.

Let us first assume that consumers' spending remains constant. If now firms reduce the amount they borrow for investment, AD is smaller. On the other hand, if firms increase their investment, AD will be larger.

FIGURE 28.2
The Level of Income Maintained through Investment

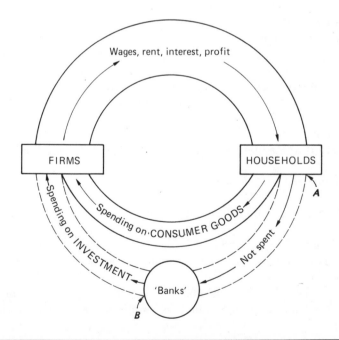

Alternatively, the amount of income spent on consumer goods may alter. Investment, we will now assume, remains unchanged. Here, if more is spent out of a given income, *AD* will increase; if less, *AD* decreases.

What it is important to recognise is that in an economy where people are free to dispose of their income as they please, and where firms are largely left to make their own investment decisions, a difference can easily exist between the amount of income which people plan to 'save' (i.e. which they do not wish to spend) and the amount which firms wish to invest. This is because, in their spending, households and firms act for different reasons and mostly independently of each other. Two questions have therefore to be asked: (i) What determines spending on consumer goods and therefore saving (at position *A*)? (ii) What determines investment spending (at position *B*)?

In our analysis, consumption, that is spending on consumer goods and services, will be given the symbol *C*; saving, i.e. income not spent on consumption, *S*; investment, i.e. spending on *net additions* to capital goods and stocks, I.

28.3 Consumption Spending

Consumption and Saving by Households: 'Personal Saving'

Income is received as wages or salaries, rent, interest and profits. With it households buy the consumer goods they need. That part of income which is not spent has been defined as 'saving'. Hence $Y=C+S$, $C=Y-S$, and $S=Y-C$.

C and *S*, therefore, are merely two sides of the same coin. Thus, whenever we consider *C* or *S*, we must examine the factors which influence both spending and thrift.

Spending decisions are more important in the short run, for a person's first concern is to maintain his standard of living. They are influenced by:

1. Size of Income

A small income leaves no margin for saving. Only when a man has satisfied what he considers are his basic needs will he save a part of his income. Indeed, if current income falls below this level, he may spend some of his past savings or borrow in order to maintain the standard of life he is accustomed to.

But we can go further. As income increases, the proportion spent tends to decrease; or, as it is often put, there is a *diminishing marginal propensity to consume*.

The above conclusions are illustrated diagrammatically in Figure 28.3, where the curve *C* shows how consumption changes with income.

Below an income of *OD* there is 'dis-saving'. At *OD* all income is consumed, the difference being covered by spending past savings or by borrowing. At higher incomes the proportion spent falls and saving occurs. This *diminishing marginal propensity to consume* is shown by the decreasing slope of the consumption curve: for any given increase in income, the extra amount spent grows successively smaller.

2. The Time-lag in Adjusting Spending Habits

It takes time for a person to adjust his standard of living as his income increases. In the short period, therefore, saving increases.

The above two factors explain the *shape* of the consumption curve – how spending changes as income changes. But we still have to account for the *position* of the curve – what determines the proportion of any given income which is spent. This amount can vary (that is, the position of the *C* curve may change) as a result of:

3. Changes in Disposable Income

We have assumed that firms have distributed all net profits and that there are no government taxation or transfers. In practice both profit distribution and government taxation will affect the size of income available for

---

FIGURE 28.3
The Relationship between Consumption and Income

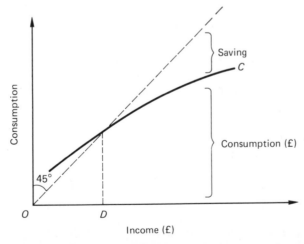

spending. Increasing direct taxation, for instance, would, by reducing disposable income, lower the *C* curve.

4. Government Policy

By its fiscal policy the government can influence the proportion of income consumed. Thus the replacement of indirect taxes by a more progressive income tax or a higher corporation tax would tend to take more from savers and less from spenders and so have the effect of increasing consumption.

5. The Size of the Wealth Owned by an Individual

6. The Distribution of Wealth in the Community

Because the proportion of income saved usually increases with income, greater equality of incomes is likely to reduce the aggregate amount saved out of a given national income. Redistributive taxation therefore tends to increase total consumption.

7. The Invention of New Consumer Goods

In recent years family cars, TV sets, hi-fi equipment, video recorders, central heating and holidays abroad have all induced spending, especially when backed by intensive advertising.

8. Hire-purchase and Other Credit Facilities

A decrease in the initial deposit or an extension of the period of repayment encourages spending. Easier bank credit does the same.

9. Anticipated Changes in the Value of Money

If people consider that the prices of goods are likely to rise, they bring forward their spending rather than save for the future.

10. The Age Distribution of the Population

Since most saving is done by people over 35 years of age, an ageing population will tend to reduce the propensity to consume of the community as a whole.

In the long period, people have some concern for their future standard of living, and *thrift* exercises a greater influence on the disposal of income.

The main factors determining thrift are:

1. Size of Income

As already shown, saving increases as income increases and at an increasing rate.

2. Psychological Attitudes

Some communities are by nature more thrifty than others, providing against sickness, unemployment and old age, and for the education of dependants. On the other hand, ostentation – the desire to 'keep up with the Joneses' – may provide a motive for a high rate of spending.

3. Social Environment

Apart from influencing the general attitude to saving, environment can be a major factor in other ways. Such institutions as savings banks, building societies, insurance companies and unit trusts encourage regular thrift, so that much saving out of income is contractual.

Political conditions, too, influence saving habits. Countries continually threatened by war or revolution do not provide the stable background necessary to encourage thrift.

4. Government Policy

The government can influence people's attitude to saving in a variety of ways. In the UK it tries to stimulate personal saving through the rate of interest offered, tax concessions (e.g. Tax Exempt Special Savings Accounts (TESSAs)) and special devices (e.g. Premium Bonds). On the other hand, a comprehensive state social-insurance and pension scheme may reduce personal saving.

At one time it was thought that people could only be induced to postpone consumption, i.e. to save, by offering interest as compensation (see p. 241). This view, however, is now largely rejected, chiefly because much saving is contractual, e.g. insurance, pension and mortgage payments. The dominant factor is the *ability* to save, i.e. the level of income.

Under our simplifying assumptions that all net profits are distributed and that there is no government taxation or spending, all saving is done by households. But saving can be achieved through retentions by firms and the government (Figure 28.4). In order to consider these, we will temporarily relax the two assumptions above.

FIGURE 28.4
Saving in the UK, 1988 (£ million)

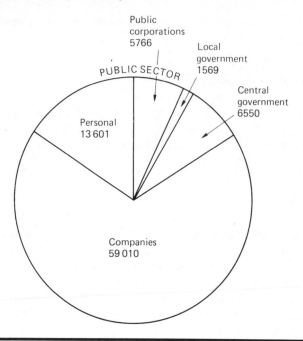

Company Saving

Saving by companies (which in volume remains fairly stable) is achieved by not distributing to shareholders all the profits made in a year. Some profits are usually retained, either to be 'ploughed back' for the expansion of the business, or to be held as liquid reserves in order to meet tax liabilities or maintain dividends when profits fluctuate. The chief factors affecting this type of saving are:

1. Profits

Transfers to reserves are dependent upon and stimulated by the level of current profits. In practice, therefore, business saving is determined principally by the level of *AD*.

2. Subjective Factors

Profits are likely to be retained when directors are expansion-minded or financially prudent.

3. Government Policy

An increased tax on *distributed* profits or a 'dividend freeze' would be likely to increase company saving.

Government Saving

Central government saving is achieved chiefly through a 'budget surplus', revenue exceeding current government expenditure. The surplus may be necessary: (i) to provide for the government's own investment and loans; and (ii) to ensure that, with personal and business saving, total saving will be sufficient to prevent an inflationary *AD* from developing (see Chapter 29). This 'saving' is shown by the *Public Sector Debt Repayment* (PSDR) (see Figure 33.1).

Public corporations are similar in many ways to ordinary businesses. But, as their operations are more directly under government control and their capital requirements are largely covered by the Treasury, their saving and investment are included under the public sector.

Local authorities, too, may have a budget surplus. In 1988 this was £1 569 m., equivalent to 2 per cent of total saving.

Thus in the public sector saving is determined chiefly by government policy, economic and political.

Conclusion

In the private sector, spending (and therefore saving) depend upon (i) the level of *Y*, i.e. the size of *AD*, and (ii) other factors influencing the amount spent out of income. In comparison with changes in *AD* these other factors are fairly stable. Hence the main factor affecting short-term changes in consumption spending is the size of *AD*!

We have therefore to look elsewhere for the reason why *AD* changes. It is to be found in the comparative instability of the other form of spending – investment.

28.4 Investment Spending

What do we Mean by 'Investment'?

Investment is spending over a given period on the production of capital goods (houses, factories, machinery, etc.) or on net additions to stocks (raw materials, consumer goods in shops, etc.).

It is important to distinguish between this definition and what is usually referred to as 'investment' by lay people. In national income analysis, investment takes place only when there is an actual net addition to capital goods or stocks. It cannot be applied to putting money in the bank or to the purchase of securities. This is true even when new securities are bought, though here there is a strong presumption that the money is required to finance real investment in factories, machinery, etc.

It should be noted that the definition above would cover 'gross investment', since it makes no allowance for the depreciation of existing capital assets. But, as already explained, we are analysing in terms of national income (net national product) *not* gross national product. Investment in our model, therefore, must be limited to *net* investment, i.e. gross investment less depreciation.

Investment in the Private Sector of the Economy

While in the private sector some investment in housing is undertaken by owner-occupiers who add garages, rooms, etc., to their property, most personal investment is by sole traders and partnerships. However, the amount of such investment is small relative to that of companies (see Figure 28.5).

The level of investment by firms is governed by the expected yield relative to cost, changes in techniques, changes in the rate of consumption and government policy.

FIGURE 28.5
Investment in the UK, 1988 (Domestic Fixed Capital Formation, £ million)

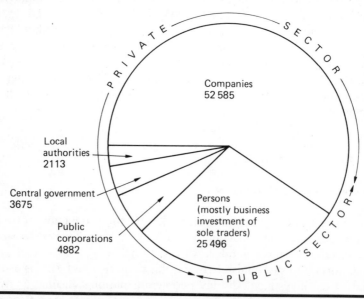

1. *Expected Yield Relative to Cost*

Entrepreneurs spend on new capital equipment when they think that the cost will be justified by the addition to revenue which will directly result. In short, marginal-revenue productivity must at least equal marginal cost.

Whereas marginal-revenue productivity in the case of labour can be estimated fairly accurately, it is not so with capital. Capital equipment lasts a long time, and the return to it is spread over many years. This involves uncertainty. Is demand for the product likely to change? Are competitors likely to enter the market? Will the present methods of production become obsolete? The return to the capital equipment over its life, therefore, can be no more definite than a series of yearly yields which the entrepreneur reasonably *expects*. It is usual to discount these yields to their present value and to express the return over the initial cost as a rate. This rate will be referred to as the *marginal efficiency of investment* (symbol MEI).

We can give more precision to this term by a simple example. Suppose a machine costs £1000. It has a working life of four years, during which the entrepreneur expects that it will add £400 each year to receipts. We could find a single rate of discount which would make the £400 received during the first year plus the £400 received during the second year plus the £400 received during the third year plus the £400 received during the fourth year just equal to the initial cost of £1000. This rate of discount is the MEI. (In our example, it is about 22 per cent.) If the MEI is greater than the rate of interest – the cost of borrowing the original £1000 – the entrepreneur will buy the machine; if it is less, he will not.

In the above example, we have shown how the marginal efficiency of a *particular* machine is determined. But what of the marginal efficiency of new capital *in general*? How will this vary as the capital equipment of the community increases or decreases?

For two reasons it can be expected that the MEI will fall as the stock of the community's capital increases. First, as more machines are produced, so will the products made by those machines increase in supply. Thus the price of those products falls, and so the expected yield of the machine will also fall. Second, producing more machines will increase the demand for the factors of production making those machines. This will increase the price of those factors, and so the supply price of the machines is likely to rise as more are produced. From the first, we have smaller expected yields to be discounted; from the second, a larger initial supply price as capital increases. Both lead to a smaller MEI as the supply of capital increases.

In other words, the curve relating MEI to the level of investment slopes downwards from left to right (Figure 28.6).

With a marginal efficiency of investment as depicted by the curve *MEI* and a rate of interest of *OR*, the level of investment will be *OM*.

FIGURE 28.6
The Determination of the Level of Investment

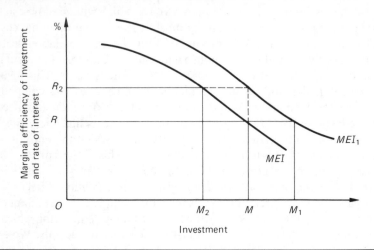

The level of investment may alter through any change in (a) the expected yield, or (b) the rate of interest. Thus if expected yield rises to MEI_1, investment will increase to OM_1. On the other hand, if the rate of interest rises to OR_2, investment will fall to OM_2. What we now have to do, therefore, is to examine the possible extent and frequency of changes in expected yield, and to see whether those changes are likely to overshadow changes in the rate of interest.

Let us look first at the *expected yield*. We have already shown that this is clouded in uncertainty because the entrepreneur will have to look far into the future to estimate changes in the demand for his product and to allow for possible changes in methods of production. Upon what can he base his estimates?

The simple answer is that he has little definite to go on. His estimate of the earning power of an investment over, say, the next five years can be only tentative, and allowance will have to be made according to the confidence he has in its accuracy. The main factors influencing his decisions are: the level of current income; the course of Stock Exchange prices; the future price level; and government policy. Let us consider each in turn.

In making his estimate, the entrepreneur will most likely commence from the position about which he does have some definite knowledge – the present. If current demand for his goods is buoyant, and has been so for some time, future prospects will probably look rosy. On the other hand, if present demand is low, he will think twice before adding to his productive capacity. But the current demand for goods as a whole depends chiefly upon the current level of *AD*. Investment is likely to be higher, therefore, the higher is *AD*.

Prices of shares on the Stock Exchange influence investment decisions in two ways. First, uncertainty in estimating the expected yield means that investment decisions are influenced considerably by prevailing moods of optimism or pessimism. An entrepreneur will be unwilling to extend his factory if current Stock Exchange prices value businesses, particularly those similar to his own, unfavourably. Second, when its share price is high, a company will find it easier and cheaper to raise capital through a 'rights' issue.

As regards the price level, if the entrepreneur thinks that prices in future are likely to be higher, then more investment is likely now. Not only will the value of the factory or machine appreciate, but expected yield will be higher through the rise in the price of the product.

Political instability and changes in government policy add to uncertainty. The former discourages investment, particularly by foreign companies operating in the country. The possibility of the latter has to be allowed for in an entrepreneur's expectations. Is corporation tax likely to be increased? Will the government carry out a disinflationary policy to curb future price rises?

This brings us to the *rate of interest*, the cost of investment. If it rises, marginal projects cease to be viable, and so the level of investment falls. This applies even if funds come from internal reserves, for the opportunity cost – the return on the best alternative, e.g. government securities – has to be considered. To Keynes, therefore, the long-term rate of interest was a major factor in determining the level of investment.

However, we must not assume a *precise* relationship. While the prevailing rate of interest could be decisive for projects where the yields extend far into the future, e.g. houses, shops and offices, and for investment by small firms, practical considerations may loom large with other investment.

For one thing investment decisions, especially for large firms, are mainly the result of long-term planning. Any alteration of plans because of a change in the rate of interest might throw the whole programme out of phase. For another, firms allow a considerable safety margin when deciding on investment, probably expecting to recover costs within five years. This margin is thus sufficient to absorb a relatively small rise in the rate of interest. Even the holding of stocks may not be affected by the rate of interest. Convenience is more likely to decide the minimum held. In any case, the rate of interest may be only a small part of the cost of holding stocks, warehousing, etc., being relatively far more important. Finally, a part of any increase in interest charges would be covered by reduced tax liability.

Nevertheless, when in 1979 interest rates rose sharply, many investment projects became marginal, and stagnation was prolonged because these could not bear the higher cost.

Even so, it is probably pessimistic expectations which are the prime cause of investment stagnation. Thus in the world depression of 1980–2, it is doubtful whether a lower rate of interest would have been significant in achieving any great increase in investment except for its psychological boost to expectations.

This implies that, *compared with entrepreneurs' expectations*, the rate of interest plays a secondary role in determining the level of investment. Moreover, uncertainty means that expected yield is subject to frequent reappraisal. In other words, changes in expectations may cause the MEI curve to change so frequently and by so much that it outweighs the effect which a movement in the rate of interest may have on the level of investment. We can illustrate from Figure 28.6. A rate of interest OR and a marginal efficiency of investment curve MEI would give a rate of investment OM. A rise in the rate of interest to OR_2 should reduce investment to OM_2. But this assumes that there is no change in the position of the MEI curve. If, for example, as the rate of interest rises to OR_2, revised expectations cause the MEI curve to move to MEI_1, investment will remain at OM. Expectations may be such that, in a slump, a low rate of interest does little to stimulate investment, while in a boom a high rate does not discourage it. It is the fickleness of business expectations which gives investment a central role in the determination of the level of employment.

2. Changes in Techniques

New technical developments, such as the internal combustion engine, nuclear energy, the microchip and North Sea gas and oil, give an added impetus to investment. On the other hand, it has to be recognised that the possibility of new techniques rendering existing capital equipment obsolete must be allowed for by the entrepreneur when estimating the MEI.

3. Changes in the Rate of Consumption: The 'Accelerator'

Our conclusion in (1) above, that the rate of investment was tied fairly closely to the size of aggregate demand, is capable of further refinement. Changes in the rate of investment are closely linked, not to the absolute level of consumption, but to changes in the *rate* of consumption. A simple example will explain.

Suppose that 1000 machines are fully employed in producing bicycle tyres and that the life of each machine is ten years. This means that 100 machines have to be replaced each year and the industry making this type of capital good must have a yearly capacity of 100.

Now suppose demand for bicycles increases so that the demand for tyres increases by 10 per cent. If there is no excess capacity for producing tyres, it can be seen that 100 new machines, in addition to the replacement requirement, are needed immediately. In this year, therefore, 200 tyre-making machines must be produced. Thus although the increased demand for consumer goods was only 10 per cent, it led to a doubling of the capacity of the industry making the machines.

If consumption of tyres now remains constant at the new level, production of the machines will have to contract sharply, for until the extra machines wear out in ten years' time, only the annual replacement of 100 machines will be required.

Taking this example as it stands, three conclusions can be drawn.

(*a*) Variations in the rate of consumption will produce changes in investment on a magnified scale. Usually changes in consumption are the result of variations in the level of *AD* (known today as recession and recoveries). But they may also be brought about by such factors as changes in hire-purchase facilities, the boom in hire-purchase commitments being followed by stagnation for two or three years while repayments are made.

(*b*) Swings in the level of production are much greater in the producer-goods industries than in the consumer-goods industries. The longer a machine lasts before it has to be replaced, the greater will be the swing. Thus in our example, if the machine for making tyres lasts for twenty years, the 10 per cent increase in demand for tyres would necessitate a trebling of the capacity of the tyre-machine industry.

(*c*) A single change in the level of consumption can produce a built-in mechanism whereby changes in the level of investment will be repeated subsequently at fairly regular intervals.

Nevertheless, when we look at the assumptions which are implicit in our example, it loses some of its precision. In the first place, although we stated that there was no excess capacity in the tyre-producing industry, the opposite was assumed in the tyre-machine-making industry – the 100 per cent increase in demand will be met by the production of 100 extra machines. If extra tyres can be produced by using idle machines or by double-shift working, then there will be no need to increase the number of machines. On the other hand, if there is no surplus capacity in the tyre-machine-making industry, the increased demand for bicycles may simply find its outlet in higher prices, and investment will not increase. Second, the model fails to allow for the expectations of entrepreneurs. An increase in the demand for bicycle tyres may have been anticipated by building up stocks or by holding excess capacity in reserve. On the other hand, it may be thought that the increase in demand is unlikely to be permanent, in which case the extra machines would not be bought.

In practice, induced investment may result, not only from an increase in consumption, but from an autonomous increase in investment. Thus it is more accurate to say that the accelerator depends upon changes in *AD* rather than simply on changes in the level of consumption.

4. Government Policy

To be complete we must again relax our assumption of no government taxation or spending. Government policy may directly influence private investment. Banks have been instructed from time to time to restrict credit for certain types of investment. Should it desire to stimulate private investment, the government may give subsidies (e.g. for restoring old houses, or improving farm buildings), raise investment or depreciation allowances in tax assessment, and revive the optimism of entrepreneurs by lowering the rate of interest and, more important, by increasing its own spending.

Investment in the Public Sector

This includes not only the capital expenditure of the central government, but also that of the nationalised industries and local authorities.

Much of central government investment is fairly stable, depending chiefly on policy commitments – road construction, school and hospital building, etc. To some extent, too, the nationalised industries, in deciding whether to invest, may be expected to consider external benefits, e.g. getting the unemployed back to work, in addition to the expected financial return.

Local authority investment, however, may react to changes in the rate of interest, especially where finance is raised on the open market. Spending on new houses in particular may vary with the rate of interest. If, after applying government grants, the cost of borrowing is not covered by the rents charged, the difference has to be found from local taxation, and this may be politically unacceptable.

The real importance of public sector investment is that, for the purpose of adjusting *AD*, it is under direct government control. Indeed, it is mostly included within the global figure of 'government spending' which can be varied to adjust *AD*.

Summary

Employment depends upon the level of *AD* – the total of spending on the goods produced. *AD* fluctuates according to the relationship between intended saving and investment.

(i) *AD* expands if:
(1) investment increases but saving remains unchanged;
(2) saving decreases but investment remains unchanged.
(ii) *AD* contracts if:
(1) investment decreases but saving remains unchanged;
(2) saving increases but investment remains unchanged.

In practice investment is more liable to frequent change than is saving. Whereas firms' expectations are highly sensitive to new conditions, people's spending habits are fairly stable. Fluctuations in the level of *AD*, and therefore of income, are thus mainly the result of changes in the level of investment.

There is another important way in which saving differs from investment in the process of income creation. Whereas an increase in investment will, other things being equal, automatically produce an increase in saving through an expansion of income, an addition to saving need not lead to an increase in investment. Indeed income merely contracts until what is saved from it equals investment.

By influencing expectations, the current level of income will play a part in determining the rate of private investment. Moreover, investment will bear some relationship to the rate of change of income.

But, in order to simplify our analysis, we shall ignore these connections between investment and the level of income and assume that all investment is autonomous. In other words, investment decisions of firms are based on a number of considerations, and changes in investment are not automatically induced by income changes.

28.5 Equilibrium Through Changes in the Level of Income

The Restoration of Equilibrium

We must now follow through what happens when, for some reason, intended saving and investment become unequal. A simple arithmetical example will help. We shall assume:

1. $Y = 10\ 000$.
2. At this level of income there are unemployed resources.
3. Consumption spending by households is $\frac{6}{10}Y$ (disposable income) at all levels of Y. (In practice, consumption is more likely to be about 90 per cent of disposable income, but our assumption will make the diagrams clearer.)
4. Any increase in Y does not affect the proportion of Y spent by any change in the distribution of Y.

5. Investment spending by firms is autonomous: that is, it is independent of the level of income. Initially the rate of investment (I) = 4000.
6. All figures are in £ million.

Initially, in period 0, the economy is in equilibrium:

$$AD = C + I = 6000 + 4000 = 10\,000$$
$$Y = C + S = 6000 + 4000 = 10\,000$$

Now suppose that, in period 1, the rate of I increases by 2000 to 6000. AD is now 12 000. The receipts of entrepreneurs rise to 12 000, and stocks of goods decrease. As a result entrepreneurs expand production – factor payments equal 12 000 = Y (Period 1). This expansion of Y has come about solely because I is greater than planned S. Similarly, a contraction of Y will occur if I is less than planned S.

FIGURE 28.7
The Effect of an Increase in the Rate of Investment on the Level of Income

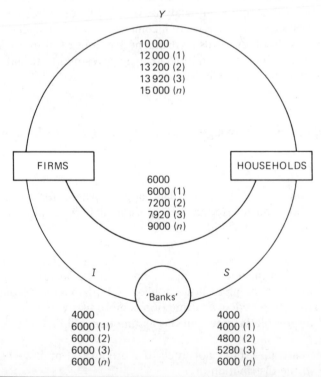

The 'Multiplier'

But this is not the end of the expansion. An increase in Y to 12 000 will mean that more workers are employed, and they, too, will have income to spend. Thus $C = \frac{6}{10} (12\ 000) = 7200$. Together with $I = 6000$, this gives a new AD of 13 200. Thus, in period 2, Y increases to 13 200. And so it continues. How the process works in real life can be illustrated from Nevil Shute's *Ruined City*. The shipyard in the town obtained an order for three tankers. 'A shop, long closed, reopened to sell meat pies . . . A man who gleaned a sack of holly in the country lanes disposed of it within an hour . . . A hot roast chesnut barrow came upon the streets, and did good trade.' In our example the process will only come to an end when Y has expanded to 15 000. At this level of income, $S = 6000$ – sufficient to match $I = 6000$. Because $S = I$, this is the new equilibrium level of Y.

The sequence outlined above is shown in Table 28.1 and in Figure 28.7.

It will be noted that the increase in Y is much larger than the original increase in I. The ratio

$$\frac{\text{Increase in } AD}{\text{Initial increase in } I}$$

is known as the 'multiplier'.

Table 28.1
The Effect of an Increase in the Rate of I on the Level of Y

Period	C	I	S	Y
0	6 000	4 000	4 000	10 000
1	6 000	6 000	4 000	12 000
2	7 200	6 000	4 800	13 200
3	7 920	6 000	5 280	13 920
4	8 352	6 000	5 568	14 352
.	.	.	.	.
.	.	.	.	.
.	.	.	.	.
n	9 000	6 000	6 000	15 000

To see what the size of the multiplier depends upon, we an concentrate on changes in C, S and Y. As we are referring to changes, we shall prefix our symbols with the sign Δ. These changes are shown in Figure 28.8.

FIGURE 28.8
Increases in Consumption, Saving and Income Resulting from an Increase in the Rate of Investment

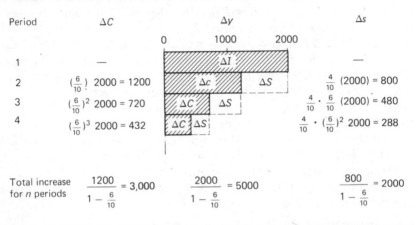

Period	ΔC	Δy	Δs
1	—		—
2	$(\frac{6}{10})$ 2000 = 1200		$\frac{4}{10}$ (2000) = 800
3	$(\frac{6}{10})^2$ 2000 = 720		$\frac{4}{10} \cdot \frac{6}{10}$ (2000) = 480
4	$(\frac{6}{10})^3$ 2000 = 432		$\frac{4}{10} \cdot (\frac{6}{10})^2$ 2000 = 288
Total increase for *n* periods	$\dfrac{1200}{1 - \frac{6}{10}} = 3{,}000$	$\dfrac{2000}{1 - \frac{6}{10}} = 5000$	$\dfrac{800}{1 - \frac{6}{10}} = 2000$

Figure 28.8 is explained as follows. The initial ΔI leads to an increase in Y. A proportion of these extra factor payments (for example, received by workers previously unemployed) is spent according to the marginal propensity to consume $(\frac{6}{10})$. The proportion not spent $(\frac{4}{10})$ is saved.

This extra spending increases AD, and therefore Y, still further. And so the process is repeated, extra increments of C going to swell the total increase in AD and therefore of Y.

These totals are shown at the foot of each column. Each is really a geometric progression of the form $a + ar + ar^2$, where r equals the marginal propensity to consume. Now the sum of a geometric progression to infinity where r is less than 1 equals $a/(1 - r)$. It follows, therefore, that:

$$\text{Total } \Delta Y = \frac{\Delta I}{1 - \text{marginal propensity to consume}}$$

The larger the marginal propensity to consume (c), the greater will be the total increase in Y. Since we defined the multiplier as $\Delta Y/\Delta I$, the value of the multiplier in this example is

$$\frac{1}{1 - c} = \frac{1}{1 - \frac{6}{10}} = 2\tfrac{1}{2}$$

This can be verified visually in Figure 28.8, where the shaded area equals the total increase in Y. If the proportion of income spent fell to $\frac{1}{2}$, the shaded areas would be smaller. Our analysis points to the reason for this. When the fraction of income consumed falls, a high proportion is saved.

Thus income does not have to expand so much in order to bring intended saving into line with investment.

This brings us to the basic difference between saving and investment in the process of income creation. Whereas an increase in investment will, other things being equal, automatically produce an increase in saving, an addition to saving need not lead to an increase in investment, income merely contracts until what is saved from it equals investment.

Diagrammatic Exposition of Changes in the Equilibrium Level of Income

Employment, we have assumed, varies directly with the level of income (AD), which itself depends upon spending on consumption and investment. If this total spending is equal to income, firms do not make losses and can continue employing the same amount of labour. If total spending is less than income, then firms make a loss because they are getting back less than their expenses of production, and so production is reduced. If total spending increases, then firms more than realise their expectations and production is expanded. This is explained in Figure 28.9.

The income–expenditure line, at an angle of 45°, traces all points where expenditure is equal to income (the same scale being chosen for both the x- and y-axes). Therefore, any point on this line will represent an equilibrium level of income.

The line C shows consumption expenditure at different levels of income. In our example $C = \frac{6}{10}Y$. To this we have to add investment expenditure of 4000 at all levels of income. Thus the line $C + I$ is vertically distant 4000 above the C line at all levels of income.

In equilibrium, $Y = AD = C + I$. The only point where this can occur is where the $C + I$ line cuts the 45° line. Here

$$AD = Y = 10\ 000$$

When I increases to 6000, the $C + I$ line moves vertically by 2000 to $C + I'$. AD immediately increases to 12 000, and so does Y. Of this income, $C = 7200$, which, with $I = 6000$, means that AD and Y increase to 13 200. This expansionary process continues until AD and Y are equal to 15 000.

Figure 28.9 (b) concentrates on leakages (S) and injections (I) as in our original approach (pp. 404–19). The equilibrium level of Y is 10 000. Less than this, Y is expanding because there is an unplanned running down of stocks. If Y exceeds 10 000, there is an unplanned accumulation of stocks, and Y decreases (eventually to 10 000) as workers are laid off.

If I increases by 2000, Y expands to 15 000.

Here the multiplier $\dfrac{\Delta Y}{\Delta I} = \dfrac{a}{b}$

FIGURE 28.9
The Effect on *Y* of a Change in *I*

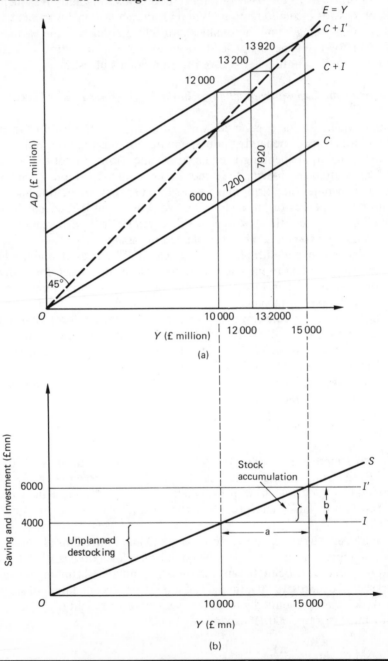

(a)

(b)

The Effect of a Diminishing Marginal Propensity to Consume

So far we have assumed that the marginal propensity to consume is constant at all levels of income. But, even if the propensity to consume diminishes as income increases, the principle of the multiplier is the same. The only difference is that the calculations are more complicated because, for each period increment, we have to apply a smaller multiplier, since the marginal propensity to consume diminishes as income increases.

28.6   The Effect of Changes in Consumption

An Autonomous Change in Consumption

So far we have analysed what happens to AD when there is an increase in autonomous investment. But the result is exactly the same if there is an autonomous increase in consumption, investment remaining unchanged.

Suppose, for instance, that C increases by 2000 at all levels of Y. That is, $C = 2000 + \frac{6}{10}Y$. This simply means that the original $C + I$ curve (Figure 28.9) would move vertically upwards by 2000 to the $C + I'$ position (as with an autonomous increase in I equal to 2000). The increase in C is subject to the same multiplier effect, and thus Y increases as before to 15 000.

The Paradox of Thrift

But what is the situation when there is a decrease in the propensity to consume, i.e. an increase in saving? Here we have what is often called the 'paradox of thrift'.

As we have seen, saving occurs because all income is not spent on consumption; people are limiting their demand for consumer goods. In real terms, they are saying that they will free factors from the production of goods for present consumption so that they can produce capital goods – houses, road, factories, power stations, machinery, etc. As we saw in Chapter 15, the acquisition of capital involves forgoing present consumption. In this respect, therefore, thrift is a virtue.

But when our peasant farmer reduced present consumption in order to make his plough (see p. 238), he automatically carried out investment with the time at his disposal. However, as we have seen, in a modern economy decisions to save and decisions to invest are carried out for different reasons by two different sets of persons – households and firms respectively. When intended saving is greater than investment, not all factors released from producing goods for present consumption are used to produce capital goods. Some are unemployed. From the community's point of view saving can only be in capital goods or additions to stocks.

When factors are unemployed there is no real saving – what they could have produced is lost to the community for ever.

What happens, as we have seen, is that income falls until it has reached that level where intended saving out of income just equals investment. Thus, if additional saving is not matched by additional investment, thrift is a curse, not a virtue, for it leads to a reduced standard of living as factors become unemployed and fewer consumer goods are produced.

Indeed, the fall in consumption is likely to have an adverse effect on firms' expectations. Therefore investment itself falls, causing an even greater fall in income. Thus the real paradox of thrift is that, in these circumstances, we can end up with less saving than we originally started with.

28.7   Government Spending and Taxation

We can now relax our assumption that there is no government activity. The government raises taxes (symbol T). T is a leak out of the circular flow of income, similar to saving.

But government spending (symbol G) is an injection into the flow of AD. Therefore, $AD = C + I + G$. This is shown in Figure 28.10.

G performs the same role as other forms of spending. Any increase in G will be subject to the multiplier. This can be illustrated from Figure 28.9. If, instead of the increase in I, the increase in AD took the form of $G = 2000$, the $C + I'$ line would be simply $C + I + G$, and the new level of Y would still be 15 000.

The effect of taxation is a little more difficult to analyse. However, we shall simplify by assuming: (a) taxes are not related to income (that is, they are imposed autonomously by the government as lump sums); (b) households spread the burden of any change in the level of taxation between consumption and saving.

Suppose $AD = C + I + G = 9000 + 4000 + 2000 = 15\,000 = Y$; assume also that there is no T. Thus disposable income still equals Y, $C = 9000$ and $S = 6000$. The government now decides to raise 2000 by taxation. Does this mean that Y falls back to 10 000? The answer is 'no'. Disposable income now equals $Y - T$: that is, there is an initial fall to 13 000. As a result there is an initial fall in $C(\frac{6}{10} \times 13\,000)$ to 7800. But this fall in C is subject to the multiplier; thus the total fall in Y equals $1200 \times \frac{10}{4} = 3000$, giving $Y = 12\,000$ with $C = 6000$, $I = 4000$ and $G = 2000$. The reason why Y does not fall to 10 000 is that part of the burden of T falls on S, which is already a leak from the circular flow of income.

Figure 28.11 illustrates the above diagrammatically. A lump sum direct tax of 2000 reduces disposable income. Consumption is therefore now only what it would be if disposable income were 2000 smaller at all levels of

FIGURE 28.10
The Circular Flow of Income and Government Spending and Taxation

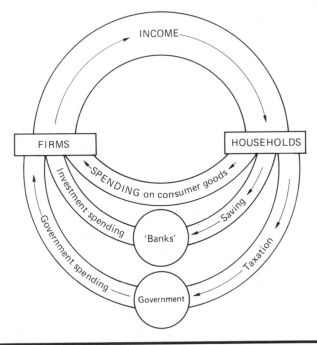

income. Thus the C curve moves downward vertically from C_0 to C_1 by 1200.

It should be noted that in moving from a budget deficit of 2000 to a balanced budget, the government has reduced Y by 3000. Similarly a budget deficit of 2000 from $Y = 12\ 000$ would increase Y by 3000. As we shall see, budgetary policy can be an important weapon in securing full employment or in combating inflation.

28.8 The Effect of Foreign Trade

We can now relax our assumption of a closed economy.

Let us assume that the production of consumer and investment goods is at a given level, and that there is unemployment. Now imagine that British firms obtain orders to supply £2000 worth of capital equipment to the USA. As a result, in the British economy AD and Y expand initially by 2000 – paid out in wages, salaries and profits, the cost being covered by entrepreneurs borrowing the money.

FIGURE 28.11
The Effect of an Increase in Taxation on Disposable Income and Consumption

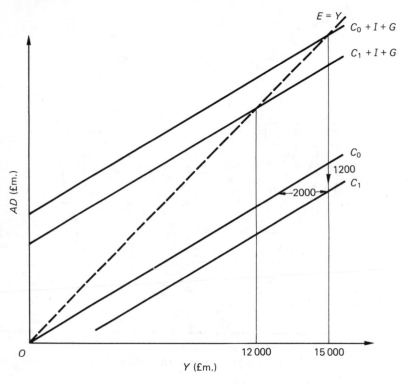

But this is not all. Of the initial 2000 increase, 1200 will be spent and 800 saved. The 1200 spent now becomes income of other persons, who in their turn spend 720 and save 480. So we could go on. The position is exactly the same as with investment – additional spending by persons abroad on British exports has a multiplier effect depending upon the marginal propensity to consume. In this case, as a result of the initial additional spending of 2000 on exports, AD increases by 5000.

Increased spending on imports, given the conditions of unemployment stipulated above, works in exactly the opposite way. There is now more spending on foreign goods, and less on British. As a result, foreign rather than British workers supply goods for the home market. Less expenditure on home-produced goods means that income is taken out of the circular flow, and AD contracts. As before, the initial loss of income is multiplied according to the marginal propensity to consume.

We can summarise the position as follows. Expenditure on exports is equivalent to an addition to investment – income is generated in producing goods which do not become available on the home market. Expenditure on imports, on the other hand, is a leak from the circular flow of income similar to a reduction of consumption (Figure 28.12).

Thus we can combine the effect on *AD* of changes in investment, exports and imports as follows:

$$\text{Increase in } AD = \frac{\text{Increase in } I + \text{Exports} - \text{Imports}}{1 - c}$$

The above explanation, however, does assume that both exports and imports are autonomous, i.e. they bear no precise relationship to the level of income. We shall continue this assumption with exports, though it could be that these decline as income expands, since it is now easier to sell on the home market.

But imports are likely to form a proportion of consumer spending and therefore of income. Thus if we assume that imports form $\frac{1}{6} C$, we can say

FIGURE 28.12
Total Leaks and Injections

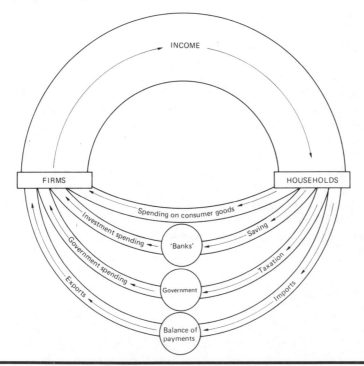

that the 'propensity to import' is $\frac{1}{10} Y$. We can now treat this import leakage in the same way as saving. Whatever the cause of the initial expansion in Y, leakages occur because some of this increased Y will be saved and some will be spent on imports. Thus, when m represents the *marginal* propensity to import, we have:

$$\text{Change in } AD = \frac{\text{Change in } I + \text{Change in exports}}{1 - c + m}$$

Suppose, for instance, that income is in equilibrium at 10 000. Up to this there is no foreign trade, and $C = 6000$ and $S = 4000$. At any income above this the marginal propensity to import is $\frac{1}{6}C = \frac{1}{10}Y$. If there are now exports of 2000, the increase in Y will be 2000 $1/(\frac{4}{10} + \frac{1}{10}) = 4000$.

The analysis of this section indicates why, during the 1930s, many countries tried to solve their unemployment problems by pushing exports (which increase income and therefore employment) and by discouraging imports (which decrease income). A little reflection will show, however, that such a restrictionist policy merely 'exports' unemployment to other countries. Nowadays we realise that countries must cooperate with one another in fighting unemployment (see pp. 523,540).

28.9   Concluding Reservation

The above analysis follows very closely Keynes's explanation of the level of activity – its dependence on an adequate level of AD.

But when we come to discuss government policy for achieving full employment, the problem is more complex. The many objectives of government stabilisation policy are interrelated and cannot be dropped into different boxes with separate measures to deal with each.

In this chapter, the model, following Keynes, has assumed a stable price level. But, as we shall see, this is unrealistic for the price level rises as AD is approached. Thus, while the maintenance of AD is essential, the model has to be extended to allow for price changes.

Furthermore, changes in the level of AD and in the price level have repercussions on the balance-of-payments situation.

These are the interrelationships which are examined in Chapters 29 and 36.

Part VI

The Government and Stabilisation Intervention

29 Full Employment

29.1 Unemployment

The Nature of Unemployment

Although today (June 1990) 5.5 per cent of the working population are unemployed, this compares favourably with the situation in pre-war Britain, where in the worst year – 1932 – the national unemployment rate was 22.1 per cent. Unemployment means that labour, machines, land and buildings stand idle; as a result, the standard of living is lower than it need be. But the real curse is the human misery that results. Many people, without work for years, lose hope of ever finding a job; in any case skills deteriorate as the period of unemployment lengthens. Thus unemployment is usually discussed in terms of labour.

Unemployment is said to occur when persons capable of and willing to work are unable to find suitable paid employment. Important points concerning and arising out of this definition, however, need to be stressed:

1. Unemployment must be involuntary; persons on strike are not reckoned as being unemployed.
2. 'Persons capable of work' must exclude the 'unemployable' – those not capable of work through mental or physical disability. On the other hand, unemployables are usually in the pool of unemployed labour seeking jobs and, where labour is scarce, more use will be made of them – provided that minimum wage regulations do not prevent this.
3. Full employment does not mean that workers will never be required to switch jobs or occupations. Changes in the conditions of demand and supply are bound to occur, and such changes will be more frequent the more dynamic the economy and the more a country is dependent on international trade.

Thus there will always be some workers unemployed. A full employment policy must identify and deal with the particular cause of the unemployment.

Interpreting Unemployment Figures

Measuring unemployment involves problems of definition. How, for example, should part-time workers be treated? Is registration at a Job-centre to be the test for inclusion?

But interpretation of the figures also necessitates subjective judgements as to the extent to which they are over or understated. When employment is buoyant, does the figure conceal 'disguised' unemployment in that firms are reluctant to release redundant workers or because some employees are working at less than their full potential? Is a high rate of job turnover adding to frictional unemployment? Are minimum wage regulations leading to unemployment? Is the rate of unemployment benefit, especially the 'poverty trap', discouraging an active search for work? In comparing unemployment rates over time should not some allowance be made for a changing age structure?

The Causes of Unemployment

1. Frictional

Unless the economy is completely static, there will always be people changing their jobs. Some merely desire a change of employment or a move to a different part of the country. In certain occupations, e.g. unskilled labour in the construction industry, workers are not employed regularly by any one employer: when a particular contract is completed, labour is made redundant. Occasionally, too, workers are discharged when a factory is being reorganised.

Unemployed workers usually register at the local Jobcentre, forming a pool of labour from which employers can fill vacancies. But how large should this pool be? If it is too large, workers remain unemployed for long periods. If it is too small, production is dislocated by bottlenecks in filling vacancies (with employers holding on to labour not currently needed), by job-switching just for the sake of change and, above all, by strikes in support of claims for higher wages.

Frictional unemployment is partly unavoidable, and the grant of unemployment benefit affords the worker some protection against its effects. Moreover, the installation of expensive machinery which must be kept fully employed has quite often had the indirect effect of 'decasual-ising' labour. In any case, it is easier to minimise unemployment when there is full employment in the economy.

2. Seasonal

Employment in some industries, e.g. building, fruit-picking and holiday catering, is seasonal in character. The difficulty is that the skills required by different seasonal jobs are not 'substitutable'. To what extent, for example, can hotel workers become shop assistants in the January sales? Seasonal employment is not completely avoidable. But it can be reduced if a small, regular labour force will work overtime during the 'season' and admit, say, students during the busy periods. Moreover, the price system may help. By offering off-season rates, hotels at holiday resorts can attract autumn conferences.

3. *International*

Because the UK is so dependent on international trade, she is particularly vulnerable to unemployment brought about by a fall in the demand for her exports. Such a fall may occur because:

(1) THE PRICES OF UK GOODS ARE TOO HIGH TO BE COMPETITIVE IN WORLD MARKETS
If home prices rise, for example because of wage increases, the export market is likely to be hit severely. The demand for exports is usually highly elastic, since substitutes are often available from competing countries. The effect on employment is shown in Figure 29.1. The wage increase moves the supply curve from S to S_1. Because demand is elastic there is a considerable fall in the demand for the good, from OM to OM_1. The industry, and therefore employment, contract.

(2) INCOMES OF MAJOR IMPORTING COUNTRIES MAY BE REDUCED BY A RECESSION
OR A DETERIORATION IN THE TERMS OF TRADE
If incomes of importing countries fall, their demand for UK goods, especially those having a high income-elasticity of demand, will be likely to

---

FIGURE 29.1
The Effect on Employment of a Wage Increase in an Export Industry

Quantity of export good demanded and supplied

---

decrease. This is what happened following the increases in the price of oil in 1973 and 1979.

4. Structural

Structural unemployment, like frictional, results largely from the immobility of labour. Ignorance of opportunities elsewhere or, more likely, obstacles to moving mean that workers do not move to available jobs in other parts of the country. Thus today local authorities in the south of England are, because of the higher cost of housing, finding it difficult to recruit from high unemployment regions.

More serious, however, is occupational immobility resulting from long-term changes in the conditions of demand and supply in certain industries, especially exporting industries.

On the demand side, there may be a change in any of the factors influencing the conditions of demand. The price of substitutes may fall (Dundee jute products have largely been replaced by plastics), or foreign buyers may switch to competitors' goods (British shipyards have been hit by Japanese competition). On the supply side, new techniques or the exhaustion of mineral deposits may make labour redundant. Automation has reduced ICI's demand for workers at Stockton; exhaustion of the better coal seams has led to the closure of pits in south Wales and mid-Scotland.

Where an industry is highly localised in a particular area, the resulting unemployment may be particularly serious (see Chapter 31).

5. Cyclical

The term 'cyclical unemployment' refers to the alternate booms and slumps in the level of industrial activity which have occurred over the last hundred years. It was the major cause of the high unemployment of the 1930s, and while we no longer speak of a 'trade cycle', we do still move between boom and recession.

This is the most serious form of unemployment and is the subject matter of the rest of this chapter.

29.2 Demand Management

Policy Implications of Keynes

As we saw in Chapter 28, Keynes considered that cylical employment was brought about by inadequate AD. The policy implication was that AD had to be expanded to, and maintained at, a level which was adequate for achieving the full employment level of output.

The analysis of Chapter 28 assumed a fixed price level. Keynes recognised that there would be some upward movement of prices as full employment was approached, but his main concern was with unemployment and so he gave little attention to remedies on the supply side. For one thing, cutting money wages generally would mean that receipts of firms from spending by workers would also fall, and so there would be no net gain. In any case, while cutting money wages to produce a fall in *real* wages would increase the demand for labour, such a cut would be resisted by workers and would therefore only be achieved after a prolonged period of unemployment.

It must be remembered that Keynes was writing his *General Theory* against the background of the high cyclical unemployment of the 1930s. For him, therefore, unemployment was the major problem.

To combat cyclical unemployment, AD must be maintained at an adequate level. The responsibility for this must rest with the government. First, only the government can exercise the powers, particularly as regards collecting the statistics and information necessary for adequate planning. Second, the government's own spending forms such a large proportion of AD that, to a great extent, it can be used to balance variations in the private sector. Third, the knowledge that the government is committed to a full-employment policy will eliminate much of the uncertainty from which cyclical fluctuations begin.

Post-war Demand Management in the UK

Britain's pre-war experience of unemployment and the solution afforded by Keynes's theory dominated economic policy during the 1950s and 1960s. The overriding aim of full employment encouraged successive governments to expand AD to the point where there were more vacancies than unemployed workers to fill them. Whereas the minimum rate of unemployment achieved by both the USA and West Germany was 3 per cent, successive UK governments maintained an AD which until 1974 (apart from 1971–2) kept unemployment below this. Whenever expansion of AD led to balance-of-payments difficulties, the government imposed temporary 'stop' policies. 'Fine-tuning' the economy in this way appeared to be working for the comparatively low inflation rate of 5 per cent seemed an acceptable price to pay for maintaining such a low rate of unemployment.

The fundamentals of the policy are outlined in Figure 29.2. Full employment requires Y to equal OE. An AD as shown by $C + I + G'$, however, will produce equilibrium where $Y = OF = OZ$. If we look at the situation from the full-employement level of Y at E, there is a deficiency of AD equal to LM – the 'deflationary' gap. The government has to raise the AD curve to $C + I + G$, chiefly by increasing its own spending. Should AD expand beyond this, the extra income of EG is unobtainable and this overheating would result in rising prices, increased imports and falling

FIGURE 29.2
Equilibrium Levels of Income

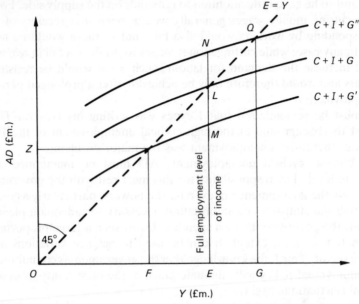

exports as home-produced goods became less price-competitive. An *AD*
represented by $C + 1 + G''$ would have to be reduced by the inflationary
gap of *NL*.

Weaknesses of the Keynesian Approach

Keynes's preoccupation with maintaining a high level of employment led
him, and in particular his followers, to underemphasise other possible
repercussions. 'Fine-tuning' the economy was in reality only dealing with
the part of the iceberg showing above the surface. The high level of
demand produced a state of 'overfull' employment, with vacancies consistently exceeding unemployed workers. The outcome was inflation,
balance-of-payments difficulties, shortages of skilled workers, high labour
turnover, firms holding on to surplus workers in case they should be
required in the future ('disguised' unemployment), underinvestment in
new equipment, a failure by industry to adopt new techniques or to switch
to the production of high-technology products and an unsatisfactory rate of
growth (see Chapter 32). As a result, British industry was in poor shape to
withstand international competition during the world recessions of 1974–5
and 1979–82.

More than that, in the 1970s the rate of inflation and the level of unemployment increased together – a situation known as 'stagflation'. Hence Keynes's views came under increasing scrutiny.

First, too little attention had been given to how supply responds to increases in AD as full employment is approached. The analysis of Chapter 28 assumed a stable price level. This is justifiable at higher rates of unemployment. Firms have spare capacity and can increase output at constant costs. Increased AD is therefore covered by increased output and the price level remains stable. But eventually, as output increases, firms experience rising costs owing to more intensive use of existing capacity and bottlenecks in obtaining variable factors. As a result prices rise.

Second, Keynes underplayed the side effects of a large PSBR which high government spending could give rise to. Keynes recognised that government deficit-spending would increase the National Debt, but since loans could be 'rolled over' as they matured, only interest had to be currently paid and, apart from overseas lenders, such payments were simply transfers from taxpayers to lenders within the UK. But servicing a large PSBR has effects unrecognised by Keynes. If it is covered by borrowing from the banks, their extra liquidity allows them to increase the supply of money. If, alternatively, it is covered by non-bank borrowing, e.g. by institutions or persons buying government bonds, the price has to be sufficiently attractive to clear the market. Thus the rate of interest rises. This could cause private investment to fall – 'crowded out' by the increased government spending!

Third, Keynes's theory of changes in the price level gave insufficient weight to the role of trade union inflationary expectations in the wage-bargaining process (see Chapter 30).

Fourth, and more important, Keynes's theory of the price level failed to recognise that increases in the money supply could have the effect of increasing AD directly (see Chapter 30).

All these criticisms will be developed as we proceed.

The Meaning of Full Employment Today

While our presentation (Chapter 28 and Figure 29.2) of the Keynesian theory of the level of activity has, for the sake of clarity, shown the full employment level of income as a single point, it is, in the real world, a too simplistic and static approach. The incompatibility of government objectives – particularly full employment and price stability – means that in practice there is no precise target full-employment level of income which can be achieved and maintained by 'fine-tuning'.

Instead the 'full-employment' position has to be decided politically according to the emphasis placed by the government on its other economic objectives. What is certain, however, is that the level of 3 per cent, which until 1970s people regarded as the maximum acceptable, has been modified by subsequent events. High rates of inflation and of unemployment have meant that most political parties now recognise that unemployment of around 5 to 6 per cent is a more realistic compromise target.

A Revised Analytical Approach

Recognition of the fact that the objective of full employment has to be considered in conjunction at least with movements in the price level means that we need a somewhat different approach from the basic Keynesian aggregate demand model outlined in Chapter 28. That assumed that the price level is unchanged. Now we have to relate changes in aggregate to demand to changes in the price level. This is achieved by paying more attention to the supply side, as follows.

29.3 Aggregate Demand and Aggregate Supply

Our task is to build a model which (1) shows how AD and AS change with respect to the price level, and (2) brings AD and AS together to determine both the level of activity and the appropriate price level.

The AD Curve

In Chapter 28 it was shown that AD consisted of the total of all *planned* spending on final goods and services in the economy; that is, consumers' expenditure + investment + government spending + (exports − imports). In terms of the symbols previously used:

$$AD = C + I + G + (X-M)$$

The AD curve shows how this total spending changes in response to changes in the price level. It is assumed that the money supply, taxation rates and the marginal propensity to consume remain constant. Since we are dealing with final goods and services, AD is the demand for real output. To simplify we will concentrate on C and I.

The AD curve slopes downwards from left to right (Figure 29.3), showing that, as the price level falls, AD expands. In other words, the lower the price level, the greater will be the total real output demanded in the economy.

The reasons for this are:

FIGURE 29.3

The Relationship of Output and the Price Level to *AD* and *AS*

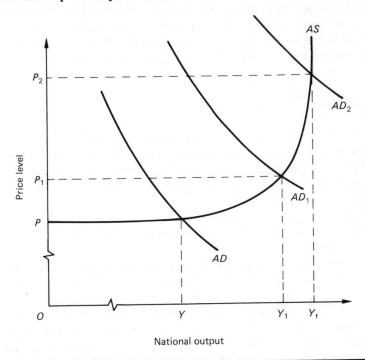

National output

1. Consumers are Wealthier

Given no change in the money supply, a fall in the price level increases the purchasing power of all balances held in cash. In other words, if all prices fall, the cash held will buy more. Thus spending on goods and services increases.

2. The Rate of Interest Falls

With no change in the money supply, a fall in prices means that there is less demand for money for transactions purposes, leaving more for the purchase of both goods and 'bonds'. This extra liquidity raises the price of 'bonds'. That is, the rate of interest falls. As a result, spending which is financed mainly by borrowing – particularly houses and cars and, above all, firms' investment – increases.

3. Home-produced Goods are More Competitive

When their price falls, home-produced goods become more competitive in foreign markets and so exports increase. Furthermore, because these goods are now relatively cheaper on the home market than imported substitutes, imports tend to decrease. Taken together, X − M increases.

Of course, the opposite effects apply for a rise in the price level.

The AS Curve

The AS curve shows the relationship between the price level and the real output of the economy. It is, however, a short-run supply curve; that is, the capital capacity of the economy as a whole is fixed so that output can only be varied by increasing or decreasing inputs of the variable factors, chiefly labour.

In general, high prices enable firms to extend output. But for analytical purposes, we have to distinguish between three broadly different situations, as follows.

At a low level of output, firms have surplus capacity; they can therefore increase output at constant costs. Equally, efficient labour can be taken on and other necessary variable inputs, such as basic materials and components, obtained at existing prices. In the economy as a whole, this increased spending by firms on resources is matched by a proportionate increase in output. Thus there is no pressure on prices to rise. The *AS* curve is perfectly elastic at the current price level, *P*, for the output *OY* (Figure 29.3).

Eventually, however, as the full employment output is approached, fixed capital equipment has to be used more intensively, and diminishing returns set in. In addition, what are usually termed 'bottlenecks' appear through skilled labour shortages, longer delivery dates for components, etc. Thus firms' marginal and average costs rise and the *AS* curve turns upwards.

The *AS* curve slopes upwards at an increasing rate the nearer output approaches OY_f. Since we are dealing with the short-run situation, output can expand no further. We have reached the maximum potential output which is attainable with given limited resources and current technology. The vertical portion is thus the equivalent of the long period *AS* curve. It can be shifted to the right only by factors which make for long-term growth (see Chapter 32). Given this absolutely inelastic AS curve, any attempt to expand output by increasing AD will be impossible and will simply find its outlet in steeply rising prices.

AD and AS Combined

Equilibrium occurs at the intersection of the *AD* and *AS* curves because at this point the output which households and firms are willing to spend on *C* and *I* equals the output which firms will supply. Thus in Figure 29.3 when aggregate demand is AD_1, real national output in OY_1 per year (still less than full employment) and the price level is P_1. Full employment can only be achieved by increasing aggregate demand to AD_2, when the price level will rise to P_2. These increases in AD have led to demand-pull inflation (see Chapter 30).

29.4 Government Full Employment Policy

The Significance of the Keynesian Approach

One conclusion to be drawn from the above analysis is that an adequate level of AD is necessary if output is to be maintained somewhere near the full employment level. The importance of Keynes was that he highlighted this essential fact.

What he failed to stress was that an inflationary situation could develop once the AS curve starts to rise if AD continues to be increased. Since he was concentrating on the high level of unemployment, he was concerned with the horizontal part of the AS curve up to OY. The assumption of a stable price level was thus by and large permissible, and so policy need only be directed to increasing AD.

But what Figure 29.3 shows is that if AD is increased beyond OY then extra employment is accompanied by rising prices and, as we show in the next chapter, this does not result in a mere inflationary situation but can develop into a process of rising prices. Since the AD and AS curves are not independent, an increase in wage-rates, for instance, moves the AS upwards. The resulting rise in prices produces further wage demands and the AD curve moves to the right.

Keynes did show, too, *how* the government can increase AD. This is no real problem, and we deal with it below.

Thus the essential part of Figure 29.3 is the AS curve between OY and OY_f (shown in Figure 29.4) for policy now involves a decision on how to reduce unemployment still further and at the same time how to deal with rising prices.

The Supply-side Approach

From this dilemma there has developed another strategy which has gained strength in recent years. Instead of concentrating entirely on AD, why not

FIGURE 29.4
Supply-side Strategy

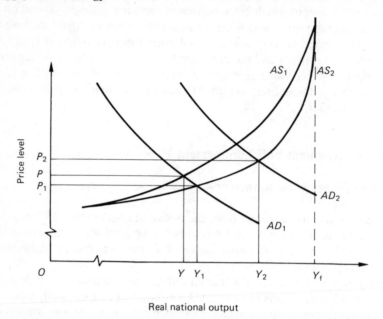

Real national output

apply policies to lower the short-run supply curve? If, for instance, such policies could lower the AS curve from AS_1 to AS_2 with aggregate demand of AD_1, employment could be increased to OY_1 at a lower price level P_1. Even if aggregate demand were increased to AD_2 to reduce unemployment to Y_2 Y_f, the price level need then only rise to P_2.

Our immediate task therefore is to fill out in more detail the policies associated with: (a) demand management; (b) supply-side economics.

The Nature of Government Intervention Policies

It must be appreciated that there is no given formula for government intervention policy. The situation which the government has to deal with is constantly changing. Furthermore, different governments react differently to similar situations.

In fact the role of the government in controlling the economy can be likened to that of the driver of a car going to work in a city. At no time can the car run on its own without some direction, and the driver has to make the necessary adjustments continuously. From time to time, too, he or she is concerned with more definite alterations, varying pressure on the accelerator and changing gear. The driver may even modify the route, making detours to avoid traffic congestions.

But in all these manoeuvres, different drivers act differently. Some use the gear lever rather than the accelerator in changing speed. Others estimate that the traffic congestion will not be so bad as to warrant a detour. Nor does the same person do exactly the same things each day. The driver knows many different routes to work and, being flexible, makes use of them as he or she thinks fit.

So it is with the government. Like the driver guessing the traffic congestion along the route, the government has to work from incomplete information in estimating what change in AD is necessary to produce the desired result and the extent to which the measures it adopts will produce that change. It has two main types of control – monetary and fiscal – but it usually has to combine them in different ways. Not only does one reinforce the other, but a different emphasis has to be placed on each at different times in order to meet the needs of the prevailing situation. Where a quick change in the direction or tempo of the economy is required, more weight must be given to those measures which begin to work immediately, e.g. a reduction of taxation to increase consumption spending.

It should be noted, however, that with all policies, timing and technique are crucial. If, for instance, reflationary action to pull the economy out of recession is taken when it has begun to turn up of its own accord, subsequent pressure on the price level may exceed that anticipated.

29.5 Policies for Managing AD

Policy prescriptions for regulating AD are basically of two kinds, monetary and fiscal.

Monetary Policy

Monetary measures are aimed at varying the cost and availability of credit.

The *cost of credit* is the rate of interest which has to be paid. Nevertheless, as noted earlier (pp. 415–6), there are doubts about its effectiveness in influencing long-term investment spending. In any case, the rate of interest does not discriminate in its operation, e.g. as between firms which export a high proportion of their output and those which do not, and projects of high social value (e.g. slum clearance) and those of less certain merit (e.g. gaming casinos). On the other hand, its impact is not neutral for it may be severe on industries the demand for whose products is particularly dependent on borrowed funds, e.g. housing construction, property development and consumer durable goods.

Nor can interest policy be operated in isolation from the general level of world rates. If, for instance, the UK retains interest rates which are low in relation to those of the rest of the world, there will be an outflow of short-term capital and a consequent lowering of the sterling exchange rate (see Chapter 35).

Even so, in recent years varying the short-term rate of interest has been the government's major weapon for adjusting AD. It can be applied quickly and to a fine degree and, if implemented early, can provide advance warning of the authorities' intentions. Indeed the psychological effects of changes are probably as important as their direct effect on investment spending.

The *availability of credit* is concerned with the *overall level of liquidity* and *selective controls*. The former is linked to the money supply. But today the monetarist view prevails: expanding the money supply to prevent the rate of interest from rising will eventually have inflationary consequences (see pp. 457–8). Thus attempts have been made to tie the overall level of liquidity to targeted ceilings for selected definitions of money (see p. 460 and pp. 580–1), the rate of interest being adjusted to bring the demand for credit into line with government present policy.

In contrast, *selective controls* are really only applicable when the interest rate is being held below the market clearing rate. Because the demand for credit exceeds supply at this lower rate, some allocation by controls becomes necessary. In the past, such credit controls have been exercised mainly by restrictions on bank advances and hire purchase.

Today, however, the government would experience difficulty in monitoring physical controls. Since the abolition of exchange control in 1979, funds can move worldwide. This has been helped by foreign banks and other intermediaries setting up branches in London, and by the development of wholesale deposit markets (particularly in Eurocurrency) and electronic dealing.

Fiscal Policy

In the context of full employment, fiscal policy refers to changes in government expenditure and taxation designed to vary the level of AD. These changes are broadly of two types: (1) those which operate automatically; (2) those which are discretionary in that they are specifically initiated by the government.

1. Automatic Stabilisers

One of the government's difficulties in maintaining the level of activity is knowing exactly when, and by how much, expenditure needs to be varied. It would be advantageous, therefore, if forces came automatically into play to correct any movements away from the full employment level of AD. To some extent this does occur, for as income expands or contracts, monetary and real forces influence consumption, investment and international trade in the desired direction.

This also happens in the public sector where increased government activity over the last sixty years has meant that its income and expenditure operate as major stabilisers.

Taxation is important in this respect. As incomes increase, so does the yield from taxation especially if taxation is progressive, e.g. income tax, or, like VAT, is applied on an *ad valorem* basis to expensive goods having a high income elasticity of demand. One important point must be made. If the stabilising effects of taxation are to work, the government must not increase its own expenditure as tax receipts rise, and vice versa.

Government spending on unemployment benefits and agricultural price support also has stabilising effects for, as unemployment increases, so do benefit payments, while there are likely to be increased subsidies to maintain farmers' incomes.

Nevertheless, built-in stabilisers cannot be relied upon solely to even out fluctuations in activity. They therefore have to be reinforced by discretionary corrective measures, which preferably should *anticipate* likely movements in AD. In fact, if not taken early, the delayed action of such measures could even accentuate fluctuations, e.g. by applying reflationary policies to counter a recession just as the economy had started to turn up of its own accord, and vice versa.

2. Discretionary Fiscal Changes

The muted built-in effect of the automatic stabilisers means that the government has to reinforce them with ad hoc fiscal policies.

Indirectly, fiscal policy can influence private consumption and investment by simply changing the *type* of taxes levied. Thus a switch from indirect taxation would tend to increase consumption, for it would mean greater spending power for poorer people (those having a high propensity to consume). Similarly, a movement away from taxes on companies would tend to increase investment through improved profitability. But altering the structure of taxation simply to effect short-term adjustments in AD is too cumbersome a weapon.

Changes in government spending increase AD directly. Much government spending, however, is more or less contractual (e.g. social welfare benefits, interest on the National Debt), while public projects, such as motorways, schools and hospitals cannot be put on ice until there is a deficiency in AD. Long-term government policy, not short-term marginal adjustments according to the level of activity, must decide priorities for such projects.

Because of these disadvantages, public spending programmes are unlikely to be sufficiently flexible for 'fine-tuning' AD. Fortunately, the government has another weapon, usually referred to as 'budgetary policy'.

Here the aim is to influence private consumption (C) by varying personal disposable income through changes in taxation. Thus a simple decrease in a direct lump-sum tax of ΔT increases disposable income by ΔT. As a result C is increased acording to the marginal propensity to consume (c) by $c\Delta T$.

This produces, via the multiplier, an increase in Y equal to $\dfrac{c\Delta T}{1-c}$ In

terms of Figure 28.11, the C curve will rise. Thus, if government spending remains unchanged, the curve $C_1 + I + G$ will rise to $C_0 + I + G$.

Attention must be paid to the phrase 'if government spending remains unchanged'. Budgetary policy is essentially one of adjusting the relationship between government taxation and expenditure. As we have seen, taxation represents an appropriation by the government of a part of private incomes. The amount so appropriated is retained in the circular flow of income only in so far as it is spent by the government. Hence AD will be increased if taxation is less than government spending and vice versa. If previously the budget were balanced, there will now be a budget deficit, and vice versa.

In other words, if AD is less than necessary to maintain full employment, the government can run a budget deficit and thus stimulate spending which, if continued from year to year will, through the multiplier, increase the size of the national income flow. Conversely, in an inflationary situation, by a combination of increasing taxation and reducing its own expenditure, the government can run a budget surplus, thereby increasing public saving to balance the deficiency in private saving.

Thus today the budget is regarded not simply as the means of raising revenue to meet the year's estimated expenditure, but as a weapon to adjust private spending power to the output which available resources can produce given the demands of the public sector. Since, as explained above, the ability to vary public expenditure is limited, it is taxation which tends to take the strain.

Such a policy is not without its difficulties. First, the convention of annual budgets tends to dictate the timing of major adjustments. However, 'mini' budgets are possible, while the 'regulator' does allow the Chancellor to vary indirect taxes by up to 25 per cent either way between budgets. Second, reducing taxes may, because of administrative difficulties, take time to be effective. With PAYE, for instance, new tax tables have to be distributed. Thus reliefs will often have to concentrate on putting extra purchasing power quickly into the hands of consumers, e.g. by reducing National Insurance contributions and indirect taxes. Taxation, too, has objectives other than that of adjusting AD – redistributing income, for instance. But a rise in taxation may have to be achieved by increasing indirect taxes because of possible disincentive effects of high income tax. Thus policies can conflict. Third, overall budgetary policy makes it difficult to direct demand into those districts and industries where unemployment is highest. Again we see the necessity of having a variety of measures which can be applied to the needs of a particular situation. Finally, the deficit may be so large and persistent that the size of the PSBR creates problems elsewhere. Not only does it increase the National Debt and thus the revenue which has to be raised to service interest payments but, and more important, if it is covered by borrowing from the banks, it increases the money supply and adds to inflationary pressure (see p. 579–80). Thus fiscal policy can only be used in conjunction with monetary policy.

Nevertheless, budgetary policy does allow the national product to be allocated between the private and public sectors according to their relative priorities. Certain tasks can be undertaken better by the State – road-building, defence, health care, etc. – and the government must decide on the proportion of the national product which shall be devoted to each of these. Taxes adjust private demand in order to release resources for the public sector. If there is full employment, excessive private demand must be reduced by increased taxation or public expenditure reduced. If, on the other hand, private demand is insufficient to employ resources not required for the public sector, taxation must be decreased.

29.6 Supply-side Economics

The Objective of Supply-side Measures

The objective of supply-side measures is to shift the short-run aggregate supply curve from AS to AS_1 (Figure 29.5). If this succeeds the government can follow policies to expand AD without incurring an unacceptable rise in the price level.

In Figure 29.5, output of the economy is originally OM and the price level at P. In order to reduce unemployment the government increases aggregate demand from AD to AD_1. At the same time, however, supply-side measures move the aggregate supply curve from AS to AS_1. Thus while unemployment is reduced by MM_1, the price level remains at P.

The advocates of supply-side economics hold that this movement of the short-run AS curve can be achieved by freeing controls over markets, introducing positive measures to lower costs and by providing incentives for greater effort and for releasing enterprise and initiative. In essence, these proposals reflect their belief in the basic efficiency of the free market system. They introduce largely microeconomic measures to deal with macroeconomic problems.

FIGURE 29.5
Supply-side Policy

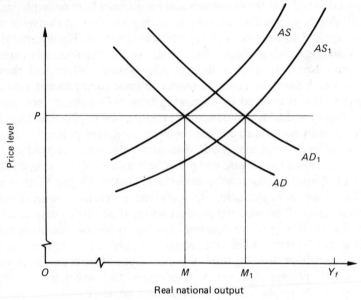

Market Freedom

Markets must be allowed to work more freely and steps taken to improve this efficiency by:

(a) freeing them from government controls (e.g. incomes policy, minimum wage regulations, pricing policies of the nationalised industries);
(b) promoting competition (e.g. in real property conveyancing, optical and financial services);
(c) restricting the power of trade unions (e.g. through precipitate and sympathetic strike action, unofficial strikes, the closed shop);
(d) the privatisation programme (see pp. 320–4);
(e) introducing competition in the natural monopolies by new devices (see pp. 323–4);
(f) removing institutional barriers in the capital market (e.g. exchange control, the Stock Exchange);
(g) using the rate of interest (the price of liquid capital) as the main weapon for adjusting aggregate demand.

Cost Reduction

Positive measures to effect a lowering of costs include:

(a) reducing national insurance contributions (an *ad valorem* tax on employing labour);
(b) improving the supply and quality of labour, e.g. by developing training schemes, encouraging flexible working hours to attract part-time workers, improving mobility, granting subsidies to firms to locate in the Assisted Areas where surplus workers are available (see p. 473).
(c) providing advisory services (e.g. on the EC's Single Market 1992).

Incentives

Incentives designed to increase effort, reward enterprise and encourage saving and investment include:

(a) an emphasis on the effect of a reduction in the marginal rate of income tax on effort, etc. even though it may reduce total tax revenue;
(b) a lower corporation tax to encourage investment and the taking of entrepreneurial risks;
(c) special help for new firms to obtain the initial capital, e.g. 'start-up' schemes, the Business Enterprise Scheme;
(d) profit-related pay (which gives employees a direct stake in the success of the company and enables pay to respond more readily to changing market conditions), share option schemes and wider share ownership generally.

The above represent a variety of measures to create conditions in which the free play of market forces can stimulate the economy to work more efficiently. They have formed a major part of the Thatcher government economic programme since 1979.

30 Maintaining Currency Stability

30.1 The Effects of Inflation

Inflation can be defined as a sustained rise in money prices generally. Today the control of inflation is given priority in government policy. To appreciate why, we have to look at the effects of rising prices or – what is the same thing – a fall in the value of money. It is then necessary to consider the causes of inflation and the possible remedies that can be applied.

Possible Benefits

At one time, a gently rising price level was not viewed with too much concern. It improved the climate for investment and so helped to maintain aggregate demand. Moreover, it tended to reduce the real burden of servicing the National Debt: while interest payments are fixed in money terms, receipts from taxation increase as money national income rises.

The snag, however, is that, once started, the rise in prices is difficult to contain. At first it becomes uncomfortable, producing undesirable results, both internal and external. Eventually the rate of inflation increases. The situation is then serious, for it is much more difficult to reverse the trend. Indeed it can develop into runaway inflation.

Internal Disadvantages

1. Income and wealth are redistributed arbitrarily, for inflation imposes a tax on those who hold money as opposed to those holding real assets. Moreover, not only does inflation reduce the standard of living of persons dependent on fixed incomes, e.g. pensioners, but it benefits debtors and penalises lenders (unless the loan is 'inflation-proofed').

452

Thus the stability upon which all lending and borrowing depends is undermined.

2. Interest rates rise, both because people require a higher reward for lending money which is falling in value and also because the government is forced to take disinflationary measures.
3. Investment is discouraged by government anti-inflation policy. In practice, controls imposed on prices are more effective than those on costs, particularly wages. The result is an erosion of profits and a disincentive to invest.
4. Saving is discouraged because postponing consumption simply means that goods cost more if bought later.
5. Inflation encourages speculation by the purchase of real assets by borrowing rather than investment by the use of resources in production. Indeed inflation discourages investment in long-term projects because possible government anti-inflation policies are difficult to forecast.
6. Inefficiency is encouraged because a buoyant sellers' market blunts competition as higher prices obtained for their products allow even inefficient firms to survive.
7. Inflation generates industrial and social unrest since there is competition for higher incomes. Thus, because of rising prices, trade unions ask for annual wage rises. Often demands exceed the rate of inflation, anticipating future rises or seeking a larger share of the national cake to improve their members' real standard of living. Those with the most 'muscle' gain at the expense of weaker groups.
8. Additional administrative costs are incurred in off-setting go-slow and work to rule disruptions, allowing for inflation in negotiating contracts and wage rates, revising price lists and labels, etc.
9. The rate of inflation tends to increase, largely because high wage settlements in anticipation of higher future prices help to bring about the very rise which people fear.

External Effects

Inflation can create serious difficulties for a country dependent on international trade, as Britain has discovered over the past thirty years.

1. Exports tend to decline because they are relatively dearer in foreign markets.
2. Imports tend to increase because foreign goods are relatively cheaper on the British market.
3. Higher money incomes in the UK increase the demand for imports and tend to decrease exports because the buoyant home market makes it less vital for manufacturers to seek outlets abroad for their goods.

4. An outward movement of capital may take place if price rises continue since foreign traders and financiers lose confidence in the pound sterling maintaining its current rate of exchange.

While the above effects are uncomfortable, it is possible to live with a moderate rise in prices. The snag is that where rising prices are thought likely to continue, people bring forward their spending, thereby producing the very price rise feared – an example of 'self-justified expectations'. So the process gathers momentum, stimulated still further by demands for higher wage increases.

30.2   Causes of Inflation: a Simplified Statement

Prices rise when there is excess purchasing power for goods available at current prices. But what brings about the excess of purchasing power? Experience of inflation over the last thirty years suggests that there is no single cause. We can begin, however, by distinguishing initiating impulses on both the demand and supply sides.

1. Demand-pull

The Keynesian analysis of the determination of the level of activity suggests that, if there is cyclical unemployment, the situation can be improved by expanding AD, e.g. from AD to AD_1 (Figure 30.1). Prices would not rise as long as output increased with the increase in AD. Eventually when bottlenecks arose, prices would begin to rise.

The really inflationary situation occurred when AD continued to expand once the position of full employment had been reached, e.g. AD_3. From henceforth any expansion of $ADDDD$ found its outlet entirely in rising prices. Any excess AD at the full employment level thus represents an inflationary gap (see p. 438).

2. Cost-push

The rise in prices can start on the supply side, e.g. through an increase in the price of imports. Thus the fivefold rise in oil prices in 1973–4 aggravated inflation in the UK, indeed worldwide.

More usually, however, cost-push inflation has followed from demand-pull. Once prices start to rise as the government pursues a full employment policy, trade unions seek compensating wage increases. Indeed, the scale of their demands tends to increase in order to allow for future price rises. Furthermore, the current practice is for such demands to be presented

FIGURE 30.1
Demand-pull Inflation

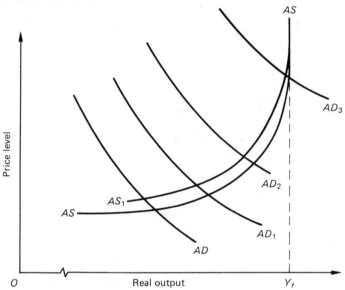

yearly, often irrespective of the rate of inflation and without any justifying increase in productivity.

Where the level of activity is high, employers tend not to resist such demands, feeling that product prices can be raised to cover them. In practice their expectations are justified, for unless the government imposes financial restraints to make it more difficult for firms to cover higher wages, the increased wages themselves provide the incomes and expenditure to justify higher prices. We have, therefore, what is termed 'cost-push' inflation – prices are being 'pushed up' by an initial increase in costs.

In all the above cases, the AS curve would shift upwards, e.g. to AS_1. This in itself shifts the AD curve further upwards e.g. from AD_1 to AD_2.

The Phillips Curve

The simple Keynesian situation where expanding output is eventually accompanied by rising prices seemed to be supported in 1958 by Professor A. W. Phillips whose research showed that in the UK over the past century there was a strong statistical negative relationship between the annual rate of inflation and the annual rate of unemployment (Figure 30.2). The policy conclusion was that a reduction in the rate of unemployment could be 'traded off' against a rise in the rate of inflation.

FIGURE 30.2
The Phillips Curve

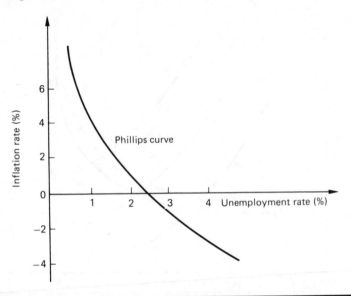

Alternatively, where the basic cause is cost-push, the government could urge or impose wage restraint, backing this with restrictions on price rises.

Stagflation

Until the mid-1960s the Phillips curve relationship held, but then both unemployment and inflation increased together, a situation described as 'stagflation'.

The weakness of the Keynesian approach is that it is too static, allowing nothing for expectations. Instead of inflation being merely a condition of excess demand at the full-employment level, it is a *process*. An initial price rise generates demands for wage increases from trade unions in key industries even though there had been little increase in productivity and irrespective of the fact that some of their members were already unemployed. Moreover, wage rises awarded in the growth industries are in practice conceded in declining industries, e.g. shipbuilding, steel, cars, etc., through the annual process of wage bargaining. Indeed, it is asserted that any norm urged by the government merely reinforces an across-the-board increase since it is interpreted as a minimum for all workers.

But increased wages push up prices still further (the *AD* curve moving, for example, from AD_1 to AD_2), thus leading to new demands for wage rises, often geared to an *expected* higher rate of inflation. In short, there is an inflationary spiral. This means that the remedy is not a simple piece of surgery to remove excess fat, but rather a fight against a cancerous growth.

Therefore, an alternative theory of inflation embodying expectations was required. This has been built up by the 'monetarists', led by Professor Milton Friedman.

30.3   Monetarism

The current monetarist explanation of inflation has three main elements: the direct connection between the money supply and AD; inflation expectations as a cause of the inflation process; and a 'natural rate of unemployment' hypothesis. We will explain each in turn.

The Money Supply and AD

It was observed that there was a positive correlation between increases in the money supply and the rate of inflation. But is there a causal connection? Does an increase in the money supply *directly* increase AD?

Keynes considered that the supply of money does not enter directly into spending decisions. In the short run these are dependent upon the level of income; over time they will be affected by long-term factors, such as social example, thrift habits, contractual commitments to regular saving, etc. Any increase in the supply of money simply increases liquidity in the economy and the rate of interest – the price paid for liquidity – therefore falls. AD will expand only indirectly, through a lower rate of interest leading to more investment spending.

In contrast, Milton Friedman holds that the demand for money, instead of adjusting to the money supply by being automatically absorbed in 'idle' balances, has a degree of stability. As a result an increase in the supply of money can lead *directly* to additional spending and thus *cause* inflation.

To a large extent it is a revival of the Quantity Theory of Money. The *Quantity Theory of Money* attributes a rise in the general price level to an increase in the supply of money. Usually it is given precision by being expressed in the form of the Fisher equation $MV = PT$, where M is the amount of money available in the economy, V is the velocity of circulation, the average number of times each unit of money changes hands in carrying out transactions, P is the general level of prices, and T the volume of transactions, the total quantity of goods and services exchanged against money.

If we are concerned with the Fisher equation as a statement of fact, there is nothing to quarrel about, for the two sides are equal by definition. MV, the amount of money multiplied by the number of times each unit changes hands in a given period, is merely the expenditure by buyers of goods and services over the period. Similarly, PT, the average price of goods multiplied by the volume, is simply the receipts of sellers. Since expenditure must be the same as receipts, MV and PT are simply different ways of expressing the same thing.

But as an explanation of what *causes* changes in the price level, the Quantity Theory is only valid if T and V can be assumed to be constant. It is regarding V – which can be looked upon as the demand for money in reverse – that Keynes and Friedman clash.

The monetarists consider that people maintain a fraction of their nominal income in cash balances. An increase in the money supply results in their having larger cash balances than they require, and so they run them down by spending. Such spending increases AD and money incomes until cash balances are equal to their former fraction. Nor does this surplus cash have to be spent on 'bonds', Keynes's omnibus term for non-money assets. Wealth can be held in many forms: cash which yields liquidity, 'bonds' which yield interest and possible capital appreciation, and the monetarists emphasise, *consumer goods* which yield utility. People distribute their spending according to their marginal preferences for those different forms of yield (which in turn can be influenced by their expectations of the future rate of inflation).

Thus any increase in the money supply is likely after a little while to lead to some increase in the demand for consumer goods, resulting in a rise in their prices.

Inflation Expectations

Once inflation expectations enter into wage negotiations, the monetarists hold that increasing AD will not achieve a *long-term* decrease in the rate of unemployment but simply result in higher inflation. In short there is no trade-off between inflation and unemployment. We return to the Phillips curve.

In Figure 30.3 we assume that the rate of inflation is 4 per cent and the rate of unemployment is 5 per cent. This position at D is stable because wage-bargainers have expected 4 per cent to be the inflation rate.

The government now decides that it wants to reduce the unemployment rate to 4 per cent and accordingly increases AD. Prices rise to 6 per cent inflation at F, but money wage rates do not rise. Thus firms, enjoying increased profitability, increase output so that initially unemployment falls to 4 per cent on curve P_4.

But this is only a short-term position depending on the fact that workers tend to concentrate on nominal money wages rather than real wages – the 'money illusion'. Eventually, however, they realise that real wages have fallen and in their next wage negotiations they obtain a 6 per cent rise in

FIGURE 30.3
The Effect of Inflation-expectations on the Rate of Unemployment

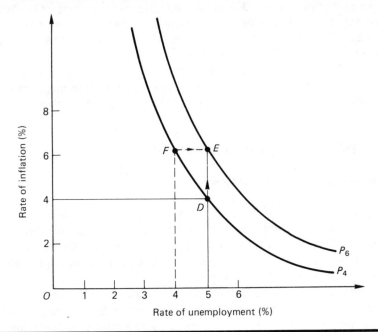

money wages (based on the previous year's inflation rate) to cover what they expect to be the rate of inflation. The recovery in real wage-rates increases costs, so that firms reduce output and unemployment reverts to 5 per cent. The Phillips curve has moved outwards to P_6 and there is a new equilibrium at E.

The 'Natural Rate of Unemployment'

In the above example, D and E represent two long-term equilibrium positions. Thus the long-term Phillips curve is a vertical straight line at 5 per cent. The monetarists would term this 5 per cent the 'natural rate of unemployment' – the rate to which unemployment will tend given the current real wage-rate. If this rate is above that which would clear the labour market when there is equilibrium *throughout the economy*, the supply of labour exceeds the demand; that is, there are workers offering their services at the current wage-rate who cannot find jobs. The natural rate of unemployment refers to this involuntary unemployment, to which must be added frictional unemployment (page 434) and structural unemployment (page 436 and Chapter 31) to account for the total level of unemployment.

Some economists dispute whether employment can be increased even in the short period by the Keynesian method of increasing *AD*. Wage-bargainers learn by experience and have available information by which they can *predict* and allow for the future rate of inflation. Thus the correct expected rate of inflation is embodied in their wage settlements. This assertion of *'rational expectations'* rather than a mere *adaptation* to an inflation rate based on the previous year's inflation rate means that the long period Phillips curve also depicts the short period situation.

30.4   Policy Implications of Monetarist Theory

Influencing Inflation Expectations

Monetarist theory originated as an explanation of how increases in the supply of money led directly to increases in *AD* and thus to rising prices. Even with cost-push inflation, extra money is necessary to accommodate wage increases. Thus the first condition for keeping inflation in check is strict control over the money supply.

A major difficulty here is that 'money' is difficult to define (see p. 341) and policy has to be based on an imperfect money index (see pp. 580–1). But, as we have seen, the theory goes further to show that expanding *AD* to reduce unemployment will only be successful for as long as there is a fall in real wage-rates. This may occur in the short period owing to the 'money illusion', but eventually labour incorporates a revised higher expected rate of inflation in its wage negotiations. Indeed, if the 'rational expectations' view applies, there is not even a short-term improvement in unemployment through an increase in *AD*.

Government policy must be directed to convincing the trade unions that the trend of the future rate of inflation is downwards. This is not easy for until wage negotiators can actually see a falling rate of inflation, they interpret a wage increase which falls short of their expected rate of inflation as a cut in real wages. Yet wage restraint is the 'least-cost' policy for controlling inflation. The difficulty is that voluntary restraint soon breaks down, and statutory wage and price freezes have to be imposed in an attempt to break the inflation spiral. But the rigidity in the economy which results means that even these cannot last long.

An alternative approach is to reduce inflation expectations by announcing strict monetary and fiscal targets for the medium-term future (see pp. 580–1). The extent to which such a policy reduces inflation expectations largely depends on how far unions are convinced of the government's resolve to hold to its targets. In this respect it should be noted that if the government sets a limit to the PSBR it virtually has to have a wages policy for the public sector, and its determination to restrict wage increases here will have its impact on the private sector.

Unfortunately, the change in the economic climate takes time to be realised especially when in the past trade union negotiators have been consistently successful in obtaining inflationary wage increases. In the meantime, there may be a sequence of unsuccessful strikes and a prolonged period of unemployment. This is the 'high cost' alternative.

Supply-side Measures

The introduction of the hypothesis of a 'natural rate of unemployment' suggests that, since expanding *AD* is ineffective in reducing unemployment, less emphasis should be placed on demand and more attention given to supply. Reducing the costs of production would mean that a greater output could be supplied at any given price level. Put in an alternative way, the objective is an eventual reduction in the natural rate of unemployment.

Policy to achieve this embraces a variety of incentives usually included under the umbrella term *'supply-side economics'*. It integrates longer-term micro measures within the overall macro policy (see pp. 449–51).

Concluding Observations

This chapter has discussed the difficulty of achieving a low rate of unemployment without making the rate of inflation uncomfortable.

The Keynesian solution puts the emphasis on reducing unemployment by expanding *AD*. Its success depends largely on achieving an effective policy to restrain rises in real wages which are not matched by increases in productivity.

In contrast, monetarist policies centre on strict control of the money supply and *supply-side* economics. The monetarist approach rests on two hypotheses – a stable demand for money and a natural rate of unemployment – both of which still require empirical verification. However, the experience of Britain and other Western economies in recent years does seem to indicate a link between an increase in the supply of money and, after a time-lag, an increase in the rate of inflation. What is certain is that without increases in the supply of money, inflation cannot continue.

Few economists, however, would go so far as to say that the increase in the supply of money was the *cause* of an inflation. As we have seen, there is no *single* cause. Excess *AD* may be generated in a number of ways apart from spending newly created money. It may come from increased government spending, or arise on the cost side through wage demands or higher import prices. The tendency, therefore, is to favour a pragmatic approach combining control of the money supply with other policies.

This is consistent with the fact that inflation cannot be considered in isolation from employment, the balance of payments and economic growth. Control of inflation may be the prior condition for a healthy economy, especially for the UK which is so dependent on maintaining exports. But in the final analysis the extent to which priority is given to inflation is a political decision.

How actual policies have varied and been implemented in the UK over the last thirty years are described in Chapter 39.

30.5   A Note on Measuring Changes in the General Level of Prices

Changes in the Value of Money and the 'Cost of Living'

Suppose a man earns £200 a week and his weekly shopping bill for food, rent, clothes, fares, cigarettes, etc., comes to £150. Now suppose his wages rise to £250 a week, but for the same goods his shopping bill increases to £210. Is he better off? In other words, has his standard of living improved?

The answer is 'no'. Although wages have increased by 25 per cent, expenditure on the same amount of goods has gone up by 40 per cent. It can be seen, therefore, that to compare *standards of living*, that is, the goods, services, and leisure enjoyed, it is necessary to adjust money income by any changes in the value of money, that is, by the cost of living.

Measuring Changes in the Value of Money over a Period

In theory, a change in the value of money would refer to a change in the level of prices in general. But different kinds of prices – wholesale prices, retail prices, capital goods prices, security prices, import prices, etc. – change differently. If we tried to measure changes in all prices, therefore, our task would be stupendous. But more than that, it would lack practical significance. Suppose, for instance, that security prices rose considerably, other prices remaining unchanged. A measurement of the general level of prices would show a rise, but this would be of little interest to the person who owns no securities.

When measuring changes in the value of money, therefore, it is usual to concentrate on changes in the prices of those goods which are of most general significance – the goods bought by the majority of people, for it is upon the prices of these that the cost of living really depends. But again, since different people spend their income differently, the value of money could be different for each.

Method of Measuring Changes in the Value of Money

Since we are mainly interested in the extent to which the value of money has altered between one date and another, it can be measured as a relative change by means of an *index number*. The steps are as follows:

1. A base year is selected. This is now referred to as the 'reference date'.
2. In order to ensure that the same goods are valued over the period under consideration, a 'basket' of goods, based on the current spending habits and income of the 'typical' family is chosen.
3. The basket is valued at reference date prices, and expressed as 100.
4. The same basket is revalued at current prices.
5. The cost of the current basket is then expressed as a percentage of the base year. Thus if the cost of living had risen by 5 per cent, the index for the current year would be 105.

In practice, the prices of the selected goods are compared, their percentage changes being 'weighted' according to the relative expenditure on the commodity at the reference date. Suppose, for instance, that there are only two commodities, bread and meat, upon which income is spent. The index between two years is calculated as follows. The price in year II is expressed as a percentage of the price in year I. This is multiplied by the appropriate weight to give a 'weighted price relative'. These weighted price relatives are then totalled and divided by the total of the weights to give the new index number.

		YEAR I				YEAR II	
	Price	*Units bought*	*Ex-pend-iture*	*Weight*	*Price*	*Year II as % of Year I*	*Weighted price relative*
Bread	30p	5	150p	10	45p	150	1,500
Meat	150p	11	1,650p	110	180p	120	13,200
				120			120 14,700

Index
Year I (base)   100
Year II   122.5

Difficulties in Calculating Index Numbers

The method outlined above of calculating changes in the value of money has obvious snags:

(1) The basket and the weighting are merely an arbitrary average. Different income groups have widely different baskets, and even within the same group the amount spent on each good varies. Thus a change in the Index of Retail Prices does not affect all people equally.

(2) The basket becomes more unreal the further we move from the reference date (at present January 13 1987 = 100). For instance, an increase in income gives a different pattern of expenditure, new goods are produced and the quality of goods changes, and spending is varied according to relative price changes. The Index of Retail Prices tries to overcome this defect by revising the weights each January on the basis of the *Family Expenditure Survey* for the previous year.

(3) Technical difficulties may arise both in choosing the reference date and in collecting information. For instance, the reference date may coincide with abnormally high prices, while the development of discount stores may upset standardised methods of collecting prices.

Thus an Index of Retail Prices is merely an indication of changes in the cost of living. But if we bear its limitations in mind, it is the most useful measurement we have of changes in the value of money.

31 Balanced Regional Development

31.1 The Regional Problem

Unemployment and the Immobility of Labour

Even where there is considerable unemployment, there will be some job vacancies. Thus, while in June 1990 the number of persons unemployed was 1,617,200 there were in existence 186,200 vacancies at Jobcentres. Why are there these unfilled vacancies?

On the one hand, conditions of demand and supply change. Tastes change, incomes rise, foreign competitors produce at a lower price, etc. As a result, demand is buoyant for some goods and slack for others. On the supply side, technological change leads to redundancies. Thus in the UK since the Second World War, we have had a buoyant demand for consumer durable goods, services, electronic equipment, high technology products, etc., and a considerably reduced demand for coal, cotton goods, iron and steel, ships, etc. The demand for factors of production is a 'derived' demand; if the demand for a good decreases, the demand for the workers producing that good will also decrease.

On the other, there are obstacles to the movement of redundant labour to vacancies in expanding industries. This labour immobility, discussed in Chapter 14, gives rise to frictional, seasonal and structural unemployment. It is the latter which is the one most closely linked to the regional problem.

Yet while labour immobility must be recognised when formulating a regional policy, it must not be overestimated. Over time there is movement; studies have shown that over a period of ten years, nearly one-quarter of all male employees move from one part of the country to another.

The Nature of the Regional Problem

In broad terms, a regional problem can arise because:

1. The Particular Region May Simply Have Poor Natural Resources

This applies, for example, to the Highlands of Scotland. More generally, with the growth of national income, an agricultural region which does not attract expanding industries – e.g. Cornwall and Devon – cannot provide its population with living standards comparable with those of the rest of the country. As a result, either any increased labour productivity is secured solely by emigration, or income per head simply remains below the level achieved in the rest of the country.

2. The Resources of the Region May not be Fully Developed, Usually Through Lack of Capital

This applies particularly to the less developed countries (see Chapter 38). The more immediate solution is for capital to be provided on favourable terms by richer regions.

In the long term an improvement in the imbalance may depend mainly on rising incomes elsewhere. Exploitation of the area's resources may now become economically viable. For example, prosperity came to Aberdeen and the Shetlands only when the rise in the price of oil and the development of modern technology made extraction of North Sea oil an economic proposition. Alternatively, rising incomes in other regions may allow tourism to be developed, e.g. North Wales, the Lake District.

3. A Region's Basic Industry is Either Stagnant or in Decline so that Economic Activity is Insufficient to Maintain Full Employment

Such a region is usually characterised by: a rising rate of unemployment; a level of income which is falling relatively to other regions; a low activity rate, particularly of female workers; a high rate of outward migration; and an inadequate infrastructure. It is thus this type of regional imbalance which creates the problem for *national* governments, and indeed the unemployment rate is normally chosen to identify depressed regions (Table 31.1).

In contrast, other regions may be expanding so rapidly that their further development results in congestion, inadequate social capital and inflationary pressures. Yet the problems of both are linked, and policies must take account of this.

The Correction of Regional Imbalance Through the Market Economy

Theoretically the market should move workers who become unemployed to other jobs. The fall in the demand for a good, and the consequent unemployment, should result in a relative wage fall. On the other hand,

Table 31.1
Percentage Rate of Unemployment (seasonally adjusted) by Region,
June 1990

United Kingdom	5.5
Region:	
South East	3.7
East Anglia	3.7
South West	4.3
West Midlands	5.8
East Midlands	4.9
Yorks and Humber	6.7
North West	7.4
North	8.5
Wales	6.4
Scotland	8.0
N. Ireland	13.9

SOURCE *Employment Gazette* (Department of Employment)

where demand is buoyant wages should rise (assuming that AD is adequate throughout the economy as a whole). Such changes in relative wages should move workers from low-wage to high-wage industries, and industries from high-wage to low-wage areas.

Weaknesses of the Market Mechanism

The attraction of the above model is that economic efficiency and the correction of an imbalance can be brought about by the free play of market forces. Yet in suggesting that a government regional policy is largely superfluous, the theory has serious weaknesses:

(a) Factor markets adjust much less perfectly than the theory implies. Not only is labour immobile, but factor prices, especially wage rates, tend to be resistant to any downward movement. Moreover, national wage-bargaining weakens the response to the price signals of regional imbalance. Finally, the information available to factor markets is often imperfect. Thus capital markets tend to be centralised in the more prosperous regions of a country. If such markets operate with a bias against, or with imperfect knowledge of, investment opportunities in the peripheral regions, there may well be no injection of investment to cover savings in these regions.

(b) The assumption of constant returns to scale which is implicit in the theory may not hold. Manufacturing in particular is characterised by increasing returns to scale over the relevant output range so that high-wage regions may also generate high returns to capital. Thus firms, like labour, may migrate to the prosperous high-wage regions. Indeed, as communications improve, these regions may gain with the progressive opening of trade at the expense of the decaying region. Thus the south-east region of England has benefited from its close connections with the EC.

Should movement be entirely outwards, the model has additional weaknesses:

(c) The theory ignores the external costs to society of (i) the loss of social capital and the disintegration of communities in the depressed regions, and (ii) the congestion and inflationary pressures generated in the expanding areas (see below).
(d) Those workers who do move from the depressed regions are mainly the better educated, most highly skilled and more enterprising young adults. As such they are often the leaders of the community. The result is that the region becomes still further depressed *and* thus unattractive to new industries.
(e) The theory follows a purely partial equilibrium approach. It ignores the fact that migration from the depressed regions leads to a loss of income there. The multiplier effect of reduced consumer spending and investment serves to depress the area still further.

It should be noted that even if, as the theory predicts, economic efficiency could be secured through market forces, government action may still be needed on the grounds of equity. The model only predicts that interregional differences in factor payments and employment *within a particular industry* will be automatically removed. Per capita *regional incomes* may not be equalised simply because differences in resource endowments and industrial structure may give some regions high-wage sectors and others low-wage sectors.

Consequences of Regional Depression

The existence of prolonged depression in certain regions has adverse consequences which can be summarised as follows:

1. An Underutilisation of Resources Through Unemployment

Not only does regional unemployment result in lost output for the community as a whole, but it can have serious social and psychological effects on the workers concerned. Moreover, significant differences in people's income between regions has equity implications.

2. A Loss of Social Capital as Towns and Cities Decay

Where the nation's population is static or falling, outward migration from depressed areas involves social costs in that schools, churches, etc. fall into decay while certain public services have to be operated below capacity. In contrast, new roads and public buildings, such as hospitals, have to be provided in the expanding areas.

However, the implied assumption that social capital should never be allowed to become obsolete has to be questioned. The stock of social capital in the high unemployment areas tends to be older and of lower quality than in the expanding areas of the south. In other words, it may be due for renewal and can be replaced as easily in another part of the country (subject to the qualification that there are no congestion or inflationary problems there).

3. External Social Costs

Migration from decaying regions results in a loss of welfare through the break-up of communities and the destruction of the 'social character' of an area. It could be, however, that having overcome their reluctance to moving away from friends, people find compensatory benefits, both economic and social, in a more pleasant environment. In any case, it is difficult to assess the loss resulting from this 'destruction of social character'.

Similarly, there may be external costs of excessive urbanisation (e.g. traffic congestion, noise, pollution and intensive housing) through migration to a prosperous region. Here again, however, the argument needs qualification. In recent years, population movement out of city centres into the surrounding countryside has exceeded other movements of population. Thus Greater London is losing population at a faster rate than any other area in the country, while areas gaining from migration, such as East Anglia, may be areas of relatively low congestion. Thus present migration may serve to reduce congestion costs as much as to increase them.

4. Differences in Unemployment Between Regions Make it More Difficult to Manage the Economy

Prosperous regions tend to become 'overheated' through the pressure of demand. This is reflected in higher wage-rates and labour shortages. Higher wage-rates tend to be transmitted even to the depressed regions through national wage agreements, the insistence on traditional wage differentials, etc. But anti-inflationary measures, both monetary and fiscal, apply nationally, thus adding to the unemployment problems of the depressed regions. It is argued, therefore, that ironing out unemployment differences between regions would not only reduce the rate of inflation but do so at a lower overall level of unemployment.

5. Economic Integration Between Nations May be Undermined by the Political Opposition of Depressed Regions Pressure Groups

The rationale of economic integration between nations, e.g. the EC, is to secure greater comparative advantages by the removal of trade barriers and increased factor mobility. However, it may exacerbate the problem of regional imbalance because certain industries, particularly in areas on the periphery, such as Northern Ireland and Scotland, find it more difficult to compete. Political pressure groups in such areas, therefore, may react by opposing integration.

31.2   Government Policy

Objectives of Government Policy

The objectives of government policy have widened in the light of experience. In brief, current regional policy seeks to:

(i)   reduce the relatively high level of unemployment in certain regions;
(ii) achieve a better balance between the population and the environment;
(iii) preserve regional cultures and identities;
(iv) relieve inflation by reducing the pressure of demand in the expanding regions;
(v)   counter possible adverse regional effects of greater international economic integration and of more open economies.

It has to be recognised, however, that these objectives are not always compatible with national economic policy. For instance, diverting firms from their optimum location to a depressed area may hamper growth, while it may be necessary to stimulate exports of goods and services produced in the more prosperous regions in order to improve the national balance of payments. Furthermore, where it is necessary to concentrate growth at particular locations within regions, greater equality between regions may only be achieved at the cost of greater inequality within regions. Finally, any regional employment policy has a better chance of success when there is full employment generally in the economy. Not only are unemployed workers encouraged to move to where there are unfilled vacancies, but firms will be more ready to go where labour is available provided it can be trained in the appropriate skills.

The Main Thrust of Government Policy

The regional problem in the UK has resulted from (a) the decline of certain major industries, particularly coal, shipbuilding and textiles, which were concentrated in specific geographical areas; and (b) the failure of the expanding industries, such as services, electrical, cars, consumer durables, light engineering and chemicals, to be attracted to these areas; and (c) the geographical immobility of labour. Government policy must concentrate on these three weaknesses.

Where an area is depressed, the government can give first aid by placing its contracts there, e.g. for defence equipment, and awarding it priority for public-works programmes – schools, new roads, hospitals, the physical regeneration of urban areas, etc. Subsidies may also be granted to secure contracts, for example, to build ships.

In the long term, however, the government must take measures that will, on the one hand, encourage the outward movement of workers, and on the other induce firms to move in to employ those workers who find it difficult to move and also to halt further degeneration of the region. The first is usually referred to as 'workers to the work', the second as 'work to the workers'.

Workers to the Work

Taking workers to the work is basically a micro approach to overcome market frictions, chiefly the immobility and imperfect knowledge of labour. In pursuing this policy, however, the government must bear in mind the following:

1. Unemployment arising through immobility is far more difficult to cure when cyclical unemployment also exists, for an unemployed person has little incentive to move if there is unemployment even in the relatively prosperous areas.
2. Other government interference in the economy may add to the problem of immobility. Thus high rates of income tax whittle away monetary inducements to move and unemployment benefit may reduce the incentive to seek a job elsewhere. Similarly, rent control and residential qualifications for local authority housing priorities lead to difficulties in finding accommodation.
3. Even owner-occupiers in depressed regions may be restricted in mobility by the much higher cost of housing in the prosperous areas.

4. Many changes of both occupation and area take place in a series of ripples. Thus an agricultural labourer may move to road construction to take the place of the labourer who transfers to the building industry.

The government's first task must be to improve occupational mobility. Entry into certain occupations should be made less difficult, e.g. by giving information on opportunities in other industries and occupations and by persuading trade unions to relax their apprenticeship rules. More important, people must be trained in the new skills required by expanding industries, e.g. through local Training and Enterprise Councils under the supervision of the National Training Task Force.

Improving the geographical mobility of workers to the more prosperous regions operates chiefly under the government's Employment Transfer Scheme. This consists of granting financial aid towards moving costs, providing information on prospects in other parts of the country and giving free fares to a place of work away from the home town.

Work to the Workers

While a 'workers-to-the-work' policy has a role to play in correcting regional imbalance, it suffers from: (i) an exclusive concern with unemployment to the neglect of other consequences of regional imbalance; (ii) a failure to recognise the macro effects of the outward movement of workers.

Thus taking work to the workers is now regarded as the policy most likely to effect a long-term solution to the problem for it reduces regional differences in income and the rate of growth as well as in unemployment. By helping the more immobile workers, such as older people and married women, it stimulates the activity rate. It also avoids forcing workers to leave areas to which they are attached, relieves the growing congestion in south-east England, and prevents the loss of social capital resulting from the depopulation of depressed areas. Above all, it works in harmony with Keynesian macro theory. The 'multiplier' operates for regional economies in much the same way as it does for the national economy. Moving unemployed workers and their families reduces spending in the area (e.g. because unemployment benefits are no longer being drawn) and this gives rise to a negative multiplier. In contrast, moving firms into the area generates spending power and producers a positive multiplier, variously calculated at between 1.25 and 1.50.

On the other hand, a policy of locating firms in depressed areas may involve them in higher costs. Their desire to establish plant in the South East is to secure location advantages, such as a supply of skilled workers, easier and less costly communications, contact with complementary firms and nearness to EC markets. The government, therefore, has to offer firms financial inducements to establish or expand in a designated Assisted Area (Figure 31.1).

New measures were introduced in 1984 by which more emphasis was put on actual job creation rather than on straight investment. There were two main types of grant.

Regional Development Grants were given *automatically* for projects in *Development Areas*. The grant was calculated in two ways according to whichever method was most favourable to the applicant:

(a) 15 per cent of eligible capital expenditure subject to a grant per job limit of £10 000 for each new job created; or
(b) £3000 for each new full-time job created.

But by 1988 it was recognised that many projects receiving *automatic* assistance made a minimal contribution to labour employment. Thus the government decided that, while schemes in the pipeline would continue to receive development grants, no further applications would be accepted. Instead there would be increased Regional Selective Assistance particularly for medium and small firms who show that they genuinely need money in order to proceed and that their projects are viable.

Regional Selective Assistance is available on a *discretionary* basis in both development areas and intermediate areas. Grants, which are negotiable, take two main forms:

(a) project grants, based on the capital cost of a project or on the number of jobs to be created within three years;
(b) training grants of up to 40 per cent of the costs of training directly associated with the viability of a project.

In addition to these grants, other incentives include:

(i) help for transferring key workers;
(ii) factories for renting on favourable terms, such as an initial rent-free period;
(iii) loans at favourable rates of interest;
(iv) grants towards the cost of reclaiming derelict land in certain designated areas.

All these incentives are in addition to the investment incentives (through tax concessions) available to manufacturing and service industries throughout the whole country.

Assistance (£2500 million to date) is also obtained from the EC's Regional Development fund, set up in 1975, and loans are available on favourable terms from the European Investment Bank and the European

FIGURE 31.1
UK Assisted Areas

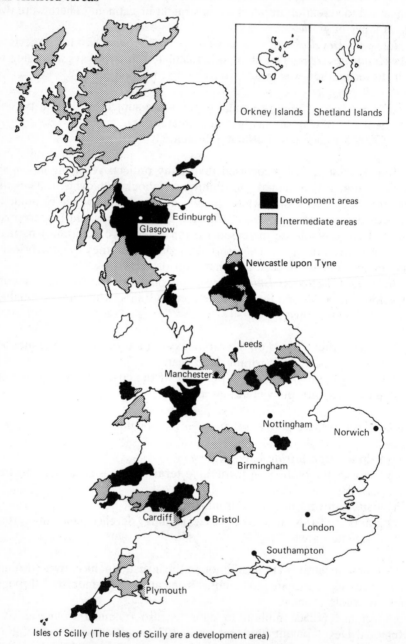

Isles of Scilly (The Isles of Scilly are a development area)

Coal and Steel Community. Depressed areas also benefit from aid given to the unemployed by the European Social Fund.

The Department of Trade and Industry controls the Industrial Estates Corporation which supervises government-sponsored industrial estates in England. Similar schemes operate in Scotland and Northern Ireland.

More recently the government has established some twenty-five 'enterprise zones' in areas of physical and economic decay, including the London docklands, Swansea, Manchester, Clydebank, Belfast and Hartlepool. Each zone covers up to 500 acres and firms there enjoy special benefits, e.g. exemption from general rates and simplified planning procedures.

In the dispersal of industry the government has set an example. Thus the Department of Social Security is centred in Newcastle, the Girobank in Bootle, and the Driving and Vehicle Licensing Centre in Swansea.

Regional Planning

While development area policy deals with special areas needing extra help, there is now a trend towards planning for larger regions each with an infrastructure which is attractive to industry and management in that it features: good executive housing; educational, cultural and recreational facilities; first-class shops and hotels; and a modern road network, rail services and airport. The aim is to secure a broad-based industrial structure, with special consideration being given to service industries.

The whole country is divided into ten regions (eight for England and one each for Scotland and Wales). Each region has an Economic Planning Board, consisting of civil servants from the main government departments concerned with regional planning, whose task is to formulate plans and coordinate the work of the various departments.

Primary responsibility for regional development lies with the Department of Trade and Industry which has an Industrial Development Unit to help with the appraisal, negotiation and monitoring of projects referred to it.

Regional Policy in the Context of the EC

A healthy integrated Community – at both economic and political levels – is possible only if progress is made towards reducing disparities in economic opportunity between regions within the Community. Indeed, while the foregoing reasons for regional policy are all relevant at the Community level, additional considerations apply:

(a) Physical controls are more difficult to apply in the EC context. Not only are they at variance with the objective of greater mobility within the EC, but firms have the option of relocating in a prosperous region of another member state.

(b) The depressed peripheral regions of Scotland, Northern Ireland, Southern Italy, etc., are more distant from the expanding centre of the Community – south-east England through to north-east France and western Germany – than they are from the centres of their own countries. This Community 'centre' forms a concentrated market to which industries are likely to be increasingly attracted, thereby adding to its dominance.

(c) The EC embraces regions exhibiting wider economic disparities than in any one member state. Moreover, regional problems are more hetero-geneous – for example, whereas the UK depressed regions are mainly industrial, Italy has many depressed agricultural areas.

These additional considerations mean that the formulation of an effect-ive EC regional policy is a difficult task. Not only must it respond quickly as new regional problems arise, but it has to be linked with, and be complementary to, the individual nation's regional policy. Indeed EC policy should also coordinate the regional policies of member states, for example, a physical control in one country must not be undermined by a firm being able to locate in another country.

It follows, therefore, that regional policy must be handled to a substan-tial degree at the Community level and be wide ranging in the measures employed so that one reinforces the others. Above all, to achieve greater equity, it must envisage substantial transfers of income through incentive funds which are in addition to those provided by the member states.

An Appraisal of Regional Policy

Although the UK has had a regional policy for over sixty years, disparities still persist in the rate of unemployment between different regions (see Table 31.1). Indeed, such disparities widen whenever unemployment is heavy for there is less incentive for firms to ease their labour problems by locating in the Assisted Areas, while workers have less inducement to move to the relatively prosperous regions for these have fewer vacancies to fill. Regeneration in Scotland has been the result of North Sea oil development rather than regional policy.

But the nature of regional policy itself has contributed to this situation. The emphasis has been on aid to manufacturing industry. Natural growth is in the service industries. Yet not until 1984 was assistance extended to include service activities.

Furthermore, the average cost of a job created has been too expensive at £38 000. For example, one-quarter of all aid since 1972 has gone to the chemical industry where investment has created hardly any new jobs.

Weighting financial incentives on the side of investment simply encourages firms to substitute capital for labour. Moreover, investment grants have encouraged investment in inherently unsuitable firms already in Development Areas. Often policy has been concerned with backing economic failure, e.g. shipbuilding, iron and steel, coal and car production. Again it was not until 1984 that expenditure was targeted on job creation.

It should be noted also that concentrating on interregional differences has diverted attention away from problems within regions. Thus London now has more unemployed than the whole of the North East region, with a rate of unemployed of up to 15 per cent in certain districts, such as Poplar.

The most favourable assessment which can be made of policy, therefore, is that without it disparities between regions would be greater.

But provided British workers and their trade unions can adapt to modern employment requirements, the outlook is hopeful. Britain's membership of the EC has encouraged firms to establish production in Development Areas, e.g. Nissan at Sunderland and Ford at Bridgend, South Wales.

32 Economic Growth

32.1 The Nature of Growth

The Meaning of 'Growth'

When there are unemployed resources, the economy's *actual* output is below its *potential* output; in terms of Figure 1.2 the economy is producing inside the production-possibility curve, say at point *A*. Here output can be increased, even in the relatively short term, by measures which absorb unemployed resources (see Chapter 29).

But, by itself, full employment of an economy's resources does not necessarily mean that the economy will grow. Growth is essentially a long-run phenomenon – the *potential* full-employment output of the economy is *increasing* over time. In terms of Figure 32.1, whereas full employment simply means that the economy is producing on a point on the production-possibility curve I, growth means that, over time, the curve is pushed outwards to II and III. Even with full employment of resources, advanced economies can achieve an *annual* growth rate of 3 per cent.

Increases in the productive capacity in the economy over time are usually measured by calculating the rate of change of real gross national product per head of the population (see Chapter 27). However, when people talk about 'growth' they are thinking chiefly of the difference it makes to the standard of living rather than to output itself. Allowances have to be made, therefore, for defects of GNP as an indication of the standard of living (see Chapter 27).

Advantages of Growth

Economic growth is the major factor for achieving improvements in the standard of living – more consumer goods, better living conditions, a shorter working week, and so on. While such improvements occur

FIGURE 32.1
Economic Growth

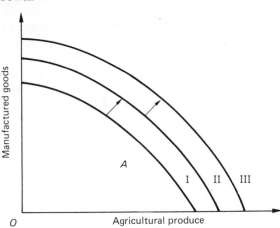

gradually and almost imperceptibly from year to year, small differences in the *annual rate* of growth produce large differences in the *speed* of growth. For instance, a rate of growth of 2.5 per cent per annum will double real GNP in twenty-eight years, whereas a 3 per cent rate doubles GNP in only twenty-four years.

In addition, growth makes it easier for the government to achieve its economic policy objectives. Revenue from taxation increases, allowing government services, e.g. education and health care, to be expanded without raising the *rates* of tax. Income can also be redistributed in favour of the poorer members of society while still allowing the standard of living of the better-off to show some improvement.

However, as noted earlier (p. 263) economic growth does have its costs (see also p. 483).

32.2   Achieving Growth

Factors Producing Growth

There are five basic causes of growth:

1. A Rise in the Productivity of Existing Factors

In the short run, productivity may be raised by improvements in organisation, which secure, for example, more division of labour and economies of large-scale production, or a more intensive use of capital equipment (e.g. the adoption of shift-working). Physical improvements for the labour force, e.g. better food and working conditions, may also increase productivity.

In the longer run, more significant increases can come with education and the acquisition of capital skills. These really represent, however, an increase in the capital invested in labour.

It is also important to draw attention to the differences in personal incentives provided by the market economy and the command economy. Compare, for instance, the growth rates of Hong Kong and Poland over the last forty years.

2. An Increase in the Available Stock of Factors of Production

(a) A RISE IN THE LABOUR INPUT
The size of the labour input can increase relative to the total population through either an increase in the number of hours worked per worker, or an increase in the ratio of the working population to the total population. The first is hardly likely to be a cause of growth in normal conditions, for as living standards improve the tendency is to demand more leisure. The second, however, may come about by an increase in the percentage of the population of working age and by changing attitudes to work (see Chapter 3).

(b) DEVELOPMENT OF NATURAL RESOURCES
North Sea natural gas and oil, for instance, have allowed Britain to obtain her fuel supplies from fewer factors of production, enabling resources to be transferred to other output and thus promoting growth.

(c) ADDITIONAL CAPITAL EQUIPMENT
Here we must distinguish between 'widening' and 'deepening' capital.

FIGURE 32.2
Factors Leading to Growth

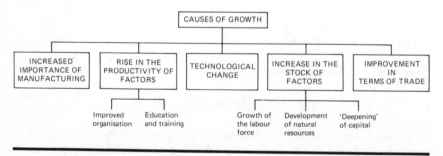

Widening capital – adding similar capital equipment – is necessary if the labour force increases, in order to maintain the existing capital-labour ratio and thus output per head. Suppose 10 men, digging a long ditch, have 5 spades between them. If the labour force is increased to 20 men the capital–labour ratio falls from 1:2 to 1:4 unless 'widening' takes place – that is, unless another 5 spades are provided to maintain the existing ratio. 'Widening' does not increase productivity; it simply prevents diminishing returns to labour setting in.

'Deepening' capital occurs when the capital-labour ratio is increased. If, for example, when there were 10 spades to 20 men, the men were given a further 10 spades, the capital–labour ratio would be raised to 1:1.

3. Technological Change

All we have done in our example so far has been to increase the stock of a given kind of capital equipment, spades. Over time, however, productivity can be raised much more significantly by technological improvements. Thus the twenty men and their spades may be replaced by a single trench-digger and its driver. Because this does the job more quickly and efficiently the remaining nineteen men are released for other kinds of work.

In practice, all three causes are usually operating at the same time to increase productivity. Thus, as the labour force or natural resources are expanded, new capital is required, and this allows for the introduction of new techniques.

The speed with which new capital and improvements are introduced also depends upon the price of capital equipment relative to the wages of the labour for which it can be substituted. Over time, wages have tended to rise relative to the cost of capital equipment. This has been marked since the Second World War; the effect has been to increase the rate of technological change in such industries as agriculture, cargo handling, transport, shipbuilding and mining.

Other factors affecting growth are:

4. Fundamental Changes in the Composition of the National Output

As a country's standard of living improves, so spending switches from agricultural to manufactured goods and then towards services. Since the opportunities for employing more capital and technical improvement are greatest in manufacturing, the growth rate increases as countries industrialise but then slows down as the relative demand for personal and government services increase.

5. A Sustained Improvement in the Terms of Trade (see p. 519)

Constraints upon Growth

In practice the UK has not succeeded in sustaining a 3 per cent annual growth rate. Thus from 1960 to 1989 it averaged only 2.5 per cent. Why is this?

First, when full employment was buoyant, consumer demand left fewer resources available for investment. Investment in capital goods involves saving, that is present sacrifice of consumer goods enjoyed. Figure 32.3 shows a production-possibility curve in terms of capital goods and consumer goods.

If society wants to move to curve II on Figure 31.1, it may choose point P (Figure 32.3). If, however, it wants the growth shown by curve III (Figure 32.1) over the same time-span, it must choose position F (Figure 32.3) giving up MM_1 consumer goods for NN_1 extra capital goods.

Second, inflation proved inimical to investment. Government disinflationary measures undermine the confidence of entrepreneurs. Trade union wage claims lead to industrial unrest and the dislocation of production. Furthermore, with wages rising faster than prices, profit margins are squeezed. Thus a low rate of return on capital together with a high rate of interest discouraged investment.

FIGURE 32.3
The Choice Between Consumer Goods and Capital Goods

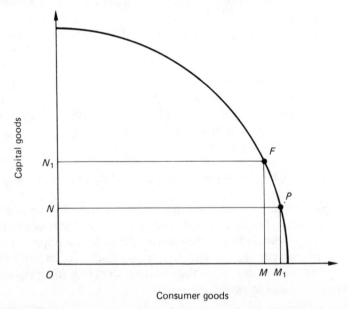

Third, at times growth has been incompatible with other government objectives. For instance, 'stop' policies have been necessary because, as the economy expands, inflationary problems arise (see p. 442) and increasing imports produce balance-of-payments difficulties (see p. 575).

Fourth, growth entails costs additional to the reduced current consumption necessary to accumulate capital. Growth usually requires change, and the more rapid the growth, the greater the change. Thus in the UK, even though the growth rate has been relatively low in recent years, coal-mines, cotton factories, shipyards and railway lines have been closed, while the electrical, plastics, aerospace, telecommunications and electronics industries have been developed. Such changes in the structure of the economy are, as we have seen, bound to lead to some unemployment, and if growth is to be achieved people must be willing to change jobs quite radically, three or four times in their working lives. This will entail retraining and probably moving around the country; and, as techniques change more rapidly, e.g. with the introduction of microchips, these processes will happen to a far greater extent than at present.

Fifth, growth is not achieved without environmental costs – pollution, noise, loss of natural beauty, destruction of wildlife habitat. And, as material wealth grows, people are inclined to question the full costs of growth with some consequent slowing down of the rate at which it can proceed.

Finally, and on the same theme, Britain's growth has been taken in forms not appearing in GNP calculations (see p. 397). Increasing welfare may mean preferring a quiet life and more leisure to the 'rat-race' and stress of accumulating material goods. Or, as John F. Kennedy put it:

> The GNP does not allow for the health of our youth, the quality of their education or the joy of their play. It does not include the beauty of our poetry or the strength of our marriages, the intelligence of our public debate or the integrity of our public officials. It measures neither our wit nor our courage, neither our wisdom nor our learning, neither our compassion nor our devotion to country. It measures everything, in short, except that which makes life worth while. (*The Times*, 10 January 1968).

32.3 The Government and Growth

Difficulties in Framing Policy

Most people look for an improvement in their standard of living. Thus one objective of the government is to secure a satisfactory rate of growth. But there are difficulties in framing policy.

(1) How is growth to be measured? We have already drawn attention to the ambiguities of GNP figures as a measure of improved living standards. Is growth to take the form of more leisure, less spending on defence, a litter-free environment, the preservation of town and rural beauty, safer and more comfortable travel?

(2) Of all the factors producing growth, which plays the greatest part – education of the population, training of labour, additional capital equipment, technological advance? There is no real means of measuring.

(3) Growth does not proceed at a *steady* rate but rather by a series of take-offs and slow-downs around an upward trend. However, if these fluctuations are too wide, uncertainty has an adverse effect on the overall rate of growth (see below).

Government Policy

Since there is no single satisfactory theory of growth, government action is confined to promoting the different factors which are essential to growth.

Growth results mainly from capital investment in its different forms. But accumulating capital involves foregoing present consumption – saving. Thus a first requirement for the government is to ensure that its policies, especially as regards taxation, will provide the amount of real saving required.

Second, additions to capital take place in both the public and private sectors. The government itself is largely responsible for investment in the public sector – the infrastructure (such as roads, hospitals, schools), education of its people and the training of the labour force.

On the other hand while all these are important as regards growth, the scale of the government's priorities must not 'crowd out' desirable private sector investment. Decisions here are based on expected profitability. Private investment can be increased, therefore, by providing a stable economic background free from 'stop–go' policies so that fixed capital formation, research and development (R & D) are not inhibited.

The major spurts in growth have come through breakthroughs in technology by innovation and the application of inventions. Most of these, e.g. aircraft, computers, antibiotics and other drugs, plant-breeding, animal selection, pesticides, etc. are the result of long-term R & D. While about a half of R & D is carried out in the private sector, the other half, particularly as regards defence, is under the control of the government, largely through government-sponsored research bodies. Here, however, it must be noted as regards civil R & D, Britain has tended to lag behind other countries, so that some transfer from defence R & D may be required.

Finally, the government has to encourage the application of the fruits of R & D so that innovation and inventions are transformed into new marketable products.

33 Government Finance

33.1 The Distribution of Income

The Government and the Redistribution of Income

At the micro level, the marginal productivity theory provides a theoretical explanation of how the owners of factors of production are rewarded. But it analyses rewards only on a functional basis – wages, interest, rent and profits. To explain the distribution of income between individual households other influences – chiefly the *ownership* of factors of production resulting from the unequal distribution of wealth – have to be taken into account.

The government is interested in the distribution of income for four main reasons:

(1) The first is 'fairness'. Especially in the richer Western economics, people's social conscience will not tolerate 'poverty in the midst of plenty'. Yet private giving through charitable institutions is irregular, unreliable and inadequate in dealing with the relative size of the problem of inequality in a 'caring society'.

(2) Second, gross inequality of income is divisive of society and disruptive of economic life, e.g. through strikes for higher pay.

(3) Third, the distribution of income affects the broad macro variables, e.g. saving and taxation yield, which the government has to take into account in formulating stabilisation policies.

(4) Fourth, the extent to which the government is successful in its stabilisation policies will, in its turn, affect income distribution, e.g. through unemployment and rising prices (and indeed these income changes will themselves generate feedbacks). The government, therefore, has a moral obligation to compensate for any failure on its part by providing unemployment benefit and 'indexing' social security benefits in line with changes in the general level of prices.

33.2   Government Expenditure

Objectives of Government Expenditure

Our survey of government policy in earlier chapters enables us to bring together a summary of the different possible objectives of government expenditure:

1. The provision of public goods and services.
2. The regulation of economic activities in the public interest, e.g. labour relations, monopoly control.
3. To influence the allocation of resources in order to improve efficiency (e.g. help to small firms), relocate to areas of high unemployment and provide for external costs.
4. Subsidise certain goods and services, e.g. agriculture, dental treatment, merit goods.
5. Social security payments to redistribute income.
6. Stabilising the level of activity, prices, the balance of payments.
7. Aid to less developed countries.

Figure 33.1 shows the main items of government expenditure and revenue.

Limits to Government Spending

Today taxation takes about 37 per cent of the gross national product – a remarkable increase since 1910, when the figure was only about 10 per cent. The government is now spending on a much wider range of activities.

Many items of government spending, e.g. pensions, National Debt interest and grants to local authorities, are unavoidable since by nature they are basically contractual. It may therefore seem that the government has merely to estimate its expenditure and imposes taxes to cover it. But this is not the case.

Since goods and services in the economy as a whole are limited, the government has cut its coat according to its cloth, asking such questions as: What can be afforded for the Arts Council? How much can be given to local authorities? Can university education be expanded? Can National Insurance Contributions be reduced? The economic problem, involving decisions at the margin, confronts private persons and the government alike. When there is full employment, the government can only secure more goods and services by allowing the private sector less. In the last resort the division rests on a political decision.

FIGURE 33.1
Public Income and Expenditure, 1988–9

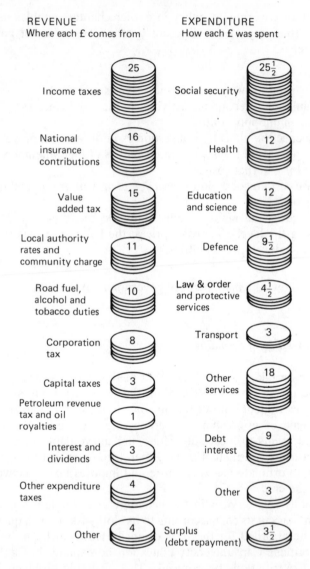

REVENUE
Where each £ comes from

EXPENDITURE
How each £ was spent

Income taxes	25
National insurance contributions	16
Value added tax	15
Local authority rates and community charge	11
Road fuel, alcohol and tobacco duties	10
Corporation tax	8
Capital taxes	3
Petroleum revenue tax and oil royalties	1
Interest and dividends	3
Other expenditure taxes	4
Other	4

Social security	$25\frac{1}{2}$
Health	12
Education and science	12
Defence	$9\frac{1}{2}$
Law & order and protective services	$4\frac{1}{2}$
Transport	3
Other services	18
Debt interest	9
Other	3
Surplus (debt repayment)	$3\frac{1}{2}$

Cash totals of revenue and expenditure £179 billion

The Distribution of Government Expenditure

Government spending can be classified under the following headings:

(i) *Defence*, which has accounted for about one-ninth of all government spending.
(ii) *Internal security* – the police, law enforcement and fire brigades.
(iii) *Social responsibilities* – education, and protection against the hazards of sickness, unemployment and old age.
(iv) *Economic policy*, covering subsidies to agriculture and industry, help for Assisted Areas, worker training and the provision of capital to the nationalised industries.
(v) *Miscellaneous*, including expenditure on diplomatic services, grants to local authorities, oversees aid and – the largest single item – interest on the National Debt.

How Government Expenditure is Financed

In the same way that firms have to pay for both variable and fixed factors, the government has to spend not only on single-use goods and services but also on goods which render services over long periods. The first, which involve regularly yearly spending, should be paid for out of regular yearly income. But capital spending, on such items as roads, loans to nationalised industries and university building, is more fairly financed by borrowing, for the repayment of the capital then partly falls on future beneficiaries.

Current expenditure is met from two main sources: (i) miscellaneous receipts, chiefly interest on loans, rents and charges on goods and services (such as medical prescriptions); and (ii) taxation, described in more detail below.

Capital expenditure is mostly covered by government borrowing, which takes the form of:

(i) Short-term loans from the sale of Treasury bills. Originally these were used to bridge the time-gap between expenditure and receipts from taxation, but – because it is cheaper to borrow short than long – they eventually became a major means of government borrowing. Nevertheless, the inflationary effects which followed forced the government to adopt a 'funding' policy (see p. 376).

(ii) Medium- and long-term loans are obtained by selling stock having a minimum currency of five years. Some, such as $3\frac{1}{2}$ per cent War Loan, are undated.

(iii) *'Non-market' borrowing*, through National Savings Certificates, Premium Savings Bonds, etc. and the National Savings Bank.

Since 1980 additional capital funds have been obtained by the 'privatisation' sales of publicly owned assets (see p. 320).

33.3　The Modern Approach to Taxation

Taxation and Government Policy

Until the end of the nineteenth century the functions of the State were concerned mainly with defence and law and order. Taxation was levied primarily for revenue purposes, those taxes regulating trade having been abolished in the previous century.

To meet the vast increase in government spending over the last fifty years, high rates of taxation have been imposed and new taxes introduced. These additions have, as we shall see, provided new means for promoting economic and social policies. Briefly, by its fiscal measures, the government can:

1. *Exercise an overall control over the economy,* mainly with the object of achieving full employment. To secure this, the government:
   (*a*) adjusts individual taxes in order to influence consumption, saving and investment;
   (*b*) varies the relationship between its own expenditure and revenue through a budget surplus or deficit. Both were discussed in Chapter 29.
2. *Promote economic growth*, by such measures as giving generous taxation allowances for investment expenditure.
3. *Modify the influence of the price system*, in order to:
   (*a*) protect an 'infant' industry;
   (*b*) develop a vital industry;
   (*c*) cushion the impact on an industry of fundamental changes in the conditions of demand and supply;
   (*d*) increase trade with the EC
   (*e*) improve the terms of trade by levying an import duty on goods whose supply is less elastic than the demand for them;
   (*f*) improve the balance of payments by imposing duties to restrict imports (these points are discussed in Chapter 34); and
   (*g*) compensate for external costs and benefits, e.g. protecting health by taxing cigarettes.
4. *Achieve greater equality in the distribution of wealth and income.*
5. *Secure minor objectives*, such as increasing individual responsibility for government (by ensuring that everybody pays some tax).

The Attributes of a Good Tax System

In his *Wealth of Nations* Adam Smith was able to confine his principles of taxation to four simple canons. Stated briefly, these were: persons should pay according to their ability; the tax should be certain and clear to everybody concerned; the convenience of the contributor should be studied as regards payment; the cost of collection should be small relative to yield.

While today the main purpose of any tax is usually to raise money, the additional uses of taxation have rendered Adam Smith's maxims inadequate. Indeed objectives other than revenue may take priority. Such objectives are now so varied that the tax system must consist of many different taxes.

Nevertheless, it is helpful to list the general attributes which a Chancellor of the Exchequer would wish his system of taxation to possess. As far as possible, his taxes should be:

1. Productive of a worthwhile revenue which the Chancellor can estimate fairly accurately.
2. Certain to the taxpayer and difficult to evade.
3. Convenient to the taxpayer as regards the time and manner of payment.
4. Equitable in the sense that:
   (a) 'the heaviest burden is borne by the broadest back';
   (b) impartial between one person and another.
5. Adjustable to changes in policy.
6. Automatic in stabilising the economy. Thus while, in order to achieve full employment or a stable price level, the chancellor can adjust taxes in his budget to influence consumer spending, it is helpful if they respond automatically in the desired direction.
7. Harmless to effort and initiative.
8. Consistent with other aspects of government policy. Although the tax structure should not change frequently, individual taxes must be constantly reviewed to see how they could be used to promote government policy. To encourage effort, should income from work be taxed at a lower rate than investment income? Will an indirect tax, by raising the cost of living, increase wage-push inflation?
9. Minimal in their effect on the optimum allocation of resources.
10. Equitable in its distribution of the tax burden. Taxes can be classified according to the proportion of a person's income which is deducted:
    (a) A *regressive* tax takes a higher proportion of the poorer person's income than of the richer. Indirect taxes, for instance, which are a fixed sum irrespective of income (e.g. television licences), are regressive.
    (b) A *proportional* tax takes a given proportion of one's income. Thus on the first £20 700 of taxable income, income tax is proportional, 25 per cent being taken from every pound of taxable income.

(c) A *progressive* tax takes a higher proportion of income as income increases (Figure 33.2). Thus income tax and capital gains tax, which have a higher rate above a certain limit, are progressive.

Justification for taxing the rich higher than the poor rests on the assumption that the law of diminishing utility applies to additional income, so that an extra £50 affords less pleasure to the rich person than to the poor person. Thus taking from the rich involves less hardship than taking from the poor. Generally this can be accepted as true, but we can never be sure, simply because there is no absolute measure of personal satisfaction.

33.4 The Structure of Taxation

Because certain objectives of taxation conflict with one another, no single tax is completely perfect. Consequently, there must be a structure of taxation, combining a number of taxes which the government can vary from time to time according to changes in emphasis on different objectives.

The following classification of taxes is based on their methods of payment.

Direct Taxes

With these taxes the person makes payment direct to the revenue authorities – the Department of Inland Revenue or the local authority. Usually each individual's tax liability is assessed separately.

FIGURE 33.2
The Difference Between Regressive, Proportional and Progressive Taxes

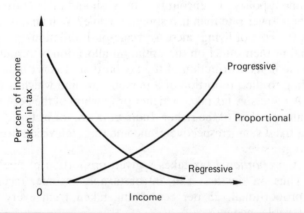

---

1. Income Tax

'Taxable income', which is subject to a basic rate of 25 per cent and a higher rate of 40 per cent above £20,700 (1990) is arrived at after allowing deductions depending on marital status and other personal circumstances.

2. Corporation Tax

All profits, whether distributed or not, are taxed at the same rate (35 per cent in 1990). A part ($\frac{1}{3}$ at an income tax rate of 25 per cent) is imputed to shareholders and deducted in advance when the dividend is paid. This advance payment is allowed against the mainstream 35 per cent corporation tax payment (which is always paid in arrears), while for the shareholder it counts as a 'tax credit', and is refundable if income tax is not paid because of low income.

3. Capital Gains Tax

A tax is now levied at 40 per cent of any capital gain when an asset is disposed of. Owner-occupied houses, cars, National Savings Certificates and goods and chattels worth less than £5000 are excluded, and losses may be offset against gains.

Where the gain does not exceed £5000 (1990) in any year, no tax is payable.

4. Inheritance Tax

Inheritance tax applies to lifetime gifts as well as to legacies, though the former generally bear only half the latter's rate of tax. The starting point is £18 000 (1990) and the rate of duty is 40 per cent. Gifts made more than seven years before death are exempt from tax.

5. Other Taxes

These consist of stamp duties (payable on financial contracts), motor-vehicle duties and a Petroleum Revenue Tax.

The Community Charge and rates on business premises levied by district councils can also be regarded as a direct tax.

This also applies to National Insurance contributions – a pay-roll tax of 10.45 per cent on employers – with a slightly lower rate paid by employees and the self-employed.

Direct taxes yield nearly two-thirds of total revenue. Their great merit is that, being progressive and assessed according to the individual's circumstances, they ensure that the heaviest burdens are placed on the broadest backs. Their progressive character also gives additional weight to their role as built-in stabilisers.

Their main disadvantage is that when the rate of tax is high there may be disincentive effects. As a result indirect taxes also have to be levied.

Indirect taxes

Indirect taxes on goods and services are so called because the revenue authority (the Department of Customs and Excise) collects them from the seller, who, as far as possible, passes the burden on to the consumer by including the duty in the final selling price of the good (see p. 506). They may be *specific* (i.e. consisting of a fixed sum irrespective of the value of the good) or *ad valorem* (i.e. consisting of a given percentage of the value of the good).

Indirect taxes may be divided into:
 (i) Customs duties levied at EC rates on goods imported from countries outside the EC.
 (ii) Excise duties on home-produced goods and services, e.g. beer, whisky, petrol, cigarettes and gambling.
(iii) Value Added Tax (VAT): an *ad valorem* tax, levied on most goods and services at each stage of production at a basic rate. Using Figure 27.1 as an example, a VAT at 15 per cent paid by the consumer on the table in the shop would be £15, making a total purchase price of £115. The VAT, however, would have been paid at each stage of production: tree-grower £4.50; saw-miller £3; table manufacturer £4.50; retailer £3. In practice each producer would pay to the Customs and Excise the full 15 per cent tax of the goods as invoiced by him *less* the VAT paid by his suppliers of materials, etc., as shown on their invoices. Thus the retailer would pay the Customs and Excise £3 – £15 minus the VAT of £12 charged to him.

Some goods, e.g. food (except meals out), coal gas, electricity, houses, books, newspapers, public transport fares, medicines on prescription, etc. are zero rated. This means that the final seller charges no VAT *and* can reclaim any VAT invoiced by intermediary producers. Other goods, e.g. rents and medical services, are 'exempt'. Here no VAT is charged by the final seller, but any VAT paid by an intermediary, e.g. for building repairs, cannot be reclaimed.

The main merit of VAT is that it is broad based, the yield increasing almost proportionately to consumer spending. Moreover, since VAT covers most forms of spending, it does not distort consumer choice as much as a highly selective tax (p. 500–1).

33.5   The Advantages and Disadvantages of Direct Taxes

We can use our survey of the attributes of a good tax to analyse the merits and demerits of the different types of tax. As regards direct taxes, the main reference will be to the income tax, but most of the arguments will apply to the other direct taxes.

As Figure 33.1 shows, direct taxes account for approximately 50 per cent of the total tax revenue, with income tax providing 23 per cent. Taxes on capital account for only 3 per cent.

Advantages

1. A High and Elastic Yield

In the UK, a 1p increase in the income tax yields approximately £1.4 billion. In comparison with yield, costs of collection are low. Indeed, through the PAYE system, the government makes use of employers as collectors, requiring them to deduct the tax each week from the worker's pay packet.

On account of its high yield, changes in the income tax are very effective when the government wishes to vary the amount of spending power in the hands of consumers.

2. Certainty

Income tax payers are usually well acquainted with the amount of tax they will be expected to pay out of a given income and when they must pay it. Moreover, it is difficult to evade payment. Workers draw their wages less PAYE deductions, while dividends and interest are received less the standard rate of income tax.

Similarly, on the government's side, the Chancellor can rely on the yield from income tax, and even when he is out in his estimates through variations in money income, the stabilising effect will be a good thing.

In the case of inheritance tax, the yield may fluctuate.

3. Convenience

Weekly PAYE tax deductions enable the tax burden to be spread over the year. Companies and self-employed persons, such as doctors, surveyors, authors, and entertainers, receive a lump-sum demand which is paid in two half-yearly instalments.

Inheritance tax is a form of wealth tax but is convenient in that the owner is able to enjoy his property throughout his life. But where the duty falls heavily on a landed estate the resulting enforced sale artificially depresses land values in the district.

4. Automatically Stabilises the Economy

Both income tax and corporation tax have an automatic effect in stabilising the economy (see p. 491).

5. Equity

In the case of income tax, equality of sacrifice is achieved in two ways:
- (a) an allowance is given for being married and for other responsibilities, e.g. a dependent aged relative;
- (b) the tax rate increases from 25 per cent to 40 per cent above £20 700 income (1990).

6. Redistributes Income and Wealth More Equally

By being progressive and giving allowances for special needs, income tax brings about greater equality in incomes. Inheritance tax works similarly as regards wealth.

Disadvantages

The simplest and fairest method of increasing revenue is to raise the rate of income tax. But here there is a major obstacle. When the rate is already high, the disadvantages of direct taxes are magnified.

1. High Rates Act as a Disincentive to Effort

When income tax is around 40 per cent, people may prefer to take their income in the form of leisure (which is not taxed) rather than in money (which is taxed).

The extent to which this occurs, however, is uncertain. If a person has fixed money commitments, e.g. hire-purchase instalments, mortgage repayments and insurance premiums, he may have to work *harder* to meet them when his income is reduced. Furthermore, if we assume that a high rate of income tax is a disincentive to effort, we infer that people always look upon work as distasteful, and leisure as a pleasurable alternative. For many, this may be true but in the high-income brackets there are some who find their work enjoyable. Last, we have to remember that most people are not free to vary their hours of work except as regards overtime. The normal working week is often an agreement on a national basis between trade unions and employers' associations.

The disincentive effect is more likely to occur when there is a sudden jump in the rate of tax between one income level and another. People reduce their effort at the higher taxed income level. This is a psychological reaction, for they are not forced to consider whether their standard of living will fall – as happens when there is a general rise in the rate of tax. In other words, the disincentive occurs when the marginal rate of tax exceeds the average rate.

2. High Direct Taxes Stifle Enterprise

A higher money reward is usually necessary to induce a person to devote time to training and study or to incur the cost of moving a home to secure promotion. It follows, therefore, that where the wage differential between skilled and unskilled labour is eroded by income tax, incentives are proportionately reduced. Similarly, firms are only prepared to accept risks if the rewards are commensurate.

3. High Rates of Tax Do not Encourage Efficiency

Companies have 35 per cent of profits taken in taxation. Thus the penalty of inefficiency is not borne entirely by the firm. Because income is smaller, less tax is paid and so a part of the cost falls on the government.

4. High Rates of Direct Taxation Encourage Tax Avoidance

Although, as we have seen above, income tax may not directly reduce effort, it is likely that people will, wherever possible, seek to reduce their tax liability in other ways. Much energy may be expended on this. Accountants are employed to advise on how tax may be legally avoided. Where possible, income is taken in kind – through share options, company cars, housing and even education for children – instead of in money, but the government is trying to tighten up in this respect.

Illegal tax evasion becomes more worthwhile, too, when the tax is high.

5. High Direct Taxes May Prevent the Optimum Allocation of Resources

Direct taxes, too, may affect the supply of factors, particularly capital, to industry. It may be that high taxation discourages saving; it certainly reduces the power to save. This is not serious for large companies, but the major source of capital for the small private company or sole proprietor is the owner's personal savings out of income. Normally firms which are making the largest profits will be the more likely to want to expand. Thus income tax and corporation tax deprive small, risky, but often progressive companies of much needed capital.

Not only that, but high direct taxes may repel foreign capital. Although the deduction of income tax on dividends may be refunded, the company still has to bear corporation tax on profits (at 35 per cent). The amount available to shareholders is therefore less, and the declared dividend correspondingly smaller. Consequently, people may prefer to invest in companies operating in countries where there is a higher return to capital – a higher return which is the result, not of superior efficiency, but simply of the lower taxes payable.

33.6   The Advantages and Disadvantages of Indirect Taxes

Advantages

1. Revenue Yield Helps to Avoid High Direct Taxes

The revenue need of the government is now so great that without the yield of indirect taxes, such a high rate would have to be borne by direct taxes that there would be serious effects on effort and initiative.

In any case, some people feel that some indirect taxes, which affect everybody, are desirable in that they foster a responsible attitude to government spending.

2. Certain and Immediate Yield

Especially when the Chancellor concentrates tax changes on goods with a fairly inelastic demand, the revenue yield can be calculated fairly accu-. rately. Indirect taxes are cheap to collect and difficult to evade.

Where the Chancellor requires immediate revenue, indirect taxes have a special advantage. Any increase in the tax produces extra revenue with little time-lag – quite different from a change in income tax.

3. Convenient to the Taxpayer

Buyers are able to spread their payments as and when purchases are actually made. Indeed, if the tax does not change frequently, buyers soon regard the combined price and tax at which the good is sold as the usual price, thereby reducing the resentment which taxation normally incites.

4. Unharmful to Effort and Initiative

While direct taxes are linked to earning, indirect taxes fall on spending. With indirect taxes, therefore, there is little disincentive to effort. It may even be that higher prices will cause people to work harder in order to maintain their customary standard of living.

On the other hand, care must be taken that certain 'incentive goods' – cars, washing machines, refrigerators, dish washers, etc. – are not taxed so heavily that they are priced beyond the reach of persons who would otherwise work overtime in order to secure them.

5. *They May Automatically Stabilise the Economy*

In as much as goods having a high income elasticity of demand (chiefly home-produced and imported luxuries) are taxed the most heavily, the yield from indirect taxes increases as incomes rise. This increase in the revenue helps to stabilise the economy in an inflationary situation (see p. 491).

Today, the Chancellor of the Exchequer is able to reinforce this automatic mechanism by the 'regulator'. He can alter an indirect tax either way by 25 per cent of the existing rate.

6. *They are Adjustable to Specific Objectives of Policy*

Selective taxes can be changed according to the particular needs of government policy. The following are examples:

(*a*) In order *to build up infant or vital defence industries*, protection from competitive foreign products may be afforded by an import duty. The British motor car, aircraft, paper, and chemicals industries have been built up in this way. In the case of an 'infant industry', it is argued that after an initial period of protection it will be able to hold its own in competition with well-established foreign rivals, but in practice this seldom occurs.

(*b*) The effects of *changes in the conditions of demand or supply on the long-term structure of an industry* may be mitigated by favourable tax concessions or by the imposition of duties on competing imports, e.g. cotton goods.

(*c*) The government may encourage the *use of certain goods* by VAT concessions, e.g. books are zero-rated.

(*d*) *Political links may be strengthened* by duties which give favourable treatment to particular countries, e.g. fellow-members of the EC.

(*e*) Citizens' health may be safeguarded by taxing certain goods, e.g. spirits, cigarettes.

(*f*) The *terms of trade may be improved* by taxing certain imports (see p. 522).

(*g*) The *balance of payments may be strengthened* by import duties on foreign goods.

Disadvantages

1. Regressive

In so far as they buy the same goods, poor persons pay exactly the same tax as the rich. More than that, purchases are made out of income left after income tax has been paid. Thus not only are indirect taxes regressive, but they undo some of the redistributive effects of direct taxation.

To some extent, the regressive nature of indirect taxes can be offset by: (*a*) imposing *ad valorem taxes* instead of *specific taxes;* (*b*) exempting from VAT such items as food, housing and children's clothing.

2. Not Completely Impartial in their Application

Although indirect taxes fulfil the requirement that all persons in the same position should pay the same tax, the concentration of taxes on a few goods – chiefly tobacco, alcoholic drink, and motoring – does penalise severely certain forms of spending. Thus a person who obtains his pleasure from walking, reading, cycling, and eating receives many benefits from state expenditure, benefits which are largely paid for by his smoking, drinking, and car-driving neighbour!

3. Possibly Harmful to Industry

Where taxes are subject to frequent variation, they may dislocate industry. This will be more marked the higher the elasticity of demand for the product (see pp. 504–6).

4. Rigidity

Protective duties and subsidies (a 'negative tax') may originally be designed to give special assistance to an industry. But the Chancellor often finds his hands tied when he wishes to reduce this form of help. Industries such as agriculture, which have come to rely on protection or subsidies, strenuously resist any such move.

5. May have Inflationary Influences

Indirect taxes, by increasing the price of goods, raise the Index of Retail Prices. This leads to a demand for wage increases.

6. Prevent Resources from Being Distributed in the Best Possible Way

The imposition of an indirect tax on a *particular* good results in resources not being perfectly allocated according to the real preferences of consumers. In the long period, under perfect competition, no supernormal profits are made – the cost of producing the good is just equal to people's valuation of it. Moreover, consumers have allocated their outlay according to their preferences, so that marginal utility relative to the price of the good is equal in all cases. A tax on one good destroys the equilibrium, for the price of the good rises (unless supply is absolutely inelastic). This results in a redistribution of consumers' expenditure and thus of the factors of production. In addition, there will be some dislocation of the industry concerned (see p. 505).

7. Result in Greater Loss to the Consumer than an Income Tax Which Raises an Equivalent Amount

Unlike an income tax, indirect taxes change the relative prices of goods. This means that consumers have to rearrange their pattern of expenditure. This substitution involves a loss of satisfaction in addition to that suffered through the reduction in income.

33.7 The Incidence of Taxation

What Do We Mean by the 'Incidence' of a Tax?

So far we have considered only the *formal* incidence of a tax – how the tax is distributed between the various taxpayers. Thus direct taxes, we saw, are progressive, falling heaviest on the higher income groups. Indirect taxes, on the other hand, are regressive as regards consumers, though the direct incidence falls on producers or distributors who actually pay the tax to the Customs and Excise.

But the economist is chiefly concerned with the *effective* incidence – how the real burden of a tax is distributed after its full effects have worked through the economy.

In the case of *direct taxes*, we have seen that, with some qualifications, both income tax and corporation tax adversely affect effort, enterprise and risk-bearing, economy in expenditure, and saving (pp. 406–7).

An increase in income tax can be passed on only by those workers who can secure some addition to their wages by way of compensation. For this to happen, they must be in a strong bargaining position. Certain conditions must be fulfilled (see p. 229), the chief one being that the demand for the good they produce is fairly inelastic. The increase in the price of the good which results from the higher wages will be borne mainly by consumers – which really means workers in other groups who are not in such a strong bargaining position.

Similarly, in the short period, when supply is fairly inelastic, an increase in a tax on profits will be borne chiefly by producers (see p. 506). But in the long period, when some entrepreneurs transfer from the riskier enterprises (which the tax hits hardest), there will be changes in the relative supply of goods, and consumers of those goods whose production involves the most risk will, according to their elasticity of demand, have to bear a part of the tax.

A tax which falls on monopoly profits, however, cannot be passed on. There has been no change in the demand or supply curves, and the monopolist is already producing where his profits are a maximum. Hence if he has to pay, say, a 20 per cent tax, his equilibrium position will be unchanged; four-fifths of maximum profits are still better than four-fifths of anything less.

With *indirect taxes*, the effective incidence can be analysed more precisely. An indirect tax may be *general* or *selective*. A sales tax levied across the board on all goods and services at a standard rate would be a *general* indirect tax. VAT comes closest to such a tax. The important point is that *relative* prices remain unchanged and the consumer cannot switch to a substitute which is relatively cheaper because it bears no tax. If the government wishes to reallocate resources, therefore, it must do so by using the proceeds of the tax to subsidize certain industries, or by imposing additional excise duties on goods whose consumption it would like to curtail, e.g. tobacco.

Any tax which is levied at a higher rate on certain goods is termed *selective*, e.g. tobacco, alcohol, cars, petrol. When a tax is selective, the following questions become important: what is the effect of imposing a selective tax on the size of the particular industry? How will the burden of such a tax be ultimately distributed between the producer and consumer?

We begin by explaining how the imposition of a tax can be shown diagrammatically.

The Diagrammatic Presentation of a Tax

Theoretically, the effect of a tax can be analysed on either the demand or the supply side. No matter which is chosen, the same new equilibrium position for price and output will result. Later we shall prefer one method to the other according to the particular problem being analysed.

Consider the following demand and supply schedules for commodity *X*.

Price of X (pence)	Demand (units)	Supply (units)
12	60	150
11	70	130
10	80	110
9	90	90
8	100	70

The equilibrium price is 9p. Now suppose a tax of 3p is charged on the producer for each unit of X he puts on the market. This means that whereas before the tax he supplied 70 000 units at a price of 8p, he will now only supply this quantity at 11p (because 3p would go in tax). Similarly, 90 000 units will only be supplied at a price of 12p instead of 9p. Thus the effect of the 3p tax can be shown by the shift in the supply curve from S to S_1 (Figure 33.3). This gives a new equilibrium price of 11p, the buyer paying 2p more and the producer receiving 1p less, the quantity traded falling from 90 000 units to 70 000 units.

The result is the same if the 3p tax is levied on purchasers. Before the tax, 100 000 units were demanded at a price of 8p. If purchasers now have to pay a 3p tax, this is equivalent to a price of 11p including tax, and so they will demand only 70 000 units. Similarly, for a price of 9p they will demand only 60 000 units instead of 90 000. Thus the effect of the 3p tax imposed on buyers can be shown by the move in the demand curve from D to D_1 (Figure 33.4). This gives a new equilibrium price of 11p (8p at which the market is cleared, plus 3p tax), and the quantity traded falls from 90 000 to 70 000.

FIGURE 33.3

The Diagrammatic Representation of a Tax on the Supply Side

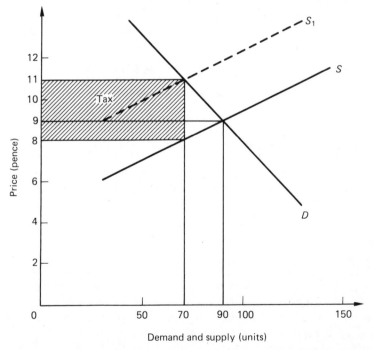

FIGURE 33.4
The Diagrammatic Representation of a Tax on the Demand Side

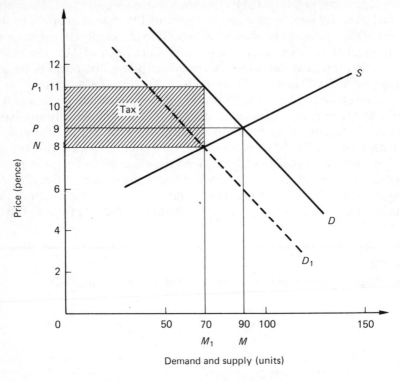

Demand and supply (units)

The Effect of an Indirect Tax on the Size of an Industry

The greater the elasticities of demand and supply, the greater will be the
effect of a tax in reducing production. We can show this diagrammatically
(Figure 33.5).

1. Elasticity of Demand

Before the tax is imposed, total output is OM. The effect of the tax is to
raise the supply curve from S to S_1. Two demand curves are shown, D_a
being less elastic than D_b at price OP. The effect of the tax is to reduce
output to OM_1 where demand is D_a, and to OM_2 where it is D_b. In the
latter case consumers switch to buying substitutes.

FIGURE 33.5
The Relationship of Elasticity of Demand and Production when a Tax is Imposed on a Good

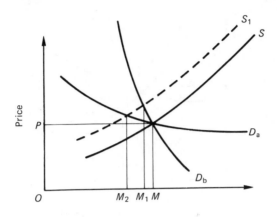

Quantity demanded and supplied

2. *Elasticity of Supply*

Before the tax is imposed, total output is OM (Figure 33.6). The effect of the tax is to lower the demand curve from D to D_1. Two supply curves are shown, S_a being less elastic than S_b at price OP. The effect of the tax is to reduce output to OM_1 where supply is S_a, and to OM_2 where it is S_b. In the latter case producers can turn to producing alternative goods.

The proposition under this heading has important practical applications.

(*a*) The government may use a subsidy (which can be illustrated by moving the supply curve to the right) to increase the production, and thus employment, of an industry. The effect will be more pronounced where demand and supply are elastic.

(*b*) Because the effect of a tax is to reduce production, even a temporary tax may be harmful to an industry. This is particularly so where home demand is elastic and production takes place under decreasing costs. Thus a higher selective tax on cars would not only reduce home demand, but, by doing so, lose economies of scale, thereby putting up prices to both home and foreign markets. Even when the tax is subsequently withdrawn, foreign markets may not be regained, for sales organisation, servicing arrangements and goodwill might all have suffered permanent harm.

FIGURE 33.6
The Relationship of Elasticity of Supply and Production when a Tax is Imposed on a Good

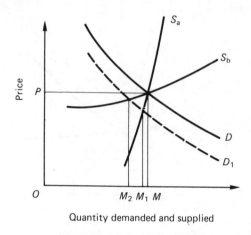

Quantity demanded and supplied

The Distribution of the Burden of a Selective Tax Between Consumers and Producers

When a good is subject to a selective tax, it does not mean that its price will rise by the full amount of the tax. Thus in Figure 33.4 the tax is 3p, but the price of X rises by only 2p. The proposition is that the amount of the tax falling on consumers as compared with that falling on producers is directly proportional to the elasticity of supply as compared with the elasticity of demand. That is:

$$\frac{\text{Consumers' share of tax}}{\text{Producers' share of tax}} = \frac{\text{Elasticity of supply}}{\text{Elasticity of demand}}$$

That this proposition is likely to be true can be seen from the following argument. When a tax is imposed, the reaction of the producer is to try to push the burden of the tax on to the consumer, while similarly the consumer tries to push it on to the producer. Who wins? Simply the one whose bargaining position is stronger. This will depend upon the ability to switch to producing substitutes if the price falls as compared with the ability to switch to buying substitutes if the price rises. Now the possibility of substitution largely determines elasticities of supply and demand. Thus the relative burden of the tax paid by producers and consumers depends upon relative elasticities of supply and demand.

The proposition can be proved geometrically as follows. As a result of the tax, price rises from OP to OP_1, and the quantity demanded and supplied falls from OM to OM_1 (Figure 33.4).

$$\text{Elasticity of supply at } OP = \frac{M_1M/OM}{NP/OP}$$

$$\text{Elasticity of demand at } OP = \frac{M_1M/OM}{PP_1/OP}$$

$$\therefore \frac{\text{Elasticity of supply}}{\text{Elasticity of demand}} = \frac{M_1M}{OM} \times \frac{OP}{NP} \times \frac{OM}{M_1M} \times \frac{PP_1}{OP}$$

$$= \frac{PP_1}{NP}$$

$$\frac{\text{Increase in price (burden of the tax) to the consumer}}{\text{Decrease in price (burden of the tax) to the producer}}$$

This proposition has a number of practical applications:

(a) A tax on a good having an inelastic demand, e.g. cigarettes, falls mainly on the consumer.

(b) Where supply is inelastic compared with demand, the tax falls mainly on the producer. Thus the imposition of VAT on the construction of new office blocks will have to be borne initially by the current landowner.

(c) Because in the long period supply tends to be more elastic than in the short period, so, as time passes, the price will tend to rise as consumers are required to bear a greater share of the tax.

(d) Where supply is inelastic even in the long period, a tax will take longer to pass on to the consumer. Thus if there are any unoccupied offices, an increase in rates will have to be borne mainly by the owners of the property.

(e) An increase in price as a result of a tax will vary according to the relationship of elasticity of supply to elasticity of demand. The greater the elasticity of supply relative to the elasticity of demand, the greater will be the price rise.

The Distribution of the Benefit of a Subsidy

The grant of a subsidy ('negative tax') can be analysed similarly by moving the demand or supply curve to the right, e.g. S to S_s (Figure 33.7).

FIGURE 33.7
The Diagrammatic Representation of a Subsidy

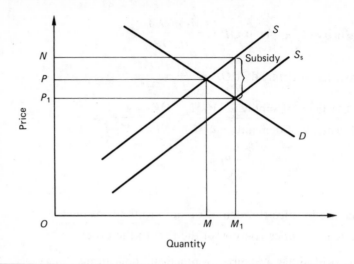

Price falls from OP to OP_1, and the quantity traded increases from OM to OM_1. As previously, it can be proved that the benefit of the subsidy to consumers as compared with that of producers is directly proportional to the elasticity of supply to the elasticity of demand. That is:

$$\frac{\text{Consumers' share of subsidy (fall in price paid)}}{\text{Producers' share of subsidy (increase in the price received)}}$$
$$= \frac{\text{Elasticity of supply}}{\text{Elasticity of demand}}$$

Part VII

International Economics

34 International Trade

34.1 Why International Trade?

How International Trade Arises

International trade arises simply because countries differ in their demand for goods and in their ability to produce them.

On the demand side, a country may be able to produce a particular good but not in the quantity it requires. The USA, for instance, is a net importer of oil. On the other hand, Kuwait does not require all the oil she can produce. Without international trade most of her deposits would remain untapped.

On the supply side, resources are not evenly distributed throughout the world. One country may have an abundance of land; another may have a skilled labour force. Capital, oil, mineral deposits, cheap unskilled labour and a tropical climate are other factors possessed by different countries in varying amounts.

Nor can these factors be transferred easily from one country to another. Climate, land and mineral deposits are obviously specific. Labour is far more immobile internationally than within its own national boundaries. Capital, too, moves less easily; exchange controls, political risks and simple ignorance of possibilities may prevent investors from moving funds abroad.

Because factors are difficult to shift, the alternative – moving the goods made by those factors – is adopted. What happens, therefore, is that countries, if the terms of trade are appropriate, specialise in producing those goods in which they have the greatest comparative advantage, exchanging them for the goods of other countries. Thus international trade arises.

Why Make a Separate Study of International Trade?

So far we have said nothing that is different in principle from trade between persons or between localities within a country. A carpenter who makes a chair exchanges it through the price mechanism for the food and other goods needed. Similarly, cars made at Sunderland are exchanged for washing machines made in South Wales. Why then, apart from the fact that longer distances are involved, do we treat separately the exchange of cars made in Britain for the wool produced in Australia?

The answer is that although the same theoretical principles apply, international trade gives rise to different problems. Exporters lack knowledge of foreign markets, find demand more difficult to predict, and have to cope with differences of language, weights and measures, government regulations, and changes of currency. Such factors tend to reduce the volume of international trade. Above all, since goods have to cross fronties and be paid for in the currency of the country selling them, international trade may be regulated by governments for both economic and political reasons (see p. 521). What we have to do, therefore, is to show the theoretical gains which result from international trade and then indicate why our theoretical argument has to be modified in practice.

34.2   The Advantages of International Trade

1. It Enables Countries to Obtain the Benefits of Specialisation

Specialisation by countries improves the standard of living for all.

(*a*) It is obvious that, without international trade, many countries would have to go without certain products. Iceland, for instance, has no coal, Britain no gold or aluminium, and Sweden no oil.

(*b*) More important, many goods can be enjoyed which, if produced at home would be available only to the very wealthy, for instance bananas, spices, oranges and peaches in Britain. But this benefit can be applied generally to all imports. The 'law of comparative costs' shows that, provided countries differ in the relative costs of producing certain goods, they can probably gain by specialisation and trade.

Suppose that there are two countries, *A* and *B*, producing just two commodities, wheat and cars. Each has the same amount of capital and the same number of labourers, but *A* has a good climate and fertile soil compared with *B*. *B*'s workers, on the other hand, are far more skilful. All factors are fully employed.

When both countries divide their factors equally between the production of wheat and cars, they can produce as follows:

Country	Wheat (units)	Cars (units)
A	500	100
B	100	500
Total production	600	600

But if *A* specialises in producing wheat and *B* cars, total production would be 1000 wheat and 1000 cars. There is thus a net gain of 400 wheat and 400 cars to be shared between them (see p. 516).

Here the gains are obvious, because *A* has an *absolute* advantage in producing wheat and *B* in producing cars. But suppose *A* also has skilled labour and capital, and is better at producing both wheat and cars, as follows:

Country	Wheat (units)	Cars (units)
A	500	300
B	400	100
Total production (no specialisation)	900	400

Are there still gains to be achieved by specialisation?

Provided the rate at which cars can be exchanged for wheat lies within certain limits (see p. 515), the answer is 'yes'. The reason for this is that *A*'s superiority in producing cars is far more pronounced than her superiority in producing wheat for with the same factors she can produce three cars for every one of *B*'s, but only one-and-a-quarter units of wheat for one of *B*'s. *Comparative*, rather than absolute, advantages are what are really important. The result is that if *A* specialises in producing cars, leaving *B* to produce wheat, total production will be 600 cars and 800 wheat.

Suppose now that world conditions of demand and supply are such that 2 wheat exchange for 1 car; that is, the price of cars is exactly twice that of wheat. *A* now exchanges 200 cars for 400 wheat, giving her a total of 400 wheat and 400 cars, and *B* 400 wheat and 200 cars.

It can be seen, therefore, that through specialisation *B* is 100 cars better off. But has specialisation improved *A*'s position? She now has 400 cars but only 400 wheat, a gain of 100 cars but a loss of 100 wheat. But by her own production she would have had to go without $166\frac{2}{3}$ wheat in order to obtain the extra 100 cars. Thus we can conclude that she too is better off.

The above arguments can be put in terms of opportunity costs. If there is no specialisation, *A* has to give up 3 cars in order to produce 5 units of wheat. On the international market, however, the terms of exchange are such that 3 cars can obtain 6 units of wheat. It will obviously pay *A*, therefore, to specialise in producing cars and to obtain her wheat by exchange. Similarly with *B*. For 4 units of wheat she can, by her own efforts, obtain only 1 car. On the world market she gets 2 cars. It will thus pay her to specialise in producing wheat and to obtain her cars by exchange.

The above explanation must be amplified to allow for:

(1) DEMAND

The law of comparative costs merely shows possibilities on the *supply* side – how two countries can specialise to advantage when their opportunity costs differ. But until we know the demand for goods we cannot say definitely whether specialisation will take place or, if it does, to what extent. Thus, although a country may be favourably placed to produce certain goods, a large home demand and thus a relatively high price may mean that it is a net importer of that good (as the USA is of oil).

(2) TRANSPORT COSTS

These reduce possible gains and therefore make for less specialisation. Indeed, it is conceivable that transport costs could so offset *A*'s superiority in making cars that *B* found it better to produce her own requirements.

(3) CHANGES IN THE CONDITIONS OF SUPPLY

Few production advantages are permanent. Climate and, to a large extent, mineral deposits persist, but new techniques can make factors more productive. Thus India now exports cotton goods to Britain!

(4) INTERFERENCE BY NATIONS WITH THE FREE MOVEMENT OF GOODS –

by customs duties, etc. (see p. 520).

(5) THE POSSIBILITY OF DIMINISHING RETURNS SETTING IN AS THE PRODUCTION OF A GOOD INCREASES

The theory as stated assumes that, at all stages of production, wheat can always be produced instead of cars by both *A* and *B* at a constant ratio. Thus at any output, *A* can have 5 wheat instead of 3 cars and *B* 4 wheat instead of 1 car. But it is likely that as *B* increases her output of wheat, diminishing returns set in, for inferior land and labour have to be used. Thus instead of getting 4 additional wheat for 1 car, she receives only 3, and later only 2, and so on. The same applies, too, as the production of cars is increased by *A*. Eventually, therefore, it pays to specialise no longer. *A* can obtain her wheat cheaper by producing herself than by buying it on the world market, and the same applies to *B* as regards cars. Diminishing returns, and thus increasing costs, usually mean in practice that there is only partial specialisation – up to the point where opportunity costs are less than those offered by the terms of trade. Thereafter it is better for a country to produce the good itself.

2. By Expanding the Market, International Trade Enables the Benefits of Large-scale Production to be Obtained

Many products, e.g. computers, drugs, aircraft and cars, are produced under conditions of decreasing cost. Here the home market is too small to exploit fully the advantages of large-scale production. This applies particularly to small countries such as Switzerland. In such cases, international trade lowers costs per unit of output.

But it is the advantages of large-scale production which mainly account for the fact that more than half the world's trade takes place between countries similarly endowed and with the same income and patterns of demand. Thus with aircraft engines, Britain both exports to and imports from the USA, but each specialises in producing different *types*.

3. International Trade Increases Competition and Thereby Promotes Efficiency in Production

As we have seen, any restriction of the market makes it easier for one seller to gain control. In contrast, international trade increases competition. A government must always consider the risk of a monopoly developing when it gives protection to the home industry by tariffs, etc.

4. International Trade Promotes Beneficial Political Links Between Countries

Examples of this are the EC and the Commonwealth, where trade is an important link.

34.3 The Terms of Trade

The Limits of the Exchange Rate

In our example, A specialises in producing cars and B in producing wheat. By her own efforts, A could have 5 wheat for 3 cars. Obviously, therefore, she will not specialise in cars if, by exchange, she receives less wheat than this. Similarly, B will not specialise in producing wheat if she has to give up more than 4 wheat for 1 car.

Thus for specialisation to be beneficial to both A and B the rate at which wheat exchanges for cars must lie somewhere between the upper limit of $\frac{5}{3}$ and the lower limit of 4.

Determination of the Exchange Rate

But how is the actual rate of exchange (which we assumed to be 2 wheat for 1 car) determined?

The answer is quite simple. When we say that 2 wheat exchange for 1 car, we are really comparing relative values. Hence the price of cars will be twice that of wheat. Their relative prices will be fixed in the market, like all other prices, by demand and supply. We can explain by developing our simplified example still further.

Suppose *A* and *B* are the only two countries engaged in trade and that only two commodities, wheat and cars, are produced. Through specialisation, but before exchange, *A* has 600 cars and *B* 800 wheat. As the relative prices of wheat and cars change, so we have the following imaginary demand and supply schedules:

Price (exchange ratio) wheat : cars	A		B	
	Wheat demanded	Cars offered	Cars demanded	Wheat offered
3 : 1	1,500	500	100	300
$2\frac{1}{4}$: 1	900	400	240	540
2 : 1	650	325	325	650
$1\frac{3}{4}$: 1	350	200	400	700

It can be seen that, given the conditions of demand and supply as shown in the above schedules, only at a price of 2 wheat to 1 car is there market equilibrium. The example could be extended to cover more than two countries and more than two commodities.

For both *A* and *B*, the rate at which wheat exchanges for cars represents the *terms of trade*. If there are changes in demand or supply, so that more wheat has to be given for a car, then the terms of trade have improved so far as *A* is concerned, but have worsened for *B*. On the other hand, if less wheat has to be given for a car, the terms of trade have improved for *B* but worsened for *A*.

Changes in the Terms of Trade

The terms of trade, therefore, are the rate at which a country exchanges its exports for imports. Where goods are traded internationally, this rate is fixed by (*a*) world conditions of demand supply, i.e. the real forces, and (*b*) the currency exchange rate, i.e. monetary influences. Long-term changes in the terms of trade are brought about by changes in the conditions of either demand or supply. Thus, in our example, if there is a large increase in *A*'s demand for wheat, the price of wheat will move nearer to the higher limit of $\frac{5}{3}$: 1. Likewise, if there is a decrease in *A*'s demand for wheat, the price will move nearer to the lower limit of 4:1. Or, if the conditions of supply change so that *A* can produce 1000 cars instead of 600, she would probably be willing to supply more cars in exchange for a given quantity of wheat, and so the price of cars falls, the terms of trade moving in favour of *B*. On the other hand, if *A*'s skilled labour emigrates and tends to be replaced by unskilled labour, she may be able to produce only 500 cars instead of 600, and the price of cars rises. The terms of trade move in favour of *A*.

Examples of how changes in the terms of trade can originate in the real world are:

1. Changes in the ·Conditions of Demand

(*a*) Demand may increase through industrial development. Thus increased demand for oil has improved the terms of trade for oil-exporting countries.

(*b*) A large increase in world demand for oil without any corresponding increase in production would improve the UK's terms of trade.

(*c*) A decrease in the demand for raw materials and basic minerals resulting from world recession when their supply is inelastic, brings about a large fall in the price. This was a factor helping to improve the UK's terms of trade in 1980.

2. Changes in the Conditions of Supply

(*a*) Technical improvements may increase supply, e.g. in agriculture during the 1970s and 1980s. Where demand is inelastic, the price of a good may, as a result, fall considerably, improving the terms of trade for net importers of foodstuffs.

(*b*) Political unrest or war in a country which is the main producer of a good, e.g. Chile (copper), may raise world prices and so improve the terms of trade for other major producers, e.g Zambia.

(*c*) Producing countries may form a successful monopoly to raise the price of their product, e.g. oil, thereby forcing up the price of their product.

How *currency* exchange rates are determined is explained in Chapter 35. Basically they reflect the relative demand for exports and imports. Thus the improvement in the sterling exchange rate in 1980 was a reflection of Britain's becoming self-sufficient in oil, enabling her to reduce imports and even to become a net exporter.

But the currency exchange rate is also influenced by capital movements. Some of the 1987 improvement in the sterling exchange rate resulted from the movement of short-term capital to London because foreigners had increasing confidence in the £ sterling as the price of oil stabilised at around $18 a barrel.

Thus a country's terms of trade can change even when there have been no real changes in the conditions of demand and supply but simply because the value of its currency has altered on the foreign exchange market.

Measurement of the Terms of Trade

The terms of trade express the relationship between the price of imports and the price of exports. In practice, however, our interest is centred on this relationship not so much at any one time but rather as it changes over a period of time. We therefore measure relative changes in the terms of trade from one period to another.

Because countries import and export many goods, and the prices of different goods move in different ways and by varying amounts, we have to measure changes in the price of imports and exports as a whole by index numbers. And, it must be remembered, these are subject to defects (p. 464).

In practice, therefore the terms of trade are measured as follows:

$$\frac{\text{Index showing average price of exports}}{\text{Index showing average price of imports}} \times \frac{100}{1}$$

Actual figures are given in Table 34.1

Table 34.1
The Terms of Trade of the UK, 1982–9 (base year 1985)

Year	Export unit-value index (1)	Import unit-value index (2)	Terms of Trade (1):(2)
1982	81.4	80.2	101.5
1983	88.0	87.8	100.2
1984	95.0	95.5	99.5
1985	100.0	100.0	100.0
1986	90.4	95.7	94.5
1987	94.2	98.5	95.7
1988	94.5	97.6	96.8
1989	101.2	103.8	97.6

SOURCE *Economic Trends*, March 1990, CSO HMSO.

When a country's exports become cheaper relative to her imports, she will have to give more goods in exchange for a given quantity of imports. It is then said that the terms of trade have 'worsened', 'moved against her', or 'become less favourable'. If the opposite occurs, the terms of trade are said to have 'improved', 'moved in her favour', or 'become more favourable'. Table 34.1 shows that the terms of trade for the UK have held fairly steady apart from a dip in 1986.

Results of Changes in the Terms of Trade

The direct effects of an improvement in a country's terms of trade are beneficial. First, she obtains more imports for a given quantity of exports. Second, her balance of payments may be improved. Suppose, for instance, that Britain's imports and exports are equal in value. Now suppose that the price of imports in sterling falls, but that the price of Britain's exports in sterling remains unchanged. If Britain's demand for imports is inelastic, the direct effect will be to improve her balance of payments, for less will be spent in sterling on imports. Similarly, if the demand for her exports were inelastic and their price in sterling rose, Britain's balance of payments would improve.

But the indirect results may make an improvement in the terms of trade, especially for a developed country, seem less desirable.

First, countries whose terms of trade have worsened may not be able to afford to buy the exports of the countries whose terms of trade have improved. For example, suppose that the price of wheat falls from £110 to £100 a tonne, but that an exporting country finds that demand increases only from 900 000 tonnes to 950 000 tonnes. Total expenditure on wheat drops, therefore, from £99m to £95m. But this expenditure equals approximately the income of farmers who are exporting the bulk of their crop. As a result of the fall in income, their demand for imports from a country such as the UK would drop.

Second, the fall in income will also mean that less is spent on home-produced goods, thereby reducing profits. To the extent that firms of these countries are owned by British shareholders, lower dividend payments reduce the UK's invisible earnings.

Third, a fall in the incomes of less developed countries may mean that the loss must be made good by increased aid.

Fourth, the economies of countries which are dependent on foreign trade may be subjected to frequent adjustments if there are swings in the terms of trade. If, for instance, the price of gold fluctuates, incomes will be greater in South Africa when the price of gold is high, and smaller when the price of gold is low, because demand is inelastic. This has far-reaching effects on a policy aimed at a stable level of income and employment.

34.4 Free Trade and Protection

Controlling International Trade

Our earlier analysis suggests that trade should be as free as possible, for only then can maximum specialisation according to the law of comparative advantage take place. In practice, however, all countries follow policies which, to varying degrees, prevent goods from moving freely in response to differences in relative prices. Methods vary.

1. Customs Duties

Customs duties, e.g. the common external tariffs of the EC, are both revenue-raising and protective. They become protective when the imported good bears a higher rate of tax than the similar home-produced good.

2. Subsidies

While countries which subscribe to the General Agreement on Tariffs and Trade (GATT) cannot follow a policy of 'dumping' exports by giving direct subsidies, the volume and pattern of international trade may be influenced indirectly by other means, e.g. government assistance to the shipbuilding industry. Less obviously, welfare benefits, e.g. child benefits and income supplements which keep down labour costs, may give one country a price advantage over another.

3. Quotas

If demand is inelastic, the increase in price resulting from a customs duty will have little effect on the quantity imported. Thus, to restrict imports of a good to a definite quantity, quotas must be imposed. Compared with duties, quotas have two main disadvantages:

(*a*) As a result of the artificial shortage of supply, the price may be increased by the foreign supplier or by the importer. Hence unless the government also introduces price control, they gain at the expense of consumers.

(*b*) Quotas make for rigidity in the economy, for they are calculated on a formula, usually based on the volume of imports over a given period, which grows increasingly out of date with time. This penalises the efficient firm wishing to expand.

To avoid having formal quotas imposed, 'voluntary' export restrictions may be agreed (e.g. on the import of Japanese cars to the UK).

4. Currency Control

A tighter check on the amount spent on imported goods can be achieved if quotas are fixed in terms of foreign currency. This necessitates some form of exchange control (see p. 539). All earnings of foreign currency or claims to foreign currency have to be handed over to the government and goods can be imported only under licence. Thus the government, not the free market, decides the priorities for imports.

5. Physical Controls

A complete ban – an embargo – may be placed on the import or export of certain goods. Thus narcotics cannot be imported, while the export of certain high technology goods and works of art require a licence. Similarly, imposing strict technical standards for certain goods (e.g. milk) and regulating the importation of live animals (e.g. cattle, dogs and parrots) make trade more difficult.

6. Minor Devices Which Divert Trade

These include: 'Buy British' campaigns, Queen's Awards for Exporting and bilateral arrangements making import purchases dependent on the exporter buying goods of equal value from the importer.

Reasons for Government Control of International Trade

In general, trade is controlled because governments think and act nationally rather than internationally. Although people as a whole lose when trade is restricted, those of a particular country may gain.

Many reasons are put forward to justify control. Occasionally they have some logical justification; more usually they stem from a narrow interest seeking to gain advantages. We can examine the arguments, therefore, under three main headings: (1) those based on strategic, political, social, and moral grounds; (2) those having some economic basis; (3) those depending on shallow economic thinking.

1. Non-economic Arguments

(a) *To encourage the production of a good of strategic importance.* Where a nation is dependent on another for a good of strategic importance, there is a danger of its supply being cut off in the event of war. Thus one argument for subsidising shipbuilding and aircraft production in the UK is to ensure the survival of plant and skilled labour.

(b) *To foster closer political ties.* As a member of the EC, Britain must impose a common external tariff as part of a movement towards political as well as economic unity.

(c) *To support political objectives.* Trade can be a weapon of foreign policy, e.g. in 1982 the USA stopped the export of high technology products to the USSR following the imposition of military rule in Poland.

(d) *To promote social policies.* Although in the past Britain has subsidised her agriculture mainly for strategic reasons, today the purposes are basically social – to avoid depression in rural districts.

2. Economic Arguments Having Some Justification

(a) *To raise revenue* (see p. 494).

(b) *To improve the terms of trade.* The incidence of a tax is shared between producer and consumer according to the relative elasticities of supply and demand (see p. 506). A government, therefore, can levy a tax on an imported good to improve the terms of trade if demand for the good is more elastic than the supply, for the increase in price is borne mainly by the producer, while the government has the proceeds of the tax. In practice this requires that: (i) the producing country has no alternative markets to which supplies can be easily diverted; (ii) her factors of production have few alternative uses; (iii) the demand for the exports of the country imposing the tariff must be unaffected by the loss of income suffered by countries who now find their sales abroad reduced.

(c) *To protect an 'infant industry'.* It may be possible to establish an industry in a country if, during its infancy, it is given protection from well-established competitors which are already producing on a large scale. It is argued that the guaranteed home market will enable it to get over its teething troubles and in time it will be so strong that it can compete on equal terms with the rest of the world. Britain's car industry, for instance, benefited from such protection.

In practice, industries tend to rely on this protection, so that tariffs are never withdrawn; for example, American duties on manufactured goods imposed in the eighteenth century still persist today. Moreover, industries are often encouraged which without protection would have no chance of survival. This leads to maldistribution of a country's resources.

(d) *To enable an industry to decline gradually.* Fundamental changes in demand for a good may severely hit an industry. Such, for instance, was the fate of the British cotton industry in 1975. Restrictions on imports can cushion the shock, but in practice many industries do not make use of the breathing space to restructure.

(e) *To correct a temporary balance-of-payments disequilibrium.* A temporary drain on gold and foreign currency reserves may be halted by controlling imports. But if the depletion of the reserves is due to fundamental and lasting causes, other measures should be used (see Chapter 36).

(*f*) *To prevent 'dumping'*. Goods may be sold abroad at a lower price than on the home market. This may be possible because: (*a*) producers are given export subsidies; (*b*) discriminating monopoly is possible (see p. 199); or (*c*) it enables the producer to obtain the advantages of decreasing costs. People in the importing country benefit directly from the lower prices. If, however, the exporter is trying to obtain a monopoly position which he can exploit once home producers have been driven out, there is a case for protecting the home market.

3. Economic Arguments Having Little Validity

(*a*) *To retaliate against tariffs of another country*. The threat of a retaliatory tariff may be used to influence another country to change its restrictive policy. Thus in 1989 the USA threatened to impose higher import duties on a number of EC goods to force a reversal of the EC's ban on beef from hormone-treated animals. Such measures are usually ineffective, for countries often retaliate by imposing still higher duties, with everybody losing.

(*b*) *To maintain home employment in a period of depression*. Countries may place restrictions on imports to promote employment in the manufacture of home-produced goods. The difficulty is that other countries retaliate, thereby leading to an all-round contraction in world trade. GATT was set up to prevent this from happening (see p. 524).

(*c*) *To protect home industries from 'unfair' foreign competition*. The demand that British workers must be protected from competition by cheap, 'sweated' foreign labour usually comes from the industry facing competition. The argument, however, has little economic justification. First, it runs counter to the principle that a country should specialise where it has the greatest advantage. That advantage may be cheap labour. Second, low wages do not necessarily denote low labour costs. Wages may be low because labour is inefficient through low productivity. What is really significant is the wage-cost per unit of output. Thus the USA can export manufactured goods to the UK even though her labour is the most highly paid in the world. The threatened industry can compete by improving productivity to reduce wage-cost per unit. Third, a tax on the goods of a poor country merely makes the country poorer and its labour cheaper. The way to raise wages (and the price of the good produced) is to increase demand in foreign markets. Indeed, if imports from poor countries are restricted, other help has to be given. They prefer 'trade to aid'. Fourth, protection, by reducing the income of the poorer countries, means that they have less to spend on Britain's exports. Last, the policy may lead to retaliation or aggressive competition elsewhere, thereby making it more difficult for the protecting country to sell abroad. One reason why Japan captured many of Britain's foreign markets for cotton goods was that her sales to Britain were restricted by protective barriers.

Conclusions

While restriction of trade tends to lower living standards, there may be benefits – economic, political and social. Thus protection may be given to an industry because home workers cannot adjust quickly to other occupations or industries. Usually, however, such economic gains are doubtful. Others cannot be measured, and it has to be left to politicians to decide where the balance of advantage lies. It must, however, always be remembered that protection creates vested interests opposed to subsequent removal.

The General Agreement on Tariffs and Trade (GATT)

The General Agreement on Tariffs and Trade, established in 1947, has three major objectives: (i) to reduce existing trade barriers; (ii) to eliminate discrimination in international trade; and (iii) to prevent the establishment of further trade barriers by getting nations to agree to consult one another rather than take unilateral action. It operates as follows.

Member nations meet together periodically to try to agree on a round of tariff reductions. Here the 'most-favoured-nation' principle applies. This means that if one country grants a tariff concession to another it must apply automatically to all the other participating countries. Thus if the EC agrees to reduce tariffs on American automatic vending machines by 5 per cent in exchange for a 5 per cent reduction in the American tariff on EC man-made fibres, then both concessions must be extended to every other member of GATT. This principle of non-discrimination also means that bilateral agreements and retaliatory tariffs against another country are out of harmony with GATT.

Today (1991) there are nearly one hundred member nations, accounting between them for four-fifths of world trade. Through the organisation, a progressive reduction in existing tariffs has been achieved, and the principle has been established that problems of international trade should be settled by cooperative discussion rather than by independent unilateral action. But difficulties have arisen.

(a) The principle of reciprocity means that low-tariff countries have to begin from an inferior bargaining position, and the concessions they can make are thus limited. Such countries may, therefore, prefer a low-tariff regional arrangement, such as the EC.

(b) In certain circumstances, the 'most-favoured-nation' principle may deter a country from making a tariff reduction to another country for the simple reason that it has to be applied to all.

(c) The Articles of the Agreement have had to be waived to allow for special circumstances – balance-of-payments difficulties, protection of agriculture, the establishment of 'infant' industries in less-developed countries, and the discriminatory character of the EC.

(d) While the GATT has been successful in dealing with tariffs and many physical barriers, it has been by-passed by the new forms of protection – voluntary restraint agreements, orderly marketing arrangements, subsidies for special groups of exports, and trading requirements as conditions for overseas investment.

(e) GATT rules will eventually have to be extended to cover *services* which now account for a quarter of world trade.

35 International Payments

35.1 The Balance of Payments

Differences in Currencies

Occasionally, international trade may take the form of a barter arrangement, one country agreeing to take so much of another country's produce in exchange for so much of its own. Normally, however, exchanges are arranged by private traders who, according to relative prices, decide whether it is profitable to export and import goods.

But each country has its own currency – Spain (pesetas), France (francs), the USA (dollars), the UK (pounds sterling), and so on. This difference is important for two reasons: (a) sufficient foreign currency has to be obtained to pay for imports; (b) a rate has to be established at which one currency will exchange for another. The first will be considered forthwith, the second in the chapter which follows; but neither is independent of the other.

Paying for Imports

Let us assume that £1 sterling exchanges for $1.60. Suppose a British merchant has imported cotton from America to the value of £10 000. The American exporter requires payment in dollars, for all his payments, e.g. his workers' wages, have to be made in dollars. Hence the importer goes to his bank, pays in £10 000, and obtains in exchange a draft for $16 000, which he sends to the exporter in the USA. The latter cashes the draft, receiving his $16 000 from the bank's branch in the USA. (Most banks have branches in foreign capitals, and where they do not, they engage local banks to act for them.) But how is it that the branch has dollars available to honour the draft?

We can see this if we imagine that another British firm has sold £10 000 worth of cars to an importer in the USA. This firm wants payment in pounds sterling. Hence the American importer of the cars pays $16 000 into his bank in the USA, receiving in exchange a draft for £10 000 which he sends to Britain. It is obvious that the two transactions – buying cotton from the USA and selling cars from Britain – balance one another. The British bank's branch has had to pay out dollars, the American sterling. The British bank has received sterling, the American bank dollars. If the two get together, their requirements match. (In practice it is more likely that they would meet their needs through the foreign exchange market.) Thus the dollars needed for paying for the cotton are obtained by selling the cars, and vice versa. In short, exports pay for imports.

'*Exports*' in its Wider Sense

In this connection the term 'exports' needs qualification. Usually it refers only to tangible goods, described as 'visibles', since they can be seen and recorded at the customs as they cross frontiers.

But there are other ways in which foreign currency can be earned – transporting foreign goods in British ships, providing for tourists visiting the UK, receiving profits and interest on sums invested by British people in firms in the USA. Such services and payments are known as 'invisibles', for there is no movement of goods which can be seen and checked (see Table 35.1).

Thus any transaction which involves a payment by somebody abroad to somebody in the UK (their nationality is irrelevant) is an 'export'. And the opposite is also true – any payment by a person in the UK to somebody abroad is an 'import'.

The Balance of Payments

Most countries give an account each year of their monetary transactions with the rest of the world. The accounts presented are known as 'the Balance of Payments'. The Balance of Payments for the UK for the year ended 31 December 1987 is given in Table 35.1.

The Current Account

The current account shows, on the one hand, the foreign currency which has been *spent* on *imported goods* and *invisibles* in the course of the year, and, on the other, the foreign currency which has been *earned* by *exporting goods* and *invisibles*.

That part of the current account which shows the payments for just the *goods* exported and imported is known as the *visible balance* (formerly the

Table 35.1
The Balance of Payments of the UK, 1988 (£ m)

CURRENT ACCOUNT
Visible trade

Exports (fob)	+80 602	
Imports (fob)	−101 428	
Visible balance		−20 826

Invisibles (net)

Government	−1 833	
Sea transport	−576	
Civil aviation	−862	
Travel	−2 042	
Financial and other services	+9 478	
Interest, profits and dividends	+5 619	
Private and government transfers	+3 575	
Invisible balance		+6 209
CURRENT BALANCE		−14 617

FINANCIAL ACCOUNT
Transactions in external assets and liabilities:

Investment abroad (net)	−12 952	
Borrowing abroad (net)	+18 047	
Official reserves, addition to	−2 761	
TOTAL	2 334	
Balancing item	12 283	
CAPITAL BALANCE		+14 617

SOURCE   Annual Abstract of Statistics

balance of trade). Where the value of goods exported exceeds the value of goods imported, we say that there is a favourable visible balance. If the opposite occurs, the visible balance is unfavourable. Too much, however, must not be read into the terms 'favourable' and 'unfavourable'. In the first place, we have to know the reasons for the unfavourable balance. It may be brought about, for instance, by an increased demand for raw materials and components as a country moves out of a recession. These will later be exported as manufactured goods. Or a less developed country may receive more aid, enabling her to import capital goods. Whereas the value of these is shown as 'imports', 'aid' will appear in the Financial Account. Secondly, a favourable or unfavourable visible balance can be reversed when the invisibles are taken into account.

When we add to the visible balance, payments and income on the invisible items, we have what is known as the *current balance*.

There is no special reason why earnings from goods and invisibles exported between 1 January and 31 December in any one year should equal expenditure on the goods and invisibles imported during that period. In fact, it would be an extraordinary coincidence if they did so. How often does what you earn during the week tally *exactly* with what you spend?

The current account, therefore, is likely to show a difference between earnings and expenditure. When the *value* of goods and invisibles exported exceeds the *value* of goods and invisibles imported, we say that there is a surplus current balance; when the reverse occurs, we say that there is a deficit. While this balance does show how far a country is paying its way, the current account is only part of the statement covering a nation's overseas financial transactions. Capital flows must also be scrutinised.

The Financial Account

The *financial account* sets out the currency flow generated by current account balances and capital movements.

If the current-account transactions were a country's only dealings with the world, the balance-of-payments accounts would be quite simple. A surplus of £100 million, for example, would add that amount to the reserves or allow the country to invest that amount overseas or to pay off short-term borrowings from the International Monetary Fund (IMF) or other foreign creditors. A deficit of £100 million would reduce the reserves by that amount or have to be financed by disinvestment or short-term borrowing abroad.

But *capital* flows also affect a country's ability to build up reserves or to pay off debts. Thus investment by private persons resident in the UK in factories or plant overseas (whether directly or by the purchase of shares), or a loan by the British government to an underdeveloped country, leads to an outflow of capital and the spending of foreign currency. Similarly, investment in the UK by persons overseas, or borrowing abroad by the British government, local authorities, nationalised industries or companies, leads to an inflow of foreign capital and the receipt of foreign currency.

Whereas the current account covers *income* earning and spending in the course of the year, 'transactions in external assets and liabilities' show the movement of *capital* in and out of the country. This capital may be short- or long-term.

Short-term capital movements arise from the transfer of liquid funds to and from Britain. Because London is a world financial market centre, foreigners hold bank balances or short-term bills there. These short-term funds can move quickly from country to country to take advantage of higher interest rates or to guard against an exchange rate depreciation. They are thus often referred to as 'hot money'.

Long-term capital investment by British residents in factories or plant overseas (whether directly or by the purchase of shares), or a loan by the British government (e.g. to a less developed country or an international institution) leads to an outflow of capital. Similarly, investment in the UK by persons overseas or borrowing from abroad by the British government, local authorities, nationalised industries or companies leads to an inflow of foreign capital.

Any movement of capital out of Britain gives rise to a demand for sterling; a movement into Britain from abroad leads to the receipt of foreign currency.

No distinction is made between short- and long-term investment in presenting the overall balance of payments. In fact much of Britain's overseas investment is financed by short-term capital borrowed from foreigners, e.g. from the pool of Eurocurrency deposited in London. To the extent that this occurs, there is no net outflow of foreign currency. Britain's overseas investment which is undertaken in order to make a profit is, in fact, like private business ventures. And, just as the shopkeeper borrows from the bank to cover the holding of stocks before Christmas, so the UK borrows to finance investment overseas in factories, plantations, oil wells, nickel-mines, etc.

Thus the UK's balance-of-payments accounts concentrate on what is really significant to Britain – the extent to which currency flows as a whole influence the £ sterling exchange rate and her reserves of gold and foreign currencies.

The balancing item arises as follows. When the total effect of recorded capital transactions is added to the current balance, the total never adds up exactly to the amount of foreign currency the country has in fact gained or lost, which is known precisely to the Bank of England. Government spending overseas, for instance, is easier to record exactly than the foreign spending of people taking holidays abroad. Exports, too, may go abroad in December, but payments for them come in the following February.

A 'balancing item' is therefore added to make up the difference between the total value of the transactions recorded and the precise acounts kept by the Bank of England. If the balancing item is '+', it means that more foreign currency has actually come in than the estimates of transactions have indicated. When there is a '−' balancing item, the opposite is the case.

FIGURE 35.1
The Balance of Payments in Outline

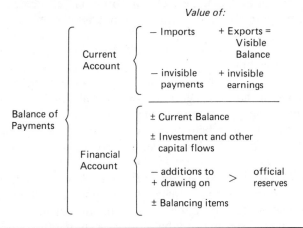

An Examination of the UK's Balance of Payments, 1988

The above explanation can be illustrated by examining the UK's Balance of Payments for 1988.

Imports exceeded exports; there was a visible balance deficit of £20 826 m. On invisibles, the UK had a favourable balance of £6209 m. The overall deficit on the Current Balance was thus £14 617 m.

In addition to the current account deficit of £14 617 m, net investment of £12 952 m abroad by Britain had to be covered. This was achieved by net borrowing of £18 047 m, together with a balancing item of £12 283 m, which allowed for an addition to the reserves of £2 761 m.

35.2   Foreign Exchange Rates

How are Exchange Rates Determined?

Trade between countries involves, as we have seen, an exchange of their currencies. But how is the rate at which one currency exchanges for another determined? Why is it that we have to give a pound note to obtain about 1.72 American dollars, 2.74 Swiss francs, 10.83 French francs, and so on?

The simple answer is that the price of the pound sterling, like all other prices, is determined by the forces of demand and supply. In this case the market is known as the 'foreign-exchange market'. It meets in no one place, but consists of all the institutions and persons – the banks of all kinds, dealers, and brokers – who are buying and selling foreign currencies. The foreign-exchange market is a world market, dealers throughout the world being in constant contact with one another by telecommunications.

Let us assume that we have 'freely fluctuating exchange rates'; that is, rates are not fixed by governments, but are free to move from day to day according to changes in the conditions of demand and supply. To discover how a change in the exchange rate can come about, we can glance once again at the mechanism of foreign payments.

When the British merchant wished to import cotton from the USA (see p. 526), he went to his bank to obtain the necessary dollars for payments. These dollars, we saw, were obtained from its branch in the USA, and this branch in its turn had received them from an American importer of cars who had deposited them in exchange for the pounds sterling he needed to pay the British motor firm. Let us assume that the existing exchange rate is $1.70 to the pound sterling and that trade is such that the same quantity of dollars is both demanded and supplied (Figure 35.2).

The situation, we will imagine, now changes. Imports of cotton from the USA increase in value, but exports of cars remain the same. The bank now finds that because more dollars are being demanded than are being deposited, its reserves of dollars are depleted. In short, the demand for

---

FIGURE 35.2
The Determination of Exchange Rates

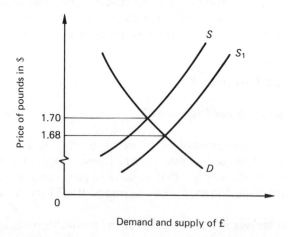

Price of pounds in $

Demand and supply of £

dollars exceeds the supply. It is possible that the bank will be able to find on the foreign-exchange market another bank or dealer who is receiving more dollars than pounds sterling. But if its experience is typical of the rest of the market, that is, there has been a general increase in the demand for dollars relative to pounds, it will be able to replenish its reserves of dollars only by offering more pounds sterling in exchange, and the supply curve moves to S_1. The dollar thus appreciates in value to \$1.68 to the pound. (As we shall see later, this will, to a large extent, bring a self-correcting mechanism into operation as regards the lack of balance between the value of imports and the value of exports.)

Arbitrage

We have concentrated our attention on the rate of exchange between the dollar and the pound. But there is also an exchange rate between the pound and the German mark, the French franc, and so on; and all these rates are linked with one another. If, for instance, £1 = \$2 and \$1 = 2 marks, then £1 must equal 4 marks. Otherwise, what are known as arbitrage operations by foreign-exchange dealers would bring the rates into line. Thus suppose in London 5 marks can be obtained for the pound. A dealer would buy marks for pounds in London, sell them for dollars in New York, and exchange the dollars for pounds, making 25p profit on the deal. This would not last for long because the world market in foreign exchange is so perfect that the increased demand for marks in London would soon bring the price there into line with the world price.

What are the Factors upon which the Demand for or Supply of Foreign Currency Depend?

It can be seen that an increased demand for dollars by people in Britain is one and the same thing as an increase in the supply of sterling being offered for dollars. An increased demand for dollars may be counteracted by an increased demand for sterling (that is, an increased supply of dollars) by Americans. For the sake of simplicity, we will concentrate our attention on the factors leading to a demand for sterling by Americans. These factors are:

1. To pay for the import of goods from Britain.
2. To pay for 'invisibles', e.g. a tour of Britain, government spending on troops in Britain, etc.
3. To meet capital movements into Britain (p. 530).

What are the Underlying Economic Forces Influencing how much Foreign Currency is Demanded and Supplied?

So far we have merely indicated the items for which foreign currency will be demand or supplied. Now we examine the economic forces which determine how large each of these items will be. They are:

1. Relative Prices

The chief factor affecting trade, both visible and invisible, is the price of home-produced goods as compared with the price of similar goods abroad. If, for example, American prices are high, Americans will wish to import cheaper British goods, whereas the British will prefer home-produced goods to American. The increased demand for sterling will, in a free exchange market, so raise the value of the pound sterling that eventually the prices of British goods are in line with those of the 'high-cost' American producer.

Some economists, notably Professor Gustav Cassel in 1922, carried this argument a stage further. They said quite categorically, in what became known as the *purchasing power parity theory*, that the value of a foreign currency in terms of another depends mainly on the relative purchasing power of the two currencies in their respective countries. In other words, the exchange rate settles at the level which makes the purchasing power of a given currency the same in whatever country it is spent.

For example, suppose that there is only one commodity, machines, and this machine sells for £200 in Britain and for $340 in the USA; then the rate of exchange would be 1.70 dollars to the pound. If now, through inflation, the price in Britain rises to £220, the rate of exchange will be 1.55 dollars to the pound. Thus a fall in the internal purchasing power of a currency through a rise in the general level of prices leads to a corresponding fall in its foreign-exchange value. Or mathematically, the purchasing power parity theory says that:

Foreign exchange price of £ (e.g. in dollars)

$$= \frac{\text{US price level}}{\text{British price level}}$$

When we are considering the long period, there is considerable truth in this theory. If, for instance, there is an inflation of prices in Britain relative to the USA, there will be less demand for British exports, but an increased demand for American imports. As a result, the price of the pound sterling falls in terms of the dollar. But, particularly in the short run, to say that overall purchasing power is the sole factor governing exchange rates is a gross oversimplification. The theory fails to allow for the following:

(*a*) Not all goods enter into international trade. Quite a number, for instance the Indian's loin-cloth, satisfy local and particular wants. Others, like houses, railway travel, gas and electricity, haircuts, and personal and professional services, cannot be transported easily from one country to another. The prices of such goods may rise considerably, whereas those of exports remain the same. Eventually, export industries will be forced by competition to pay higher wages, etc., but owing to immobility and imperfections of the market, this may take a very long time to come about. In the meantime, exchange rates will not be affected – in spite of the statistical rise in the general level of prices.

(*b*) Such factors as indirect taxes, subsidies, and transport costs may change the prices of goods within a country but not affect exchange rates in the way the theory predicts. Suppose a £100 per cent tariff is placed on an important import, the demand for which is not absolutely inelastic. The price in the home market would rise, but since less *foreign* currency would be spent on it, the exchange rate would tend to improve!

(*c*) A change in the exchange rate may originate in factors quite independent of the internal price level. When national income rises, for instance, imports are likely to increase in value relative to exports. As a result, the external value of the currency will depreciate. Similarly, a change in the terms of trade may affect the exchange rate. For instance, the 1986 fall in the price of oil led to a depreciation of the £ sterling on the foreign-exchange market.

(*d*) The theory ignores the effect of movements of capital upon the exchange rates, an influence which is particularly important in the short period (see p. 536).

The purchasing power parity theory, therefore is not a complete explanation of what determines exchange rates. In particular, it disregards the effect of capital movements both for investment and speculative purposes, and overlooks the fact that prices in the export industries may move differently from prices in other industries. But this does not mean that the theory has no value. Since imports and exports are the major items in a country's balance of payments, it draws attention to what, in the long run, is the dominant influence on exchange rates – how the internal price level moves relative to that of other countries. Indeed, there is a close link between this and the movement of capital for speculative purposes, for the latter is likely to reinforce changes in the exchange rates originating in the current account of the balance of payments.

2. Relative Money Incomes

When a country's money income expands, its demand for imports increases. Potential exports also tend to be diverted to the home market.

3. Long-term Investment Prospects

People can invest capital in foreign countries either by buying the bonds of foreign governments or the equities of companies there, or directly by building factories abroad as offshoots of parent companies in the UK. The chief factor influencing such investment decisions is how the prospective yield compares with that which could be obtained elsewhere.

Political risks, e.g. of default on loans, or possible changes in government policy, e.g. of a swingeing increase in corporation tax, have also to be assessed by those investing overseas.

4. The Rate of Interest

Short-term capital moves from one country to another as changes take place in the rate of interest being offered by each. The government can therefore vary interest rates to attract or repel foreign capital as it sees fit.

5. Expected Future Movements of the Exchange Rate

Inflation in a country will be interpreted by foreign holders of its currency as being likely to lead also to a fall in the external value of the currency. Selling of the currency follows, thereby helping to bring about the fulfilment of those expectations!

6. Government Expenditure

Military expenditure and economic aid abroad now provide large sources of supply of certain currencies, e.g. the American dollar and the pound sterling, to foreigners.

It can be seen, therefore, that exchange rates are not dependent on any single factor. The only safe generalisation which can be made is that the value of a currency depends upon all the forces which give rise to the purchase or sale of that currency in the foreign-exchange market.

36

The Correction of a Balance-of-Payments Disequilibrium

36.1   Alternative Approaches

When do Corrective Measures Become Necessary?

Taken as a whole, the balance of payments must always balance. Foreign currency necessary for making payments abroad must have come from somewhere. If there is an outward total currency flow, the balance must be achieved by drawing on the gold and foreign currency reserves or by official borrowing.

In the short period, a withdrawal from the reserves may not be serious. It could easily happen that, just prior to 31 December, the date usually chosen for drawing up the accounts, imports of raw materials were running at a high rate. Later, when the goods manufactured from these raw materials are sold abroad, the reserves will be replenished. Reserves of gold and foreign currencies are held for this very purpose – to provide a 'cushion' when current earnings are temporarily insufficient to cover payments abroad. Even individuals usually carry spare cash to bridge the gap between income and spending.

Alternatively, a less developed country may run an adverse current balance for a number of years. The deficit is covered, not by drawing on reserves, but by borrowing, both private and official. Loans are used to buy capital equipment. Eventually, this equipment will allow her to export goods which will cover the interest due on the loan and then the repayment of the loan itself. Once again, the balance-of-payments deficit need not be frowned upon; it is just good business – like a firm obtaining a loan from the bank.

But the situation is different when year after year a country is running a current balance deficit and there is little likelihood of its being able to reverse the trend. This disequilibrium between credits and debits is then said to be of a 'fundamental nature'. If not corrected, reserves will run out (see p. 576). Other countries will refuse to lend to the country in difficulties – they doubt whether the spendthrift will ever be in a position to repay. Action has to be taken, therefore, to remedy the situation.

A Broad Analysis of the Problem

A first-aid measure is for the authorities to force up the short-term rate of interest in order to reverse the outward flow of short-term capital. Furthermore, reserves could be strengthened by borrowing from the IMF and the other central banks. This would help to restore confidence in the currency.

Eventually, however, exports must be increased in value and/or imports decreased in value.

There are two basic policies which can be followed: (1) reducing expenditure on imports; (2) switching expenditure, so that foreigners spend more on British exports and Britons spend less on imports in favour of home-produced goods. Both policies can be followed simultaneously (though with a different emphasis on each), but it is easier to clarify the issues by considering them separately.

36.2 Reducing Expenditure on Imports: Deflation

The difficulty of increasing exports

A government may adopt policies to promote exports. Thus the British government guarantees payment through the Export Credits Guarantee Department and provides information on the possibility of developing markets abroad. Moreover, banks may be asked to discriminate in favour of exporters when granting loans. Although under the terms of GATT it is impossible to grant direct tax reliefs, incentives can be incorporated in indirect taxes; for example, zero-rating VAT on exports.

Increasing the value of exports by such means, however, takes time and is largely only marginal to the problem. The main thrust would need to be made on reducing expenditure on imports. This may be achieved by both physical controls and the deflation of home income.

Physical Controls

Physical controls may be exercised by import duties, quotas and exchange controls.

1. Import Duties and Quotas

Tariffs may be levied to increase the price of imports. But if demand is inelastic, imports will not be greatly discouraged or expenditure on them in terms of foreign currency greatly decreased. Sometimes, therefore, an import quota in terms of volume is imposed. As a result, however, the advantages of free trade are reduced, while the efficiency of home industry may be impaired by its protection from foreign competition. Moreover, tariffs displease other countries, and are likely to attract retaliation.

2. Exchange Control

Exchange control may be introduced for the following purposes:

(*a*) to limit the amount of foreign currency spent on imports;
(*b*) to discriminate against those countries whose currencies are 'hard' (that is, cannot easily be earned by exporting to them), and to favour those countries whose currencies are 'soft' (because they buy exports from the country concerned);
(*c*) to distinguish between essential and non-essential imports;
(*d*) to control the export of capital.

Exchange control is essential when a country's currency is overvalued – that is, its declared exchange rate is higher than it would be if it were determined by demand and supply on the foreign-exchange market. What this really means is that foreign currencies are valued below the market price – and so they have to be rationed.

Pegging the rate at a high level, however, may be advantageous to the country concerned, particularly if her demand for imports and supply of exports are inelastic. In such circumstances, the balance of payments might not be improved by reducing the external value of the currency (see pp. 545–8).

Nevertheless, exchange control suffers from many of the disadvantages associated with rationing. Inefficient home firms are protected from foreign competition. Regulations are evaded and 'black markets' in the currencies occur. Many administrators are needed who could be more productively employed elsewhere. Moreover, it can lead to uncertainty in international trade. Countries may find their regular markets closed, and firms cannot plan ahead because of uncertainty as to whether they will be allowed to purchase their raw materials from a hard-currency area. Furthermore, the confidence of foreigners is impaired if any attempt is made to prohibit the movement of their funds out of a country. Finally, when people are prevented from buying in hard-currency countries, it often means that they are forced to purchase dearer or inferior goods elsewhere.

Deflation of Home Income

Since imports increase as income expands, one way in which the value of imports can be brought into line with that of exports is by reducing income. Figure 36.1 explains the situation.

We assume an economy with no government spending or taxation, injections consisting of autonomous investment and exports, and leaks of saving and imports related to income. At the current level of income, Y, there is a current balance-of-payments deficit, DF. Assuming exports are maintained, this deficit can be eliminated by bringing down the level of investment to I' reducing income to Y'.

Such a deflationary policy would also tend to put a brake on any rise in home prices. More important, it allows adjustment to take place without altering currency-exchange rates (see below). This has the advantage that it facilitates international trade by removing the uncertainty associated with fluctuating exchange rates when negotiating long-term contracts or making loans.

But there are serious disadvantages:

1. Unless home prices are flexible downwards, a deflationary policy can only succeed at the expense of creating unemployment. Thus in Figure 36.1 if Y were the full employment level of income, the fall to Y' would represent a rise in unemployment. In practice costs, particularly wage rates, prove to be rigid, so that home prices are sticky.
2. There is a low income-elasticity of demand for many imports, e.g. basic foodstuffs, raw materials and manufactured components.
3. Any reduction of imports to Britain represents a loss of exports by other countries. Deflationary effects on their economies may result in a reduction in their demand for imports, thereby reducing British exports. In short, deflation is a 'beggar-my-neighbour' policy where the benefit is uncertain even to the deflating country.

The Gold Standard

The old gold standard was basically such a deflationary mechanism for correcting a balance-of-payments deficit. All major currencies had a declared value in terms of gold. If, for instance, Britain had a balance-of-payments deficit, foreign currency would be demanded. But the sterling exchange rate could not fall a great deal because it soon became cheaper to pay for imports with gold.

FIGURE 36.1
Achieving Balance-of-payments Equilibrium by Deflation

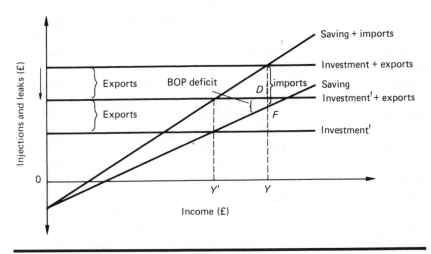

Purchases of gold were paid for by cheques drawn on the commercial banks, who drew gold from the Bank of England. This lowered their cash reserve and so, unless the Bank of England restored the position by buying securities on the open market, the commercial banks had to reduce their lending activities.

Furthermore, the Bank of England's power to issue notes was limited by its gold reserves and the fiduciary issue. Hence, in order to protect its reserves, the Bank raised the bank rate. Other interest rates moved in sympathy.

Higher rates of interest attracted foreign capital, thereby halting the export of gold. But, by discouraging investment, they also set in motion a deflationary process. It was assumed that the contraction of income would result in a fall in costs, and thus lower home prices. In practice, as noted above, this proved difficult. As a result, restoration of balance-of-payments equilibrium was achieved, not so much by expanding exports but, as incomes fell, by a reduction in imports. Eventually the unemployment which resulted did produce a fall in costs and, as exports became cheaper relative to foreign goods, the flow of trade was reversed.

In the meantime, however, the deflationary process caused severe suffering. Rather than continue with this, the UK and most other countries abandoned the gold standard in the 1930s.

36.3   Expenditure-switching: Depreciation of the Exchange Rate

Expenditure-switching by Exchange Rate Adjustment

The great merit of the gold standard was that, in maintaining stable exchange rates, it facilitated trade. Its big disadvantage was that a country could not follow an independent internal monetary policy in order to promote full employment.

But balance-of-payments policy can take the form of expenditure-switching, with foreigners spending more on British exports and Britain spending less on imports. While some switching can be enforced by government control of import expenditure (p. 539), the most effective method is to alter the relative prices of imports and home-produced goods.

Prices of internationally traded goods are composed of: (1) the home producer's price, and (2) the exchange rate. Thus British exports can be made more competitive in world markets by lowering the rate at which the £ sterling exchanges for foreign currencies. Because fewer units of foreign currency have now to be given up to obtain a £ sterling, foreigners can buy British exports more cheaply. Similarly, imports to Britain now cost more in terms of sterling, encouraging Britons to switch to the relatively cheaper home-produced goods. Provided that, taken together, the demand for both exports and imports is sufficiently elastic, there will be a correction of Britain's balance-of-payments deficit (see pp. 546–7).

Such corrective exchange-rate adjustments occur automatically through the forces of demand and supply in a freely operating foreign-exchange market. Thus if the USA's exports to Britain are greater in value than her imports from Britain, the demand for dollars will increase, for British importers will be wanting them to pay for the USA goods. Consequently the exchange rate will move against sterling. This will raise the price in sterling of Britain's imports from the USA, and lower the price in dollars of British exports to the USA. Demand responses to these price changes tend to bring about equality in value of British imports and exports.

Advantages and Disadvantages of Exchange Depreciation as a Means of Correcting a Balance-of-payments Disequilibrium

Exchange depreciation has the advantage that this correction is effected without the tribulations of deflation. Instead a country can follow its own internal monetary policy – even reflating if it thinks that this is desirable in the interests of reducing unemployment.

Moreover, with freely fluctuating exchange rates (when the value of the currency 'floats'), the correction is secured without the many controls which are often necessary when the exchange rate is 'pegged' (see p. 539) because reserves do not have to be protected. Indeed there is less pressure on a country to carry gold and foreign currency reserves.

Unfortunately, fluctuating exchange rates are themselves not without disadvantages.

First, the demand for exports and imports may be so inelastic that the balance-of-payments disequilibrium is made worse by depreciation rather than better (see p. 546). Supply, too, may be so inelastic that a country cannot take advantage of the expanded demand for its exports which follows a fall in the exchange value of its currency (see p. 547). It should be emphasised, however, that such conditions are possible rather than likely in the real world.

Second, fluctuating exchange rates may deflect a government from pursuing policies to maintain the internal purchasing power of its currency. Instead export prices are made competitive by foreign exchange depreciation. Unfortunately, such depreciation tends to be continuous for, as the prices of imports also rise, home costs and prices are increased, giving a push to further inflation through wage demands, etc.

Third, freely fluctuating exchange rates encourage speculation, thereby making movements more frequent and pronounced. Speculative capital moves according to the holder's estimate of the future value of currencies. Similar speculation occurs with trade. Foreign importers of British goods who expect the price of sterling to depreciate delay paying for the goods as long as possible, a situation described as 'lags'. British importers of foreign goods make their payments in foreign currency as soon as possible, described as 'leads'. The importance of speculation is that it can bring about the very rise or fall in the exchange rate that was expected. On the other hand, dealers who quote fixed 'future' prices for foreign currencies on the 'forward' market serve, to some extent, to even out exchange rate fluctuations.

Fourth, fluctuating exchange rates add to the normal uncertainties associated with foreign trade for this usually involves granting credit and even entering into long-term contracts. By the time an exporter receives payment for his goods, the exchange rate may have moved so adversely that the expected profit has been turned into a loss. In such circumstances the exporter may prefer not to take the risk of an adverse movement in the exchange rate. Although this risk can usually be transferred to a foreign exchange dealer by a 'forward' exchange arrangement (that is, the foreign currency can be obtained at a given future date at an agreed price), trade may still not be worthwhile through the additional cost involved.

Finally, fluctuating exchange rates can similarly discourage long-term investment overseas.

36.4 Managed Flexibility

The Exchange Equalisation Account

When Britain left the gold standard in 1931, she followed a policy of flexible exchange rates. Nevertheless, to cancel out fluctuations in the exchange rate brought about by movements of short-term capital, the government set up the Exchange Equalisation Account.

The Account operates by the simple application of the laws of price. It has a stock of gold and foreign currencies (mostly borrowed against Treasury bills), and this stock is either replenished or offered on the market according to whether short-term capital is moving into or out of London. For instance, a movement of capital into London from the USA would increase the demand for the £ sterling and drive up its price; the Account can prevent this rise by offering pounds in exchange for dollars. The value of the pound would not change but the Account would add to its stock of dollars. On the other hand, if there were a movement of capital out of London, the Account would offer dollars in exchange for pounds, thereby reducing its stock of dollars and increasing its holding of pounds.

The knowledge that such an Account exists to even out exchange fluctuations has done much to prevent speculation in the value of the pound. Provided it has adequate reserves of foreign currency, the Account can allow that value to appreciate or depreciate within its discretion, and this it now does according to the policy of the monetary authorities (see p. 544).

The International Monetary Fund (IMF)

The major defect of a system of freely fluctuating exchange rates is that it tends to discourage international trade. Countries, therefore, attempted to stabilise the exchange value of their currencies and an international code of behaviour to achieve this was drawn up at the Bretton Woods Conference in 1944. This established the International Monetary Fund (IMF) and the International Bank for Reconstruction and Development (IBRD, the 'World Bank').

A system of 'managed flexibility' was operated through the IMF. Each member country (140 in 1987) agreed that eventually it would maintain free convertibility of its currency at an agreed rate and contribute its quota of currency to a pool held by the IMF. From these reserves, the IMF could make foreign currency available to a country running a short-term balance of payments deficit. Should this balance-of-payments disequilibrium prove to be 'fundamental', devaluation of the country's currency was possible under agreed rules.

The Bretton Woods agreement worked tolerably well for twenty-five years. But it suffered from two main weaknesses:

1. The pressure of exchange adjustment fell almost entirely on debtor nations (who were forced to devalue) rather than on creditor nations (who could have eased part of the burden by revaluing).
2. In spite of Keynes's arguments at Bretton Woods, little provision was made for the expansion of international liquidity necessary to service an increasing world trade.

We can consider each in turn.

Exchange Adjustment

While the UK and, later, the USA were frequent 'persistent debtor' nations, Germany and Japan were 'persistent creditor' countries. Both the latter countries, however, proved reluctant to revalue their currencies, fearing that the rise in the price of their exports which this would entail would make them uncompetitive in world markets.

The result was that, in order to maintain the existing exchange rate, the UK in particular had to deflate her economy whenever balance-of-payments difficulties arose. To some extent this could be regarded as the just penalty which she had to pay for her inability to prevent prices rising as her economy expanded. Furthermore, the 'stop' policy had to be carried further since an initial weakness of the pound gathered momentum because sterling was held as a reserve currency (see p. 576).

The decisive step was taken in June 1972, when once again sterling came under pressure as the British economy expanded. The Heath government would not allow the maintenance of a fixed exchange rate to stand in the way of economic expansion. Thus the 'pegged' pound was abandoned: instead the pound was allowed to 'float', its value being arrived at according to the day-to-day demand for and supply of sterling on the foreign exchange market. Eventually all other major trading countries adopted floating exchange rates, though these are not completely market-determined. Instead they are influenced by the operations of each country's equivalent of the UK's Exchange Equalisation Account.

Conditions Necessary for Successful Exchange Depreciation/Devaluation

Where countries maintain an agreed rate of exchange between their currencies (e.g. as in the European Monetary System, p. 554), depreciation takes the form of a once-for-all reduction in the value of a country's currency by definite government decision and is known as *devaluation*. But both depreciation (through the mechanism of the foreign exchange market) and devaluation involve a reduction in the rate at which a country's currency exchanges for other currencies, so that, in examining the effects, the same broad principles apply.

Let us suppose that the UK trades only with the USA and that she has a persistent balance-of-payments deficit. The value of the pound falls from $1.65 to $1.50. Whether such depreciation is successful or not will depend upon the answers to the following questions.

1. What is the Elasticity of Demand for Exports and Imports?

The effect of the depreciation will be to make British exports cheaper in terms of dollars to the American buyer and imports from America dearer in terms of pounds to the British buyer.

A British good formerly selling in the USA for $1.65 need now cost only $1.50. This fall in price should lead to more British goods being demanded, and if elasticity of demand is greater than unity, more dollars will be earned.

Similarly, an American good worth $1.65 formerly cost the British buyer £1. After the depreciation, the price will rise to £1.10. But will this mean that we have to spend more *dollars* on our imports? The answer is 'no'. (Suppose that you are on a camping holiday in the USA and that the pound is devalued. Will your bread, camp site, etc. change in price?) The worst possible situation is when demand for imports is absolutely inelastic; then the same quantity of imports will be demanded and the same amount of dollars spent on them. Otherwise there will be some contraction of demand (because the price in terms of pounds has risen) and then expenditure in dollars will fall.

The two elasticities of demand for exports and imports must be considered together. Even if the demand for imports is absolutely inelastic (so that the same amount of foreign currency is spent on them), the balance of payments will not deteriorate provided that there is a gain of foreign currency from an increased demand for exports.

What is the probable situation in the real world for the UK as regards the elasticities of demand for imports and exports? Demand for imports is likely to be fairly inelastic, consisting, for instance, of raw-materials, essential components and tropical foodstuffs. Indeed, if her exports expand, demand for raw materials and components will increase. Offsetting this is a likely fall in British demand for luxuries and foreign travel on account of the greater cost, home-produced goods and holidays now being more competitive.

On the other hand, the demand for British exports as a whole is probably elastic. Not only could she undersell exporting competitors, e.g. in aero engines, electrical equipment, etc., but the lower export price resulting from the depreciation would convert what were formerly 'potential exports' into real exports. Moreover, such items as tourism are likely to have a highly elastic demand. But it must be remembered that the price of exported goods will not fall by the entire amount of the depreciation. Their home price will rise when they are made from imported raw materials or components.

2. What is the Elasticity of Supply of Exports?

It is on the supply side that the greatest obstacles to a successful depreciation are likely to be encountered. The fall in the price of exports will probably lead to an expansion of demand, but this will provide no lasting cost advantage if the supply of exports cannot be increased without the home price rising. Here the reaction of labour to the effects of depreciation is crucial. The increase in the cost of imports raises the cost of living. There is thus a strong temptation to demand wage increases. Moreover, labour is in a strong position, because demand for exports should increase following the devaluation. If the trade unions exploit their position, the resultant rise in wages could soon wipe out the cost advantage which Britain had gained and further depreciation would occur.

It should be noted, however, that where demand for British exports is inelastic, then inelasticity of supply may not be detrimental. The exporter can maintain his price *in terms of foreign currency* to foreign importers, and British earnings of foreign currency may not fall.

3. What is the Elasticity of Supply of Imports?

If foreigners are dependent on the British market, and supply is inelastic, then they may be willing to reduce their prices. This may reduce Britain's expenditure of foreign currency, although in volume imports are almost as great.

4. What is the Nature of British and American Investments with Each Other?

Suppose British investments in the USA are mostly in the form of shares in companies there. Profits will be earned in dollars and so there will be no loss of foreign currency after depreciation.

On the other hand, if American investments in the UK are in stock with interest fixed in sterling, the USA will lose by depreciation of the pound for she gets fewer dollars than formerly in invisible earnings.

5. Will Countries Fear Further Depreciation?

Depreciation reduces the value of sterling securities held by foreigners, including the sterling balances held in London. In the first place, this may destroy confidence in sterling, undermining London's position as a banking centre. Business is transferred elsewhere, and invisible earnings are lost. Second, unless positive measures are taken to correct the underlying inflation, foreigners will fear further depreciation and so hasten to remove their capital from London, bringing about what they fear.

The above arguments suggest that, for a country like Britain, depreciation provides no escape from dealing with inflation. It may entail a serious deterioration in the terms of trade, a large amount of additional exports having to be given to achieve a small gain in the balance of payments. Indeed, where demand for both imports and exports is highly inelastic or where supply is inelastic, depreciation may cause the balance of payments to deteriorate still further. In this case, a country has to resort to physical controls to reduce imports.

36.5 International Liquidity

Just as money in our pockets or at the bank is necessary to finance our everyday purchases, so people dealing in international markets require reserves of an acceptable form to finance international trade.

The one form that is always acceptable is gold. Unfortunately, the supply of gold is not increasing fast enough to keep pace with the expansion of world trade and the corresponding need for larger reserves. In the past, the difficulty has been overcome by holding reserves in other currencies – dollars and sterling. These were convertible into gold, and were known as 'reserve currencies'. Holding reserve currencies instead of gold had the additional advantage that a rate of interest was earned, whereas there is no return on holding gold.

The willingness to hold a reserve currency, however, only lasts as long as there is little possibility of the reserve currency being devalued. Persistent balance-of-payments deficits undermine confidence in the currency concerned, and there will then be a tendency to move out of the reserve currency. This is what happened in 1972 and 1973, first to the pound sterling, and then to the dollar.

To some extent the shortage of international liquidity has been made good by economising in the reserves through pooling arrangements, e.g. in the IMF and by the central banks of the Group of Ten. But such pooling arrangements proved inadequate in the speculation against the pound in

June 1972. A new form of reserve to provide *additional* assets became essential.

Special Drawing Rights (SDRs) – in contrast to the ordinary drawing rights of the IMF – are such an addition. Beginning in 1970, they have been issued by the IMF as a line of credit to members in proportion to their quotas. The value of SDRs is expressed in terms of a basket of sixteen major currencies weighted according to their international importance and calculated according to their daily value on the foreign exchange market.

Both the IMF and its members have agreed to honour SDRs. Thus a member country can use them to purchase foreign currency in order to support its exchange rate, and the countries with a strong balance of payments can be required to accept SDRs up to twice their own quota allocation.

At present (1991), with the general adoption of floating exchange rates, there is no pressure on international liquidity. But the creation of SDRs has established an important principle – that internationally created credit could be used to finance world trade – and the creation of SDRs is likely to be the major source of extra international reserves in the future. Indeed, it has been suggested that SDRs could be created as a means of giving aid to the less developed countries.

37 The European Community

37.1 Background to the European Community

Supranational Organisations

The two world wars convinced statesmen in Western European countries that some form of political unity was desirable, and in 1949 the Council of Europe was created – the basis, it was hoped, of a European parliament. But organisations with definite functions – the Organisation for European Economic Cooperation (founded in 1948), the North Atlantic Treaty Organisation (1949) and the Western European Union (1954) proved more fruitful than did the Council of Europe with its broad aims.

Although these organisations involved cooperation, they were merely voluntary associations, not federal bodies exercising supranational powers in the interests of members as a whole. While federation was the ultimate aim of European statesmen, they realised that it could only proceed piecemeal and on a functional basis. The first supranational organisation, the European Coal and Steel Community (ECSC) was formed in 1951 to control the whole of the iron, steel and coal resources of the six member countries – France, West Germany, Italy, Holland, Belgium and Luxembourg. The old divisions created by inward-looking national interests were thus broken down.

The success of the ECSC led to the setting up in 1957 of the Atomic Energy Community (EURATOM), a similar organisation for the peaceful use of atomic energy, and the European Economic Community (EEC), an organisation to develop a 'common market' between the six member countries. All three communities have now been brought within the European Community (EC).

Britain's Attitude to the EC

When first offered membership of these organisations, Britain refused to join. Not only would joining the EEC have weakened Commonealth ties, but she was also unwilling to forgo the right to follow independent policies in economics and defence. Instead, with six other nations, she joined the looser European Free Trade Area (EFTA).

Contrary to Britain's expectations, the EEC grew in strength, for difficulties were resolved as they arose. Moreover, Britain's trade with EEC countries increased at a faster rate than that with EFTA, since her goods were more complementary to their economies. Accordingly, after protracted negotiations, the UK joined the EEC in 1973. The other members are now: France, Germany, Italy, Belgium, the Netherlands, Luxembourg, Denmark, the Irish Republic, Greece, Spain and Portugal.

37.2   The Institutions of the EC

The essential point to grasp is that the 1957 Treaty of Rome set up a 'Community' with its own form of government and institutions.

There are four main institutions:

1. The Commission

This is the most important organ of the EC. Its seventeen members (two from the UK) serve for four years. Once chosen, however, the members of the Commission act as an independent body in the interests of the Community as a whole, and not as representatives of the individual governments that have nominated them.

The Commission is responsible for formulating policy proposals, promoting the Community interest, trying to reconcile national viewpoints and implementing Community decisions.

2. The Council of Ministers

Each member country sends a cabinet minister (usually the Foreign Secretary) to the Council of Ministers. This is the supreme decision-making body. Its task is to harmonise the Commission's draft Community policies with the wishes of member governments. Proposals and compromise plans are exchanged between the Council and the Commission. If the Council becomes deadlocked, the Commission reconsiders the proposal in order to accommodate the views of the opposing countries. Originally it was intended that the Council decisions should be on a weighted majority basis, but proposals affecting vital national interests now have usually to be unanimous.

3. The Court of Justice

This consists of ten judges appointed for a six-year term by agreement among member governments. Its task is to interpret the Rome Treaty and adjudicate on complaints, whether from member states, private enterprises or the institutions themselves. Its rulings are binding on member countries, community institutions, and individuals.

4. The Assembly or European Parliament

This is a body of 518 elected members (81 from the UK). Members sit according to party affiliation, not nationality. The Assembly debates Community policies and examines the Community's budget. It can dismiss the Commission by a two-thirds majority.

5. Special Institutions

Apart from the four main institutions above, there are also special institutions to deal with particular policies, e.g. the Economic and Social Committee, the European Investment Bank.

The *European Council* is a meeting of the heads of member states three times a year. The major problems confronting them are reviewed in an informal and pragmatic way. The object is to suggest loosely defined strategies so that each member can take into account the impact of its own policies on the others.

37.3 Economic Objectives of the EC

The overriding aim of the EC is to integrate the policies of its member countries. Its economic policy is based on two main principles: (1) a customs union, and (2) a common market.

1. A Customs Union

We have to distinguish between a free-trade area and a customs union. The former simply removes tariff barriers between member countries but allows individual members to impose their own rates of duty against outsiders. A customs union goes further. While it too has internal free trade, it also imposes common external tariffs.

The EC has a customs union, since this is essential for an integrated common market. Otherwise goods would enter the market through low-duty countries and be resold in those imposing higher rates.

2. A Common Market

In essence the common market of the EC envisages goods and factors of production moving freely within the Community through the operation of the price system; only in this way can the full benefits of the larger market be realised.

However, it is recognised that this takes time to accomplish. Member countries had already developed their own individual taxes, welfare benefits, monopoly policies, methods of removing balance-of-payments imbalances, full employment policies and so on. Such differences could disrupt the working of the price system because they would give some members advantages over others. For example, suppose Britain taxed refrigerators but not binoculars. This would weight the possibilities of trade against Italy (which has a comparative advantage in producing refrigerators) and in favour of Germany (which has a comparative advantage in producing high-grade binoculars).

Alternatively, the comparative advantage of some countries may lie in the expertise of the professional services they can provide. Usually this means that such services have to be taken to where the customer is (e.g. know-how regarding property development). There must therefore be mobility of labour within the market, e.g. for property developers.

Policy has therefore been directed towards the gradual introduction of 'harmonisation' measures, examples of which are:

(a) *A Common External Tariff* (CET) by which members impose tariffs on imports from non-member countries at the same rates. However, some countries, e.g. members of the European Free Trade Area and developing countries, are given preferential treatment by concessions on tariffs.

(b) *A common agricultural policy* (CAP) – see below.

(c) *Removing barriers to trade and the movement of persons and capital between countries.*

(d) *Uniform rules on competition.* To prevent the distortion of competition in trade, uniform regulations have been introduced to cover price-fixing, sharing of markets and patent rights.

(e) *A common transport policy.* By regulating such items as freight rates, licences, taxation and working conditions, the EC can seek to ensure that transport undertakings compete on an equal footing. Any hidden advantages enjoyed by one country would distort the free movement of goods within the Community.

(f) *Harmonisation of tax systems.* As has already been shown, some standardisation of taxation is necessary in order to remove any 'hidden' barriers to trade. This applies particularly to indirect taxes. In the EC value added tax (VAT) is the basic form of indirect tax, and it is proposed that eventually all member countries will levy it at the same rates.

No proposals exist for harmonising income taxes, but most countries have adopted the 'imputation' system of corporation tax (see p. 493).

(g) *Complete monetary integration.* As we have seen, countries can adjust the prices of imports and exports by varying the exchange rate. If this were allowed within the EC, it could enable a member to obtain a competitive advantage over others by depreciating its currency. Thus through the European Monetary System (EMS) – the 'snake' – all currencies have fixed exchange rates within narrow limits. To date (1989) the UK has not seen her way clear to join (see below).

The importance of stability of exchange rates can be seen in the operation of the CAP. The essence of the latter is a common price support system. Prices are fixed in advance in terms of a common unit – the European Currency Unit (ECU) – and are then translated into national currencies using a reference rate (in the case of sterling, the 'Green Pound').

If exchange rates are fixed, this raises no difficulties. But if the exchange rate varies – as sterling does since Britain is outside the European Monetary System – an appreciation, say, of sterling would leave the Green Pound undervalued. The intervention price when converted into sterling would now be high in Britain. Therefore, to discourage other EC farmers exporting to Britain, border taxes, known as Monetary Compensatory Amounts (MCA), are levied. Similarly, to restore his competitive position, the British farmer is given MCAs for his exports to other EC countries.

In the above case, if the Green Pound were revalued in line with its value on the foreign exchange market, MCAs would be eliminated. This would lower food prices in Britain, but would reduce the incomes of British farmers.

(h) *A common regional policy.* Just as one nation cannot allow depressed areas to persist, so the EC is expected to help regions of high unemployment. Northern Ireland and southern Italy are two such regions. Apart from the establishment of a regional development fund, however, little has so far been done to integrate policies designed to encourage industries to go to problem areas.

37.4   Advantages for the UK of Belonging to the EC

Several advantages can accrue to countries by forming a common market.

First, it increases the possibility of specialisation. The EC provides a market of 320 million people, larger than that of the USA. This allows economies of scale to be achieved, especially as regards sophisticated products requiring high initial research expenditure, e.g. computers, drugs, nuclear reactors, supersonic aircraft and modern weapons. These economies should enable EC firms to compete more effectively in world markets.

Second, keener competition in the larger market can result in greater efficiency. Within the EC there are no trade barriers which in effect protect inefficient firms. Free trade means that goods and services can compete freely in all parts of the market and that factors of production can move to their most efficient uses, not merely within but also between countries. On the other hand, it must be recognised that protective duties may reduce competition from outside the market.

Third, a faster rate of growth may be achieved. In the EC's first fifteen years the GNPs of the six original members grew twice as fast as that of the UK, giving them (Italy apart) a higher GNP per head than Britain's. To a large extent this faster rate of growth was the result of increased economies of scale and competition enjoyed by the EC countries. But it is also possible that the EC generates growth by increasing the *prospects* of growth.

Fourth, there could be significant political benefits. As already explained, the ultimate objective of the original advocates of European cooperation was some form of political union. A Western Europe which could speak with one voice would carry weight when dealing with other major powers, particularly the USA and the USSR. Moreover, the integration of defence forces and strategy would give its members far greater security. Such benefits, it is held, more than compensate for any loss of political sovereignty (see p. 515).

Fifth, because she is a member of the EC and has a stable political background, the UK will attract investment from countries outside (particularly the USA and Japan) who are anxious to obtain the advantages of producing inside the EC.

Sixth, the dynamic growth of the EC will enable assistance to be given to the poorer regions (including the UK) and to the less developed countries of the world.

37.5 Problems Facing the UK as a Member of the EC

While Britain's membership of the EC can secure important benefits and allow her to influence its future development, it does pose special problems.

1. The CET Could Lead to the Diversion of Trade Towards Less Efficient EC Suppliers

The duties imposed by the customs union may allow firms within the common market to compete in price with more efficient firms outside.

Suppose, for instance, that the same machine can be produced by both the USA and Germany but, because the American firm is more efficient, its machine is 10 per cent cheaper than the German. In these circumstances, Britain would, other things being equal, import from the USA. As a member of EC, however, Britain would have to discriminate against the American machine by the appropriate CET, say 20 per cent. This would make the German machine cheaper, and so trade would be diverted to the less efficient producer.

2. The CAP is a Drain on the Community Funds

Before joining the EC Britain imported food at the lowest world price that could be found. In so far as the UK producer could not make an adequate living by selling at free market prices, British policy consisted of granting *deficiency payments* (financed out of taxation) sufficient to raise the price received by the producer to a level set out in an Annual Review. The consumer paid a low price for food and the world had free access to the UK market. The taxpayer paid for the farmers' support.

But because the Community could not function satisfactorily if the cost of food to consumers differed appreciably in various parts of it, there has to be some equalisation of prices. However, if this occurred through competition between producing countries it could destroy many small farmers, particularly in France and Germany. In addition, because demand for agricultural products tends to be inelastic, changes in the conditions of supply can have far-reaching effects on the incomes of farmers.

The CAP seeks to support farmers' incomes by maintaining prices on the home market through a variety of protective devices at the Community's external frontier. Three prices are fixed for each product:

(*a*) a *target price*, which, it is estimated, will give farmers an adequate return in a normal year;
(*b*) a *threshold price*, which is the basis for assessing levies on imports when the world price is 10 per cent below the target price, and;

(c) the *intervention price*, at which surplus supplies are bought up by various agencies to prevent the price falling more than 8 per cent below the target price and which are disposed of outside the EC, e.g. butter sold to the Soviet Union.

In practice, however, giving farmers a guaranteed price above the market clearing price for all they can produce simply encourages over-production, since stocks accumulate and far exceed what are necessary to draw on in the event of a poor harvest (see p. 58).

In Figure 37.1, the market-clearing price would be OP. However, if the guaranteed intervention price is OP_1, the demand curve becomes hori-zontal, D_i, at this price. At price P_1, consumers take OQ_1 but farmers supply OQ_2. There is thus an excess supply of Q_1Q_2 which is bought for storage by the authorities of a cost of $P_1 \times Q_1Q_2$. The increase in farmer's incomes is shown by the shaded area.

If these stores were used as buffer stocks to make good deficiencies in supply when harvests were poor, at least some of the costs could be recouped. In practice, however, the artificially high price has encouraged additional supplies as techniques have improved. The result has been embarrassing butter mountains, beef and corn stocks and milk and wine lakes. These have to be sold off on the world market at a low price.

FIGURE 37.1
The Effect on Supply of a Guaranteed 'Intervention' Price

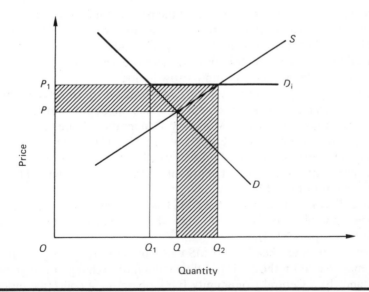

In addition, the distortion of the normal pattern of international trade in foodstuffs widens the gap between the rich and poor countries because the latter are often food producers.

Obviously the CAP confers greater benefits on countries in which agriculture is important (e.g. France) compared with countries which are relatively more dependent on manufacturing (e.g. the UK, Germany).

3. There is Insufficient Control over the Community Budget

A Community budget is necessary to meet the costs of administration and policies requiring expenditure, e.g. CAP and regional assistance. There are three main sources – agricultural levies, import duties on non-Community goods and a VAT of just over 1 per cent.

Today, over 70 per cent of the budget is spent on agricultural support, and this is increasing. As a result, annual Community expenditure exceeds receipts, necessitating a rise in the VAT yield.

Some revision of the CAP system is essential but this is politically difficult for countries where the farming lobby is important. Yet Britain can see that, unless firm action is taken to deal with the CAP problem, there will be a continuous increase in the VAT rate and spending on other Community policies, e.g. the regional and social funds, will suffer.

4. The Ultimate Development of the European Monetary System may not be in Britain's Best Interests

As we have seen, countries can adjust the prices of imports and exports by varying the exchange rate. If this were allowed within the EC, it could enable a member to obtain a competitive advantage over others by depreciating its currency. It is agreed, therefore, that all currencies should have fixed exchange rates within narrow limits.

The *European Monetary System (EMS)* was set up to achieve this. At present it is simply the arrangement by which member countries put their currencies into a European Monetary Cooperation Fund, out of which emerges the European Currency Unit (ECU). The ECU is a weighted average of these currencies (at present worth about 67p). Sterling is one of the component currencies, but at present (1990) this is the limit of the UK's involvement in the EMS.

So far the main objective of the EMS has been to stabilise exchange rates between member countries through the Exchange Rate Mechanism (ERM) (see pp. 583–4).

Looking further ahead, the EMS could provide: (a) a single European currency (based on the ECU) as the medium of exchange throughout the EC; and (b) a Central Community Bank operating a collective monetary policy. This does raise the problem, however, of whether Britain would be wise to relinquish control over her monetary policy to a supranational body.

5. The UK Could Face an Unacceptable Loss of Political Sovereignty

Certain members would like the community to develop into a political union of federated states. Mrs Thatcher, in particular, has held that this goes beyond the original intention of the Treaty of Rome, and would mean that policies would be increasingly decided in Brussels rather than at Westminster.

37.6   The Single Market: 1992

Measures Essential to Creating a Single Market

'1992' has become the shorthand for the EC programme of measures due to be completed by the end of that year which are necessary to achieve the single, unified European market envisaged in the Treaty of Rome 1957.

Although tariffs between members have already been scrapped, non-tariff barriers to free and fair trade still remain. These can take the form of:

(a) frontier delays, e.g. in checking documents, collecting excise duties;
(b) transport control, e.g. licences, national safety rules, lorry weights;
(c) differences in national product standards and in national trade mark and patent laws;
(d) restrictions on public purchasing;
(e) exchange control over capital movements and restrictions on financial services offered across national frontiers by banks, insurance companies, etc;
(f) state subsidies to industry and agriculture;
(g) different rates of VAT, corporation tax, and of depreciation and other tax allowances;
(h) the friction of changing currencies.

Many of these non-tariff barriers can be overcome by harmonisation of national requirements, e.g. as regards transport safety rules, product standards, acceptable professional standards. For example, a new trading form, the Single Administrative Document, has replaced about 100 different documents for the export, import and transit of goods over EC frontiers. Alternatively, the Commission can persuade states to remove national restrictions, e.g. on public purchasing and capital movements. In the last resort major areas of the programme can be implemented by qualified majority voting, although matters of vital national interest, such as taxation, require unanimity.

As far as possible the Commission seeks to eliminate controls through deregulation generally rather than dealing with each control individually. For instance, if one state imposed an excise duty on a good which was higher than that of another state the market would automatically transfer trade in that good from the dearer country to the cheaper, so that no regulation on duties would be necessary.

It should also be noted that liberalisation policies are really only an extension of national supply-side measures to the Community level.

Economic Benefits of the Single Market

Removing restrictions on trade will allow the full benefits of free trade to be achieved within a market of 320 million people, one of the biggest and richest in the world. More than that, countries outside will also benefit from the increased economic growth of the market since it will make exporting easier for them.

A report prepared by economists for the Commission in 1985 considered that, as a result of:

(a) the removal of frontier barriers affecting trade;
(b) the removal of barriers affecting overall production, e.g. through different standards;
(c) economies of scale; and
(d) intensified competition,

the real GNP of the Community should increase by 5 per cent over a six- to eight-year period. Furthermore, as activity responded to the removal of production restrictions, 2 million new jobs could be created. Other employment could result through investment by firms outside the Community seeking to win for themselves the advantages of servicing this large market.

Consumers, too, would benefit from lower prices and more choice, especially as regards electrical goods, motor vehicles, pharmaceuticals, food and drink, airlines and financial services.

Conclusions

While the Single Market offers increased opportunities, the tougher competition presents challenges. Large-scale, low-cost producers will benefit at the expense of smaller higher-cost producers, some of whom could be taken over or go out of business. Even the larger British firms, with their greater reliance for expansion on equity finance through the capital market, may be more vulnerable to take-over or merger.

Certain regions, too, may find the readjustment painful, and the EC must provide extra finance through its Regional, Social and Agricultural Guidance Funds to promote the development of the poorer regions.

For its part the Community has to decide whether it closes in on itself, secure from competition behind the common external tariff – 'fortress Europe' as this looking inwards has been termed. Or alternatively, whether it should maintain and develop a liberal policy of trading with the rest of the world allowing them to share in the benefits of growth.

The importance of the Single Market to the UK cannot be overemphasised. In value 50 per cent of the UK's exports go to the EC and 52 per cent of her imports come from there. Hence the government has launched a 'Europe Open for Business' campaign to alert UK companies to the implications of the Single Market and to encourage them to act now to meet the opportunities and challenges it presents. A number of fact sheets summarise the most important developments and identify sources of more detailed information and advice.

38 Aid to Less Developed Countries

38.1 Why Give Aid?

What do We Mean by a 'Less Developed Country' (LDC)?

When used in this way, the term 'less developed' suggests that such countries have not fully exploited their natural resources. They are poor simply because they lack the essential capital. Their low standards of living could be raised considerably, therefore, if external help enabled them to obtain machines, fertilizers, hydroelectric power plants, irrigation works and social capital, such as a transport system, telecommunications, schools and hospitals.

Nevertheless, although theoretically sound, this line of approach is impracticable as a criterion upon which aid should be given. Not all poor countries have untapped natural resources; if aid was restricted to those having sound investment potential, many would remain poor. Moreover, no country in the world can be said to be 'fully developed'. Development is a matter of degree, dependent upon current demand and existing technical knowledge. If capital spending were to be determined solely by its yield, the more advanced countries themselves, such as the USA, Britain and France, would probably yield the highest returns from research and advanced technology. Thus we must accept a broader concept of the term 'less developed'.

The peoples of the world can be divided into the 'haves' and the 'have nots'. One-fifth of the world's population, having 80 per cent of the world's income is in the former category; almost the whole of the remaining four-fifths in the latter. Thus for the purposes of giving aid, 'less developed' must mean quite simply that a country is very poor.

What is Aid?

The main object of aid must be to raise living standards in the very poor countries. Any help which the richer countries can give them in the form of capital, technical assistance, export credits, education grants, etc. works to this end, irrespective of whether it comes from private sources or governments, or whether it is given on a commercial basis or simply as a gift. For the purposes of measuring the aid given, therefore, the most useful approach is to include all sources and all forms. What we must recognise is that, for reasons discussed later, help available on a commercial basis is insufficient. Thus an increasing amount of help must be given by way of 'special aid', and it is this which we have chiefly in mind when discussing aid. But we do distinguish between military and non-military aid, for the former usually only benefits the receiving country indirectly, if at all.

What are the Reasons for Giving Aid?

Special aid is now given by the richer countries to the less developed regions of the world for the following reasons:

1. To Relieve Poverty

People in the less developed countries (LDCs) are living on the margin of subsistence. For example, in 1987 the UK's GNP per head (in US dollars) was $10 430, India was only $300. The situation is aggravated by population pressure. While the birth rate is high, improved medical services have so reduced the death rate, that in such countries as Kenya and Botswana, the natural rate of increase is over 3 per cent per annum. Population in such areas, therefore, could double over the next thirty years. Humanitarianism demands that the richer countries should help the LDCs.

2. To Allow LDCs to 'Take-off' into Self-sustained Economic Growth

In economics it often follows that 'to him that hath shall be given'. Where people are living at the starvation level, there is little margin to reduce consumption in order to accumulate capital. Thus growth is possible only when output is more than necessary to sustain subsistence living standards.

Furthermore, export earnings are usually insufficient to buy imports essential for industrial development. Tanzania's oil imports, for instance, account for one-half of her foreign currency earnings.

The situation is like comparing two frogs, one which can jump 8 inches, and one 10 inches. There may not be much between them but on a stairway of 9 inch steps one (like Hong Kong or Taiwan) will leave the other (like Ethiopia or Kenya) far behind.

3. To Provide Donor Countries with Markets, Especially for Capital Goods

In the long run, aid, by speeding up the economic growth of LDCs will extend international trade, and so all countries will benefit. But in the short run, only by tying export credits to the import of specific goods will there be any direct gain. Indirectly, if a country supplies capital goods, it may find that there will be a demand for spare parts later.

4. To Further Political Ideologies

Both Russia and the West have given aid as a weapon in the Cold War. Russia has used it as a means of extending her influence; the West, apart from altruistic motives, has given aid to prevent the spread of Communism.

Criticisms of Aid

However, aid to LDCs is not without its critics. Some feel that it might undermine self-help, and point to the preference for leisure or the small contribution made by a few wealthy inhabitants of some of the LDCs. Others condemn aid which is wasted on such status symbols as steel mills and airlines. Finally, influential critics, such as Professor P. T. Bauer, consider that aid tends to concentrate power with governments in both the giving and receiving countries. The former tax private persons and companies to raise aid; the latter centrally plan the distribution of aid and thereby restrict private enterprise. Nevertheless, it must be recognised that although we may consider a country is making mistakes or is even downright ungrateful, our moral obligations must still be fulfilled.

The Basic Difficulties of LDCs

The difficulties of LDCs have common features.

First, there is a high dependence on subsistence agriculture. For many, low incomes are the result of poor soil and climatic conditions. The pressure of population and the limited supply of land results in a low average product. For some, however, a considerable increase in production is possible by the adoption of new techniques or the construction of irrigation works.

Second, only one or two cash crops or a basic mineral are often the sole sources of the foreign exchange which is required to pay for imports of capital equipment. But an inelastic world demand means that any change in their conditions of supply causes fluctuations in foreign exchange earnings.

Third, the combination of a high birth rate and a falling death rate has led to rapidly increasing populations. There is thus considerable 'disguised unemployment' on family farms, but this also means that any new manufacturing industries could be supplied with labour without decreasing food output.

Fourth, owing to the shortage of capital, production is labour-intensive. Nevertheless, to some extent this is the economic response to relatively cheap labour, and thus has to be accepted.

Fifth, labour generally is of low quality, the result of poor health and the lack of education and training. In particular, there is an acute shortage of managers and technical experts.

Sixth, the basic infrastructure necessary to sustain modern industry and urban living – transport and communications, energy, a good water supply and sewage works – is woefully inadequate. Private investment is unlikely to be forthcoming for such projects.

What Forms Can Aid Take?

Assistance to LDCs can take the following forms:

1. Direct Gifts of Consumer Goods

The provision of consumer goods releases resources of the poor countries for the production of capital goods. However, aid in this form has been relatively small, and has mostly been forthcoming when the USA has wished to dispose of surplus stockpiles of perishable foodstuffs.

But the direct provision of consumer goods has disadvantages. First, surplus foodstuffs of the developed countries are often unsuitable or uneconomic. Wheat given by the USA to the Chinese immediately after the war could be cooked only with difficulty, because people who normally lived on rice had no ovens. In any case, many of the richer peoples' foodstuffs are unnecessarily extravagant for persons whose main concern is to obtain sufficient calories for survival. Second, from an economic point of view, it is better for the richer countries to concentrate their resources on the production of capital goods in which they have the greater relative advantage, leaving it to the LDCs to increase the production of their own foodstuffs. Third, the release of supplies from stockpiles disrupts the normal pattern of world production, creating difficulties for established producers. Fourth, if consumer goods are given, there is no guarantee that factors will be released to produce capital goods. Where people are living on a starvation level, the pressure is to meet immediate needs. If this happens, the provision of consumer goods is simply a short-term gain. It is summed up in the Chinese proverb: 'If you give a man a fish, you feed him for one day; if you teach him to fish, you feed him for many days.'

2. Pre-investment Surveys

The object of pre-investment surveys is to reveal the potential of LDCs and to assess which are the most worthwhile projects. Often, for instance, a deficiency of trained personnel means that a scheme requiring high technology capital is, for the time being, inadvisable. Capital which creates a demand for labour, particularly in agriculture, is usually the most appropriate. Pre-investment surveys are undertaken by the United Nations Special Fund at the request of the government of an LDC. In order to avoid frivolous requests, these governments are required to subscribe part of the cost.

3. The Provision of Capital Equipment

Capital equipment can be given directly or by line of credit either in the form of loans or grants. Actual machines or implements probably impress more than a credit, for real goods can be seen. On the other hand, a line of credit gives choice in the allocation of funds to the receiving country, e.g. on irrigation schemes, power plants, etc. As compared with grants, the danger is that loans may incur a burden of interest and debt repayments far beyond the capacity of the LDC to repay from a balance-of-payments surplus.

4. Technical Assistance

Technical know-how and skill are just as important as the machines themselves. Aid, therefore, must cover the provision of technical experts both to operate the capital equipment and to train local technicians. Technical assistance is also necessary to suggest how existing productive assets can be used to better advantage.

5. Education

Not only is education essential for the people generally to increase their literacy, but administrators, doctors, teachers, and other professional persons have to be trained if they are to advance their social services and develop economically.

Educational help can often be given by sending instructors to teach locally. But for more advanced studies, it may be necessary to award scholarships in the universities and schools of the richer countries. The latter method has the advantage that, provided students are welcomed, they can learn something of the way of life and the government institutions of democratic countries.

6. Liberal Trade Policies

Increasing the productive capacity of the LDCs and expecting them to repay interest on loans is self-defeating if barriers to trade prevent them from selling their products abroad. Their main asset is usually their cheap, unskilled labour, and so it would be quite wrong to impose tariffs and quotas against goods produced by the newly industrialised countries such as Singapore, Taiwan, India and Hong Kong. Trade is the corollary to aid, and can even replace aid, since it makes use of the comparative cost advantages of the LDCs (as opposed to import substitution, which is economically inefficient). Indeed, the LDCs prefer trade to aid, for it carries no strings or taint of charity.

As regards trade with the LDCs, we must note certain important points. (a) The world demand for primary products is rather inelastic; this suggests that, to increase their earnings of foreign currency, these countries will have to produce and export manufactured goods, mainly those which are labour intensive in production. (b) To maintain demand for the goods of the poorer countries, the advanced countries will have to follow a policy of full employment at home. (c) The encouragement of the production of foodstuffs and basic materials by subsidies in the advanced countries depresses the world prices of such commodities to the detriment of the poor countries whose income is largely dependent upon them. Thus increased production of rice in the USA means that Burma receives a lower price for the rice she exports – though here other LDCs are the chief beneficiaries. (d) An improvement in the terms of trade for the advanced countries is only a mixed blessing. It means a worsening of the terms of trade for the poorer countries, and the difference may have to be made up by increased aid.

38.2 Who Shall be Responsible for Giving Aid?

There are three main channels of aid: (1) private sources; (2) national governments; (3) international bodies.

1. Private Sources

Aid in the form of gifts from private sources has been relatively infinitesimal. Missionary societies have built and run hospitals, churches, and schools, and the Ford Foundation, the Rockefeller Trust, Oxfam and Save the Children Fund have subscribed to specific projects.

A larger amount of aid has come through loans floated on behalf of the governments of these LDCs in New York and European capitals. Export credits are also given by firms. While this may stimulate the import of capital goods, it increases total debt and may fund the wrong products.

However, the chief form of private investment has been that of companies seeking to make a profit. Thus jute and cotton mills have been set up in India, oil-wells sunk in the Persian Gulf, tin mines worked in Malaysia, and tea plantations established in Ceylon. Such projects raise productivity and real wages, create employment opportunities, provide revenue from the taxation of corporate profits, stimulate auxiliary industries and extend the expertise available to other sectors.

2. National Governments

Private investment, however, is not sufficient to provide capital on the scale required by the LDCs. Much of the overseas investment undertaken by international companies has been directed to North America and Western Europe, countries having a high income elasticity of demand for their particular products. Above all, prospective yield from investment in LDCs has to be discounted owing to the political risks. Governments in many of the emergent countries tend to be ephemeral, while those that are stable often possess socialist inclinations, frequently revealed in the nationalisation of major industries. Private enterprise has burned its fingers in Egypt, Indonesia, Iraq, Cuba and Tanzania, to mention only a few countries.

In practice, private sources of capital have proved rather inelastic. Yet the demand for capital has increased, the LDCs seeing it as the road to rapid advancement. Furthermore, private capital has been concentrated on certain countries and on particular types of production. Thus the oil-producing Gulf States and Zambia absorbed a disproportionate part, as investment was directed towards the production of raw materials for processing overseas. Only a small proportion went to agricultural development or to the production of local consumer goods.

Hence additional capital has had to be provided, either as gifts or loans, by national governments. The USA has been the major source, being responsible for two-thirds of all the economic aid given in public loans or grants. The UK and France have directed their assistance to their former colonial empires. Britain gives aid directly through its Overseas Development Administration, while indirectly private investment has been encouraged through the Export Credits Guarantee Department. The advantages of giving aid through national governments, as opposed to international bodies, are:

(*a*) People in the donating countries are more willing to shoulder the extra taxation required if they feel that they have some direct control over the aid.

(*b*) It is possible to channel aid in specific directions, e.g. the Commonwealth.

(*c*) Aid can be tied to the exports of the donating country. In practice it may well be that tying aid increases the total amount of aid given. First, countries are not so apprehensive about the effect on their balance of payments, for they do not have to find hard currencies when the aid is spent on other countries' goods. Second, as Germany is a major exporter, she gains automatically when untied aid is given by other countries. Tying aid would be a means, therefore, of forcing Germany to give aid more liberally herself in order to maintain her exports to the LDCs. Third, spending aid on machinery does mean that spare parts and replacements will have to come from that country later.

(*d*) Where aid takes the form of education in the donating country, leaders of the developing nations can be influenced in particular attitudes.

(*e*) It creates a favourable impression when aid can be seen to come from a definite country.

But aid through national governments has major disadvantages:

(*a*) It tends to pander to narrow national interests.

(*b*) It offends the extremely nationalistic outlook of many of the emergent countries. 'Aid with strings' is resented because it savours of a refined form of colonial exploitation (neo-colonialism).

(*c*) Because individual countries decide their own priorities, aid may not be directed to the best possible advantage, some countries being entirely neglected. Thus for political and strategic reasons, Taiwan and South Korea have received a disproportionate share of American aid.

3. *International Bodies*

To make technical cooperation and assistance more effective, many governments have grouped themselves on a regional basis. Examples are the Colombo Plan, the EC Development Fund, the OPEC Countries and the Commission for Technical Cooperation in Africa South of the Sahara. But even with these schemes there is no real planning, and each member country retains responsibility for preparing and administering its own development programme.

If the disadvantages of giving assistance on a national basis are really to be overcome, aid must be channelled through the United Nations and its agencies. Only the United Nations can promote a unified development programme for all the LDCs. It can advise countries receiving aid as to which projects should have priority, and because these countries are represented in the United Nations they are more willing to accept advice. Thus they can be steered away from 'status symbols', while susceptibilities regarding 'political strings' and the acceptance of second-hand capital equipment can more easily be allayed. Moreover, the United Nations can encourage the advanced countries to open their markets to the products of the LDCs. Finally, through its function of helping the LDCs, especially in the distribution of aid, the authority of the United Nations is strengthened generally.

The main United Nations agencies responsible for aid are:

(*a*) *Lending agencies:* The *World Bank* refers to two legally and financially distinct entities: the International Bank for Reconstruction and Development (IBRD) and the International Development Association (IDA). Both have three related functions: to lend funds long term for reconstruction and development, to provide economic advice and technical assistance, to encourage investment by others.

Funds are obtained by: (1) a 'quota' subscribed by member nations roughly in proportion to their national incomes: (2) borrowing on the international market by the issue of bonds backed by the quotas of members. Countries which can satisfy the Bank that they have economically sound projects may borrow from the Bank for a period of five to twenty-five years at a rate of interest which is as low as possible having regard to the Bank's ability to borrow.

The *IBRD* finances its lending operations primarily from borrowings in the world capital markets. Thus, to cover its costs, its loans have to consider the prospective return to the investment and the creditworthiness of the borrower. This has meant in practice that help has tended to go to the comparatively richer, semi-developed countries rather than to the really poor, though recently there has been a switch to the LDCs.

The *IDA* extends assistance to the poorest countries on easier terms, largely from resources provided by its wealthier members. Funds from such other sources as governments, commercial banks, export credit agencies, and other multilateral institutions are increasingly being paired with World Bank funds to co-finance projects. The World Bank also provides loans to help developing countries adjust their economic policies and structures in the face of structural problems that threaten continuing development.

The *International Finance Corporation* (IFC), an affiliate of the World Bank, seeks to promote growth in the private sector of developing countries by mobilising foreign and domestic capital to invest alongside its own funds in commercial enterprises.

(*b*) *The United Nations Development Programme* was set up in 1966 with the merger of the United Nations Special Fund and its Technical

Assistance Board. Its purpose is mainly to help LDCs, through pre-investment surveys, to obtain the basic knowledge indispensable for economic development. Its spending is through the specialised agencies of the United Nations.

(*c*) *Specialized agencies of the United Nations*, such as the Food and Agriculture Organisation (FAO) and the World Health Organisation (WHO), have their own regular budgets but also receive additional finance from the United Nations Development Programme.

What Conclusions can be Drawn Concerning Aid?

1. Aid is Insufficient

In 1968 the UN Conference on Trade and Development agreed that the developed countries should give aid equal to 1 per cent of their national income, but this has not been achieved. Indeed, the rise in the price of oil harmed both the donating countries and the LDCs. Moreover, lenders are concerned about the ability of the LDCs to repay the huge debts accumulated.

Thus the *Brandt Commission* put forward in 1980 a wide-ranging programme to help poor countries. Among its recommendations were: (*a*) aid to LDCs should be doubled; (*b*) the establishment of a World Development Fund to complement the IMF and World Bank; (*c*) sources of funds to include taxes on trade, air travel and arms transfers of the developed countries; (*d*) an increase in the export of the LDCs' manufactured goods by the developed countries liberalising trade and restructuring industry for new technology.

2. More Aid Should be Given Through the United Nations

At present only about one-twentieth of all aid is distributed through the United Nations, and therefore the effectiveness of the spending has been reduced. On the other hand, it might be better if all aid were administered by *one* responsible UN agency, for at present there is competition between the agencies for aid. Squabbling also occurs between the recipients, who want aid in the same proportion from year to year, thereby producing a static pattern.

3. More Coordination in the Distribution of Aid is Desirable

This is necessary in order to ensure: (*a*) an order of priority; (*b*) more labour-intensive schemes to employ local resources; (*c*) technical and teacher training so that there are the personnel to work and repair equipment; (*d*) aid for agricultural improvement, e.g. fertilizers, soil conservation, better animal management, improved seeds, pesticides, irrigation, which would probably show a higher return than industrial equipment.

4. Since Aid is Strictly Limited, It May be Necessary to Influence How It is Employed

Ideally aid should be without strings, with the receiving country working out its own form of government. But it is necessary to recognise the risk that aid given may be applied to furthering, directly or indirectly, the political aims of the recipient government.

To offset this difficulty, agencies could direct more aid through voluntary bodies working in the field. Governments would continue to be responsible for major infrastructure projects, such as roads, railways, schools and hospitals, which cannot be left to a market economy. But the most successful LDCs, e.g. Taiwan, South Korea, Kenya, have been those which have recognised the economic efficiency of markets in relating preferences to costs and providing incentives for private enterprise. This means that more aid should be directed to supporting smaller projects in the private sector.

5. Acceptance of Birth Control Should be Encouraged

Without birth control, the increase in population will mean that aid can make little impression on living standards within the foreseeable future. Thus if current trends continue, the 500 million population of sub-Saharan Africa will double by 2010, and economic growth is unlikely to exceed this. The World Bank commented in 1989: 'Africans are almost as poor today as they were 30 years ago.' Without birth control that is likely to be the position over the next thirty years.

The LDCs and the World Economy

While LDCs have benefitted from the fall in the world price of oil, other adverse economic factors have arisen. These include:

(*a*) a rise in world interest rates, making it more difficult to service interest payments on accumulated debt;

(*b*) a deterioration in the terms of trade, resulting from the fall in the prices of basic commodities as the growth rate of the Western economies has slowed down;

(*c*) the possible diversion of a proportion of the limited aid funds to support the economies of the East European countries recently freed from USSR domination.

Part VIII

Current Economic Problems

39 Current Problems and Policies of the UK

39.1 Introduction

The theoretical analysis set out in this book indicates that to some extent the main objectives of government stabilisation policy – full employment, a stable price level, a healthy balance of payments and a satisfactory rate of growth – are mutually incompatible, for success in one creates difficulties for others. Full employment, for instance, requires an adequate level of aggregate demand. But when aggregate demand is increased, so spending on imports rises and home-produced goods are diverted from exports to the home market. Thus the balance-of-payments position becomes less favourable. Full employment also means that eventually less efficient labour has to be employed, bottlenecks occur in the supply of certain factors of production, and trade unions are in a stronger position to bargain for wage increases. Thus, on the cost side alone, there are forces which make for a rise in the price level as full employment is approached.

In essence, therefore, the government is somewhat like a juggler who is endeavouring to keep four balls in the air simultaneously. At any given moment, one is going up, a second has reached its peak, a third is on the way down and the fourth is being passed from one hand to the other to be given a new upward thrust.

Nevertheless, other developed economies are in the same position, and it has to be admitted that most of them, particularly Germany and Japan, have been more successful than Britain in achieving these objectives. Why is this?

As we shall see there is no single cause, but a general phrase which would cover Britain's post-war attitude is that she has tried too hard 'to get a quart out of a pint pot'. Fundamental conditions have not been observed: price stability to maintain exports; wage restraint to avoid rising wage-unit costs; restructuring industry to promote employment. We now examine these weaknesses in the light of recent history.

575

39.2   Balance-of-Payments Difficulties

Post-war Problems

Throughout the twentieth century Britain has been losing her share of international trade as other countries have industrialised and competed in world markets. But for a time net income from overseas investments which were accumulated during the prosperous nineteenth century covered the deficit on visible trade.

The two world wars aggravated Britain's difficulties. Overseas investments were sold and external debts incurred to pay for essential imports. Furthermore, when peace came, Britain's industry, which had been geared to the war effort, needed time to readjust and re-equip.

To make matters worse, although sterling was still used by foreigners as a reserve currency, Britain's gold and foreign currency reserves were too small to provide an adequate cushion when confidence in sterling faltered through a balance-of-payments weakness. At first, in order to protect the reserves and the value of the pound, deflationary measures – the 'stop-go' policy – had to be taken. Eventually, in 1972, the pound was 'floated', and since then its value has been determined by the day-to-day conditions of demand and supply on the foreign exchange market.

The rise in the world price of oil in 1973 added £900 million to the UK's annual import bill. Furthermore, since all oil-importing countries were in the same position, they, too, had less to spend on other goods. Only if the oil-producing countries had spent their increased revenues on goods from the rest of the world would incomes have been maintained. In practice, this 'recycling' was only partly successful; the oil-producing countries, with their small populations, could not spend anything like enough on imports to use up their vast revenues. With the world recession which followed, it became more difficult for Britain to increase exports. A persistent balance-of-payments deficit was covered by borrowing, chiefly from foreign governments and the IMF (see p. 579).

The Effect of North Sea Oil

The discovery and successful extraction of North Sea oil transformed the situation. By 1979 the UK was self-sufficient in oil, and in this respect had some protection from the quadrupling in the world price of oil. Later, as the UK became a net exporter, surpluses on the balance of payments were used to accumulate overseas assets, which rose from £5 bn in 1979 to £140 bn by 1987. Net returns on these assets are currently providing £8 bn a year invisible earnings.

Nevertheless, the emergence of the pound sterling as a petrocurrency was not without snags, for it meant that the sterling exchange rate became closely related to the price of oil, appreciating to $2.50 when in 1984 the price of oil rose above $30 a barrel. This made it still more difficult for British exports to compete, and manufacturing industries in particular were forced to cut capacity. By 1983 trade in manufactured goods had moved from surplus to deficit. Similarly, when in 1986 the price of oil fell to $10 a barrel, the exchange value of the pound fell to $1.50.

The Present Balance of Payments Position

But North Sea oil reserves are limited. Since 1986 the value of the oil trade balance has been falling, partly through a drop in the world price of oil from $35 to under $20 a barrel, and partly through reduced UK production. Without the discovery of fresh reserves, it is estimated that by the end of the century net oil exports will make no contribution to the balance of payments and that once again Britain will be a net importer.

While earnings from oil exports have dwindled, the rate of growth of the economy from 1985 rose to a high of 4 per cent per annum, resulting in a considerable increase in the value of imports. To make matters worse, net earnings from invisibles started to fall. As explained later, government measures to dampen down an overheating economy were not taken soon enough. In 1989, the balance-of-payments current account deficit was over £20 billion, equivalent to 4 per cent of the GNP.

Thus the UK is back to what has been the recurrent restraint on growth – the balance of payments. As the economy expands, imports increase at a faster rate than exports. It has been estimated that Britain's *income* elasticity of demand for imports is 1.7, compared with a world elasticity of demand for British exports of 1.0. If the yawning deficit in the balance of payments is to be eliminated without the UK going into recession, it is essential she effects a major improvement in the competitiveness of her exports.

Some economists think this is best brought about by a depreciation of sterling and import controls. This would avoid severe deflation and unemployment. But depreciation benefits all exporting firms, efficient and inefficient, alike. Efficient firms have tended to hold their own in world markets because they have modernised their methods and concentrated on the right products. Moreover, past devaluations have only provided a short-term benefit, since depreciation adds to inflationary pressures by raising the prices of imported consumer goods and of the import content of home-produced goods (e.g. raw materials, basic metals, manufactured components).

Nor do import controls, as advocated by other economists, appear to present a viable alternative. Not only do they offend the spirit of international economic cooperation which has been so laboriously fostered over the last forty years, but, more important, they invite retaliation.

Two vital steps are necessary for a long-term solution: (a) controlling the rate of inflation below that of competitors; (b) restructuring British industry to provide a strong export base. It is to a consideration of these to which we now turn.

39.3 Inflation

Background to Present Government Policy

Government policy faces the difficulty of achieving a low rate of unemployment without making the rate of inflation uncomfortable.

The Keynesian solution puts the emphasis on reducing unemployment by expanding AD. Its success depends largely on achieving an effective policy to restrain rises in real wages which are not matched by increases in productivity.

In contrast, monetarist policies centre on strict control of the money supply and *supply-side* economics. While the theories supporting these policies still require empirical verification, the experience of Britain and other Western economies in recent years does seem to indicate a link between an increase in the supply of money and, after a time-lag, an increase in the rate of inflation. What is certain is that without increases in the supply of money, inflation cannot continue.

Few economists, however, would go so far as to say that the increase in the supply of money was the *cause* of an inflation. As we have seen, there is no *single* cause. Excess *AD* may be generated in a number of ways apart from spending newly created money. It may come from increased government spending, or arise on the cost side through wage demands or higher import prices. The tendency, therefore, is to favour a pragmatic approach combining control of the money supply with other policies, such as reducing government spending and supply-side economics.

This is consistent with the fact that inflation cannot be considered in isolation from employment and economic growth. Control of inflation may be the prior condition for a healthy economy, especially for the UK which is so dependent on maintaining exports. But in the final analysis the extent to which priority is given to inflation is a political decision.

Britain's Anti-inflation Policy, 1974–9

Although the Labour government increased food and housing subsidies to keep down the cost of living, during 1974 there was a leap in money wage-rates. Furthermore, world inflation resulted from the 1973 rise in the price of oil, and the price of British imports rose. By the end of 1974 inflation in Britain was running at the rate of 27 per cent.

To combat this, the Labour government placed the emphasis on the 'social contract'. On the one hand, trade unions limited their demand for wage increases; on the other, the government agreed to maintain as far as possible the level of employment and the real value of social benefits and to legislate to improve the conditions of employment.

However, the high level of *AD* led to a 1975 current balance-of-payments deficit of nearly £1700 million. The value of sterling fell, and this was accentuated by the withdrawal of sterling balances. Not only did this raise the price of imports (thereby adding to inflation) but, to prevent the exchange rate falling still further, the Bank of England had to spend heavily from the reserves. By the end of 1976 Britain had to exercise her final borrowing facility with the IMF of £2350 million.

But this loan was only advanced on condition that Britain introduced acceptable economic measures. The IMF was concerned over the inflationary implications (see below) of a PSBR running at £9000 million, largely the result of increased government spending under the social contract. Britain therefore had to agree to cut the PSBR by at least £2500 million in each of the following two years. Government policy, although imposed by the IMF, was now reflecting the views of the monetarists.

Even the announcement of these measures eased pressure on the exchange rate, and the rate of inflation fell to 8 per cent. By 1978, however, the trade unions were in no mood to limit their wage demands to the government norm of 5 per cent and they achieved increases of almost 15 per cent. The rate of inflation moved once more into double figures.

The Inflationary Implications of a High PSBR

Reducing a PSBR by higher taxation faces difficulties. Higher rates of direct taxes may have disincentive effects, while higher indirect taxes could prove inflationary by leading to demands for higher wages. In this situation the PSBR can only be covered by creating money or by borrowing.

Initially, an excess of government spending over taxation is achieved by the government's paying its employees and contractors from its deposits at the Bank of England. Eventually this extra cash finds its way into the joint-stock banks, allowing them to expand their total deposits, including advances.

But resorting to the 'printing press' in this way cannot be a permanent solution. The government has to cover its PSBR by borrowing. Even so, if it does this by the cheapest method – the sale of Treasury bills – it runs into difficulties. The major holders of Treasury bills are the joint-stock banks, and they buy them as the increased offering by the authorities forces up the yield. Such purchases, however, directly add to the banks' liquid assets, allowing them, as above, to increase their deposits. In other words, short-term borrowing involves an inflationary increase in the money supply.

As a result, the government has to rely on long-term borrowing, selling medium- and long-term bonds in the market to the *non-bank* sector, the institutions and private purchasers. Since such sources of funds rely mainly on current saving, this method is not inflationary. The difficulty, however, is that extra bonds can only be disposed of at a lower price – that is, by a rise in the long-term rate of interest. This has the overall effect of discouraging investment, thereby increasing unemployment and retarding the rate of growth. Nor is this all. Interest payments on this borrowing add to the PSBR. Furthermore, inasmuch as higher interest rates attract funds from abroad, the money supply is increased.

Monetarism under Mrs Thatcher

Mrs Thatcher's government of 1979 considered that bringing inflation under control was necessary if other objectives, particularly a high level of employment, were to be achieved. 'Fine-tuning' the economy by adjusting *AD* had failed. Instead it was replaced by naked monetarism, and its strategy followed that outlined above.

Strict control of the money supply was to follow a *medium-term financial strategy (MTFS)*. This set targets for four years ahead to: (a) limit increases in M3; and (b) reduce the PSBR as a percentage of GDP. Each year these projections were amended in the light of past experience.

The main weapon for *controlling* M3 is the rate of interest, on the assumption that higher interest rates would reduce the demand for credit (reflected in M3). In practice M3 did not prove to be interest-elastic – indeed at times firms had to *increase* their borrowing when the rate of interest rose in order to tide them over the deflationary squeeze. Moreover, because of the increasing habit of credit-card buying, higher rates often had a muted effect on borrowing. For their part the banks could still lend because the abolition of exchange control in 1979 and the development of the wholesale deposit markets enabled the banks to obtain funds at a price. Finally, the definition of M3 can produce difficulties, a switch in the source of mortgages from building societies to banks, for instance, increases M3 since building society deposits are excluded from it.

While M0, which is virtually coins and notes, appears to be a more consistent aggregate, it simply *reflects* changes in GDP since cash is always made available on demand by the Bank of England; there is no *causal* connection between M0 and *AD* in the way that there is with M3.

The reality is that, because there is such a wide range of assets having some 'moneyness', there is no single aggregate which can be measured as representing the money suply. The result was that in March 1987 the Chancellor of the Exchequer announced that he would stop setting targets for £M3, but would retain M0 and also have regard to the wider aggregates when exercising his discretion as to the degree of monetary restraint required.

While £M3 consistently overran its target, the government was more successful in *reducing the PSBR* and since 1988 borrowing has been replaced by debt repayment (PSDR). This has been achieved by (a) an increase in tax receipts as the economy expanded; and (b) the sale of government assets (see p. 321). The latter, however, is simply a one-off method, but by reducing the need to borrow it relieves the pressure of increases in the money supply and a higher rate of interest which bank and public borrowing could give rise to (see p. 449).

The changed role of fiscal policy should also be noted. Instead of being the main weapon of Keynesian demand management, it is now merely a support to monetary policy in that budgetary policy to hold back consumer spending enables liquidity to be controlled at a lower rate of interest than would otherwise be necessary.

Other Aspects of Thatcher Monetarism

A policy for wages was implicitly embodied in the MTFS: instead of playing an active role in wage settlements, the government leaves employers to negotiate terms with the trade unions. It was hoped that holding to a MTFS would convince the unions that wage demands should be based on a *lower* expected rate of inflation. Alternatively, any inflationary wage increases which the unions did obtain would not be financed by an increase in the money supply. Instead firms' profits would fall, and unemployment follow. To limit the possibility of 'blood-letting' strikes and consequent damage to the economy, the government introduced legislation curtailing the powers of the unions.

The situation was somewhat different as regards labour in the public sector where output is not related to profits. Here, therefore, the government had virtually to impose a wages policy, and its strategy of limiting public sector spending helped to influence the unions in their wage demands.

In addition to controlling the money supply, the Thatcher government took on board the politico–economic views of Friedman. He considers that the expansion of the public sector in most Western economies has undermined the willingness to accept risk-bearing and thus the ability to increase wealth. This view bore fruit in the privatisation policy. It is augmented by other measures to improve performance on the supply side (see p. 449).

Assessment of Thatcher Monetarism

The abandonment of £M3 as a monitor of the money supply virtually represented the ending of an attempt to link the money supply to set targets – the core of monetarist policy. In its place, the Chancellor of the Exchequer has adopted a pragmatic approach which takes account of the wider aggregates as he exercises his discretion as to the degree of monetary restraint required. Moreover, the objective of varying the interest rate shifted to maintaining the sterling exchange rate (at about 3.20 Deutschmarks). In short, an implicit commitment to monetary discipline replaced an explicit target.

This should not imply that the Thatcher monetarist policy has failed. Instead the strategy must be regarded as a whole. The fall in the rate of inflation from 18 per cent in 1980 to less than 4 per cent in 1987 provided a framework of stability within which the longer-term supply-side measures could more easily become effective.

But while monetarism provided the theoretical background for the government's policies, it is arguable whether it was the control of the money supply which actually produced the fall in the rate of inflation.

Until 1981 sterling appreciated, the result of the high price received for North Sea oil and the relatively high UK rate of interest. This reduced the cost of imported raw materials and components. Furthermore, as a result of the world recession of 1980–2, the price of raw materials fell.

Nor must we overlook that the deflationary effect of reduced government spending has meant that the lower inflation rate was achieved at a high cost in unemployment, which rose to $3\frac{1}{4}$ million in 1986. Some Keynesians claim that it was this weakening of labour's bargaining position rather than control of the money supply which was responsible for the fall in the rate of inflation.

The Re-emergence of Inflation

The abandonment of monetary targets in favour of shadowing the DM exchange rate was a major mistake for it permitted an alarming increase in the money supply. More than that, the DM is a strong currency compared with the pound sterling. Not only are German exports buoyant, but the government pursues monetary control uncompromisingly, raising the rate of interest at the first hint of excessive expansion.

Worse still, the UK's interest policy was relaxed just when, in hindsight, it should have been tightened, the Chancellor fearing that the stock market crash of October 1987 would result in severe worldwide deflation as happened in 1929. When this fear proved groundless, there was no real reason for maintaining the comparatively low rate of interest. Furthermore, successive budgets had decreased direct taxation, a popular policy but one which can generate a spending philosophy.

The result was that the rate of inflation started to rise, almost doubling to 7.7 per cent in two years and causing workers to seek wage rises in excess of this. The rate of interest was raised, the banks' base rate reaching 15 per cent in October 1989. This had the effect of squeezing consumer demand, especially as house mortgage rates rose to 15.4 per cent, and of halting firms' investment plans. There will thus be, at best, some reduction in the rate of growth, at worst, a serious recession. The eventual outcome may largely depend on how organised labour responds. It is possible that the traumatic experience of unemployment during the first half of the 1980s will have a long-term follow-through on the climate of negotiations so that wage demands are moderated.

Inflation and the Exchange Rate Mechanism (ERM)

At present (January 1990) there is strong pressure on the UK to join the Exchange Rate Mechanism (ERM) which is at the hub of the EMS.

All members of the Community, except the UK, Greece and Portugal, have put their currencies in the ERM and pledged to keep their exchange rate fixed against each others' within a narrow band (2.25 per cent each side, except for Italy and Spain whose limit is 6 per cent). A weak currency would initially be supported from a country's reserves, but where these are insufficient it can be supported by mutual help. This would come by borrowing from the central bank or another participating country or from the European Monetary Cooperative Fund to which all EC countries have contributed (see p. 558). Where these measures prove insufficient, a controlled devaluation of the exchange rate is arranged.

In as much as it succeeds in stabilising exchange rates, the ERM promotes international trade by removing uncertainties. More than that, fixed exchange rates would facilitate the operation of other Community policies, e.g. the CAP.

In itself the ERM does not *impose* any discipline, but it does provide a measuring post by which members are expected to be guided in formulating their internal monetary policy. Indeed the exchange rate may be a more reliable monitor of inflationary pressure than money aggregates, e.g. M3. Furthermore, the commitment to the measuring post helps to alleviate speculation against a country's currency, and this is strengthened by the knowledge that mutual support is available.

Finally, although a country's interest rate would be more volatile as it took the strain of defending the exchange rate, it would be likely to move in a narrower range. For instance, by removing the uncertainty regarding exchange rate policy, holders of the currency would not require a 'risk premium' in the required rate of interest, which could therefore be lower.

The Thatcher government is committed to joining the ERM 'when the time is ripe', but so far (September, 1990) no date has been fixed. Various factors explain this reluctance to join. In 1979, Britain was a major supplier of oil. Thus sterling was a 'petro-currency' in that its value depended significantly on the prevailing world oil price, which in turn was largely determined by OPEC decisions. More recently, Britain has indicated she will not play ball until there is a level playing-field. More specifically, France, Italy, Greece and Spain must remove their exchange controls over capital movements and remove certain industrial subsidies which are regarded as being unfair in comparison with Britain's open market.

But what has probably most influenced Mrs Thatcher is the feeling that the UK's inflation is insufficiently under control to maintain an agreed exchange rate for long. The price would be too high in terms of deflation and unemployment. Germany's stringent monetary policies, her low inflation rate of $2\frac{1}{2}$ per cent, and her success in exporting has resulted in the ERM being virtually a DM dominated bloc. Moreover, with any weakness of the dollar, reserves tend to move into the DM, causing its exchange rate to rise relative to other currencies. In practice, however, adjustment is not symmetrical by being expansionary for Germany and deflationary for the rest. There is thus a deflationary bias in the system, and Mrs Thatcher is as yet unwilling to anchor the UK rate of inflation to the low German rate.

Thus Britain has preferred a pragmatic approach, obtaining most of the advantages of ERM membership without sacrificing the flexibility of exchange rate adjustment. The former was achieved in the late 1980s by the pound shadowing movements in the DM. However, when in 1989 the DM appreciated strongly against all currencies, Britain allowed the pound sterling change rate to fall rather than raise interest rates still further.

But while the economic arguments for and against Britain joining the ERM may be finely balanced, there is also a political dimension to be considered. By joining the ERM, Britain would signal her commitment to the united European ideal and so indirectly stimulate the willingness of members generally to assist in overcoming her other difficulties, e.g. regional imbalance.

39.4   Unemployment

Post-war Experience

Although unemployment in the UK has been almost halved over the past four years and now (June 1990) stands at 1.6 million, 5.5 per cent of the working population, it is still too high. Indeed, as a result of the high interest rate policy to fight inflation, the fear is that unemployment will start to turn up again.

An appropriate policy will not emerge, however, unless we heed the lessons of Britain's post-war economic experience. As already explained (pp. 437–40), fine-tuning the economy to adjust *AD* in accordance with Keynesian theory seemed to be working. From 1974, however, unemployment began to rise, and it was accompanied by a worrying rate of inflation. By 1986, the number of persons unemployed was 3.2 million, 11.6 per cent of the working population.

Some economists will see the remedy as increased spending in some form or the other to expand *AD* – with import controls being imposed if necessary to avoid a balance-of-payments deficit as the economy expands. But, as a *long-term* policy, reflation has not proved effective for the following reasons. First, expanding *AD* may simply increase the rate of inflation. Second, it takes no account of the influence of foreign economies on the UK position. Third, in concentrating on *AD*, it overlooks measures which could be taken on the supply side. Fourth, it fails to recognise that much of the unemployment is structural. We will deal with each point in turn.

Unemployment and Inflation

In the past a policy of expanding *AD* to boost the economy has eventually led to inflation. The concept of a natural rate of unemployment forms the basis of a theoretical explanation (see Chapter 30). The balance-of-payments difficulties which inflation produced resulted in the pattern of 'stop–go' which was the feature of government policy until 1980.

North Sea oil provided only temporary relief from the balance-of-payments constraint. As noted above, the UK now has a serious deficit on her current balance of payments. This is the problem that must be solved if a high level of employment is to be sustained. Policy must be directed to (a) preventing the UK costs of production from rising relative to those of foreign competitors; and (b) restructuring British industry so as to provide a strong export base (see below).

Unemployment and International Pressures

Expanding *AD* is not a solution to unemployment in the UK if this results from weaknesses in the economies of other countries, especially if these are significant importers of British goods. A striking example of this is the world economic depression which followed the tenfold increase in the price of oil between 1973 and 1979. Because demand for oil is price inelastic, world spending on oil increased. Thus oil users had less to spend on other goods. Instead spending power was transferred to the oil producers, who were unable to increase their spending commensurately. Thus, in spite of the efforts made to 'recycle' the oil revenues by borrowing and reinvest-

reinvestment, a shortfall was 'saved', i.e. lost to the circular flow of world income. This produced a recession in 1980–3 in the world economy with prices in general rising and the non-oil countries having an aggregate balance-of-payments deficit with the oil-producing countries.

These world recessions reduced international trade, reflected in the downturn in the demand for ships, steel, air transport, cars, etc. Thus all the major industrial countries experienced a rise in unemployment.

Although the world economy has now recovered the problem has presented itself to Britain in a modified form. Since 1985 the British annual average rate of growth of 3.5 per cent has exceeded that of other countries. Thus while spending on imports rose, increasing exports to pay for them became relatively more difficult. Consequently, her rate of growth has had to be reduced to 2.5 per cent.

Unemployment and Wage Rises

Until 1980 manufacturers were able to compensate for increased costs by raising prices. The Thatcher monetarist policy, by squeezing AD, prevented this. Instead employers, faced with a squeeze on profits, had to show greater resistance to wage demands, reducing output and shedding labour in response to wage increases.

To a large extent the implications of this change in government policy have now been recognised by organised labour. Demands for wage increases have moderated. Moreover, the elimination of overmanning produced increased productivity of some 4 per cent per annum, but this was a special case. It is unlikely that future improved labour productivity will be sufficient to sustain annual increases in real earnings in manufacturing of around 9.5 per cent, and since 1985 the increases in labour costs per unit per annum has accelerated from 3.5 per cent to 5 per cent – higher than that of our competitors.

There is evidence that, in broad terms, a 1 per cent change in the average level of real earnings will in time make a difference of 0.5 to 1.0 per cent in the level of employment in the UK. This means that if average earnings are kept in line with price rises (instead of rising by 3 per cent more), something like $1\frac{1}{2}$ million extra jobs would be created over three years, and these would be in addition to those created as the economy expands and supply-side measures bear fruit.

By its supply-side policies the government has recognised the desirability of integrating micro measures with its macro policies. Expanding AD is in itself not sufficient to produce full employment for the price level also rises. Thus current unemployment in the UK is confined mostly to the unskilled. In contrast, there are severe shortages in technologists and technicians. Training the unskilled is part of the overall supply-side policy.

Unemployment and the Structure of British Industry

The danger of overemphasising the effect of 'monetarism' on the level of unemployment is that it may divert attention from Britain's basic problem – the structural weaknesses of the industrial sector through low productivity, lack of growth and the decay of the old basic industries.

Growth in British industry is essential to raise living standards and to employ the proportionately larger working population produced by increased female participation. Yet growth has been limited by lack of investment – the result of 'stop-go' policies, the diversion of resources to the public sector, the failure to develop export markets, and the reluctance to change the structure of British industry. It is the latter which is the long-term unemployment problem.

Until the 1960s the older basic industries – coal, steel, shipbuilding, textiles, engineering and vehicles, on which Britain's nineteenth-century prosperity had been based – were fully employed in making good the shortages created by the war. But there emerged newly industrialised countries of the Third World (e.g. Brazil, South Korea and Taiwan), while others grew rapidly (e.g. Japan). These adopted new techniques, and Britain lost its early comparative advantages in production. Management was slow to revise the methods which had served so well in the past. Governments seeking a policy that would allow long-term industrial change without causing short-term political embarrassment, continued to support these industries with generous subsidies. As a result, resources were diverted from the new and expanding industries.

Britain's task is to identify and develop those industries which have a high income-elasticity of demand – especially those which can keep down import penetration, and at the same time, increase exports, e.g. chemicals, soap and detergents, industrial plant and electrical engineering, aerospace, electronics. It is noticeable that, even in the world economic recession of 1980–2, the last four more than held their own in export markets.

Index